New Perspectives on

MICROSOFT® ACCESS 2002

Introductory

New Perspectives on Microsoft® Access 2002—Introductory
is published by Course Technology.

Managing Editor:
Greg Donald

Technology Product Manager:
Amanda Young

Production Editor:
Daphne Barbas

Senior Editor:
Donna Gridley

Editorial Assistant:
Jessica Engstrom

Composition:
GEX Publishing Services

Senior Product Manager:
Kathy Finnegan

Marketing Manager:
Sean Teare

Text Designer:
Meral Dabcovich

Product Manager:
Melissa Hathaway

Developmental Editor:
Jessica Evans

Cover Designer:
Efrat Reis

New Perspectives on

MICROSOFT®
ACCESS 2002

Introductory

JOSEPH J. ADAMSKI
Grand Valley State University

KATHLEEN T. FINNEGAN

COURSE
TECHNOLOGY

THOMSON LEARNING™

Australia • Canada • Mexico • Singapore • Spain • United Kingdom • United States

APPROVED COURSEWARE

What does this logo mean?

It means this courseware has been approved by the Microsoft Office User Specialist Program to be among the finest available for learning Microsoft Access 2002. It also means that upon completion of this courseware, you may be prepared to become a Microsoft Office User Specialist.

What is a Microsoft Office User Specialist?

A Microsoft Office User Specialist is an individual who has certified his or her skills in one or more of the Microsoft Office desktop applications of Microsoft Word, Microsoft Excel, Microsoft PowerPoint, Microsoft Outlook or Microsoft Access, or in Microsoft Project. The Microsoft Office User Specialist Program typically offers certification exams at the "Core" and "Expert" skill levels*. The Microsoft Office User Specialist Program is the only Microsoft approved program in the world for certifying proficiency in Microsoft Office desktop applications and Microsoft Project. This certification can be a valuable asset in any job search or career advancement.

More Information:

To learn more about becoming a Microsoft Office User Specialist, visit **www.mous.net**

To purchase a Microsoft Office User Specialist certification exam, visit **www.DesktopIQ.com**

To learn about other Microsoft Office User Specialist approved courseware from Course Technology, visit **www.course.com/NewPerspectives/TeachersLounge/mous.cfm**

Preface

Course Technology is the world leader in information technology education. The New Perspectives Series is an integral part of Course Technology's success. Visit our Web site to see a whole new perspective on teaching and learning solutions.

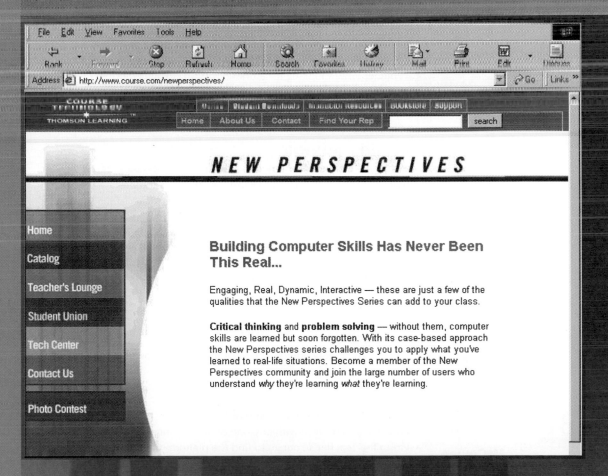

File Edit View Favorites Tools Help

Back | Forward | Stop | Refresh | Home | Search | Favorites | History | Mail | Print | Edit | Discuss

Address http://www.course.com/newperspectives/

COURSE TECHNOLOGY
THOMSON LEARNING

Series | Student Downloads | Instructor Resources | Bookstore | Support

Home | About Us | Contact | Find Your Rep | search

NEW PERSPECTIVES

- Home
- Catalog
- Teacher's Lounge
- Student Union
- Tech Center
- Contact Us
- Photo Contest

Building Computer Skills Has Never Been This Real...

Engaging, Real, Dynamic, Interactive — these are just a few of the qualities that the New Perspectives Series can add to your class.

Critical thinking and **problem solving** — without them, computer skills are learned but soon forgotten. With its case-based approach the New Perspectives series challenges you to apply what you've learned to real-life situations. Become a member of the New Perspectives community and join the large number of users who understand *why* they're learning *what* they're learning.

New Perspectives—Building Computer Skills Has Never Been This Real

Why New Perspectives will work for you.

Critical thinking and problem solving—without them, computer skills are learned but soon forgotten. With its case-based approach, the New Perspectives Series challenges students to apply what they've learned to real-life situations. Become a member of the New Perspectives community and watch your students not only master computer skills, but also retain and carry this knowledge into the world.

New Perspectives catalog
Our online catalog is never out of date! Go to the Catalog button on our Web site to check out our available titles, request a desk copy, download a book preview, or locate online files.

Complete system of offerings
Whether you're looking for a Brief book, an Advanced book, or something in between, we've got you covered. Go to the Catalog button on our Web site to find the level of coverage that's right for you.

Instructor materials
We have all the tools you need—data files, solution files, figure files, a sample syllabus, and ExamView, our powerful testing software package.

How well do your students know Microsoft Office?
Find out with performance-based testing software that measures your students' proficiency in the application. Click the Tech Center button to learn more.

Get certified
If you want to get certified, we have the titles for you. Find out more by clicking the Teacher's Lounge button.

Interested in distance learning?
Enhance your course with any one of our distance learning platforms. Go to the Teacher's Lounge to find the platform that's right for you.

Your link to the future is at
www.course.com/NewPerspectives

What you need to know about this book.

- Student Online Companion takes students to the Web for additional work.

- ExamView testing software gives you the option of generating a printed test, LAN-based test, or test over the Internet.

- New Perspectives Labs provide students with self-paced practice on computer-related topics.

- All cases are NEW to this edition!

- Our clear and concise coverage of database concepts provides students with the solid foundation they need as they progress to creating and working with database objects.

- Students will appreciate the in-depth explanation of creating and modifying queries, which proceeds logically from simple to more complex queries involving calculated fields, domain aggregate functions, pattern matches, and parameters.

- This text takes students beyond the basics, as they learn how to design and create professional-looking forms and reports that contain subforms/subreports and are sourced from multiple queries

- Students also design and create data access pages with PivotTables and PivotCharts, and work with XML files and hyperlinks to other programs.

- The scenarios in our end-of-tutorial exercises will hold students' interest, and the number of exploratory exercises will challenge students and give them a sense of accomplishment.

- This book is certified at the MOUS Core level for Access 2002!

CASE	TROUBLE?	SESSION 1.1	QUICK CHECK	RW
Tutorial Case Each tutorial begins with a problem presented in a case that is meaningful to students. The case sets the scene to help students understand what they will do in the tutorial.	**TROUBLE? Paragraphs** These paragraphs anticipate the mistakes or problems that students may have and help them continue with the tutorial.	**Sessions** Each tutorial is divided into sessions designed to be completed in about 45 minutes each. Students should take as much time as they need and take a break between sessions.	**Quick Check Questions** Each session concludes with conceptual Quick Check questions that test students' understanding of what they learned in the session.	**Reference Windows** Reference Windows are succinct summaries of the most important tasks covered in a tutorial. They preview actions students will perform in the steps to follow.

BRIEF CONTENTS

Preface   v

Microsoft Office XP   OFF 1

Tutorial 1 *Introducing Microsoft Office XP*   OFF 3
Preparing Promotional Materials for Delmar Office Supplies

Microsoft Access 2002—Level I Tutorials   AC 1.01

Tutorial 1 *Introduction to Microsoft Access 2002*   AC 1.03
Viewing and Working with a Table Contraining Employer Data

Tutorial 2 *Creating and Maintaining a Database*   AC 2.01
Creating the Northeast Database, and Creating, Modifying, and Updating the Position Table

Tutorial 3 *Querying a Database*   AC 3.01
Retrieving Information About Employers and Their Positions

Tutorial 4 *Creating Forms and Reports*   AC 4.01
Creating a Position Data Form, an Employer Positions Form, and an Employers and Positions Report

Microsoft Access 2002—Level II Tutorials   AC 5.01

Tutorial 5 *Enhancing a Table's Design,
and Creating Advanced Queries and Custom Forms*   AC 5.03
Making the Jobs Database Easier to Use

Tutorial 6 *Creating Custom Reports*   AC 6.01
Creating a Potential Income Report

Tutorial 7 *Integrating Access with the Web and with Other
Programs*   AC 7.01
Creating Web-Enabled and Integrated Information for the Jobs Database

Appendix *Relational Databases and Database Design*   RD 1

Index   1

Task Reference   10

Certification Grid   16

File Finder   21

TABLE OF CONTENTS

Preface	v
Microsoft Office XP	**OFF 1**
Read This Before You Begin	OFF 2

Tutorial 1 — OFF 3

Introducing Microsoft Office XP

Preparing Promotional Materials for Delmar Office Supplies

Exploring Microsoft Office XP	OFF 4
Integrating Programs	OFF 7
Starting Office Programs	OFF 9
Switching Between Open Programs and Files	OFF 12
Using Personalized Menus and Toolbars	OFF 13
Using Speech Recognition	OFF 15
Saving and Closing a File	OFF 16
Opening a File	OFF 18
Printing a File	OFF 20
Getting Help	OFF 21
Exiting Programs	OFF 23
Quick Check	OFF 23
Review Assignments	OFF 23
Quick Check Answers	OFF 24

Microsoft Access 2002	
Level I Tutorials	**AC 1.01**
Read This Before You Begin	AC 1.02

Tutorial 1 — AC 1.03

Introduction to Microsoft Access 2002

Viewing and Working with a Table Containing Employer Data

SESSION 1.1	**AC 1.04**
Introduction to Database Concepts	AC 1.04
Organizing Data	AC 1.04
Databases and Relationships	AC 1.04
Relational Database Management Systems	AC 1.06
Opening an Existing Database	AC 1.07
The Access and Database Windows	AC 1.10
Opening an Access Table	AC 1.10
Navigating an Access Datasheet	AC 1.11
Saving a Database	AC 1.12
Session 1.1 Quick Check	AC 1.13
SESSION 1.2	**AC 1.13**
Working with Queries	AC 1.13
Opening an Existing Query	AC 1.13
Creating, Sorting, and Navigating a Query	AC 1.15
Creating and Navigating a Form	AC 1.18
Creating, Previewing, and Navigating a Report	AC 1.20
Managing a Database	AC 1.23
Backing Up and Restoring a Database	AC 1.23
Compacting and Repairing a Database	AC 1.24
Compacting a Database Automatically	AC 1.24
Converting an Access 2000 Database	AC 1.25
Session 1.2 Quick Check	AC 1.26
Review Assignments	AC 1.27
Case Problems	AC 1.28
Lab Assignments	AC 1.31
Internet Assignments	AC 1.32
Quick Check Answers	AC 1.32

Tutorial 2 — AC 2.01

Creating and Maintaining a Database

Creating the Northeast Database, and Creating, Modifying, and Updating the Position Table

SESSION 2.1	**AC 2.02**
Guidelines for Designing Databases	AC 2.02
Guidelines for Setting Field Properties	AC 2.04
Naming Fields and Objects	AC 2.04
Assigning Field Data Types	AC 2.05
Setting Field Sizes	AC 2.06
Creating a New Database	AC 2.07
Creating a Table	AC 2.08
Defining Fields	AC 2.09
Specifying the Primary Key	AC 2.16
Saving the Table Structure	AC 2.17
Session 2.1 Quick Check	AC 2.18
SESSION 2.2	**AC 2.19**
Adding Records to a Table	AC 2.19
Modifying the Structure of an Access Table	AC 2.22
Deleting a Field	AC 2.23
Moving a Field	AC 2.24
Adding a Field	AC 2.24
Changing Field Properties	AC 2.26
Obtaining Data from Another Access Database	AC 2.29
Copying Records from Another Access Database	AC 2.29
Importing a Table from Another Access Database	AC 2.32
Updating a Database	AC 2.33

Deleting Records   AC 2.33
Changing Records   AC 2.34
Session 2.2 Quick Check   AC 2.35
Review Assignments   AC 2.36
Case Problems   AC 2.37
Internet Assignments   AC 2.42
Quick Check Answers   AC 2.42

Tutorial 3   AC 3.01

Querying a Database

Retrieving Information About Employers and Their Positions

SESSION 3.1   AC 3.01
Introduction to Queries   AC 3.02
Query Window   AC 3.02
Creating and Running a Query   AC 3.05
Updating Data Using a Query   AC 3.07
Defining Table Relationships   AC 3.08
    One-to-Many Relationships   AC 3.08
    Referential Integrity   AC 3.09
    Defining a Relationship Between Two Tables   AC 3.09
Creating a Multi-table Query   AC 3.13
Sorting Data in a Query   AC 3.14
    Using a Toolbar Button to Sort Data   AC 3.15
    Sorting Multiple Fields in Design View   AC 3.16
Filtering Data   AC 3.19
Session 3.1 Quick Check   AC 3.21

SESSION 3.2   AC 3.22
Defining Record Selection Criteria for Queries   AC 3.22
    Specifying an Exact Match   AC 3.22
    Changing a Datasheet's Appearance   AC 3.25
    Using a Comparison Operator to Match
        a Range of Values   AC 3.26
Defining Multiple Selection Criteria for Queries   AC 3.28
    The And Logical Operator   AC 3.29
    Using Multiple Undo and Redo   AC 3.30
    The Or Logical Operator   AC 3.31
Performing Calculations   AC 3.33
    Creating a Calculated Field   AC 3.34
    Using Aggregate Functions   AC 3.38
    Using Record Group Calculations   AC 3.40
Session 3.2 Quick Check   AC 3.41
Review Assignments   AC 3.42
Case Problems   AC 3.43

Internet Assignments   AC 3.46
Quick Check Answers   AC 3.46

Tutorial 4   AC 4.01

Creating Forms and Reports

Creating a Position Data Form, an Employer Positions Form, and an Employers and Positions Report

SESSION 4.1   AC 4.02
Creating a Form Using the Form Wizard   AC 4.02
Changing a Form's AutoFormat   AC 4.05
Finding Data Using a Form   AC 4.08
Previewing and Printing Selected Form Records   AC 4.11
Maintaining Table Data Using a Form   AC 4.12
Checking the Spelling of Table Data Using a Form   AC 4.14
Session 4.1 Quick Check   AC 4.16

SESSION 4.2   AC 4.16
Creating a Form with a Main Form and a Subform   AC 4.16
    Modifying a Form in Design View   AC 4.19
Creating a Report Using the Report Wizard   AC 4.22
Inserting a Picture in a Report   AC 4.30
Session 4.2 Quick Check   AC 4.34
Review Assignments   AC 4.34
Case Problems   AC 4.36
Internet Assignments   AC 4.40
Quick Check Answers   AC 4.40

Microsoft Access 2002

Level II Tutorials	AC 5.01
Read This Before You Begin	AC 5.02

Tutorial 5   AC 5.03

Enhancing a Table's Design, and Creating Advanced Queries and Custom Forms

Making the Jobs Database Easier to Use

SESSION 5.1   AC 5.04
Creating a Lookup Wizard Field   AC 5.04
Displaying Related Records in a Subdatasheet   AC 5.09
Using the Input Mask Wizard   AC 5.10
Defining Data Validation Criteria   AC 5.13
Using a Pattern Match in a Query   AC 5.15
Using a List-of-Values Match in a Query   AC 5.17

Using a Nonmatching Value in a Query	AC 5.18
Using Both the And and Or Operators in the Same Query	AC 5.19
Creating a Parameter Query	AC 5.20
Session 5.1 Quick Check	AC 5.22
SESSION 5.2	**AC 5.23**
Creating a Custom Form	AC 5.23
Designing a Custom Form	AC 5.23
The Form Window in Design View	AC 5.25
Adding Fields to a Form	AC 5.28
Selecting and Moving Controls	AC 5.29
Changing a Label's Caption	AC 5.31
Resizing Controls	AC 5.33
Using Form Headers and Form Footers	AC 5.35
Adding a Label to a Form	AC 5.37
Adding a Picture to a Form	AC 5.39
Changing the Background Color of a Form Control	AC 5.40
Session 5.2 Quick Check	AC 5.42
SESSION 5.3	**AC 5.42**
Creating a Multi-page Form Using Tab Controls	AC 5.42
Adding a Subform Using Control Wizards	AC 5.48
Using a Filter with a Form	AC 5.53
Using Filter By Form	AO 5.53
Saving a Filter as a Query	AC 5.56
Applying a Filter Saved as a Query	AC 5.57
Session 5.3 Quick Check	AC 5.58
Review Assignments	AC 5.58
Case Problems	AC 5.61
Internet Assignments	AC 5.69
Quick Check Answers	AC 5.69

Tutorial 6   AC 6.01

Creating Custom Reports

Creating a Potential Income Report

SESSION 6.1	**AC 6.02**
Creating a Custom Report	AC 6.02
Designing a Custom Report	AC 6.04
Reviewing and Creating Queries for a Custom Report	AC 6.05
Assigning a Conditional Value to a Calculated Field	AC 6.08
Report Window in Design View	AC 6.10

Sorting and Grouping Data in a Report	AC 6.12
Adding Fields to a Report	AC 6.14
Working with Controls	AC 6.15
Changing the Caption Property	AC 6.15
Moving and Resizing Controls	AC 6.17
Aligning Controls	AC 6.19
Session 6.1 Quick Check	AC 6.21
SESSION 6.2	**AC 6.22**
Adding a Subreport Using Control Wizards	AC 6.22
Modifying a Subreport	AC 6.23
Adding Lines to a Report	AC 6.27
Hiding Duplicate Values in a Report	AC 6.28
Calculating Group Totals	AC 6.29
Defining Conditional Formatting Rules	AC 6.32
Using Domain Aggregate Functions	AC 6.36
Session 6.2 Quick Check	AC 6.40
SESSION 6.3	**AC 6.41**
Adding the Date to a Report	AC 6.41
Adding Page Numbers to a Report	AC 6.43
Adding a Title to a Report	AC 6.45
Creating Mailing Labels	AC 6.50
Session 6.3 Quick Check	AC 6.57
Review Assignments	AC 6.57
Case Problems	AC 6.58
Internet Assignments	AC 6.67
Quick Check Answers	AC 6.68

Tutorial 7   AC 7.01

Integrating Access with the Web and with Other Programs

Creating Web-Enabled and Integrated Information for the Jobs Database

SESSION 7.1	**AC 7.02**
Using the Web	AC 7.02
Exporting an Access Query to an HTML Document	AC 7.02
Viewing an HTML Document Using Internet Explorer	AC 7.05
Creating a Data Access Page for an Access Table	AC 7.08
Updating Data on a Data Access Page Using Internet Explorer	AC 7.11
Using a Data Access Page to Sort and Filter Records	AC 7.13
Creating a Custom Data Access Page	AC 7.14

Creating a Blank Data Access Page
    in Design View   AC 7.14

Adding Fields to a Data Access Page   AC 7.16

Deleting, Moving, and Resizing Controls
    on a Data Access Page   AC 7.19

Resizing a Section and Applying a Special Effect   AC 7.20

Selecting a Theme   AC 7.21

Saving and Viewing a Data Access Page   AC 7.22

Session 7.1 Quick Check   AC 7.24

SESSION 7.2   **AC 7.25**

Creating and Using a PivotTable
    on a Data Access Page   AC 7.25

Adding a PivotTable to a Data Access Page   AC 7.26

Adding Fields to a PivotTable   AC 7.28

Using a PivotTable in Page View   AC 7.30

Adding a Total Field to a PivotTable   AC 7.33

Creating and Using a PivotChart
    on a Data Access Page   AC 7.37

Session 7.2 Quick Check   AC 7.46

SESSION 7.3   **AC 7.46**

Using XML   AC 7.46

Importing an XML File as an Access Table   AC 7.46

Exporting an Access Table as an XML File   AC 7.49

Exporting an Access Query as an Excel Worksheet   AC 7.51

Saving the Worksheet and Exiting Excel   AC 7.54

Creating Hyperlinks to Other Office XP Documents   AC 7.54

Creating a Hyperlink Field in a Table   AC 7.55

Entering Hyperlink Field Values   AC 7.56

Using a Hyperlink   AC 7.58

Session 7.3 Quick Check   AC 7.59

Review Assignments   AC 7.60

Case Problems   AC 7.61

Internet Assignments   AC 7.69

Quick Check Answers   AC 7.70

Appendix   **RD 1**

*Relational Databases and
Database Design*

Relations   RD 2

Keys   RD 3

Relationships   RD 5

One-to-One   RD 6

One-to-Many   RD 6

Many-to-Many   RD 7

Entity Subtype   RD 8

Entity-Relationship Diagrams   RD 9

Integrity Constraints   RD 11

Dependencies and Determinants   RD 12

Anomalies   RD 14

Normalization   RD 15

First Normal Form   RD 15

Second Normal Form   RD 17

Third Normal Form   RD 19

Review Questions   RD 21

Index   **1**

Task Reference   **10**

Certification Grid   **16**

File Finder   **21**

Acknowledgments

I would like to thank the following reviewers for their helpful and thorough feedback: Lorraine Bergkvist, College of Notre Dame; Michael Feiler, Merritt College; Eric Johnston, Vatterott College; Donna Occhifinto, County College of Morris; and Rebekah Tidwell, Carson Newman College and Lee University. Many thanks to all the Course Technology staff, especially Greg Donald and Donna Gridley for their leadership and encouragement; Melissa Hathaway and Jessica Engstrom for their tireless support and good humor; Daphne Barbas for her excellent management of the production process; and John Bosco, John Freitas, and Marianne Broughey for ensuring the quality and accuracy of this text. Special thanks to Jessica Evans for her exceptional editorial and technical skills in developing this text and her willingness to go the extra mile; and to Joe Adamski for his continued guidance and expertise. This book is dedicated with love to my two terrific sons, Connor and Devon, who always keep me both hopping and grounded at the same time.

Kathleen T. Finnegan

Thank you to all the people who contributed to developing and completing this book, with special thanks to Susan Solomon, who started it all and asked me to join the team nearly ten years ago; Greg Donald for making a smooth transition to the team; the marketing staff for supporting the series over the years; Kathy Finnegan for her many contributions; Jessica Evans for her thoughtfulness, attention to quality, perseverance, friendship, and exceptional skills; and Judy for making it all worthwhile.

Joseph J. Adamski

New Perspectives on

MICROSOFT®
OFFICE XP

TUTORIAL 1 OFF 3

Introducing Microsoft Office XP

Delmar Office Supplies
Exploring Microsoft Office XP   4
Starting Office Programs   9
Using Personalized Menus and Toolbars   13
Saving and Closing a File   16
Opening a File   18
Printing a File   20
Getting Help   21
Exiting Programs   23

Read This Before You Begin

To the Student

Data Disks

To complete this tutorial and the Review Assignments, you need one Data Disk. Your instructor will either provide you with the Data Disk or ask you to make your own.

If you are making your own Data Disk, you will need **one** blank, formatted high-density disk. You will need to copy a set of files and/or folders from a file server, standalone computer, or the Web onto your disk. Your instructor will tell you which computer, drive letter, and folder contain the files you need. You could also download the files by going to **www.course.com** and following the instructions on the screen.

The information below shows you which folder goes on your disk, so that you will have enough disk space to complete the tutorial and Review Assignments:

Data Disk 1

Write this on the disk label:
Data Disk 1: Introducing Office XP

Put this folder on the disk:
Tutorial.01

When you begin the tutorial, be sure you are using the correct Data Disk. Refer to the "File Finder" chart at the back of this text for more detailed information on which files are used in the tutorial. See the inside front or inside back cover of this book for more information on Data Disk files, or ask your instructor or technical support person for assistance.

Using Your Own Computer

If you are going to work through this tutorial using your own computer, you need:

- ■ **Computer System** Microsoft Windows 98, NT, 2000 Professional, or higher must be installed on your computer. This book assumes a typical installation of Microsoft Office XP.

- ■ **Data Disk** You will not be able to complete this tutorial or Review Assignments using your own computer until you have your Data Disk.

Visit Our World Wide Web Site

Additional materials designed especially for you are available on the World Wide Web.
Go to **www.course.com/NewPerspectives**.

To the Instructor

The Data Disk Files are available on the Instructor's Resource Kit for this title. Follow the instructions in the Help file on the CD-ROM to install the programs to your network or standalone computer. For information on creating the Data Disk, see the "To the Student" section above.

You are granted a license to copy the Data Disk Files to any computer or computer network used by students who have purchased this book.

In this tutorial you will:

- Explore the programs that comprise Microsoft Office

- Explore the benefits of integrating data between programs

- Start programs and switch between them

- Use personalized menus and toolbars

- Save and close a file

- Open an existing file

- Print a file

- Get Help

- Close files and exit programs

INTRODUCING MICROSOFT OFFICE XP

Preparing Promotional Materials for Delmar Office Supplies

CASE

Delmar Office Supplies

Delmar Office Supplies, a company in Wisconsin founded by Nicole Delmar in 1996, sells recycled office supplies to businesses and home-based offices around the world. The demand for quality recycled papers, reconditioned toner cartridges, and renovated office furniture has been growing each year. Nicole and all her employees use Microsoft Office XP, which provides everyone in the company the power and flexibility to store a variety of information, create consistent documents, and share data. In this tutorial, you'll review some of the latest documents the company's employees have created using Microsoft Office XP.

Exploring Microsoft Office XP

Microsoft Office XP, or simply **Office**, is a collection of the most popular Microsoft programs: Word, Excel, PowerPoint, Access, and Outlook. Each Office program contains valuable tools to help you accomplish many tasks, such as composing reports, analyzing data, preparing presentations, and compiling information.

Microsoft Word 2002, or simply **Word**, is a **word processing program** you use to create text documents. The files you create in Word are called **documents**. Word offers many special features that help you compose and update all types of documents, ranging from letters and newsletters to reports, fliers, faxes, and even books—all in attractive and readable formats. You also can use Word to create, insert, and position figures, tables, and other graphics to enhance the look of your documents. Figure 1 shows a business letter that a sales representative composed with Word.

Figure 1   **LETTER COMPOSED IN A WORD DOCUMENT**

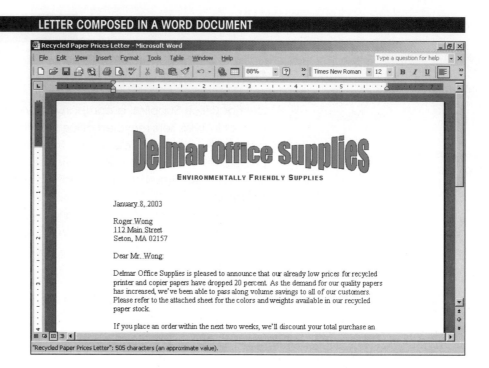

Microsoft Excel 2002, or simply **Excel**, is a **spreadsheet program** you use to display, organize, and analyze numerical information. You can do some of this in Word with tables, but Excel provides many more tools for performing calculations than Word does. Its graphics capabilities also enable you to display data visually. You might, for example, generate a pie chart or bar chart to help readers quickly see the significance of and the connections between information. The files you create in Excel are called **workbooks**. Figure 2 shows an Excel workbook with a line chart that the Operations Department uses to track the company's financial performance.

Figure 2   FINANCIAL DATA IN AN EXCEL WORKBOOK

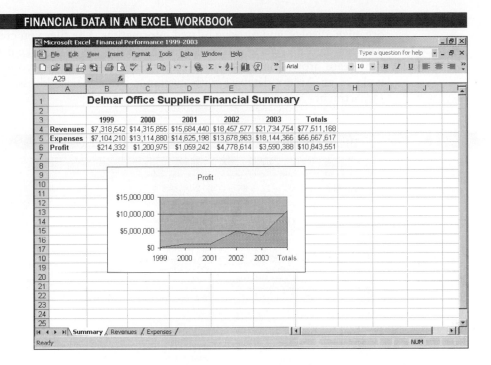

Microsoft PowerPoint 2002, or simply **PowerPoint**, is a **presentation graphics program** you use to create a collection of "slides" that can contain text, charts, pictures, and so on. The files you create in PowerPoint are called **presentations**. You can show these presentations on your computer monitor, project them onto a screen as a slide show, print them, share them over the Internet, or display them on the World Wide Web. You also can use PowerPoint to generate presentation-related documents such as audience handouts, outlines, and speakers' notes. Figure 3 shows an effective slide presentation the Sales Department created with PowerPoint to promote the latest product line.

Figure 3   SLIDE PRESENTATION CREATED IN POWERPOINT

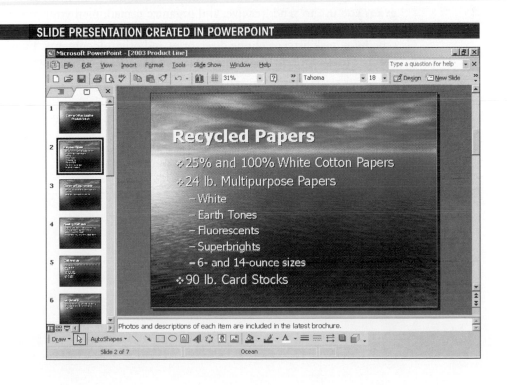

Microsoft Access 2002, or simply **Access**, is a **database program** you use to enter, organize, display, and retrieve related information. The files you create in Access are called **databases**. With Access you can create data entry forms to make data entry easier, and you can create professional reports to improve the readability of your data. Figure 4 shows a table in an Access database with customer names and addresses compiled by the Sales Department.

Figure 4   CUSTOMER ADDRESSES COMPILED IN AN ACCESS DATABASE

Customer Num	Name	Street	City	State/Prov	Postal Code
201	Wonder Supplies	5499 Alpine Lane	Gardner	MA	01440
285	The Best Supplies	2837 Commonwealth Avenue	Cambridge	MA	02142
129	Office World	95 North Bay Boulevard	Warwick	RI	02287
135	Supplies Plus	2840 Cascade Road	Laconia	NH	03246
104	American Office	Pond Hill Road	Millinocket	ME	04462
515	Pens and Paper	8200 Baldwin Boulevard	Burlington	VT	05406
165	Pen and Ink	1935 Snow Street	Nagatuck	CT	06770
423	Wonderful World of Work	H 1055	Budapest	Hungary	1/A
83	Sophia's Supplies	87 Weeping Willow Road	Brooklyn	NY	11201
17	Supplies and More	132-A Old Country Road	Bellport	NY	11763
322	Supply Closet	114 Lexington	Plattsburgh	NY	12901
302	Blackburg's Stationers	4489 Perlman Avenue	Blacksburg	VA	24060
136	Home Office Needs	4090 Division Stret NW	Fort Lauderdale	FL	33302
131	Supplies 4 U	14832 Old Bedford Trail	Mishawaka	IN	46544
122	VIP Stationery	8401 E. Fletcher Road	Clare	MI	48617
164	Supply Depot	1355 39th Street	Roscommon	MI	48653
325	Max Office Supplies	56 Four Mile Road	Grand Rapids	MI	49505
133	Supply Your Office	2874 Western Avenue	Sioux Falls	SD	57057
107	A+ Supplies	82 Mix Avenue	Bonners Ferry	ID	83805
203	Discount Supplies	28320 Fruitland Street	Studio City	CA	94106
536	One Stop Shop	31 Union Street	San Francisco	CA	94123
82	Supply Stop	2159 Causewayside	Edinburgh	Scotland	EH9 1PH
202	Office Products	3130 Edgwood Parkway	Thunder Bay	Ontario	L5B 1X2
407	Paper and More	44 Tower Lane	Leeds	England	LS12 3SD
394	The Office Store	397 Pine Road	Toronto	Ontario	M4J1R5

Microsoft Outlook 2002, or simply **Outlook**, is an **information management program** you use to send, receive, and organize e-mail; plan your schedule; arrange meetings; organize contacts; create a to-do list; and jot down notes. You also can use Outlook to print schedules, task lists, or phone directories and other documents. Figure 5 shows how Nicole Delmar uses Outlook to plan her schedule and create a to-do list.

Figure 5	CALENDAR AND TASKS IN OUTLOOK

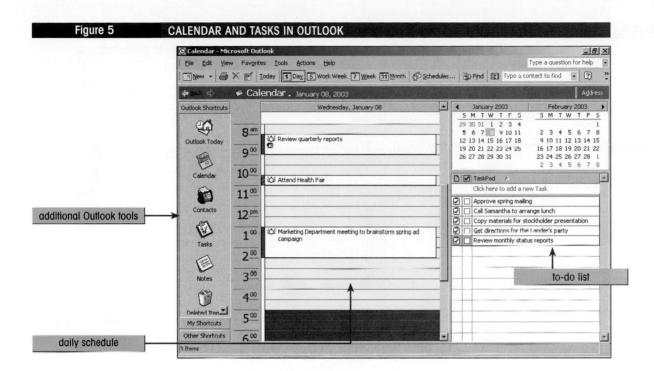

additional Outlook tools

to-do list

daily schedule

Although each Office program individually is a strong tool, their potential is even greater when used together.

Integrating Programs

One of the main advantages of Office is **integration**, the ability to share information between programs. Integration ensures consistency and accuracy, and it saves time because you don't have to re-enter the same information in several Office programs. The staff at Delmar Office Supplies uses the integration features of Office daily, including the following examples:

■ The Accounting Department created an Excel bar chart on the last two years' fourth-quarter results, which they inserted into the quarterly financial report, created in Word. They added a hyperlink to the Word report that employees can click to open the Excel workbook and view the original data. See Figure 6.

Figure 6   WORD DOCUMENT WITH AN EXCEL CHART

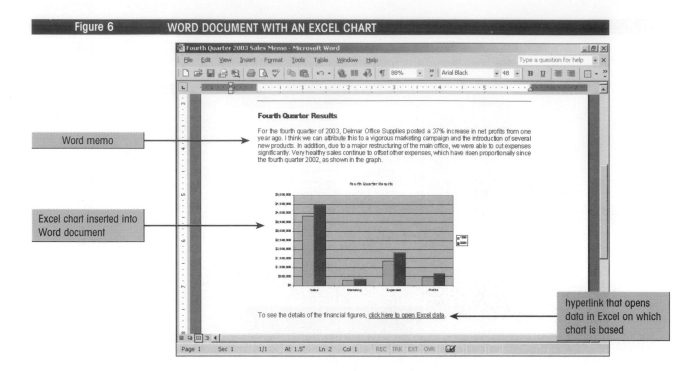

Word memo

Excel chart inserted into Word document

hyperlink that opens data in Excel on which chart is based

■ An Excel pie chart of sales percentages by divisions of Delmar Office Supplies can be duplicated on a PowerPoint slide. The slide is part of the Operations Department's presentation to stockholders. See Figure 7.

Figure 7   POWERPOINT PRESENTATION WITH AN EXCEL CHART

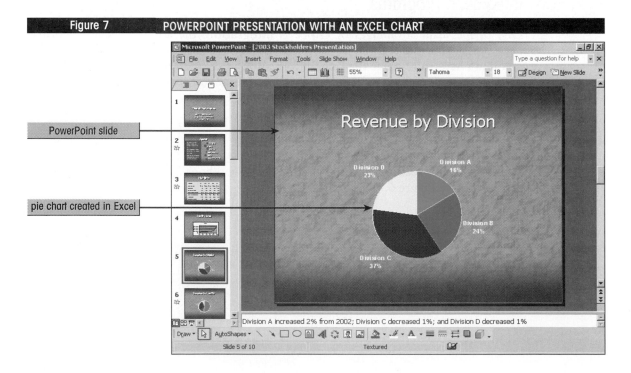

PowerPoint slide

pie chart created in Excel

■ An Access database or an Outlook contact list that stores the names and addresses of customers can be combined with a form letter that the Marketing Department created in Word, to produce a mailing promoting the company's newest products. See Figure 8.

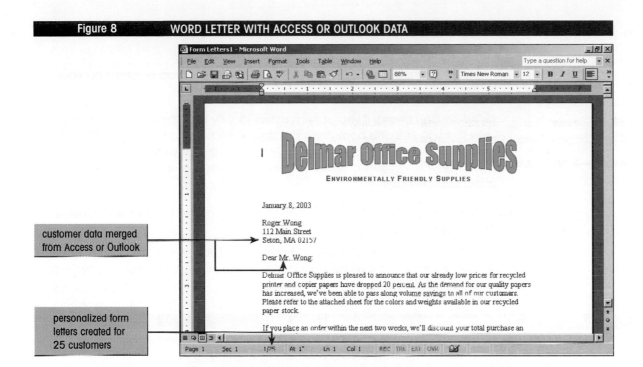

Figure 8   WORD LETTER WITH ACCESS OR OUTLOOK DATA

customer data merged from Access or Outlook

personalized form letters created for 25 customers

These are just a few examples of how you can take information from one Office program and integrate it into another.

Starting Office Programs

All Office programs start the same way—from the Programs menu on the Start button. You select the program you want, and then the program starts so you can immediately begin to create new files or work with existing ones.

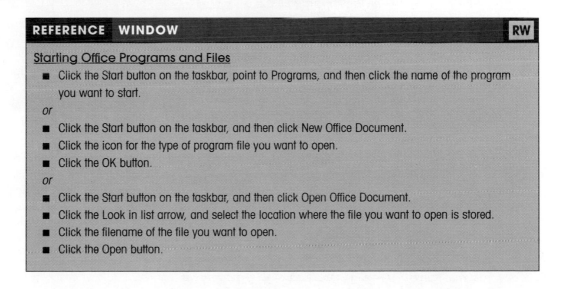

REFERENCE   WINDOW   RW

Starting Office Programs and Files

- Click the Start button on the taskbar, point to Programs, and then click the name of the program you want to start.

or

- Click the Start button on the taskbar, and then click New Office Document.
- Click the icon for the type of program file you want to open.
- Click the OK button.

or

- Click the Start button on the taskbar, and then click Open Office Document.
- Click the Look in list arrow, and select the location where the file you want to open is stored.
- Click the filename of the file you want to open.
- Click the Open button.

You'll start Excel using the Start button.

To start Excel and open a new, blank workbook from the Start menu:

1. Make sure your computer is on and the Windows desktop appears on your screen.

   TROUBLE? Don't worry if your screen differs slightly from those shown in the figures. The figures in this book were created while running Windows 2000 in its default settings, but Office runs equally well using Windows 98 or later or Windows NT 4 with Service Pack 5. These operating systems share the same basic user interface.

2. Click the **Start** button on the taskbar, and then point to **Programs** to display the Programs menu.

3. Point to **Microsoft Excel** on the Programs menu. See Figure 9. Depending on how your computer is set up, your desktop and menu might contain different icons and commands.

Figure 9	START MENU WITH PROGRAMS MENU DISPLAYED

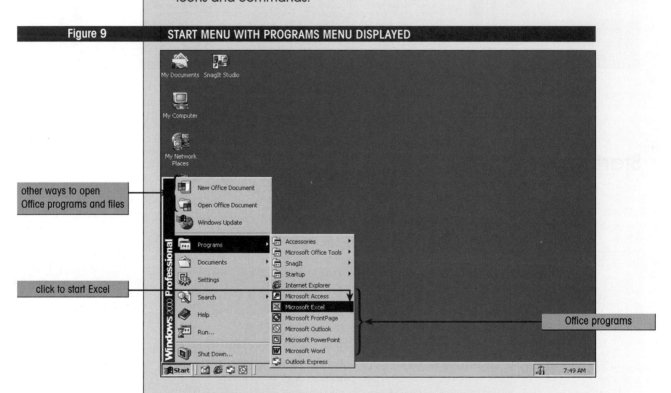

other ways to open Office programs and files

click to start Excel

Office programs

   TROUBLE? If you don't see Microsoft Excel on the Programs menu, point to Microsoft Office, and then point to Microsoft Excel. If you still don't see Microsoft Excel, ask your instructor or technical support person for help.

4. Click **Microsoft Excel** to start Excel and open a new, blank workbook. See Figure 10.

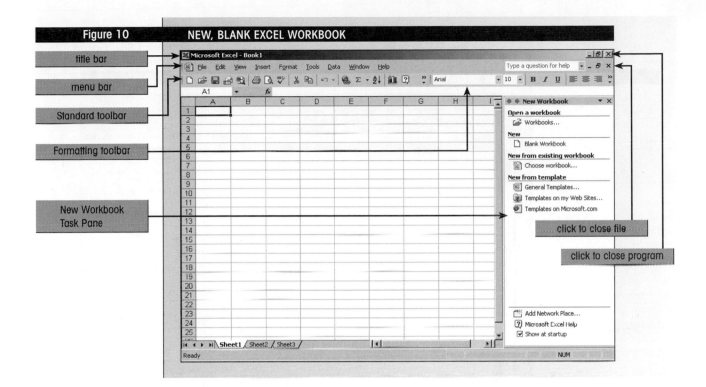

Figure 10   NEW, BLANK EXCEL WORKBOOK

An alternate method for starting programs with a blank file is to click the New Office Document command on the Start menu; the kind of file you choose determines which program opens. You'll use this method to start Word and open a new, blank document.

To start Word and open a new, blank document with the New Office Document command:

1. Leaving Excel open, click the **Start** button on the taskbar, and then click **New Office Document**. The New Office Document dialog box opens, providing another way to start Office programs. See Figure 11.

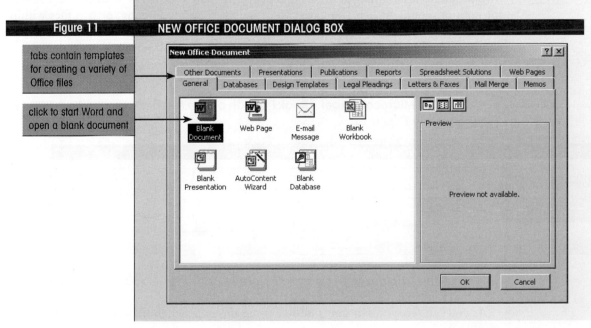

Figure 11   NEW OFFICE DOCUMENT DIALOG BOX

2. If necessary, click the **General** tab, click the **Blank Document** icon, and then click the **OK** button. Word opens with a new, blank document. See Figure 12.

Figure 12	NEW, BLANK DOCUMENT IN WORD

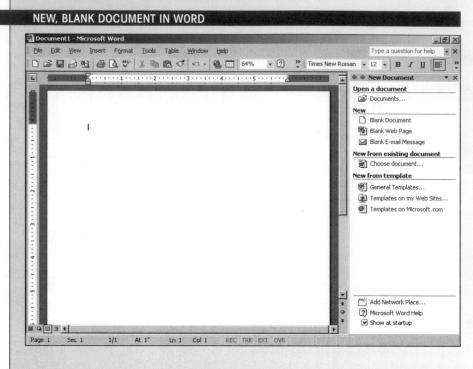

TROUBLE? If you don't see the New Document Task Pane, click File on the Word menu bar, and then click New.

You've tried two ways to start a program. There are several methods for performing most tasks in Office. This flexibility enables you to use Office in the way that fits how you like to work.

Switching Between Open Programs and Files

Two programs are running at the same time—Excel and Word. The taskbar contains buttons for both programs. When you have two or more programs running, or two files within the same program open, you can use the taskbar buttons to switch from one program or file to another. The employees at Delmar Office Supplies often work in several programs at once.

To switch between Word and Excel:

1. Click the **Microsoft Excel – Book1** button on the taskbar to switch from Word to Excel. See Figure 13.

Figure 13	EXCEL AND WORD PROGRAMS OPENED

button appears pressed to show it is the active program

taskbar

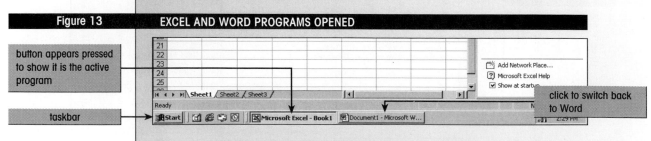

click to switch back to Word

2. Click the **Document1 – Microsoft Word** button on the taskbar to return to Word.

As you can see, you can start multiple programs and switch between them in seconds.

The Office programs also share many features, so once you've learned one program, it's easy to learn the others. One of the most visible similarities among all the programs is the "personalized" menus and toolbars.

Using Personalized Menus and Toolbars

In each Office program, you perform tasks using a menu command, a toolbar button, or a keyboard shortcut. A **menu command** is a word on a menu that you click to execute a task; a **menu** is a group of related commands. For example, the File menu contains commands for managing files, such as the Open command and the Save command. A **toolbar** is a collection of **buttons** that correspond to commonly used menu commands. For example, the Standard toolbar contains an Open button and a Save button. **Keyboard shortcuts** are combinations of keys you press to perform a command. For example, Ctrl+S is the keyboard shortcut for the Save command (you hold down the Ctrl key while you press the S key). Keyboard shortcuts are displayed to the right of many menu commands.

When you first use a newly installed Office program, the menus and toolbars display only the basic and most commonly used commands and buttons, streamlining the program window. The other commands and buttons are available, but you have to click an extra button to see them (the double-arrow button on a menu and the Toolbar Options button on a toolbar). As you select commands and click buttons, the ones you use often are put on the short, personalized menu and on the visible part of the toolbars. The ones you don't use remain available on the full menus and toolbars. This means that the Office menus and toolbars might display different commands and buttons on each person's computer.

To view a personalized and full menu:

1. Click **Insert** on the Word menu bar to display the short, personalized menu. See Figure 14. The Bookmark command, for example, does not appear on the short menu.

| Figure 14 | SHORT, PERSONALIZED MENU |

double-arrow button

TROUBLE? If the Insert menu displays different commands than shown in Figure 14, you need to reset the menus. Click Tools on the menu bar, click Customize (you might need to pause until the full menu appears to see that command), and then click the Options tab in the Customize dialog box. Click the Always show full menus check box to remove the check mark if necessary, and then click the Show full menus after a short delay check box to insert a check mark if necessary. Click the Reset my usage data button, and then click the Yes button to confirm that you want to reset the commands. Click the Close button. Repeat Step 1.

You can display the full menu in one of three ways: (1) pause until the full menu appears, which might happen as you read this; (2) click the double-arrow button at the bottom of the menu; or (3) double-click the menu name on the menu bar.

2. Pause until the full Insert menu appears, as shown in Figure 15. The Bookmark command and other commands are now visible.

Figure 15 **EXPANDED, FULL MENU**

commands with light border appear on short menu

commands with dark border appear only on full menu

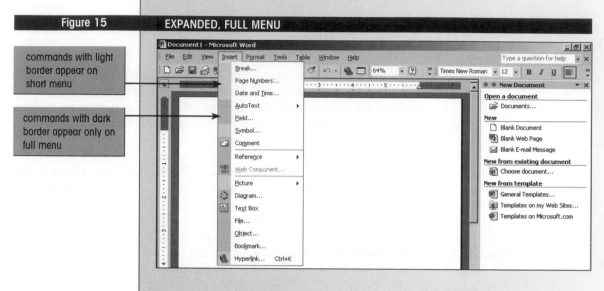

3. Click the **Bookmark** command. A dialog box opens when you click a command whose name is followed by an ellipsis (…). In this case, the Bookmark dialog box opens.

4. Click the **Cancel** button to close the Bookmark dialog box.

5. Click **Insert** on the menu bar again to display the short, personalized menu. The Bookmark command appears on the short, personalized menu because you used it.

6. Press the **Esc** key to close the menu.

As you can see, the menu changed based on your actions. Over time, only the commands you use frequently will appear on the personalized menu. The toolbars work similarly.

To use the personalized toolbars:

1. Observe that the Standard and Formatting toolbars appear side by side below the menu bar.

TROUBLE? If the toolbars appear on two rows, you need to reset them. Click Tools on the menu bar, click Customize, and then click the Options tab in the Customize dialog box. Click the Show Standard and Formatting toolbars on two rows check box to remove the check mark. Click the Reset my data usage button, and then click the Yes button to confirm you want to reset the commands. Click the Close button. Repeat Step 1.

The Formatting toolbar sits to the right of the Standard toolbar. You can see most of the Standard toolbar buttons, but only a few Formatting toolbar buttons.

2. Click the **Toolbar Options** button ⊠ at the right side of the Standard toolbar. See Figure 16.

Figure 16	TOOLBAR OPTIONS LIST

Toolbar Options button

Bullets button

click to move toolbars onto separate rows

drag from here to resize side-by-side toolbars

TROUBLE? If you see different buttons on the Toolbar Options list, your side-by-side toolbars might be resized differently than the ones shown in Figure 16. Continue with Step 3.

3. Click the **Bullets** button. The Bullets button moves to the visible part of the Formatting toolbar, and another button is moved onto the Toolbar Options list to make room for the new button.

   TROUBLE? If the Bullets button already appears on the Formatting toolbar, click another button on the Toolbar Options list. Then click that same button again in Step 4 to turn off that formatting.

4. Click again to turn off the Bullets formatting.

Some people like that the menus and toolbars change to meet their work habits. Others prefer to see all the menu commands or to display the toolbars on different rows so that all the buttons are always visible. You'll change the toolbar setting now.

To turn off the personalized toolbars:

1. Click the **Toolbar Options** button at the right side of the Standard toolbar.

2. Click the **Show Buttons on Two Rows command**. The toolbars move to separate rows (the Standard toolbar on top) and you can see all the buttons on each toolbar.

You can easily access any button on the toolbars with one mouse click. The drawback is that the toolbars take up more space in the program window.

Using Speech Recognition

Another way to perform tasks in Office is with your voice. Office's **speech recognition technology** enables you to say the names of the toolbar buttons, menus, menu commands, dialog box items, and so forth, rather than clicking the mouse or pressing keys to select them. The Language toolbar includes the Speech Balloon, which displays the voice command equivalents of a selected button or command. If you switch from Voice mode to Dictation mode, you can dictate the contents of your files rather than typing the text or numbers. For better accuracy, complete the Training Wizard, which helps Office learn your vocal quality, rate of talking, and speech patterns. To start using speech recognition, click Tools on the menu bar in any Office program, and then click Speech. The first time you start this feature, the Training Wizard guides you through the setup process.

Saving and Closing a File

As you create and modify Office files, your work is stored only in the computer's temporary memory, not on disk. If you were to exit the programs, turn off your computer, or experience a power failure, your work would be lost. To prevent losing work, frequently save your file to a disk—at least every ten minutes. You can save files to the hard disk located inside your computer or to portable storage disks, such as CD-ROMs, Zip disks, or floppy disks.

The first time you save a file, you need to name it. This name is called a **filename**. When you choose a filename, select a descriptive one that accurately reflects the content of the document, workbook, presentation, or database, such as "Shipping Options Letter" or "Fourth Quarter Financial Analysis." Filenames can include a maximum of 255 letters, numbers, hyphens, or spaces in any combination. Office appends a **file extension** to the filename, which identifies the program in which that file was created. The file extensions are .doc for Word, .xls for Excel, .ppt for PowerPoint, and .mdb for Access. Whether you see file extensions depends on how Windows is set up for your computer.

You also need to decide where you'll save the file—on which disk and in what folder. Choose a logical location that you'll remember whenever you want to use the file again.

REFERENCE WINDOW   **RW**

Saving a File

- Click the Save button on the Standard toolbar (*or* click File on the menu bar, and then click Save or Save As).
- Click the Save in list arrow, and then select the location where you want to save the file.
- Type a filename in the File name text box.
- Click the Save button.
- To resave the named file to the same location, click the Save button on the Standard toolbar (*or* click File on the menu bar, and then click Save).

Nicole has asked you to start working on the agenda for the stockholder meeting. You enter text in a Word document by typing. After you type some text, you'll save the file.

To enter text in a document:

1. Type **Delmar Office Supplies**, and then press the **Enter** key. The text you typed appears on one line in the Word document.

   TROUBLE? If you make a typing error, press the Backspace key to delete the incorrect letters, and then retype the text.

2. Type **Stockholder Meeting Agenda**, and then press the **Enter** key. The text you typed appears on the second line.

The two lines of text you typed are not yet saved on disk. You'll do that now.

To save a file for the first time:

1. Insert your Data Disk in the appropriate drive.

TROUBLE? If you don't have a Data Disk, you need to get one before you can proceed. Your instructor or technical support person will either give you one or ask you to make your own by following the instructions on the "Read This Before You Begin" page at the beginning of this tutorial. See your instructor or technical support person for more information.

2. Click the **Save** button 💾 on the Standard toolbar. The Save As dialog box opens. See Figure 17. The first few words of the first line appear in the File name text box, as a suggested filename. You'll replace this with a more descriptive filename.

Figure 17	SAVE AS DIALOG BOX

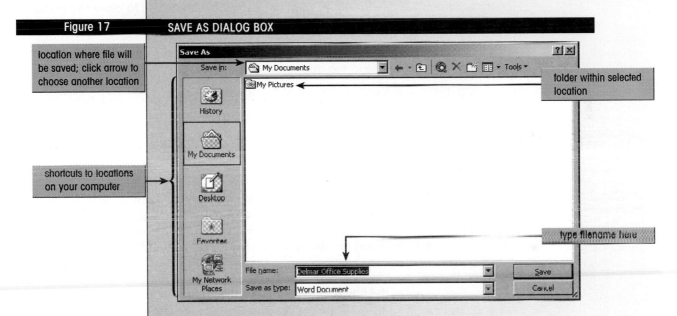

location where file will be saved; click arrow to choose another location

shortcuts to locations on your computer

folder within selected location

type filename here

TROUBLE? If the .doc file extension appears after the filename, then your computer is configured to show file extensions. Just continue with Step 3.

3. Type **Stockholder Meeting Agenda** in the File name text box.

4. Click the **Save in** list arrow, and then click the drive that contains your Data Disk.

5. Double-click the **Tutorial.01** folder in the list box, and then double-click the **Tutorial** folder. This is the location where you want to save the document.

6. Click the **Save** button. The Save As dialog box closes, and the name of your file appears in the program window title bar.

The saved file includes everything in the document at the time you saved. Any edits or additions you then make to the document exist only in the computer's memory and are not saved in the file on the disk. As you work, remember to save frequently so that the file is updated to reflect the latest content of the document.

Because you already named the document and selected a storage location, the second and subsequent times you save, the Save As dialog box doesn't open. If you wanted to save a copy of the file with a different filename or to a different location, you would reopen the Save As dialog box by clicking File on the menu bar, and then clicking Save As. The previous version of the file remains on your disk as well.

You need to add your name to the agenda. Then you'll save your changes and close the file. You can close a file by clicking the Close command on the File menu or by clicking the Close Window button in the upper-right corner of the menu bar.

To modify, save, and close a file:

1. Type your name, and then press the **Enter** key. The text you typed appears on the next line.

2. Click the **Save** button 🔲 on the Standard toolbar.

   The updated document is saved to the file. When you're done with a file, you can close it. Although you can keep multiple files open at one time, you should close any file you are no longer working on to conserve system resources.

3. Click the **Close Window** button ⊠ on the Word menu bar to close the document. Word is still running, but no documents are open.

   TROUBLE? If a dialog box opens and asks whether you want to save the changes you made to the document, you modified the document since you last saved. Click the Yes button to save the current version and close it.

Opening a File

Once you have a program open, you can create additional new files for the open programs or you can open previously created and saved files. You can do both of these from the New Task Pane. The New Task Pane enables you to create new files and open existing ones. The name of the Task Pane varies, depending on the program you are using: Word has the New Document Task Pane, Excel has the New Workbook Task Pane, PowerPoint has the New Presentation Task Pane, and Access has the New File Task Pane.

When you want to work on a previously created file, you must open it first. Opening a file transfers a copy of the file from the storage disk (either a hard disk or a portable disk) to the computer's memory and displays it on your screen. The file is then in your computer's memory and on the disk.

REFERENCE WINDOW   RW

Opening an Existing or New File

- Click File on the menu bar, click New, and then (depending on the program) click the More documents, More workbooks, More presentations, or More files link in the New Task Pane (or click the Open button on the Standard toolbar or click File on the menu bar, and then click Open).
- Click the Look in list arrow, and then select the storage location of the file you want to open.
- Click the filename of the file you want to open.
- Click the Open button.

or

- Click File on the menu bar, click New, and then (depending on the program) click the Blank Document, Blank Workbook, Blank Presentation, or Blank Database link in the New Task Pane (or click the New button on the Standard toolbar).

Nicole asks you to print the agenda. To do that, you'll reopen the file. Because Word is still open, you'll use the New Document Task Pane.

To open an existing file:

1. If necessary, click **File** on the menu bar, and then click **New** to display the New Document Task Pane. See Figure 18.

Figure 18	NEW DOCUMENT TASK PANE

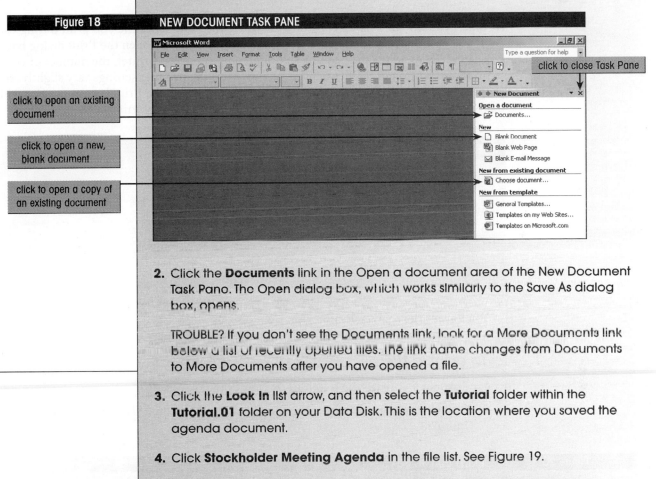

click to open an existing document

click to open a new, blank document

click to open a copy of an existing document

click to close Task Pane

2. Click the **Documents** link in the Open a document area of the New Document Task Pane. The Open dialog box, which works similarly to the Save As dialog box, opens.

   TROUBLE? If you don't see the Documents link, look for a More Documents link below a list of recently opened files. The link name changes from Documents to More Documents after you have opened a file.

3. Click the **Look In** list arrow, and then select the **Tutorial** folder within the **Tutorial.01** folder on your Data Disk. This is the location where you saved the agenda document.

4. Click **Stockholder Meeting Agenda** in the file list. See Figure 19.

Figure 19	OPEN DIALOG BOX

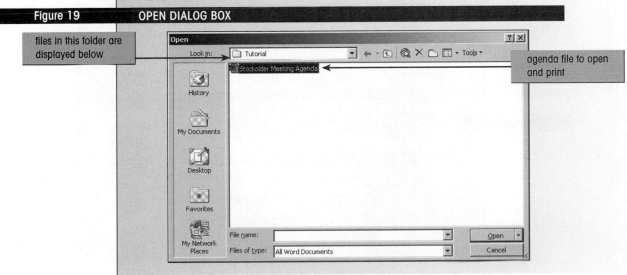

files in this folder are displayed below

agenda file to open and print

5. Click the **Open** button. The file you saved earlier reopens in the Word program window, and the New Document Task Pane closes.

After the file is open, you can view, edit, print, or resave it.

Printing a File

At times, you'll want a paper copy of your Office file. The first time you print during each computer session, you should use the Print menu command to open the Print dialog box so you can verify or adjust the printing settings. You can select a printer, the number of copies to print, the portion of the file to print, and so forth; the printing settings vary slightly from program to program. For subsequent print jobs you can use the Print button to print without opening the dialog box, if you want to use the same default settings.

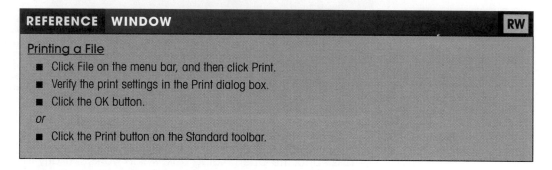

REFERENCE WINDOW   RW

Printing a File
- Click File on the menu bar, and then click Print.
- Verify the print settings in the Print dialog box.
- Click the OK button.
or
- Click the Print button on the Standard toolbar.

You'll print the agenda document.

To print a file:

1. Make sure your printer is turned on and contains paper.

2. Click **File** on the menu bar, and then click **Print**. The Print dialog box opens. See Figure 20.

Figure 20   PRINT DIALOG BOX

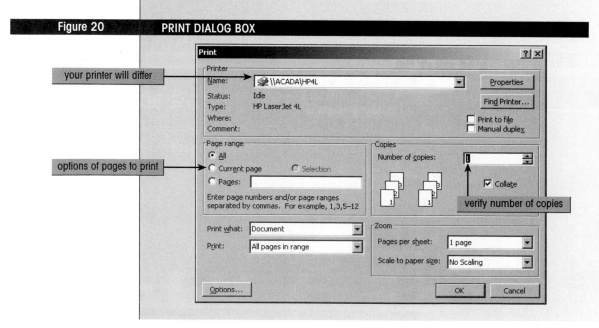

3. Verify that the correct printer appears in the Name list box. If the wrong printer appears, click the **Name** list arrow, and then click the correct printer from the list of available printers.

4. Verify that **1** appears in the Number of copies text box.

5. Click the **OK** button to print the document. See Figure 21.

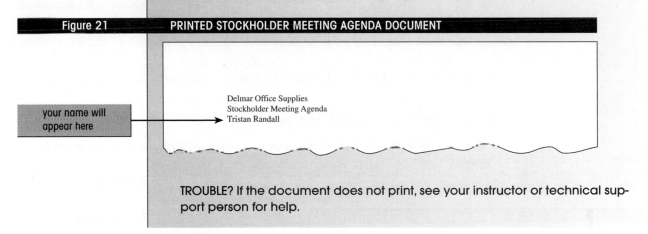

| Figure 21 | PRINTED STOCKHOLDER MEETING AGENDA DOCUMENT |

your name will appear here

Delmar Office Supplies
Stockholder Meeting Agenda
Tristan Randall

TROUBLE? If the document does not print, see your instructor or technical support person for help.

Another important aspect of Office is the ability to get help right from your computer.

Getting Help

If you don't know how to perform a task or want more information about a feature, you can turn to Office itself for information on how to use it. This information, referred to simply as **Help**, is like a huge encyclopedia stored on your computer. You can access it in a variety of ways.

There are two fast and simple methods you can use to get Help about objects you see on the screen. First, you can position the mouse pointer over a toolbar button to view its **ScreenTip**, a yellow box with the button's name. Second, you can click the **What's This?** command on the Help menu to change the pointer to ⬚?, which you can click on any toolbar button, menu command, dialog box option, worksheet cell, or anything else you can see on your screen to view a brief description of that item.

For more in-depth help, you can use the **Ask a Question** box, located on the menu bar of every Office program, to find information in the Help system. You simply type a question using everyday language about a task you want to perform or a topic you need help with, and then press the Enter key to search the Help system. The Ask a Question box expands to show Help topics related to your query. You click a topic to open a Help window with step-by-step instructions that guide you through a specific procedure and explanations of difficult concepts in clear, easy-to-understand language. For example, you might ask how to format a cell in an Excel worksheet; a list of Help topics related to the words you typed will appear. The Help window also has Contents, Answer Wizard, and Index tabs, which you can use to look up information directly from the Help window.

If you prefer, you can ask questions of the **Office Assistant**, an interactive guide to finding information from the Help system. In addition, the Office Assistant can provide Help topics and tips on tasks as you work. For example, it might offer a tip when you select a menu command instead of clicking the corresponding toolbar button. You can turn on or off the tips, depending on your personal preference.

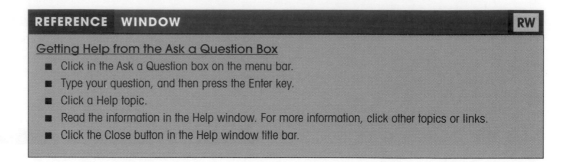

REFERENCE   WINDOW   RW

Getting Help from the Ask a Question Box
- Click in the Ask a Question box on the menu bar.
- Type your question, and then press the Enter key.
- Click a Help topic.
- Read the information in the Help window. For more information, click other topics or links.
- Click the Close button in the Help window title bar.

You'll use the Ask a Question box to obtain more information about Help.

To use the Ask a Question box:

1. Click in the **Ask a Question** box on the menu bar, and then type **How do I search help?**.

2. Press the **Enter** key to retrieve a list of topics, as shown in Figure 22.

Figure 22	ASK A QUESTION BOX WITH HELP TOPICS

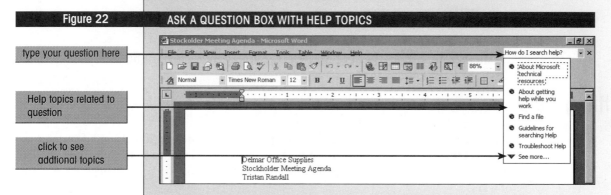

type your question here

Help topics related to question

click to see addtional topics

3. Click the **See more** link, review the additional Help topics, and then click the **See previous** link.

4. Click **About getting help while you work** to open the Help window and learn more about the various ways to obtain assistance in Office. See Figure 23.

Figure 23	HELP WINDOW

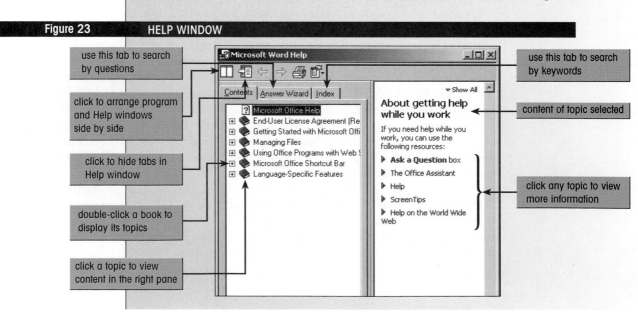

use this tab to search by questions

click to arrange program and Help windows side by side

click to hide tabs in Help window

double-click a book to display its topics

click a topic to view content in the right pane

use this tab to search by keywords

content of topic selected

click any topic to view more information

5. Click **Help** in the right pane to display information about that topic.

6. Click the other links about Help features and read the information.

7. When you're done, click the **Close** button ☒ in the Help window title bar to return to the Word window.

The Help features enable the staff at Delmar Office Supplies to get answers to questions they have about any task or procedure when they need it. The more you practice getting information from the Help system, the more effective you will be at using Office to its full potential.

Exiting **Programs**

Whenever you finish working with a program, you should exit it. As with many other aspects of Office, you can exit programs with a button or from a menu. You'll use both methods to close Word and Excel.

To exit a program:

1. Click the **Close** button ☒ in the upper-right corner of the screen to exit Word. Word exits, and the Excel window is visible again on your screen.

   TROUBLE? If a dialog box opens, asking whether you want to save the document, you may have inadvertently made a change to the document. Click the No button.

2. Click **File** on the menu bar, and then click **Exit**. The Excel program exits.

Exiting programs after you are done using them keeps your Windows desktop uncluttered for the next person using the computer, frees up your system's resources, and prevents data from being lost accidentally.

QUICK CHECK

1. Which Office program would you use to write a letter?
2. Which Office programs could you use to store customer names and addresses?
3. What is integration?
4. Explain the difference between Save As and Save.
5. What is the purpose of the New Task Pane?
6. When would you use the Ask a Question box?

REVIEW ASSIGNMENTS

Before the stockholders meeting at Delmar Office Supplies, you'll open and print documents for the upcoming presentation.

1. Start PowerPoint using the Start button and the Programs menu.

2. Use the Ask a Question box to learn how to change the toolbar buttons from small to large, and then do it. Use the same procedure to change the buttons back to regular size. Close the Help window when you're done.

3. Open a blank Excel workbook using the New Office Document command on the Start menu.

Explore   4. Switch to the PowerPoint window using the taskbar, and then close the presentation but leave open the PowerPoint program. (*Hint:* Click the Close Window button in the menu bar.)

Explore   5. Open a new, blank PowerPoint presentation from the New Presentation Task Pane. (*Hint:* Click Blank Presentation in the New area of the New Presentation Task Pane.)

6. Close the PowerPoint presentation and program using the Close button in the PowerPoint title bar; do not save changes if asked.

Explore   7. Open a copy of the Excel **Finances** workbook located in the **Review** folder within the **Tutorial.01** folder on your Data Disk using the New Workbook Task Pane. (*Hint:* Click File on the Excel menu bar and then click New to open the Task Pane. Click Choose Workbook in the New from existing workbook area of the New Workbook Task Pane; the dialog box functions similarly to the Open dialog box.)

8. Type your name, and then press the Enter key to insert your name at the top of the worksheet.

9. Save the worksheet as **Delmar Finances** in the **Review** folder within the **Tutorial.01** folder on your Data Disk.

10. Print one copy of the worksheet using the Print command on the File menu.

11. Exit Excel using the File menu.

Explore   12. Open the **Letter** document located in the **Review** folder within the **Tutorial.01** folder on your Data Disk using the Open Office Document command on the Start menu.

13. Use the Save As command to save the document with the filename **Delmar Letter** in the **Review** folder within the **Tutorial.01** folder on your Data Disk.

Explore   14. Press and hold the Ctrl key, press the End key, and then release both keys to move the insertion point to the end of the letter, and then type your name.

15. Use the Save button on the Standard toolbar to save the change to the Delmar Letter document.

16. Print one copy of the document, and then close the document.

17. Exit the Word program using the Close button on the title bar.

QUICK | CHECK ANSWERS

1. Word
2. Access or Outlook
3. the ability to share information between programs
4. Save As enables you to change the filename and save location of a file. Save updates a file to reflect its latest contents using its current filename and location.
5. enables you to create new files and open existing files
6. when you don't know how to perform a task or want more information about a feature

New Perspectives on

MICROSOFT®
ACCESS 2002

TUTORIAL 1   AC 1.03

Introduction to Microsoft Access 2002
Viewing and Working with a Table Containing Employer Data

TUTORIAL 2   AC 2.01

Creating and Maintaining a Database
Creating the Northeast Database, and Creating, Modifying, and Updating the Position Table

TUTORIAL 3   AC 3.01

Querying a Database
Retrieving Information About Employers and Their Positions

TUTORIAL 4   AC 4.01

Creating Forms and Reports
Creating a Position Data Form, an Employer Positions Form, and an Employers and Positions Report

Read This Before You Begin

To the Student

Data Disks

To complete the Level I tutorials, Review Assignments, and Case Problems, you need six Data Disks. Your instructor will either provide you with these Data Disks or ask you to make your own.

If you are making your own Data Disks, you will need **six** blank, formatted high-density disks. You will need to copy a set of files and/or folders from a file server, standalone computer, or the Web onto your disks. Your instructor will tell you which computer, drive letter, and folders contain the files you need. You could also download the files by going to www.course.com and following the instructions on the screen.

The information below shows you which folders go on each of your disks, so that you will have enough disk space to complete all the tutorials, Review Assignments, and Case Problems:

Data Disk 1
Write this on the disk label:
Data Disk 1: Access Tutorial Files
Put this folder on the disk:
Tutorial

Data Disk 2
Write this on the disk label:
Data Disk 2: Access Review Assignments
Put this folder on the disk:
Review

Data Disk 3
Write this on the disk label:
Data Disk 3: Access Case Problem 1
Put this folder on the disk:
Cases

Data Disk 4
Write this on the disk label:
Data Disk 4: Access Case Problem 2
Put this folder on the disk:
Cases

Data Disk 5
Write this on the disk label:
Data Disk 5: Access Case Problem 3
Put this folder on the disk:
Cases

Data Disk 6
Write this on the disk label:
Data Disk 6: Access Case Problem 4
Put this folder on the disk:
Cases

When you begin each tutorial, be sure you are using the correct Data Disk. Refer to the "File Finder" chart at the back of this text for more detailed information on which files are used in which tutorials, and make sure you carefully read the note above the chart. See the inside front or inside back cover of this book for more information on Data Disk files, or ask your instructor or technical support person for assistance.

Course Labs

The Access Level I tutorials feature an interactive Course Lab to help you understand database concepts. There are Lab Assignments at the end of Tutorial 1 that relate to this Lab.

To start a Lab, click the **Start** button on the Windows taskbar, point to **Programs**, point to **Course Labs**, point to **New Perspectives Course Labs**, and then click the name of the Lab you want to use.

Using Your Own Computer

If you are going to work through this book using your own computer, you need:

- **Computer System** Microsoft Windows 98, NT, 2000 Professional, or higher must be installed on your computer. This book assumes a typical installation of Microsoft Access.

- **Data Disks** You will not be able to complete the tutorials or exercises in this book using your own computer until you have your Data Disks.

- **Course Labs** See your instructor or technical support person to obtain the Course Lab software for use on your own computer.

Visit Our World Wide Web Site

Additional materials designed especially for you are available on the World Wide Web.
Go to www.course.com/NewPerspectives.

To the Instructor

The Data Disk Files and Course Labs are available on the Instructor's Resource Kit for this title. Follow the instructions in the Help file on the CD-ROM to install the programs to your network or standalone computer. For information on creating Data Disks or the Course Labs, see the "To the Student" section above.

You are granted a license to copy the Data Files and Course Labs to any computer or computer network used by students who have purchased this book.

OBJECTIVES

In this tutorial you will:

- Define the terms field, record, table, relational database, primary key, and foreign key

- Open an existing database

- Identify the components of the Access and Database windows

- Open and navigate a table

- Learn how Access saves a database

- Open an existing query, and create, sort, and navigate a new query

- Create and navigate a form

- Create, preview, and navigate a report

- Learn how to manage a database by backing up, restoring, compacting, and converting a database

LAB

Databases

INTRODUCTION TO MICROSOFT ACCESS 2002

Viewing and Working with a Table Containing Employer Data

CASE

Northeast Seasonal Jobs International (NSJI)

During her high school and college years, Elsa Jensen spent her summers working as a lifeguard for some of the most popular beaches on Cape Cod, Massachusetts. Throughout those years, Elsa met many foreign students who had come to the United States to work for the summer, both at the beaches and at other seasonal businesses, such as restaurants and hotels. Elsa formed friendships with several students and kept in contact with them beyond college. Through discussions with her friends, Elsa realized that foreign students often have a difficult time finding appropriate seasonal work, relying mainly on "word-of-mouth" references to locate jobs. Elsa became convinced that there must be an easier way.

Several years ago, Elsa founded Northeast Seasonal Jobs, a small firm located in Boston that served as a job broker between foreign students seeking part-time, seasonal work and resort businesses located in New England. Recently Elsa expanded her business to include resorts in the eastern provinces of Canada, and consequently she changed her company's name to Northeast Seasonal Jobs International (NSJI). At first the company focused mainly on summer employment, but as the business continued to grow, Elsa increased the scope of operations to include all types of seasonal opportunities, including foliage tour companies in the fall and ski resorts in the winter.

Elsa depends on computers to help her manage all areas of NSJI's operations, including financial management, sales, and information management. Several months ago the company upgraded to Microsoft Windows and **Microsoft Access 2002** (or simply **Access**), a computer program used to enter, maintain, and retrieve related data in a format known as a database. Elsa and her staff use Access to maintain data such as information about employers, positions they have available for seasonal work, and foreign students seeking employment. Elsa recently created a database named Seasonal to track the company's employer customers and data about their available positions. She asks for your help in completing and maintaining this database.

SESSION 1.1

In this session, you will learn key database terms and concepts, open an existing database, identify components of the Access and Database windows, open and navigate a table, and learn how Access saves a database.

Introduction to Database Concepts

Databases

Before you begin working on Elsa's database and using Access, you need to understand a few key terms and concepts associated with databases.

Organizing Data

Data is a valuable resource to any business. At NSJI, for example, important data includes employers' names and addresses, and available positions and wages. Organizing, storing, maintaining, retrieving, and sorting this type of data are critical activities that enable a business to find and use information effectively. Before storing data on a computer, however, you first must organize the data.

Your first step in organizing data is to identify the individual fields. A **field** is a single characteristic or attribute of a person, place, object, event, or idea. For example, some of the many fields that NSJI tracks are employer ID, employer name, employer address, employer phone number, position, wage, and start date.

Next, you group related fields together into tables. A **table** is a collection of fields that describe a person, place, object, event, or idea. Figure 1-1 shows an example of an Employer table consisting of four fields: EmployerID, EmployerName, EmployerAddress, and PhoneNumber.

Figure 1-1 **DATA ORGANIZATION FOR A TABLE OF EMPLOYERS**

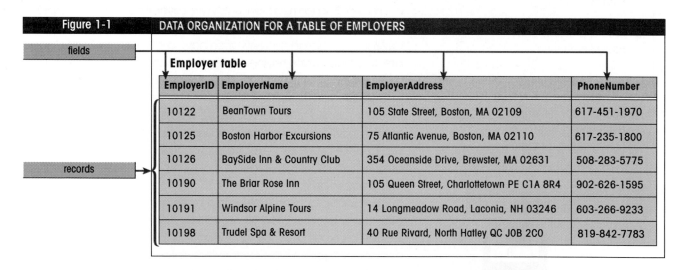

fields

Employer table

records

EmployerID	EmployerName	EmployerAddress	PhoneNumber
10122	BeanTown Tours	105 State Street, Boston, MA 02109	617-451-1970
10125	Boston Harbor Excursions	75 Atlantic Avenue, Boston, MA 02110	617-235-1800
10126	BaySide Inn & Country Club	354 Oceanside Drive, Brewster, MA 02631	508-283-5775
10190	The Briar Rose Inn	105 Queen Street, Charlottetown PE C1A 8R4	902-626-1595
10191	Windsor Alpine Tours	14 Longmeadow Road, Laconia, NH 03246	603-266-9233
10198	Trudel Spa & Resort	40 Rue Rivard, North Hatley QC J0B 2C0	819-842-7783

The specific value, or content, of a field is called the **field value**. In Figure 1-1, the first set of field values for EmployerID, EmployerName, EmployerAddress, and PhoneNumber are, respectively: 10122; BeanTown Tours; 105 State Street, Boston, MA 02109; and 617-451-1970. This set of field values is called a **record**. In the Employer table, the data for each employer is stored as a separate record. Figure 1-1 shows six records; each row of field values is a record.

Databases and Relationships

A collection of related tables is called a **database**, or a **relational database**. NSJI's Seasonal database contains two related tables: the Employer and NAICS tables, which Elsa created. (The NAICS table contains North American Industry Classification System codes, which are used to classify businesses by the type of activity in which they are engaged.) In Tutorial 2, you will create a Position table to store information about the available positions at NSJI's employer clients.

Sometimes you might want information about employers and their available positions. To obtain this information, you must have a way to connect records in the Employer table to records in the Position table. You connect the records in the separate tables through a **common field** that appears in both tables.

In the sample database shown in Figure 1-2, each record in the Employer table has a field named EmployerID, which is also a field in the Position table. For example, BaySide Inn & Country Club is the third employer in the Employer table and has an EmployerID of 10126. This same EmployerID field value, 10126, appears in three records in the Position table. Therefore, BaySide Inn & Country Club is the employer with these three positions available.

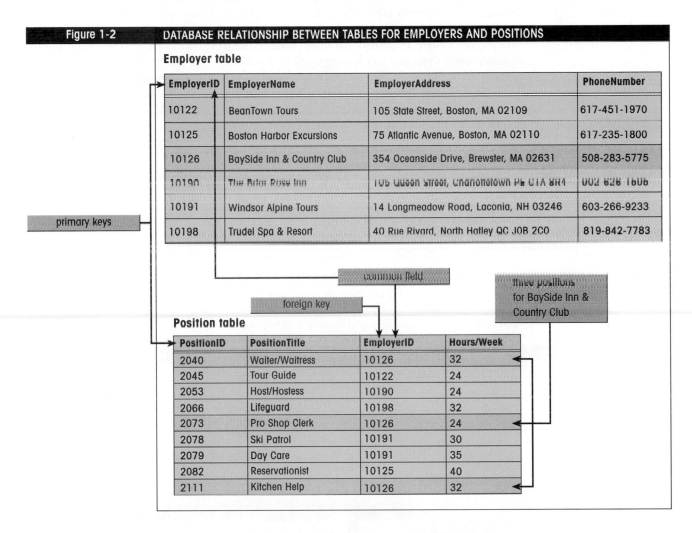

| Figure 1-2 | DATABASE RELATIONSHIP BETWEEN TABLES FOR EMPLOYERS AND POSITIONS |

Employer table

EmployerID	EmployerName	EmployerAddress	PhoneNumber
10122	BeanTown Tours	105 State Street, Boston, MA 02109	617-451-1970
10125	Boston Harbor Excursions	75 Atlantic Avenue, Boston, MA 02110	617-235-1800
10126	BaySide Inn & Country Club	354 Oceanside Drive, Brewster, MA 02631	508-283-5775
10190	The Briar Rose Inn	105 Queen Street, Charlottetown PE C1A 8R4	002 626 1606
10191	Windsor Alpine Tours	14 Longmeadow Road, Laconia, NH 03246	603-266-9233
10198	Trudel Spa & Resort	40 Rue Rivard, North Hatley QC J0B 2C0	819-842-7783

primary keys

common field

foreign key

three positions for BaySide Inn & Country Club

Position table

PositionID	PositionTitle	EmployerID	Hours/Week
2040	Waiter/Waitress	10126	32
2045	Tour Guide	10122	24
2053	Host/Hostess	10190	24
2066	Lifeguard	10198	32
2073	Pro Shop Clerk	10126	24
2078	Ski Patrol	10191	30
2079	Day Care	10191	35
2082	Reservationist	10125	40
2111	Kitchen Help	10126	32

Each EmployerID in the Employer table must be unique, so that you can distinguish one employer from another and identify the employer's specific positions available in the Position table. The EmployerID field is referred to as the primary key of the Employer table. A **primary key** is a field, or a collection of fields, whose values uniquely identify each record in a table. In the Position table, PositionID is the primary key.

When you include the primary key from one table as a field in a second table to form a relationship between the two tables, it is called a **foreign key** in the second table, as shown in Figure 1-2. For example, EmployerID is the primary key in the Employer table and a foreign key in the Position table. Although the primary key EmployerID has unique values in the Employer table, the same field as a foreign key in the Position table does not have unique values. The EmployerID value 10126, for example, appears three times in the Position table because the BaySide Inn & Country Club has three available positions. Each foreign key value, however, must match one of the field values for the primary key in the other table. In the example shown in Figure 1-2, each EmployerID value in the Position table must match an EmployerID value in the Employer table. The two tables are related, enabling users to connect the facts about employers with the facts about their employment positions.

Relational Database Management Systems

To manage its databases, a company purchases a database management system. A **database management system (DBMS)** is a software program that lets you create databases and then manipulate data in them. Most of today's database management systems, including Access, are called relational database management systems. In a **relational database management system**, data is organized as a collection of tables. As stated earlier, a relationship between two tables in a relational DBMS is formed through a common field.

A relational DBMS controls the storage of databases on disk by carrying out data creation and manipulation requests. Specifically, a relational DBMS provides the following functions, which are illustrated in Figure 1-3:

- It allows you to create database structures containing fields, tables, and table relationships.
- It lets you easily add new records, change field values in existing records, and delete records.
- It contains a built-in query language, which lets you obtain immediate answers to the questions you ask about your data.
- It contains a built-in report generator, which lets you produce professional-looking, formatted reports from your data.
- It provides protection of databases through security, control, and recovery facilities.

| Figure 1-3 | RELATIONAL DATABASE MANAGEMENT SYSTEM |

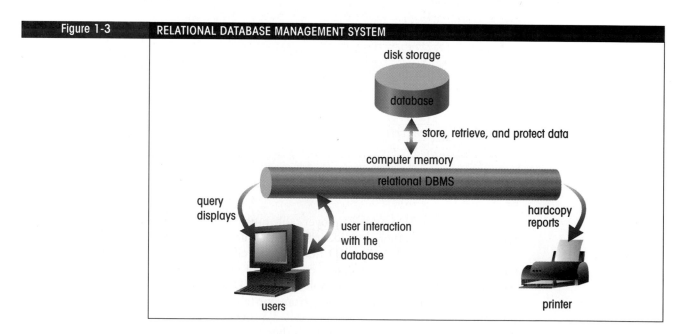

A company such as NSJI benefits from a relational DBMS because it allows users working in different departments to share the same data. More than one user can enter data into a database, and more than one user can retrieve and analyze data that was entered by others. For example, NSJI will store only one copy of the Employer table, and all employees will be able to use it to meet their specific requests for employer information.

Finally, unlike other software programs, such as spreadsheets, a DBMS can handle massive amounts of data and can easily form relationships among multiple tables. Each Access database, for example, can be up to two gigabytes in size and can contain up to 32,768 objects (tables, queries, and so on).

Opening an Existing Database

Now that you've learned some database terms and concepts, you're ready to start Access and open the Seasonal database.

> ### To start Access and open the Seasonal database:
>
> **1.** Click the **Start** button on the taskbar, point to **Programs**, and then point to **Microsoft Access**. See Figure 1-4.

| Figure 1-4 | STARTING MICROSOFT ACCESS |

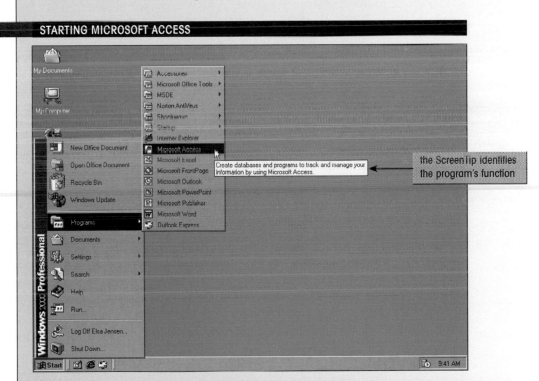

the ScreenTip identifies the program's function

> **TROUBLE?** If your screen differs slightly from the figure, don't worry. Although the figures in this tutorial were created on a computer running Windows 2000 in its default settings, the different Windows operating systems share the same basic user interface, and Microsoft Access runs equally well using Windows 98, Windows NT, or Windows 2000.
>
> **TROUBLE?** If you don't see the Microsoft Access option on the Programs menu, you might need to click the double arrow on the Programs menu to display more options. If you still cannot find the Microsoft Access option, ask your instructor or technical support person for help.

2. Click **Microsoft Access** to start Access. After a short pause, the Access copyright information appears in a message box and remains on the screen until the Access window opens. See Figure 1-5.

Figure 1-5	MICROSOFT ACCESS WINDOW

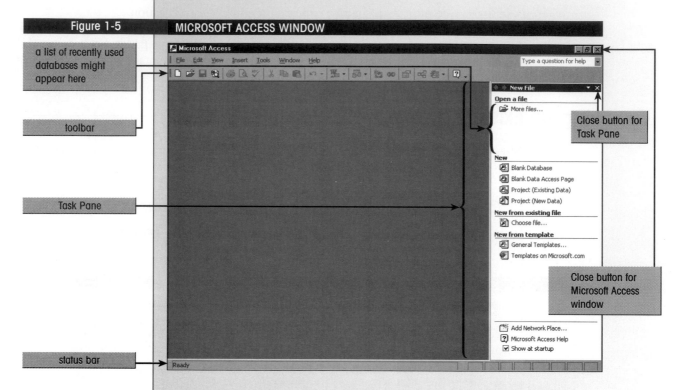

a list of recently used databases might appear here

toolbar

Close button for Task Pane

Task Pane

Close button for Microsoft Access window

status bar

When you start Access, the Access window contains a Task Pane that allows you to create a new database or to open an existing database. You can click the "Blank Database" option in the "New" section of the Task Pane to create a new database on your own, or you can click the "General Templates" option in the "New from template" section of the Task Pane to let Access guide you through the steps for creating one of the standard databases provided by Microsoft. In this case, you need to open an existing database.

To open an existing database, you can select the name of a database in the list of recently opened databases (if the list appears), or you can click the "More files" option to open a database not listed. You need to open an existing database—the Seasonal database on your Data Disk.

3. Make sure you have created your copy of the Access Data Disk, and then place your Data Disk in the appropriate disk drive.

TROUBLE? If you don't have a Data Disk, you need to get one before you can proceed. Your instructor will either give you one or ask you to make your own. (See your instructor for more information.) In either case, be sure that you have made a backup copy of your Data Disk before you begin working, so that the original Data Files will be available on the copied disk in case you need to start over because of an error or problem.

4. In the "Open a file" section of the Task Pane, click the **More files** option. The Open dialog box is displayed. See Figure 1-6.

Figure 1-6	OPEN DIALOG BOX

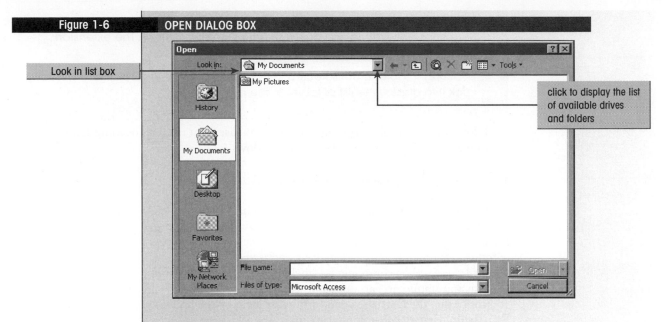

TROUBLE? The list of folders and files on your screen might be different from the list in Figure 1-6.

5. Click the **Look in** list arrow, and then click the drive that contains your Data Disk.

6. Click **Tutorial** in the list box (if necessary), and then click the **Open** button to display a list of the files in the Tutorial folder.

7. Click **Seasonal** in the list box, and then click the **Open** button. The Seasonal database opens in the Access window. See Figure 1-7.

Figure 1-7	ACCESS AND DATABASE WINDOWS

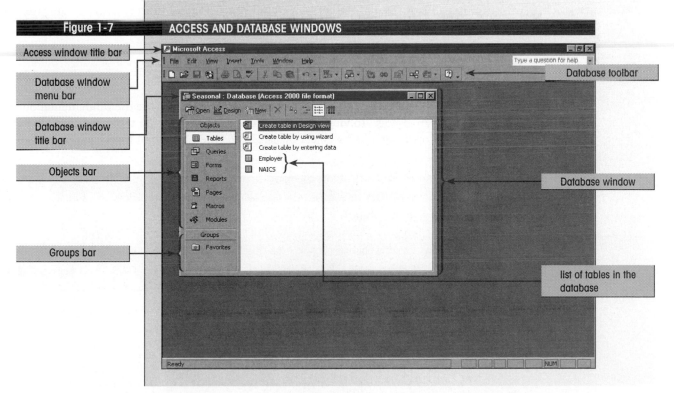

> **TROUBLE?** The filename on your screen might be Seasonal.mdb instead of Seasonal, depending on your computer's default settings. The extension ".mdb" identifies the file as a Microsoft Access database.
>
> **TROUBLE?** If Tables is not selected in the Objects bar of the Database window, click it to display the list of tables in the database.

Before you can begin working with the database, you need to become familiar with the components of the Access and Database windows.

The Access and Database Windows

The **Access window** is the program window that appears when you start the program. The **Database window** appears when you open a database; this window is the main control center for working with an open Access database. Except for the Access window title bar, all screen components now on your screen are associated with the Database window (see Figure 1-7). Most of these screen components—including the title bars, window sizing buttons, menu bar, toolbar, and status bar—are the same as the components in other Windows programs.

Notice that the Database window title bar includes the notation "(Access 2000 file format)." By default, databases that you create in Access 2002 use the Access 2000 database file format. This feature ensures that you can use and share databases originally created in Access 2002 without converting them to Access 2000, and vice versa. (You'll learn more about database file formats and converting databases later in this tutorial.)

The Database window provides a variety of options for viewing and manipulating database objects. Each item in the **Objects bar** controls one of the major object groups—such as tables, queries, forms, and reports—in an Access database. The **Groups bar** allows you to organize different types of database objects into groups, with shortcuts to those objects, so that you can work with them more easily. The Database window also provides buttons for quickly creating, opening, and managing objects, as well as shortcut options for some of these tasks.

Elsa has already created the Employer and NAICS tables in the Seasonal database. She asks you to open the Employer table and view its contents.

Opening an Access Table

As noted earlier, tables contain all the data in a database. Tables are the fundamental objects for your work in Access. To view, add, change, or delete data in a table, you first open the table. You can open any Access object by using the Open button in the Database window.

REFERENCE WINDOW	RW

Opening an Access Object
- In the Objects bar of the Database window, click the type of object you want to open.
- If necessary, scroll the object list box until the object name appears, and then click the object name.
- Click the Open button in the Database window.

You need to open the Employer table, which is one of two tables in the Seasonal database.

To open the Employer table:

1. In the Database window, click **Employer** to select it.

2. Click the **Open** button in the Database window. The Employer table opens in Datasheet view on top of the Database and Access windows. See Figure 1-8.

Figure 1-8	EMPLOYER TABLE DISPLAYED IN DATASHEET VIEW

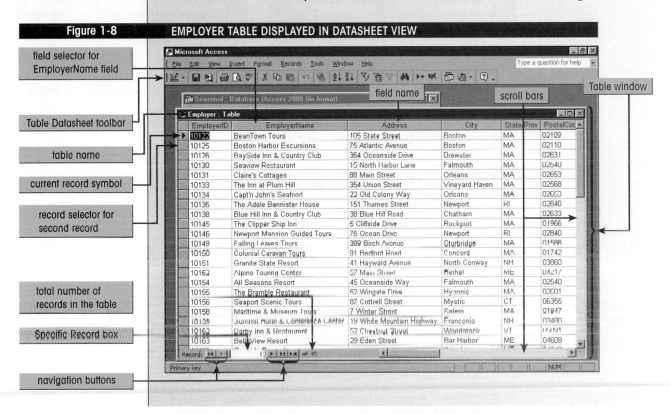

Datasheet view shows a table's contents as a **datasheet** in rows and columns, similar to a table or spreadsheet. Each row is a separate record in the table, and each column contains the field values for one field in the table. Each column is headed by a field name inside a field selector, and each row has a record selector to its left. Clicking a **field selector** or a **record selector** selects that entire column or row (respectively), which you then can manipulate. A field selector is also called a **column selector**, and a record selector is also called a **row selector**.

Navigating an Access Datasheet

When you first open a datasheet, Access selects the first field value in the first record. Notice that this field value is highlighted and that a darkened triangle symbol, called the current record symbol, appears in the record selector to the left of the first record. The **current record symbol** identifies the currently selected record. Clicking a record selector or field value in another row moves the current record symbol to that row. You can also move the pointer over the data on the screen and click one of the field values to position the insertion point.

The Employer table currently has 13 fields and 45 records. To view fields or records not currently visible in the datasheet, you can use the horizontal and vertical scroll bars shown in Figure 1-8 to navigate through the data. The **navigation buttons**, also shown in Figure 1-8, provide another way to move vertically through the records. Figure 1-9 shows which record becomes the current record when you click each navigation button. The **Specific Record box**, which appears between the two sets of navigation buttons, displays the current record number. The total number of records in the table appears to the right of the navigation buttons.

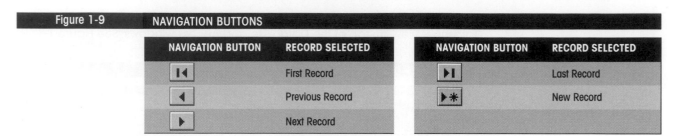

Figure 1-9	NAVIGATION BUTTONS

NAVIGATION BUTTON	RECORD SELECTED	NAVIGATION BUTTON	RECORD SELECTED
◄	First Record	►►	Last Record
◄	Previous Record	►✳	New Record
►	Next Record		

Elsa suggests that you use the various navigation techniques to move through the Employer table and become familiar with its contents.

To navigate the Employer datasheet:

1. Click the right scroll arrow in the horizontal scroll bar a few times to scroll to the right and view the remaining fields in the Employer table.

2. Drag the scroll box in the horizontal scroll bar all the way to the left to return to the previous display of the datasheet.

3. Click the **Next Record** navigation button [►]. The second record is now the current record, as indicated by the current record symbol in the second record selector. Also, notice that the second record's value for the EmployerID field is highlighted, and "2" (for record number 2) appears in the Specific Record box.

4. Click the **Last Record** navigation button [►►]. The last record in the table, record 45, is now the current record.

5. Click the **Previous Record** navigation button [◄]. Record 44 is now the current record.

6. Click the **First Record** navigation button [◄◄]. The first record is now the current record.

Saving a Database

Notice the Save button [🖫] on the Table Datasheet toolbar. Unlike the Save buttons in other Windows programs, this Save button does not save the active document (database) to your disk. Instead, you use the Save button to save the design of an Access object, such as a table, or to save datasheet format changes. Access does not have a button or option you can use to save the active database.

Access saves changes to the active database to your disk automatically, when a record is changed or added and when you close the database. If your database is stored on a disk in drive A, you should never remove the disk while the database file is open. If you remove the disk, Access will encounter problems when it tries to save the database, which might damage the database.

Now that you've viewed the Employer table, you can exit Access.

To exit Access:

1. Click the **Close** button ☒ on the Access window title bar. The Employer table and the Seasonal database close, Access closes, and you return to the Windows desktop.

Now that you've become familiar with Access and the Seasonal database, in the next session, you'll be ready to work with the data stored in the database.

Session 1.1 QUICK CHECK

1. A(n) _____ is a single characteristic of a person, place, object, event, or idea.

2. You connect the records in two separate tables through a(n) _____ that appears in both tables.

3. The _____, whose values uniquely identify each record in a table, is called a(n) _____ when it is placed in a second table to form a relationship between the two tables.

4. In a table, the rows are also called _____, and the columns are also called _____.

5. The _____ identifies the selected record in an Access table.

6. Describe two methods for navigating through a table.

SESSION 1.2

In this section, you will open an existing query and create and navigate a new query; create and navigate a form; and create, preview, and navigate a report. You will also learn how to manage databases by backing up and restoring, compacting and repairing, and converting databases.

Working with Queries

A **query** is a question you ask about the data stored in a database. In response to a query, Access displays the specific records and fields that answer your question. When you create a query, you tell Access which fields you need and what criteria Access should use to select the records. Then Access displays only the information you want, so you don't have to navigate through the entire database for the information.

Before creating a new query, you will open a query that Elsa created recently so that she could view information in the Employer table in a different way.

Opening an Existing Query

Queries that you create and save appear in the Queries list of the Database window. To see the results of a query, you simply open, or run, the query. Elsa created and saved a query named "Contacts" in the Seasonal database. This query shows all the fields from the Employer table, but in a different order. Elsa suggests that you open this query to see its results.

To open the Contacts query:

1. Insert your Data Disk into the appropriate disk drive.

2. Start Access, and then click the **More files** option in the Task Pane to display the Open dialog box.

3. Click the **Look in** list arrow, click the drive that contains your Data Disk, click **Tutorial** in the list box, and then click the **Open** button to display the list of files in the Tutorial folder.

4. Click **Seasonal** in the list box, and then click the **Open** button.

5. Click **Queries** in the Objects bar of the Database window to display the Queries list. The Queries list box contains one object—the Contacts query. See Figure 1-10.

Figure 1-10	LIST OF QUERIES IN THE SEASONAL DATABASE

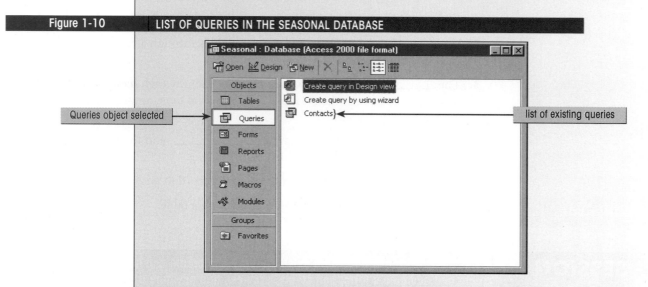

Now you will run the Contacts query by opening it.

6. Click **Contacts** to select it, and then click the **Open** button in the Database window. Access displays the results of the query in Datasheet view. See Figure 1-11.

Figure 1-11	RESULT OF RUNNING THE CONTACTS QUERY

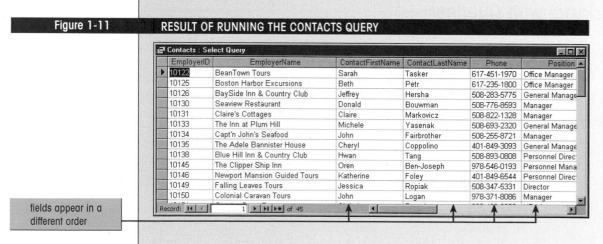

Notice that the query displays the fields from the Employer table, but in a different order. For example, the first and last names of each contact, as well as the contact's phone number, appear next to the employer name. This arrangement lets Elsa view pertinent contact information without having to scroll through the table. Rearranging the display of table data is one task you can perform with queries, so that table information appears in a different order to suit how you want to work with the information.

7. Click the **Close** button ☒ on the Query window title bar to close the Contacts query.

Even though a query can display table information in a different way, the information still exists in the table as it was originally entered. If you opened the Employer table, it would still show the fields in their original order.

Zack Ward, the director of marketing at NSJI, wants a list of all employers so that his staff can call them to check on their satisfaction with NSJI's services and recruits. He doesn't want the list to include all the fields in the Employer table (such as PostalCode and NAICSCode). To produce this list for Zack, you need to create a query using the Employer table.

Creating, Sorting, and Navigating a Query

You can design your own queries or use an Access **Query Wizard**, which guides you through the steps to create a query. The Simple Query Wizard allows you to select records and fields quickly, and it is an appropriate choice for producing the employer list Zack wants. You can choose this Wizard either by clicking the New button, which opens a dialog box from which you can choose among several different Wizards to create your query, or by double-clicking the "Create query by using wizard" option, which automatically starts the Simple Query Wizard.

To start the Simple Query Wizard:

1. Double-click **Create query by using wizard**. The first Simple Query Wizard dialog box opens. See Figure 1-12.

Figure 1-12   FIRST SIMPLE QUERY WIZARD DIALOG BOX

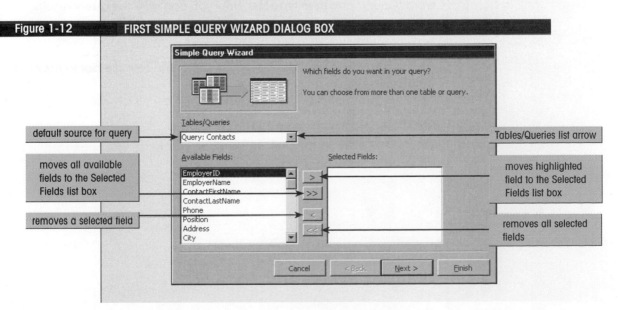

Because Contacts is the only query object currently in the Seasonal database, it is listed in the Tables/Queries box by default. You need to base the query you're creating on the Employer table.

2. Click the **Tables/Queries** list arrow, and then click **Table: Employer** to select the Employer table as the source for the new query. The Available Fields list box now lists the fields in the Employer table.

You need to select fields from the Available Fields list to include them in the query. To select fields one at a time, click a field and then click the `>` button. The selected field moves from the Available Fields list box on the left to the Selected Fields list box on the right. To select all the fields, click the `>>` button. If you change your mind or make a mistake, you can remove a field by clicking it in the Selected Fields list box and then clicking the `<` button. To remove all selected fields, click the `<<` button.

Each Wizard dialog box contains buttons on the bottom that allow you to move to the previous dialog box (Back button), move to the next dialog box (Next button), or cancel the creation process (Cancel button) and return to the Database window. You can also finish creating the object (Finish button) and accept the Wizard's defaults for the remaining options.

Zack wants his list to include data from only the following fields: EmployerName, City, State/Prov, ContactFirstName, ContactLastName, and Phone. You need to select these fields to include them in the query.

To create the query using the Simple Query Wizard:

1. Click **EmployerName** in the Available Fields list box, and then click the `>` button. The EmployerName field moves to the Selected Fields list box.

2. Repeat Step 1 for the fields **City**, **State/Prov**, **ContactFirstName**, **ContactLastName**, and **Phone**, and then click the **Next** button. The second, and final, Simple Query Wizard dialog box opens and asks you to choose a name for your query. This name will appear in the Queries list in the Database window. You'll change the suggested name (Employer Query) to "Employer List."

3. Click at the end of the highlighted name, use the Backspace key to delete the word "Query," and then type **List**. Now you can view the query results.

4. Click the **Finish** button to complete the query. Access displays the query results in Datasheet view.

5. Click the **Maximize** button 🔲 on the Query window title bar to maximize the window. See Figure 1-13.

Figure 1-13   **QUERY RESULTS**

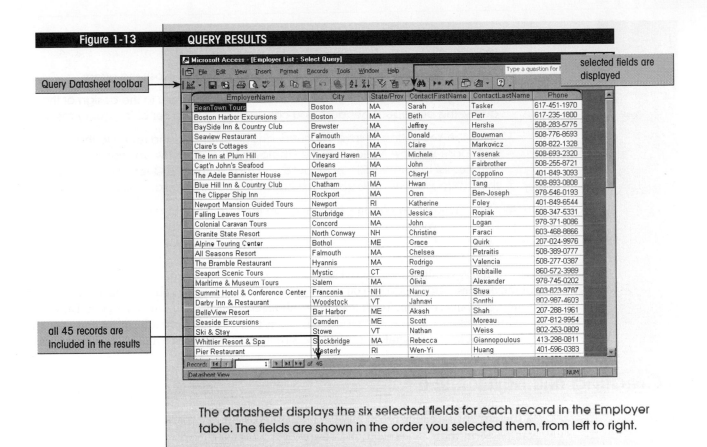

Query Datasheet toolbar

selected fields are displayed

all 45 records are included in the results

The datasheet displays the six selected fields for each record in the Employer table. The fields are shown in the order you selected them, from left to right.

The records are currently listed in order by the primary key field (EmployerID from the Employer table). This is true even though the EmployerID field is not included in the display of the query results. Zack prefers the records listed in order by state or province, so that his staff members can focus on all records for the employers in a particular state or province. To display the records in the order Zack wants, you need to sort the query results by the State/Prov field.

To sort the query results:

1. Click to position the insertion point anywhere in the State/Prov column. This establishes the State/Prov column as the current field.

2. Click the **Sort Ascending** button ⬆ on the Query Datasheet toolbar. Now the records are sorted in ascending alphabetical order by the values in the State/Prov field. All the records for Connecticut (CT) are listed first, followed by the records for Massachusetts (MA), Maine (ME), and so on.

   Notice that the navigation buttons are located at the bottom of the window. You navigate through a query datasheet in the same way that you navigate through a table datasheet.

3. Click the **Last Record** navigation button ▶❙ . The last record in the query datasheet, for the Darby Inn & Restaurant, is now the current record.

4. Click the **Previous Record** navigation button ◀ . Record 44 in the query datasheet is now the current record.

5. Click the **First Record** navigation button ◄. The first record is now the current record.

6. Click the **Close Window** button ☒ on the menu bar to close the query.

   A dialog box opens and asks if you want to save changes to the design of the query. This box opens because you changed the sort order of the query results.

7. Click the **Yes** button to save the query design changes and return to the Database window. Notice that the Employer List query now appears in the Queries list box. In addition, because you maximized the Query window, now the Database window is also maximized. You need to restore the window.

8. Click the **Restore Window** button 🗗 on the menu bar to restore the Database window.

The query results are not stored in the database; however, the query design is stored as part of the database with the name you specified. You can re-create the query results at any time by running the query again. You'll learn more about creating and running queries in Tutorial 3.

After Zack views the query results, Elsa then asks you to create a form for the Employer table so that her staff members can use the form to enter and work with data in the table easily.

Creating and Navigating a Form

A **form** is an object you use to maintain, view, and print records in a database. Although you can perform these same functions with tables and queries, forms can present data in many customized and useful ways.

In Access, you can design your own forms or use a Form Wizard to create your forms automatically. A **Form Wizard** is an Access tool that asks you a series of questions, and then creates a form based on your answers. The quickest way to create a form is to use an **AutoForm Wizard**, which places all the fields from a selected table (or query) on a form automatically, without asking you any questions, and then displays the form on the screen.

Elsa wants a form for the Employer table that will show all the fields for one record at a time, with fields listed one below another in a column. This type of form will make it easier for her staff to focus on all the data for a particular employer. You'll use the AutoForm: Columnar Wizard to create the form.

To create the form using an AutoForm Wizard:

1. Click **Forms** in the Objects bar of the Database window to display the Forms list. The Forms list box does not contain any forms yet.

2. Click the **New** button in the Database window to open the New Form dialog box. See Figure 1-14.

Figure 1-14   NEW FORM DIALOG BOX

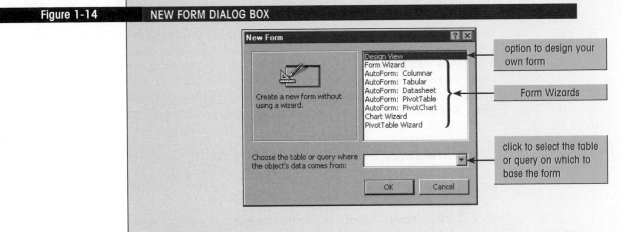

The top list box provides options for designing your own form or creating a form using one of the Form Wizards. In the bottom list box, you choose the table or query that will supply the data for the form.

3. Click **AutoForm: Columnar** to select this AutoForm Wizard.

4. Click the list arrow for choosing the table or query on which to base the form, and then click **Employer**.

5. Click the **OK** button. The AutoForm Wizard creates the form and displays it in Form view. See Figure 1-15.

Figure 1-15   FORM CREATED BY THE AUTOFORM: COLUMNAR WIZARD

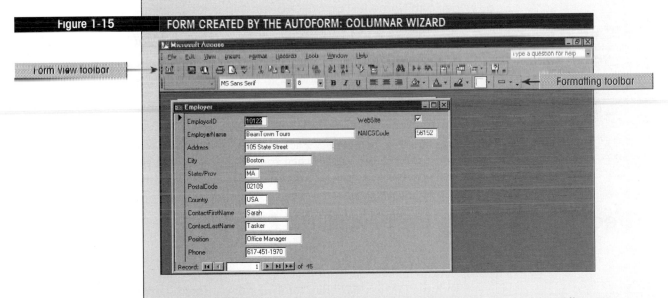

TROUBLE? The background of your form might look different from the one shown in Figure 1-15, depending on your computer's settings. If so, don't worry. You will learn how to change the form's style later in this text. For now, continue with the tutorial.

The form displays one record at a time in the Employer table. Access displays the field values for the first record in the table and selects the first field value (EmployerID). Each field name appears on a separate line (spread over two columns) and on the same line as its field value, which appears in a box. The widths of the boxes are different to accommodate the different sizes of the displayed field values; for example, compare the small box for the State/Prov field value with the larger box for the EmployerName field value. The AutoForm: Columnar Wizard automatically placed the field names and values on the form and supplied the background style.

To view and maintain data using a form, you must know how to move from field to field and from record to record. Notice that the Form window contains navigation buttons, similar to those available in Datasheet view, which you can use to display different records in the form. You'll use these now to navigate through the form; then you'll save and close the form.

To navigate, save, and close the form:

1. Click the **Next Record** navigation button ▶ . The form now displays the values for the second record in the Employer table.

2. Click the **Last Record** navigation button ▶I to move to the last record in the table. The form displays the information for record 45, Lighthouse Tours.

3. Click the **Previous Record** navigation button ◀ to move to record 44.

4. Click the **First Record** navigation button I◀ to return to the first record in the Employer table.

   Next, you'll save the form with the name "Employer Data" in the Seasonal database. Then the form will be available for later use. You'll learn more about creating and customizing forms in Tutorial 4.

5. Click the **Save** button 🖫 on the Form View toolbar. The Save As dialog box opens.

6. In the Form Name text box, click at the end of the highlighted word "Employer," press the **spacebar**, type **Data**, and then press the **Enter** key. Access saves the form as Employer Data in the Seasonal database and closes the dialog box.

7. Click the **Close** button ✕ on the Form window title bar to close the form and return to the Database window. Note that the Employer Data form is now listed in the Forms list box.

After attending a staff meeting, Zack returns with another request. He wants the same employer list you produced earlier when you created the Employer List query, but he'd like the information presented in a more readable format. You'll help Zack by creating a report.

Creating, Previewing, and Navigating a Report

A **report** is a formatted printout (or screen display) of the contents of one or more tables in a database. Although you can print data appearing in tables, queries, and forms, reports provide you with the greatest flexibility for formatting printed output. As with forms, you can design your own reports or use a Report Wizard to create reports automatically.

Zack wants a report showing the same information contained in the Employer List query that you created earlier. However, he wants the data for each employer to be grouped together, with one employer record below another, as shown in the report sketch in Figure 1-16.

Figure 1-16   SKETCH OF ZACK'S REPORT

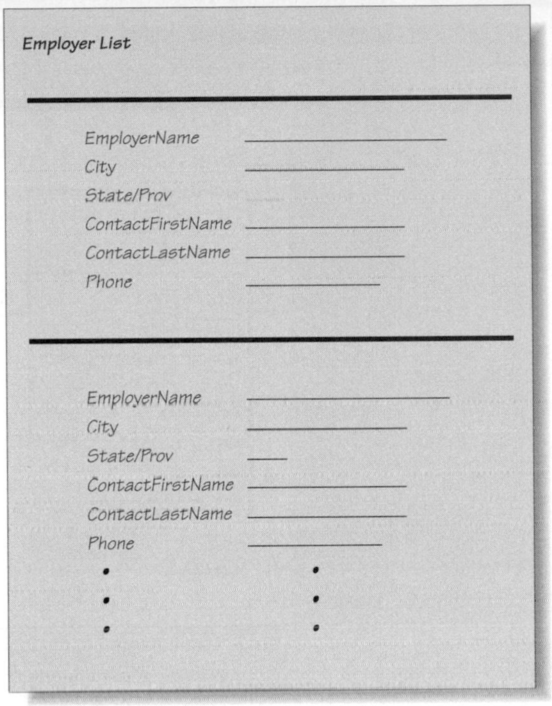

Employer List

EmployerName _____
City _____
State/Prov _____
ContactFirstName _____
ContactLastName _____
Phone _____

EmployerName _____
City _____
State/Prov ___
ContactFirstName _____
ContactLastName _____
Phone _____

To produce the report for Zack, you'll use the AutoReport: Columnar Wizard, which is similar to the AutoForm: Columnar Wizard you used earlier when creating the Employer Data form.

To create the report using the AutoReport: Columnar Wizard:

1. Click **Reports** in the Objects bar of the Database window, and then click the **New** button in the Database window to open the New Report dialog box, which is similar to the New Form dialog box you saw earlier.

2. Click **AutoReport: Columnar** to select this Wizard for creating the report.

   Because Zack wants the same data as in the Employer List query, you need to choose that query as the basis for the report.

3. Click the list arrow for choosing the table or query on which to base the report, and then click **Employer List**.

4. Click the **OK** button. The AutoReport Wizard creates the report and displays it in Print Preview, which shows exactly how the report will look when printed.

   To view the report better, you'll maximize the window and change the Zoom setting so that you can see the entire page.

5. Click the **Maximize** button ▢ on the Report window title bar, click the **Zoom** list arrow (to the right of the value 100%) on the Print Preview toolbar, and then click **Fit**. The entire first page of the report is displayed in the window. See Figure 1-17.

| Figure 1-17 | FIRST PAGE OF THE REPORT IN PRINT PREVIEW |

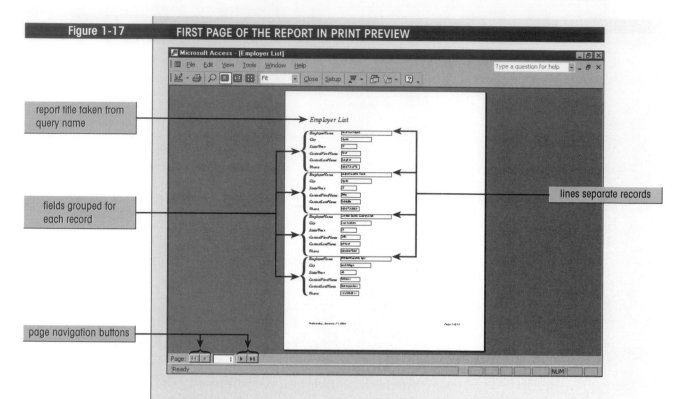

report title taken from query name

fields grouped for each record

page navigation buttons

lines separate records

TROUBLE? The fonts used in your report might look different from the ones shown in Figure 1-17, depending on your computer's settings. If so, don't worry. You will learn how to change the report's style later in this text.

Each field from the Employer List query appears on its own line, with the corresponding field value to the right and in a box. Horizontal lines separate one record from the next, visually grouping all the fields for each record. The name of the query—Employer List—appears as the report's title.

Notice that the Print Preview window provides page navigation buttons at the bottom of the window, similar to the navigation buttons you've used to move through records in a table, query, and form. You use these buttons to move through the pages of a report.

6. Click the **Next Page** navigation button [▶]. The second page of the report is displayed in Print Preview.

7. Click the **Last Page** navigation button [▶I] to move to the last page of the report. Note that this page contains the fields for only one record. Also note that the box in the middle of the navigation buttons displays the number "12"; there are 12 pages in this report.

TROUBLE? Depending on the printer you are using, your report might have more or fewer pages. If so, don't worry. Different printers format reports in different ways, sometimes affecting the total number of pages.

8. Click the **First Page** navigation button [I◀] to return to the first page of the report.

At this point, you could close the report without saving it because you can easily re-create it at any time. In general, it's best to save an object—report, form, or query—only if you anticipate using the object frequently or if it is time-consuming to create, because these objects use considerable storage space on your disk. However, Zack wants to show the report to his staff members, so he asks you to save it.

To close and save the report:

1. Click the **Close Window** button ☒ on the menu bar. *Do not* click the Close button on the Print Preview toolbar.

   TROUBLE? If you clicked the Close button on the Print Preview toolbar, you switched to Design view. Simply click the Close Window button ☒ on the menu bar, and then continue with the steps.

   A dialog box opens and asks if you want to save the changes to the report design.

2. Click the **Yes** button. The Save As dialog box opens.

3. Click to the right of the highlighted text in the Report Name text box, press the **spacebar** once, type **Report**, and then click the **OK** button. Access saves the report as "Employer List Report" and returns to the Database window.

You'll learn more about creating and customizing reports in Tutorial 4.

Managing a Database

One of the main tasks involved in working with database software is managing your databases and the data they contain. By managing your databases, you can ensure that they operate in the most efficient way, that the data they contain is secure, and that you can work with the data effectively. Some of the activities involved in database management include backing up and restoring a database, compacting and repairing a database, and converting a database for use in other versions of Access.

Backing Up and Restoring a Database

You make a backup copy of a database file to protect your database against loss or damage. You can make the backup copy using one of several methods: Windows Explorer, My Computer, Microsoft Backup, or other backup software. If you back up your database file to a floppy disk, and the file size exceeds the size of the disk, you cannot use Windows Explorer or My Computer; you must use Microsoft Backup or some other backup software so that you can copy the file over more than one disk.

To restore a backup database file, choose the same method you used to make the backup copy. For example, if you used the Microsoft Backup tool (which is one of the System Tools available from the Programs menu and Accessories submenu in Windows 2000), you must choose the Restore option for this tool to copy the database file to your database folder. If the existing database file and the backup copy have the same name, restoring the backup copy might replace the existing file. If you want to save the existing file, rename it before you restore it.

Compacting and Repairing a Database

Whenever you open an Access database and work in it, the size of the database increases. Likewise, when you delete records and when you delete or replace database objects—such as queries, forms, and reports—the space that had been occupied on the disk by the deleted or replaced records or objects does not become available for other records or objects. To make the space available, you must compact the database. **Compacting** a database rearranges the data and objects in a database to decrease its file size. Unlike making a copy of a database file, which you do to protect your database against loss or damage, you compact a database to make it smaller, thereby making more space available on your disk and speeding up the process of opening and closing the database. Figure 1-18 illustrates the compacting process; the orange colored elements in the figure represent database records and objects.

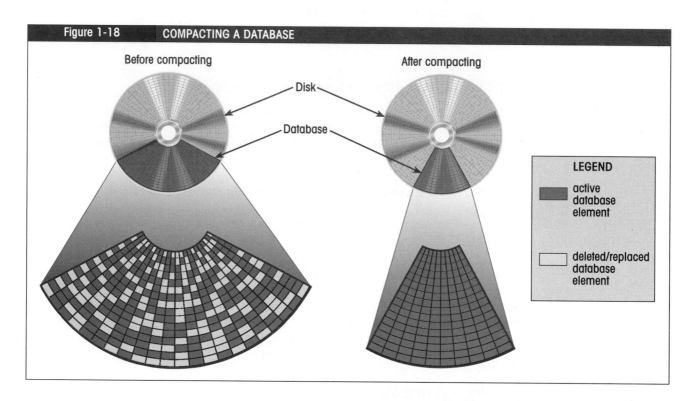

Figure 1-18   COMPACTING A DATABASE

When you compact a database, Access repairs the database at the same time. In many cases, Access detects that a database is damaged when you try to open it and gives you the option to compact and repair it at that time. If you think your database might be damaged because it is behaving unpredictably, you can use the "Compact and Repair Database" option to fix it. With your database file open, point to the Database Utilities option on the Tools menu, and then choose the Compact and Repair Database option.

Compacting a Database Automatically

Access also allows you to set an option for your database file so that every time you close the database, it will be compacted automatically.

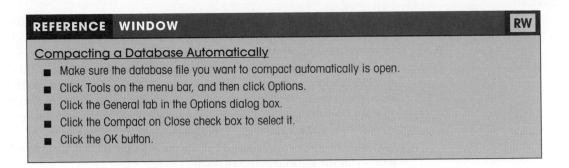

Compacting a Database Automatically

- Make sure the database file you want to compact automatically is open.
- Click Tools on the menu bar, and then click Options.
- Click the General tab in the Options dialog box.
- Click the Compact on Close check box to select it.
- Click the OK button.

You'll set the compact option now for the Seasonal database. Then, every time you subsequently close the Seasonal database, Access will compact the database file for you. After setting this option, you'll exit Access.

To set the option for compacting the Seasonal database:

1. Make sure the Seasonal Database window is open on your screen.

2. Click **Tools** on the menu bar, and then click **Options**. The Options dialog box opens.

3. Click the **General** tab in the dialog box, and then click the **Compact on Close** check box to select it. See Figure 1-19.

Figure 1-19	GENERAL TAB OF THE OPTIONS DIALOG BOX

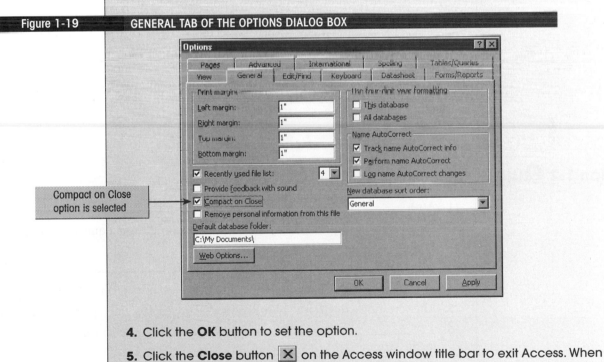

Compact on Close option is selected

4. Click the **OK** button to set the option.

5. Click the **Close** button ☒ on the Access window title bar to exit Access. When you exit, Access closes the Seasonal database file and compacts it automatically.

Converting an Access 2000 Database

Another important database management task is converting a database so that you can work with it in a different version of Access. As noted earlier in this tutorial, the default file format for databases you create in Access 2002 is Access 2000. This enables you to work with the database in either the Access 2000 or 2002 versions of the software, without having to convert it. This compatibility makes it easy for multiple users working with different versions of the software to share the same database and work more efficiently.

Sometimes, however, you might need to convert an Access 2000 database to another version. For example, if you needed to share an Access 2000 database with a colleague who worked on a laptop computer with Access 97 installed on it, you could convert the Access 2000 database to the Access 97 format. Likewise, you might want to convert an Access 2000 database to the Access 2002 file format if the database becomes very large in size. Access 2002 is enhanced so that large databases run faster in the Access 2002 file format, making it more efficient for you to work with the information contained in them.

To convert a database, follow these steps:

1. Make sure the database you want to convert is closed and the Access window is open.

2. Click Tools on the menu bar, point to Database Utilities, point to Convert Database, and then choose the format you want to convert to—To Access 97 File Format, To Access 2000 File Format, or To Access 2002 File Format.

3. In the Database to Convert From dialog box, select the name of the database you want to convert, and then click the Convert button.

4. In the Convert Database Into dialog box, enter a new name for the converted database in the File name text box, and then click the Save button.

After converting a database, you can use it in the version of Access to which you converted the file. Note, however, that when you convert to a previous file format, such as converting from the Access 2000 file format to the Access 97 file format, you might lose some of the advanced features of the newer version and you might need to make some adjustments to the converted database.

With the Employer and NAICS tables in place, Elsa can continue to build the Seasonal database and use it to store, manipulate, and retrieve important data for NSJI. In the following tutorials, you'll help Elsa complete and maintain the database, and you'll use it to meet the specific information needs of other NSJI employees.

Session 1.2 QUICK CHECK

1. A(n) _____ is a question you ask about the data stored in a database.

2. Unless you specify otherwise, the records resulting from a query are listed in order by the _____.

3. The quickest way to create a form is to use a(n) _____.

4. Describe the form created by the AutoForm: Columnar Wizard.

5. After creating a report, the AutoReport Wizard displays the report in _____.

6. _____ a database rearranges the data and objects in a database to decrease its file size.

REVIEW ASSIGNMENTS

In the Review Assignments, you'll work with the **Seasons** database, which is similar to the database you worked with in the tutorial. Complete the following:

1. Make sure your Data Disk is in the disk drive.

2. Start Access and open the **Seasons** database, which is located in the Review folder on your Data Disk.

Explore
3. Open the Microsoft Access Help window, and then display the Contents tab. Double-click the topic "Microsoft Access Help" (if necessary), and then double-click the topic "Queries," and then click "About types of queries." Read the displayed information, and then click "Select queries." Read the displayed information. In the Contents tab, double-click the topic "Forms," and then click the topic "About forms." Read the displayed information. In the Contents tab, scroll down and double-click the topic "Reports and Report Snapshots," and then click the topic "About reports." Read the displayed information. When finished reading all the topics, close the Microsoft Access Help window. Use Notepad, Word, or some other text editor to write a brief summary of what you learned.

Explore
4. Use the "Ask a Question" box to ask the following question: "How do I rename an object?" Click the topic "Rename a database object" and read the displayed information. Close the Microsoft Access Help window. Then, in the **Seasons** database, rename the **Table1** table as **Employers**.

5. Open the **Employers** table.

Explore
6. Open the Microsoft Access Help window, and then display the Index tab. Type the keyword "print" in the Type keywords text box, and then click the Search button. Click the topic "Set page setup options for printing" and then click "For a table, query, form, or report." Read the displayed information. Close the Microsoft Access Help window. Set the option for printing in landscape orientation, and then print the first page only of the **Employers** table datasheet. Close the **Employers** table.

Explore
7. Use the Simple Query Wizard to create a query that includes the City, EmployerName, ContactFirstName, ContactLastName, and Phone fields (in that order) from the **Employers** table. Name the query **Employer Phone List**. Sort the query results in ascending order by City. Set the option for printing in landscape orientation, and then print the second page only of the query results. Close and save the query.

8. Use the AutoForm: Columnar Wizard to create a form for the **Employers** table.

Explore
9. Use context-sensitive Help to find out how to move to a particular record and display it in the form. Click the What's This? command from the Help menu, and then use the Help pointer to click the number 1 in the Specific Record box at the bottom of the form. Read the displayed information. Click to close the Help box, and then use the Specific Record box to move to record 42 (for Whitney's Resort & Spa) in the **Employers** table.

Explore
10. Print the form for the current record (42). (*Hint:* Click the Selected Record(s) option in the Print dialog box to print the current record.)

11. Save the form as **Employer Info**, and then close the form.

Explore
12. Use the AutoReport: Tabular Wizard to create a report based on the **Employers** table. Print the first page of the report, and then close and save the report as **Employers**.

13. Set the option for compacting the **Seasons** database on close.

Explore ▶ 14. Convert the **Seasons** database to Access 2002 file format, saving the converted file as **Seasons2002** in the Review folder. Then convert the **Seasons** database to Access 97 file format, saving the converted file as **Seasons97** in the Review folder. Using Windows Explorer or My Computer, view the contents of your Review folder, and note the file sizes of the three versions of the **Seasons** database. Describe the results.

15. Exit Access.

CASE PROBLEMS

Case 1. Lim's Video Photography Several years ago, Youngho Lim left his position at a commercial photographer's studio and started his own business, Lim's Video Photography, located in San Francisco, California. Youngho quickly established a reputation as one of the area's best videographers, specializing in digital video photography. Youngho offers customers the option of storing edited videos on CD or DVD. His video shoots include weddings and other special events, as well as recording personal and commercial inventories for insurance purposes.

As his business continues to grow, Youngho relies on Access to keep track of information about clients, contracts, and so on. Youngho recently created an Access database named **Videos** to store data about his clients. You'll help Youngho complete and maintain the **Videos** database. Complete the following:

1. Make sure your Data Disk is in the disk drive.

2. Start Access and open the **Videos** database, which is located in the Cases folder on your Data Disk.

3. Open the **Client** table, print the table datasheet, and then close the table.

4. Use the Simple Query Wizard to create a query that includes the ClientName, Phone, and City fields (in that order) from the **Client** table. Name the query **Client List**. Print the query results, and then close the query.

Explore ▶ 5. Use the AutoForm: Tabular Wizard to create a form for the **Contract** table. Print the form, save it as **Contract Info**, and then close it.

Explore ▶ 6. Use the AutoReport: Columnar Wizard to create a report based on the **Contract** table. Maximize the Report window and change the Zoom setting to Fit. Use the Two Pages button on the Print Preview toolbar to view the first two pages of the report in Print Preview. Print the first page of the report, and then close and save it as **Contracts**.

7. Set the option for compacting the **Videos** database on close.

Explore ▶ 8. Convert the **Videos** database to Access 2002 file format, saving the converted file as **Videos2002** in the Cases folder. Then convert the **Videos** database to Access 97 file format, saving the converted file as **Videos97** in the Cases folder. Using Windows Explorer or My Computer, view the contents of your Cases folder, and note the file sizes of the three versions of the **Videos** database. Describe the results.

9. Exit Access.

Case 2. DineAtHome.course.com After working as both a concierge in a local hotel and a manager of several restaurants, Claire Picard founded DineAtHome.course.com in Naples, Florida. Her idea for this e-commerce company was a simple one: to provide people with an easy-to-use, online service that would allow them to order meals from one or more area restaurants and have the meals delivered to their homes. DineAtHome acts as a sort of broker between restaurants and customers. The participating restaurants offer everything from simple fare to gourmet feasts. Claire's staff performs a variety of services, from simply picking up and delivering the meals to providing linens and table service for more formal occasions.

Claire created the **Meals** database in Access to maintain information about participating restaurants and their menu offerings. She needs your help in working with this database. Complete the following:

1. Make sure your Data Disk is in the disk drive.

2. Start Access and open the **Meals** database, which is located in the Cases folder on your Data Disk.

Explore ▶ 3. Open the **Restaurant** table, print the table datasheet in landscape orientation, and then close the table.

4. Use the Simple Query Wizard to create a query that includes the RestaurantName, OwnerFirstName, OwnerLastName, and City fields (in that order) from the **Restaurant** table. Name the query **Owner List**.

Explore ▶ 5. Sort the query results in descending order by the City field. (*Hint*: Use a toolbar button.)

Explore ▶ 6. Use the "Ask a Question" box to ask the following question: "How do I select multiple records?" Click the topic "Select fields and records," and then click the topic "Select fields and records in a datasheet." Read the displayed information, and then close the Help window. Select the four records with "Marco Island" as the value in the City field, and then print just the selected records. (*Hint*: Use the Selected Record(s) option in the Print dialog box to print them.) Close the query, and save your changes to the design.

Explore ▶ 7. Use the AutoForm: Columnar Wizard to create a form for the **Restaurant** table. Use context-sensitive Help to find out how to move to a particular record and display it in the form. Click the What's This? command from the Help menu, and then use the Help pointer to click the number 1 in the Specific Record box at the bottom of the form. Read the displayed information. Click to close the Help box, use the Specific Record box to move to record 11 (for The Gazebo), and then print the form for the current record only. (*Hint*: Use the Selected Record(s) option in the Print dialog box to print the current record.) Save the form as **Restaurant Info**, and then close the form.

8. Use the AutoReport: Columnar Wizard to create a report based on the **Restaurant** table. Maximize the Report window and change the Zoom setting to Fit.

Explore ▶ 9. Use the View menu to view all eight pages of the report at the same time in Print Preview.

10. Print just the first page of the report, and then close and save the report as **Restaurants**.

11. Set the option for compacting the **Meals** database on close.

Explore ▶ 12. Convert the **Meals** database to Access 2002 file format, saving the converted file as **Meals2002** in the Cases folder. Then convert the **Meals** database to Access 97 file format, saving the converted file as **Meals97** in the Cases folder. Using Windows Explorer or My Computer, view the contents of your Cases folder, and note the file sizes of the three versions of the **Meals** database. Describe the results.

13. Exit Access.

Case 3. Redwood Zoo The Redwood Zoo is a small zoo located in the picturesque city of Gig Harbor, Washington, on the shores of Puget Sound. The zoo is ideally situated, with the natural beauty of the site providing the perfect backdrop for the zoo's varied exhibits. Although there are larger zoos in the greater Seattle area, the Redwood Zoo is considered to have some of the best exhibits of marine animals. The newly constructed polar bear habitat is a particular favorite among patrons.

Michael Rosenfeld is the director of fundraising activities for the Redwood Zoo. The zoo relies heavily on donations to fund both ongoing exhibits and temporary displays, especially those involving exotic animals. Michael created an Access database named **Redwood** to keep track of information about donors, their pledges, and the status of funds. You'll help Michael maintain the **Redwood** database. Complete the following:

1. Make sure your Data Disk is in the disk drive.

2. Start Access and open the **Redwood** database, which is located in the Cases folder on your Data Disk.

3. Open the **Donor** table, print the table datasheet, and then close the table.

Explore   4. Use the Simple Query Wizard to create a query that includes all the fields in the **Donor** table *except* the MI field. (*Hint*: Use the `>>` and `<` buttons to select the necessary fields.) Name the query **Donors**.

Explore   5. Sort the query results in descending order by the Class field. (*Hint*: Use a toolbar button.) Print the query results, and then close and save the query.

Explore   6. Use the AutoForm: Columnar Wizard to create a form for the **Fund** table. Use context-sensitive Help to find out how to move to a particular record and display it in the form. Click the What's This? command from the Help menu, and then use the Help pointer to click the number 1 in the Specific Record box at the bottom of the form. Read the displayed information. Click to close the Help box, use the Specific Record box to move to record 7 (Polar Bear Park), and then print the form for the current record only. (*Hint:* Use the Selected Record(s) option in the Print dialog box to print the current record.) Save the form as **Fund Info**, and then close it.

7. Use the AutoReport: Columnar Wizard to create a report based on the **Donor** table. Maximize the Report window and change the Zoom setting to Fit.

Explore   8. Use the View menu to view all seven pages of the report at the same time in Print Preview.

9. Print just the first page of the report, and then close and save the report as **Donors**.

10. Set the option for compacting the **Redwood** database on close.

Explore   11. Convert the **Redwood** database to Access 2002 file format, saving the converted file as **Redwood2002** in the Cases folder. Then convert the **Redwood** database to Access 97 file format, saving the converted file as **Redwood97** in the Cases folder. Using Windows Explorer or My Computer, view the contents of your Cases folder, and note the file sizes of the three versions of the **Redwood** database. Describe the results.

12. Exit Access.

Case 4. Mountain River Adventures   Several years ago, Connor and Siobhan Dempsey moved to Boulder, Colorado, drawn by their love of the mountains and their interest in outdoor activities of all kinds. This interest led them to form the Mountain River Adventures center. The center began as a whitewater rafting tour provider, but quickly grew to encompass other activities, such as canoeing, hiking, camping, fishing, and rock climbing.

From the beginning, Connor and Siobhan have used computers to help them manage all aspects of their business. They recently installed Access and created a database named **Trips** to store information about clients, equipment, and the types of guided tours they provide. You'll work with the **Trips** database to manage this information. Complete the following:

1. Make sure your Data Disk is in the disk drive.

2. Start Access and open the **Trips** database, which is located in the Cases folder on your Data Disk.

3. Open the **Client** table.

Explore 4. Print the **Client** table datasheet in landscape orientation, and then close the table.

5. Use the Simple Query Wizard to create a query that includes the ClientName, City, State/Prov, and Phone fields (in that order) from the **Client** table. Name the query **Client Info**.

Explore 6. Sort the query results in descending order by State/Prov. (*Hint*: Use a toolbar button.)

7. Print the query results, and then close and save the query.

Explore 8. Use the AutoForm: Columnar Wizard to create a form for the **Client** table. Use context-sensitive Help to find out how to move to a particular record and display it in the form. Click the What's This? command from the Help menu, and then use the Help pointer to click the number 1 in the Specific Record box at the bottom of the form. Read the displayed information. Click to close the Help box, use the Specific Record box to move to record 18, and then print the form for the current record only. (*Hint:* Use the Selected Record(s) option in the Print dialog box to print the current record.) Save the form as **Client Info**, and then close it.

Explore 9. Use the AutoReport: Tabular Wizard to create a report based on the **Client** table. Maximize the Report window and change the Zoom setting to Fit. Use the Two Pages button on the Print Preview toolbar to view both pages of the report in Print Preview. Print the first page of the report in landscape orientation, and then close and save the report as **Clients**.

10. Set the option for compacting the **Trips** database on close.

Explore 11. Convert the **Trips** database to Access 2002 file format, saving the converted file as **Trips2002** in the Cases folder. Then convert the **Trips** database to Access 97 file format, saving the converted file as **Trips97** in the Cases folder. Using Windows Explorer or My Computer, view the contents of your Cases folder, and note the file sizes of the three versions of the **Trips** database. Describe the results.

12. Exit Access.

Databases

LAB ASSIGNMENTS

These Lab Assignments are designed to accompany the interactive Course Lab called Databases. To start the Databases Lab, click the Start button on the Windows taskbar, point to Programs, point to Course Labs, point to New Perspectives Applications, and then click Databases. If you do not see Course Labs on your Programs menu, see your instructor or technical support person.

Databases This Databases Lab demonstrates the essential concepts of file and database management systems. You will use the Lab to search, sort, and report the data contained in a file of classic books.

1. Click the Steps button to review basic database terminology and to learn how to manipulate the classic books database. As you proceed through the Steps, answer all of the Quick Check questions that appear. After you complete the Steps, you will see a Quick Check summary report. Follow the instructions on the screen to print this report.

2. Click the Explore button. Make sure you can apply basic database terminology to describe the classic books database by answering the following questions:
   a. How many records does the file contain?
   b. How many fields does each record contain?

   c. What are the contents of the Catalog # field for the book written by Margaret Mitchell?

   d. What are the contents of the Title field for the record with Thoreau in the Author field?

   e. Which field has been used to sort the records?

3. In Explore, manipulate the database as necessary to answer the following questions:

   a. When the books are sorted by title, what is the first record in the file?

   b. Use the Search button to search for all the books in the West location. How many do you find?

   c. Use the Search button to search for all the books in the Main location that are checked in. What do you find?

4. Use the Report button to print out a report that groups the books by Status and sorts them by Title. On your report, circle the four field names. Draw a box around the summary statistics showing which books are currently checked in and which books are currently checked out.

INTERNET ASSIGNMENTS

Student Union

The purpose of the Internet Assignments is to challenge you to find information on the Internet that you can use to create effective documents. The actual assignments are updated and maintained on the Course Technology Web site. Log on to the Internet and use your Web browser to go to the Student Union on the New Perspectives Series site at **www.course.com/NewPerspectives/studentunion**. Click the Online Companions link, and then click the link for this text.

QUICK CHECK ANSWERS

Session 1.1

1. field

2. common field

3. primary key; foreign key

4. records; fields

5. current record symbol

6. Use the horizontal and vertical scroll bars to view fields or records not currently visible in the datasheet; use the navigation buttons to move vertically through the records.

Session 1.2

1. query

2. primary key

3. AutoForm Wizard

4. The form displays each field name to the left of its field value, which appears in a box; the widths of the boxes represent the size of the fields.

5. Print Preview

6. Compacting

OBJECTIVES

In this tutorial you will:

- Learn the guidelines for designing databases and setting field properties

- Create a new database

- Create and save a table

- Define fields and specify a table's primary key

- Add records to a table

- Modify the structure of a table

- Delete, move, and add fields

- Change field properties

- Copy records and import tables from another Access database

- Delete and change records

CREATING
AND MAINTAINING
A DATABASE

Creating the Northeast Database, and Creating, Modifying, and Updating the Position Table

CASE

Northeast Seasonal Jobs International (NSJI)

The Seasonal database contains two tables—the Employer table and the NAICS table. These tables store data about NSJI's employer customers and the NAICS codes for pertinent job positions, respectively. Elsa Jensen also wants to track Information about each position that is available at each employer's place of business. This information includes the position title and wage. Elsa asks you to create a third table, named Position, in which to store the position data.

Because this is your first time creating a new table, Elsa suggests that you first create a new database, named "Northeast," and then create the new Position table in this database. This will keep the Seasonal database intact. Once the Position table is completed, you then can import the Employer and NAICS tables from the Seasonal database into your new Northeast database.

Some of the position data Elsa needs is already stored in another NSJI database. After creating the Position table and adding some records to it, you'll copy the records from the other database into the Position table. Then you'll maintain the Position table by modifying it and updating it to meet Elsa's specific data requirements.

SESSION 2.1

In this session, you will learn the guidelines for designing databases and setting field properties. You'll also learn how to create a new database, create a table, define the fields for a table, select the primary key for a table, and save the table structure.

Guidelines for Designing Databases

A database management system can be a useful tool, but only if you first carefully design the database so that it meets the needs of its users. In database design, you determine the fields, tables, and relationships needed to satisfy the data and processing requirements. When you design a database, you should follow these guidelines:

- **Identify all the fields needed to produce the required information.** For example, Elsa needs information about employers, NAICS codes, and positions. Figure 2-1 shows the fields that satisfy these information requirements.

Figure 2-1	ELSA'S DATA REQUIREMENTS

EmployerID	ContactFirstName
PositionID	ContactLastName
PositionTitle	Position
EmployerName	Wage
Address	Hours/Week
City	NAICSCode
State/Prov	NAICSDesc
PostalCode	StartDate
Country	EndDate
Phone	ReferredBy
Openings	WebSite

- **Group related fields into tables.** For example, Elsa grouped the fields relating to employers into the Employer table and the fields related to NAICS codes into the NAICS table. The other fields are grouped logically into the Position table, which you will create, as shown in Figure 2-2.

Figure 2-2	ELSA'S FIELDS GROUPED INTO TABLES

Employer table	NAICS table	Position table
EmployerID	NAICSCode	PositionID
EmployerName	NAICSDesc	PositionTitle
Address		Wage
City		Hours/Week
State/Prov		Openings
PostalCode		ReferredBy
Country		StartDate
ContactFirstName		EndDate
ContactLastName		
Position		
Phone		
WebSite		

■ **Determine each table's primary key.** Recall that a primary key uniquely identifies each record in a table. Although a primary key is not mandatory in Access, it's usually a good idea to include one in each table. Without a primary key, selecting the exact record that you want can be a problem. For some tables, one of the fields, such as a Social Security or credit card number, naturally serves the function of a primary key. For other tables, two or more fields might be needed to function as the primary key. In these cases, the primary key is referred to as a **composite key**. For example, a school grade table would use a combination of student number and course code to serve as the primary key. For a third category of tables, no single field or combination of fields can uniquely identify a record in a table. In these cases, you need to add a field whose sole purpose is to serve as the table's primary key.

For Elsa's tables, EmployerID is the primary key for the Employer table, NAICSCode is the primary key for the NAICS table, and PositionID will be the primary key for the Position table.

■ **Include a common field in related tables.** You use the common field to connect one table logically with another table. For example, Elsa's Employer and Position tables will include the EmployerID field as a common field. Recall that when you include the primary key from one table as a field in a second table to form a relationship, the field is called a foreign key in the second table; therefore, the EmployerID field will be a foreign key in the Position table. With this common field, Elsa can find all positions available at a particular employer; she can use the EmployerID value for an employer and search the Position table for all records with that EmployerID value. Likewise, she can determine which employer has a particular position available by searching the Employer table to find the one record with the same EmployerID value as the corresponding value in the Position table.

■ **Avoid data redundancy.** Data redundancy occurs when you store the same data in more than one place. With the exception of common fields to connect tables, you should avoid redundancy because it wastes storage space and can cause inconsistencies, if, for instance, you type a field value one way in one table and a different way in the same table or in a second table. Figure 2-3, which contains portions of potential data to be stored in the Employer and Position tables, shows an example of incorrect database design that has data redundancy in the Position table; the EmployerName field is redundant, and one value was entered incorrectly, in three different ways.

Figure 2-3   INCORRECT DATABASE DESIGN WITH DATA REDUNDANCY

Employer table

EmployerID	EmployerName	Address	Phone
10122	BeanTown Tours	105 State Street, Boston, MA 02109	617-451-1970
10125	Boston Harbor Excursions	75 Atlantic Avenue, Boston, MA 02110	617-235-1800
10126	BaySide Inn & Country Club	354 Oceanside Drive, Brewster, MA 02631	508-283-5775
10190	The Briar Rose Inn	105 Queen Street, Charlottetown PE C1A 8R4	902-626-1595
10191	Windsor Alpine Tours	14 Longmeadow Road, Laconia, NH 03246	603-266-9233
10198	Trudel Spa & Resort	40 Rue Rivard, North Hatley QC J0B 2C0	819-842-7783

data redundancy

Position table

PositionID	EmployerID	EmployerName	PositionTitle	Hours/Week
2040	10126	DaySide Inn & Country Club	Waiter/Waitress	32
2045	10122	BeanTown Tours	Tour Guide	24
2053	10190	The Briar Rose Inn	Host/Hostess	24
2066	10198	Trudel Spa & Resort	Lifeguard	32
2073	10126	Baside Inn & Country Club	Pro Shop Clerk	24
2078	10191	Windsor Alpine Tours	Ski Patrol	30
2079	10191	Windsor Alpine Tours	Day Care	35
2082	10125	Boston Harbor Excursions	Reservationist	40
2111	10126	BaySide Inn Club	Kitchen Help	32

inconsistent data

■ **Determine the properties of each field.** You need to identify the **properties**, or characteristics, of each field so that the DBMS knows how to store, display, and process the field values. These properties include the field's name, maximum number of characters or digits, description, valid values, and other field characteristics. You will learn more about field properties later in this tutorial.

The Position table you need to create will contain the fields shown in Figure 2-2, plus the EmployerID field as a foreign key. Before you create the new Northeast database and the Position table, you first need to learn some guidelines for setting field properties.

Guidelines for Setting Field Properties

As just noted, the last step of database design is to determine which values to assign to the properties, such as the name and data type, of each field. When you select or enter a value for a property, you **set** the property. Access has rules for naming fields, choosing data types, and setting other properties for fields.

Naming Fields and Objects

You must name each field, table, and other object in an Access database. Access then stores these items in the database, using the names you supply. It's best to choose a field or object name that describes the purpose or contents of the field or object, so that later you can easily remember what the name represents. For example, the three tables in the Northeast database will be named Employer, NAICS, and Position, because these names suggest their contents.

The following rules apply to naming fields and objects:

- A name can be up to 64 characters long.
- A name can contain letters, numbers, spaces, and special characters, except for a period (.), exclamation mark (!), accent grave (`), and square brackets ([ ]).
- A name cannot start with a space.
- A table or query name must be unique within a database. A field name must be unique within a table, but it can be used again in another table.

In addition, experienced users of databases follow these conventions for naming fields and objects:

- Capitalize the first letter of each word in the name.
- Avoid extremely long names because they are difficult to remember and reference.
- Use standard abbreviations, such as Num for Number, Amt for Amount, and Qty for Quantity.
- Do not use spaces in field names because these names will appear in column headings on datasheets and on labels in forms and reports. By not using spaces, you'll be able to show more fields in these objects at one time.

Assigning Field Data Types

You must assign a data type for each field. The **data type** determines what field values you can enter for the field and what other properties the field will have. For example, the Position table will include a StartDate field, which will store date values, so you will assign the date/time data type to this field. Then Access will allow you to enter and manipulate only dates or times as values in the StartDate field.

Figure 2-4 lists the 10 data types available in Access, describes the field values allowed for each data type, explains when you should use each data type, and indicates the field size of each data type.

Figure 2-4	DATA TYPES FOR FIELDS	
DATA TYPE	**DESCRIPTION**	**FIELD SIZE**
Text	Allows field values containing letters, digits, spaces, and special characters. Use for names, addresses, descriptions, and fields containing digits that are not used in calculations.	0 to 255 characters; 50 characters default
Memo	Allows field values containing letters, digits, spaces, and special characters. Use for long comments and explanations.	1 to 65,535 characters; exact size is determined by entry
Number	Allows positive and negative numbers as field values. Numbers can contain digits, a decimal point, commas, a plus sign, and a minus sign. Use for fields that you will use in calculations, except calculations involving money.	1 to 15 digits
Date/Time	Allows field values containing valid dates and times from January 1, 100 to December 31, 9999. Dates can be entered in mm/dd/yy (month, day, year) format, several other date formats, or a variety of time formats, such as 10:35 PM. You can perform calculations on dates and times, and you can sort them. For example, you can determine the number of days between two dates.	8 bytes
Currency	Allows field values similar to those for the number data type. Unlike calculations with number data type decimal values, calculations performed using the currency data type are not subject to round-off error.	Accurate to 15 digits on the left side of the decimal separator and to 4 digits on the right side

Figure 2-4	DATA TYPES FOR FIELDS, CONTINUED	
DATA TYPE	**DESCRIPTION**	**FIELD SIZE**
AutoNumber	Consists of integers with values controlled by Access. Access automatically inserts a value in the field as each new record is created. You can specify sequential numbering or random numbering, which guarantees a unique field value, so that such a field can serve as a table's primary key.	9 digits
Yes/No	Limits field values to yes and no, on and off, or true and false. Use for fields that indicate the presence or absence of a condition, such as whether an order has been filled or whether an employee is eligible for the company dental plan.	1 character
OLE Object	Allows field values that are created in other programs as objects, such as photographs, video images, graphics, drawings, sound recordings, voice-mail messages, spreadsheets, and word-processing documents. These objects can be linked or embedded.	1 gigabyte maximum; exact size depends on object size
Hyperlink	Consists of text used as a hyperlink address. A hyperlink address can have up to three parts: the text that appears in a field or control; the path to a file or page; and a location within the file or page. Hyperlinks help you to connect your application easily to the Internet or an intranet.	Up to 64,000 characters total for the three parts of a hyperlink data type
Lookup Wizard	Creates a field that lets you look up a value in another table or in a predefined list of values.	Same size as the primary key field used to perform the lookup

Setting Field Sizes

The **Field Size** property defines a field value's maximum storage size for text, number, and AutoNumber fields only. The other data types have no Field Size property because their storage size is either a fixed, predetermined amount or is determined automatically by the field value itself, as shown in Figure 2-4. A text field has a default field size of 50 characters; you can also set its field size by entering a number from 0 to 255. For example, the PositionTitle and ReferredBy fields in the Position table will be text fields with a size of 30 each.

When you use the number data type to define a field, you should set the field's Field Size property based on the largest value that you expect to store in that field. Access processes smaller data sizes faster using less memory, so you can optimize your database's performance and its storage space by selecting the correct field size for each field. For example, it would be wasteful to use the Long Integer setting when defining a field that will store only whole numbers ranging from 0 to 255, because the Long Integer setting will use four bytes of storage space. A better choice would be the Byte setting, which uses one byte of storage space to store the same values. Field Size property settings for number fields are as follows:

- **Byte:** Stores whole numbers (numbers with no fractions) from 0 to 255 in one byte
- **Integer:** Stores whole numbers from −32,768 to 32,767 in two bytes
- **Long Integer** (default): Stores whole numbers from −2,147,483,648 to 2,147,483,647 in four bytes
- **Single:** Stores positive and negative numbers to precisely seven decimal places and uses four bytes
- **Double:** Stores positive and negative numbers to precisely 15 decimal places and uses eight bytes
- **Replication ID:** Establishes a unique identifier for replication of tables, records, and other objects and uses 16 bytes
- **Decimal:** Stores positive and negative numbers to precisely 28 decimal places and uses 12 bytes

Elsa documented the design for the new Position table by listing each field's name, data type, size (if applicable), and description, as shown in Figure 2-5. Note that Elsa assigned the text data type to the PositionID, PositionTitle, EmployerID, and ReferredBy fields; the currency data type to the Wage field; the number data type to the Hours/Week and Openings fields; and the date/time data type to the StartDate and EndDate fields.

Figure 2-5	DESIGN FOR THE POSITION TABLE			
Field Name	Data Type	Field Size	Description
PositionID	Text	4	Primary key
PositionTitle	Text	30	
EmployerID	Text	5	Foreign key
Wage	Currency		Rate per hour
Hours/Week	Number	Integer	Work hours per week
Openings	Number	Integer	Number of openings
ReferredBy	Text	30	
StartDate	Date/Time		Month and day
EndDate	Date/Time		Month and day

With Elsa's design in place, you're ready to create the new Northeast database and the Position table.

Creating a New Database

Access provides two ways for you to create a new database: using a Database Wizard or creating a blank database. When you use a Wizard, the Wizard guides you through the database creation process and provides the necessary tables, forms, and reports for the type of database you choose — all in one operation. Using a Database Wizard is an easy way to start creating a database, but only if your data requirements closely match one of the supplied templates. When you choose to create a blank database, you need to add all the tables, forms, reports, and other objects after you create the database file. Creating a blank database provides the most flexibility, allowing you to define objects in the way that you want, but it does require that you define each object separately. Whichever method you choose, you can always modify or add to your database after you create it.

The following steps outline the process for creating a new database using a Database Wizard:

1. If necessary, click the New button on the Database toolbar to display the Task Pane.

2. In the "New from template" section of the Task Pane, click General Templates. The Templates dialog box opens.

3. Click the Databases tab, and then choose the Database Wizard that most closely matches the type of database you want to create. Click the OK button.

4. In the File New Database dialog box, choose the location in which to save the new database, specify its name, and then click the Create button.

5. Complete each of the Wizard dialog boxes, clicking the Next button to move through them after making your selections.

6. Click the Finish button when you have completed all the Wizard dialog boxes.

None of the Database Wizards matches the requirements of the new Northeast database, so you'll use the Blank Database option to create it.

To create the Northeast database:

1. Place your Data Disk in the appropriate disk drive, and then start Access.

2. In the New section of the Task Pane, click **Blank Database**. The File New Database dialog box opens. This dialog box is similar to the Open dialog box.

3. Click the **Save in** list arrow, and then click the drive that contains your Data Disk.

4. Click **Tutorial** in the list box, and then click the **Open** button.

5. In the File name text box, double-click the text **db1** to select it, and then type **Northeast**.

   TROUBLE? Your File name text box might contain an entry other than "db1." Just select whatever text is in this text box, and continue with the steps.

6. Click the **Create** button. Access creates the Northeast database in the Tutorial folder on your Data Disk, and then displays the Database window for the new database with the Tables object selected.

Now you can create the Position table in the Northeast database.

Creating a Table

Creating a table consists of naming the fields and defining the properties for the fields, specifying a primary key (and a foreign key, if applicable) for the table, and then saving the table structure. You will use Elsa's design (Figure 2-5) as a guide for creating the Position table in the Northeast database.

To begin creating the Position table:

1. Click the **New** button in the Database window. The New Table dialog box opens. See Figure 2-6.

| Figure 2-6 | NEW TABLE DIALOG BOX |

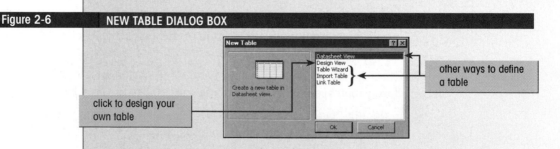

TROUBLE? If the Task Pane opens and displays "New File" at the top, you clicked the New button on the Database toolbar instead of the New button in the Database window. Click the Close button to close the Task Pane, and then repeat Step 1.

In Access, you can create a table from entered data (Datasheet View), define your own table (Design View), use a Wizard to automate the table creation process (Table Wizard), or use a Wizard to import or link data from another database or other data source (Import Table or Link Table). For the Position table, you will define your own table.

2. Click **Design View** in the list box, and then click the **OK** button. The Table window opens in Design view. (Note that you can also double-click the "Create table in Design view" option in the Database window to open the Table window in Design view.) See Figure 2-7.

Figure 2-7	TABLE WINDOW IN DESIGN VIEW

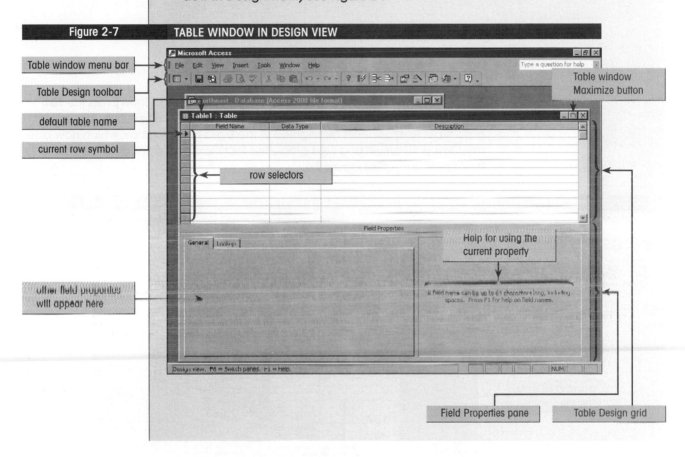

You use Design view to define or modify a table structure or the properties of the fields in a table. If you create a table without using a Wizard, you enter the fields and their properties for your table directly in the Table window in Design view.

Defining Fields

Initially, the default table name, Table1, appears on the Table window title bar, the current row symbol is positioned in the first row selector of the Table Design grid, and the insertion point is located in the first row's Field Name box. The purpose or characteristics of the current property (Field Name, in this case) appear in the right side of the Field Properties pane. You can display more complete information about the current property by pressing the F1 key.

You enter values for the Field Name, Data Type, and Description field properties in the Table Design grid. You select values for all other field properties, most of which are optional, in the Field Properties pane. These other properties will appear when you move to the first row's Data Type text box.

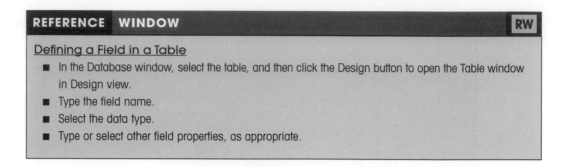

REFERENCE WINDOW   RW

Defining a Field in a Table

- In the Database window, select the table, and then click the Design button to open the Table window in Design view.
- Type the field name.
- Select the data type.
- Type or select other field properties, as appropriate.

The first field you need to define is PositionID.

To define the PositionID field:

1. Type **PositionID** in the first row's Field Name text box, and then press the **Tab** key (or press the **Enter** key) to advance to the Data Type text box. The default data type, Text, appears highlighted in the Data Type text box, which now also contains a list arrow, and field properties for a text field appear in the Field Properties pane. See Figure 2-8.

Figure 2-8	TABLE WINDOW AFTER ENTERING THE FIRST FIELD NAME

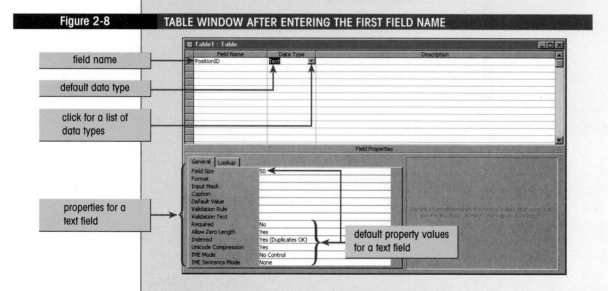

Notice that the right side of the Field Properties pane now provides an explanation for the current property, Data Type.

TROUBLE? If you make a typing error, you can correct it by clicking the mouse to position the insertion point, and then using either the Backspace key to delete characters to the left of the insertion point or the Delete key to delete characters to the right of the insertion point. Then type the correct text.

Because the PositionID numbers will not be used in calculations, you will assign the text data type (as opposed to the number data type) to the PositionID field.

2. Press the **Tab** key to accept Text as the data type and to advance to the Description text box.

Next you'll enter the Description property value as "Primary key." You can use the Description property to enter an optional description for a field to explain its purpose or usage. A field's Description property can be up to 255 characters long, and its value appears on the status bar when you view the table datasheet.

3. Type **Primary key** in the Description text box.

Notice the Field Size property for the text field. The default setting of "50" is displayed. You need to change this number to "4" because all PositionID values at NSJI contain only 4 digits. (Refer to the Access Help system for a complete description of all the properties available for the different data types.)

4. Double-click the number **50** in the Field Size property box to select it, and then type **4**. The definition of the first field is completed. See Figure 2-9.

Figure 2-9	PositionID FIELD DEFINED

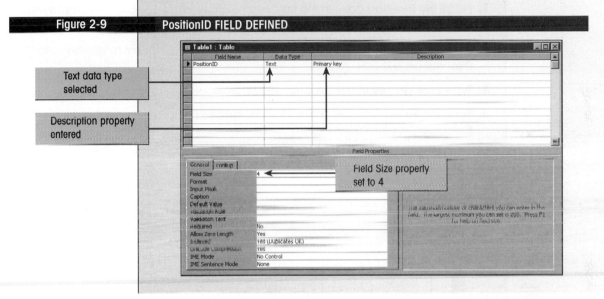

Elsa's Position table design shows PositionTitle as the second field. You will define PositionTitle as a text field with a Field Size of 30, which is a sufficient length for any title values that will be entered.

To define the PositionTitle field:

1. Place the insertion point in the second row's Field Name text box, type **PositionTitle** in the text box, and then press the **Tab** key to advance to the Data Type text box.

2. Press the **Tab** key to accept Text as the field's data type.

According to Elsa's design (Figure 2-5), you do not need to enter a description for this field. If you've assigned a descriptive field name and the field does not fulfill a special function (such as primary key), you usually do not enter a value for the optional Description property. PositionTitle is a field that does not require a value for its Description property.

Next, you'll change the Field Size property to 30. Note that when defining the fields in a table, you can move between the Table Design grid and the Field Properties pane of the Table window by pressing the F6 key.

3. Press the **F6** key to move to the Field Properties pane. The current entry for the Field Size property, 50, is highlighted.

4. Type **30** to set the Field Size property. You have completed the definition of the second field.

The third field in the Position table is the EmployerID field. Recall that this field will serve as the foreign key in the Position table, allowing you to relate data from the Position table to data in the Employer table. The field must be defined in the same way in both tables—that is, a text field with a field size of 5.

To define the EmployerID field:

1. Place the insertion point in the third row's Field Name text box, type **EmployerID** in the text box, and then press the **Tab** key to advance to the Data Type text box.

2. Press the **Tab** key to accept Text as the field's data type and to advance to the Description text box.

3. Type **Foreign key** in the Description text box.

4. Press the **F6** key to move to the Field Properties pane. The current entry for the Field Size property, 50, is highlighted.

5. Type **5** to set the Field Size property. You have completed the definition of the third field. See Figure 2-10.

Figure 2-10	TABLE WINDOW AFTER DEFINING THE FIRST THREE FIELDS

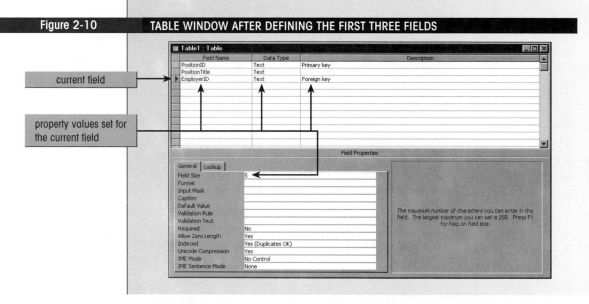

The fourth field is the Wage field, which will display values in the currency format.

To define the Wage field:

1. Place the insertion point in the fourth row's Field Name text box, type **Wage** in the text box, and then press the **Tab** key to advance to the Data Type text box.

2. Click the **Data Type** list arrow, click **Currency** in the list box, and then press the **Tab** key to advance to the Description text box.

3. Type **Rate per hour** in the Description text box.

   Elsa wants the Wage field values to be displayed with two decimal places, and she does not want any value to be displayed by default for new records. So, you need to set the Decimal Places and Default Value properties accordingly.

4. Click the **Decimal Places** text box to position the insertion point there. A list arrow appears on the right side of the Decimal Places text box.

   When you position the insertion point or select text in many Access text boxes, Access displays a list arrow, which you can click to display a list box with options. You can display the list arrow and the list box simultaneously if you click the text box near its right side.

5. Click the **Decimal Places** list arrow, and then click **2** in the list box to specify two decimal places for the Wage field values.

   Next, notice the Default Value property, which specifies the value that will be automatically entered into the field when you add a new record. Currently this property has a setting of 0. Elsa wants the Wage field to be empty (that is, to contain *no* default value) when a new record is added. Therefore, you need to change the Default Value property to the setting "Null." Setting the Default Value property to "Null" tells Access to display no value in the Wage field, by default.

6. Select **0** in the Default Value text box either by dragging the pointer or double-clicking the mouse, and then type **Null**.

The next two fields in the Position table—Hours/Week and Openings—are number fields with a field size of Integer. Also, for each of these fields, Elsa wants the values displayed with no decimal places, and she does not want a default value displayed for the fields when new records are added. You'll define these two fields next.

To define the Hours/Week and Openings fields:

1. Position the insertion point in the fifth row's Field Name text box, type **Hours/Week** in the text box, and then press the **Tab** key to advance to the Data Type text box.

2. Click the **Data Type** list arrow, click **Number** in the list box, and then press the **Tab** key to advance to the Description text box.

3. Type **Work hours per week** in the Description text box.

4. Click the right side of the **Field Size** text box, and then click **Integer** to choose this setting. Recall that the Integer field size stores whole numbers in two bytes.

5. Click the right side of the **Decimal Places** text box, and then click **0** to specify no decimal places.

6. Select the value **0** in the Default Value text box, and then type **Null**.

7. Repeat Steps 1 through 6 to define the **Openings** field as the sixth field in the Position table. For the Description, enter the text **Number of openings**.

According to Elsa's design (Figure 2-5), the final three fields to be defined in the Position table are ReferredBy, a text field, and StartDate and EndDate, both date/time fields. You'll define these three fields next.

To define the ReferredBy, StartDate, and EndDate fields:

1. Position the insertion point in the seventh row's Field Name text box, type **ReferredBy** in the text box, press the **Tab** key to advance to the Data Type text box, and then press the **Tab** key again to accept the default Text data type.

2. Change the default Field Size of 50 to **30** for the ReferredBy field.

3. Position the insertion point in the eighth row's Field Name text box, type **StartDate**, and then press the **Tab** key to advance to the Data Type text box.

4. Click the **Data Type** list arrow, click **Date/Time** to select this type, press the **Tab** key, and then type **Month and day** in the Description text box.

   Elsa wants the values in the StartDate field to be displayed in a format showing only the month and day, as in the following example: 03/11. You use the Format property to control the display of a field value.

5. In the Field Properties pane, click the right side of the **Format** text box to display the list of predefined formats. As noted in the right side of the Field Properties pane, you can either choose a predefined format or enter a custom format.

   TROUBLE? If you see a list arrow instead of a list of predefined formats, click the list arrow to display the list.

   None of the predefined formats matches the layout Elsa wants for the StartDate values. Therefore, you need to create a custom date format. Figure 2-11 shows some of the symbols available for custom date and time formats. (A complete description of all the custom formats is available in Help.)

Figure 2-11	SYMBOLS FOR SOME CUSTOM DATE FORMATS

SYMBOL	DESCRIPTION
/	date separator
d	day of the month in one or two numeric digits, as needed (1 to 31)
dd	day of the month in two numeric digits (01 to 31)
ddd	first three letters of the weekday (Sun to Sat)
dddd	full name of the weekday (Sunday to Saturday)
w	day of the week (1 to 7)
ww	week of the year (1 to 53)
m	month of the year in one or two numeric digits, as needed (1 to 12)
mm	month of the year in two numeric digits (01 to 12)
mmm	first three letters of the month (Jan to Dec)
mmmm	full name of the month (January to December)
yy	last two digits of the year (01 to 99)
yyyy	full year (0100 to 9999)

Elsa wants the dates to be displayed with a two-digit month (mm) and a two-digit day (dd). You'll enter this custom format now.

6. Click the **Format** list arrow to close the list of predefined formats, and then type **mm/dd** in the Format text box. See Figure 2-12.

Figure 2-12   SPECIFYING THE CUSTOM DATE FORMAT

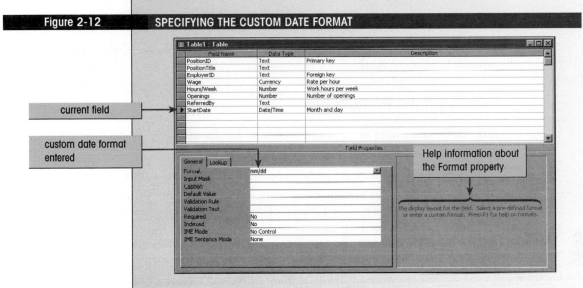

current field

custom date format entered

Help information about the Format property

Next, you'll define the ninth and final field, EndDate. This field will have the same definition and properties as the StartDate field.

7. Place the insertion point in the ninth row's Field Name text box, type **EndDate**, and then press the **Tab** key to advance to the Data Type text box.

You can select a value from the Data Type list box as you did for the StartDate field. Alternately, you can type the property value in the text box or type just the first character of the property value.

8. Type **d**. The value in the ninth row's Data Type text box changes to "date/Time," with the letters "ate/Time" highlighted. See Figure 2-13.

Figure 2-13   SELECTING A VALUE FOR THE DATA TYPE PROPERTY

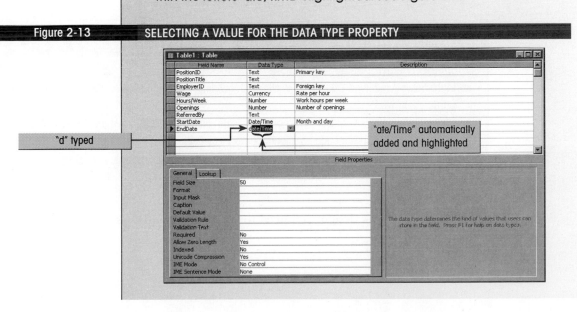

"d" typed

"ate/Time" automatically added and highlighted

9. Press the **Tab** key to advance to the Description text box, and then type **Month and day**. Note that Access changes the value for the Data Type property to Date/Time.

10. In the Format text box, type **mm/dd** to specify the custom date format for the EndDate field.

You've finished defining the fields for the Position table. Next, you need to specify the primary key for the table.

Specifying the Primary Key

Although Access does not require a table to have a primary key, including a primary key offers several advantages:

- A primary key uniquely identifies each record in a table.
- Access does not allow duplicate values in the primary key field. If a record already exists with a PositionID value of 1320, for example, Access prevents you from adding another record with this same value in the PositionID field. Preventing duplicate values ensures the uniqueness of the primary key field.
- When a primary key has been specified, Access forces you to enter a value for the primary key field in every record in the table. This is known as **entity integrity**. If you do not enter a value for a field, you have actually given the field what is known as a **null value**. You cannot give a null value to the primary key field because entity integrity prevents Access from accepting and processing that record.
- Access stores records on disk in the same order as you enter them but displays them in order by the field values of the primary key. If you enter records in no specific order, you are ensured that you will later be able to work with them in a more meaningful, primary key sequence.
- Access responds faster to your requests for specific records based on the primary key.

REFERENCE WINDOW   **RW**

Specifying a Primary Key for a Table

- In the Table window in Design view, click the row selector for the field you've chosen to be the primary key.
- If the primary key will consist of two or more fields, press and hold down the Ctrl key, and then click the row selector for each additional primary key field.
- Click the Primary Key button on the Table Design toolbar.

According to Elsa's design, you need to specify PositionID as the primary key for the Position table.

To specify PositionID as the primary key:

1. Position the pointer on the row selector for the PositionID field until the pointer changes to a ➡ shape. See Figure 2-14.

Figure 2-14	SPECIFYING PositionID AS THE PRIMARY KEY

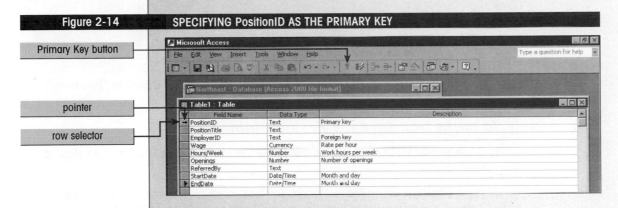

2. Click the mouse button. The entire first row of the Table Design grid is highlighted.

3. Click the **Primary Key** button 🔑 on the Table Design toolbar, and then click a row other than the first to deselect the first row. A key symbol appears in the row selector for the first row, indicating that the PositionID field is the table's primary key. See Figure 2-15.

Figure 2-15	PositionID SELECTED AS THE PRIMARY KEY

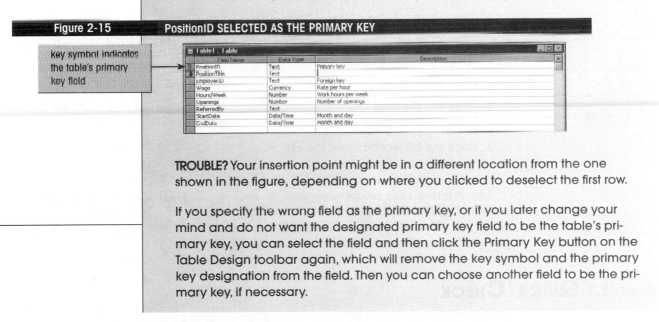

TROUBLE? Your insertion point might be in a different location from the one shown in the figure, depending on where you clicked to deselect the first row.

If you specify the wrong field as the primary key, or if you later change your mind and do not want the designated primary key field to be the table's primary key, you can select the field and then click the Primary Key button on the Table Design toolbar again, which will remove the key symbol and the primary key designation from the field. Then you can choose another field to be the primary key, if necessary.

You've defined the fields for the Position table and specified its primary key, so you can now save the table structure.

Saving the Table Structure

The last step in creating a table is to name the table and save the table's structure on disk. Once the table is saved, you can use it to enter data in the table.

> ### REFERENCE WINDOW   RW
>
> Saving a Table Structure
> - Click the Save button on the Table Design toolbar.
> - Type the name of the table in the Table Name text box of the Save As dialog box.
> - Click the OK button (or press the Enter key).

According to Elsa's plan, you need to save the table you've defined as "Position."

> ### To name and save the Position table:
>
> 1. Click the **Save** button 🖫 on the Table Design toolbar. The Save As dialog box opens.
>
> 2. Type **Position** in the Table Name text box, and then press the **Enter** key. Access saves the table with the name Position in the Northeast database on your Data Disk. Notice that Position now appears instead of Table1 in the Table window title bar.

Recall that in Tutorial 1 you set the Compact on Close option for the Seasonal database so that it would be compacted automatically each time you closed it. Now you'll set this option for your new Northeast database, so that it will be compacted automatically.

> ### To set the option for compacting the Northeast database automatically:
>
> 1. Click **Tools** on the menu bar, and then click **Options**. The Options dialog box opens.
>
> 2. Click the **General** tab in the dialog box, and then click the **Compact on Close** check box to select it.
>
> 3. Click the **OK** button to set the option.

The Position table is now complete. In Session 2.2, you'll continue to work with the Position table by entering records in it, modifying its structure, and maintaining data in the table. You will also import two tables, Employer and NAICS, from the Seasonal database into the Northeast database.

Session 2.1 QUICK | CHECK

1. What guidelines should you follow when designing a database?

2. What is the purpose of the Data Type property for a field?

3. For which three types of fields can you assign a field size?

4. In Design view, which key do you press to move between the Table Design grid and the Field Properties pane?

5. You use the _____ property to control the display of a field value.

6. A(n) _____ value, which results when you do not enter a value for a field, is not permitted for a primary key.

SESSION 2.2

In this session, you will add records to a table; modify the structure of an existing table by deleting, moving, and adding fields and changing field properties; copy records from another Access database; import tables from another Access database; and update an existing database by deleting and changing records.

Adding Records to a Table

You can add records to an Access table in several ways. A table datasheet provides a simple way for you to add records. As you learned in Tutorial 1, a datasheet shows a table's contents in rows and columns. Each row is a separate record in the table, and each column contains the field values for one field in the table. If you are currently working in Design view, you first must change from Design view to Datasheet view in order to view the table's datasheet.

Elsa asks you to add the two records shown in Figure 2-16 to the Position table. These two records contain data for positions that have recently become available at two employers.

Figure 2-16   RECORDS TO BE ADDED TO THE POSITION TABLE

PositionID	PositionTitle	EmployerID	Wage	Hours/Week	Openings	ReferredBy	StartDate	EndDate
2021	Waiter/Waitress	10155	9.50	30	1	Sue Brown	6/30	9/15
2017	Tour Guide	10149	15.00	20	1	Ed Curran	9/21	11/1

To add the records in the Position table datasheet:

1. If you took a break after the previous session, make sure that Access is running and that the Position table of the Northeast database is open in Design view. To open the table in Design view from the Database window, right-click the **Position** table, and then click **Design View** on the shortcut menu.

   Access displays the fields you defined for the Position table in Design view. Now you need to switch to Datasheet view so that you can enter the two records for Elsa.

2. Click the **View** button for Datasheet view 🔲 on the Table Design toolbar. The Table window opens in Datasheet view. See Figure 2-17.

Figure 2-17   TABLE WINDOW IN DATASHEET VIEW

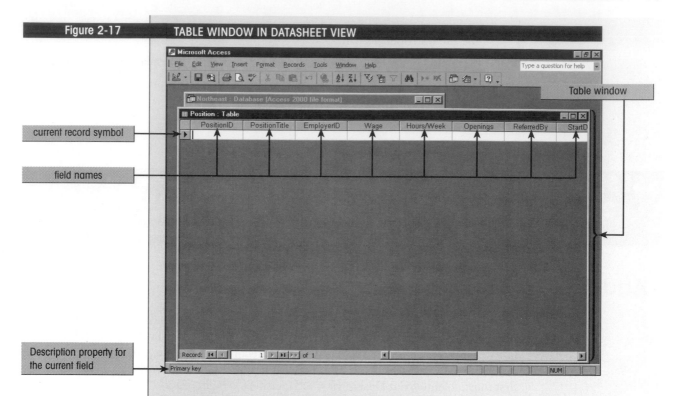

current record symbol

field names

Description property for
the current field

The table's nine field names appear at the top of the datasheet. Some of the
field names might not be visible. The current record symbol in the first row's
record selector identifies the currently selected record, which contains no data
until you enter the first record. The insertion point is located in the first row's
PositionID field, whose Description property appears on the status bar.

3. Type **2021**, which is the first record's PositionID field value, and then press the
Tab key. Each time you press the Tab key, the insertion point moves to the right
to the next field in the record. See Figure 2-18.

Figure 2-18   DATASHEET FOR POSITION TABLE AFTER ENTERING THE FIRST FIELD VALUE

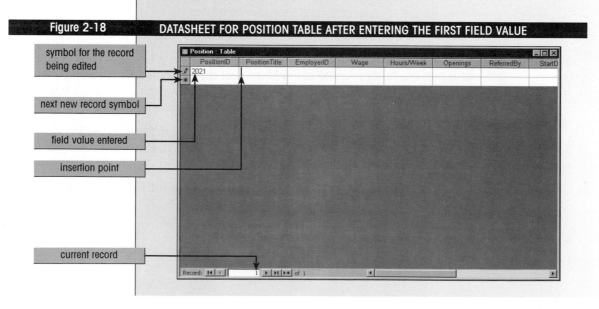

symbol for the record
being edited

next new record symbol

field value entered

insertion point

current record

TROUBLE? If you make a mistake when typing a value, use the Backspace key to delete characters to the left of the insertion point or the Delete key to delete characters to the right of the insertion point. Then type the correct value. If you want to correct a value by replacing it entirely, double-click the value to select it, and then type the correct value.

The pencil symbol in the first row's record selector indicates that the record is being edited. The star symbol in the second row's record selector identifies the second row as the next one available for a new record. Notice that all the fields are initially empty; this occurs because you set the Default Value property for the fields (as appropriate) to Null.

4. Type **Waiter/Waitress** in the PositionTitle field, and then press the **Tab** key. The insertion point moves to the EmployerID field.

5. Type **10155** and then press the **Tab** key. The insertion point moves to the right side of the Wage field.

   Recall that the PositionID, PositionTitle, and EmployerID fields are all text fields and that the Wage field is a currency field. Field values for text fields are left-aligned in their boxes, and field values for number, date/time, and currency fields are right-aligned in their boxes.

6. Type **9.5** and then press the **Tab** key. Access displays the field value with a dollar sign and two decimal places ($9.50), as specified by the currency format. You do not need to type the dollar sign, commas, or decimal point (for whole dollar amounts) because Access adds these symbols automatically for you.

7. In the Hours/Week field, type **30**, press the **Tab** key, type **1** in the Openings field, and then press the **Tab** key.

8. Type **Sue Brown** in the ReferredBy field, and then press the **Tab** key. Depending on your monitor's resolution and size, the display of the datasheet might shift so that the next field, StartDate, is completely visible.

9. Type **6/30** in the StartDate field, and then press the **Tab** key. Access displays the value as 06/30, as specified by the custom date format (mm/dd) you set for this field. The insertion point moves to the final field in the table, EndDate.

10. Type **9/15** in the EndDate field, and then press the **Tab** key. Access displays the value as 09/15, shifts the display of the datasheet back to the left, stores the first completed record in the Position table, removes the pencil symbol from the first row's record selector, advances the insertion point to the second row's PositionID text box, and places the current record symbol in the second row's record selector.

   Now you can enter the values for the second record.

11. Refer to Figure 2-16, and repeat Steps 3 through 10 to add the second record to the table. Access saves the record in the Position table, and moves the insertion point to the beginning of the third row. See Figure 2-19.

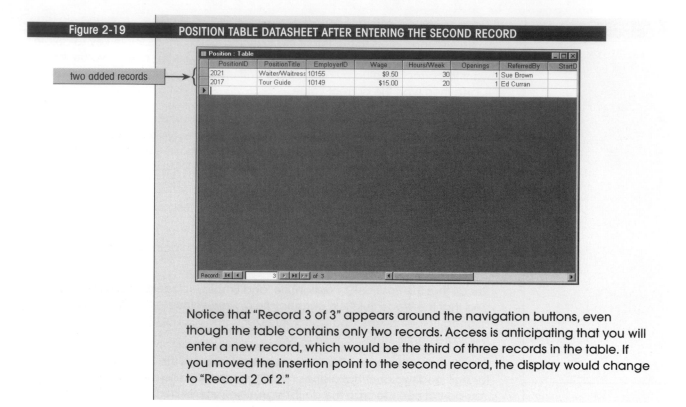

Figure 2-19 **POSITION TABLE DATASHEET AFTER ENTERING THE SECOND RECORD**

two added records

Notice that "Record 3 of 3" appears around the navigation buttons, even though the table contains only two records. Access is anticipating that you will enter a new record, which would be the third of three records in the table. If you moved the insertion point to the second record, the display would change to "Record 2 of 2."

Notice that the two records are currently listed in the order in which you entered them. However, once you close the table or change to another view, and then redisplay the table datasheet, the records will be listed in primary key order by the values in the PositionID field.

Modifying the Structure of an Access Table

Even a well-designed table might need to be modified. For example, the government at all levels and competitors place demands on a company to track more data and to modify the data it already tracks. Access allows you to modify a table's structure in Design view: you can add and delete fields, change the order of fields, and change the properties of the fields.

After holding a meeting with her staff members and reviewing the structure of the Position table and the format of the field values in the datasheet, Elsa has several changes she wants you to make to the table. First, she has decided that it's not necessary to keep track of the name of the person who originally requested a particular position, so she wants you to delete the ReferredBy field. Also, she thinks that the Wage field should remain a currency field, but she wants the dollar signs removed from the displayed field values in the datasheet. She also wants the Openings field moved to the end of the table. Finally, she wants you to add a new yes/no field, named Experience, to the table to indicate whether the available position requires that potential recruits have prior experience in that type of work. The Experience field will be inserted between the Hours/Week and StartDate fields. Figure 2-20 shows Elsa's modified design for the Position table.

Figure 2-20	MODIFIED DESIGN FOR THE POSITION TABLE			
Field Name	Data Type	Field Size	Description	
PositionID	Text	4	Primary key	
PositionTitle	Text	30		
EmployerID	Text	5	Foreign key	
Wage	Currency		Rate per hour	
Hours/Week	Number	Integer	Work hours per week	
Experience	Yes/No		Experience required	
StartDate	Date/Time		Month and day	
EndDate	Date/Time		Month and day	
Openings	Number	Integer	Number of openings	

You'll begin modifying the table by deleting the ReferredBy field.

Deleting a Field

After you've defined a table structure and added records to the table, you can delete a field from the table structure. When you delete a field, you also delete all the values for the field from the table. Therefore, you should make sure that you need to delete a field and that you delete the correct field.

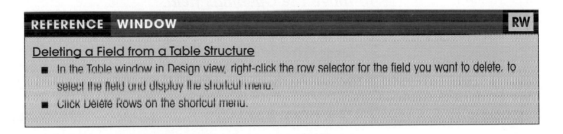

REFERENCE WINDOW   RW

Deleting a Field from a Table Structure
- In the Table window in Design view, right-click the row selector for the field you want to delete, to select the field and display the shortcut menu.
- Click Delete Rows on the shortcut menu.

You need to delete the ReferredBy field from the Position table structure.

To delete the ReferredBy field:

1. Click the **View** button for Design view ![icon] on the Table Datasheet toolbar. The Table window for the Position table opens in Design view.

2. Position the pointer on the row selector for the ReferredBy field until the pointer changes to a ➡ shape.

3. Right-click to select the entire row for the ReferredBy field and display the shortcut menu, and then click **Delete Rows**.

   A dialog box opens asking you to confirm the deletion.

4. Click the **Yes** button to close the dialog box and to delete the field and its values from the table. See Figure 2-21.

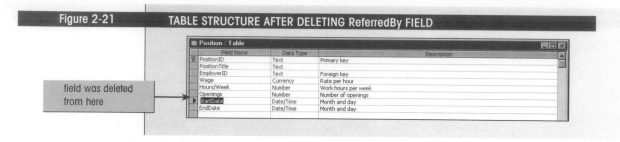

Figure 2-21 TABLE STRUCTURE AFTER DELETING ReferredBy FIELD

field was deleted from here

You have deleted the ReferredBy field in the Table window, but the change doesn't take place in the table on disk until you save the table structure. Because you have other modifications to make to the table, you'll wait until you finish them all before saving the modified table structure to disk.

Moving a Field

To move a field, you use the mouse to drag it to a new location in the Table window in Design view. Your next modification to the Position table structure is to move the Openings field to the end of the table, as Elsa requested.

To move the Openings field:

1. Click the **row selector** for the Openings field to select the entire row.

2. Place the pointer in the row selector for the Openings field, click the ⬚ pointer, and then drag the ⬚ pointer to the row selector below the EndDate row selector. See Figure 2-22.

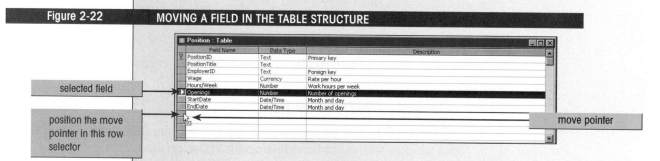

Figure 2-22 MOVING A FIELD IN THE TABLE STRUCTURE

selected field

position the move pointer in this row selector

move pointer

3. Release the mouse button. Access moves the Openings field below the EndDate field in the table structure.

TROUBLE? If the Openings field did not move, repeat Steps 1 through 3, making sure you firmly hold down the mouse button during the drag operation.

Adding a Field

Next, you need to add the Experience field to the table structure between the Hours/Week and StartDate fields. To add a new field between existing fields, you must insert a row. You begin by selecting the field that will be below the new field you want to insert.

Adding a Field Between Two Existing Fields

- In the Table window in Design view, right-click the row selector for the row above which you want to add a new field, to select the field and display the shortcut menu.
- Click Insert Rows on the shortcut menu.
- Define the new field by entering the field name, data type, description (optional), and any property specifications.

To add the Experience field to the Position table:

1. Right-click the **row selector** for the StartDate field to select this field and display the shortcut menu, and then click **Insert Rows**. Access adds a new, blank row between the Hours/Week and StartDate fields. See Figure 2-23.

| Figure 2-23 | AFTER INSERTING A ROW IN THE TABLE STRUCTURE |

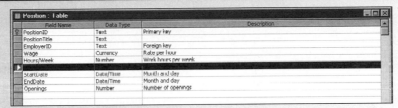

You'll define the Experience field in the new row of the Position table. Access will add this new field to the Position table structure between the Hours/Week and StartDate fields.

2. Click the **Field Name** text box for the new row, type **Experience**, and then press the **Tab** key.

   The Experience field will be a yes/no field that will specify whether prior work experience is required for the position.

3. Type **y**. Access completes the data type as "yes/No."

4. Press the **Tab** key to select the yes/no data type and to move to the Description text box.

   Notice that Access changes the value in the Data Type text box from "yes/No" to "Yes/No."

5. Type **Experience required** in the Description text box.

   Elsa wants the Experience field to have a Default Value property value of "No," so you need to set this property.

6. In the Field Properties pane, click the **Default Value** text box, type **no**, and then click somewhere outside of the Default Value text box to deselect the value. Notice that Access changes the Default Value property value from "no" to "No." See Figure 2-24.

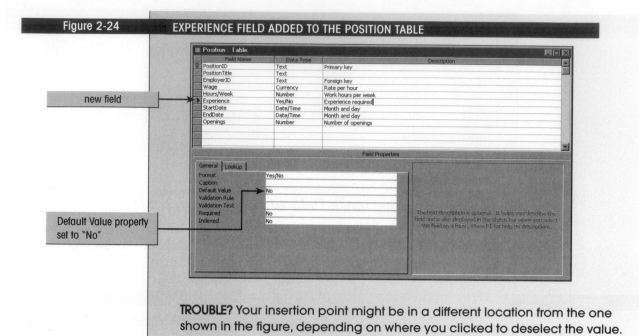

Figure 2-24   EXPERIENCE FIELD ADDED TO THE POSITION TABLE

new field

Default Value property set to "No"

TROUBLE? Your insertion point might be in a different location from the one shown in the figure, depending on where you clicked to deselect the value.

You've completed adding the Experience field to the Position table in Design view. As with the other changes you've made in Design view, however, the Experience field is not added to the Position table in the Northeast database until you save the changes to the table structure.

Changing Field Properties

Elsa's last modification to the table structure is to remove the dollar signs from the Wage field values displayed in the datasheet—repeated dollar signs are unnecessary and they clutter the datasheet. As you learned earlier when defining the StartDate and EndDate fields, you use the Format property to control the display of a field value.

To change the Format property of the Wage field:

1. Click the **Description** text box for the Wage field. The Wage field is now the current field.

2. Click the right side of the **Format** text box to display the Format list box. See Figure 2-25.

Figure 2-25	FORMAT LIST BOX FOR THE WAGE FIELD

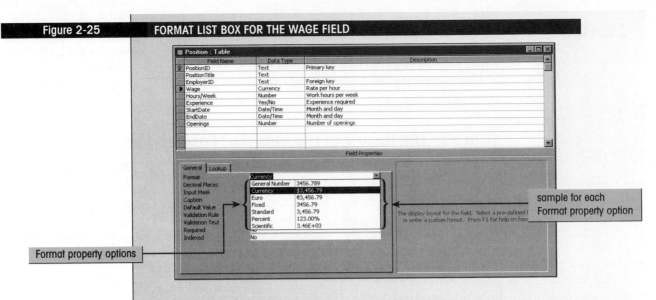

Format property options

sample for each Format property option

To the right of each Format property option is a field value whose appearance represents a sample of the option. The Standard option specifies the format Elsa wants for the Wage field.

3. Click **Standard** in the Format list box to accept this option for the Format property.

Elsa wants you to add a third record to the Position table datasheet. Before you can add the record, you must save the modified table structure, and then switch to the Position table datasheet.

To save the modified table structure, and then switch to the datasheet:

1. Click the **Save** button 🖫 on the Table Design toolbar. The modified table structure for the Position table is stored in the Northeast database. Note that if you forget to save the modified structure and try to close the table or switch to another view, Access will prompt you to save the table before you can continue.

2. Click the **View** button for Datasheet view 🔲 on the Table Design toolbar. The Position table datasheet opens. See Figure 2-26.

Figure 2-26	DATASHEET FOR THE MODIFIED POSITION TABLE

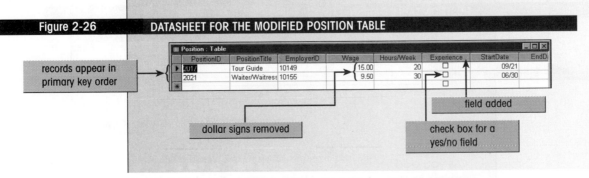

records appear in primary key order

field added

dollar signs removed

check box for a yes/no field

Notice that the ReferredBy field no longer appears in the datasheet, the Openings field is now the rightmost column (you might need to scroll the datasheet to see it), the Wage field values do not contain dollar signs, and the Experience field appears between the Hours/Week and StartDate fields. The Experience column contains check boxes to represent the yes/no field values. Empty check boxes signify "No," which is the default value you assigned to the Experience field. A check mark in the check box indicates a "Yes" value. Also notice that the records appear in ascending order based on the value in the PositionID field, the Position table's primary key, even though you did not enter the records in this order.

Elsa asks you to add a third record to the table. This record is for a position that requires prior work experience.

To add the record to the modified Position table:

1. Click the **New Record** button ▶* on the Table Datasheet toolbar. The insertion point moves to the PositionID field for the third row, which is the next row available for a new record.

2. Type **2020**. The pencil symbol appears in the row selector for the third row, and the star appears in the row selector for the fourth row. Recall that these symbols represent a record being edited and the next available record, respectively.

3. Press the **Tab** key. The insertion point moves to the PositionTitle field.

4. Type **Host/Hostess**, press the **Tab** key to move to the EmployerID field, type **10163**, and then press the **Tab** key. The Wage field is now the current field.

5. Type **18.5** and then press the **Tab** key. Access displays the value as "18.50" (with no dollar sign).

6. Type **32** in the Hours/Week field, and then press the **Tab** key. The Experience field is now the current field.

   Recall that the default value for this field is "No," which means the check box is initially empty. For yes/no fields with check boxes, you press the Tab key to leave the check box unchecked; you press the spacebar or click the check box to add or remove a check mark in the check box. Because this position requires experience, you need to insert a check mark in the check box.

7. Press the **spacebar**. A check mark appears in the check box.

8. Press the **Tab** key, type **6/15** in the StartDate field, press the **Tab** key, and then type **10/1** in the EndDate field.

9. Press the **Tab** key, type **1** in the Openings field, and then press the **Tab** key. Access saves the record in the Position table and moves the insertion point to the beginning of the fourth row. See Figure 2-27.

Figure 2-27	POSITION TABLE DATASHEET WITH THIRD RECORD ADDED

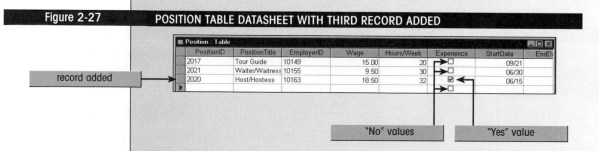

As you add records, Access places them at the end of the datasheet. If you switch to Design view and then return to the datasheet, or if you close the table and then open the datasheet, Access will display the records in primary key sequence.

For many of the fields, the columns are wider than necessary for the field values. You can resize the datasheet columns so that they are only as wide as needed to display the longest value in the column, including the field name. Resizing datasheet columns to their best fit improves the display of the datasheet and allows you to view more fields at the same time.

To resize the Position datasheet columns to their best fit:

1. Place the pointer on the line between the PositionID and PositionTitle field names until the pointer changes to a ✛ shape.

2. Double-click the pointer. The PositionID column is resized so that it is only as wide as the longest value in the column (the field name, in this case).

3. Double-click the ✛ pointer on the line to the right of each remaining field name to resize all the columns in the datasheet to their best fit. See Figure 2-28.

Figure 2-28   DATASHEET AFTER RESIZING ALL COLUMNS TO THEIR BEST FIT

PositionID	PositionTitle	EmployerID	Wage	Hours/Week	Experience	StartDate	EndDate	Openings
2017	Tour Guide	10149	15.00	20	☐	09/21	11/01	1
2020	Host/Hostess	10163	18.50	32	☑	06/15	10/01	1
2021	Waiter/Waitress	10155	9.50	30	☐	06/30	09/15	1
					☐			

Notice that all nine fields in the Position table are now visible in the datasheet.

You have modified the Position table structure and added one record. Next you need to obtain the rest of the records for this table from another database, and then import the two tables from the Seasonal database (Employer and NAICS) into your Northeast database.

Obtaining Data from Another Access Database

Sometimes the data you need for your database might already exist in another Access database. You can save time in obtaining this data by copying and pasting records from one database table into another or by importing an entire table from one database into another.

Copying Records from Another Access Database

You can copy and paste records from a table in the same database or in a different database only if the tables have the same structure—that is, the tables contain the same fields in the same order. Elsa's NEJobs database in the Tutorial folder on your Data Disk has a table named Available Positions that has the same table structure as the Position table. The records in the Available Positions table are the records Elsa wants you to copy into the Position table.

Other programs, such as Microsoft Word and Microsoft Excel, allow you to have two or more documents open at a time. However, you can have only one Access database open at a time. Therefore, you need to close the Northeast database, open the Available Positions table in the NEJobs database, select and copy the table records, close the NEJobs database, reopen the Position table in the Northeast database, and then paste the copied records. (*Note*: If you have a database open and then open a second database, Access will automatically close the first database for you.)

To copy the records from the Available Positions table:

1. Click the **Close** button ☒ on the Table window title bar to close the Position table. A message box opens asking if you want to save the changes to the layout of the Position table. This box appears because you resized the datasheet columns to their best fit.

2. Click the **Yes** button in the message box.

3. Click ☒ on the Database window title bar to close the Northeast database.

4. Click the **Open** button 🗁 on the Database toolbar to display the Open dialog box.

5. If necessary, display the list of files on your Data Disk, and then open the **Tutorial** folder.

6. Open the database file named **NEJobs**. The Database window opens. Notice that the NEJobs database contains only one table, the Available Positions table. This table contains the records you need to copy.

7. Click **Available Positions** in the Tables list box (if necessary), and then click the **Open** button in the Database window. The datasheet for the Available Positions table opens. See Figure 2-29. Note that this table contains a total of 62 records.

Figure 2-29	DATASHEET FOR THE NEJobs DATABASE'S AVAILABLE POSITIONS TABLE

click here to select all records

total number of records in the table

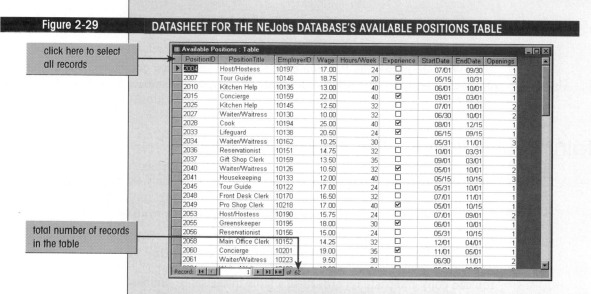

Elsa wants you to copy all the records in the Available Positions table. You can select all records by clicking the row selector for the field name row.

8. Click the **row selector** for the field name row (see Figure 2-29). All the records in the table are now highlighted, which means that Access has selected all of them.

9. Click the **Copy** button 📋 on the Table Datasheet toolbar. All the records are copied to the Windows Clipboard.

   TROUBLE? If a Clipboard panel opens in the Task Pane, click its Close button to close it, and then continue with Step 10.

10. Click ☒ on the Table window title bar. A dialog box opens asking if you want to save the data you copied to the Windows Clipboard.

11. Click the **Yes** button in the dialog box. The dialog box closes, and then the table closes.

12. Click ☒ on the Database window title bar to close the NEJobs database.

To finish copying and pasting the records, you must open the Position table and paste the copied records into the table.

To paste the copied records into the Position table:

1. Click **File** on the menu bar, and then click **Northeast** in the list of recently opened databases. The Database window opens, showing the tables for the Northeast database.

2. In the Tables list box, click **Position** (if necessary), and then click the **Open** button in the Database window. The datasheet for the Position table opens.

   You must paste the records at the end of the table.

3. Click the **row selector** for row four, which is the next row available for a new record.

4. Click the **Paste** button 🖺 on the Table Datasheet toolbar. A dialog box opens asking if you are sure you want to paste the records (62 in all)

5. Click the **Yes** button. All the records are pasted from the Windows Clipboard, and the pasted records remain highlighted. See Figure 2-30. Notice that the table now contains a total of 65 records—the three original records plus the 62 copied records.

Figure 2-30   TABLE AFTER COPYING AND PASTING RECORDS

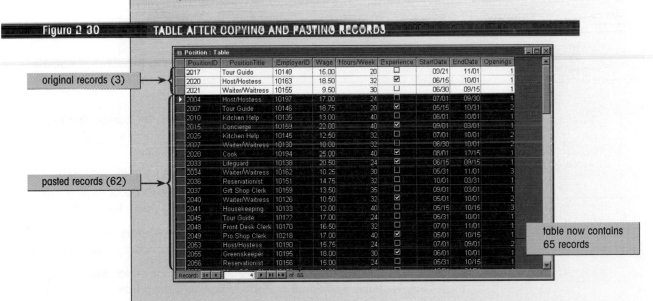

original records (3)

pasted records (62)

table now contains 65 records

6. Click the **Close** button ☒ on the Table window title bar to close the Position table.

Importing a Table from Another Access Database

When you import a table from one Access database to another, you place a copy of the table—including its structure, field definitions, and field values—in the database into which you import it. There are two ways to import a table from another Access database into your current database: using the Get External Data option on the File menu, or using the Import Table Wizard, which is available in the New Table dialog box. You'll use both methods to import the two tables from the Seasonal database into your Northeast database.

To import the Employer and NAICS tables:

1. Make sure the Northeast Database window is open on your screen.

2. Click **File** on the menu bar, position the pointer on the double-arrow at the bottom of the File menu to display the full menu (if necessary), point to **Get External Data**, and then click **Import**. The Import dialog box opens. This dialog box is similar to the Open dialog box.

3. Display the list of files in your Tutorial folder, click **Seasonal**, and then click the **Import** button. The Import Objects dialog box opens. See Figure 2-31.

| Figure 2-31 | IMPORT OBJECTS DIALOG BOX |

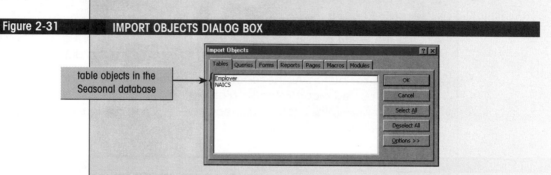

table objects in the Seasonal database

The Tables tab of the dialog box lists both tables in the Seasonal database—Employer and NAICS. Note that you can import other objects as well (queries, forms, reports, and so on).

4. Click **Employer** in the list of tables, and then click the **OK** button. The Import Objects dialog box closes, and the Employer table is now listed in the Northeast Database window.

Now you'll use the Import Table Wizard to import the NAICS table. (Note that you could also use the Select All button in the Import Objects dialog box to import all the objects listed on the current tab at the same time.)

5. Click the **New** button in the Database window, click **Import Table** in the New Table dialog box, and then click the **OK** button. The Import dialog box opens.

6. If necessary, display the list of files in your Tutorial folder, click **Seasonal**, and then click the **Import** button. The Import Objects dialog box opens, again displaying the tables in the Seasonal database.

7. Click **NAICS** in the list of tables, and then click the **OK** button to import the NAICS table into the Northeast database.

Now that you have all the records in the Position table and all three tables in the Northeast database, Elsa examines the records to make sure they are correct. She finds one record in the Position table that she wants you to delete and another record that needs changes to its field values.

Updating a Database

Updating, or maintaining, a database is the process of adding, changing, and deleting records in database tables to keep them current and accurate. You've already added records to the Position table. Now Elsa wants you to delete and change records.

Deleting Records

To delete a record, you need to select the record in Datasheet view, and then delete it using the Delete Record button on the Table Datasheet toolbar or the Delete Record option on the shortcut menu.

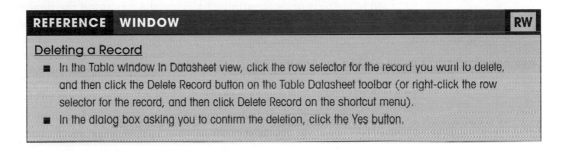

REFERENCE WINDOW   **RW**

Deleting a Record
- In the Table window in Datasheet view, click the row selector for the record you want to delete, and then click the Delete Record button on the Table Datasheet toolbar (or right-click the row selector for the record, and then click Delete Record on the shortcut menu).
- In the dialog box asking you to confirm the deletion, click the Yes button.

Elsa asks you to delete the record whose PositionID is 2015 because this record was entered in error; the position for this record does not exist. The fourth record in the table has a PositionID value of 2015. This record is the one you need to delete.

To delete the record:

1. Open the Position table in Datasheet view.

2. Right-click the **row selector** for row four. Access selects the fourth record and displays the shortcut menu. See Figure 2-32.

Figure 2-32   **DELETING A RECORD**

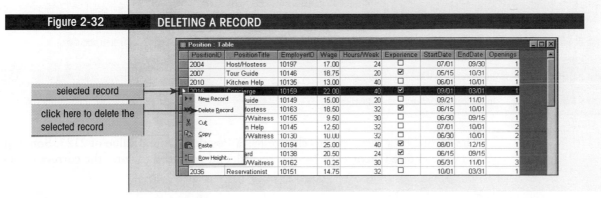

3. Click **Delete Record** on the shortcut menu. Access deletes the record and opens a dialog box asking you to confirm the deletion. Because the deletion of a record is permanent and cannot be undone, Access prompts you to make sure that you want to delete the record.

TROUBLE? If you selected the wrong record for deletion, click the No button. Access ends the deletion process and continues to display the selected record. Repeat Steps 2 and 3 to delete the correct record.

4. Click the **Yes** button to confirm the deletion and close the dialog box.

Elsa's final update to the Position table involves changes to field values in one of the records.

Changing Records

To change the field values in a record, you first must make the record the current record. Then you position the insertion point in the field value to make minor changes or select the field value to replace it entirely. In Tutorial 1, you used the mouse with the scroll bars and the navigation buttons to navigate through the records in a datasheet. You can also use keystroke combinations and the F2 key to navigate a datasheet and to select field values.

The **F2 key** is a toggle that you use to switch between navigation mode and editing mode:

- In **navigation mode**, Access selects an entire field value. If you type while you are in navigation mode, your typed entry replaces the highlighted field value.
- In **editing mode**, you can insert or delete characters in a field value based on the location of the insertion point.

Figure 2-33 shows some of the navigation mode and editing mode keystroke techniques.

Figure 2-33	NAVIGATION MODE AND EDITING MODE KEYSTROKE TECHNIQUES	
PRESS	**TO MOVE THE SELECTION IN NAVIGATION MODE**	**TO MOVE THE INSERTION POINT IN EDITING MODE**
←	Left one field value at a time	Left one character at a time
→	Right one field value at a time	Right one character at a time
Home	Left to the first field value in the record	To the left of the first character in the field value
End	Right to the last field value in the record	To the right of the last character in the field value
↑ or ↓	Up or down one record at a time	Up or down one record at a time and switch to navigation mode
Tab or Enter	Right one field value at a time	Right one field value at a time and switch to navigation mode
Ctrl + Home	To the first field value in the first record	To the left of the first character in the field value
Ctrl + End	To the last field value in the last record	To the right of the last character in the field value

The record Elsa wants you to change has a PositionID field value of 2125. Some of the values were entered incorrectly for this record, and you need to enter the correct values.

To modify the record:

1. Make sure the PositionID field value for the fourth record is still highlighted, indicating that the table is in navigation mode.

2. Press **Ctrl + End**. Access displays records from the end of the table and selects the last field value in the last record. This field value is for the Openings field.

3. Press the **Home** key. The first field value in the last record is now selected. This field value is for the PositionID field.

4. Press the ↑ key. The PositionID field value for the previous record (PositionID 2125) is selected. This record is the one you need to change.

   Elsa wants you to change these field values in the record: PositionID to 2124, EmployerID to 10163, Wage to 14.50, Experience to "Yes" (checked), and EndDate to 10/15.

5. Type **2124**, press the **Tab** key twice, type **10163**, press the **Tab** key, type **14.5**, press the **Tab** key twice, press the **spacebar** to insert a check mark in the Experience check box, press the **Tab** key twice, and then type **10/15**. The changes to the record are complete. See Figure 2-34.

| Figure 2-34 | TABLE AFTER CHANGING FIELD VALUES IN A RECORD |

field values changed

You've completed all of Elsa's updates to the Position table. Now you can exit Access.

6. Click the **Close** button ☒ on the Access window title bar to close the Position table and the Northeast database, and to exit Access.

Elsa and her staff members approve of the revised table structure for the Position table. They are confident that the table will allow them to easily track position data for NSJI's employer customers.

Session 2.2 QUICK CHECK

1. What does a pencil symbol in a datasheet's row selector represent? A star symbol?

2. What is the effect of deleting a field from a table structure?

3. How do you insert a field between existing fields in a table structure?

4. A field with the _____ data type can appear in the table datasheet as a check box.

5. Describe the two ways in which you can display the Import dialog box, so that you can import a table from one Access database to another.

6. In Datasheet view, what is the difference between navigation mode and editing mode?

REVIEW ASSIGNMENTS

Elsa needs a database to track data about the students recruited by NSJI and about the recruiters who find jobs for the students. She asks you to create the database by completing the following:

1. Make sure your Data Disk is in the appropriate disk drive, and then start Access.

2. Create a new, blank database named **Recruits** and save it in the Review folder on your Data Disk.

Explore

3. Use the Table Wizard to create a new table named **Recruiter** in the **Recruits** database, as follows:
   a. Base the new table on the Employees sample table, which is one of the sample tables in the Business category.
   b. Add the following fields to your table (in the order shown): SocialSecurityNumber, Salary, FirstName, MiddleName, and LastName.
   c. Click SocialSecurityNumber in the "Fields in my new table" list, and then use the Rename Field button to change the name of this field to SSN. Click the Next button.
   d. Name the new table **Recruiter**, and choose the option for setting the primary key yourself. Click the Next button.
   e. Specify SSN as the primary key field and accept the default data type. Click the Next button.
   f. In the final Table Wizard dialog box, click the Finish button to display the table in Datasheet view. (*Note:* The field names appear with spaces between words; this is how the Table Wizard is set up to format these field names when they appear in Datasheet view.)

4. Add the recruiter records shown in Figure 2-35 to the **Recruiter** table. (*Note:* You do not have to type the dashes in the SSN field values or commas in the Salary field values; the Table Wizard formatted these fields so that these symbols are entered automatically for you.)

Figure 2-35

SSN	Salary	First Name	Middle Name	Last Name
892-77-1201	40,000	Kate	Teresa	Foster
901-63-1554	38,500	Paul	Michael	Kirnicki
893-91-0178	40,000	Ryan	James	DuBrava

5. Make the following changes to the structure of the **Recruiter** table:
   a. Move the Salary field so that it appears after the LastName field.
   b. Add a new field between the LastName and Salary fields, using the following properties:
Field Name:	BonusQuota
Data Type:	Number
Description:	Number of recruited students needed to receive bonus
Field Size:	Byte
Decimal Places:	0
   c. Change the format of the Salary field so that commas are displayed, dollar signs are not displayed, and no decimal places are displayed in the field values.
   d. Save the revised table structure.

6. Use the **Recruiter** datasheet to update the database as follows:
   a. Enter these BonusQuota values for the three records: 60 for Kate Foster; 60 for Ryan DuBrava; and 50 for Paul Kirnicki.
   b. Add a record to the **Recruiter** datasheet with the following field values:
SSN:	899-40-2937
First Name:	Sonia
Middle Name:	Lee
Last Name:	Xu
BonusQuota:	50
Salary:	39,250

7. Close the **Recruiter** table, and then set the option for compacting the **Recruits** database on close.

8. Elsa created a database with her name as the database name. The **Recruiter Employees** table in that database has the same format as the **Recruiter** table you created. Copy all the records from the **Recruiter Employees** table in the **Elsa** database (located in the Review folder on your Data Disk) to the end of the **Recruiter** table in the **Recruits** database.

Explore 9. Because you added a number of records to the database, its size has increased. Compact the database manually using the Compact and Repair Database option.

10. Delete the MiddleName field from the **Recruiter** table structure, and then save the table structure.

11. Resize all columns in the datasheet for the **Recruiter** table to their best fit.

12. Print the **Recruiter** table datasheet, and then save and close the table.

13. Create a table named **Student** using the Import Table Wizard. The table you need to import is named **Student**, which is one of the tables in the **Elsa** database located in the Review folder on your Data Disk.

14. Make the following modifications to the structure of the **Student** table in the **Recruits** database:
   a. Enter the following Description property values:
      StudentID: Primary key
      SSN: Foreign key value of the recruiter for this student
   b. Change the Field Size property for both the FirstName field and the LastName field to 15.
   c. Move the BirthDate field so that it appears between the Nation and Gender fields.
   d. Change the format of the BirthDate field so that it displays only two digits for the year instead of four.
   e. Save the table structure changes. (Answer "Yes" to any warning messages about property changes and lost data.)

15. Switch to Datasheet view, and then resize all columns in the datasheet to fit the data.

16. Delete the record with the StudentID DRI9901 from the **Student** table.

17. Save, print, and then close the **Student** datasheet.

18. Close the **Recruits** database, and then exit Access.

CASE PROBLEMS

Case 1. Lim's Video Photography Youngho Lim uses the **Videos** database to maintain information about the clients, contracts, and events for his video photography business. Youngho asks you to help him maintain the database by completing the following:

1. Make sure your Data Disk is in the appropriate disk drive.

2. Start Access and open the **Videos** database located in the Cases folder on your Data Disk.

Explore 3. Use Design view to create a table using the table design shown in Figure 2-36.

Figure 2-36

Field Name	Data Type	Description	Field Size	Other Properties
Shoot#	Number	Primary key	Long Integer	Decimal Places: 0 Default Value: Null
ShootType	Text		2	
ShootTime	Date/Time			Format: Medium Time
Duration	Number	# of hours	Single	Default Value: Null
Contact	Text	Person who booked shoot	30	
Location	Text		30	
ShootDate	Date/Time			Format: mm/dd/yyyy
Contract#	Number	Foreign key	Integer	Decimal Places: 0 Default Value: Null

4. Specify Shoot# as the primary key, and then save the table as **Shoot**.

5. Add the records shown in Figure 2-37 to the **Shoot** table.

Figure 2-37

Shoot#	ShootType	ShootTime	Duration	Contact	Location	ShootDate	Contract#
927032	AP	4:00 PM	3.5	Ellen Quirk	Elm Lodge	9/27/2003	2412
103031	HP	9:00 AM	3.5	Tom Bradbury	Client's home	10/30/2003	2611

6. Youngho created a database named **Events** that contains a table with shoot data named **Shoot Events**. The **Shoot** table you created has the same format as the **Shoot Events** table. Copy all the records from the **Shoot Events** table in the **Events** database (located in the Cases folder on your Data Disk) to the end of the **Shoot** table in the **Videos** database.

7. Modify the structure of the **Shoot** table by completing the following:

   a. Delete the Contact field.

   b. Move the ShootDate field so that it appears between the ShootType and ShootTime fields.

8. Switch to Datasheet view and resize all columns in the datasheet for the **Shoot** table to their best fit.

9. Use the **Shoot** datasheet to update the database as follows:

   a. For Shoot# 421032, change the ShootTime value to 7:00 PM, and change the Location value to Le Bistro.

   b. Add a record to the **Shoot** datasheet with the following field values:
      Shoot#:   913032
      ShootType: SE
      ShootDate: 9/13/2003
      ShootTime: 1:00 PM
      Duration: 2.5
      Location: High School football field
      Contract#:   2501

10. Switch to Design view, and then switch back to Datasheet view so that the records appear in primary key sequence by Shoot#. Resize any datasheet columns to their best fit, as necessary.

11. Print the **Shoot** table datasheet, and then save and close the table.

Explore

12. Create a table named **ShootDesc**, based on the data shown in Figure 2-38 and according to the following steps:

Figure 2-38

ShootType	ShootDesc
AP	Anniversary Party
BM	Bar/Bat Mitzvah
BP	Birthday Party
CP	Insurance Commercial Property
DR	Dance Recital
GR	Graduation
HP	Insurance Home Property
LS	Legal Services
RC	Religious Ceremony
SE	Sports Event
WE	Wedding

   a. Select the Datasheet View option in the New Table dialog box.

   b. Enter the 11 records shown in Figure 2-38. (Do *not* enter the field names at this point.)

   c. Switch to Design view, supply the table name, and then answer "No" if asked if you want to create a primary key.

    d. Type the following field names and set the following properties for the two text fields:

ShootType
Description:	Primary key
Field Size:	2

ShootDesc
Description:	Description of shoot
Field Size:	30

    e. Specify the primary key, save the table structure changes, and then switch back to Datasheet view. If you receive any warning messages, answer "Yes" to continue.

    f. Resize both datasheet columns to their best fit; then save, print, and close the datasheet.

13. Close the **Videos** database, and then exit Access.

Case 2. DineAtHome.course.com Claire Picard uses the **Meals** database to track information about local restaurants and orders placed at the restaurants by the customers of her e-commerce business. You'll help her maintain this database by completing the following:

1. Make sure your Data Disk is in the appropriate disk drive.

2. Start Access and open the **Meals** database located in the Cases folder on your Data Disk.

3. Use Design view to create a table using the table design shown in Figure 2-39.

Figure 2-39

Field Name	Data Type	Description	Field Size	Other Properties
Order#	Number	Primary key	Long Integer	Decimal Places: 0 Default Value: Null
Restaurant#	Number	Foreign key	Long Integer	Decimal Places: 0
OrderAmt	Currency	Total amount of order		Format: Fixed

4. Specify Order# as the primary key, and then save the table as **Order**.

5. Add the records shown in Figure 2-40 to the **Order** table.

Figure 2-40

Order#	Restaurant#	OrderAmt
3117	131	155.35
3123	115	45.42
3020	120	85.50

Explore

6. Modify the structure of the **Order** table by adding a new field between the Restaurant# and OrderAmt fields, with the following properties:
Field Name:	OrderDate
Data Type:	Date/Time
Format:	Long Date

7. Use the revised **Order** datasheet to update the database as follows:

    a. Enter the following OrderDate values for the three records: 1/15/03 for Order# 3020, 4/2/03 for Order# 3117, and 5/1/03 for Order# 3123.

    b. Add a new record to the **Order** datasheet with the following field values:
Order#:	3045
Restaurant#:	108
OrderDate:	3/16/03
OrderAmt:	50.25

8. Claire created a database named **Customer** that contains a table with order data named **Order Records**. The **Order** table you created has the same format as the **Order Records** table. Copy all the records from the **Order Records** table in the **Customer** database (located in the Cases folder on your Data Disk) to the end of the **Order** table in the **Meals** database.

9. Resize all columns in the datasheet for the **Order** table to their best fit.

10. For Order# 3039, change the OrderAmt value to 87.30.

11. Delete the record for Order# 3068.

12. Print the **Order** table datasheet, and then save and close the table.

13. Close the **Meals** database, and then exit Access.

Case 3. Redwood Zoo Michael Rosenfeld continues to track information about donors, their pledges, and the status of funds to benefit the Redwood Zoo. Help him maintain the **Redwood** database by completing the following:

1. Make sure your Data Disk is in the appropriate disk drive.

2. Start Access and open the **Redwood** database located in the Cases folder on your Data Disk.

3. Create a table named **Pledge** using the Import Table Wizard. The table you need to import is named **Pledge Records**, which is located in the **Pledge** database in the Cases folder on your Data Disk.

Explore   4. After importing the **Pledge Records** table, use the shortcut menu to rename the table to **Pledge** in the Database window.

Explore   5. Modify the structure of the **Pledge** table by completing the following:

a. Enter the following Description property values:

Pledge#:	Primary key
DonorID:	Foreign key
FundCode:	Foreign key

b. Change the format of the PledgeDate field to mm/dd/yyyy.

c. Change the Data Type of the TotalPledged field to Currency with the Standard format.

d. Specify a Default Value of B for the PaymentMethod field.

e. Specify a Default Value of F for the PaymentSchedule field.

f. Save the modified table structure.

6. Switch to Datasheet view, and then resize all columns in the datasheet to their best fit.

7. Use the **Pledge** datasheet to update the database as follows:

a. Add a new record to the **Pledge** table with the following field values:

Pledge#:	2695
DonorID:	59045
FundCode:	P15
PledgeDate:	7/11/2003
TotalPledged:	1000
PaymentMethod:	B
PaymentSchedule:	M

b. Change the TotalPledged value for Pledge# 2499 to 150.

c. Change the FundCode value for Pledge# 2332 to B03.

8. Print the **Pledge** table datasheet, and then save and close the table.

9. Close the **Redwood** database, and then exit Access.

Case 4. Mountain River Adventures Connor and Siobhan Dempsey use the **Trips** database to track the data about the guided tours they provide. You'll help them maintain this database by completing the following:

1. Make sure your Data Disk is in the appropriate disk drive.

2. Start Access and open the **Trips** database located in the Cases folder on your Data Disk.

Explore   3. Use the Import Spreadsheet Wizard to create a new table named **Rafting Trip**. The data you need to import is contained in the **Rafting** workbook, which is a Microsoft Excel file located in the Cases folder on your Data Disk.

a. Select the Import Table option in the New Table dialog box.

b. Change the entry in the Files of type list box to display the list of Excel workbook files in the Cases folder.

c. Select the **Rafting** file and then click the Import button.

d. In the Import Spreadsheet Wizard dialog boxes, choose the Sheet1 worksheet; choose the option for using column headings as field names; select the option for choosing your own primary key; specify Trip# as the primary key; and enter the table name (**Rafting Trip**). Otherwise, accept the Wizard's choices for all other options for the imported data.

4. Open the **Rafting Trip** table and resize all datasheet columns to their best fit.

5. Modify the structure of the **Rafting Trip** table by completing the following:

a. For the Trip# field, enter a Description property of "Primary key", change the Field Size to Long Integer, and set the Decimal Places property to 0.

b. For the River field, change the Field Size to 45.

c. For the TripDistance field, enter a Description property of "Distance in miles", change the Field Size to Integer, and set the Decimal Places property to 0.

d. For the TripDays field, enter a Description property of "Number of days for the trip", and change the Field Size to Single.

e. For the Fee/Person field, change the Data Type to Currency and set the Format property to Fixed.

f. Save the table structure. If you receive any warning messages about lost data or integrity rules, click the Yes button.

6. Use the **Rafting Trip** datasheet to update the database as follows:

a. For Trip# 3142, change the TripDistance value to 20.

b. Add a new record to the **Rafting Trip** table with the following field values:

Trip#:   3675
River·   Colorado River (Grand Canyon)
TripDistance: 110
TripDays: 2.5
Fee/Person: 215

c. Delete the record for Trip# 3473

7. Print the **Rafting Trip** table datasheet, and then close the table.

8. Use Design view to create a new table named **Booking** using the table design shown in Figure 2-41.

Figure 2-41

Field Name	Data Type	Description	Field Size	Other Properties
Booking#	Number	Primary key	Long Integer	Decimal Places: 0 Default Value: Null
Client#	Number	Foreign key	Integer	Decimal Places: 0
TripDate	Date/Time			Format: Short Date
Trip#	Number	Foreign key	Long Integer	Decimal Places: 0
People	Number	Number of people in the group	Byte	Decimal Places: 0

9. Specify Booking# as the primary key, and then save the table as **Booking**.

10. Add the records shown in Figure 2-42 to the **Booking** table.

Figure 2-42

Booking#	Client#	TripDate	Trip#	People
410	330	6/5/03	3529	4
403	315	7/1/03	3107	7
411	311	7/5/03	3222	5

11. Connor created a database named **Groups** that contains a table with booking data named **Group Info**. The **Booking** table you created has the same format as the **Group Info** table. Copy all the records from the **Group Info** table in the **Groups** database (located in the Cases folder on your Data Disk) to the end of the **Booking** table in the **Trips** database.

12. Resize all columns in the **Booking** datasheet to their best fit.

13. Print the **Booking** datasheet, and then save and close the table.

14. Close the **Trips** database, and then exit Access.

INTERNET ASSIGNMENTS

Student Union

The purpose of the Internet Assignments is to challenge you to find information on the Internet that you can use to create effective documents. The actual assignments are updated and maintained on the Course Technology Web site. Log on to the Internet and use your Web browser to go to the Student Union on the New Perspectives Series site at **www.course.com/NewPerspectives/studentunion**. Click the Online Companions link, and then click the link for this text.

QUICK CHECK ANSWERS

Session 2.1

1. Identify all the fields needed to produce the required information, group related fields into tables, determine each table's primary key, include a common field in related tables, avoid data redundancy, and determine the properties of each field.

2. The Data Type property determines what field values you can enter for the field and what other properties the field will have.

3. text, number, and AutoNumber fields

4. F6

5. Format

6. null

Session 2.2

1. the record being edited; the next row available for a new record

2. The field and all its values are removed from the table.

3. In Design view, right-click the row selector for the row above which you want to insert the field, click Insert Rows on the shortcut menu, and then define the new field.

4. yes/no

5. Make sure the database into which you want to import a table is open, click the File menu, point to Get External Data, and then click Import; or, click the New button in the Database window, click Import Table in the New Table dialog box, and then click the OK button.

6. In navigation mode, the entire field value is selected, and anything you type replaces the field value; in editing mode, you can insert or delete characters in a field value based on the location of the insertion point.

OBJECTIVES

In this tutorial you will:

- Learn how to use the Query window in Design view

- Create, run, and save queries

- Update data using a query

- Define a relationship between two tables

- Sort data in a query

- Filter data in a query

- Specify an exact match condition in a query

- Change a datasheet's appearance

- Use a comparison operator to match a range of values

- Use the And and Or logical operators

- Use multiple undo and redo

- Perform calculations in a query using calculated fields, aggregate functions, and record group calculations

QUERYING A DATABASE

Retrieving Information About Employers and Their Positions

CASE

Northeast Seasonal Jobs International (NSJI)

At a recent company meeting, Elsa Jensen and other NSJI employees discussed the importance of regularly monitoring the business activity of the company's employer clients. For example, Zack Ward and his marketing staff track employer activity to develop new strategies for promoting NSJI's services. Matt Griffin, the manager of recruitment, needs to track information about available positions, so that he can find student recruits to fill those positions. In addition, Elsa is interested in analyzing other aspects of the business, such as the wage amounts paid for different positions at different employers. All of these informational needs can be satisfied by queries that retrieve information from the Northeast database.

SESSION 3.1

In this session, you will use the Query window in Design view to create, run, and save queries; update data using a query; define a one-to-many relationship between two tables; sort data with a toolbar button and in Design view; and filter data in a query datasheet.

Introduction to Queries

As you learned in Tutorial 1, a query is a question you ask about data stored in a database. For example, Zack might create a query to find records in the Employer table for only those employers located in a specific state or province. When you create a query, you tell Access which fields you need and what criteria Access should use to select the records.

Access provides powerful query capabilities that allow you to:

- display selected fields and records from a table
- sort records
- perform calculations
- generate data for forms, reports, and other queries
- update data in the tables in a database
- find and display data from two or more tables

Most questions about data are generalized queries in which you specify the fields and records you want Access to select. These common requests for information, such as "Which employers are located in Quebec?" or "How many waiter/waitress positions are available?" are called **select queries**. The answer to a select query is returned in the form of a datasheet. The result of a query is also referred to as a **recordset**, because the query produces a set of records that answers your question.

More specialized, technical queries, such as finding duplicate records in a table, are best formulated using a Query Wizard. A Query Wizard prompts you for information by asking a series of questions and then creates the appropriate query based on your answers. In Tutorial 1, you used the Simple Query Wizard to display only some of the fields in the Employer table; Access provides other Query Wizards for more complex queries. For common, informational queries, it is easier for you to design your own query than to use a Query Wizard.

Zack wants you to create a query to display the employer ID, employer name, city, contact first name, contact last name, and Web site information for each record in the Employer table. He needs this information for a market analysis his staff is completing on NSJI's employer clients. You'll open the Query window to create the query for Zack.

Query Window

You use the Query window in Design view to create a query. In Design view, you specify the data you want to view by constructing a query by example. When you use **query by example** (**QBE**), you give Access an example of the information you are requesting. Access then retrieves the information that precisely matches your example.

For Zack's query, you need to display data from the Employer table. You'll begin by starting Access, opening the Northeast database, and displaying the Query window in Design view.

To start Access, open the Northeast database, and open the Query window in Design view:

1. Place your Data Disk in the appropriate disk drive.

2. Start Access and open the **Northeast** database located in the Tutorial folder on your Data Disk. The Northeast database is displayed in the Database window.

3. Click **Queries** in the Objects bar of the Database window, and then click the **New** button. The New Query dialog box opens. See Figure 3-1.

Figure 3-1	NEW QUERY DIALOG BOX

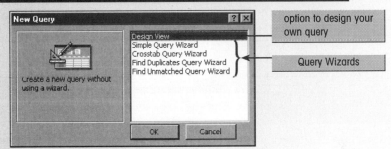

You'll design your own query instead of using a Query Wizard.

4. If necessary, click **Design View** in the list box.

5. Click the **OK** button. Access opens the Show Table dialog box on top of the Query window. (Note that you could also have double clicked the "Create query in Design view" option in the Database window.) Notice that the title bar of the Query window shows that you are creating a select query.

   The query you are creating will retrieve data from the Employer table, so you need to add this table to the Select Query window.

6. Click **Employer** in the Tables list box (if necessary), click the **Add** button, and then click the **Close** button. Access places the Employer table's field list in the Select Query window and closes the Show Table dialog box.

   To display more of the fields you'll be using for creating queries, you'll maximize the Select Query window.

7. Click the **Maximize** button ▢ on the Select Query window title bar. See Figure 3-2.

Figure 3-2   SELECT QUERY IN DESIGN VIEW

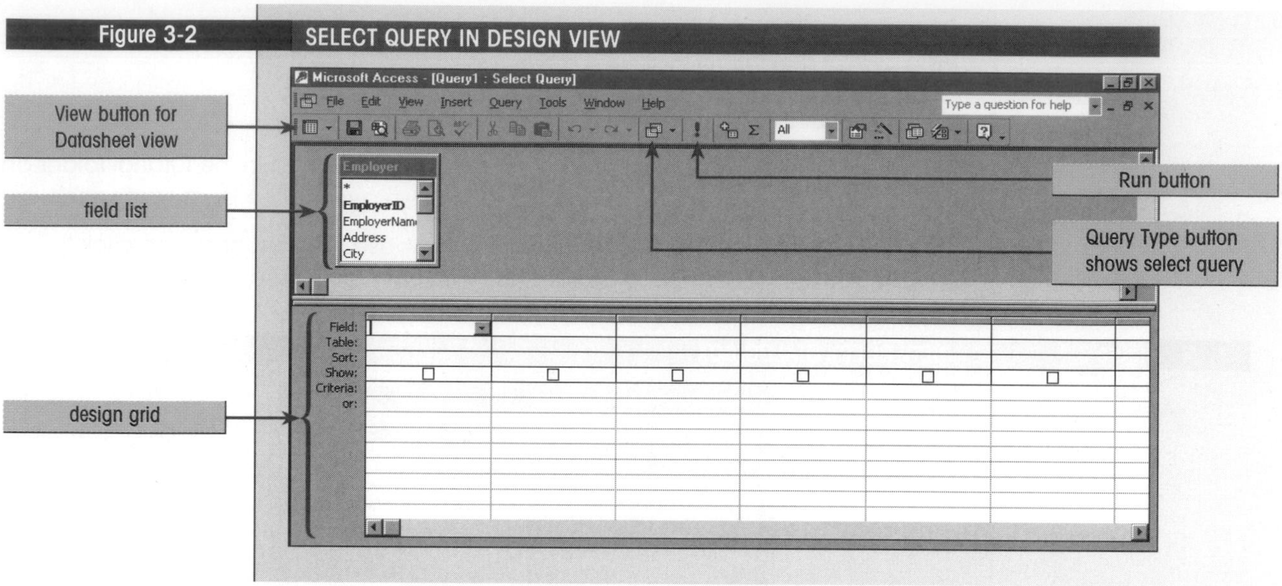

In Design view, the Select Query window contains the standard title bar, the menu bar, the status bar, and the Query Design toolbar. On the toolbar, the Query Type button shows a select query; the icon on this button changes according to the type of query you are creating. The title bar on the Select Query window displays the query type (Select Query) and the default query name (Query1). You'll change the default query name to a more meaningful one later when you save the query.

The Select Query window in Design view contains a field list and the design grid. The **field list** contains the fields for the table you are querying. The table name appears at the top of the list box, and the fields are listed in the order in which they appear in the table. You can scroll the field list to see more fields; or, you can expand the field list to display all the fields and the complete field names by resizing the field list box.

In the **design grid**, you include the fields and record selection criteria for the information you want to see. Each column in the design grid contains specifications about a field you will use in the query. You can choose a single field for your query by dragging its name from the field list to the design grid in the lower portion of the window. Alternatively, you can double-click a field name to place it in the next available design grid column.

When you are constructing a query, you can see the query results at any time by clicking the View button or the Run button on the Query Design toolbar. In response, Access displays the datasheet, which contains the set of fields and records that results from answering, or **running**, the query. The order of the fields in the datasheet is the same as the order of the fields in the design grid. Although the datasheet looks just like a table datasheet and appears in Datasheet view, a query datasheet is temporary, and its contents are based on the criteria you establish in the design grid. In contrast, a table datasheet shows the permanent data in a table. However, you can update data while viewing a query datasheet, just as you can when working in a table datasheet or form.

If the query you are creating includes every field from the specified table, you can use one of the following three methods to transfer all the fields from the field list to the design grid:

- Click and drag each field individually from the field list to the design grid. Use this method if you want the fields in your query to appear in an order that is different from the order in the field list.

■ Double-click the asterisk in the field list. Access places the table name followed by a period and an asterisk (as in "Employer.*") in the design grid, which signifies that the order of the fields will be the same in the query as it is in the field list. Use this method if you don't need to sort the query or specify conditions for the records you want to select. The advantage of using this method is that you do not need to change the query if you add or delete fields from the underlying table structure. Such changes are reflected automatically in the query.

■ Double-click the field list title bar to highlight all the fields, and then click and drag one of the highlighted fields to the design grid. Access places each field in a separate column and arranges the fields in the order in which they appear in the field list. Use this method when you need to sort your query or include record selection criteria.

Now you'll create and run Zack's query to display selected fields from the Employer table.

Creating and Running a Query

The default table datasheet displays all the fields in the table, in the same order as they appear in the table. In contrast, a query datasheet can display selected fields from a table, and the order of the fields can be different from that of the table.

Zack wants the Employer table's EmployerID, EmployerName, City, ContactFirstName, ContactLastName, and WebSite fields to appear in the query results. You'll add each of these fields to the design grid.

To select the fields for the query, and then run the query:

1. Drag **EmployerID** from the Employer field list to the design grid's first column Field text box, and then release the mouse button. See Figure 3-3.

Figure 3-3	FIELD ADDED TO THE DESIGN GRID

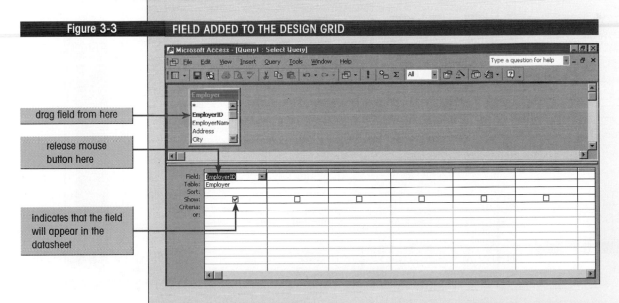

drag field from here

release mouse button here

indicates that the field will appear in the datasheet

In the design grid's first column, the field name EmployerID appears in the Field text box, the table name Employer appears in the Table text box, and the check mark in the Show check box indicates that the field will be displayed in the datasheet when you run the query. Sometimes you might not want to display a field and its values in the query results. For example, if you are creating a query to show all employers located in Massachusetts, and you assign the name "Employers in Massachusetts" to the query, you do not need to include the State/Prov field value for each record in the query results—every State/Prov field value would be "MA" for Massachusetts. Even if you choose not to include a field in the display of the query results, you can still use the field as part of the query to select specific records or to specify a particular sequence for the records in the datasheet.

2. Double-click **EmployerName** in the Employer field list. Access adds this field to the second column of the design grid.

3. Scrolling the Employer field list as necessary, repeat Step 2 for the **City**, **ContactFirstName**, **ContactLastName**, and **WebSite** fields to add these fields to the design grid in that order.

   TROUBLE? If you double-click the wrong field and accidentally add it to the design grid, you can remove the field from the grid. Select the field's column by clicking the pointer ↓ on the bar above the Field text box for the field you want to delete, and then press the Delete key (or click Edit on the menu bar, and then click Delete Columns).

   Having selected the fields for Zack's query, you now can run the query.

4. Click the **Run** button [!] on the Query Design toolbar. Access runs the query and displays the results in Datasheet view. See Figure 3-4.

Figure 3-4	DATASHEET DISPLAYED AFTER RUNNING THE QUERY

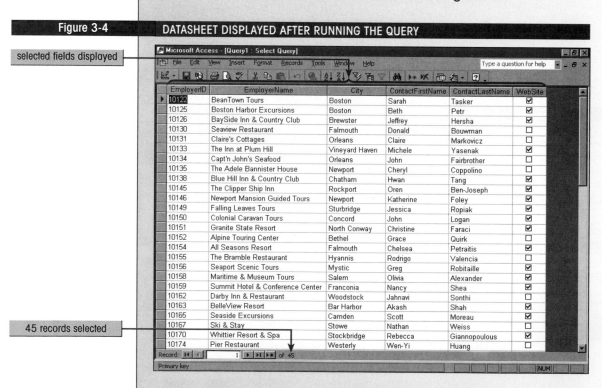

The six fields you added to the design grid appear in the datasheet, and the records are displayed in primary key sequence by EmployerID. Access selected a total of 45 records for display in the datasheet.

Zack asks you to save the query as "Employer Analysis" so that he can easily retrieve the same data again.

5. Click the **Save** button 🔲 on the Query Datasheet toolbar. The Save As dialog box opens.

6. Type **Employer Analysis** in the Query Name text box, and then press the **Enter** key. Access saves the query with the specified name in the Northeast database on your Data Disk and displays the name in the title bar.

When viewing the results of the query, Zack noticed a couple of changes that need to be made to the data in the Employer table. The Adele Bannister House recently developed a Web site, so the WebSite field for this record needs to be updated. In addition, the contact information has changed for the Alpine Touring Center.

Updating Data Using a Query

Although a query datasheet is temporary and its contents are based on the criteria in the query design grid, you can update the data in a table using a query datasheet. In this case, Zack has changes he wants you to make to records in the Employer table. Instead of making the changes in the table datasheet, you can make them in the Employer Analysis query datasheet. The underlying Employer table will be updated with the changes you make.

To update data using the Employer Analysis query datasheet:

1. For the record with EmployerID 10135 (The Adele Bannister House), click the check box in the WebSite field to place a check mark in it.

2. For the record with EmployerID 10162 (Alpine Touring Center), change the ContactFirstName field value to **Mary** and change the ContactLastName field value to **Grant**.

3. Click the **Close Window** button ☒ on the menu bar to close the query. Note that the Employer Analysis query appears in the list of queries.

4. Click the **Restore Window** button 🗗 on the menu bar to return the Database window to its original size.

   Now you will check the Employer table to verify that the changes you made in the query datasheet were also made to the Employer table records.

5. Click **Tables** in the Objects bar of the Database window, click **Employer** in the list of tables, and then click the **Open** button. The Employer table datasheet opens.

6. For the record with EmployerID 10135, scroll the datasheet to the right to verify that the WebSite field contains a check mark. For the record with EmployerID 10152, scroll to the right to see the new contact information (Mary Grant).

7. Click the **Close** button ☒ on the Employer table window to close it.

Matt also wants to view specific information in the Northeast database. However, he needs to see data from both the Employer table and the Position table at the same time. To view data from two tables at the same time, you need to define a relationship between the tables.

Defining **Table Relationships**

One of the most powerful features of a relational database management system is its ability to define relationships between tables. You use a common field to relate one table to another. The process of relating tables is often called performing a **join**. When you join tables that have a common field, you can extract data from them as if they were one larger table. For example, you can join the Employer and Position tables by using the EmployerID field in both tables as the common field. Then you can use a query, a form, or a report to extract selected data from each table, even though the data is contained in two separate tables, as shown in Figure 3-5. In the Positions query shown in Figure 3-5, the PositionID, PositionTitle, and Wage columns are fields from the Position table, and the EmployerName and State/Prov columns are fields from the Employer table. The joining of records is based on the common field of EmployerID. The Employer and Position tables have a type of relationship called a one-to-many relationship.

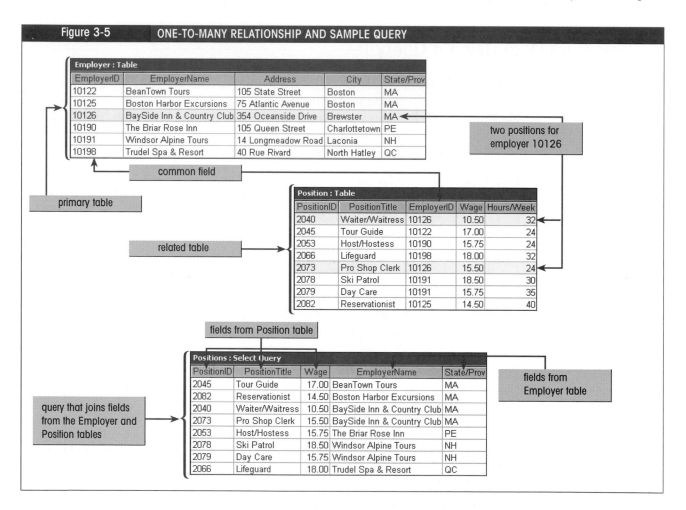

Figure 3-5   ONE-TO-MANY RELATIONSHIP AND SAMPLE QUERY

One-to-Many Relationships

A **one-to-many relationship** exists between two tables when one record in the first table matches zero, one, or many records in the second table, and when one record in the second table matches exactly one record in the first table. For example, as shown in Figure 3-5, employers 10126 and 10191 each have two available positions, and employers 10122, 10125, 10190, and 10198 each have one available position. Every position has a single matching employer.

Access refers to the two tables that form a relationship as the primary table and the related table. The **primary table** is the "one" table in a one-to-many relationship; in Figure 3-5, the Employer table is the primary table because there is only one employer for each available position. The **related table** is the "many" table; in Figure 3-5, the Position table is the related table because there can be many positions offered by each employer.

Because related data is stored in two tables, inconsistencies between the tables can occur. Consider the following scenarios:

- Matt adds a position record to the Position table for a new employer, Glen Cove Inn, using EmployerID 10132. Matt did not first add the new employer's information to the Employer table, so this position does not have a matching record in the Employer table. The data is inconsistent, and the position record is considered to be an **orphaned** record.

- Matt changes the EmployerID in the Employer table for BaySide Inn & Country Club from 10126 to 10128. Two orphaned records for employer 10126 now exist in the Position table, and the database is inconsistent.

- Matt deletes the record for Boston Harbor Excursions, employer 10125, in the Employer table because this employer is no longer an NSJI client. The database is again inconsistent; one record for employer 10125 in the Position table has no matching record in the Employer table.

You can avoid these problems by specifying referential integrity between tables when you define their relationships.

Referential Integrity

Referential integrity is a set of rules that Access enforces to maintain consistency between related tables when you update data in a database. Specifically, the referential integrity rules are as follows:

- When you add a record to a related table, a matching record must already exist in the primary table, thereby preventing the possibility of orphaned records.

- If you attempt to change the value of the primary key in the primary table, Access prevents this change if matching records exist in a related table. However, if you choose the **cascade updates** option, Access permits the change in value to the primary key and changes the appropriate foreign key values in the related table, thereby eliminating the possibility of inconsistent data.

- When you delete a record in the primary table, Access prevents the deletion if matching records exist in a related table. However, if you choose the **cascade deletes** option, Access deletes the record in the primary table and also deletes all records in related tables that have matching foreign key values.

Now you'll define a one-to-many relationship between the Employer and Position tables so that you can use fields from both tables to create a query that will retrieve the information Matt needs. You will also define a one-to-many relationship between the NAICS (primary) table and the Employer (related) table.

Defining a Relationship Between Two Tables

When two tables have a common field, you can define a relationship between them in the Relationships window. The **Relationships window** illustrates the relationships among a database's tables. In this window, you can view or change existing relationships, define new relationships between tables, and rearrange the layout of the tables in the window.

You need to open the Relationships window and define the relationship between the Employer and Position tables. You'll define a one-to-many relationship between the two tables, with Employer as the primary table and Position as the related table, and with EmployerID as the common field (the primary key in the Employer table and a foreign key in the Position table). You'll also define a one-to-many relationship between the NAICS and Employer tables, with NAICS as the primary table and Employer as the related table, and with NAICSCode as the common field (the primary key in the NAICS table and a foreign key in the Employer table).

To define the one-to-many relationship between the Employer and Position tables:

1. Click the **Relationships** button on the Database toolbar. The Show Table dialog box opens on top of the Relationships window. See Figure 3-6.

Figure 3-6	SHOW TABLE DIALOG BOX

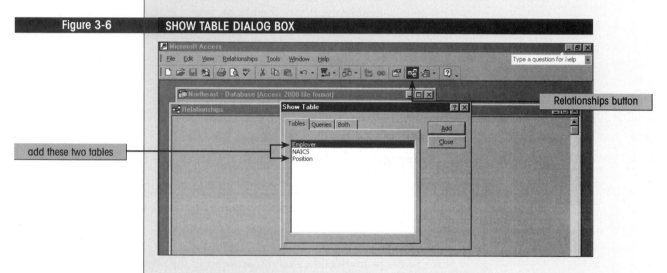

add these two tables

Relationships button

You must add each table participating in a relationship to the Relationships window.

2. Click **Employer** (if necessary), and then click the **Add** button. The Employer field list is added to the Relationships window.

3. Click **Position**, and then click the **Add** button. The Position field list is added to the Relationships window.

4. Click the **Close** button in the Show Table dialog box to close it and reveal the entire Relationships window.

   To form the relationship between the two tables, you drag the common field of EmployerID from the primary table to the related table. Then Access opens the Edit Relationships dialog box, in which you select the relationship options for the two tables.

5. Click **EmployerID** in the Employer field list, and drag it to **EmployerID** in the Position field list. When you release the mouse button, the Edit Relationships dialog box opens. See Figure 3-7.

Figure 3-7   EDIT RELATIONSHIPS DIALOG BOX

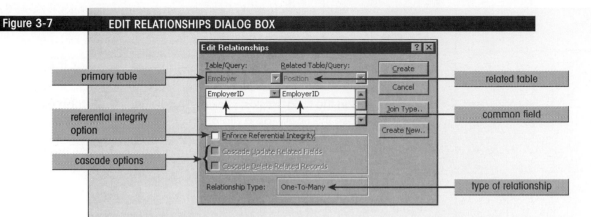

The primary table, related table, and common field appear at the top of the dialog box. The type of relationship, One-To-Many, appears at the bottom of the dialog box. When you click the Enforce Referential Integrity check box, the two cascade options become available. If you select the Cascade Update Related Fields option, Access will change the appropriate foreign key values in the related table when you change a primary key value in the primary table. If you select the Cascade Delete Related Records option, when you delete a record in the primary table, Access will delete all records in the related table that have a matching foreign key value.

6. Click the **Enforce Referential Integrity** check box, click the **Cascade Update Related Fields** check box, and then click the **Cascade Delete Related Records** check box. You now have selected all the necessary relationship options.

7. Click the **Create** button to define the one-to-many relationship between the two tables and to close the dialog box. The completed relationship appears in the Relationships window. See Figure 3-8.

Figure 3-8   DEFINED RELATIONSHIP IN THE RELATIONSHIPS WINDOW

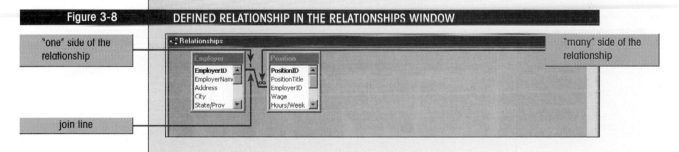

The **join line** connects the EmployerID fields, which are common to the two tables. The common field joins the two tables, which have a one-to-many relationship. The "one" side of the relationship has the digit 1 at its end, and the "many" side of the relationship has the infinity symbol ∞ at its end. The two tables are still separate tables, but you can use the data in them as if they were one table.

Now you need to define the one-to-many relationship between the NAICS and Employer tables. In this relationship, NAICS is the primary ("one") table because there is only one code for each employer. Employer is the related ("many") table because there are multiple employers with the same NAICS code.

To define the one-to-many relationship between the NAICS and Employer tables:

1. Click the **Show Table** button on the Relationship toolbar. The Show Table dialog box opens on top of the Relationships window.

2. Click **NAICS** in the list of tables, click the **Add** button, and then click the **Close** button to close the Show Table dialog box. The NAICS field list appears in the Relationships window to the right of the Position field list. To make it easier to define the relationship, you'll move the NAICS field list below the Employer and Position field lists.

3. Click the NAICS field list title bar and drag the list until it is below the Position table (see Figure 3-9), and then release the mouse button.

4. Scroll the Employer field list until the NAICSCode field is visible. Because the NAICS table is the primary table in this relationship, you need to drag the NAICSCode field from the NAICS field list to the Employer field list. Notice that the NAICSCode field in the NAICS table appears in a bold font; this indicates that the field is the table's primary key. On the other hand, the NAICSCode field in the Employer table is not bold, which is a reminder that this field is the foreign key in this table.

5. Click and drag the **NAICSCode** field in the NAICS field list to the **NAICSCode** field in the Employer field list. When you release the mouse button, the Edit Relationships dialog box opens.

6. Click the **Enforce Referential Integrity** check box, click the **Cascade Update Related Fields** check box, and then click the **Cascade Delete Related Records** check box. You now have selected all the necessary relationship options.

7. Click the **Create** button to define the one-to-many relationship between the two tables and close the dialog box. The completed relationship appears in the Relationships window. See Figure 3-9.

Figure 3-9	BOTH RELATIONSHIPS DEFINED

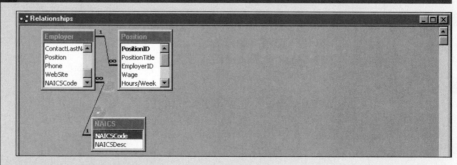

With both relationships defined, you have connected the data among the three tables in the Northeast database.

8. Click the **Save** button on the Relationship toolbar to save the layout in the Relationships window.

9. Click the **Close** button on the Relationships window title bar. The Relationships window closes, and you return to the Database window.

Creating a Multi-table Query

Now that you have joined the Employer and Position tables, you can create a query to produce the information Matt wants. To help him determine his recruiting needs, Matt wants a query that displays the EmployerName, City, and State/Prov fields from the Employer table and the Openings, PositionTitle, StartDate, and EndDate fields from the Position table.

To create, run, and save the query using the Employer and Position tables:

1. Click **Queries** in the Objects bar of the Database window, and then double-click **Create query in Design view**. The Show Table dialog box opens on top of the Query window in Design view.

   You need to add the Employer and Position tables to the Query window.

2. Click **Employer** in the Tables list box (if necessary), click the **Add** button, click **Position**, click the **Add** button, and then click the **Close** button. The Employer and Position field lists appear in the Query window, and the Show Table dialog box closes. Note that the one-to-many relationship that exists between the two tables is shown in the Query window. Also, notice that the join line is thick at both ends; this signifies that you selected the option to enforce referential integrity. If you had not selected this option, the join line would be thin at both ends and neither the "1" nor the infinity symbol would appear, even though there is a one-to-many relationship between the two tables.

   You need to place the EmployerName, City, and State/Prov fields from the Employer field list into the design grid, and then place the Openings, PositionTitle, StartDate, and EndDate fields from the Position field list into the design grid.

3. Double-click **EmployerName** in the Employer field list to place EmployerName in the design grid's first column Field text box.

4. Repeat Step 3 to add the **City** and **State/Prov** fields from the Employer table, so that these fields are placed in the second and third columns of the design grid.

5. Repeat Step 3 to add the **Openings**, **PositionTitle**, **StartDate**, and **EndDate** fields (in that order) from the Position table, so that these fields are placed in the fourth through seventh columns of the design grid.

   The query specifications are completed, so you now can run the query.

6. Click the **Run** button ▣ on the Query Design toolbar. Access runs the query and displays the results in the datasheet.

7. Click the **Maximize** button ▣ on the Query window title bar. See Figure 3-10.

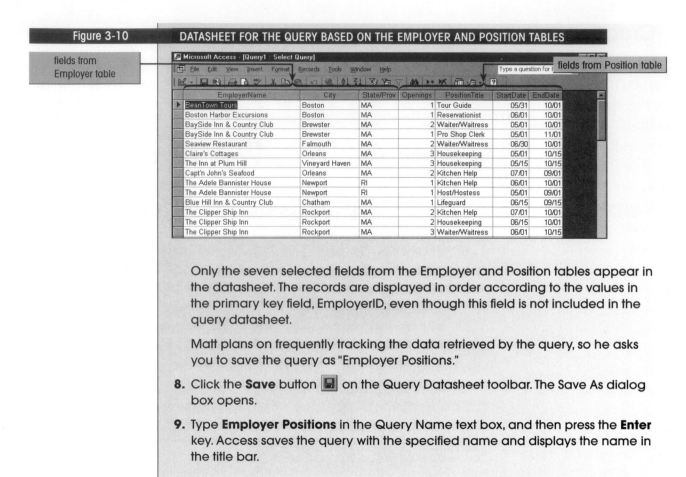

Figure 3-10 — DATASHEET FOR THE QUERY BASED ON THE EMPLOYER AND POSITION TABLES

fields from Employer table

fields from Position table

Only the seven selected fields from the Employer and Position tables appear in the datasheet. The records are displayed in order according to the values in the primary key field, EmployerID, even though this field is not included in the query datasheet.

Matt plans on frequently tracking the data retrieved by the query, so he asks you to save the query as "Employer Positions."

8. Click the **Save** button 🔲 on the Query Datasheet toolbar. The Save As dialog box opens.

9. Type **Employer Positions** in the Query Name text box, and then press the **Enter** key. Access saves the query with the specified name and displays the name in the title bar.

Matt decides he wants the records displayed in alphabetical order by employer name. Because the query displays data in order by the field value of EmployerID, which is the primary key for the Employer table, you need to sort the records by EmployerName to display the data in the order Matt wants.

Sorting Data in a Query

Sorting is the process of rearranging records in a specified order or sequence. Sometimes you might need to sort data before displaying or printing it to meet a specific request. For example, Matt might want to review position information arranged by the StartDate field because he needs to know which positions are available earliest in the year. On the other hand, Elsa might want to view position information arranged by the Openings field for each employer, because she monitors employer activity for NSJI.

When you sort data in a query, you do not change the sequence of the records in the underlying tables. Only the records in the query datasheet are rearranged according to your specifications.

To sort records, you must select the **sort key**, which is the field used to determine the order of records in the datasheet. In this case, Matt wants the data sorted by the employer name, so you need to specify the EmployerName field as the sort key. Sort keys can be text, number, date/time, currency, AutoNumber, yes/no, or Lookup Wizard fields, but not memo, OLE object, or hyperlink fields. You sort records in either ascending (increasing) or descending (decreasing) order. Figure 3-11 shows the results of each type of sort for different data types.

Figure 3-11	SORTING RESULTS FOR DIFFERENT DATA TYPES	
DATA TYPE	**ASCENDING SORT RESULTS**	**DESCENDING SORT RESULTS**
Text	A to Z	Z to A
Number	lowest to highest numeric value	highest to lowest numeric value
Date/Time	oldest to most recent date	most recent to oldest date
Currency	lowest to highest numeric value	highest to lowest numeric value
AutoNumber	lowest to highest numeric value	highest to lowest numeric value
Yes/No	yes (check mark in check box) then no values	no then yes values

Access provides several methods for sorting data in a table or query datasheet and in a form. One method, clicking a toolbar sort button, lets you sort the displayed records quickly.

Using a Toolbar Button to Sort Data

The **Sort Ascending** and **Sort Descending** buttons on the toolbar allow you to sort records immediately, based on the values in the selected field. First you select the column on which you want to base the sort, and then you click the appropriate sort button on the toolbar to rearrange the records in either ascending or descending order. Unless you save the datasheet or form after you've sorted the records, the rearrangement of records is temporary.

Recall that in Tutorial 1 you used the Sort Ascending button to sort query results by the State/Prov field. You'll use this same button to sort the Employer Positions query results by the EmployerName field.

To sort the records using a toolbar sort button:

1. Click any visible EmployerName field value to establish the field as the current field (if necessary).

2. Click the **Sort Ascending** button  on the Query Datasheet toolbar. The records are rearranged in ascending order by employer name. See Figure 3-12.

Figure 3-12	SORTING RECORDS ON A SINGLE FIELD IN A DATASHEET

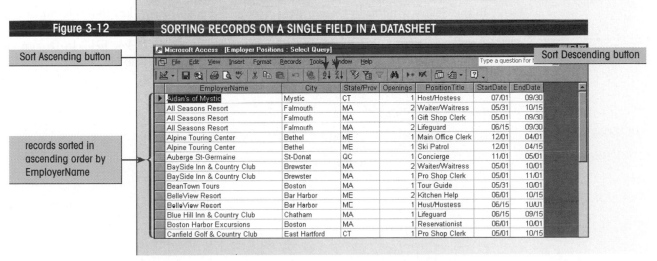

Sort Ascending button

Sort Descending button

records sorted in ascending order by EmployerName

After viewing the query results, Matt decides that he'd prefer to see the records arranged by the value in the PositionTitle field, so that he can identify the types of positions he needs to fill. He also wants to display the records in descending order according to the value of the Openings field, so that he can easily see how many openings there are for each position. To do this you need to sort using two fields.

Sorting Multiple Fields in Design View

Sort keys can be unique or nonunique. A sort key is **unique** if the value of the sort key field for each record is different. The EmployerID field in the Employer table is an example of a unique sort key because each employer record has a different value in this field. A sort key is **nonunique** if more than one record can have the same value for the sort key field. For example, the PositionTitle field in the Position table is a nonunique sort key because more than one record can have the same PositionTitle value.

When the sort key is nonunique, records with the same sort key value are grouped together, but they are not in a specific order within the group. To arrange these grouped records in a specific order, you can specify a **secondary sort key**, which is a second sort key field. The first sort key field is called the **primary sort key**. Note that the primary sort key is *not* the same as a table's primary key field. A table has at most one primary key, which must be unique, whereas any field in a table can serve as a primary sort key.

Access lets you select up to 10 different sort keys. When you use the toolbar sort buttons, the sort key fields must be in adjacent columns in the datasheet. You highlight the adjacent columns, and Access sorts first by the first column and then by each other highlighted column in order from left to right.

Matt wants the records sorted first by the PositionTitle field and then by the Openings field. The two fields are adjacent, but not in the correct left-to-right order, so you cannot use the toolbar buttons to sort them. You could move the Openings field to the right of the PositionTitle field in the query datasheet. However, you can specify only one type of sort—either ascending or descending—for selected columns in the query datasheet. This is not what Matt wants; he wants the PositionTitle field values to be sorted in ascending alphabetical order and the Openings field values to be sorted in descending order.

In this case, you need to specify the sort keys for the query in Design view. Any time you want to sort on multiple fields that are nonadjacent or in the wrong order, but do not want to rearrange the columns in the query datasheet to accomplish the sort, you must specify the sort keys in Design view.

In the Query window in Design view, Access first uses the sort key that is leftmost in the design grid. Therefore, you must arrange the fields you want to sort from left to right in the design grid, with the primary sort key being the leftmost sort key field. In Design view, multiple sort fields do not have to be adjacent to each other, as they do in Datasheet view; however, they must be in the correct left-to-right order.

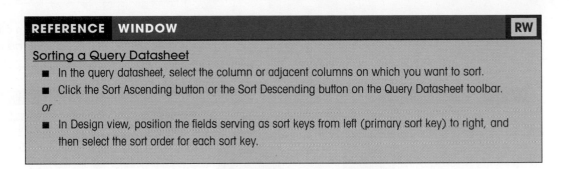

<u>Sorting a Query Datasheet</u>
- In the query datasheet, select the column or adjacent columns on which you want to sort.
- Click the Sort Ascending button or the Sort Descending button on the Query Datasheet toolbar.

or

- In Design view, position the fields serving as sort keys from left (primary sort key) to right, and then select the sort order for each sort key.

To achieve the results Matt wants, you need to switch to Design view, move the Openings field to the right of the EndDate field, and then specify the sort order for the two fields.

To select the two sort keys in Design view:

1. Click the **View** button for Design view 🔲 on the Query Datasheet toolbar to open the query in Design view.

   First, you'll move the Openings field to the right of the EndDate field. Remember, in Design view, the sort fields do not have to be adjacent, and non-sort key fields can appear between sort key fields. So, you will move the Openings field to the end of the query design, following the EndDate field.

2. If necessary, click the right arrow in the design grid's horizontal scroll bar a few times to scroll to the right so that both the Openings and EndDate fields are completely visible.

3. Position the pointer in the Openings field selector until the pointer changes to a ⬇ shape, and then click to select the field. See Figure 3-13

Figure 3-13   **SELECTED OPENINGS FIELD**

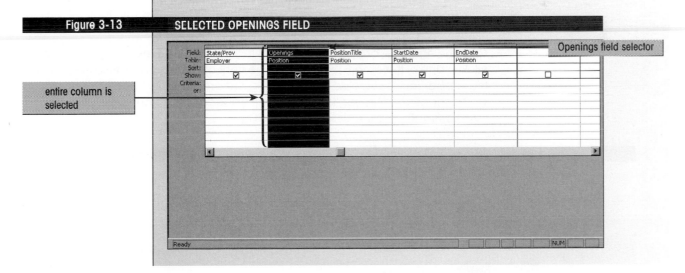

Openings field selector

entire column is selected

4. Position the pointer in the Openings field selector, and then click and drag the pointer 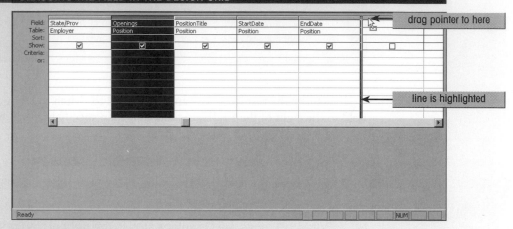 to the right until the vertical line on the right of the EndDate field is highlighted. See Figure 3-14.

Figure 3-14   **DRAGGING THE FIELD IN THE DESIGN GRID**

5. Release the mouse button. The Openings field moves to the right of the EndDate field.

The fields are now in the correct order for the sort. Next, you need to specify an ascending sort order for the PositionTitle field and a descending sort order for the Openings field.

6. Click the right side of the **PositionTitle Sort** text box to display the list arrow and the sort options, and then click **Ascending**. You've selected an ascending sort order for the PositionTitle field, which will be the primary sort key. The PositionTitle field is a text field, and an ascending sort order will display the field values in alphabetical order.

7. Click the right side of the **Openings Sort** text box, click **Descending**, and then click in one of the empty text boxes to the right of the Openings field to deselect the setting. You've selected a descending sort order for the Openings field, which will be the secondary sort key, because it appears to the right of the primary sort key (PositionTitle) in the design grid. See Figure 3-15.

Figure 3-15   **SELECTING TWO SORT KEYS IN DESIGN VIEW**

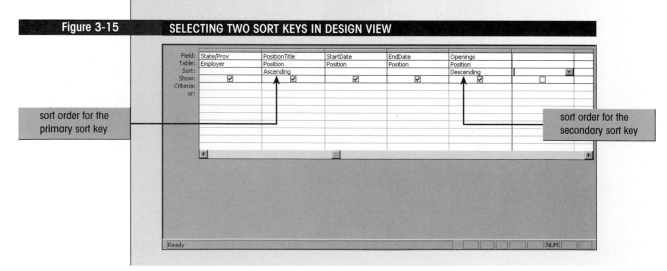

You have finished your query changes, so now you can run the query and then save the modified query with the same query name.

8. Click the **Run** button ⚠ on the Query Design toolbar. Access runs the query and displays the query datasheet. The records appear in ascending order, based on the values of the PositionTitle field. Within groups of records with the same PositionTitle field value, the records appear in descending order by the values of the Openings field. See Figure 3-16.

| Figure 3-16 | DATASHEET SORTED ON TWO FIELDS |

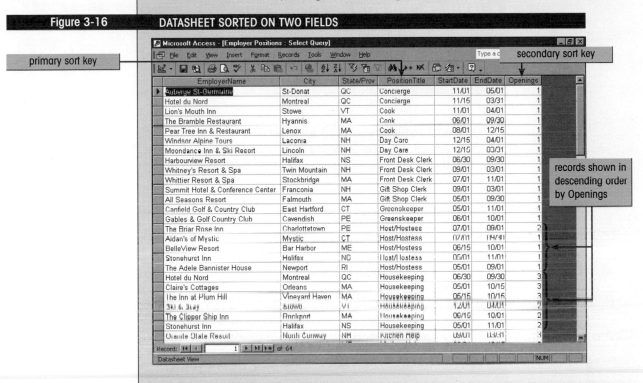

primary sort key

secondary sort key

records shown in descending order by Openings

When you save the query, all of your design changes—including the selection of the sort keys—are saved with the query. The next time Matt runs the query, the records will appear sorted by the primary and secondary sort keys.

9. Click the **Save** button 🖫 on the Query Datasheet toolbar to save the revised Employer Positions query.

Matt wants to concentrate on the positions in the datasheet with a start date sometime in May, to see how many recruits he will need to fill these positions. Selecting only the records with a StartDate field value in May is a temporary change that Matt wants in the datasheet, so you do not need to switch to Design view and change the query. Instead, you can apply a filter.

Filtering Data

A **filter** is a set of restrictions you place on the records in an open datasheet or form to *temporarily* isolate a subset of the records. A filter lets you view different subsets of displayed records so that you can focus on only the data you need. Unless you save a query or form with a filter applied, an applied filter is not available the next time you run the query or open the form.

The simplest technique for filtering records is Filter By Selection. **Filter By Selection** lets you select all or part of a field value in a datasheet or form, and then display only those records that contain the selected value in the field. Another technique for filtering records is to use **Filter By Form**, which changes your datasheet to display empty fields. Then you can select a value from the list arrow that appears when you click any blank field to apply a filter that selects only those records containing that value.

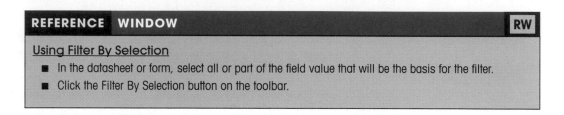

REFERENCE WINDOW   RW

Using Filter By Selection
- In the datasheet or form, select all or part of the field value that will be the basis for the filter.
- Click the Filter By Selection button on the toolbar.

For Matt's request, you need to select just the beginning digits "05" in the StartDate field, to view all the records with a May start date, and then use Filter By Selection to display only those query records with this same partial value.

To display the records using Filter By Selection:

1. In the query datasheet, locate the first occurrence of a May date in the StartDate field, and then select **05** in that field value.

2. Click the **Filter By Selection** button 🕎 on the Query Datasheet toolbar. Access displays the filtered results. Only the 17 query records that have a StartDate field value with the beginning digits "05" appear in the datasheet. The status bar's display (FLTR), the area next to the navigation buttons, and the selected Remove Filter button on the toolbar all indicate that the records have been filtered. See Figure 3-17.

Figure 3-17   USING FILTER BY SELECTION

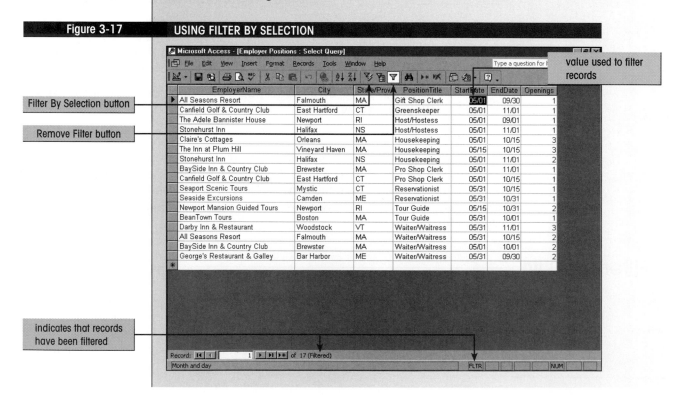

Next, Matt wants to view only those records with a StartDate value of 05/01, because he needs to fill those positions before the other May positions. So, you need to filter by the complete field value of 05/01.

3. Click in any StartDate field value of **05/01**, and then click 🔽. The filtered display now shows only the 9 records with a value of 05/01 in the StartDate field.

Now you can redisplay all the query records by clicking the Remove Filter button; this button works as a toggle to switch between the filtered and nonfiltered displays.

4. Click the **Remove Filter** button 🔽 on the Query Datasheet toolbar. Access redisplays all the records in the query datasheet.

5. Click the **Save** button 💾 on the Query Datasheet toolbar, and then click the **Close Window** button ✕ on the menu bar to save and close the query and return to the Database window.

6. Click the **Restore Window** button 🗗 on the menu bar to return the Database window to its original size.

The queries you've created will help NSJI employees retrieve just the information they want to view. In the next session, you'll continue to create queries to meet their information needs.

Session 3.1 QUICK CHECK

1. What is a select query?

2. Describe the field list and the design grid in the Query window in Design view.

3. How are a table datasheet and a query datasheet similar? How are they different?

4. The _____ is the "one" table in a one-to-many relationship, and the _____ is the "many" table in the relationship.

5. _____ is a set of rules that Access enforces to maintain consistency between related tables when you update data in a database.

6. For a date/time field, how do the records appear when sorted in ascending order?

7. When must you define multiple sort keys in Design view instead of in the query datasheet?

8. A(n) _____ is a set of restrictions you place on the records in an open datasheet or form to isolate a subset of records temporarily.

SESSION 3.2

In this session, you will specify an exact match condition in a query, change a datasheet's appearance, use a comparison operator to match a range of values, use the And and Or logical operators to define multiple selection criteria for queries, use multiple undo and redo, and perform calculations in queries.

Defining Record Selection Criteria for Queries

Matt wants to display employer and position information for all positions with a start date of 07/01, so that he can plan his recruitment efforts accordingly. For this request, you could create a query to select the correct fields and all records in the Employer and Position tables, select a StartDate field value of 07/01 in the query datasheet, and then click the Filter By Selection button to filter the query results to display only those positions starting on July 1. However, a faster way of displaying the data Matt needs is to create a query that displays the selected fields and only those records in the Employer and Position tables that satisfy a condition.

Just as you can display selected fields from a database in a query datasheet, you can display selected records. To tell Access which records you want to select, you must specify a condition as part of the query. A **condition** is a criterion, or rule, that determines which records are selected. To define a condition for a field, you place the condition in the field's Criteria text box in the design grid.

A condition usually consists of an operator, often a comparison operator, and a value. A **comparison operator** asks Access to compare the value in a database field to the condition value and to select all the records for which the relationship is true. For example, the condition >15.00 for the Wage field selects all records in the Position table having Wage field values greater than 15.00. Figure 3-18 shows the Access comparison operators.

Figure 3-18	ACCESS COMPARISON OPERATORS	

OPERATOR	MEANING	EXAMPLE
=	equal to (optional; default operator)	="Hall"
<	less than	<#1/1/99#
<=	less than or equal to	<=100
>	greater than	>"C400"
>=	greater than or equal to	>=18.75
<>	not equal to	<>"Hall"
Between ... And...	between two values (inclusive)	Between 50 And 325
In ()	in a list of values	In ("Hall", "Seeger")
Like	matches a pattern that includes wildcards	Like "706*"

Specifying an Exact Match

For Matt's request, you need to create a query that will display only those records in the Position table with the value 07/01 in the StartDate field. This type of condition is called an **exact match** because the value in the specified field must match the condition exactly in order for the record to be included in the query results. You'll use the Simple Query Wizard to create the query, and then you'll specify the exact match condition.

To create the query using the Simple Query Wizard:

1. If you took a break after the previous session, make sure that Access is running, the Northeast database is open, and the Queries object is selected in the Database window.

2. Double-click **Create query by using wizard**. Access opens the first Simple Query Wizard dialog box, in which you select the tables (or queries) and fields for the query.

3. Click the **Tables/Queries** list arrow, and then click **Table: Position**. The fields in the Position table appear in the Available Fields list box. Except for the PositionID and EmployerID fields, you will include all fields from the Position table in the query.

4. Click the ⟩⟩ button. All the fields from the Available Fields list box move to the Selected Fields list box.

5. Scroll up and click **PositionID** in the Selected Fields list box, click the ⟨ button to move the PositionID field back to the Available Fields list box, click **EmployerID** in the Selected Fields list box, and then click the ⟨ button to move the EmployerID field back to the Available Fields list box.

   Matt also wants certain information from the Employer table included in the query results. Because he wants the fields from the Employer table to appear in the query datasheet to the right of the fields from the Position table fields, you need to click the last field in the Selected Fields list box so that the new Employer fields will be inserted below it in the list.

6. Click **Openings** in the Selected Fields list box.

7. Click the **Tables/Queries** list arrow, and then click **Table: Employer**. The fields in the Employer table now appear in the Available Fields list box. Notice that the fields you selected from the Position table remain in the Selected Fields list box.

8. Click **EmployerName** in the Available Fields list box, and then click the ⟩ button to move EmployerName to the Selected Fields list box, below the Openings field.

9. Repeat Step 8 to move the **State/Prov**, **ContactFirstName**, **ContactLastName**, and **Phone** fields into the Selected Fields list box. (Note that you can also double-click a field to move it from the Available Fields list box to the Selected Fields list box.)

10. Click the **Next** button to open the second Simple Query Wizard dialog box, in which you choose whether the query will display records from the selected tables or a summary of those records. Summary options show calculations such as average, minimum, maximum, and so on. Matt wants to view the details for the records, not a summary.

11. Make sure the **Detail (shows every field of every record)** option button is selected, and then click the **Next** button to open the last Simple Query Wizard dialog box, in which you choose a name for the query and complete the Wizard. You need to enter a condition for the query, so you'll want to modify the query's design.

12. Type **July 1 Positions**, click the **Modify the query design** option button, and then click the **Finish** button. Access saves the query as July 1 Positions and opens the query in Design view. See Figure 3-19.

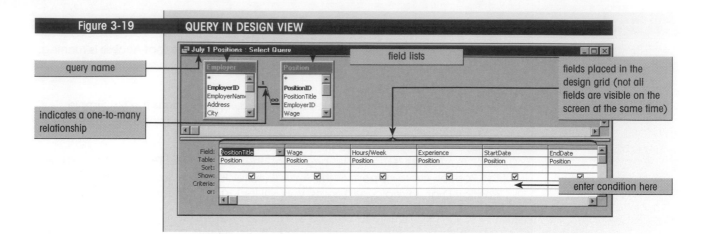

Figure 3-19   QUERY IN DESIGN VIEW

The field lists for the Employer and Position tables appear in the top portion of the window, and the join line indicating a one-to-many relationship connects the two tables. The selected fields appear in the design grid. Not all of the fields are visible in the grid; to see the other selected fields, you need to scroll to the right using the horizontal scroll bar.

To display the information Matt wants, you need to enter the condition for the StartDate field in its Criteria text box. Matt wants to display only those records with a start date of 07/01.

To enter the exact match condition, and then run the query:

1. Click the **StartDate Criteria** text box, type **7/01**, and then press the **Enter** key. The condition changes to #7/01/2003#.

   TROUBLE? If your date is displayed with a two-digit year, don't worry. You can customize Windows to display different date formats.

   TROUBLE? If the year in your date is different, don't worry. The StartDate field values do not contain digits for the year, so the year value will not affect the query you are creating.

   Access automatically placed number signs (#) before and after the condition. You must place date and time values inside number signs when using these values as selection criteria. If you omit the number signs, however, Access will include them automatically.

2. Click the **Run** button on the Query Design toolbar. Access runs the query and displays the selected field values for only those records with a StartDate field value of 07/01. A total of 9 records are selected and displayed in the datasheet. See Figure 3-20.

Figure 3-20	DATASHEET DISPLAYING SELECTED FIELDS AND RECORDS

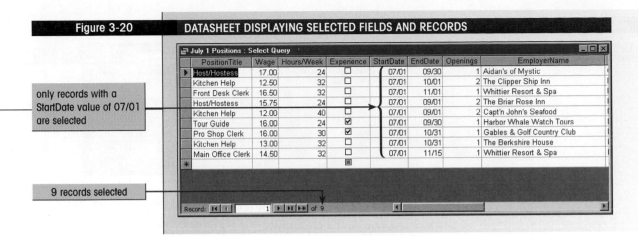

only records with a
StartDate value of 07/01
are selected

9 records selected

Matt would like to see more fields and records on the screen at one time. He asks you to maximize the datasheet, change the datasheet's font size, and resize all the columns to their best fit.

Changing a Datasheet's Appearance

You can change the characteristics of a datasheet, including the font type and size of text in the datasheet, to improve its appearance or readability. As you learned in Tutorial 2, you can also resize the datasheet columns to view more columns on the screen at the same time.

You'll maximize the datasheet, change the font size from the default 10 points to 8, and then resize the datasheet columns.

To change the font size and resize columns in the datasheet:

1. Click the **Maximize** button ▢ on the Query window title bar.

2. Click **Format** on the menu bar, and then click **Font** to open the Font dialog box.

3. Scroll the Size list box, click **8**, and then click the **OK** button. The font size for the entire datasheet changes to 8.

   Next you need to resize the columns to their best fit, so that each column is just wide enough to fit the longest value in the column. Instead of resizing each column individually, as you did in Tutorial 2, you'll select all the columns and resize them at the same time.

4. Position the pointer in the PositionTitle field selector. When the pointer changes to a ↓ shape, click to select the entire column.

5. Click the right arrow on the horizontal scroll bar until the Phone field is fully visible, and then position the pointer in the Phone field selector until the pointer changes to a ↓ shape.

6. Press and hold the **Shift** key, and then click the mouse button. All the columns are selected. Now you can resize all of them at once.

7. Position the pointer at the right edge of the Phone field selector until the pointer changes to a ↔ shape. See Figure 3-21.

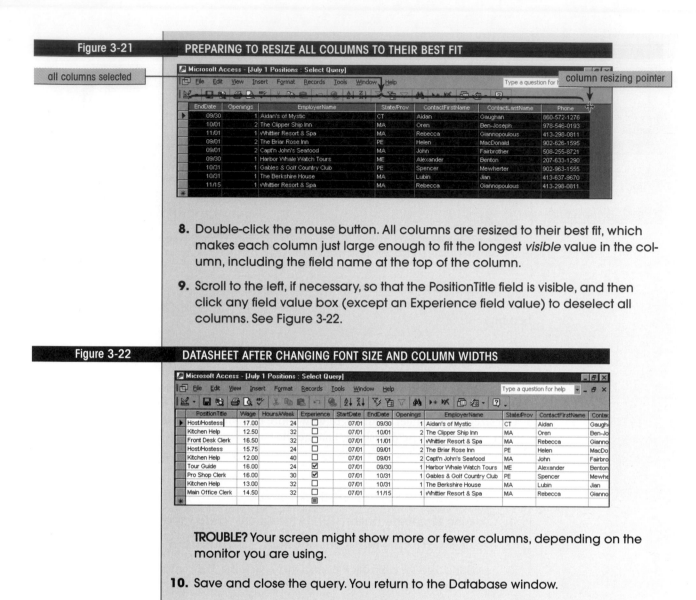

Figure 3-21   PREPARING TO RESIZE ALL COLUMNS TO THEIR BEST FIT

all columns selected

column resizing pointer

8. Double-click the mouse button. All columns are resized to their best fit, which makes each column just large enough to fit the longest *visible* value in the column, including the field name at the top of the column.

9. Scroll to the left, if necessary, so that the PositionTitle field is visible, and then click any field value box (except an Experience field value) to deselect all columns. See Figure 3-22.

Figure 3-22   DATASHEET AFTER CHANGING FONT SIZE AND COLUMN WIDTHS

TROUBLE? Your screen might show more or fewer columns, depending on the monitor you are using.

10. Save and close the query. You return to the Database window.

After viewing the query results, Matt decides that he would like to see the same fields, but only for those records whose Wage field value is equal to or greater than 17.00. He needs this information when he recruits students who will require a higher wage per hour for the available positions. To create the query needed to produce these results, you need to use a comparison operator to match a range of values—in this case, any Wage value greater than or equal to 17.00.

Using a Comparison Operator to Match a Range of Values

Once you create and save a query, you can click the Open button to run it again, or you can click the Design button to change its design. Because the design of the query you need to create next is similar to the July 1 Positions query, you will change its design, run the query to test it, and then save the query with a new name, which keeps the July 1 Positions query intact.

To change the July 1 Positions query design to create a new query:

1. Click the **July 1 Positions** query in the Database window (if necessary), and then click the **Design** button to open the July 1 Positions query in Design view.

2. Click the **Wage Criteria** text box, type **>=17**, and then press the **Tab** key three times. See Figure 3-23.

Figure 3-23	CHANGING A QUERY'S DESIGN TO CREATE A NEW QUERY

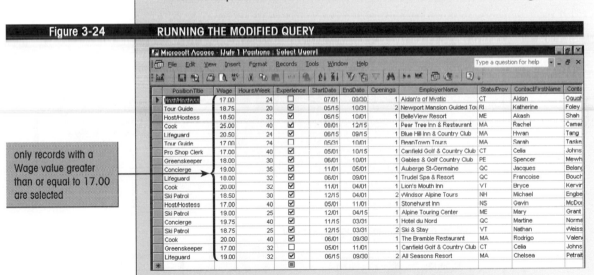

new condition

condition to delete

Matt's new condition specifies that a record will be selected only if its Wage field value is 17.00 or higher. Before you run the query, you need to delete the condition for the StartDate field.

3. With the StartDate field condition highlighted, press the **Delete** key. Now there is no condition for the StartDate field.

4. Click the **Run** button on the Query Design toolbar. Access runs the query and displays the selected fields for only those records with a Wage field value greater than or equal to 17.00. A total of 19 records are selected. See Figure 3-24.

Figure 3-24	RUNNING THE MODIFIED QUERY

Microsoft Access - [July 1 Positions : Select Query]

only records with a Wage value greater than or equal to 17.00 are selected

PositionTitle	Wage	Hours/Week	Experience	StartDate	EndDate	Openings	EmployerName	State/Prov	ContactFirstName	Conta
Host/Hostess	17.00	24	☐	07/01	09/30	1	Aidan's of Mystic	CT	Aidan	Cough
Tour Guide	18.75	20	☑	05/15	10/31	2	Newport Mansion Guided Tou	RI	Katherine	Foley
Host/Hostess	18.50	32	☑	06/15	10/01	1	BelleView Resort	ME	Akash	Shah
Cook	25.00	40	☑	09/01	12/15	1	Pear Tree Inn & Restaurant	MA	Rachel	Camer
Lifeguard	20.50	24	☑	06/15	09/15	1	Blue Hill Inn & Country Club	MA	Hwan	Tang
Tour Guide	17.00	24	☐	05/31	10/01	1	BeanTown Tours	MA	Sarah	Taske
Pro Shop Clerk	17.00	40	☑	05/01	10/15	1	Canfield Golf & Country Club	CT	Celia	Johns
Greenskeeper	18.00	30	☑	06/01	10/01	1	Gables & Golf Country Club	PE	Spencer	Mewh
Concierge	19.00	35	☑	11/01	05/01	1	Auberge St-Germaine	QC	Jacques	Belan
Lifeguard	18.00	32	☑	06/01	09/01	1	Trudel Spa & Resort	QC	Francoise	Bouch
Cook	20.00	32	☑	11/01	04/01	1	Lion's Mouth Inn	VT	Bryce	Kervir
Ski Patrol	18.50	30	☑	12/15	04/01	2	Windsor Alpine Tours	NH	Michael	Engbe
Host/Hostess	17.00	40	☑	05/01	11/01	1	Stonehurst Inn	NS	Gavin	McDor
Ski Patrol	19.00	25	☑	12/01	04/15	1	Alpine Touring Center	ME	Mary	Grant
Concierge	19.75	40	☑	11/15	03/31	1	Hotel du Nord	QC	Martine	Norma
Ski Patrol	18.75	25	☑	12/15	03/31	2	Ski & Stay	VT	Nathan	Weiss
Cook	20.00	40	☑	06/01	09/30	1	The Bramble Restaurant	MA	Rodrigo	Valeni
Greenskeeper	17.00	32	☐	05/01	11/01	1	Canfield Golf & Country Club	CT	Celia	Johns
Lifeguard	19.00	32	☑	06/15	09/30	2	All Seasons Resort	MA	Chelsea	Petrait

So that Matt can display this information again, as necessary, you'll save the query as High Wage Amounts.

5. Click **File** on the menu bar, click the double-arrow at the bottom of the menu to display the full menu (if necessary), and then click **Save As** to open the Save As dialog box.

6. In the text box for the new query name, type **High Wage Amounts**. Notice that the As text box specifies that you are saving the data as a query.

7. Click the **OK** button to save the query using the new name. The new query name appears in the title bar.

8. Close the Query window and return to the Database window.

Elsa asks Matt for a list of the positions with a start date of 07/01 for only the employers in Prince Edward Island. She wants to increase NSJI's business activity throughout eastern Canada (Prince Edward Island in particular), especially in the latter half of the year. To produce this data, you need to create a query containing two conditions—one for the position's start date and another to specify only the employers in Prince Edward Island (PE).

Defining Multiple Selection Criteria for Queries

Multiple conditions require you to use **logical operators** to combine two or more conditions. When you want a record selected only if two or more conditions are met, you need to use the **And logical operator**. In this case, Elsa wants to see only those records with a StartDate field value of 07/01 *and* a State/Prov field value of PE. If you place conditions in separate fields in the *same* Criteria row of the design grid, all conditions in that row must be met in order for a record to be included in the query results. However, if you place conditions in *different* Criteria rows, a record will be selected if at least one of the conditions is met. If none of the conditions is met, Access does not select the record. When you place conditions in different Criteria rows, you are using the **Or logical operator**. Figure 3-25 illustrates the difference between the And and Or logical operators.

Figure 3-25	LOGICAL OPERATORS And AND Or FOR MULTIPLE SELECTION CRITERIA

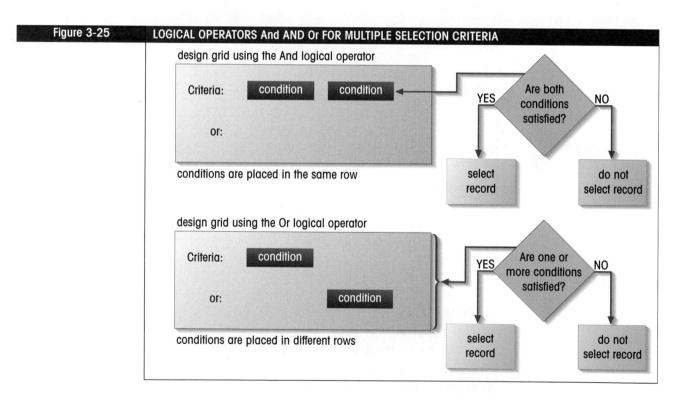

The And Logical Operator

To create Elsa's query, you need to modify the existing July 1 Positions query to show only the records for employers located in Prince Edward Island and offering positions starting on 07/01. For the modified query, you must add a second condition in the same Criteria row. The existing condition for the StartDate field finds records for positions that start on July 1; the new condition "PE" in the State/Prov field will find records for employers in Prince Edward Island. Because the conditions appear in the same Criteria row, the query will select records only if both conditions are met.

After modifying the query, you'll save it and then rename it as "PE July 1 Positions," overwriting the July 1 Positions query, which Matt no longer needs.

To modify the July 1 Positions query and use the And logical operator:

1. With the Queries object selected in the Database window, click **July 1 Positions** (if necessary), and then click the **Design** button to open the query in Design view.

2. Scroll the design grid to the right, click the **State/Prov Criteria** text box, type **PE**, and then press the ↓ key. See Figure 3-26.

Figure 3-26   QUERY TO FIND POSITIONS IN PE THAT START ON 07/01

And logical operator; conditions entered in the same row

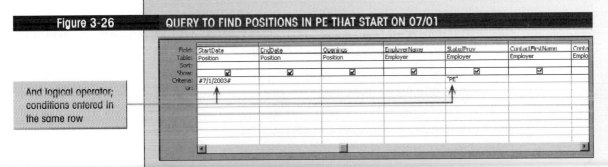

Notice that Access added quotation marks around the entry "PE"; you can type the quotation marks when you enter the condition, but if you forget to do so, Access will add them for you automatically.

The condition for the StartDate field is already entered, so you can run the query.

3. Run the query. Access displays in the datasheet only those records that meet both conditions: a StartDate field value of 07/01 and a State/Prov field value of PE. Two records are selected. See Figure 3-27.

Figure 3-27   RESULTS OF QUERY USING THE AND LOGICAL OPERATOR

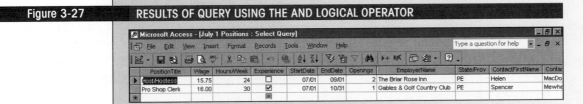

Now you can save the changes to the query and rename it.

4. Save and close the query. You return to the Database window.

5. Right-click **July 1 Positions** in the Queries list box, and then click **Rename** on the shortcut menu.

6. Click to position the insertion point to the left of the word "July," type **PE**, press the **spacebar**, and then press the **Enter** key. The query name is now PE July 1 Positions.

Using Multiple Undo and Redo

In previous versions of Access, you could not undo certain actions. Now Access allows you to undo and redo multiple actions when you are working in Design view for tables, queries, forms, reports, and so on. For example, when working in the Query window in Design view, if you specify multiple selection criteria for a query, you can use the multiple undo feature to remove the criteria—even after you run and save the query.

To see how this feature works, you will reopen the PE July 1 Positions query in Design view, delete the two criteria, and then reinsert them using multiple undo.

To modify the PE July 1 Positions query and use the multiple undo feature:

1. Open the **PE July 1 Positions** query in Design view.

2. Select the StartDate Criteria value, **#7/1/2003#**, and then press the **Delete** key. The StartDate Criteria text box is now empty.

3. Press the **Tab** key four times to move to and select **"PE"**, the State/Prov Criteria value, and then press the **Delete** key.

4. Run the query. Notice that the results display all records for the fields specified in the query design grid.

5. Switch back to Design view.

   Now you will use multiple undo to reverse the edits you made and reinsert the two conditions.

6. Click the **list arrow** for the Undo button 🔄 on the Query Design toolbar. A menu appears listing the actions you can undo. See Figure 3-28.

Figure 3-28	USING MULTIPLE UNDO

Undo list arrow

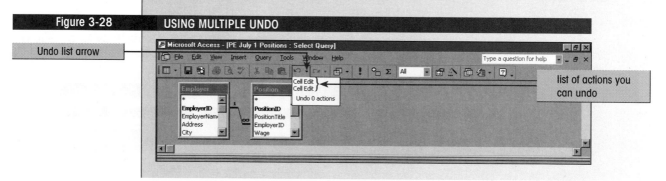

list of actions you can undo

Two items, both named "Cell Edit," are listed in the Undo list box. These items represent the two changes you made to the query design—first deleting the StartDate condition and then deleting the State/Prov condition. If you select an action that is below other items in the list, you will undo all the actions above the one you select, in addition to the one you select. Currently no actions are selected, so the list box indicates "Undo 0 actions."

7. Position the pointer over the second occurrence of **Cell Edit** in the list. Notice that both undo actions are highlighted, and the list box indicates that you can undo two actions.

8. Click the second occurrence of **Cell Edit**. Both actions are "undone," and the two conditions are redisplayed in the query design grid. The multiple undo feature makes it easy for you to test different criteria for a query and, when necessary, to undo your actions based on the query results.

   Notice that the Redo button and list arrow are now available. You can redo the actions you've just undone.

9. Click the **list arrow** for the Redo button 🔲 on the Query Design toolbar. The Redo list box indicates that you can redo the two cell edits.

10. Click the **list arrow** for the Redo button 🔲 again to close the Redo list box without selecting any option.

11. Close the query. Click the **No** button in the message box that opens, asking if you want to save your changes. You return to the Database window.

Matt has another request for information. He knows that it can be difficult to find student recruits for positions that offer fewer than 30 hours of work per week or that require prior work experience. So that his staff can focus on such positions, Matt wants to see a list of those positions that provide less than 30 hours of work or that require experience. To create this query, you need to use the Or logical operator.

The Or Logical Operator

For Matt's request, you need a query that selects a record when either one of two conditions is satisfied or when both conditions are satisfied. That is, a record is selected if the Hours/Week field value is less than 30 *or* if the Experience field value is "Yes" (checked). You will enter the condition for the Hours/Week field in one Criteria row and the condition for the Experience field in another Criteria row, thereby using the Or logical operator.

To display the information Matt wants to view, you'll create a new query containing the EmployerName and City fields from the Employer table and the PositionTitle, Hours/Week, and Experience fields from the Position table. Then you'll specify the conditions using the Or logical operator.

To create the query and use the Or logical operator:

1. In the Database window, double-click **Create query in Design view**. The Show Table dialog box opens on top of the Query window in Design view.

2. Click **Employer** in the Tables list box (if necessary), click the **Add** button, click **Position**, click the **Add** button, and then click the **Close** button. The Employer and Position field lists appear in the Query window and the Show Table dialog box closes.

3. Double-click **EmployerName** in the Employer field list to add the EmployerName field to the design grid's first column Field text box.

4. Repeat Step 3 to add the **City** field from the Employer table, and then add the **PositionTitle**, **Hours/Week**, and **Experience** fields from the Position table.

   Now you need to specify the first condition, <30, in the Hours/Week field.

5. Click the **Hours/Week Criteria** text box, type **<30** and then press the **Tab** key.

   Because you want records selected if either of the conditions for the Hours/Week or Experience fields is satisfied, you must enter the condition for the Experience field in the "or" row of the design grid.

6. Press the ↓ key, and then type **Yes** in the "or" text box for Experience. See Figure 3-29.

Figure 3-29	QUERY WINDOW WITH THE OR LOGICAL OPERATOR

	EmployerName	City	PositionTitle	Hours/Week	Experience	
Field:	EmployerName	City	PositionTitle	Hours/Week	Experience	
Table:	Employer	Employer	Position	Position	Position	
Sort:						
Show:	☑	☑	☑	☑	☑	☐
Criteria:				<30		
or:					Yes	

Or logical operator; conditions entered in different rows

7. Run the query. Access displays only those records that meet either condition: an Hours/Week field value less than 30 or an Experience field value of "Yes" (checked). A total of 35 records are selected.

   Matt wants the list displayed in alphabetical order by EmployerName. The first record's EmployerName field is highlighted, indicating the current field.

8. Click the **Sort Ascending** button 🔼 on the Query Datasheet toolbar.

9. Resize all datasheet columns to their best fit. Scroll through the entire datasheet to make sure that all values are completely displayed. Deselect all columns when you are finished resizing them, and then return to the top of the datasheet. See Figure 3-30.

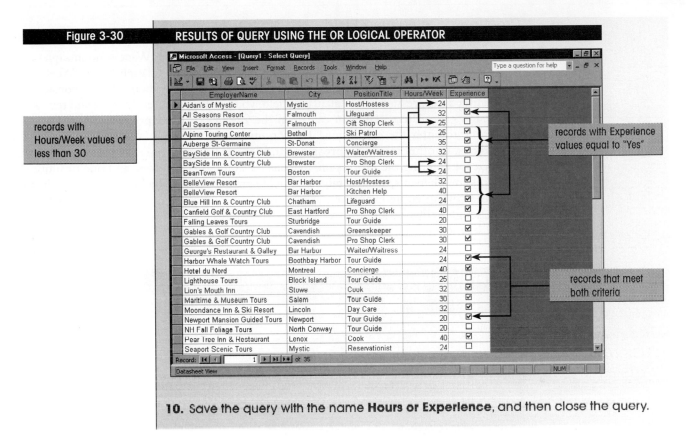

Figure 3-30   **RESULTS OF QUERY USING THE OR LOGICAL OPERATOR**

records with Hours/Week values of less than 30

records with Experience values equal to "Yes"

records that meet both criteria

10. Save the query with the name **Hours or Experience**, and then close the query.

Next, Elsa wants to use the Northeast database to perform calculations. She is considering offering a 2% bonus per week to the student recruits in higher paid positions, based on employer recommendation, and she wants to know exactly what these bonuses would be.

Performing Calculations

In addition to using queries to retrieve, sort, and filter data in a database, you can use a query to perform calculations. To perform a calculation, you define an **expression** containing a combination of database fields, constants, and operators. For numeric expressions, the data types of the database fields must be number, currency, or date/time; the constants are numbers such as .02 (for the 2% bonus); and the operators can be arithmetic operators (+ − * /) or other specialized operators. In complex expressions, you can enclose calculations in parentheses to indicate which one should be performed first. In expressions without parentheses, Access calculates in the following order of precedence: multiplication and division before addition and subtraction. When operators have equal precedence, Access calculates them in order from left to right.

To perform a calculation in a query, you add a calculated field to the query. A **calculated field** is a field that displays the results of an expression. A calculated field appears in a query datasheet or in a form or report; however, it does not exist in a database. When you run a query that contains a calculated field, Access evaluates the expression defined by the calculated field and displays the resulting value in the datasheet, form, or report.

Creating a Calculated Field

To produce the information Elsa wants, you need to open the High Wage Amounts query and create a calculated field that will multiply each Wage field value by each Hours/Week value, and then multiply that amount by .02 to determine the 2% weekly bonus Elsa is considering.

To enter an expression for a calculated field, you can type it directly in a Field text box in the design grid. Alternately, you can open the Zoom box or Expression Builder and use either one to enter the expression. The **Zoom box** is a large text box for entering text, expressions, or other values. **Expression Builder** is an Access tool that contains an expression box for entering the expression, buttons for common operators, and one or more lists of expression elements, such as table and field names. Unlike a Field text box, which is too small to show an entire expression at one time, the Zoom box and Expression Builder are large enough to display lengthy expressions. In most cases, Expression Builder provides the easiest way to enter expressions.

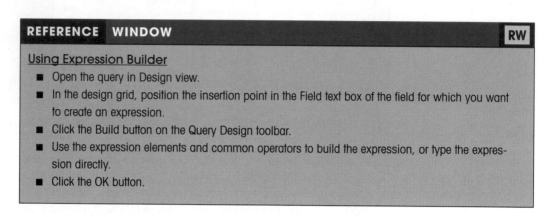

REFERENCE WINDOW   RW

Using Expression Builder
- Open the query in Design view.
- In the design grid, position the insertion point in the Field text box of the field for which you want to create an expression.
- Click the Build button on the Query Design toolbar.
- Use the expression elements and common operators to build the expression, or type the expression directly.
- Click the OK button.

You'll begin by copying, pasting, and renaming the High Wage Amounts query, keeping the original query intact. You'll name the new query "High Wages with Bonus." Then you'll modify this query in Design view to show only the information Elsa wants to view.

To copy the High Wage Amounts query and paste the copy with a new name:

1. Right-click the **High Wage Amounts** query in the list of queries, and then click **Copy** on the shortcut menu.

2. Right-click an empty area of the Database window, and then click **Paste** on the shortcut menu. The Paste As dialog box opens.

3. Type **High Wages with Bonus** in the Query Name text box, and then press the **Enter** key. The new query appears in the query list, along with the original High Wage Amounts query.

Now you're ready to modify the High Wages with Bonus query to create the calculated field for Elsa.

To modify the High Wages with Bonus query:

1. Open the **High Wages with Bonus** query in Design view.

   Elsa wants to see only the EmployerName, PositionTitle, and Wage fields in the query results. First, you'll delete the unnecessary fields, and then you'll move the EmployerName field so that it appears first in the query results.

2. Scroll the design grid to the right until the Hours/Week and EmployerName fields are visible at the same time.

3. Position the pointer on the Hours/Week field until the pointer changes to a ⬇ shape, click and hold down the mouse button, drag the mouse to the right to highlight the Hours/Week, Experience, StartDate, EndDate, and Openings fields, and then release the mouse button.

4. Press the **Delete** key to delete the five selected fields.

5. Repeat Steps 3 and 4 to delete the State/Prov, ContactFirstName, ContactLastName, and Phone fields from the query design grid.

   Next you'll move the EmployerName field to the left of the PositionTitle field so that the Wage values will appear next to the calculated field values in the query results.

6. Scroll the design grid back to the left (if necessary), select the **EmployerName** field, and then use the pointer ⩏ to drag the field to the left of the PositionTitle field. See Figure 3-31.

| Figure 3-31 | MODIFIED QUERY BEFORE ADDING THE CALCULATED FIELD |

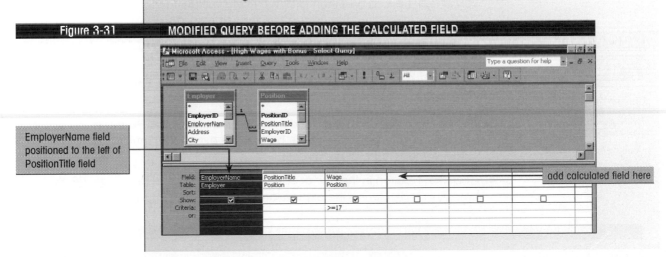

EmployerName field positioned to the left of PositionTitle field

add calculated field here

Now you're ready to use Expression Builder to enter the calculated field in the High Wages with Bonus query.

To add the calculated field to the High Wages with Bonus query:

1. Position the insertion point in the Field text box to the right of the Wage field, and then click the **Build** button ⚒ on the Query Design toolbar. The Expression Builder dialog box opens. See Figure 3-32.

Figure 3-32   INITIAL EXPRESSION BUILDER DIALOG BOX

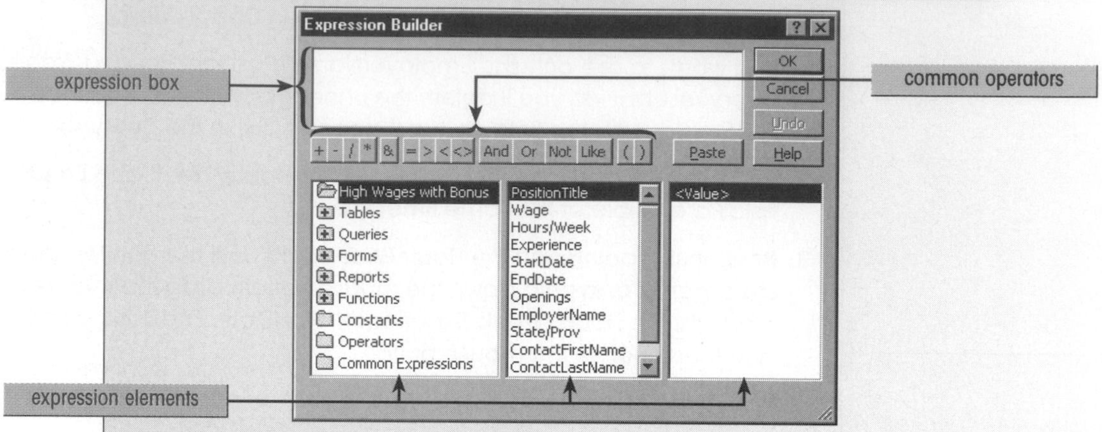

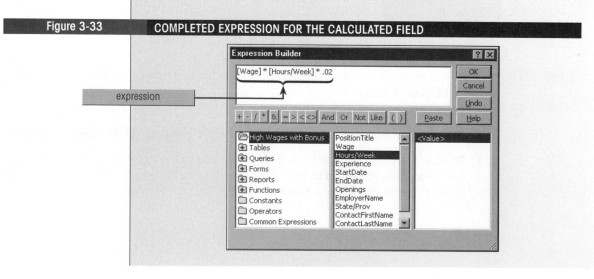

You use the common operators and expression elements to help you build an expression. Note that the High Wages with Bonus query is already selected in the list box on the lower left; the fields included in the original version of the query are listed in the center box.

The expression for the calculated field will multiply the Wage field values by the Hours/Week field values, and then multiply that amount by the numeric constant .02 (which represents a 2% bonus). To include a field in the expression, you select the field and then click the Paste button. To include a numeric constant, you simply type the constant in the expression.

2. Click **Wage** in the field list, and then click the **Paste** button. [Wage] appears in the expression box.

   To include the multiplication operator in the expression, you click the asterisk (*) button.

3. Click the * button in the row of common operators, click **Hours/Week** in the field list, and then click the **Paste** button. The expression multiplies the Wage values by the Hours/Week values.

4. Click the * button in the row of common operators, and then type **.02**. You have finished entering the expression. See Figure 3-33.

Figure 3-33   COMPLETED EXPRESSION FOR THE CALCULATED FIELD

Note that you also could have typed the expression directly into the expression box, instead of clicking the field names and the operator.

5. Click the **OK** button. Access closes the Expression Builder dialog box and adds the expression to the design grid in the Field text box for the calculated field.

   Next, you need to specify a name for the calculated field as it will appear in the query results.

6. Press the **Home** key to position the insertion point to the left of the expression.

   You'll enter the name WeeklyBonus, which is descriptive of the field's contents; then you'll run the query.

7. Type **WeeklyBonus:**. *Make sure you include the colon following the field name.* The colon is needed to separate the field name from its expression.

8. Run the query. Access displays the query datasheet, which contains the three specified fields and the calculated field with the name "WeeklyBonus." Resize all datasheet columns to their best fit. See Figure 3-34.

Figure 3-34	DATASHEET DISPLAYING THE CALCULATED FIELD

Notice the WeeklyBonus value for Ski & Stay; the value appears with three decimal places (9.375). Currency values should have only two decimal places, so you need to format the WeeklyBonus calculated field so that all values appear in the Fixed format with two decimal places.

To format the calculated field:

1. Switch to Design view.

2. Right-click the **WeeklyBonus** calculated field in the design grid to open the shortcut menu, and then click **Properties**. The property sheet for the selected field opens. The property sheet for a field provides options for changing the display of field values in the datasheet.

3. Click the right side of the **Format** text box to display the list of formats, and then click **Fixed**.

4. Click the right side of the **Decimal Places** text box, and then click **2**.

5. Click in the **Description** text box to deselect the Decimal Places setting. See Figure 3-35.

Figure 3-35	PROPERTY SHEET SETTINGS TO FORMAT THE CALCULATED FIELD

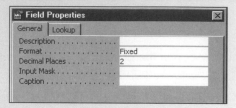

Now that you have formatted the calculated field, you can run the query.

6. Close the Field Properties window, and then save and run the query. The value for Ski & Stay now correctly appears as 9.38.

7. Close the query.

Elsa prepares a report on a regular basis that includes a summary of information about the wages paid to student recruits. She lists the minimum hourly wage paid, the average wage amount, and the maximum hourly wage paid. She asks you to create a query to determine these statistics from data in the Position table.

Using Aggregate Functions

You can calculate statistical information, such as totals and averages, on the records selected by a query. To do this, you use the Access aggregate functions. **Aggregate functions** perform arithmetic operations on selected records in a database. Figure 3-36 lists the most frequently used aggregate functions. Aggregate functions operate on the records that meet a query's selection criteria. You specify an aggregate function for a specific field, and the appropriate operation applies to that field's values for the selected records.

Figure 3-36	FREQUENTLY USED AGGREGATE FUNCTIONS	
AGGREGATE FUNCTION	**DETERMINES**	**DATA TYPES SUPPORTED**
Avg	Average of the field values for the selected records	AutoNumber, Currency, Date/Time, Number
Count	Number of records selected	AutoNumber, Currency, Date/Time, Memo, Number, OLE Object, Text, Yes/No
Max	Highest field value for the selected records	AutoNumber, Currency, Date/Time, Number, Text
Min	Lowest field value for the selected records	AutoNumber, Currency, Date/Time, Number, Text
Sum	Total of the field values for the selected records	AutoNumber, Currency, Date/Time, Number

To display the minimum, average, and maximum of all the wage amounts in the Position table, you will use the Min, Avg, and Max aggregate functions for the Wage field.

To calculate the minimum, average, and maximum of all wage amounts:

1. Double-click **Create query in Design view**, click **Position**, click the **Add** button, and then click the Close button. The Position field list is added to the Query window and the Show Table dialog box closes.

   To perform the three calculations on the Wage field, you need to add the field to the design grid three times.

2. Double-click **Wage** in the Position field list three times to add three copies of the field to the design grid.

   You need to select an aggregate function for each Wage field. When you click the Totals button on the Query Design toolbar, a row labeled "Total" is added to the design grid. The Total row provides a list of the aggregate functions that you can select.

3. Click the **Totals** button Σ on the Query Design toolbar. A new row labeled "Total" appears between the Table and Sort rows in the design grid. See Figure 3-37.

Figure 3-37	TOTAL ROW INSERTED IN THE DESIGN GRID

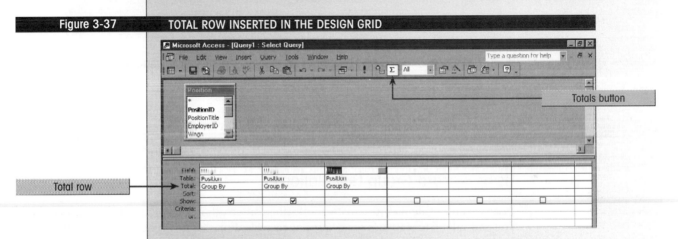

Totals button

Total row

   In the Total row, you specify the aggregate function you want to use for a field.

4. Click the right side of the first column's **Total** text box, and then click **Min**. This field will calculate the minimum amount of all the Wage field values.

   When you run the query, Access automatically will assign a datasheet column name of "MinOfWage" for this field. You can change the datasheet column name to a more descriptive or readable name by entering the name you want in the Field text box. However, you must also keep the field name Wage in the Field text box, because it identifies the field whose values will be calculated. The Field text box will contain the datasheet column name you specify followed by the field name (Wage) with a colon separating the two names.

5. Position the insertion point to the left of Wage in the first column's Field text box, and then type **MinimumWage:**. Be sure that you type the colon.

6. Click the right side of the second column's **Total** text box, and then click **Avg**. This field will calculate the average of all the Wage field values.

7. Position the insertion point to the left of Wage in the second column's Field text box, and then type **AverageWage:**.

8. Click the right side of the third column's **Total** text box, and then click **Max**. This field will calculate the maximum amount of all the Wage field values.

9. Position the insertion point to the left of Wage in the third column's Field text box, and then type **MaximumWage**:.

The query design is completed, so you can run the query.

10. Run the query. Access displays one record containing the three aggregate function values. The single row of summary statistics represents calculations based on the 64 records selected by the query.

You need to resize the three columns to their best fit to see the column names.

11. Resize all columns to their best fit, and then position the insertion point in the field value in the first column. See Figure 3-38.

Figure 3-38	RESULTS OF THE QUERY USING AGGREGATE FUNCTIONS

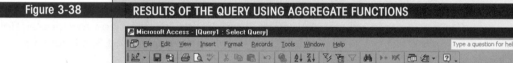

12. Save the query as **Wage Statistics**, and then close the query.

Elsa also wants her report to include the same wage statistics (minimum, average, and maximum) for each type of position. She asks you to display the wage statistics for each different PositionTitle value in the Position table.

Using Record Group Calculations

In addition to calculating statistical information on all or selected records in selected tables, you can calculate statistics for groups of records. For example, you can determine the number of employers in each state or province, or the average wage amount by position.

To create a query for Elsa's latest request, you can modify the current query by adding the PositionTitle field and assigning the Group By operator to it. The **Group By operator** divides the selected records into groups based on the values in the specified field. Those records with the same value for the field are grouped together, and the datasheet displays one record for each group. Aggregate functions, which appear in the other columns of the design grid, provide statistical information for each group.

You need to modify the current query to add the Group By operator for the PositionTitle field. This will display the statistical information grouped by position for the 64 selected records in the query. As you did earlier, you will copy the Wage Statistics query and paste it with a new name, keeping the original query intact, to create the new query.

To copy and paste the query, and then add the PositionTitle field with the Group By operator:

1. Right-click the **Wage Statistics** query in the list of queries, and then click **Copy** on the shortcut menu.

2. Right-click an empty area of the Database window, and then click **Paste** on the shortcut menu.

3. Type **Wage Statistics by Position** in the Query Name text box, and then press the **Enter** key.

Now you're ready to modify the query design.

4. Open the **Wage Statistics by Position** query in Design view.

5. Double-click **PositionTitle** in the Position field list to add the field to the design grid. Group By, which is the default option in the Total row, appears for the PositionTitle field.

You've completed the query changes, so you can run the query.

6. Run the query. Access displays 16 records—one for each PositionTitle group. Each record contains the three aggregate function values and the PositionTitle field value for the group. Again, the summary statistics represent calculations based on the 64 records selected by the query. See Figure 3-39.

| Figure 3-39 | AGGREGATE FUNCTIONS GROUPED BY PositionTitle |

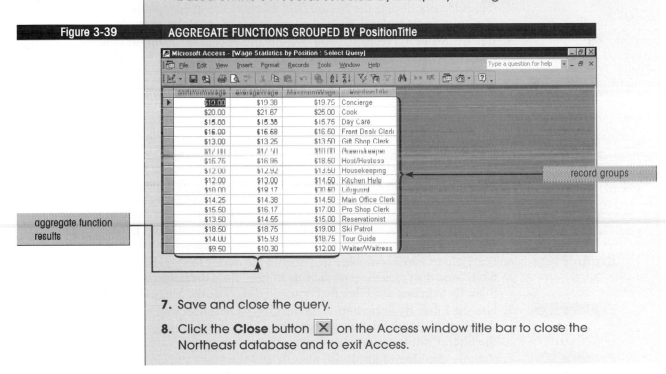

7. Save and close the query.

8. Click the **Close** button ⊠ on the Access window title bar to close the Northeast database and to exit Access.

The queries you've created and saved will help Elsa, Zack, Matt, and other employees to monitor and analyze the business activity of NSJI's employer customers. Now any NSJI staff member can run the queries at any time, modify them as needed, or use them as the basis for designing new queries to meet additional information requirements.

Session 3.2 QUICK CHECK

1. A(n) _____ is a criterion, or rule, that determines which records are selected for a query datasheet.

2. In the design grid, where do you place the conditions for two different fields when you use the And logical operator? The Or logical operator?

3. To perform a calculation in a query, you define a(n) _____ containing a combination of database fields, constants, and operators.

4. How does a calculated field differ from a table field?

5. What is an aggregate function?

6. The _____ operator divides selected records into groups based on the values in a field.

REVIEW ASSIGNMENTS

Elsa needs information from the **Recruits** database, and she asks you to query the database by completing the following:

1. Make sure your Data Disk is in the appropriate disk drive, start Access, and then open the **Recruits** database located in the Review folder on your Data Disk.

2. Create a select query based on the **Student** table. Display the StudentID, FirstName, and LastName fields in the query results; sort in ascending order based on the LastName field values; and select only those records whose Nation value equals Ireland. (*Hint*: Do not display the Nation field values in the query results.) Save the query as **Students from Ireland**, run the query, and then print the query datasheet.

3. Use the **Students from Ireland** datasheet to update the **Student** table by changing the FirstName field value for StudentID OMA9956 to Richard. Print the query datasheet, and then close the query.

4. Define a one-to-many relationship between the primary **Recruiter** table and the related **Student** table. Select the referential integrity option and both cascade options for the relationship.

5. Use Design view to create a select query based on the **Recruiter** and **Student** tables. Select the fields FirstName (from the **Student** table), LastName (from the **Student** table), City, Nation, BonusQuota, Salary, and SSN (from the **Student** table), in that order. Sort in ascending order based on the Nation field values. Select only those records whose SSN equals "977071798." (*Hint*: Do not type the dashes for the SSN criterion, and do not display the SSN field values in the query results.) Save the query as **Wolfe Recruits**, and then run the query. Resize all columns in the datasheet to fit the data. Print the datasheet, and then save the query.

Explore 6. Use Help to learn about Filter By Form. In the Ask a Question box, type, "How do I create a filter?" and then click the topic "Create a filter." Read the portions of the topic pertaining to Filter By Selection and Filter By Form, and then close the Microsoft Access Help window.

Explore 7. Use the Filter By Form button on the Query Datasheet toolbar to filter the records in the **Wolfe Recruits** datasheet that have a Nation field value of "Spain," and then apply the filter. Print the query datasheet.

Explore 8. Remove the filter to display all records, and then save and close the query.

Explore 9. Use Design view to create a query based on the **Recruiter** table that shows all recruiters with a BonusQuota field value between 40 and 50, and whose Salary field value is greater than 35000. (*Hint*: Refer to Figure 3-18 to determine the correct comparison operator to use.) Display all fields except SSN from the **Recruiter** table. Save the query as **Bonus Info**, and then run the query.

Explore 10. Switch to Design view for the **Bonus Info** query. Create a calculated field named RaiseAmt that displays the net amount of a 3% raise to the Salary values. Display the results in descending order by RaiseAmt. Save the query as **Salaries with Raises**, run the query, resize all columns in the datasheet to fit the data, print the query datasheet, and then save and close the query.

11. In the Database window, copy the **Students from Ireland** query, and then paste it with the new name **Students from Holland Plus Younger Students**. Open the new query in Design view. Modify the query to display only those records with a Nation field value of Holland or with a BirthDate field value greater than 1/1/84. Also, modify the query to include the Nation field values in the query results. Save and run the query. Resize all columns in the datasheet to fit the data, print the query datasheet, and then save and close the query.

12. Create a new query based on the **Recruiter** table. Use the Min, Max, and Avg aggregate functions to find the lowest, highest, and average values in the Salary field. Name the three aggregate fields LowestSalary, HighestSalary, and AverageSalary, respectively. Save the query as **Salary Statistics**, and then run the query. Resize all columns in the datasheet to fit the data, print the query datasheet, and then save and close the query.

13. Open the **Salary Statistics** query in Design view. Modify the query so that the records are grouped by the BonusQuota field. Save the query as **Salary Statistics by BonusQuota**, run the query, print the query datasheet, and then close the query.

14. Close the **Recruits** database, and then exit Access.

CASE PROBLEMS

Case 1. Lim's Video Photography Youngho Lim wants to view specific information about his clients and video shoot events. He asks you to query the **Videos** database by completing the following:

1. Make sure your Data Disk is in the appropriate disk drive, start Access, and then open the **Videos** database located in the Cases folder on your Data Disk.

Explore

2. Define the necessary one-to-many relationships between the database tables, as follows: between the primary **Client** table and the related **Contract** table, between the primary **Contract** table and the related **Shoot** table, and between the primary **ShootDesc** table and the related **Shoot** table. (*Hint*: Add all four tables to the Relationships window, and then define the three relationships.) Select the referential integrity option and both cascade options for each relationship.

3. Create a select query based on the **Client** and **Contract** tables. Display the ClientName, City, ContractDate, and ContractAmt fields, in that order. Sort in ascending order based on the ClientName field values. Run the query, save the query as **Client Contracts**, and then print the datasheet.

4. Use Filter By Selection to display only those records with a City field value of Oakland in the **Client Contracts** datasheet. Print the datasheet and then remove the filter. Save and close the query.

5. Open the **Client Contracts** query in Design view. Modify the query to display only those records with a ContractAmt value greater than or equal to 600. Run the query, save the query as **Contract Amounts**, and then print the datasheet.

6. Switch to Design view for the **Contract Amounts** query. Modify the query to display only those records with a ContractAmt value greater than or equal to 600 and with a City value of San Francisco. Also modify the query so that the City field values are not displayed in the query results. Run the query, save it as **SF Contract Amounts**, print the datasheet, and then close the query.

7. Close the **Videos** database, and then exit Access.

Case 2. DineAtHome.course.com Claire Picard is completing an analysis of the orders placed at restaurants that use her company's services. To help her find the information she needs, you'll query the **Meals** database by completing the following:

1. Make sure your Data Disk is in the appropriate disk drive, start Access, and then open the **Meals** database located in the Cases folder on your Data Disk.

2. Define a one-to-many relationship between the primary **Restaurant** table and the related **Order** table. Select the referential integrity option and both cascade options for the relationship.

3. Use Design view to create a select query based on the **Restaurant** and **Order** tables. Display the fields RestaurantName, City, OrderAmt, and OrderDate, in that order. Sort in descending order based on the OrderAmt field values. Select only those records whose OrderAmt is greater than 150. Save the query as **Large Orders**, and then run the query.

4. Use the **Large Orders** datasheet to update the **Order** table by changing the OrderAmt value for the first record in the datasheet to 240.25. Print the datasheet, and then close the query.

5. Use Design view to create a select query based on the **Restaurant** and **Order** tables. For all orders placed on 03/21/2003, display the Order#, OrderAmt, OrderDate, and RestaurantName fields. Save the query as **March 21 Orders**, and then run the query. Switch to Design view, modify the query so that the OrderDate values do not appear in the query results, and then save the modified query. Run the query, print the query results, and then close the query.

6. Use Design view to create a select query based on the **Restaurant** table. For all restaurants that have a Website and are located in Naples, display the RestaurantName, OwnerFirstName, OwnerLastName, and Phone fields. Save the query as **Naples Restaurants with Websites**, run the query, print the query results, and then close the query.

7. Use Design view to create a select query based on the **Restaurant** and **Order** tables. For all orders placed on 03/14/2003 or 03/15/2003, display the fields OrderDate, OrderAmt, RestaurantName, and Restaurant# (from the **Restaurant** table). Display the results in ascending order by OrderDate and then in descending order by OrderAmt. Save the query as **Selected Dates**, run the query, print the query datasheet, and then close the query.

Explore   8. Use the **Order** table to display the highest, lowest, total, average, and count of the OrderAmt field for all orders. Then do the following:

   a. Specify column names of HighestOrder, LowestOrder, TotalOrders, AverageOrder, and #Orders. Use the property sheet for each column (except #Orders) to format the results as Fixed with two decimal places. Save the query as **Order Statistics**, and then run the query. Resize all datasheet columns to their best fit, save the query, and then print the query results.

   b. Change the query to display the same statistics grouped by RestaurantName. (*Hint*: Use the Show Table button on the Query Design toolbar to add the **Restaurant** table to the query.) Save the query as **Order Statistics by Restaurant**. Run the query, print the query results, and then close the query.

9. Close the **Meals** database, and then exit Access.

Case 3. *Redwood Zoo*   Michael Rosenfeld wants to find specific information about the donors and their pledge amounts for the Redwood Zoo. You'll help them find the information in the **Redwood** database by completing the following:

1. Make sure your Data Disk is in the appropriate disk drive, start Access, and then open the **Redwood** database located in the Cases folder on your Data Disk.

Explore   2. Define the necessary one-to-many relationships between the database tables, as follows: between the primary **Donor** table and the related **Pledge** table, and between the primary **Fund** table and the related **Pledge** table. (*Hint*: Add all three tables to the Relationships window, and then define the two relationships.) Select the referential integrity option and both cascade options for each relationship.

3. Use Design view to create a select query that, for all pledges with a TotalPledged field value of greater than 200, displays the DonorID (from the **Donor** table), FirstName, LastName, Pledge#, TotalPledged, and FundName fields. Sort the query in ascending order by TotalPledged. Save the query as **Large Pledges**, and then run the query.

4. Use the **Large Pledges** datasheet to update the **Pledge** table by changing the TotalPledged field value for Pledge# 2976 to 750. Print the query datasheet, and then close the query.

5. Use Design view to create a select query that, for all donors who pledged less than $150 or who donated to the Whale Watchers fund, displays the Pledge#, PledgeDate, TotalPledged, FirstName, and LastName fields. Save the revised query as **Pledged or Whale Watchers**, run the query, and then print the query datasheet. Change the query to select all donors who pledged less than $150 and who donated to the Whale Watchers fund. Save the revised query as **Pledged and Whale Watchers**, and then run the query. Close the query.

Explore   6. Use Design view to create a select query that displays the DonorID (from the **Donor** table), TotalPledged, PaymentMethod, PledgeDate, and FundName fields. Save the query as **Pledges after Costs**. Create a calculated field named Overhead that displays the results of multiplying the TotalPledged field values by 15% (to account for overhead costs). Save the query, and then create a second calculated field named NetPledge that displays the results of subtracting the Overhead field values from the TotalPledged field values.

Format the calculated fields as Fixed. Display the results in ascending order by TotalPledged. Save the modified query, and then run the query. Resize all datasheet columns to their best fit, print the query results, and then save and close the query.

Explore Use the **Pledge** table to display the sum, average, and count of the TotalPledged field for all pledges. Then do the following:

a. Specify column names of TotalPledge, AveragePledge, and #Pledges.

b. Change properties so that the values in the TotalPledge and AveragePledge columns display two decimal places and the Fixed format.

c. Save the query as **Pledge Statistics**, run the query, resize all datasheet columns to their best fit, and then print the query datasheet. Save the query.

d. Change the query to display the sum, average, and count of the TotalPledged field for all pledges by FundName. (*Hint*: Use the Show Table button on the Query Design toolbar to add the **Fund** table to the query.) Save the query as **Pledge Statistics by Fund**, run the query, print the query datasheet, and then close the query.

8. Close the **Redwood** database, and then exit Access.

Case 4. Mountain River Adventures Connor and Siobhan Dempsey want to analyze data about their clients and the rafting trips they take. Help them query the **Trips** database by completing the following:

1. Make sure your Data Disk is in the appropriate disk drive, start Access, and then open the **Trips** database located in the Cases folder on your Data Disk.

Explore 2. Define the necessary one-to-many relationships between the database tables, as follows: between the primary **Client** table and the related **Booking** table, and between the primary **Rafting Trip** table and the related **Booking** table. (*Hint*: Add all three tables to the Relationships window, and then define the two relationships.) Select the referential integrity option and both cascade options for each relationship.

3. For all clients, display the ClientName, City, State/Prov, Booking#, and TripDate fields. Save the query as **Client Trip Dates**, and then run the query. Resize all datasheet columns to their best fit. In Datasheet view, sort the query results in ascending order by the TripDate field. Print the query datasheet, and then save and close the query.

4. For all clients from Colorado (CO), display the ClientName, City, State/Prov, Trip#, People, and TripDate fields. Sort the query in ascending order by City. Save the query as **Colorado Clients**, and then run the query. Modify the query to remove the display of the State/Prov field values from the query results. Save the modified query, run the query, print the query datasheet, and then close the query.

Explore 5. For all clients who are not from Colorado or who are taking a rafting trip in the month of July 2003, display the ClientName, City, State/Prov, Booking#, TripDate, and Trip# fields. (*Hint*: Refer to Figure 3-18 to determine the correct comparison operators to use.) Sort the query in descending order by TripDate. Save the query as **Out of State or July**, run the query, and then print the query datasheet. Change the query to select all clients who are not from Colorado and who are taking a rafting trip in the month of July 2003. Sort the query in ascending order by State/Prov. Save the query as **Out of State and July**, run the query, print the query datasheet, and then close the query.

6. For all bookings, display the Booking#, TripDate, Trip# (from the **Booking** table), River, People, and Fee/Person fields. Save the query as **Trip Cost**. Then create a calculated field named TripCost that displays the results of multiplying the People field values by the Fee/Person field values. Display the results in descending order by TripCost. Run the query, resize all datasheet columns to their best fit, print the query datasheet, and then save and close the query.

Explore 7. Use the **Rafting Trip** table to determine the minimum, average, and maximum Fee/Person for all trips. Use the Ask a Question box to ask the question, "What is a caption?" and then click the topic "Change a field name in a query." Read the displayed information, and then click and read the subtopic "Change a field's caption."

Close the Help window. Set the Caption property of the three fields to Lowest Fee, Average Fee, and Highest Fee, respectively. Also set the properties so that the results of the three fields are displayed as Fixed with two decimal places. Save the query as **Fee Statistics**, run the query, resize all datasheet columns to their best fit, print the query datasheet, and then save the query again. Revise the query to show the fee statistics grouped by People. (*Hint*: Use the Show Table button on the Query Design toolbar to display the Show Table dialog box.) Save the revised query as **Fee Statistics by People**, run the query, print the query datasheet, and then close the query.

Explore

8. Use the Ask a Question box to ask the following question: "How do I create a Top Values query?" Click the topic "Show only the high or low values in a query." Read the displayed information, and then close the Help window. Open the **Trip Cost** query in Design view, and then modify the query to display only the top five values for the TripCost field. Save the query as **Top Trip Cost**, run the query, print the query datasheet, and then close the query.

9. Close the **Trips** database, and then exit Access.

INTERNET ASSIGNMENTS

Student Union

The purpose of the Internet Assignments is to challenge you to find information on the Internet that you can use to create effective documents. The actual assignments are updated and maintained on the Course Technology Web site. Log on to the Internet and use your Web browser to go to the Student Union on the New Perspectives Series site at **www.course.com/NewPerspectives/studentunion**. Click the Online Companions link, and then click the link for this text.

QUICK CHECK ANSWERS

Session 3.1

1. a general query in which you specify the fields and records you want Access to select
2. The field list contains the table name at the top of the list box and the table's fields listed in the order in which they appear in the table; the design grid displays columns that contain specifications about a field you will use in the query.
3. A table datasheet and a query datasheet look the same, appearing in Datasheet view, and can be used to update data in a database. A table datasheet shows the permanent data in a table, whereas a query datasheet is temporary and its contents are based on the criteria you establish in the design grid.
4. primary table; related table
5. Referential integrity
6. oldest to most recent date
7. when you want to perform different types of sorts (both ascending and descending, for example) on multiple fields, and when you want to sort on multiple fields that are nonadjacent or in the wrong order, but you do not want to rearrange the columns in the query datasheet to accomplish the sort
8. filter

Session 3.2

1. condition
2. in the same Criteria row; in different Criteria rows
3. expression
4. A calculated field appears in a query datasheet, form, or report but does not exist in a database, as does a table field.
5. a function that performs an arithmetic operation on selected records in a database
6. Group By

OBJECTIVES

In this tutorial you will:

- Create a form using the Form Wizard

- Change a form's AutoFormat

- Find data using a form

- Preview and print selected form records

- Maintain table data using a form

- Check the spelling of table data using a form

- Create a form with a main form and a subform

- Create a report using the Report Wizard

- Insert a picture in a report

- Preview and print a report

CREATING FORMS AND REPORTS

Creating a Position Data Form, an Employer Positions Form, and an Employers and Positions Report

CASE

Northeast Seasonal Jobs International (NSJI)

Elsa Jensen wants to continue enhancing the Northeast database to make it easier for NSJI employees to find and maintain data. In particular, she wants the database to include a form based on the Position table to make it easier for employees to enter and change data about available positions. She also wants the database to include a form that shows data from both the Employer and Position tables at the same time. This form will show the position information for each employer along with the corresponding employer data, providing a complete picture of NSJI's employer clients and their available positions.

In addition, Zack Ward would like the database to include a formatted report of employer and position data so that his marketing staff members will have printed output when completing market analyses and planning strategies for selling NSJI's services to employer clients. He wants the information to be formatted attractively, perhaps by including a picture or graphic image on the report for visual interest.

SESSION 4.1

In this session, you will create a form using the Form Wizard, change a form's AutoFormat, find data using a form, preview and print selected form records, maintain table data using a form, and check the spelling of table data using a form.

Creating a Form Using the Form Wizard

As you learned in Tutorial 1, a form is an object you use to maintain, view, and print records in a database. In Access, you can design your own forms or use a Form Wizard to create them for you automatically.

Elsa asks you to create a new form that her staff can use to view and maintain data in the Position table. In Tutorial 1, you used the AutoForm Wizard to create the Employer Data form in the Seasonal database. The AutoForm Wizard creates a form automatically, using all the fields in the selected table or query. To create the form for the Position table, you'll use the Form Wizard. The **Form Wizard** allows you to choose some or all of the fields in the selected table or query, choose fields from other tables and queries, and display the selected fields in any order on the form. You can also apply an existing style to the form to format its appearance quickly.

To open the Northeast database and activate the Form Wizard:

1. Place your Data Disk in the appropriate disk drive.

2. Start Access and open the **Northeast** database located in the Tutorial folder on your Data Disk.

3. Click **Forms** in the Objects bar of the Database window.

4. Click the **New** button in the Database window. The New Form dialog box opens.

5. Click **Form Wizard**, click the list arrow for choosing a table or query, click **Position** to select this table as the source for the form, and then click the **OK** button. The first Form Wizard dialog box opens. See Figure 4-1.

Figure 4-1	FIRST FORM WIZARD DIALOG BOX

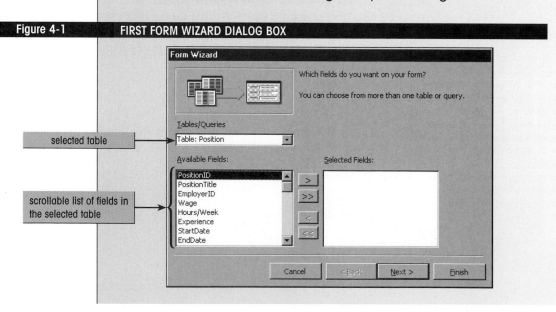

selected table

scrollable list of fields in the selected table

Elsa wants the form to display all the fields in the Position table, but in a different order. She would like the Experience field to appear at the bottom of the form so that it stands out more, making it easier to determine if a position requires prior work experience.

To finish creating the form using the Form Wizard:

1. Click **PositionID** in the Available Fields list box (if necessary), and then click the **>** button to move the field to the Selected Fields list box.

2. Repeat Step 1 to select the **PositionTitle**, **EmployerID**, **Wage**, **Hours/Week**, **StartDate**, **EndDate**, **Openings**, and **Experience** fields, in that order. Remember, you can also double-click a field to move it from the Available Fields list box to the Selected Fields list box.

3. Click the **Next** button to display the second Form Wizard dialog box, in which you select a layout for the form. See Figure 4-2.

Figure 4-2	CHOOSING A LAYOUT FOR THE FORM

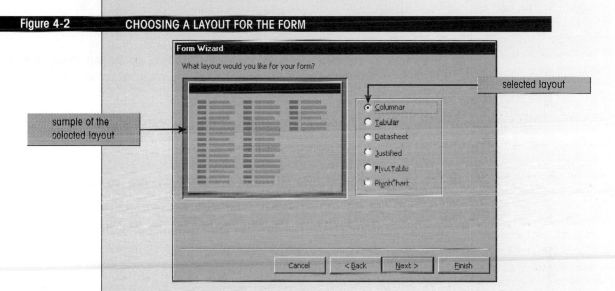

The layout choices are Columnar, Tabular, Datasheet, Justified, PivotTable, and PivotChart. A sample of the selected layout appears on the left side of the dialog box.

4. Click each of the option buttons and review the corresponding sample layout.

   The Tabular and Datasheet layouts display the fields from multiple records at one time, whereas the Columnar and Justified layouts display the fields from one record at a time. The PivotTable and PivotChart layouts display summary and analytical information. Elsa thinks the Columnar layout is the appropriate arrangement for displaying and updating data in the table, so you'll choose this layout.

5. Click the **Columnar** option button (if necessary), and then click the **Next** button. Access displays the third Form Wizard dialog box, in which you choose a style for the form. See Figure 4-3.

Figure 4-3   CHOOSING A STYLE FOR THE FORM

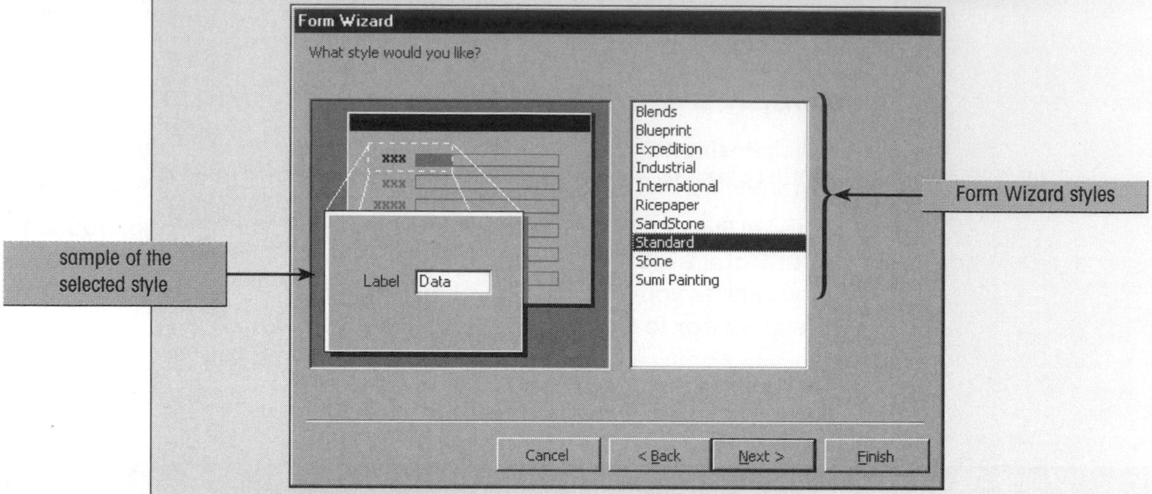

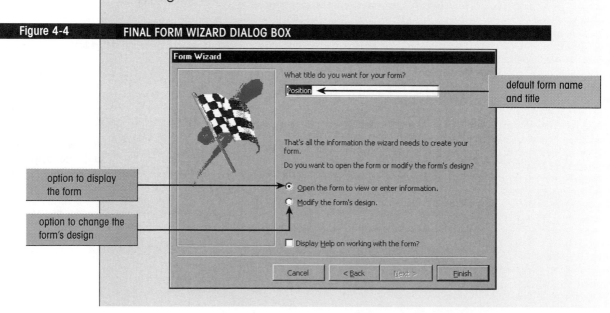

A sample of the selected style appears in the box on the left. If you choose a style, which is called an **AutoFormat**, and decide you'd prefer a different one after the form is created, you can change it.

TROUBLE? Don't worry if a different form style is selected in your dialog box instead of the one shown in Figure 4-3. The dialog box displays the most recently used style, which might be different on your computer.

6. Click each of the styles and review the corresponding sample.

Elsa likes the Expedition style and asks you to use it for the form.

7. Click **Expedition** and then click the **Next** button. Access displays the final Form Wizard dialog box and shows the Position table's name as the default form name. "Position" is also the default title that will appear in the form's title bar. See Figure 4-4.

Figure 4-4   FINAL FORM WIZARD DIALOG BOX

You'll use "Position Data" as the form name and, because you don't need to change the form's design at this point, you'll display the form.

8. Click the insertion point to the right of Position in the text box, press the **spacebar**, type **Data**, and then click the **Finish** button. The completed form opens in Form view. See Figure 4-5.

Figure 4-5   **COMPLETED FORM FOR THE POSITION TABLE**

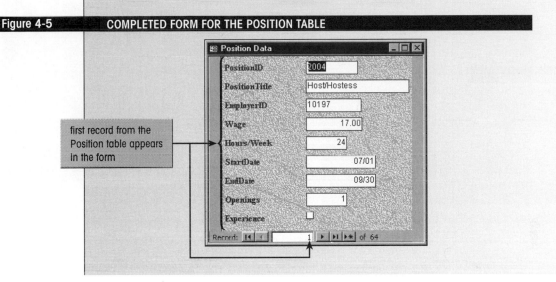

first record from the Position table appears in the form

After viewing the form, Elsa decides that she doesn't like the form's style; the background makes the field names a bit difficult to read. She asks you to change the form's style.

Changing a Form's AutoFormat

You can change a form's appearance by choosing a different AutoFormat for the form. As you learned when you created the Position Data form, an AutoFormat is a predefined style for a form (or report). The AutoFormats available for a form are the ones you saw when you selected the form's style using the Form Wizard. To change an AutoFormat, you must switch to Design view.

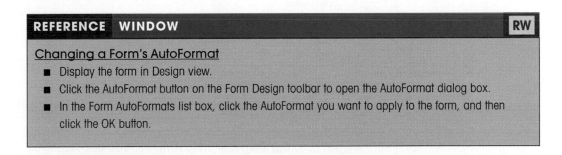

REFERENCE   WINDOW   **RW**

Changing a Form's AutoFormat
- Display the form in Design view.
- Click the AutoFormat button on the Form Design toolbar to open the AutoFormat dialog box.
- In the Form AutoFormats list box, click the AutoFormat you want to apply to the form, and then click the OK button.

To change the AutoFormat for the Position Data form:

1. Click the **View** button for Design view ![icon] on the Form View toolbar. The form is displayed in Design view. See Figure 4-6.

Figure 4-6   FORM DISPLAYED IN DESIGN VIEW

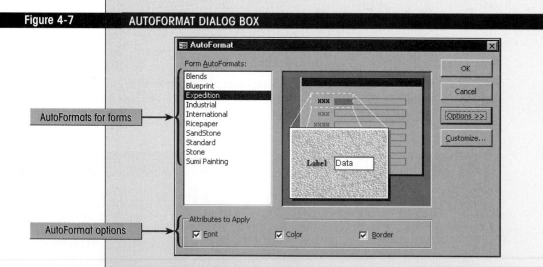

Form window

AutoFormat button

TROUBLE? If your screen displays any window other than those shown in Figure 4-6, click the Close button ☒ on the window's title bar to close it.

You use Design view to modify an existing form or to create a form from scratch. In this case, you need to change the AutoFormat for the Position Data form.

2. Click the **AutoFormat** button 📙 on the Form Design toolbar. The AutoFormat dialog box opens.

3. Click the **Options** button to display the AutoFormat options. See Figure 4-7.

Figure 4-7   AUTOFORMAT DIALOG BOX

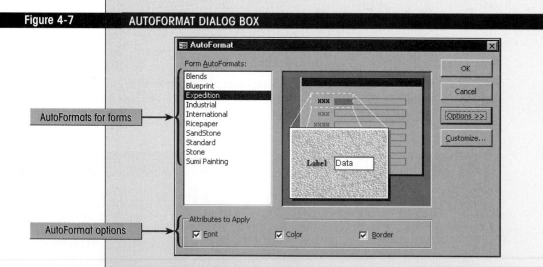

AutoFormats for forms

AutoFormat options

A sample of the selected AutoFormat appears to the right of the Form AutoFormats list box. The options at the bottom of the dialog box let you apply the selected AutoFormat or just its font, color, or border.

Elsa decides that she prefers the Standard AutoFormat, because its field names and field values are easy to read.

4. Click **Standard** in the Form AutoFormats list box, and then click the **OK** button. The AutoFormat dialog box closes, the Standard AutoFormat is applied to the form, and the Form window in Design view becomes the active window.

5. Click the **View** button for Form view 🔲 on the Form Design toolbar. The form is displayed in Form view with the new AutoFormat. See Figure 4-8.

Figure 4-8	FORM DISPLAYED WITH THE NEW AUTOFORMAT

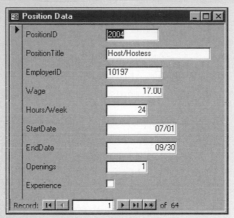

You have finished modifying the format of the form and can now save it.

6. Click the **Save** button 🔲 on the Form View toolbar to save the modified form.

Elsa wants to use the Position Data form to view some data in the Position table. To view data, you need to navigate through the form. As you learned in Tutorial 1, you navigate through a form in the same way that you navigate through a table datasheet. Also, the navigation mode and editing mode keystroke techniques you used with datasheets in Tutorial 2 are the same when navigating a form.

To navigate through the Position Data form:

1. Press the **Tab** key to move to the PositionTitle field value, and then press the **End** key to move to the Experience field. Because the Experience field is a yes/no field, its value is not highlighted; instead, a dotted outline appears around the field name to indicate that it is the current field.

2. Press the **Home** key to move back to the PositionID field value. The first record in the Position table still appears in the form.

3. Press **Ctrl + End** to move to the Experience field for record 64, which is the last record in the table. The record number for the current record appears in the Specific Record box between the navigation buttons at the bottom of the form.

4. Click the **Previous Record** navigation button 🔲 to move to the Experience field in record 63.

5. Press the ↑ key twice to move to the EndDate field in record 63.

6. Click the insertion point between the numbers "1" and "5" in the EndDate field value to switch to editing mode, press the **Home** key to move the insertion point to the beginning of the field value, and then press the **End** key to move the insertion point to the end of the field value.

7. Click the **First Record** navigation button ⏮ to move to the EndDate field value in the first record. The entire field value is highlighted because you have switched from editing mode to navigation mode.

8. Click the **Next Record** navigation button ▶ to move to the EndDate field value in record 2, the next record.

Elsa asks you to display the records for The Clipper Ship Inn, whose EmployerID is 10145, because she wants to review the available positions for this employer.

Finding Data Using a Form

The **Find** command lets you search for data in a form or datasheet so you can display only those records you want to view. You choose a field to serve as the basis for the search by making that field the current field; then you enter the value you want Access to match in the Find and Replace dialog box. You can use the Find command by clicking the toolbar Find button or by using the Edit menu.

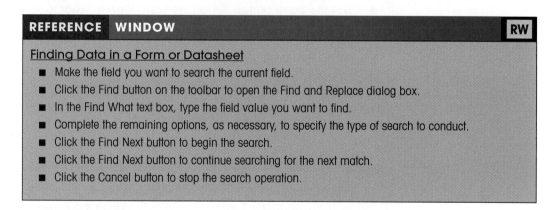

REFERENCE	WINDOW	RW

Finding Data in a Form or Datasheet
- Make the field you want to search the current field.
- Click the Find button on the toolbar to open the Find and Replace dialog box.
- In the Find What text box, type the field value you want to find.
- Complete the remaining options, as necessary, to specify the type of search to conduct.
- Click the Find Next button to begin the search.
- Click the Find Next button to continue searching for the next match.
- Click the Cancel button to stop the search operation.

You need to find all records in the Position table for The Clipper Ship Inn, whose EmployerID is 10145.

To find the records using the Position Data form:

1. Click in the **EmployerID** field value box. This is the field that you will search for matching values.

2. Click the **Find** button 🔍 on the Form View toolbar. The Find and Replace dialog box opens. Note that the Look In list box shows the name of the field that Access will search (in this case, the current EmployerID field), and the Match list box indicates that Access will find values that match the entire entry in the field. You could choose to match only part of a field value or only the beginning of each field value.

3. If the Find and Replace dialog box covers the form, move the dialog box by dragging its title bar. If necessary, move the Position Data form window so that you can see both the dialog box and the form at the same time. See Figure 4-9.

| Figure 4-9 | FIND AND REPLACE DIALOG BOX |

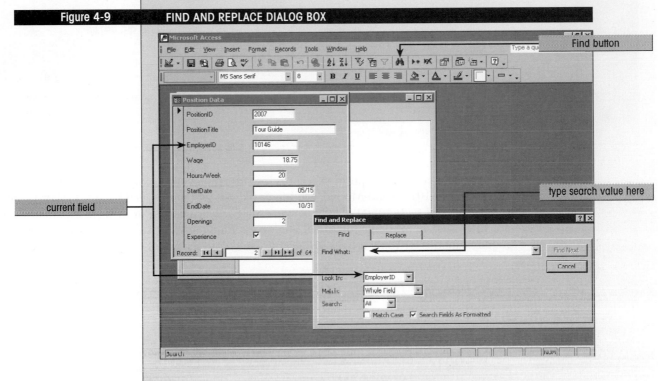

4. In the Find What text box, type **10145** and then click the **Find Next** button. Access displays record 7, which is the first record for EmployerID 10145.

5. Click the **Find Next** button. Access displays record 47, which is the second record for EmployerID 10145.

6. Click the **Find Next** button. Access displays record 48, which is the third record for EmployerID 10145.

7. Click the **Find Next** button. Access displays a dialog box informing you that the search is finished.

8. Click the **OK** button to close the dialog box.

The search value you enter can be an exact value, such as the EmployerID 10145 you just entered, or it can include wildcard characters. A **wildcard character** is a placeholder you use when you know only part of a value or when you want to start or end with a specific character or match a certain pattern. Figure 4-10 shows the wildcard characters you can use when finding data.

Figure 4-10	WILDCARD CHARACTERS	
WILDCARD CHARACTER	**PURPOSE**	**EXAMPLE**
*	Match any number of characters. It can be used as the first and/or last character in the character string.	th* finds *the, that, this, therefore,* and so on
?	Match any single alphabetic character.	a?t finds *act, aft, ant, apt,* and *art*
[]	Match any single character within the brackets.	a[fr]t finds *aft* and *art* but not *act, ant,* and *apt*
!	Match any character not within brackets.	a[!fr]t finds *act, ant,* and *apt* but not *aft* and *art*
-	Match any one of a range of characters. The range must be in ascending order (a to z, not z to a).	a[d-p]t finds *aft, ant,* and *apt* but not *act* and *art*
#	Match any single numeric character.	#72 finds *072, 172, 272, 372,* and so on

Elsa wants to view the position records for two employers: George's Restaurant & Galley (EmployerID 10180) and Moondance Inn & Ski Resort (EmployerID 10185). Matt Griffin, the manager of recruitment, knows of some student recruits with prior work experience who are interested in working for these employers. Elsa wants to see which positions, if any, require experience. You'll use the * wildcard character to search for these employers' positions.

To find the records using the * wildcard character:

1. Click **10145** in the Find What text box to select the entire value, and then type **1018***.

   Access will match any field value in the EmployerID field that starts with the digits 1018.

2. Click the **Find Next** button. Access displays record 64, which is the first record found for EmployerID 10185. Note that the Experience field value is unchecked, indicating that this position does not require experience.

3. Click the **Find Next** button. Access displays record 25, which is the first record found for EmployerID 10180. Again, the Experience field value is unchecked.

4. Click the **Find Next** button. Access displays record 42, which is the second record found for EmployerID 10185. In this case, the Experience field value is checked, indicating that this position requires prior work experience.

5. Click the **Find Next** button. Access displays a dialog box informing you that the search is finished.

6. Click the **OK** button to close the dialog box.

7. Click the **Cancel** button to close the Find and Replace dialog box.

Of the three positions, only one requires experience—PositionID 2089. Elsa asks you to use the form to print the data for record 42, which is for PositionID 2089, so that she can give the printout to Matt.

Previewing and Printing Selected Form Records

Access prints as many form records as can fit on a printed page. If only part of a form record fits on the bottom of a page, the remainder of the record prints on the next page. Access allows you to print all pages or a range of pages. In addition, you can print the currently selected form record.

Before printing record 42, you'll preview the form record to see how it will look when printed. Notice that the current record number (in this case, 42) appears in the Specific Record box at the bottom of the form.

To preview the form and print the data for record 42:

1. Click the **Print Preview** button 🔍 on the Form View toolbar. The Print Preview window opens, showing the form records for the Position table in miniature. If you clicked the Print button now, all the records for the table would be printed, beginning with the first record.

2. Click the **Maximize** button 🗖 on the form's title bar.

3. Click the **Zoom** button 🔍 on the Print Preview toolbar, and then use the vertical scroll bar to view the entire page. Each record from the Position table appears in a separate form. See Figure 4-11.

| Figure 4-11 | PRINT PREVIEW WINDOW DISPLAYING FORM RECORDS |

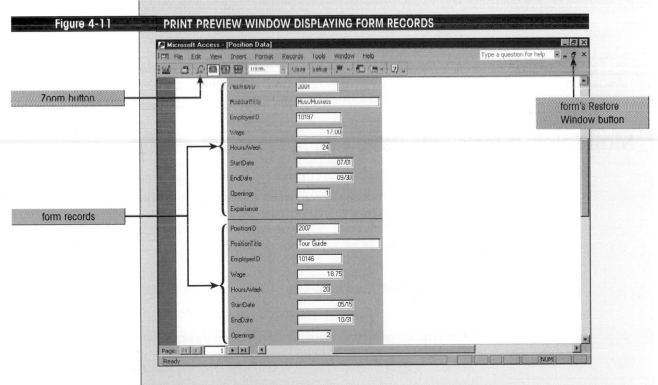

4. Click the **Restore Window** button 🗗 on the Print Preview menu bar, and then click the **Close** button on the Print Preview toolbar to return to the table in Form view.

The record that you need to print, PositionID 2089, appears in the form. To print selected records you need to use the Print dialog box.

5. Click **File** on the menu bar, and then click **Print**. The Print dialog box opens.

6. Click the **Selected Record(s)** option button to print the current form record (record 42).

7. Click the **OK** button to close the dialog box and to print the selected record.

Elsa has identified several updates, as shown in Figure 4-12, that she wants you to make to the Position table. You'll use the Position Data form to update the data in the Position table.

Figure 4-12	UPDATES TO THE POSITION TABLE

PositionID	Update Action
2033	Change Hours/Week to 35
	Change StartDate to 6/30
2072	Delete record
2130	Add new record for PositionID 2130:
	PositionTitle = Housekeeping
	EmployerID = 10151
	Wage = 12.50
	Hours/Week = 30
	StartDate = 6/1
	EndDate = 10/15
	Openings = 2
	Experience = No

Maintaining Table Data Using a Form

Maintaining data using a form is often easier than using a datasheet, because you can concentrate on all the changes required to a single record at one time. You already know how to navigate a form and find specific records. Now you'll make the changes Elsa requested to the Position table, using the Position Data form.

First, you'll update the record for PositionID 2033.

To change the record using the Position Data form:

1. Make sure the Position Data form is displayed in Form view.

When she reviewed the position data to identify possible corrections, Elsa noted that 10 is the record number for PositionID 2033. If you know the number of the record you want to display, you can type the number in the Specific Record box and press the Enter key to go directly to that record.

2. Select **42** in the Specific Record box, type **10**, and then press the **Enter** key. Record 10 (PositionID 2033) is now the current record.

You need to change the Hours/Week field value to 35 and the StartDate field value to 6/30 for this record.

3. Click the insertion point to the left of the number 2 in the Hours/Week field value, press the **Delete** key twice, and then type **35**. Note that the pencil symbol appears in the upper-left corner of the form, indicating that the form is in editing mode.

4. Press the **Tab** key to move to and select the StartDate field value, type **6/30**, and then press the **Enter** key. See Figure 4-13.

Figure 4-13	POSITION RECORD AFTER CHANGING FIELD VALUES

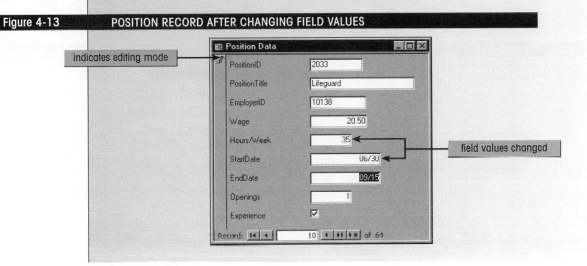

You have completed the changes for PositionID 2033. Elsa's next update is to delete the record for PositionID 2072. The employer client recently informed Elsa that a full-time, permanent employee has been hired for this position, so it is no longer available for student recruits

To delete the record using the Position Data form:

1. Click anywhere in the PositionID field value to make it the current field.

2. Click the **Find** button 🔍 on the Form View toolbar. The Find and Replace dialog box opens.

3. Type **2072** in the Find What text box, click the **Find Next** button, and then click the **Cancel** button. The record for PositionID 2072 is now the current record.

4. Click the **Delete Record** button 🗙 on the Form View toolbar. A dialog box opens, asking you to confirm the record deletion.

5. Click the **Yes** button. The dialog box closes, and the record for PositionID 2072 is deleted from the table.

Elsa's final maintenance change is to add a record for a new position available at the Granite State Resort.

To add the new record using the Position Data form:

1. Click the **New Record** button ▶* on the Form View toolbar. Record 64, the next record available for a new record, becomes the current record. All field value boxes are empty, and the insertion point is positioned at the beginning of the field value box for PositionID.

2. Refer to Figure 4-14 and enter the value shown for each field. Press the **Tab** key to move from field to field.

Figure 4-14	COMPLETED FORM FOR THE NEW RECORD

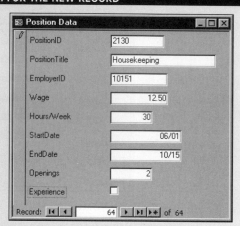

TROUBLE? Compare your screen with Figure 4-14. If any field value is wrong, correct it now, using the methods described earlier for editing field values.

3. After entering the value for Openings, press the **Tab** key twice (if necessary). Record 65, the next record available for a new record, becomes the current record, and the record for PositionID 2130 is saved in the Position table.

You've completed Elsa's changes to the Position table, so you can close the Position Data form.

4. Click the **Close** button ✕ on the form's title bar. The form closes and you return to the Database window. Notice that the Position Data form is listed in the Forms list box.

Checking the Spelling of Table Data Using a Form

You can check the spelling of table data using a table or query datasheet or a form that displays the table data. The Spelling feature searches through the data and identifies any words that are not included in its dictionary. Sometimes the word is misspelled, and you can correct it; other words are spelled correctly, but they are not listed in the spelling dictionary.

Elsa wants to make sure that the position data contains no spelling errors. You'll use the Position Data form to check the spelling of data in the Position table.

To check the spelling of data using the Position Data form:

1. Double-click **Position Data** to open the form in Form view. The form displays data for the first record.

2. Click the **Spelling** button on the Form View toolbar. The Spelling dialog box opens, identifying the word "Reservationist" as not in its dictionary. See Figure 4-15.

Figure 4-15   SPELLING DIALOG BOX

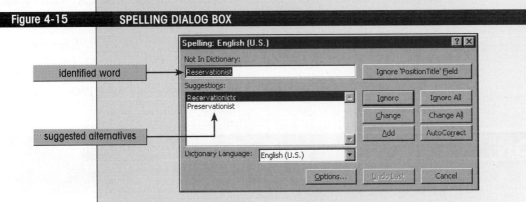

TROUBLE? If the word "Reservationist" is not identified by the Spelling feature, it was probably added to your dictionary. Just continue with the steps.

Note that the dialog box provides buttons for ignoring the word or changing it to one of the suggested alternatives, plus an option for ignoring all entries in the selected field (PositionTitle, in this case). The word is spelled correctly, so you will ignore all occurrences of this word in the Position table.

3. Click the **Ignore All** button. Next, the Spelling dialog box identifies the word "Greenskeeper" as not in its dictionary, and suggests the spelling should be two words, "Greens keeper." You'll change to the suggested spelling.

4. Click the **Change All** button. All occurrences of the word "Greenskeeper" are changed to the words "Greens keeper" in the Position table.

A dialog box opens, informing you that the spell check is complete.

5. Click the **OK** button to close the dialog box.

6. Close the form.

You can customize how the Spelling feature works in Access by changing the settings on the Spelling tab of the Options dialog box, which you open by choosing Options from the Tools menu. For example, you can choose another language for the main dictionary, and you can create custom dictionaries to contain words or phrases specific to the type of data in your database. Adding frequently used words to a custom dictionary will prevent the Spelling feature from identifying those words as not in its dictionary, thereby speeding up the spell check process.

The Position Data form will enable Elsa and her staff to enter and maintain data easily in the Position table. In the next session, you'll create another form for working with data in both the Position and Employer tables at the same time. You'll also create a report showing data from both tables.

Session 4.1 QUICK CHECK

1. Describe the difference between creating a form using the AutoForm Wizard and creating a form using the Form Wizard.

2. What is an AutoFormat, and how do you change one for an existing form?

3. Which table record is displayed in a form when you press Ctrl + End while you are in navigation mode?

4. You can use the Find command to search for data in a form or _____.

5. Which wildcard character matches any single alphabetic character?

6. How many form records does Access print by default on a page?

SESSION 4.2

In this session, you will create a form with a main form and a subform, modify a form in Design view, create a report using the Report Wizard, insert a picture in a report, and preview and print a report.

Elsa would like you to create a form so that she can view the data for each employer and its available positions at the same time. The type of form you need to create will include a main form and a subform.

Creating a Form with a Main Form and a Subform

To create a form based on two tables, you must first define a relationship between the two tables. In Tutorial 3, you defined a one-to-many relationship between the Employer (primary) and Position (related) tables, so you are ready to create the form based on both tables.

When you create a form containing data from two tables that have a one-to-many relationship, you actually create a main form for data from the primary table and a subform for data from the related table. Access uses the defined relationship between the tables to join the tables automatically through the common field that exists in both tables.

Elsa and her staff will use the form when contacting employers about their available positions. The main form will contain the employer ID and name, contact first and last names, and phone number for each employer. The subform will contain the position ID and title, wage, hours/week, experience, start and end dates, and number of openings for each position.

You'll use the Form Wizard to create the form.

To create the form using the Form Wizard:

1. If you took a break after the previous session, make sure that Access is running and the Northeast database is open.

2. Make sure the Forms object is selected in the Database window, and then click the **New** button. The New Form dialog box opens.

   When creating a form based on two tables, you first choose the primary table and select the fields you want to include in the main form; then you choose the related table and select fields from it for the subform.

3. Click **Form Wizard**, click the list arrow for choosing a table or query, click **Employer** to select this table as the source for the main form, and then click the **OK** button. The first Form Wizard dialog box opens, in which you select fields in the order you want them to appear on the main form.

Elsa wants the form to include only the EmployerID, EmployerName, ContactFirstName, ContactLastName, and Phone fields from the Employer table.

4. Click **EmployerID** in the Available Fields list box (if necessary), and then click the ▷ button to move the field to the Selected Fields list box.

5. Repeat Step 4 for the **EmployerName**, **ContactFirstName**, **ContactLastName**, and **Phone** fields.

The EmployerID field will appear in the main form, so you do not have to include it in the subform. Otherwise, Elsa wants the subform to include all the fields from the Position table.

6. Click the **Tables/Queries** list arrow, and then click **Table: Position**. The fields from the Position table appear in the Available Fields list box. The quickest way to add the fields you want to include is to move all the fields to the Selected Fields list box, and then to remove the only field you don't want to include (EmployerID).

7. Click the ▷▷ button to move all the fields from the Position table to the Selected Fields list box.

8. Click **Position.EmployerID** in the Selected Fields list box, and then click the ◁ button to move the field back to the Available Fields list box. Note that the table name (Position) is included in the field name to distinguish it from the same field (EmployerID) in the Employer table.

9. Click the **Next** button. The next Form Wizard dialog box opens. See Figure 4-16.

Figure 4-16   CHOOSING A MAIN/SUBFORM FORMAT

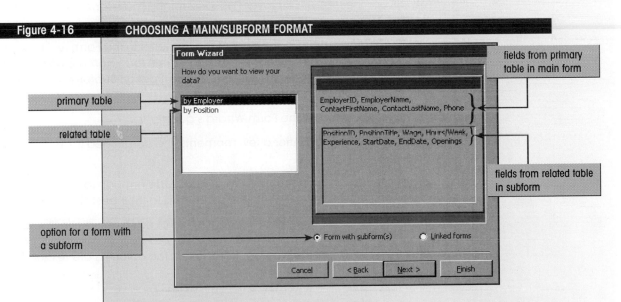

In this dialog box, the list box on the left shows the order in which you will view the selected data: first by data from the primary Employer table, and then by data from the related Position table. The form will be displayed as shown in the right side of the dialog box, with the fields from the Employer table at the top in the main form, and the fields from the Position table at the bottom in the subform. The selected option button specifies a main form with a subform. The Linked forms option creates a form structure where only the main form fields are displayed. A button with the subform's name on it appears on the main form; you can click this button to display the associated subform records.

The default options shown in Figure 4-16 are correct for creating a form with Employer data in the main form and Position data in the subform.

To finish creating the form:

1. Click the **Next** button. The next Form Wizard dialog box opens, in which you choose the subform layout.

   The Tabular layout displays subform fields as a table, whereas the Datasheet layout displays subform fields as a table datasheet. The PivotTable and PivotChart layouts display summary and analytical information. The layout choice is a matter of personal preference. You'll use the Datasheet layout.

2. Click the **Datasheet** option button (if necessary), and then click the **Next** button. The next Form Wizard dialog box opens, in which you choose the form's style.

   Elsa wants all forms in the Northeast database to have the same style, so you will choose Standard, which is the same style you applied to the Position Data form.

3. Click **Standard** (if necessary), and then click the **Next** button. The next Form Wizard dialog box opens, in which you choose names for the main form and the subform.

   You will use the name "Employer Positions" for the main form and the name "Position Subform" for the subform.

4. Click the insertion point to the right of the last letter in the Form text box, press the **spacebar**, and then type **Positions**. The main form name is now Employer Positions. Note that the default subform name, Position Subform, is the name you want, so you don't need to change it.

   You have answered all the Form Wizard's questions.

5. Click the **Finish** button. After a few moments, the completed form opens in Form view.

   Some of the columns in the subform are not wide enough to display the field names entirely. You need to resize the columns to their best fit.

6. Double-click the pointer ++ at the right edge of each column in the subform, scrolling the subform to the right, as necessary, to display additional columns. Scroll the subform all the way back to the left. The columns are resized to their best fit. See Figure 4-17.

Figure 4-17	MAIN FORM WITH SUBFORM IN FORM VIEW

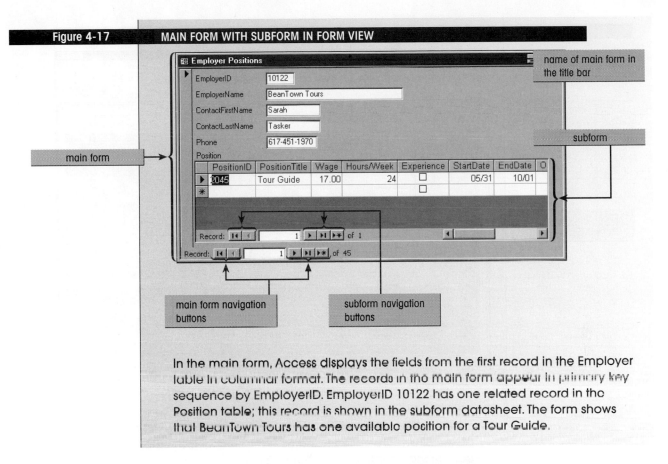

In the main form, Access displays the fields from the first record in the Employer table in columnar format. The records in the main form appear in primary key sequence by EmployerID. EmployerID 10122 has one related record in the Position table; this record is shown in the subform datasheet. The form shows that BeanTown Tours has one available position for a Tour Guide.

Notice that the subform is not wide enough to display all the fields from the Position table. Although the subform includes a horizontal scroll bar, which allows you to view the other fields, Elsa wants all the fields from the Position table to be visible in the subform at the same time. Even if you maximized the Form window, the subform would still not display all of the fields. You need to widen the main form and the subform in Design view.

Modifying a Form in Design View

Just as you use Design view to modify the format and content of tables and queries, you use Design view to modify a form. You can change the fields that are displayed on a form, and modify their size, location, format, and so on. You need to open the Employer Positions form in Design view and resize the Position subform to display all the fields at the same time.

To widen the Position subform:

1. Click the **View** button for Design view ⬕ on the Form View toolbar to display the form in Design view.

2. Click the **Maximize** button ☐ to enlarge the window. See Figure 4-18.

Figure 4-18   FORM DISPLAYED IN DESIGN VIEW

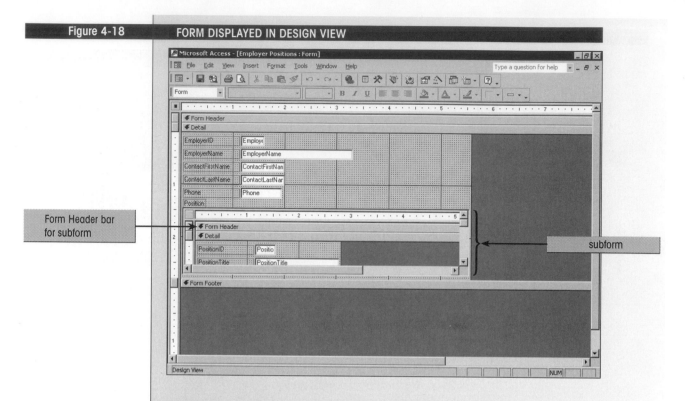

Form Header bar for subform

subform

3. Click the **Form Header** bar for the subform (refer to Figure 4-18) to select the subform. Notice that small boxes appear around the subform's border. These boxes, which are called **handles**, indicate that the subform is selected and can be manipulated. See Figure 4-19.

Figure 4-19   SUBFORM SELECTED IN DESIGN VIEW

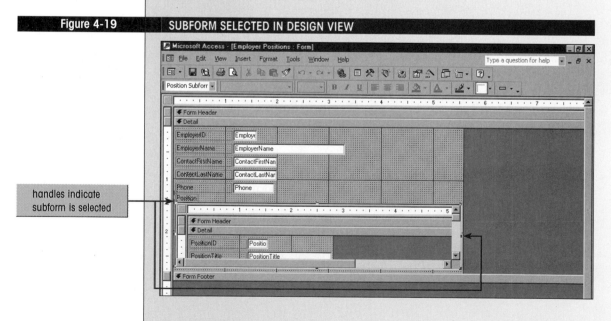

handles indicate subform is selected

4. Position the pointer on the right-center sizing handle so it changes to a ↔ shape, and then click and drag the handle to the right to the **6.5**-inch mark on the horizontal ruler. See Figure 4-20.

Figure 4-20 **RESIZING THE POSITION SUBFORM**

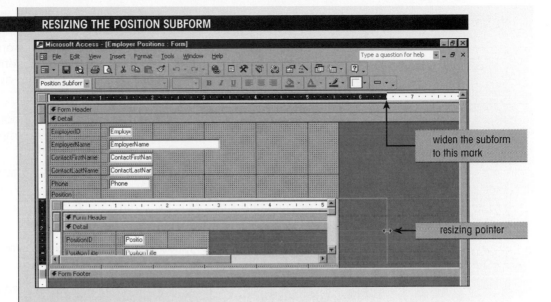

widen the subform to this mark

resizing pointer

5. Release the mouse button. The subform section is resized. Notice that the main form section is also resized.

6. Switch back to Form view. Notice that all the field names in the Position Subform are now visible.

7. Click the **Restore Window** button on the menu bar to restore the form to its original size. Now you need to resize the Form window in Form view so that all the fields will be displayed when the Form window is not maximized.

8. Position the pointer on the right edge of the form so it changes to a ↔ shape, and then click and drag the right edge of the form to resize it so that it matches the form shown in Figure 4-21.

Figure 4-21 **FORM WITH ALL SUBFORM FIELDS VISIBLE**

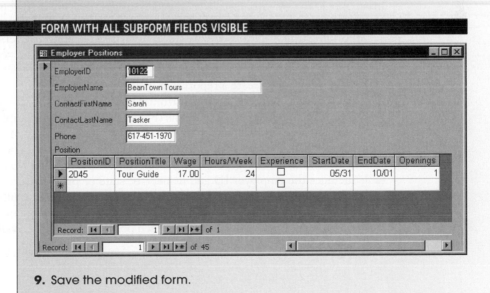

9. Save the modified form.

Two sets of navigation buttons appear at the bottom of the Form view window. You use the top set of navigation buttons to select records from the related table in the subform, and the bottom set to select records from the primary table in the main form.

You'll use the navigation buttons to view different records.

To navigate to different main form and subform records:

1. Click the **Last Record** navigation button [▶|] in the main form. Record 45 in the Employer table for Lighthouse Tours becomes the current record in the main form. The subform shows that this employer has one available Tour Guide position.

2. Click the **Previous Record** navigation button [◀] in the main form. Record 44 in the Employer table for Harbor Whale Watch Tours becomes the current record in the main form.

3. Select **44** in the Specific Record box for the main form, type **32**, and then press the **Enter** key. Record 32 in the Employer table for Windsor Alpine Tours becomes the current record in the main form. This employer has two available positions.

4. Click the **Last Record** navigation button [▶|] in the subform. Record 2 in the Position table becomes the current record in the subform.

   You have finished your work with the form, so you can close it.

5. Close the form. Notice that both the main form, Employer Positions, and the subform, Position Subform, appear in the Forms list box.

Zack would like a report showing data from both the Employer and Position tables so that all the pertinent information about employer clients and their positions is available in one place. To satisfy Zack's request, you'll create the report using the Report Wizard.

Creating a Report Using the Report Wizard

As you learned in Tutorial 1, a report is a formatted printout of the contents of one or more tables in a database. In Access, you can create your own reports or use the Report Wizard to create them for you. Like the Form Wizard, the **Report Wizard** asks you a series of questions and then creates a report based on your answers. Whether you use the Report Wizard or design your own report, you can change the report's design after you create it.

Zack wants you to create a report that includes selected employer data from the Employer table and all the available positions from the Position table for each employer. Zack has sketched a design of the report he wants (Figure 4-22). Like the Employer Positions form you just created, which includes a main form and a subform, the report will be based on both tables, which are joined in a one-to-many relationship through the common EmployerID field. As shown in the sketch in Figure 4-22, the selected employer data from the primary Employer table includes the employer ID and name, city, state or province, contact first and last names, and phone number. Below the data for each employer, the report will include the position ID and title, wage, hours/week, experience, start and end dates, and openings data from the related Position table. The set of field values for each position is called a **detail record**.

| Figure 4-22 | REPORT SKETCH FOR THE EMPLOYERS AND POSITIONS REPORT |

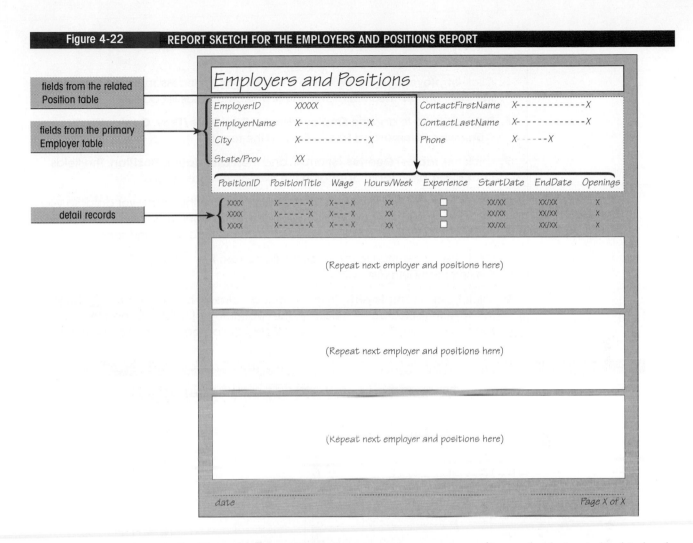

You'll use the Report Wizard to create the report according to the design in Zack's sketch.

To start the Report Wizard and select the fields to include in the report:

1. Click **Reports** in the Objects bar of the Database window to display the Reports list box. You have not yet created any reports.

2. Click the **New** button in the Database window. The New Report dialog box opens.

   As was the case when you created the form with a subform, initially you can choose only one table or query to be the data source for the report. Then you can include data from other tables. You will select the primary Employer table in the New Report dialog box.

3. Click **Report Wizard**, click the list arrow for choosing a table or query, and then click **Employer**.

4. Click the **OK** button. The first Report Wizard dialog box opens.

   In the first Report Wizard dialog box, you select fields in the order you want them to appear on the report. Zack wants the EmployerID, EmployerName, City,

State/Prov, ContactFirstName, ContactLastName, and Phone fields from the Employer table to appear on the report.

5. Click **EmployerID** in the Available Fields list box (if necessary), and then click the ⟩ button. The field moves to the Selected Fields list box.

6. Repeat Step 5 to add the **EmployerName**, **City**, **State/Prov**, **ContactFirstName**, **ContactLastName**, and **Phone** fields to the report.

7. Click the **Tables/Queries** list arrow, and then click **Table: Position**. The fields from the Position table appear in the Available Fields list box.

The EmployerID field will appear on the report with the employer data, so you do not have to include it in the detail records for each position. Otherwise, Zack wants all the fields from the Position table to be included in the report.

8. Click the ⟩⟩ button to move all the fields from the Available Fields list box to the Selected Fields list box.

9. Click **Position.EmployerID** in the Selected Fields list box, click the ⟨ button to move the selected field back to the Available Fields list box, and then click the **Next** button. The second Report Wizard dialog box opens. See Figure 4-23.

Figure 4-23	CHOOSING A GROUPED OR UNGROUPED REPORT

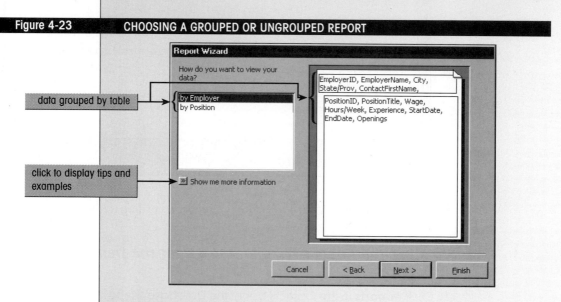

You can choose to arrange the selected data grouped by table, which is the default, or ungrouped. For a grouped report, the data from a record in the primary table appears as a group, followed on subsequent lines of the report by the joined records from the related table. For the report you are creating, data from a record in the Employer table appears in a group, followed by the related records for each employer from the Position table. An example of an ungrouped report would be a report of records from the Employer and Position tables in order by PositionID. Each position and its associated employer data would appear together on one or more lines of the report; the data would not be grouped by table.

You can display tips and examples for the choices in the Report Wizard dialog box by clicking the "Show me more information" button ⟩⟩ .

To display tips about the options in the Report Wizard dialog box:

1. Click the ⟫ button. The Report Wizard Tips dialog box opens. Read the information shown in the dialog box.

You can display examples of different grouping methods by clicking the ⟫ button ("Show me examples").

2. Click ⟫ . The Report Wizard Examples dialog box opens. See Figure 4-24.

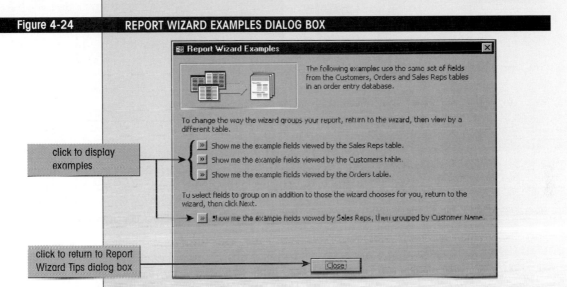

You can display examples of different grouping methods by clicking the ⟫ buttons.

3. Click each ⟫ button in turn, review the displayed example, and then click the **Close** button to return to the Report Wizard Examples dialog box.

4. Click the **Close** button to return to the Report Wizard Tips dialog box, and then click the **Close** button to return to the second Report Wizard dialog box.

The default options shown on your screen are correct for the report Zack wants, so you can continue responding to the Report Wizard questions.

To finish creating the report using the Report Wizard:

1. Click the **Next** button. The next Report Wizard dialog box opens, in which you choose additional grouping levels.

Two grouping levels are shown: one for an employer's data, and the other for an employer's positions. Grouping levels are useful for reports with multiple levels, such as those containing monthly, quarterly, and annual totals, or for those containing city and country groups. Zack's report contains no further grouping levels, so you can accept the default options.

2. Click the **Next** button. The next Report Wizard dialog box opens, in which you choose the sort order for the detail records. See Figure 4-25.

Figure 4-25   CHOOSING THE SORT ORDER FOR DETAIL RECORDS

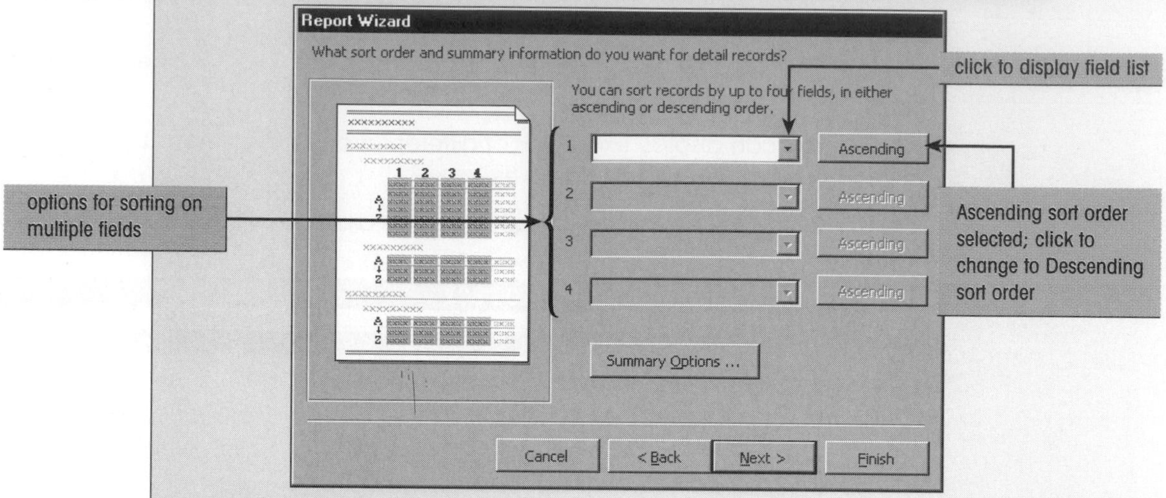

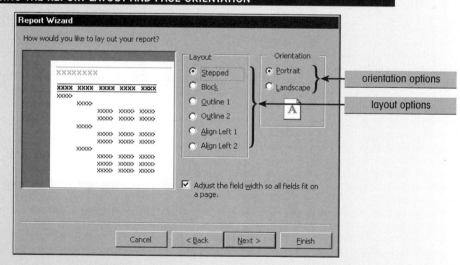

options for sorting on multiple fields

click to display field list

Ascending sort order selected; click to change to Descending sort order

The records from the Position table for an employer represent the detail records for Zack's report. He wants these records to appear in increasing, or ascending, order by the value in the PositionID field. The Ascending option is already selected by default. To change to descending order, you simply click this button, which acts as a toggle between the two sort orders. Also, notice that you can sort on multiple fields, as you can with queries.

3. Click the **1** list arrow, click **PositionID**, and then click the **Next** button. The next Report Wizard dialog box opens, in which you choose a layout and page orientation for the report. See Figure 4-26.

Figure 4-26   CHOOSING THE REPORT LAYOUT AND PAGE ORIENTATION

orientation options

layout options

A sample of each layout appears in the box on the left.

4. Click each layout option and examine each sample that appears.

You'll use the Outline 2 layout option because it resembles the layout shown in Zack's sketch of the report. Also, because of the number of fields in the Position table, the information would fit better in a wide format; therefore, you'll choose the landscape orientation.

5. Click the **Outline 2** option button, click the **Landscape** option button, and then click the **Next** button. The next Report Wizard dialog box opens, in which you choose a style for the report.

A sample of the selected style, or AutoFormat, appears in the box on the left. You can always choose a different AutoFormat after you create the report, just as you can when creating a form. Zack likes the appearance of the Corporate AutoFormat, so you'll choose this one for your report.

6. Click **Corporate** (if necessary), and then click the **Next** button. The last Report Wizard dialog box opens, in which you choose a report name, which also serves as the printed title on the report.

According to Zack's sketch, the report title you need to specify is "Employers and Positions."

7. Type **Employers and Positions** and then click the **Finish** button. The Report Wizard creates the report based on your answers and saves it as an object in the Northeast database. Then Access opens the Employers and Positions report in Print Preview.

To view the report better, you need to maximize the Report window.

8. Click the **Maximize** button ☐ on the Employers and Positions title bar.

To view the entire page, you need to change the Zoom setting.

9. Click the **Zoom** list arrow on the Print Preview toolbar, and then click **Fit**. The first page of the report is displayed in Print Preview. See Figure 4-27.

| Figure 4-27 | REPORT DISPLAYED IN PRINT PREVIEW |

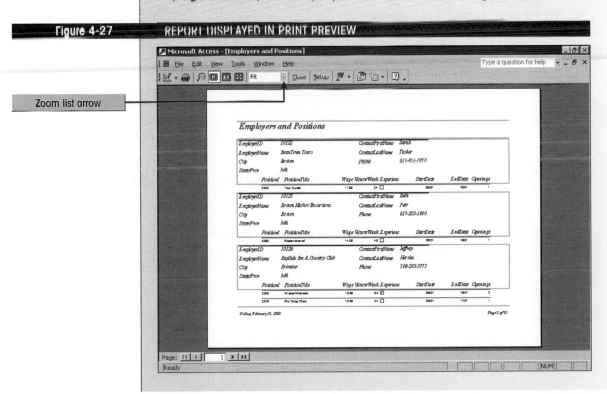

When a report is displayed in Print Preview, you can use the pointer to toggle between a full-page display and a close-up display of the report. Zack asks you to check the report to see if any adjustments need to be made. For example, some of the field titles or values might not be displayed completely, or you might need to move fields to enhance the report's appearance. To do so, you need to view a close-up display of the report.

To view a close-up display of the report and make any necessary corrections:

1. Click the pointer 🔍 at the top center of the report. The display changes to show a close-up view of the report. See Figure 4-28.

Figure 4-28	CLOSE-UP VIEW OF THE REPORT

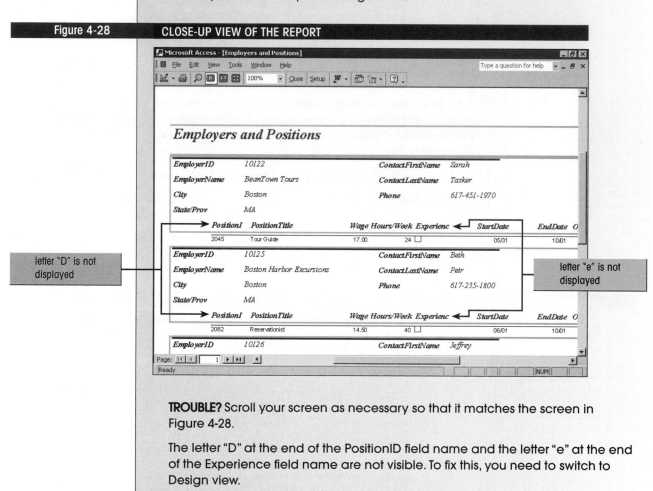

letter "D" is not displayed

letter "e" is not displayed

TROUBLE? Scroll your screen as necessary so that it matches the screen in Figure 4-28.

The letter "D" at the end of the PositionID field name and the letter "e" at the end of the Experience field name are not visible. To fix this, you need to switch to Design view.

2. Click the **View** button for Design view 🖉 on the Print Preview toolbar. Access displays the report in Design view. See Figure 4-29.

| Figure 4-29 | REPORT DISPLAYED IN DESIGN VIEW |

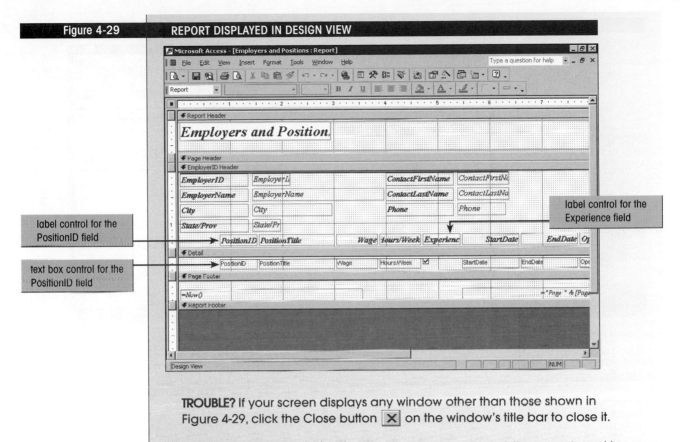

TROUBLE? If your screen displays any window other than those shown in Figure 4-29, click the Close button ☒ on the window's title bar to close it.

You use the Report window in Design view to modify existing reports and to create custom reports.

Each item on a report in Design view is called a **control**. For example, the PositionID field consists of two controls: the label "PositionID," which appears on the report to identify the field value, and the PositionID text box, in which the actual field value appears. You need to widen the label control for the PositionID field so that the entire field name is visible in the report.

3. Click the label control for the PositionID field to select it. Handles appear on the border around the control, indicating that the control is selected and can be manipulated.

4. Position the pointer on the center-left handle of the PositionID label control until the pointer changes to a ↔ shape. See Figure 4-30.

Figure 4-30   RESIZING THE PositionID LABEL CONTROL

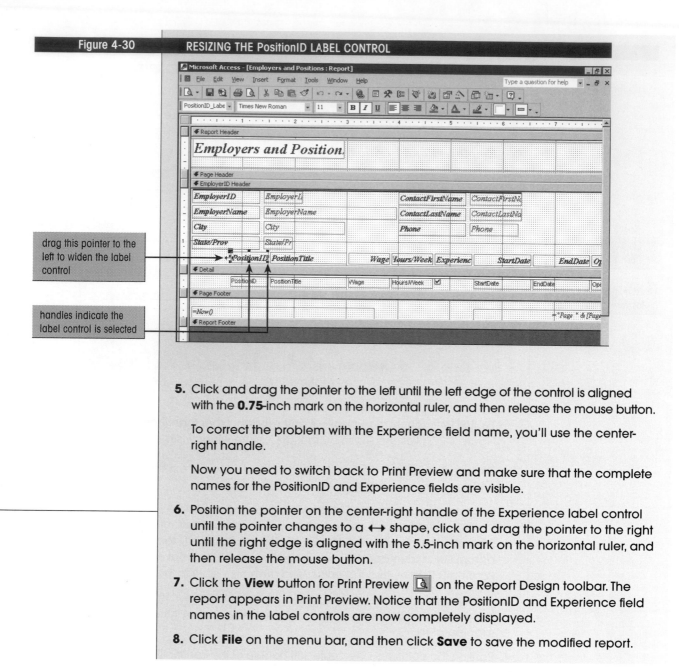

drag this pointer to the left to widen the label control

handles indicate the label control is selected

5. Click and drag the pointer to the left until the left edge of the control is aligned with the **0.75**-inch mark on the horizontal ruler, and then release the mouse button.

   To correct the problem with the Experience field name, you'll use the center-right handle.

   Now you need to switch back to Print Preview and make sure that the complete names for the PositionID and Experience fields are visible.

6. Position the pointer on the center-right handle of the Experience label control until the pointer changes to a ↔ shape, click and drag the pointer to the right until the right edge is aligned with the 5.5-inch mark on the horizontal ruler, and then release the mouse button.

7. Click the **View** button for Print Preview ▣ on the Report Design toolbar. The report appears in Print Preview. Notice that the PositionID and Experience field names in the label controls are now completely displayed.

8. Click **File** on the menu bar, and then click **Save** to save the modified report.

Zack decides that he wants the report to include a graphic image to the right of the report title, for visual interest. You can add the graphic to the report by inserting a picture.

Inserting a Picture in a Report

In Access, you can insert a picture or other graphic image in a report or form to enhance the appearance of the report or form. Sources of graphic images include files created in Microsoft Paint and other drawing programs, and scanned files. The file containing the picture you need to insert is named Globe, and it is located in the Tutorial folder on your Data Disk.

To insert the picture in the report:

1. Click the **Close** button on the Print Preview toolbar to display the report in Design view. See Figure 4-31.

| Figure 4-31 | INSERTING A PICTURE IN DESIGN VIEW |

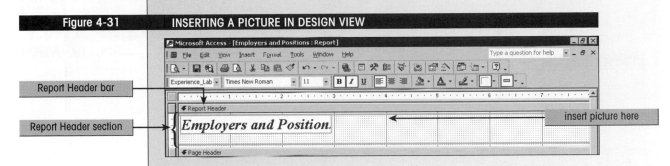

Zack wants the picture to appear on the first page of the report only; therefore, you need to insert the picture in the Report Header section (see Figure 4-31). Any text or picture placed in this section appears once at the beginning of the report.

2. Click the **Report Header** bar to select this section of the report. The bar is highlighted to indicate that the section is selected.

3. Click **Insert** on the menu bar, and then click **Picture**. The Insert Picture dialog box opens. If necessary, open the **Tutorial** folder on your Data Disk. See Figure 4-32.

| Figure 4-32 | INSERT PICTURE DIALOG BOX |

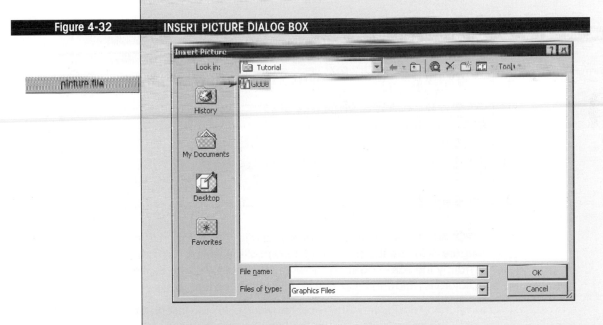

4. Click **Globe** to select the picture for the report, and then click the **OK** button. The picture is inserted in the left side of the Report Header section, covering some of the report title text. See Figure 4-33.

Figure 4-33

PICTURE INSERTED IN THE REPORT

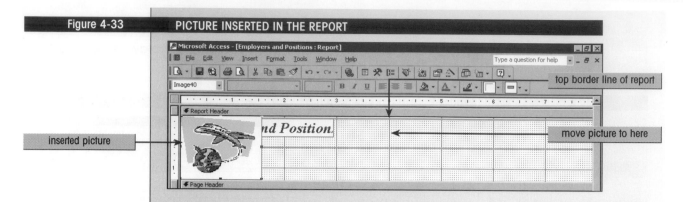

inserted picture

top border line of report

move picture to here

Notice that handles appear around the picture's border, indicating that the picture is selected and can be manipulated.

Zack wants the picture to appear to the right of the report title, so you need to move the picture using the mouse.

5. Position the pointer on the picture until the pointer changes to a 🖑 shape, and then click and drag the mouse to move the picture to the right so that its left edge aligns with the 4-inch mark on the horizontal ruler and its top edge is just below the top border line above the report title (see Figure 4-33).

6. Release the mouse button. The picture appears in the new position. Notice that the height of the Report Header section increased slightly to accommodate the picture. See Figure 4-34.

Figure 4-34

REPOSITIONED PICTURE IN THE REPORT

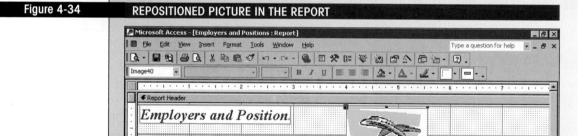

TROUBLE? If your picture appears in a different location from the one shown in Figure 4-34, use the pointer 🖑 to reposition the picture until it is in approximately the same position shown in the figure. Be sure that the top edge of the picture is below the top border line of the report.

7. Switch to Print Preview. The report now includes the inserted picture. If necessary, click the **Zoom** button 🔍 on the Print Preview toolbar to display the entire report page. See Figure 4-35.

| Figure 4-35 | PRINT PREVIEW OF REPORT WITH PICTURE |

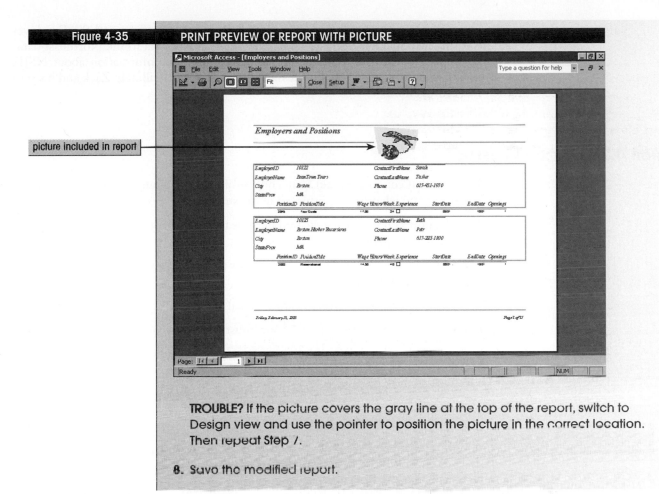

picture included in report

TROUBLE? If the picture covers the gray line at the top of the report, switch to Design view and use the pointer to position the picture in the correct location. Then repeat Step 7.

8. Save the modified report.

The report is now completed. You'll print just the first page of the report so that Zack can review the report layout and the inserted picture.

To print page 1 of the report:

1. Click **File** on the menu bar, and then click **Print**. The Print dialog box opens.

2. In the Print Range section, click the **Pages** option button. The insertion point now appears in the From text box so that you can specify the range of pages to print.

3. Type **1** in the From text box, press the **Tab** key to move to the To text box, and then type **1**. These settings specify that only page 1 of the report will be printed.

4. Click the **OK** button. The Print dialog box closes, and the first page of the report is printed.

   Zack approves of the report layout and contents, so you can close the report.

5. Click the **Close Window** button [X] on the menu bar.

   TROUBLE? If you click the Close button on the Print Preview toolbar by mistake, you switch to Design view. Click the Close Window button [X] on the menu bar.

6. Exit Access.

Elsa is satisfied that the forms you created—the Position Data form and the Employer Positions form—will make it easier to enter, view, and update data in the Northeast database. The Employers and Positions report presents important information about NSJI's employer clients in an attractive and professional format, which will help Zack and his staff in their marketing efforts.

Session 4.2 QUICK CHECK

1. In a form that contains a main form and a subform, what data is displayed in the main form and what data is displayed in the subform?

2. Describe how you use the navigation buttons to move through a form containing a main form and a subform.

3. When you use the Report Wizard, the report name is also used as the _____.

4. Each item on a report in Design view is called a(n) _____.

5. To insert a picture in a report, the report must be displayed in _____.

6. Any text or pictures placed in the _____ section of a report will appear only on the first page of the report.

REVIEW ASSIGNMENTS

Elsa wants to enhance the **Recruits** database with forms and reports, and she asks you to complete the following:

1. Make sure your Data Disk is in the appropriate disk drive, start Access, and then open the **Recruits** database located in the Review folder on your Data Disk.

2. If your **Recruits** database is stored on drive A, you will need to delete the files **Seasons97.mdb** and **Seasons2002.mdb** from your disk so you will have enough room to complete the steps. If your database is stored on a hard or network drive, no action is necessary.

3. Use the Form Wizard to create a form based on the **Student** table. Select all fields for the form, the Columnar layout, the SandStone style, and the title **Student Data** for the form.

4. Use the form you created in the previous step to print the fifth form record. Change the AutoFormat to Sumi Painting, save the changed form, and then print the fifth form record again.

5. Use the **Student Data** form to update the **Student** table as follows:

   a. Use the Find command to move to the record with StudentID STO1323. Change the field values for FirstName to Nathaniel, City to Perth, and BirthDate to 4/2/85 for this record.

   b. Use the Find command to move to the record with StudentID KIE2760, and then delete the record.

   c. Add a new record with the following field values:
      StudentID: SAN2540
      FirstName: Pedro
      LastName: Sandes

City:	Barcelona
Nation:	Spain
BirthDate:	5/1/85
Gender:	M
SSN:	977-07-1798

d. Print only this form record, and then close the form.

Explore   6. Use the AutoForm: Columnar Wizard to create a form based on the **Salaries with Raises** query. Save the form as **Salaries with Raises**, and then close the form.

Explore   7. Use the Form Wizard to create a form containing a main form and a subform. Select the FirstName, LastName, and SSN fields from the **Recruiter** table for the main form, and select all fields except SSN from the **Student** table for the subform. Use the Datasheet layout and the Sumi Painting style. Specify the title **Recruiter Students** for the main form and the title **Student Subform** for the subform. Resize all columns in the subform to their best fit. Use Design view to resize the main form and the subform so that all fields are visible in the subform at the same time. Resize the Form window in Form view, as necessary, so that all fields are visible at the same time. Print the fourth main form record and its subform records. Save and close the form.

Explore   8. Use the Report Wizard to create a report based on the primary **Recruiter** table and the related **Student** table. Select all fields from the **Recruiter** table, and select all fields from the **Student** table except SSN, in the following order: FirstName, LastName, City, Nation, BirthDate, Gender, StudentID. In the third Report Wizard dialog box, specify the Nation field as an additional grouping level. Sort the detail records in ascending order by City. Choose the Align Left 2 layout and the Formal style for the report. Specify the title **Recruiters and Students** for the report.

Explore   9. Display the **Recruiters and Students** report in Design view and maximize the Report window. In the Nation Header section, change the Student_FirstName label control to "FirstName" and change the Student_LastName label control to "LastName." Widen both the Gender and StudentID label controls so that the labels are fully visible in the report. (*Hint*: You can resize the Gender control to both the left and the right, and the borders of adjacent controls can touch each other.)

10. Insert the **Travel** picture, which is located in the Review folder on your Data Disk, in the Report Header section of the **Recruiters and Students** report. Position the picture so that its left edge aligns with the 4-inch mark on the horizontal ruler and its top edge is just below the top border line of the report.

11. Print only the first page of the report, and then close and save the modified report.

12. If your database is stored on drive A, you will need to turn off the Compact on Close feature before closing the **Recruits** database because there isn't enough room on the disk to compact the database. If your database is stored on a hard or network drive, no action is necessary.

13. Close the **Recruits** database, and then exit Access.

CASE PROBLEMS

Case 1. Lim's Video Photography   Youngho Lim wants the **Videos** database to include forms and reports that will help him track and view information about his clients and their video shoot events. You'll create the necessary forms and reports by completing the following:

1. Make sure your Data Disk is in the appropriate disk drive, start Access, and then open the **Videos** database located in the Cases folder on your Data Disk.

2. Use the Form Wizard to create a form based on the **Client** table. Select all fields for the form, the Columnar layout, and the Blends style. Specify the title **Client Data** for the form.

3. Change the AutoFormat for the **Client Data** form to Standard.

4. Use the Find command to move to the record with Client# 338, and then change the Address field value for this record to 2150 Brucewood Avenue.

5. Use the **Client Data** form to add a new record with the following field values:

Client#:	351
ClientName:	Peters, Amanda
Address:	175 Washington Street
City:	Berkeley
State:	CA
Zip:	94704
Phone:	510-256-1007

    Print only this form record, and then save and close the form.

6. Use the Form Wizard to create a form containing a main form and a subform. Select all the fields from the **Client** table for the main form, and select all fields except Client# from the **Contract** table for the subform. Use the Tabular layout and the Standard style. Specify the title **Contracts by Client** for the main form and the title **Contract Subform** for the subform.

7. Print the seventh main form record and its subform records, and then close the **Contracts by Client** form.

8. Use the Report Wizard to create a report based on the primary **Client** table and the related **Contract** table. Select all the fields from the **Client** table, and select all the fields from the **Contract** table except Client#. Sort the detail records in ascending order by Contract#. Choose the Align Left 2 layout and the Casual style. Specify the title **Client Contracts** for the report.

9. Insert the **Camcord** picture, which is located in the Cases folder on your Data Disk, in the Report Header section of the **Client Contracts** report. Position the picture so that its left edge aligns with the 4-inch mark on the horizontal ruler and its top edge is just below the top border line of the report.

10. Print only the first page of the report, and then close and save the modified report.

11. Close the **Videos** database, and then exit Access.

Case 2. DineAtHome.course.com   Claire Picard continues her work with the **Meals** database to track and analyze the business activity of the restaurants she works with and their customers. To help her, you'll enhance the **Meals** database by completing the following:

1. Make sure your Data Disk is in the appropriate disk drive, start Access, and then open the **Meals** database located in the Cases folder on your Data Disk.

2. Use the Form Wizard to create a form containing a main form and a subform. Select the Restaurant#, RestaurantName, City, Phone, and Website fields from the **Restaurant** table for the main form, and select all fields except Restaurant# from the **Order** table for the subform. Use the Datasheet layout and the Industrial style. Specify the title **Restaurant Orders** for the main form and the title **Order Subform** for the subform. Resize all columns in the subform to their best fit. Print the first main form record and its displayed subform records.

3. For the form you just created, change the AutoFormat to SandStone, save the changed form, and then print the first main form record and its subform records.

4. Navigate to the third record in the subform for the first main record, and then change the OrderAmt field value to 107.80.

5. Use the Find command to move to the record with the Restaurant# 118, and then delete the record. Answer Yes to any warning messages about deleting the record.

Explore 6. Use the appropriate wildcard character to find all records with the word "House" anywhere in the restaurant name. (*Hint*: You must enter the wildcard character before and after the text you are searching for.) How many records did you find? Close the **Restaurant Orders** form.

Explore 7. Use the Report Wizard to create a report based on the primary **Restaurant** table and the related **Order** table. Select the Restaurant#, RestaurantName, Street, City, OwnerFirstName, and OwnerLastName fields from the **Restaurant** table, and select all fields from the **Order** table except Restaurant#. In the third Report Wizard dialog box, specify the OrderDate field as an additional grouping level. Sort the detail records by OrderAmt in *descending* order. Choose the Align Left 1 layout and the Bold style for the report. Specify the title **Orders by Restaurants** for the report.

8. Insert the **Server** picture, which is located in the Cases folder on your Data Disk, in the Report Header section of the **Orders by Restaurants** report. Leave the picture in its original position at the left edge of the Report Header section.

Explore 9. Use the Ask a Question box to ask the following question: "How do I move a control in front of or behind other controls?" Click the topic "Move one or more controls to a new position," and then click the subtopic "Move a control in front of or behind other controls." Read the information and then close the Help window. Make sure the **Server** picture is still selected, and then move it behind the Orders by Restaurants title.

Explore 10. Use the Ask a Question box to ask the following question: "How do I change the background color of a control?" Click the topic "Change the background color of a control or section." Read the information and then close the Help window. Select the Orders by Restaurant title object, and then change its background color to Transparent.

11. Display the report in Print Preview. Print just the first page of the report, and then close and save the report.

12. Close the **Meals** database, and then exit Access.

Case 3. Redwood Zoo Michael Rosenfeld wants to create forms and reports for the **Redwood** database. You'll help him create these database objects by completing the following:

1. Make sure your Data Disk is in the appropriate disk drive, start Access, and then open the **Redwood** database located in the Cases folder on your Data Disk.

2. If your **Redwood** database is stored on drive A, you will need to delete the files **Redwood97.mdb** and **Redwood2002.mdb** from your disk so you will have enough room to complete the steps. If your database is stored on a hard or network drive, no action is necessary.

3. Use the Form Wizard to create a form based on the **Pledge** table. Select all fields for the form, the Columnar layout, and the Blueprint style. Specify the title **Pledge Info** for the form.

4. Use the **Pledge Info** form to update the **Pledge** table as follows:

   a. Use the Find command to move to the record with Pledge# 2490, and then change the FundCode to B11 and the TotalPledged amount to 75.

   b. Add a new record with the following values:

Pledge#:	2977
DonorID:	59021
FundCode:	M23
PledgeDate:	12/15/2003
TotalPledged:	150
PaymentMethod:	C
PaymentSchedule:	S

   c. Print just this form record.

   d. Delete the record with Pledge# 2900.

5. Change the AutoFormat of the **Pledge Info** form to Expedition, save the changed form, and then use the form to print the last record in the **Pledge** table. Close the form.

6. Use the Form Wizard to create a form containing a main form and a subform. Select all the fields from the **Donor** table for the main form, and select the Pledge#, FundCode, PledgeDate, and TotalPledged fields from the **Pledge** table for the subform. Use the Tabular layout and the Expedition style. Specify the title **Donors and Pledges** for the main form and the title **Pledge Subform** for the subform.

7. Display record 11 in the main form. Print the current main form record and its subform records, and then close the **Donors and Pledges** form.

Explore
8. Use the Report Wizard to create a report based on the primary **Donor** table and the related **Pledge** table. Select the DonorID, FirstName, LastName, and Class fields from the **Donor** table, and select all fields from the **Pledge** table except DonorID. In the third Report Wizard dialog box, specify the FundCode field as an additional grouping level. Sort the detail records in *descending* order by TotalPledged. Choose the Align Left 2 layout, Landscape orientation, and the Soft Gray style. Specify the title **Donors and Pledges** for the report.

9. Insert the **Animals** picture, which is located in the Cases folder on your Data Disk, in the Report Header section of the **Donors and Pledges** report. Position the picture so that its left edge aligns with the 4-inch mark on the horizontal ruler and its top edge is just below the top border line of the report.

Explore
10. Use the Ask a Question box to ask the following question: "How do I add a special effect to an object?" Click the topic "Make a control appear raised, sunken, shadowed, chiseled, or etched." Read the information, and then close the Help window. Add the Shadowed special effect to the **Animals** picture, and then save the report.

Explore
11. Print only pages 1 and 7 of the report, and then close it.

12. If your database is stored on drive A, you will need to turn off the Compact on Close feature before closing the **Redwood** database because there isn't enough room on the disk to compact the database. If your database is stored on a hard or network drive, no action is necessary.

13. Close the **Redwood** database, and then exit Access.

Case 4. Mountain River Adventures   Connor and Siobhan Dempsey want to create forms and reports that will help them track and analyze data about their customers and the rafting trips they take. Help them enhance the **Trips** database by completing the following:

1. Make sure your Data Disk is in the appropriate disk drive, start Access, and then open the **Trips** database located in the Cases folder on your Data Disk.

2. Use the Form Wizard to create a form containing a main form and a subform. Select the Client#, ClientName, City, State/Prov, and Phone fields from the **Client** table for the main form, and select all fields except Client# from the **Booking** table for the subform. Use the Datasheet layout and the Standard style. Specify the title **Clients and Bookings** for the main form and the title **Booking Subform** for the subform. Resize all columns in the subform to their best fit. Print the ninth main form record and its subform records.

3. For the form you just created, change the AutoFormat to Stone, save the changed form, and then print the ninth main form record and its subform records.

4. Navigate to the second record in the subform for the ninth main record, and then change the People field value to 7.

5. Use the Find command to move to the record with Client# 330, and then delete the record. Answer Yes to any warning messages about deleting the record.

6. Use the appropriate wildcard character to find all records with a City value that begins with the letter "D." How many records did you find? Close the form.

7. Use the Report Wizard to create a report based on the primary **Client** table and the related **Booking** table. Select all fields from the **Client** table, and select all fields except Client# from the **Booking** table. Sort the detail records by the TripDate field in ascending order. Choose the Outline 1 layout and the Compact style. Specify the title **Client Bookings** for the report.

Explore ▶ 8. Display the **Client Bookings** report in Design view, and then widen the Phone text box control so that the Phone field values are completely displayed in the report.

9. Insert the **Raft** picture, which is located in the Cases folder on your Data Disk, in the Report Header section of the **Client Bookings** report. Position the picture so that its left edge aligns with the 2-inch mark on the horizontal ruler and its top edge is just below the top border line of the report. (If the picture blocks part of the bottom border line of the header, that is fine.)

Explore ▶ 10. Insert the same **Raft** picture in the Report Footer section of the **Client Bookings** report. (Items placed in the Report Footer section appear only once, at the end of the report.) Position the picture so that its right edge aligns with the right edge of the report, at approximately the 6.5-inch mark on the horizontal ruler. Save the report.

Explore ▶ 11. View the first two pages of the report in Print Preview at the same time. (*Hint*: Use a toolbar button.) Use the Page navigation buttons to move through the report, displaying two pages at a time. Print only the first and last pages of the report, and then close the report.

12. Close the **Trips** database, and then exit Access.

INTERNET ASSIGNMENTS

Student Union

The purpose of the Internet Assignments is to challenge you to find information on the Internet that you can use to create effective documents. The actual assignments are updated and maintained on the Course Technology Web site. Log on to the Internet and use your Web browser to go to the Student Union on the New Perspectives Series site at **www.course.com/NewPerspectives/studentunion**. Click the Online Companions link, and then click the link for this tutorial.

QUICK CHECK ANSWERS

Session 4.1

1. The AutoForm Wizard creates a form automatically using all the fields in the selected table or query; the Form Wizard allows you to choose some or all of the fields in the selected table or query, choose fields from other tables and queries, and display fields in any order on the form.

2. An AutoFormat is a predefined style for a form (or report). To change a form's AutoFormat, display the form in Design view, click the AutoFormat button on the Form Design toolbar, click the new AutoFormat in the Form AutoFormats list box, and then click the OK button.

3. the last record in the table

4. datasheet

5. the question mark (?)

6. as many form records as can fit on a printed page

Session 4.2

1. The main form displays the data from the primary table, and the subform displays the data from the related table.

2. You use the top set of navigation buttons to select and move through records from the related table in the subform, and the bottom set to select and move through records from the primary table in the main form.

3. report title

4. control

5. Design view

6. Report Header

New Perspectives on

MICROSOFT®
ACCESS 2002

TUTORIAL 5   AC 5.03

Enhancing a Table's Design, and Creating Advanced Queries and Custom Forms
Making the Jobs Database Easier to Use

TUTORIAL 6   AC 6.01

Creating Custom Reports
Creating a Potential Income Report

TUTORIAL 7   AC 7.01

Integrating Access with the Web and with Other Programs
Creating Web-Enabled and Integrated Information for the Jobs Database

APPENDIX   RD 1

Relational Databases and Database Design

Read This Before You Begin

To the Student

Data Disks

To complete the Level II tutorials, Review Assignments, and Case Problems, you will need to store your Data Disk files on your computer's hard drive or on a personal network drive. Your instructor will either provide you with these Data Disk files or ask you to obtain them.

If you are obtaining your own Data Disk files, you will need to copy a set of files and/or folders from a file server, standalone computer, or the Web onto your drives. Your instructor will tell you which computer, drive letter, and folders contain the files you need. You could also download the files by going to www.course.com and following the instructions on the screen.

If you will store your original Data Disk files on floppy disks, you will need **two** blank, formatted high-density disks. The information below shows you which folders go on each of your disks. After making your Data Disks, you can copy the files to your hard drive or personal network drive, and then retain the Data Disks as a backup.

Data Disk 1

Write this on the disk label:
Data Disk 1: Tutorial Files (Tutorials 5-7)
Review Assignments (Tutorials 5-7)

Put this folder on the disk:
Tutorial
Review

Data Disk 2

Write this on the disk label:
Data Disk 2: Case Problems 1-5 (Tutorials 5-7)

Put this folder on the disk:
Cases

When you begin each tutorial, be sure you are using the correct files. Refer to the "File Finder" chart at the back of this text for more detailed information on which files are used in which tutorials. These Access Level II tutorials use the same files for Tutorials 5-7. If you are completing the Level III tutorials (Tutorials 8-11), you will need to obtain new Data Disk files for those tutorials. See the inside front or inside back cover of this book for more information on Data Disk files, or ask your instructor or technical support person for assistance.

Using Your Own Computer

If you are going to work through this book using your own computer, you need:

■ **Computer System** Microsoft Windows 98, NT, 2000 Professional, or higher must be installed on your computer. This book assumes a typical installation of Microsoft Access. You will also need Microsoft Internet Explorer 5.0 or higher (or another comparable Web browser), Microsoft Excel, and Microsoft Word to complete Tutorial 7.

■ **Data Disk Files** You will not be able to complete the tutorials or exercises in this book using your own computer until you have your Data Disk files.

Visit Our World Wide Web Site

Additional materials designed especially for you are available on the World Wide Web.
Go to www.course.com/NewPerspectives.

To the Instructor

The Data Disk files are available on the Instructor's Resource Kit for this title. Follow the instructions in the Help file on the CD-ROM to install the files to your network or standalone computer. For information on creating Data Disks, see the "To the Student" section above.

You are granted a license to copy the Data Files to any computer or computer network used by students who have purchased this book.

OBJECTIVES

In this tutorial you will:

- Create a Lookup Wizard field in a table

- Display related table records in a subdatasheet

- Create an input mask for a table field

- Define data validation criteria

- Use the In, Like, and Not operators in queries

- Use both the And and Or logical operators in the same query

- Create a parameter query

- Design and create a custom form

- Add, select, move, resize, delete, and rename controls

- Add form headers and footers

- Add a graphic image to a form

- Use Control Wizards to create a multi-page form with a subform

- Use Filter By Form

ENHANCING

A TABLE'S DESIGN, AND CREATING ADVANCED QUERIES AND CUSTOM FORMS

Making the Jobs Database Easier to Use

CASE

Northeast Seasonal Jobs International (NSJI)

Several years ago, Elsa Jensen founded Northeast Seasonal Jobs International (NSJI), a small Boston firm that serves as a job broker between foreign students seeking part-time, seasonal work and resort businesses located in New England and the eastern provinces of Canada. At first the company focused mainly on summer employment, but as the business continued to grow, Elsa increased the scope of operations to include all types of seasonal opportunities, including foliage tour companies in the fall and ski resorts in the winter.

Elsa incorporated the use of computers in all aspects of the business, including financial management, payroll, accounts payable, and student recruitment. Her company developed the Jobs database of employer and position data and uses **Microsoft Access 2002** (or simply **Access**) to manage it.

The Jobs database contains tables, queries, forms, and reports that Zack Ward, director of marketing, and Matt Griffin, manager of recruitment, use to track employers and their positions.

Elsa, Zack, and Matt are pleased with the information they get from the Jobs database. They are interested in taking better advantage of the power of Access to make the database easier to use and to create more sophisticated queries and custom forms. For example, Zack wants to obtain lists of employers with certain area codes, and Matt needs a list of positions in a specified state or province. Elsa wants to change the design of the Employer table. She wants to make entering the NAICS code value for an Employer record easier, improve the appearance of Phone field values, verify the correct entry of country values, and learn more about subdatasheets. (NAICS codes are the North American Industry Classification System codes used to classify businesses by the type of activity in which they are engaged.) In this tutorial, you'll make the necessary modifications and customizations to the Jobs database.

SESSION 5.1

In this session, you will change the NAICSCode field in the Employer table to a Lookup Wizard field, display related Position table records as a subdatasheet in the Employer table, create an input mask for the Phone field in the Employer table, and specify data validation values for the Country field in the Employer table. You will also create a pattern match query, a list-of-values query, and a query selecting nonmatching values. Finally, you will construct complex selection criteria using the And with Or operators, and you'll create a parameter query.

Creating a Lookup Wizard Field

The Employer table in the Jobs database contains information about the seasonal businesses with available jobs that NSJI fills with qualified foreign students. Elsa wants to make entering data in the table easier for her staff. In particular, data entry is easier if they do not need to remember the correct NAICS code for each employer. So, Elsa wants to change the NAICSCode field in the Employer table to a Lookup Wizard field. A **Lookup Wizard field** lets the user select a value from a list of possible values. For the NAICSCode field, the user will be able to select from the list of NAICS codes in the NAICS table rather than having to remember the correct code. The NAICSCode field in the Employer table will store the NAICS code, but the NAICS code description will appear in Datasheet view. This arrangement makes entering codes easier for the user and guarantees that the NAICS code is valid.

Elsa asks you to change the NAICSCode field in the Employer table to a Lookup Wizard field. You begin by opening the Jobs database and then opening the Employer table in Design view.

To change the NAICSCode field to a Lookup Wizard field:

1. Make sure you have created your copy of the Access Data Disk, and then place your Data Disk in the appropriate disk drive.

   TROUBLE? If you don't have a Data Disk, you need to get one before you can proceed. Your instructor or technical support person will either give you one or ask you to make your own. (See your instructor for information.) In either case, make sure you have a copy of your Data Disk before you begin, so that the original Data Disk files are available on the copied disk in case you need to start over because of an error or problem.

   TROUBLE? If you are not sure which disk drive to use for your Data Disk, read the "Read This Before You Begin" page on page AC 5.02 or ask your instructor for help.

2. Start Access, open the **Jobs** database located in the Tutorial folder on your Data Disk, and then open the **Employer** table in Design view.

3. Scroll down (if necessary) to the NAICSCode field, click the right side of the **Data Type** text box for the NAICSCode field, and then click **Lookup Wizard**. The first Lookup Wizard dialog box opens. See Figure 5-1.

Figure 5-1   **FIRST LOOKUP WIZARD DIALOG BOX**

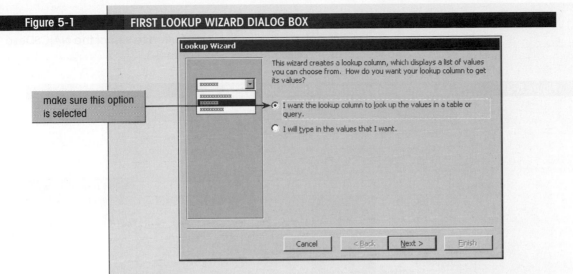

make sure this option is selected

This dialog box lets you specify a list of allowed values for the NAICSCode field in a record in the Employer table. You can specify a table or query from which users select the value, or you can enter a new list of values. You want the NAICSCode value to come from the NAICS table.

4. Make sure the option for looking up the values in a table or query is selected, and then click the **Next** button to display the next Lookup Wizard dialog box.

5. Make sure **Table: NAICS** is selected, and then click the **Next** button to display the next Lookup Wizard dialog box. See Figure 5-2.

Figure 5-2   **SELECTING THE NAICS TABLE FIELDS**

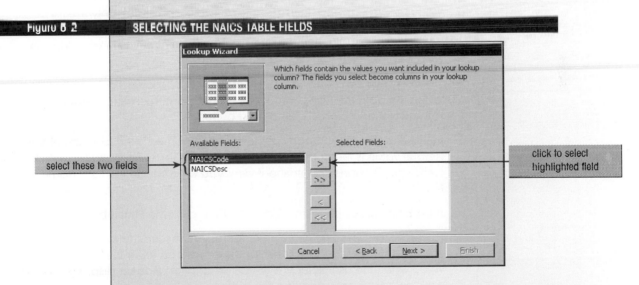

select these two fields

click to select highlighted field

This dialog box lets you select the lookup fields from the NAICS table. You need to select the NAICSCode field because it's the common field that links the NAICS and Employer tables. You also must select the NAICSDesc field because Elsa wants the user to be able to select from a list of NAICS descriptions when entering a new employer record.

6. Click the ⬚>⬚ button to select the NAICSCode field from the NAICS table so the lookup column will include it, click the ⬚>⬚ button to select the NAICSDesc field, and then click the **Next** button. See Figure 5-3.

Figure 5-3   **ADJUSTING THE WIDTH OF THE LOOKUP FIELD**

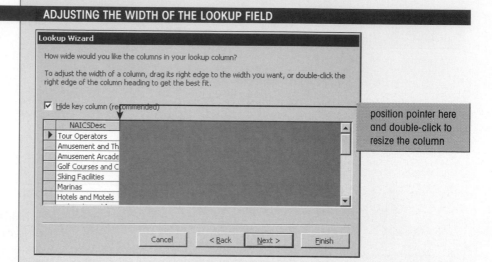

In this dialog box, you can adjust the width of the NAICSDesc column. This column will appear when a user enters a NAICSCode for the employer in the Employer table. The user can select a NAICSDesc, and Access will enter the correct NAICSCode for the selected NAICSDesc value automatically. The selected "Hide key column (recommended)" option means that the list of NAICSCode values will not appear in the Employer table datasheet; only the list of NAICSDesc values will appear. If you uncheck this option, both lists of field values will appear in the Employer table datasheet when you select a value for the field.

7. Place the pointer on the right edge of the NAICSDesc field column heading. When the pointer changes to a ↔ shape, double-click to resize the column to fit the data, and then click the **Next** button.

In this dialog box, you can specify the field name for the lookup field. The default value is the current field name, NAICSCode. Because the field will show NAICS descriptions in Datasheet view, you will change the field name to NAICSDesc.

8. Type **NAICSDesc** in the text box, and then click the **Finish** button.

To create the Lookup Wizard field, Access must save the table design and create the necessary relationship, so Access can enter the correct NAICSCode value when the user selects a NAICS description. Access displays a dialog box asking you to confirm saving the table.

9. Click the **Yes** button. Access creates the Lookup Wizard field, and you return to the Employer table in Design view. See Figure 5-4.

Figure 5-4	LOOKUP WIZARD FIELD DEFINED

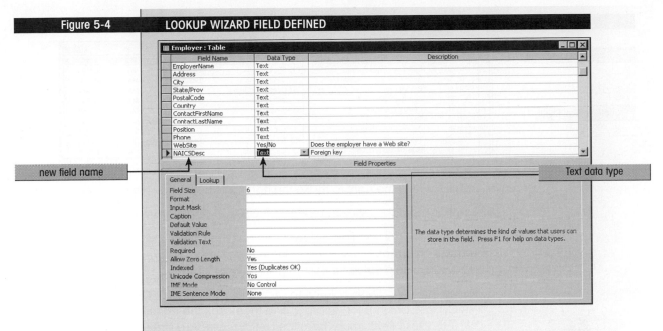

new field name   Text data type

The Data Type value for the NAICSDesc field still is Text because this field contains text data. However, Access now uses the NAICSCode field value to look up and display NAICS descriptions from the NAICS table.

Elsa just discovered that the NAICSCode field value stored in the Employer table for Boston Harbor Excursions is incorrect. She asks you to run the new Lookup Wizard field to select the correct code. To do so, you need to switch to Datasheet view.

To change the NAICSCode Lookup Wizard field value:

1. Switch to Datasheet view.

   The NAICSCode field values, which now have NAICSDesc for a column heading in the datasheet, are in column 13. After you scroll to the right to view the NAICSDesc column, you'll no longer be able to verify that you're changing the correct field value because the EmployerID and EmployerName fields will be hidden. You'll freeze those two columns so they'll remain visible in the datasheet as you scroll to the right.

2. Click the **EmployerID** column selector, press and hold down the **Shift** key, click the **EmployerName** column selector to select both columns, and then release the **Shift** key.

3. Click **Format** on the menu bar, click **Freeze Columns**, and then click anywhere in the datasheet to deselect the first two columns. A dark vertical line now separates the two leftmost columns from the other columns. The line indicates that these two columns will remain visible no matter where you scroll in the datasheet. See Figure 5-5.

| Figure 5-5 | FREEZING THE FIRST TWO DATASHEET COLUMNS |

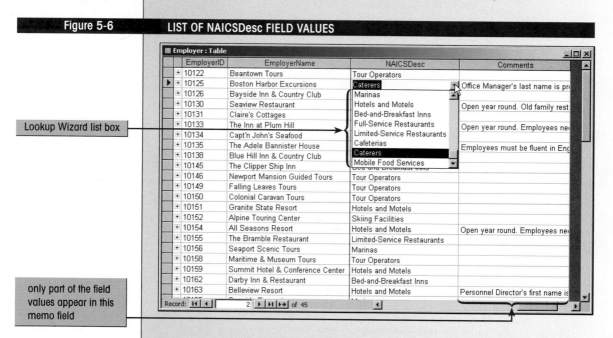

frozen columns

dark vertical line

EmployerID	EmployerName	Address	City	State/Prov	PostalC
+ 10122	Beantown Tours	105 State Street	Boston	MA	02109
+ 10125	Boston Harbor Excursions	75 Atlantic Avenue	Boston	MA	02110
+ 10126	Bayside Inn & Country Club	354 Oceanside Drive	Brewster	MA	02631
+ 10130	Seaview Restaurant	15 North Harbor Lane	Falmouth	MA	02540
+ 10131	Claire's Cottages	88 Main Street	Orleans	MA	02653
+ 10133	The Inn at Plum Hill	354 Union Street	Vineyard Haven	MA	02568
+ 10134	Capt'n John's Seafood	22 Old Colony Way	Orleans	MA	02653
+ 10135	The Adele Bannister House	151 Thames Street	Newport	RI	02840
+ 10138	Blue Hill Inn & Country Club	38 Blue Hill Road	Chatham	MA	02633

You'll scroll to the right to make the rightmost columns in the datasheet visible.

4. Scroll to the right until you see the NAICSDesc and Comments columns.

Because NAICSDesc field values replaced the NAICSCode field values in column 13, you should resize the column to its best fit before you change the NAICSDesc field value for Boston Harbor Excursions.

5. Resize the NAICSDesc column to its best fit, double-click **Caterers** in the NAICSDesc column for record 2, and then click the list arrow to display the list of NAICSDesc field values from the NAICS table. See Figure 5-6.

| Figure 5-6 | LIST OF NAICSDesc FIELD VALUES |

Lookup Wizard list box

only part of the field values appear in this memo field

EmployerID	EmployerName	NAICSDesc	Comments
+ 10122	Beantown Tours	Tour Operators	
+ 10125	Boston Harbor Excursions	Caterers	Office Manager's last name is pr
+ 10126	Bayside Inn & Country Club	Marinas	
+ 10130	Seaview Restaurant	Hotels and Motels	Open year round. Old family rest
+ 10131	Claire's Cottages	Bed-and-Breakfast Inns	
+ 10133	The Inn at Plum Hill	Full-Service Restaurants	Open year round. Employees ne
+ 10134	Capt'n John's Seafood	Limited-Service Restaurants	
+ 10135	The Adele Bannister House	Cafeterias	Employees must be fluent in Eng
+ 10138	Blue Hill Inn & Country Club	Caterers	
+ 10145	The Clipper Ship Inn	Mobile Food Services	
+ 10146	Newport Mansion Guided Tours	Tour Operators	
+ 10149	Falling Leaves Tours	Tour Operators	
+ 10150	Colonial Caravan Tours	Tour Operators	
+ 10151	Granite State Resort	Hotels and Motels	
+ 10152	Alpine Touring Center	Skiing Facilities	
+ 10154	All Seasons Resort	Hotels and Motels	Open year round. Employees ne
+ 10155	The Bramble Restaurant	Limited-Service Restaurants	
+ 10156	Seaport Scenic Tours	Marinas	
+ 10158	Maritime & Museum Tours	Tour Operators	
+ 10159	Summit Hotel & Conference Center	Hotels and Motels	
+ 10162	Darby Inn & Restaurant	Bed-and-Breakfast Inns	
+ 10163	Belleview Resort	Hotels and Motels	Personnel Director's first name is

Record: 2 of 45

6. Click **Marinas** to select this field value. The list box closes and Marinas appears in the NAICSDesc text box. However, it is the value 71393, which is the NAICSCode field value for Marinas, that is stored in the Employer table for this column.

The Comments column is a memo field that NSJI staff members use to store explanations about the employer, its contact, and its positions. The Comments field values are partially hidden because the datasheet column is not wide enough. You'll increase the datasheet row height so more of the Comments field values will be visible.

7. Place the pointer between the row selectors for rows 2 and 3, and, when the pointer changes to a ✚ shape, drag the edge down to the approximate position shown in Figure 5-7. Note that you could have increased the row height by placing the pointer between any two row selectors.

Figure 5-7	DATASHEET ROWS RESIZED

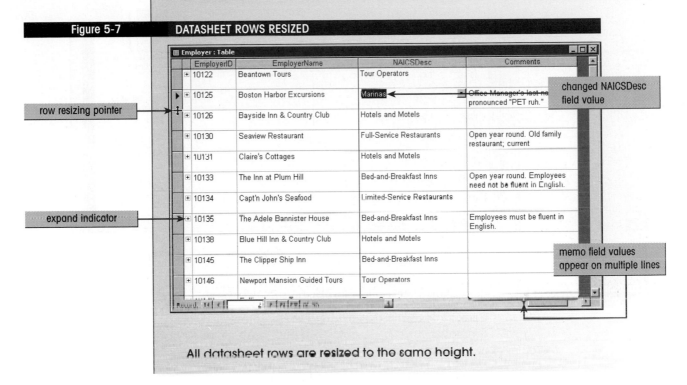

All datasheet rows are resized to the same height.

Elsa notices that a plus symbol appears to the left of the EmployerID field in the Employer table datasheet and asks what function it serves. You investigate and find that when you defined the one-to-many relationship between the Employer and Position tables in Tutorial 3, Access automatically added plus symbols to the Employer datasheet. These plus symbols let you view an employer's related Position table records in a subdatasheet.

Displaying **Related Records in a Subdatasheet**

For tables such as the Employer and Position tables, which have a one-to-many relationship, you can display records from the related table—the Position table in this case—as a **subdatasheet** in the primary table's datasheet—the Employer table in this case. When you first open a table (or query) datasheet, its subdatasheets are not expanded. To display the position subdatasheet for a specific employer, you click the **expand indicator** ➕ in the row for that employer. Next, you'll display the position subdatasheet for Beantown Tours.

To display Position table records in a subdatasheet:

1. Click the **expand indicator** ➕ for Beantown Tours, which is EmployerID 10122. The subdatasheet for Beantown Tours opens. See Figure 5-8.

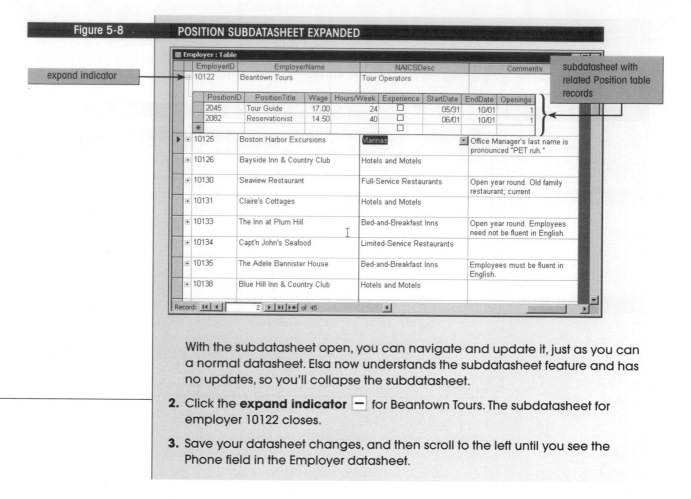

Figure 5-8   POSITION SUBDATASHEET EXPANDED

With the subdatasheet open, you can navigate and update it, just as you can a normal datasheet. Elsa now understands the subdatasheet feature and has no updates, so you'll collapse the subdatasheet.

2. Click the **expand indicator** ─ for Beantown Tours. The subdatasheet for employer 10122 closes.

3. Save your datasheet changes, and then scroll to the left until you see the Phone field in the Employer datasheet.

Elsa asks you to change the appearance of the Phone field in the Employer table to a standard telephone number format.

Using the Input Mask Wizard

The Phone field in the Employer table is a 10-digit number that's difficult to read because it appears with none of the special formatting characters usually associated with a telephone number. For example, the Phone field value for Beantown Tours, which appears as 6174511970, would be more readable in any of the following formats: 617-451-1970, 617.451.1970, 617/451-1970, or (617) 451-1970. Elsa asks you to use the 617-451-1970 style for the Phone field.

Elsa wants hyphens to appear as literal display characters whenever users enter Phone field values. **Literal display characters** are the special characters that automatically appear in specific positions of a field value; users don't need to type literal display characters. To include these characters, you need to create an **input mask**, a predefined format used to enter and display data in a field. An easy way to create an input mask is to use the **Input Mask Wizard**, an Access tool that guides you in creating a predefined format for a field. You must use the Input Mask Wizard in Design view.

To use the Input Mask Wizard for the Phone field:

1. Switch to Design view, and then click the **Field Name** text box for the Phone field to make it the current field and to display its Field Properties options.

2. Click the **Input Mask** text box in the Field Properties pane. A Build button [...] appears to the right of the Input Mask text box.

3. Click the **Build** button [...] next to the Input Mask text box. The first Input Mask Wizard dialog box opens. See Figure 5-9.

Figure 5-9	INPUT MASK WIZARD DIALOG BOX

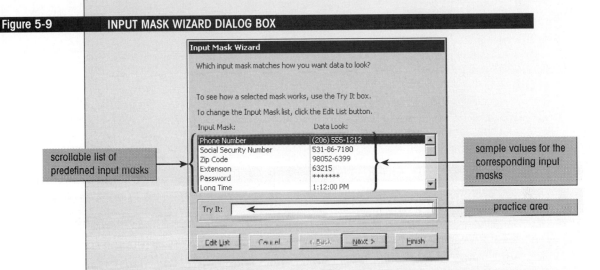

scrollable list of predefined input masks

sample values for the corresponding input masks

practice area

TROUBLE? If a dialog box opens and tells you that this feature is not installed, insert your Office XP CD into the correct drive, and then click the Yes button. If you do not have an Office XP CD, ask your instructor or technical support person for help.

You can scroll the Input Mask list box, select the input mask you want, and then enter representative values to practice using the input mask.

4. If necessary, click **Phone Number** in the Input Mask list box to select it.

5. Click the far left side of the **Try It** text box. (__) __-__ appears in the Try It text box. As you type a phone number, Access replaces the underscores, which are placeholder characters.

TROUBLE? If your insertion point is not immediately to the right of the left parenthesis, press the Left Arrow key until it is.

6. Type **9876543210** to practice entering a sample phone number. The input mask makes the typed value appear as (987) 654-3210.

7. Click the **Next** button. The next Input Mask Wizard dialog box opens. In it, you can change the input mask and placeholder character. Because changing an input mask is easier after the Input Mask Wizard finishes, you'll accept all Wizard defaults.

8. Click the **Finish** button. The Input Mask Wizard creates the default phone number input mask, placing it in the Input Mask text box for the Phone field. See Figure 5-10.

Figure 5-10	INPUT MASK CREATED BY THE INPUT MASK WIZARD

The characters preceding the first semicolon represent the input mask. The symbols in the default phone number input mask of !(999) 000-0000;;_ have the meanings shown in Figure 5-11.

Figure 5-11	INPUT MASK CHARACTERS

INPUT MASK CHARACTER	DESCRIPTION
!	Causes the input mask to display from right to left, rather than the default of left to right. Characters typed in the mask always fill in from left to right.
9	Digit or space can be entered. Entry is not required.
0	Digit only can be entered. Entry is required.
;;	The character between the first and second semicolon determines whether to store in the database the literal display characters such as the hyphen and parentheses. If left blank or set to a value of 1, do not store the literal characters. If set to a value of 0, store the literal characters.
_ (underscore)	Placeholder character because it follows the second semicolon.
( ) -	Literal display characters

Elsa wants to view the Phone field with the default input mask before you change it for her.

To view and change the input mask for the Phone field:

1. Save your table design changes, and then switch to Datasheet view.

2. Scroll the table to the right until the Phone field is visible. The Phone field values now have the format specified by the input mask.

3. Switch to Design view.

   The input mask changed from !(999) 000-0000;;_ to !\(999") "000\-0000;;_. The backslash character (\) causes the character that follows it to appear as a literal character. Characters enclosed in quotation marks also appear as literal characters.

4. Change the input mask to **!999\-000\-0000;;_** in the Input Mask text box for the Phone field.

5. Save your table design changes, and then switch to Datasheet view.

6. Scroll the table to the right until the Phone field is visible. The Phone field values now have the format Elsa requested. See Figure 5-12.

Figure 5-12	AFTER CHANGING THE PHONE FIELD INPUT MASK

Phone field with input mask

EmployerID	EmployerName	Position	Phone	WebSite	NAICSDes
10122	Beantown Tours	Office Manager	617-451-1970	☑	Tour Operators
10125	Boston Harbor Excursions	Office Manager	617-235-1800	☑	Marinas
10126	Bayside Inn & Country Club	General Manager	508-283-5775	☑	Hotels and Motels
10130	Seaview Restaurant	Manager	508-776-8593	☐	Full-Service Restaur
10131	Claire's Cottages	Manager	508-822-1328	☐	Hotels and Motels
10133	The Inn at Plum Hill	General Manager	508-693-2320	☑	Bed-and-Breakfast Ir

Elsa wants to limit the entry of Country field values in the Employer table to Canada and USA because NSJI employer clients are located in only these two countries. She's concerned that typing errors might produce incorrect query results and cause other problems. To provide this data-entry capability, you'll set validation properties for the Country field.

Defining Data Validation Criteria

To prevent a user from entering a value other than Canada or USA, you can set the Validation Rule and the Validation Text properties for the Country field in the Employer table. The **Validation Rule** property value specifies the valid values that users can enter in a field. The **Validation Text** property value will be displayed in a dialog box if the user enters an invalid value (in this case, a value other than Canada or USA). After you set these two Country field properties in the Employer table, Access will prevent users from entering an invalid Country field value in all current and future forms and queries.

You'll now set the Validation Rule and Validation Text properties for the Country field in the Employer table.

To set the Validation Rule and Validation Text properties for the Country field:

1. Switch to Design view, and then click the **Country Field Name** text box to make that row the current row.

To make sure that the only values entered in the Country field are Canada or USA, you'll specify a list of valid values in the Validation Rule text box.

2. Click the **Validation Rule** text box, type **Canada or USA**, and then press the **Tab** key.

When you pressed the Tab key, the Validation Rule changed to "Canada" Or "USA". You can set the Validation Text property to a value that appears in a dialog box that opens if a user enters a value not listed in the Validation Rule text box.

3. Type **Must be Canada or USA** in the Validation Text text box. See Figure 5-13.

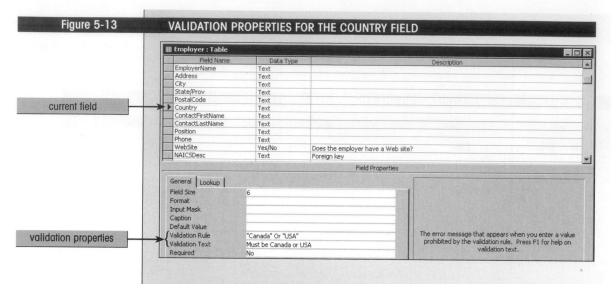

Figure 5-13   **VALIDATION PROPERTIES FOR THE COUNTRY FIELD**

You can now save the table design changes and then test the validation properties.

4. Save your table design changes, and click the **Yes** button when asked if you want to test the existing Country field values in the Employer table against the new validation rule.

Next, you'll test the validation rule.

5. Switch to Datasheet view, and then scroll the table to the right until the Country field is visible.

6. Double-click **USA** in the first row's Country field text box, type **Spain**, and then press the **Tab** key. A dialog box opens containing the message "Must be Canada or USA," which is the Validation Text property setting you created in Step 3.

7. Click the **OK** button, and then click the **Undo typing** button [image] on the Table Datasheet toolbar. The first row's Country field value again has its original value, USA.

8. Close the Employer table, and click the **Yes** button if asked to save the table design changes.

You defined the validation criteria for the Country field and completed your design changes to the Employer table. You are now ready to create the queries that Elsa, Matt, and Zack requested. You are already familiar with queries that use an exact match or a range of values (for example, queries that use the >= and < comparison operators) to select records. Access provides many other operators for creating select queries. These operators let you create more complicated queries that are difficult or impossible to create with exact match or range of values selection criteria.

Elsa, Matt, and Zack created a list of questions they want to answer using the Jobs database:

■ Which employers have the 508 area code?

■ What is the employer information for employers located in Maine (ME), New Hampshire (NH), or Vermont (VT)?

■ What is the position information for all positions *except* those positions with the titles Lifeguard or Ski Patrol?

■ What is the position information for those Waiter/Waitress or Kitchen Help positions located in Massachusetts (MA) or New Hampshire (NH)?

■ What is the position information for positions in a particular state or province? For this query, the user needs to be able to specify the state or province.

Next, you will create the queries necessary to answer these questions. To do so, you'll use the Query window in Design view.

Using a Pattern Match in a Query

Zack wants to view the records for all employers within the 508 area code. He plans to travel in their area next week and wants to contact them. To answer Zack's question, you can create a query that uses a pattern match. A **pattern match** selects records with a value for the selected field that matches the pattern of the simple condition value, in this case, employers with the 508 area code. You do this using the Like comparison operator.

The **Like comparison operator** selects records by matching field values to a specific pattern that includes one or more of these wildcard characters: asterisk (*), question mark (?), and number symbol (#). The asterisk represents any string of characters, the question mark represents any single character, and the number symbol represents any single digit. Using a pattern match is similar to using an exact match, except that a pattern match includes wildcard characters.

To create the query, you must first place the Employer table field list in the Query window in Design view.

To create the pattern match query in Design view:

1. Click **Queries** in the Objects bar of the Database window, and then click the **New** button. The New Query dialog box opens.

2. Click **Design View** in the list box (if necessary), and then click the **OK** button. The Show Table dialog box opens on top of the Query window.

3. Click **Employer** in the Tables list box (if necessary), click the **Add** button, and then click the **Close** button. Access places the Employer table field list in the Query window.

4. Double-click the **title bar** of the Employer field list to highlight all the fields, and then drag one of the highlighted fields to the first column's Field text box in the design grid. Access places each field in a separate column in the design grid, in the same order that the fields appear in the table. See Figure 5-14.

Figure 5-14	ADDING THE FIELDS FOR THE QUERY

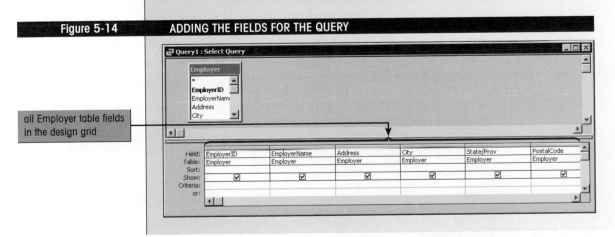

all Employer table fields in the design grid

> **TROUBLE?** If Employer.* appears in the first column's Field text box, you dragged the * from the field list instead of one of the highlighted fields. Press the Delete key, and then repeat Step 4.

Now you will enter the pattern match condition Like "508*" for the Phone field. Access will select records with a Phone field value of 508 in positions one through three. The asterisk (*) wildcard character specifies that any characters can appear in the remaining positions of the field value.

To specify records that match the specified pattern:

1. Scroll the design grid until the Phone field is visible.

2. Click the **Phone Criteria** text box, and then type **Like "508*"**. See Figure 5-15. (*Note*: If you omit the Like operator, Access automatically adds it when you run the query.)

Figure 5-15	RECORD SELECTION BASED ON MATCHING A SPECIFIC PATTERN

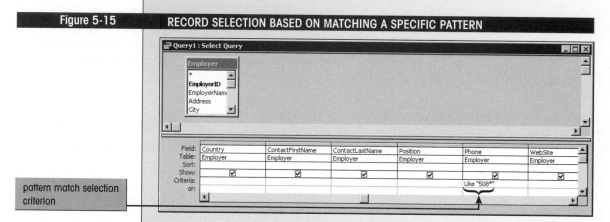

pattern match selection criterion

3. Click the **Run** button **!** on the Query Design toolbar, scroll the window until the Phone field is visible, and then reduce the row height, as shown in Figure 5-16. The query results display the nine records with the area code 508 in the Phone field.

Figure 5-16	EMPLOYER RECORDS FOR AREA CODE 508

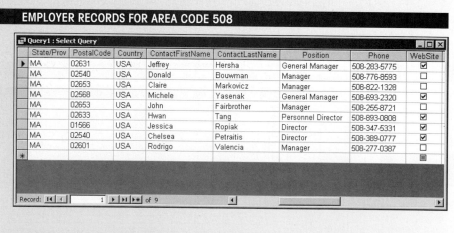

Now you can save the query.

4. Click the **Save** button 🖫 on the Query Datasheet toolbar. The Save As dialog box opens.

5. Type **508 Area Code** in the Query Name text box, and then press the **Enter** key. Access saves the query in the Jobs database on your Data Disk.

Next, Zack asks you to create a query that displays information about employers in the states of Maine (ME), New Hampshire (NH), or Vermont (VT). He wants a printout of the employer data for his administrative aide, who will contact these employers. To produce the results Zack wants, you'll create a query using a list-of-values match.

Using a List-of-Values Match in a Query

A **list-of-values match** selects records whose value for the selected field matches one of two or more simple condition values. You could accomplish this by including several Or conditions in the design grid, but the In comparison operator provides an easier way to do this. The **In comparison operator** lets you define a condition with two or more values. If a record's field value matches one value from the list of defined values, then Access selects and includes that record in the query results.

To display the information Zack requested, you want records selected if their State/Prov field value equals ME, NH, or VT. These are the values you will use with the In comparison operator.

To create the query using a list-of-values match:

1. Switch to Design view.

First you need to delete the condition for the previous query you created.

2. Click the **Phone Criteria** text box, press the **F2** key to highlight the entire condition, and then press the **Delete** key to remove the condition.

Now you can enter the criteria for the new query using the In comparison operator. When you use this operator, you must enclose the list of values you want to match within parentheses and separate the values with commas. In addition, for Text data types you must enclose each value in quotation marks, but you don't use the quotation marks for Number data type fields.

3. Scroll the design grid to the left to display the State/Prov column, click the **State/Prov Criteria** text box, and then type **In ("ME","NH","VT")**. See Figure 5-17.

Figure 5-17	RECORD SELECTION BASED ON MATCHING FIELD VALUES TO A LIST OF VALUES

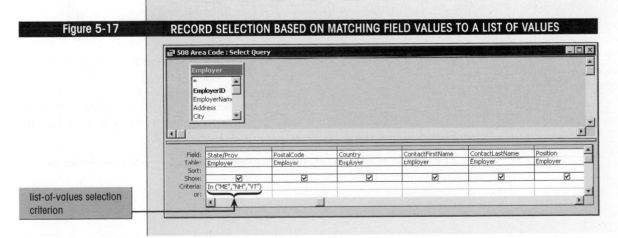

list-of-values selection criterion

4. Run the query. Access displays the query results, which show the 14 records with ME, NH, or VT in the State/Prov field.

Now you can print the query results for Zack. Because Zack doesn't need this information again, you don't have to save this query.

5. Click the **Print** button 🖨 on the Query Datasheet toolbar, and then close the query without saving your design changes.

Matt recruited several students who qualify for any position except Lifeguard and Ski Patrol. You can provide Matt with this information by creating a query with a nonmatching condition.

Using a Nonmatching Value in a Query

A **nonmatching value** selects records whose value for the selected field does not match the simple condition value. You create the selection criterion using the Not logical operator. The **Not logical operator** negates a criterion. For example, if you enter Not = "CT" in the Criteria text box for the State/Prov field in the Employer table, the query results show records that do not have the State/Prov field value CT; that is, records of all employers not located in Connecticut.

To create Matt's query, you will combine the Not operator with the In operator to select positions whose PositionTitle field value is not in the list ("Lifeguard","Ski Patrol"). The Weekly Wages query has the fields that Matt needs to see in the query results.

To create the query using a nonmatching value:

1. Open the **Weekly Wages** query in Design view.

2. Click the **PositionTitle Criteria** text box, and then type **Not In ("Lifeguard","Ski Patrol")** for the condition. See Figure 5-18.

Figure 5-18	RECORD SELECTION BASED ON NOT MATCHING A LIST OF VALUES

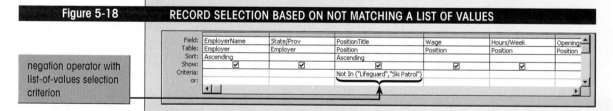

negation operator with list-of-values selection criterion

TROUBLE? Your screen might show only part of the criterion in the PositionTitle Criteria text box.

3. Run the query. Access displays only those records with a PositionTitle field value that is not Lifeguard and is not Ski Patrol. The query results include a total of 58 of the 64 position records.

4. Scroll down the datasheet to make sure that no Lifeguard and Ski Patrol positions appear in your results.

Matt wants a printed copy of the query results.

5. Switch to Print Preview, and use the navigation buttons to preview the report. Notice that two pages are required to print all seven columns, so you'll change to landscape orientation.

6. Click the **Setup** button on the Print Preview toolbar to open the Page Setup dialog box, click the **Page** tab, click the **Landscape** option button, and then click the **OK** button.

7. Print the query results.

   Now you can close the query without saving it, because Matt does not need to run this query again.

8. Close the query without saving your design changes.

You now are ready to create the query to answer Matt's question about Waiter/Waitress or Kitchen Help positions located in Massachusetts (MA) or New Hampshire (NH).

Using **Both the And and Or Operators in the Same Query**

Matt wants to see the employer names, states/provinces, position titles, wages, hours per week, number of openings, and weekly wages for employers in Massachusetts or New Hampshire that have openings for Waiter/Waitress or Kitchen Help positions. To create this query, you must use both the And and the Or logical operators to create two compound conditions. That is, you will create conditions that select records for employers located in Massachusetts *or* in New Hampshire *and* have Waiter/Waitress positions *or* Kitchen Help positions. Because Matt wants to see the same fields used in the Weekly Wages query, you will use this query as the basis for your new query.

To create the query using the And logical operator with the Or logical operator:

1. Open the **Weekly Wages** query In Design view.

   Matt wants to view data for employers in Massachusetts (MA) or New Hampshire (NH). You have several choices for specifying the required Or logical operator. One choice is to type "MA" in the State/Prov Criteria text box and then type "NH" in the State/Prov or text box. A second choice is to type "MA" Or "NH" in the State/Prov Criteria text box. A third choice, and the one you'll use, is the In comparison operator.

2. Click the **State/Prov Criteria** text box, type **In (MA,NH)** and then press the **Enter** key. The State/Prov condition changed to In ("MA","NH") because Access adds quotation marks automatically to fields defined with the Text data type.

   To use the And logical operator, you need to enter the condition for the PositionTitle field in the same row as the State/Prov condition. This time you'll use the Or logical operator for the condition in the PositionTitle column.

3. Type **"Waiter/Waitress" Or "Kitchen Help"** in the PositionTitle Criteria text box, and then press the **Enter** key. See Figure 5-19.

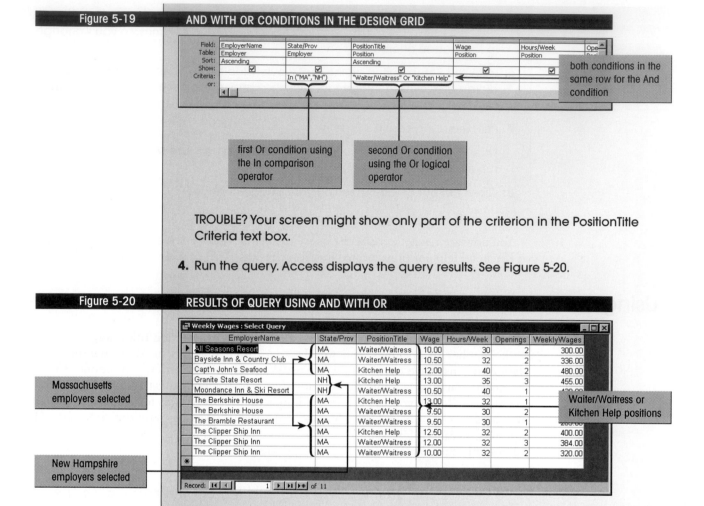

Figure 5-19 AND WITH OR CONDITIONS IN THE DESIGN GRID

first Or condition using the In comparison operator

second Or condition using the Or logical operator

both conditions in the same row for the And condition

TROUBLE? Your screen might show only part of the criterion in the PositionTitle Criteria text box.

4. Run the query. Access displays the query results. See Figure 5-20.

Figure 5-20 RESULTS OF QUERY USING AND WITH OR

Massachusetts employers selected

New Hampshire employers selected

Waiter/Waitress or Kitchen Help positions

The query results show records for employers in Massachusetts or New Hampshire that have either Waiter/Waitress or Kitchen Help positions. Next, you'll save the query with a new name (to keep the original query intact), and then you'll close the query.

5. Click **File** on the menu bar, click **Save As**, type **MA and NH Special Positions** in the Save Query text box, and then press the **Enter** key.

6. Close the query.

TROUBLE? If necessary, scroll the Queries list box to the left to display all the queries.

You are now ready to create the query to satisfy Matt's request for information about positions in a particular state or province.

Creating a Parameter Query

Matt's final query asks for records in the Weekly Wages query for employers in a particular state or province. For this query, he wants to specify the state or province, such as RI (Rhode Island), QC (Quebec), or NS (Nova Scotia).

To create this query, you will modify the existing Weekly Wages query. You could create a simple condition using an exact match for the State/Prov field, but you would need to change it in Design view every time you run the query. Instead, you will create a parameter query. A **parameter query** prompts you for information when the query runs. In this case, you want to create a query that prompts you for the state or province of the employers to select from the table. You enter the prompt in the Criteria text box for the State/Prov field.

When Access runs the query, it will open a dialog box and prompt you to enter the state or province. Access then creates the query results, just as if you had changed the criteria in Design view.

REFERENCE WINDOW   **RW**

Creating a Parameter Query
- Create a select query that includes all fields to appear in the query results. Also choose the sort keys and set the criteria that do not change when you run the query.
- Decide which fields will use prompts when the query runs. In the Criteria text box for each of these fields, type the prompt you want to appear in a message box when you run the query, and enclose the prompt in brackets.

Now you can open the Weekly Wages query in Design view and change its design to create the parameter query.

To create the parameter query based on an existing query:

1. Open the **Weekly Wages** query in Design view.

   Next you must enter the criteria for the parameter query. In this case, Matt wants the query to prompt users to enter the state or province for the position information they want to view. So, you need to enter the prompt in the Criteria text box for the State/Prov field. Brackets must enclose the text of the prompt.

2. Click the **State/Prov Criteria** text box, type **[Enter the state or province:]** and then press the **Enter** key. See Figure 5-21.

Figure 5-21   SPECIFYING THE PROMPT FOR THE PARAMETER QUERY

Field:	EmployerName	State/Prov	PositionTitle	Wage	Hours/Week	Openings
Table:	Employer	Employer	Position	Position	Position	Position
Sort:	Ascending		Ascending			
Show:	☑	☑	☑	☑	☑	
Criteria:		[Enter the state or province:]				
or:						

prompt text

TROUBLE? Your screen might show only part of the criterion in the State/Prov Criteria text box.

3. Run the query. Access displays a dialog box prompting you for the name of the state or province. See Figure 5-22.

Figure 5-22	ENTER PARAMETER VALUE DIALOG BOX

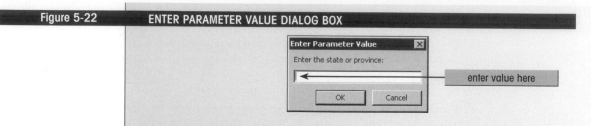

enter value here

The text you specified in the Criteria text box of the State/Prov field appears above a text box, in which you must type a State/Prov field value. You must enter the value so that it matches the spelling of a State/Prov field value in the table, but you can enter the value in either lowercase or uppercase letters. Matt wants to see all positions in Nova Scotia (NS).

4. Type **NS**, and then press the **Enter** key. Access displays the data for the three positions in Nova Scotia. See Figure 5-23.

Figure 5-23	RESULTS OF THE PARAMETER QUERY

Nova Scotia positions selected

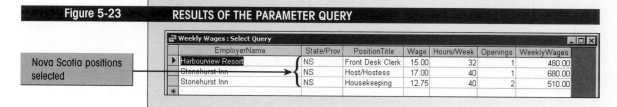

Matt plans to run this query frequently to monitor available positions by state or province, so he asks you to save it with a new name.

5. Click **File** on the menu bar, and then click **Save As**. The Save As dialog box opens.

6. Press the **End** key, press the **spacebar**, type **Parameter**, press the **Enter** key, and then close the query.

The Employer table design changes you made and the queries you created will make the Jobs database easier to use. In the next session, you will create a custom form for the database to help NSJI employees enter and maintain data more easily.

Session 5.1 QUICK CHECK

1. What is a Lookup Wizard field?

2. What is a subdatasheet?

3. A(n) _____ is a predefined format you use to enter data in a field.

4. Define the Validation Rule property, and give an example of when you would use it.

5. Define the Validation Text property, and give an example of when you would use it.

6. Which comparison operator selects records based on a specific pattern?

7. What is the purpose of the asterisk (*) in a pattern match query?

8. When do you use the In comparison operator?

9. How do you negate a selection criterion?

10. When do you use a parameter query?

SESSION 5.2

In this session, you will create a custom form for employer information. You will work in Design view to add form controls; select, move, resize, delete, and rename the controls; create a form header with a title and a picture, and add color to the background of the form.

Creating a Custom Form

Elsa has been using the Employer Positions form to enter and view information about NSJI's employers and their positions. She likes having the information on a single form, but she prefers to display all fields from the Employer table instead of only a few. Also, Elsa would prefer to have the fields rearranged and a picture added to the form. To make the form easier to read, she wants the employer and position information on separate pages, like the tabs in a dialog box. She asks you to create a new form to display information this way. Because this form differs significantly from the Employer Positions form, you will create a new custom form.

To create a **custom form**, you can modify an existing form or design and create a form from scratch. In either case, you create a custom form in the Form window in Design view. You can design a custom form to match a paper form, to display some fields side by side and others top to bottom, to highlight certain sections with color, or to add special buttons and list boxes. A multi-page form displays the form on more than one page on a single screen. Each page is labeled with a tab; by clicking a tab, you can display the information on that page.

Designing a Custom Form

Whether you want to create a simple or complex custom form, planning the form's content and appearance first is always best. Figure 5-24 shows Elsa's design for the custom form she wants you to create.

Figure 5-24   ELSA'S DESIGN FOR THE MULTI-PAGE CUSTOM FORM

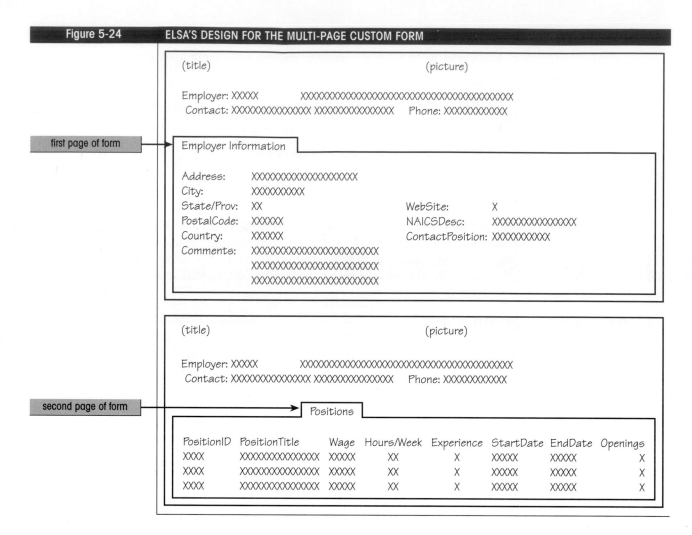

Notice that the top of the form displays a title and picture. Below these items are field values from the Employer table—the first employer line displays the EmployerID and EmployerName field values; and the second employer line displays the ContactFirstName, ContactLastName, and Phone field values. Also, notice that Elsa's form contains two pages. The first page, labeled "Employer Information," displays the employer's address information, comments, and miscellaneous information. The second page, labeled "Positions," displays position information for the employer. Each field value from the Employer table is to appear in a text box, with identifying labels placed to the left of most field values. Each label will be the value of the field's Caption property (if any) or the field name. In Elsa's form design, a series of Xs indicates the locations and approximate lengths of each field value. For example, the five Xs following the Employer field label indicate that the field value (for the EmployerID field) is approximately five characters. The Position table fields appear in a **subform**, a separate form contained within another form, on the second page. Unlike the Employer table data, which appears on the first page with identifying labels to the left of the field values in text boxes, the Position table data appears in datasheet format with identifying labels above field values.

With the design for the custom form in place, you are ready to create it. You could use an AutoForm Wizard or the Form Wizard to create a basic form and then customize it in Design view. However, to create the form Elsa wants, you would need to make many modifications to a basic form, so you will design the entire form directly in Design view.

The Form Window in Design View

You use the Form window in Design view to create and modify forms. To create Elsa's custom form, you'll create a blank form based on the Employer table and then add the Position table fields in a subform.

REFERENCE WINDOW   **RW**

Creating a Form in Design View
- In the Database window, click Forms in the Objects bar to display the Forms list.
- Click the New button to open the New Form dialog box, and then click Design View.
- Select the table or query on which to base the form, and then click the OK button.
- Place the necessary controls in the Form window in Design view. Modify the size, position, and other control properties as necessary.
- Click the Save button on the Form Design toolbar, and then enter a name for the form.

Now you'll create a blank form based on the Employer table.

To create a blank form in Design view:

1. If you took a break after the previous session, make sure that Access is running and that the **Jobs** database from the Tutorial folder on your Data Disk is open.

2. Click **Forms** in the Objects bar of the Database window, and then click the **New** button. The New Form dialog box opens.

3. Click **Design View** (if necessary), click the list arrow for choosing a table or query, click **Employer**, and then click the **OK** button. Access opens the Form window in Design view.

4. Click the **Maximize** button [□] on the Form window to maximize the window. See Figure 5-25.

Figure 5-25	FORM WINDOW IN DESIGN VIEW

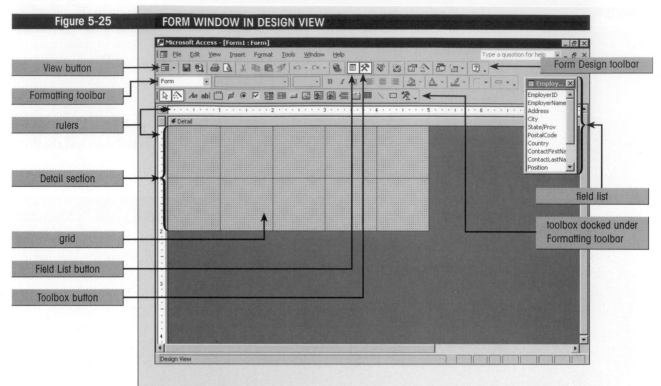

TROUBLE? If the rulers, grid, or toolbox do not appear, click View on the menu bar, and then click Ruler, Grid, or Toolbox to display the missing component. If the grid is still invisible, ask your instructor or technical support person for assistance. If the toolbox is not positioned as in Figure 5-25, click the Toolbox window's title bar and then drag it to the position shown.

TROUBLE? If the field list is not visible, click the Field List button 🖿 on the Form Design toolbar to display it. If the field list is not positioned as in Figure 5-25, click the field list title bar and then drag it to the position shown. If necessary, resize the field list window so it matches the one shown Figure 5-25.

TROUBLE? If the Form Design toolbar or the Formatting toolbar does not appear, click View on the menu bar, point to Toolbars, and then click Form Design or Formatting (Form/Report) to display the missing toolbar.

TROUBLE? If the Form Design and Formatting toolbars appear on the same line, drag the Formatting toolbar's move handle ▮ below the Form Design toolbar to the position shown in Figure 5-25.

The Form window in Design view contains the tools necessary to create a custom form. You create the form by placing objects on the blank form in the window. Each object—such as a text box, list box, rectangle, or command button—that you place on a form is called a **control**. You can place three kinds of controls on a form:

- A **bound control** is linked, or bound, to a field in the underlying table or query. You use a bound control to display table field values.

- An **unbound control** is not linked to a field in the underlying table or query. You use an unbound control to display text, such as a form title or instructions; to display lines and rectangles; or to display graphics and pictures created using other software programs. An unbound control that displays text is called a **label**.

■ A **calculated control** displays a value calculated using data from one or more fields.

To create a bound control, you use the Field List button on the Form Design toolbar to display a list of fields available from the underlying table or query. Then you drag fields from the field list box to the Form window, and place the bound controls where you want them to appear on the form.

To place other controls on a form, you use the buttons on the toolbox. The **toolbox** is a specialized toolbar containing buttons that represent the tools you use to place controls on a form or report. ScreenTips are available for each tool. If you want to show or hide the toolbox, click the Toolbox button on the Form Design toolbar. Figure 5-26 describes the tools available on the toolbox. (*Note*: You'll learn about Control Wizards later in this tutorial.)

Figure 5-26	**SUMMARY OF BUTTONS AVAILABLE ON THE TOOLBOX FOR A FORM OR REPORT**		
BUTTON	**BUTTON NAME**	**PURPOSE ON A FORM OR A REPORT**	**CONTROL WIZARD AVAILABLE?**
	Bound Object Frame	Display a frame for enclosing a bound OLE object stored in an Access database table	Yes
	Check Box	Display a check box control bound to a yes/no field	Yes
	Combo Box	Display a control that combines the features of a list box and a text box; you can type in the text box or select an entry in the list box to add a value to an underlying field	Yes
	Command Button	Display a control button you can use to link to an action, such as finding a record, printing a record, or applying a form filter	Yes
	Control Wizards	Activate Control Wizards for certain other toolbox tools	No
	Image	Display a graphic image	Yes
	Label	Display text, such as title or instructions; an unbound control	No
	Line	Display a line	No
	List Box	Display a control that contains a scrollable list of values	Yes
	More Controls	Display a list of all available controls	No
	Option Button	Display an option button control bound to a yes/no field	Yes
	Option Group	Display a group frame containing toggle buttons, options buttons, or check boxes	Yes
	Page Break	Begin a new screen on a form or a new page on a report	No
	Rectangle	Display a rectangle	No
	Select Objects	Select, move, size, and edit controls	No
	Subform/Subreport	Display data from a related table	Yes
	Tab Control	Display a tab control with multiple pages	No
	Text Box	Display a label attached to a text box that contains a bound control or a calculated control	No
	Toggle Button	Display a toggle button control bound to a yes/no field	Yes
	Unbound Object Frame	Display a frame for enclosing an unbound OLE object, such as a Microsoft Excel spreadsheet	Yes

The Form window in Design view also contains a **Detail section**, which appears as a light gray rectangle. In this section, you place the fields, labels, and values for your form. You can change the size of the Detail section by dragging its edges. The **grid** consists of the dots that appear in the Detail section to help you position controls precisely on a form.

Rulers at the top and left edge of the Detail section define the horizontal and vertical dimensions of the form and serve as guides for placing controls on a form.

Your first task is to add bound controls to the Detail section for the EmployerID, EmployerName, ContactFirstName, ContactLastName, and Phone fields from the Employer table.

Adding Fields to a Form

When you add a bound control to a form, Access adds a text box and, to its left, a label. The text box displays the field values from the underlying table or query on which the form is based, and the label identifies the values. To create a bound control, you display the field list by clicking the Field List button on the Form Design toolbar. Then you select one or more fields from the field list and drag the fields to place them on the form. You select a single field by clicking that field. You select two or more fields by holding down the Ctrl key and clicking each field; you select all fields by double-clicking the field list title bar.

Next, you will add bound controls to the Detail section for five of the fields in the field list.

To add bound controls from the Employer table to the grid:

1. Click **EmployerID** in the field list, press and hold the **Ctrl** key, click (scrolling as necessary) **EmployerName**, **ContactFirstName**, **ContactLastName**, and **Phone** in the field list, and then release the **Ctrl** key. You selected all five fields.

2. Click one highlighted field and then drag it to the form's Detail section. Release the mouse button when the pointer ⌷ is positioned at the 1.5-inch mark on the horizontal ruler and at the top of the Detail section. Access adds five bound controls—one for the each of the five selected fields in the Employer field list—in the Detail section of the form. See Figure 5-27.

Figure 5-27	ADDING TEXT BOXES AND ATTACHED LABELS AS BOUND CONTROLS TO A FORM

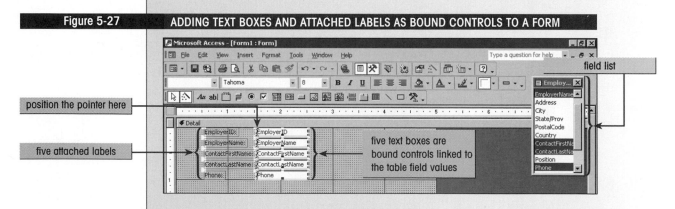

TROUBLE? You do not need to place your controls in exactly the same position as the controls in Figure 5-27. However, you should place them in approximately the same position. If you did not position the bound controls properly in the Detail section, click the Undo button ↶ on the Form Design toolbar to delete the text boxes and labels from the Detail section. Then repeat Step 2 to add and position the bound controls.

3. Click the **Close** button ☒ on the field list to close it.

   Comparing the form's Detail section with Elsa's design, notice that you need only three of the five labels, so you'll decide to delete two labels.

4. Click the darker gray area outside the Detail section to deselect all controls.

5. Right-click the **EmployerName label** to select it, and then click **Cut** on the shortcut menu.

6. Repeat Step 5 to delete the **ContactLastName label**.

Working on a form in Design view might seem awkward at first. With practice you will become comfortable with creating a custom form. Remember that you can always click the Undo button one or more times immediately after you make one or more errors or make undesired form adjustments.

Comparing the form's Detail section with Elsa's design, notice that you need to arrange the labels and text boxes in two rows. To do so, you must select and move the controls.

Selecting and Moving Controls

Five text boxes now appear in the form's Detail section, one below the other. Each text box is a bound control linked to a field in the underlying table. Three text boxes have labels attached to their left. Each text box and each label is a control on the form. When you select a control, square boxes appear on its corners and edges. Called **sizing handles**, these boxes let you move or resize the control. The handle in a control's upper-left corner is its **move handle**, which you use to move the control.

REFERENCE WINDOW   **RW**

Selecting and Moving Controls
- Click the control to select it. To select several controls at once, press and hold down the Shift key while clicking each control. Handles appear around all selected controls.
- To move a single selected control, drag the control's move handle to its new position.
- To move a group of selected controls, click any selected control (but do not click any of its handles), and then drag the group of selected controls to its new position.

For Elsa's custom form, you must select the EmployerID and ContactFirstName controls and move them to the far left edge of the Detail section. Each control consists of a field-value text box and a corresponding label to its left.

To select the EmployerID and ContactFirstName controls:

1. Hold down the **Shift** key, click the **EmployerID** text box, click the **ContactFirstName** text box, and then release the **Shift** key. Move handles, which are the larger handles, appear on the upper-left corners of the two selected text boxes and their attached labels. Sizing handles also appear, but only on the two text boxes. See Figure 5-28.

Figure 5-28   SELECTING TWO BOUND CONTROLS

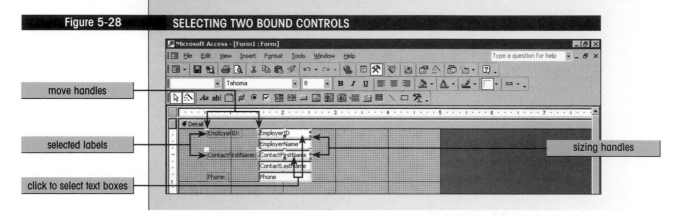

You can move a text box and its attached label together. To move them, place the pointer anywhere on the border of the text box, but not on a move handle or a sizing handle. When the pointer changes to a 🖐 shape, you can drag the text box and its attached label to the new location. As you move the controls, their outline moves to show you the changing position.

You can also move either the text box or its label individually. If you want to move the text box but not its label, for example, place the pointer on the text box's move handle. When the pointer changes to a 🖐 shape, drag the text box to the new location. You use the label's move handle in a similar way to move just the label.

You'll now arrange the controls to match Elsa's design.

To rearrange the controls in the Detail section:

1. Position the pointer on the EmployerID text box, but not on a move handle or a sizing handle. When the pointer changes to a 🖐 shape, drag the control as far left as you can, and then release the mouse button. When the EmployerID and ContactFirstName labels reach the left edge of the Detail section, you won't be able to move the labels and text boxes any further left. See Figure 5-29.

Figure 5-29   AFTER MOVING THE EmployerID AND ContactFirstName BOUND CONTROLS

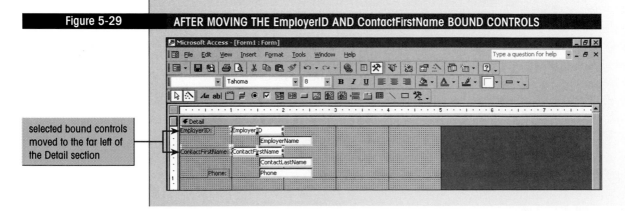

Next, you'll move the EmployerName text box to the right of the EmployerID text box.

2. Click the **EmployerName** text box, and then position the pointer on its move handle. When the pointer changes to a ⬛ shape, drag the control to the top of the Detail section, so its left edge is on the 2.125-inch mark on the horizontal ruler, and then release the mouse button.

   TROUBLE? If other form controls moved with the EmployerName text box, these other controls were also selected when you moved the EmployerName text box. To return the controls to their original positions, click the Undo button 🔙 on the Form Design toolbar, and then click the gray area outside the Detail section to deselect all selected controls. Repeat Step 2 to move the EmployerName text box.

According to Elsa's design, the three bound controls should be captioned "Employer:", "Contact:", and "Phone:". Before you finish arranging the controls in the Detail section, you'll modify the label text. To change the label text, you'll change each label's caption.

Changing a Label's Caption

The text in a label on a form is defined by the column name used for the associated text box in the underlying table or query. If you want the label to display different text, you need to change the label's Caption property value.

REFERENCE WINDOW   **RW**

Changing a Label's Caption
- Right-click the label to select it and to display the shortcut menu, and then click Properties to display the property sheet.
- If necessary, click the All tab to display the All page of the property sheet.
- Edit the existing label in the Caption text box, or double-click the Caption text box to select the current value, and then type a new caption.
- Click the property sheet Close button to close it.

EmployerID, ContactFirstName, and Phone are the field names in the Employer table for the three bound controls in the report that still have attached labels. The "Phone:" label in the report matches Elsa's form design, but Elsa wants the other two labels to be "Employer:" and "Contact:", so you'll change the Caption property for these two labels.

To change the Caption property value for the two labels:

1. Right-click the **EmployerID label** to select it and to display the shortcut menu, and then click **Properties** on the shortcut menu. The property sheet for the EmployerID label opens.

2. If necessary, click the property sheet title bar and drag the property sheet down to the lower-right corner of your screen, so that all controls in the Detail section are visible.

3. If necessary, click the **All** tab to display all properties for the selected EmployerID label.

   TROUBLE? If you do not see the word "Label" on your title bar or if EmployerID: is not the Caption property value, then you selected the wrong control in Step 1. Click the EmployerID label to change to the property sheet for this control.

4. Position the insertion point between the "D" and the colon in EmployerID: in the Caption text box, and then press the **Backspace** key twice. The Caption property value should now be Employer:. See Figure 5-30.

Figure 5-30   **CHANGING THE CAPTION PROPERTY FOR THE LABEL**

TROUBLE? The property sheet title bar, the Object list box, and the Name property on your screen might have a value other than the one shown in Figure 5-30. Also, if your label's position slightly differs from the position shown in the figure, some property values on your screen, such as the Left and Top property values, might differ. These differences cause no problems.

The property sheet title bar displays the object type (Label) and the Name property value (Label5—yours might differ). For most form controls, Access sets the Name property to the object type followed by a number; you can set the Name property to another value at any time.

5. Click the **ContactFirstName label** to select it. The property sheet now displays the properties for the ContactFirstName label, and the EmployerID label in the Detail section now displays Employer:.

6. Change the Caption property value for the label to **Contact:**.

7. Click the **Close** button [X] on the property sheet to close it. The ContactFirstName label in the Detail section now displays Contact:.

As you create a form, you should periodically check your progress by displaying the form in Form view. You might find you want to make adjustments to your form in Design view. Next, you'll save the current form design and then view the form in Form view.

To save the form and switch to Form view:

1. Click the **Save** button on the Form Design toolbar. The Save As dialog box opens.

2. Type **Employer Information Multi-page**, and then press the **Enter** key. Access saves the form in the Jobs database.

3. Click the **View** button for Form view on the Form Design toolbar. Access closes the Form window in Design view and displays the form in Form view. See Figure 5-31.

Figure 5-31	FORM WINDOW IN FORM VIEW

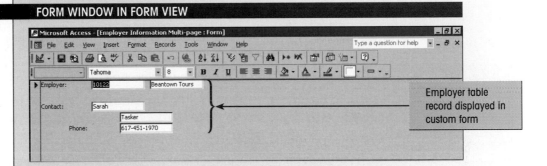

Access displays the EmployerID, EmployerName, ContactFirstName, ContactLastName, and Phone field values for the first record in the Employer table (Beantown Tours). You can use the navigation buttons to view other records from the table in the form.

4. Click the **Last Record** navigation button to view record 45 in the Employer table (Lighthouse Tours), and then click the **Previous Record** navigation button to view record 44 (Harbor Whale Watchers).

Form view reveals that you need to make some adjustments to the form design. The EmployerID, ContactFirstName, ContactLastName, and Phone text boxes are too large for the field values they contain; and the EmployerName field-value text box is too small for the field value it contains. To correct these design problems, you will resize all five text boxes in Design view.

Resizing Controls

A selected control displays seven sizing handles: one on each side of the control and one at each corner except the upper-left corner. The upper-left corner displays the move handle. Positioning the pointer over a sizing handle changes the pointer to a two-headed arrow; the directions in which the arrows point indicate in which direction you can resize the selected control. When you drag a sizing handle, you resize the control. As you resize the control, a thin line appears between the sizing handle to guide you in completing the task accurately.

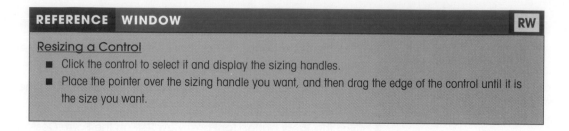

REFERENCE WINDOW   RW

<u>Resizing a Control</u>
- Click the control to select it and display the sizing handles.
- Place the pointer over the sizing handle you want, and then drag the edge of the control until it is the size you want.

You'll begin by resizing the EmployerID text box, which is much larger than necessary to display the five-digit EmployerID field value. Then you'll resize the other four controls appropriately.

To resize the text boxes:

1. Switch to Design view, and then click the **EmployerID** text box to select it.

2. Place the pointer on the middle-right handle. When the pointer changes to a ◄──► shape, drag the right border horizontally to the left until the text box is approximately the size shown in Figure 5-32.

   TROUBLE? If you accidentally change the vertical size of the text box, click the Undo button [↩] on the Form Design toolbar, and then repeat Step 2.

   Now you will move the EmployerName control to its correct position and then resize the EmployerName text box.

3. Click the **EmployerName** text box to select it. Place the pointer on the EmployerName text box, but not on a move handle or a sizing handle. When the pointer changes to a 🖐 shape, drag the control to the left until its left edge is at the 1.75-inch mark on the horizontal ruler.

4. Place the pointer on the middle-right handle of the EmployerName text box control. When the pointer changes to a ◄──► shape, drag the right border horizontally to the right until the right edge of the text box is at the 3.75-inch mark on the horizontal ruler. See Figure 5-32.

| Figure 5-32 | EmployerID AND EmployerName CONTROLS MOVED AND RESIZED |

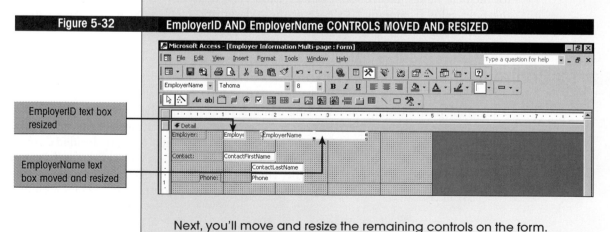

EmployerID text box resized

EmployerName text box moved and resized

Next, you'll move and resize the remaining controls on the form.

5. Select the **ContactFirstName** text box, move it and its attached label up until their top edges are at the 0.25-inch mark on the vertical ruler, and then drag the right edge of the ContactFirstName text box to the left until its right edge is at the 1.75-inch mark on the horizontal ruler. See Figure 5-33.

6. Select the **ContactLastName** text box, move it until its top edge is at the 0.25-inch mark on the vertical ruler and its left edge is at the 1.875-inch mark on the horizontal ruler, and then drag the right edge of the ContactLastName text box to the left until its right edge is at the 2.75-inch mark on the horizontal ruler. See Figure 5-33.

7. Select the **Phone** text box, and then move it and its attached label up until their top edges are at the 0.25-inch mark on the vertical ruler and the left edge of the label is at the 3-inch mark on the horizontal ruler. See Figure 5-33.

8. Place the pointer on the **Phone** text box move handle and, when the pointer changes to a 🖑 shape, drag the control to the left to the 3.5-inch mark on the horizontal ruler. Make sure the top edge of the control remains at the 0.25-inch mark on the vertical ruler. See Figure 5-33.

9. Resize the Phone text box by dragging its right edge to the left to the 4.25-inch mark on the horizontal ruler. See Figure 5-33.

Figure 5-33   **AFTER MOVING AND RESIZING ALL CONTROLS**

10. Save your design changes, and then switch to Form view to view the controls on the form. Navigate through the first several records, and notice that the text boxes are now the appropriate sizes for displaying the field values.

Now you will add the title and picture to the top of the form.

Using **Form Headers and Form Footers**

The Form Header and Form Footer sections let you add titles, instructions, command buttons, and other information to the top and bottom of your form, respectively. Controls placed in the Form Header or Form Footer sections remain on the screen whenever the form is displayed; they do not change when the contents of the Detail section change. To add either a header or footer to your form, you must first add both the Form Header and Form Footer sections as a pair to the Form window in Design view. If your form needs one of these sections but not the other, you can remove a section by setting its height to zero, which is the same method you would use to remove any form section.

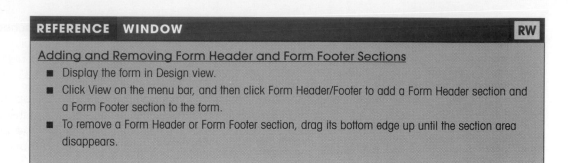

REFERENCE WINDOW   **RW**

Adding and Removing Form Header and Form Footer Sections
- Display the form in Design view.
- Click View on the menu bar, and then click Form Header/Footer to add a Form Header section and a Form Footer section to the form.
- To remove a Form Header or Form Footer section, drag its bottom edge up until the section area disappears.

Elsa's design includes a title and a picture at the top of the form. Because these two controls will not change as you navigate through the form records, you will add them to a Form Header section in the form.

To add Form Header and Form Footer sections to the form:

1. Switch to Design view.

2. Click **View** on the menu bar, and then click **Form Header/Footer**. Access inserts a Form Header section above the Detail section and a Form Footer section below the Detail section. See Figure 5-34.

| Figure 5-34 | ADDING THE FORM HEADER AND FORM FOOTER SECTIONS |

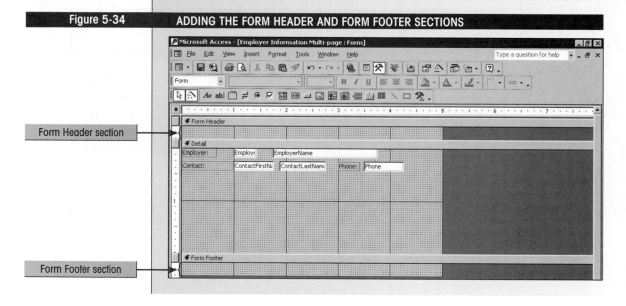

Elsa's form design does not include any items on the bottom of each form, so you don't need the Form Footer section. You'll remove it by changing its height to zero.

To remove the Form Footer section:

1. Place the pointer at the bottom edge of the Form Footer section. When the pointer changes to a ╪ shape, drag the bottom edge of the section up until it disappears. Even though the words "Form Footer" remain, the area defining the section is set to zero, so the section will not appear in the form. If a future form design change makes adding controls to the Form Footer section necessary, you can restore the section by using the pointer to drag its bottom edge back down.

You can now add the title to the Form Header section using the Label tool on the toolbox.

Adding a Label to a Form

The form design shows a title at the top of the form. You can add a title or other text to a form by using the Label tool on the toolbox.

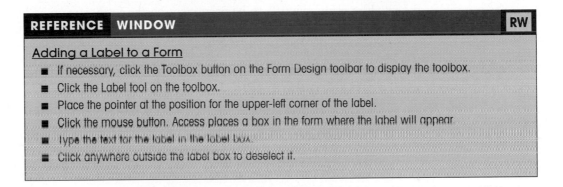

REFERENCE WINDOW   **RW**

<u>Adding a Label to a Form</u>

- If necessary, click the Toolbox button on the Form Design toolbar to display the toolbox.
- Click the Label tool on the toolbox.
- Place the pointer at the position for the upper-left corner of the label.
- Click the mouse button. Access places a box in the form where the label will appear.
- Type the text for the label in the label box.
- Click anywhere outside the label box to deselect it.

You'll begin by placing a label box for the title in the Form Header section.

To place a label on the form:

1. Click the **Label** tool [Aa] on the toolbox.

2. Move the pointer to the Form Header section. The pointer changes to a $^+$A shape.

3. Position the center of the + portion of the pointer on the grid dot in the upper-left corner of the Form Header section. This is the location for the upper-left corner of the label.

4. Click the mouse button. Access inserts a small label box in the Form Header section and places the insertion point in the label box.

5. Type **NSJI Employer Information** in the label box, and then click anywhere outside the label box to deselect it. See Figure 5-35.

Figure 5-35   LABEL PLACED IN THE FORM HEADER SECTION

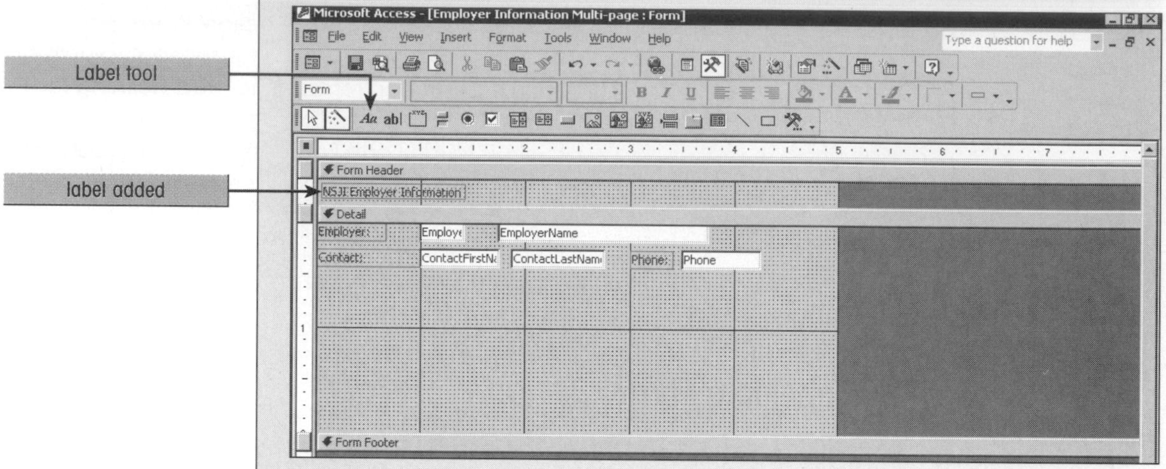

Label tool

label added

Elsa wants the title to be prominent on the form, so you will change the format of the label text to increase its font size and change its font weight to bold. You do this by using the buttons on the Formatting toolbar.

To change the font size and weight for the title:

1. Click the title label control to select it. Sizing handles appear on the control.

2. Click the **Font Size** list arrow on the Formatting toolbar, and then click **14**.

3. Click the **Bold** button **B** on the Formatting toolbar. See Figure 5-36.

Figure 5-36   SETTING THE PROPERTIES FOR THE TITLE LABEL CONTROL

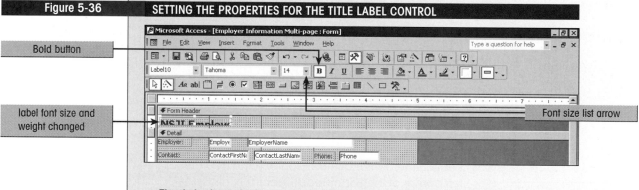

Bold button

label font size and weight changed

Font size list arrow

The label control now displays the title in 14-point, bold text. However, the label control is not large enough to display the entire title. You need to resize the label control so that it is large enough to display all the text. You could use the sizing handles to resize the label. However, using the Format menu is faster.

4. Click **Format** on the menu bar, point to **Size**, and then click **To Fit**. The resized label control displays the entire title. In addition, the Form Header's size automatically increased to accommodate the new label size. See Figure 5-37.

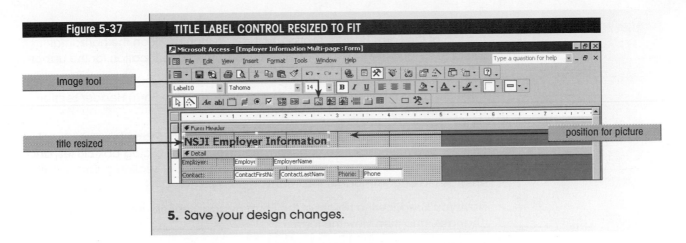

| Figure 5-37 | TITLE LABEL CONTROL RESIZED TO FIT |

5. Save your design changes.

Elsa also wants a picture at the top of the form. You will now add the picture to the Form Header section.

Adding a Picture to a Form

Access lets you use files and data created by other software programs. To enhance the appearance of a form or report, for example, you can include a picture or another graphic image on the form or report. To do so, you use the Image tool on the toolbox.

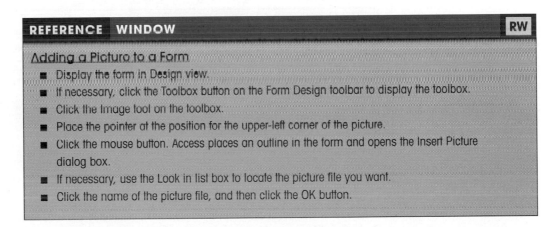

REFERENCE WINDOW   **RW**

Adding a Picture to a Form
- Display the form in Design view.
- If necessary, click the Toolbox button on the Form Design toolbar to display the toolbox.
- Click the Image tool on the toolbox.
- Place the pointer at the position for the upper-left corner of the picture.
- Click the mouse button. Access places an outline in the form and opens the Insert Picture dialog box.
- If necessary, use the Look in list box to locate the picture file you want.
- Click the name of the picture file, and then click the OK button.

Elsa's picture was created in a graphics program and saved in a file named Plane. Now you'll add this picture to the upper-right of the form.

To place the picture on the form:

1. Click the **Image** tool 🖾 on the toolbox.

2. Move the pointer to the Form Header section. The pointer changes to a
    🖾 shape.

3. Using the ruler as a guide, position the + portion of the pointer slightly below the top of the Form Header section, at the 3.25-inch mark on the horizontal ruler. (See Figure 5-37 for the correct position.) This is the location for the upper-left corner of the picture.

4. Click the mouse button. Access places an outline in the Form Header section and opens the Insert Picture dialog box.

5. Make sure **Tutorial** appears in the Look in list box, click **Plane** to select the picture file, and then click the **OK** button. The Insert Picture dialog box closes, and Access inserts the picture on the form. The Form Header section automatically enlarges to accommodate the image.

   Now, you'll reduce the height of the Form Header section, save your form changes, and then view the form.

6. Drag the bottom edge of the Form Header section up to the 0.875-inch mark on the vertical ruler.

7. Save your form changes, and then switch to Form view to view the form. See Figure 5-38.

| Figure 5-38 | VIEWING THE FORM WITH THE NEW HEADER |

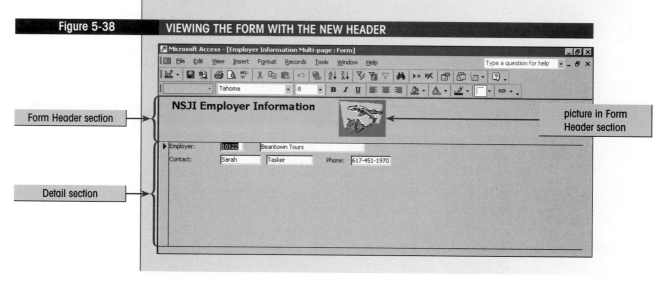

Elsa views the form and confirms that you correctly placed, formatted, and sized the title and picture. However, she wants you to change the background color of the form to dark teal to match the outline color of the picture, so that the picture will blend in better with the form.

Changing the Background Color of a Form Control

You can change the background color of a form or of a specific section or control on the form by using tools available in Design view.

> ### REFERENCE WINDOW   **RW**
>
> Changing the Background Color of a Control
> - In Design view, click the control to select it.
> - Click the Fill/Back Color list arrow on the Form Design toolbar to display the palette of available colors.
> - Click the box of the color you want to apply to the control.

You need to change the background color of the Form Header and Detail sections of the form to match the outline color of the picture. This will cause the picture to blend in with the form.

To change the background color of the Detail and Form Header sections:

1. Switch to Design view.

2. Click an empty area of the Detail section to make the Detail section the selected control.

3. Click the list arrow for the **Fill/Back Color** button 🖉 on the Formatting toolbar. Access displays the palette of available colors. See Figure 5-39.

Figure 5-39   **CHANGING THE BACKGROUND COLOR OF THE FORM SECTIONS**

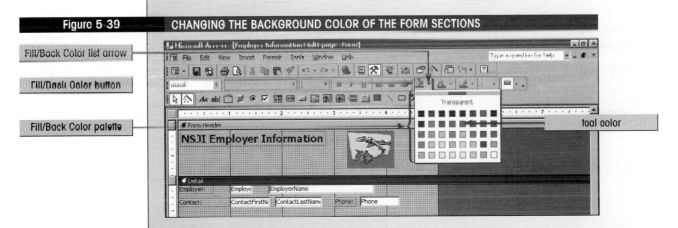

Fill/Back Color list arrow
Fill/Back Color button
Fill/Back Color palette
teal color

4. Click the **teal** box in the color palette, the box in row 2, column 5. (See Figure 5-39.) The background color of the Detail section changes to teal.

   Now you need to apply the same color to the Form Header section. To do so, you do not have to redisplay the color palette; once you select a color from the palette, you can apply the color to other objects by simply clicking the Fill/Back Color button.

5. Click an empty area of the Form Header section to make the Form Header section the selected control.

6. Click the **Fill/Back Color** button 🖉 (not the list arrow) on the Formatting toolbar. The Form Header section now appears with the teal background.

   Now you can save the form and view your changes in Form view.

7. Save your design changes, and then switch to Form view to view the form. See Figure 5-40.

Figure 5-40   **FORM WITH NEW BACKGROUND COLOR**

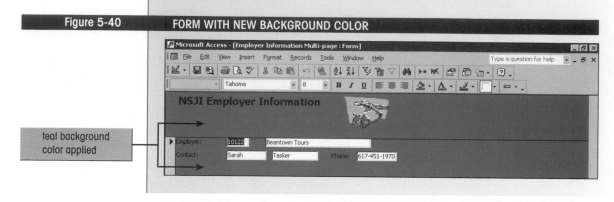

teal background color applied

In the next session, you will add the two pages to the form to display employer address and miscellaneous information on one page and the position information on the other.

Session 5.2 QUICK | CHECK

1. What is the difference between a bound control and an unbound control?

2. The _____ consists of the dots that appear in the Detail section to help you position controls precisely on a form.

3. The _____ is a specialized toolbar containing buttons that represent the tools you use to place controls on a form or a report.

4. The handle in an object's upper-left corner is the _____ handle.

5. How do you move a selected control and its label at the same time?

6. How do you change a label's caption?

7. How do you resize a control?

8. What is the Form Header section?

9. How do you add a picture created using another software program to a form?

SESSION 5.3

In this session, you will create a multi-page form and use Control Wizards to add a subform. You will also use the custom form to filter the data and save the filter as a query.

Creating a Multi-page Form Using Tab Controls

You can create a multi-page form in two ways: by inserting a page break control in the form or by using a tab control. If you insert a page break control in a form, the user can move between pages by pressing the Page Up and Page Down keys. If you use a tab control, the control appears with tabs at the top, with one tab for each page. The user can switch between pages by clicking the tabs.

Elsa wants to include a tab control with two pages on the Employer Information Multi-page form. The first page of the tab control will contain employer information, such as the employer address from the Employer table. The second page of the tab control will contain a subform with position information for that employer.

First, you will resize the Detail section of the form to make room for the tab control.

To resize the Detail section:

1. If you took a break after the previous session, make sure that Access is running, that the **Jobs** database from the Tutorial folder on your Data Disk is open, that the **Employer Information Multi-page** form is open in Form view, and that the window is maximized.

2. Switch to Design view.

3. Place the pointer on the right edge of the Detail section. When the pointer changes to a ↔ shape, drag the section's edge to the right until it is at the 6.5-inch mark on the horizontal ruler.

Now you can place the tab control on the form.

To place the tab control on the form:

1. Click the **Tab Control** tool 🔲 on the toolbox.

2. Position the + portion of the pointer at the left edge of the Detail section, approximately 0.5-inch below the top of the Detail section, and then click the mouse button. (Refer to Figure 5-41 for the correct position of the tab control.) Access places a tab control in the Detail section.

   Now you will resize the tab control so that it is wide enough to display the remaining fields for the form.

3. Drag the middle-right sizing handle of the tab control to the right until it is three grid dots from the right edge of the form. See Figure 5-41.

| Figure 5-41 | TAB CONTROL PLACED IN THE DETAIL SECTION AND RESIZED |

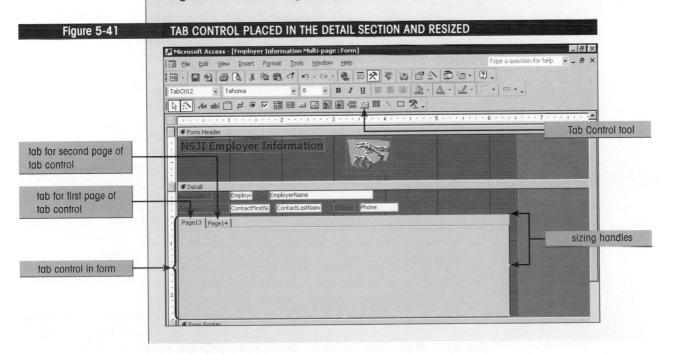

tab for second page of tab control

tab for first page of tab control

tab control in form

Tab Control tool

sizing handles

TROUBLE? The page tabs on your screen might show different page numbers in the labels, depending on how you completed the previous steps. This does not affect the form. Just continue with the tutorial.

The top of the tab control displays two tabs. Each tab indicates a separate page on the form. On the first page, you will place the controls for the fields from the Employer table. On the second page, you will place a subform displaying the fields from the Position table for that employer. The user can move between the two pages by clicking the tabs.

First, you'll add the fields from the Employer table to the first page of the tab control.

To add the fields from the Employer table to the tab control:

1. Click the **Field List** button 🗐 on the Form Design toolbar to display the field list.

2. Click the **Address** field in the field list, scroll to the end of the field list, press and hold down the **Shift** key, click the **Comments** field, and then release the **Shift** key. You selected all fields in the list, except EmployerID and EmployerName.

   The ContactFirstName, ContactLastName, and Phone fields are already in the form, so you'll remove these three fields from your selection.

3. Press and hold down the **Ctrl** key, click the **ContactFirstName** field, click the **ContactLastName** field, click the **Phone** field, and then release the **Ctrl** key.

   Next, you'll drag the selected fields to the first page of the tab control. When you drag the fields over the central portion of the tab control, the central portion changes color and the area near the borders remains gray; as you drag the fields near a tab control border, the entire tab control turns gray again. The area that changes color shows you where you can release the mouse button to make sure the bound controls fit within the tab control.

4. Drag the selected fields to the tab control, and release the mouse button when the tab control changes color and when the pointer is approximately at the 1-inch mark on the horizontal ruler and at the 0.75-inch mark on the vertical ruler, making sure the pointer is still positioned in the area that changes color.

   Text boxes for the selected fields are added in a column to the tab control with each text box's associated label to its left. To fit all the added bound controls to the tab control, Access increased the height of the tab control at its bottom automatically.

5. Close the field list, and then click a blank area of the tab control to deselect the bound controls.

   Now you need to move and resize the controls to match Elsa's form design.

6. Click the **NAICSDesc** text box to select it, and then position the pointer on one of its borders. When the pointer changes to a 🖑 shape, drag the bound control up and to the right until the left edge of the outline is at the 3-inch mark on the horizontal ruler and the top edge is at the 1.5-inch mark on the vertical ruler. Refer to Figure 5-42 for help in positioning the bound control.

   Next, you'll resize the NAICSDesc text box and align the top of the NAICSDesc bound control with the top of the PostalCode bound control.

7. Place the pointer on the middle-right handle of the **NAICSDesc** text box. When the pointer changes to a ↔ shape, drag the right border to the right until the right edge of the text box is at the 5.75-inch mark on the horizontal ruler.

8. Press and hold down the **Shift** key, click the **PostalCode** text box, click the **NAICSDesc label** (the PostalCode text box and the NAICSDesc text box and label should all have handles on their borders), click the **PostalCode** label, release the **Shift** key, click **Format** on the menu bar, point to **Align**, and then click **Top**. You aligned the top edges of the two bound controls.

   TROUBLE? If the NAICSDesc label is not aligned with the other three controls, deselect all controls, select the NAICSDesc label and the PostalCode label, click Format on the menu bar, point to Align, and then click Top.

   All the labels, except the WebSite label, have colons, so you'll add the colon to its caption, and then resize the label to fit.

9. Open the property sheet for the **WebSite label**, add a colon at the end of the control's Caption property, close the property sheet, and then size the control to fit.

   Unlike the other labels, the WebSite label is to the right of its associated text box, so you'll move the two WebSite controls independently.

10. Make sure the WebSite label is still selected, and then position the pointer on its move handle in the upper-left corner. When the pointer changes to a ✋ shape, drag the label above the NAICSDesc label, align their left edges, and then align the bottom edges of the WebSite and State/Prov labels. (See Figure 5-42.)

11. Click the **WebSite** text box, move the control above the NAICSDesc text box, align the two controls on their left edges, and then align the top edges of the WebSite label and the WebSite text box. (See Figure 5-42.)

12. Move, resize, and align the remaining controls. Use Figure 5-42 as a guide for positioning, sizing, and aligning the controls. Make sure to use the Align command on the Format menu to position pairs or larger groups of controls, aligning the controls on their top, left, or other edges.

| Figure 5-42 | EMPLOYER FIELDS PLACED IN THE TAB CONTROL |

controls arranged and sized on the first page of the tab control

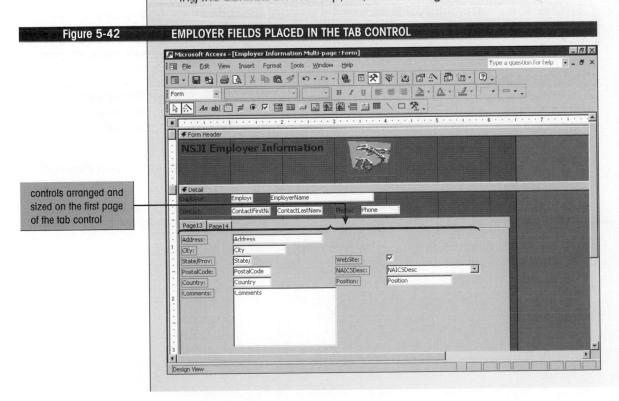

> **TROUBLE?** You do not have to position your controls exactly where the controls appear in Figure 5-42. However, you should place them in approximately the same position. If you placed the controls incorrectly, move, resize, and align them now.

Elsa refers back to her form design and identifies two more changes. The Position label needs its Caption property changed to "ContactPosition:". Also, you must size the Employer and Contact labels above the tab control to fit and then move them to the right so that they are closer to their associated text boxes. Finally, Elsa's design shows these labels as right-aligned. To align them, you will select all labels in a column and use the shortcut menu.

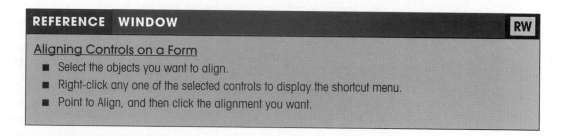

REFERENCE WINDOW   **RW**

Aligning Controls on a Form
- Select the objects you want to align.
- Right-click any one of the selected controls to display the shortcut menu.
- Point to Align, and then click the alignment you want.

Now you can change the Position label's Caption property and then resize, move, and align the two labels above the tab control.

To change the Caption property and then resize, move, and right-align the labels:

1. Open the property sheet for the **Position label**, set the Caption property to **ContactPosition:**, close the property sheet, and then size the control to fit.

2. Deselect all controls, press and hold down the **Shift** key, click the **Employer label**, click the **Contact label**, release the **Shift** key, and then size both controls to fit.

3. Place the pointer on the Employer label's move handle in the upper-left corner. When the pointer changes to a ✥ shape, drag the **Employer label** to the right until its left edge is at the 0.375-inch mark on the horizontal ruler. Refer to Figure 5-43 for help in positioning the label.

4. Make sure the Employer and Contact labels are still selected, and then right-click either of the selected label boxes to display the shortcut menu.

5. Point to **Align**, and then click **Right**. Access aligns the right edges of the label boxes. See Figure 5-43.

Figure 5-43	SIZING AND ALIGNING LABEL BOXES

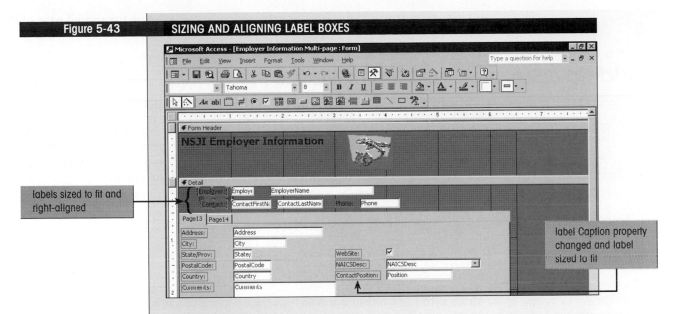

labels sized to fit and right-aligned

label Caption property changed and label sized to fit

TROUBLE? If the text boxes also were aligned, click the Undo button 🔄 on the Form Design toolbar, make sure that you select only the Employer and Contact labels (and that no other controls have sizing handles), and then repeat Steps 4 and 5.

6. Save your design changes, and then switch to Form view to view the form. See Figure 5-44.

Figure 5-44	FIRST RECORD IN FORM VIEW

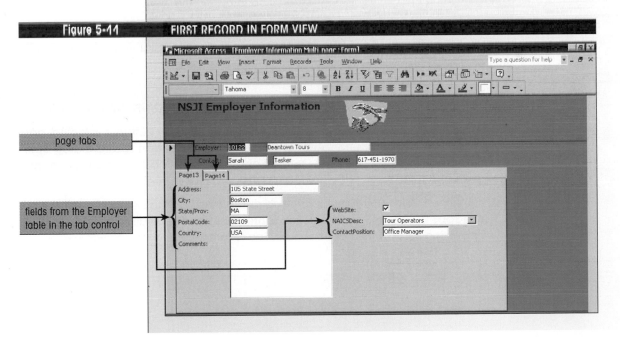

page tabs

fields from the Employer table in the tab control

You are now ready to add the Position table fields as a subform on the second page of the tab control.

Adding a Subform Using Control Wizards

You use the Subform/Subreport tool on the toolbox to add a subform to a form. If you want help when defining the subform, you can select one of the Access Control Wizards. A **Control Wizard** asks a series of questions and then uses your answers to create a control on a form or report. Access offers Control Wizards for the Combo Box, List Box, Option Group, Command Button, and Subform/Subreport tools, among others.

You will use the Subform/Subreport Wizard to add the subform for the Position table records to the second page of the tab control.

To add the subform to the tab control:

1. Switch to Design view.

2. Make sure the **Control Wizards** tool ⬛ on the toolbox is selected.

3. Click the tab for the second page (the tab on the right) to select it.

4. Click the **Subform/Subreport** tool ⬛ on the toolbox.

5. Position the + portion of the pointer near the upper-left corner of the tab control, just below the 1-inch mark on the vertical ruler and at the 0.5-inch mark on the horizontal ruler, and then click the mouse button. Access places a subform control in the tab control and opens the first SubForm Wizard dialog box.

You can use an existing table, query, or form as the source for a new subform. You'll use the Position table as the basis for the new subform.

To use the SubForm Wizard to add the subform to the form:

1. Make sure the **Use existing Tables and Queries** option button is selected, and then click the **Next** button. Access opens the next SubForm Wizard dialog box. This dialog box lets you select a table or query as the basis for the subform and then select the fields from that table or query.

2. Click the **Tables/Queries** list arrow to display the list of tables and queries in the Jobs database, and then click **Table: Position**. The Available Fields list box shows the fields in the Position table. See Figure 5-45.

Figure 5-45	SELECTING THE TABLE AND FIELDS FOR THE SUBFORM

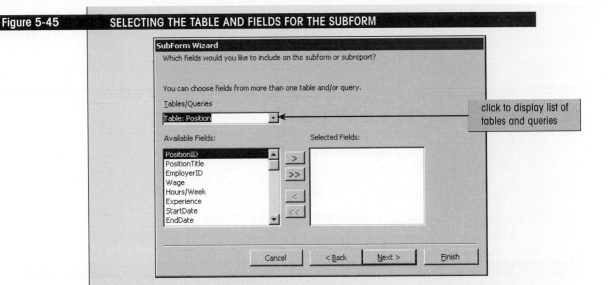

Elsa's design includes all fields from the Position table in the subform, except the EmployerID field, which is already placed on the form from the Employer table.

3. Click the **>>** button to move all available fields to the Selected Fields list box, click **EmployerID** in the Selected Fields list box, click the **<** button, and then click the **Next** button. See Figure 5-46.

Figure 5-46	SELECTING THE LINKING FIELD

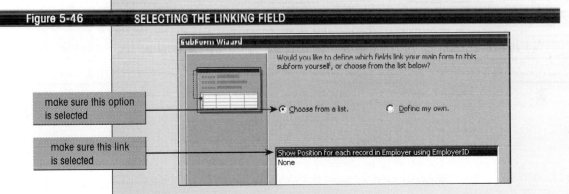

This dialog box lets you select the link between the Employer table and the Position table. EmployerID, as the common field between the two tables, links the two tables. Access uses the EmployerID field to display a record in the main form, which displays data from the Employer table, and to select and display the related records for that employer in the subform, which displays data from the Position table.

4. Make sure the **Choose from a list** option button is selected and that the first link is highlighted, and then click the **Next** button. The next SubForm Wizard dialog box lets you specify a name for the subform.

5. Type **Employer Information Subform** and then click the **Finish** button. Access inserts a subform object in the tab control. This is where the Position records will appear.

6. Maximize the Form window, and then close the field list.

7. Save your form changes, and then switch to Form view.

   The tab control shows the employer information on the first page. You can view the position information for the employer by clicking the second page tab.

8. Click the page tab on the right to display the position information. The subform displays the position data in a datasheet. See Figure 5-47.

| Figure 5-47 | VIEWING THE SUBFORM ON THE TAB CONTROL |

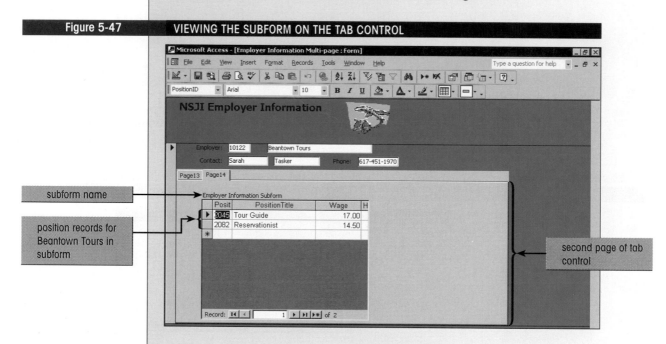

subform name

position records for Beantown Tours in subform

second page of tab control

TROUBLE? If the size of the columns in your datasheet differs, don't worry. You'll resize all columns to their best fit later.

After viewing the form, Elsa identifies several modifications she wants you to make. The subform is not properly sized and the columns in the subform are not sized to their best fit. She wants you to resize the subform and its columns, so that the columns are entirely visible. Also, she asks you to delete the Employer Information Subform label and to edit the labels for the tabs in the tab control, so that they indicate the contents of each page.

You can resize the subform and edit the labels in Design view. Then you can resize the subform columns in Form view. You'll begin by resizing the subform and editing the labels in Design view.

To resize the subform, delete its label, and edit the labels for the tabs:

1. Switch to Design view. Notice that in Design view, the subform data does not appear in a datasheet as it does in Form view. That difference causes no problem; you should ignore it.

2. If necessary, scroll down until you see the bottom of the subform. If necessary, click the right tab to select it.

   If you click a tab, you select the tab control, and sizing handles appear on its edges. If you want to select a subform positioned in a tab control, you should click the right or bottom edge of the subform; sizing handles disappear from the tab control and appear on the edges of the subform, indicating that it's selected.

3. Select and then resize the subform on the right and left, so that the subform extends horizontally from the 0.25-inch mark to the 6.25-inch mark on the horizontal ruler. Then drag the bottom of the subform up to the 3-inch mark on the vertical ruler.

4. Click anywhere in the light gray area of the tab control to deselect the subform, right-click the label for the subform control (make sure the subform no longer has sizing handles), and then click **Cut** on the shortcut menu to delete the label.

   Next, you'll change the labels on the tabs. To do so, you need to set the Caption property for each tab.

5. Right-click the subform page tab, and then click **Properties** on the shortcut menu to open the property sheet.

6. Click the **All** tab (if necessary), and then type **Positions** in the Caption text box. See Figure 5-48.

Figure 5-48	SETTING THE CAPTION PROPERTY VALUE FOR THE PAGE TAB

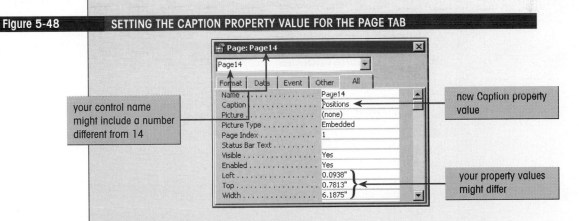

your control name might include a number different from 14

new Caption property value

your property values might differ

7. Click the page tab on the left, set the Caption property to **Employer Information**, and then close the property sheet.

Now you can view the form, and then resize the columns in the subform.

To view the form and resize the columns in the subform:

1. Switch to Form view, and then click the **Positions** tab. The second page of the multi-page form displays the Position table records for Beantown Tours.

   Before you resize the columns in the Positions subform, you'll change the font size in the subform datasheet.

2. Make sure the PositionID field in the datasheet is the current field, and then change the font size to **9**. All text in the datasheet changes to Arial 9.

3. Resize all datasheet columns to their best fit. The form is complete. See Figure 5-49.

Figure 5-49	POSITION COLUMNS AFTER RESIZING

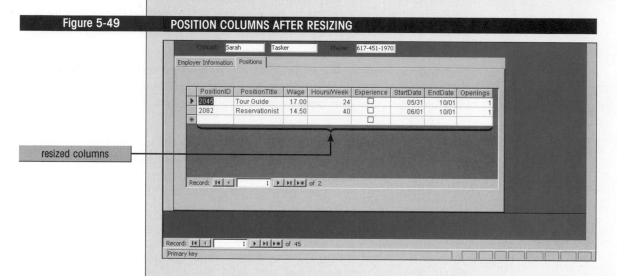

resized columns

4. Practice navigating through the Employer and Position table records using the form. When you finish, click the **Employer Information** tab, and then click the main form's **First Record** navigation button to display the employer information for Beantown Tours.

   Now you can save the completed form.

5. Save your form changes.

Elsa has a new request. She wants to see information for all employers in Massachusetts and Rhode Island that are tour operators. She wants to view this information using the Employer Information Multi-page form. To display the results she wants, you need to use a filter with the form.

Using a Filter with a Form

Recall that a **filter** is a set of criteria that describes the records you want to see, in a datasheet or a form, and their sequence. A filter is like a query, but it applies only to the current datasheet or form. If you want to use a filter at another time, you can save the filter as a query.

Four filter tools let you specify and apply filters: Filter By Selection, Filter By Form, Filter For Input, and Advanced Filter/Sort. With Filter By Selection, Filter By Form, and Filter For Input, you specify the record selection criteria directly in the form. **Filter By Selection** finds records that match a particular field value or a portion of a field value. **Filter By Form** and **Filter For Input** find records that match multiple selection criteria using the same Access logical and comparison operators used in queries. After applying a filter by selection or by form or for input, you can use the Sort Ascending or Sort Descending toolbar buttons to rearrange the records, if necessary.

Advanced Filter/Sort lets you specify multiple selection criteria and specify a sort order for selected records in the Advanced Filter/Sort window, in the same way you specify record selection criteria and sort orders for a query in Design view.

To produce the results Elsa wants, you'll use Filter By Form.

Using Filter By Form

Because the Employer Information Multi-page form already shows all the employer information, you can use Filter By Form to display information for only employers in Massachusetts and Rhode Island that are tour operators.

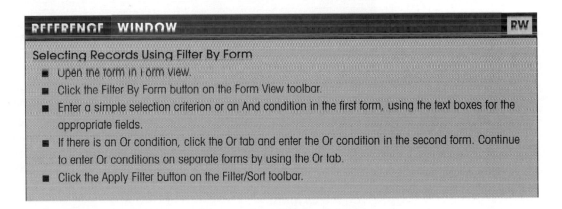

REFERENCE WINDOW RW

Selecting Records Using Filter By Form

- Open the form in Form View.
- Click the Filter By Form button on the Form View toolbar.
- Enter a simple selection criterion or an And condition in the first form, using the text boxes for the appropriate fields.
- If there is an Or condition, click the Or tab and enter the Or condition in the second form. Continue to enter Or conditions on separate forms by using the Or tab.
- Click the Apply Filter button on the Filter/Sort toolbar.

To answer Elsa's question, the multiple selection criteria you will enter are: Massachusetts *and* Tour Operators *or* Rhode Island *and* Tour Operators.

To select the records using Filter By Form:

1. Click the **Filter By Form** button [icon] on the Form View toolbar. Access displays a blank form. See Figure 5-50.

Figure 5-50	BLANK FORM FOR FILTER BY FORM

Clear Grid button

Or tab

enter selection criteria for first And condition on blank form

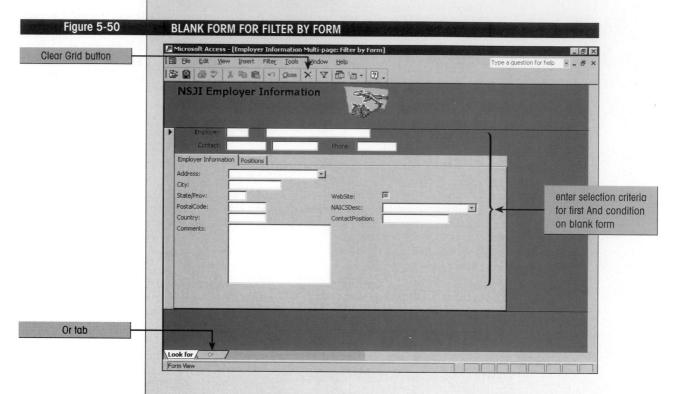

On this blank form, you specify multiple selection criteria by entering conditions in the text boxes for the fields in a record. If you enter criteria in more than one field, you create the equivalent of an And condition—Access selects any record that matches all criteria. To create an Or condition, you enter the criteria for the first part of the condition in the field on the first (Look for) blank form, and then click the Or tab to display a new blank form. You enter the criteria for the second part of the condition on the "Or" blank form. Access selects any record that matches all criteria on the Look for form *or* all criteria on the Or form.

2. Click the **State/Prov** text box, click the list arrow that appears, and then click **MA**. Access adds the criterion "MA" to the State/Prov text box.

3. Click the **NAICSDesc** list arrow, and then click **Tour Operators**. Access adds the criterion "Tour Operators" to the NAICSDesc text box.

You specified the logical operator (And) for the condition "Massachusetts and Tour Operators." To add the rest of the criteria, you need to display the Or form.

4. Click the **Or** tab to display a second blank form. The insertion point is in the text box for the NAICSDesc field. Notice that a third tab, also labeled "Or," is now available in case you need to specify another Or condition.

5. Click the **NAICSDesc** list arrow, and then click **Tour Operators**.

6. Click the **State/Prov** text box, click the list arrow, and then click **RI**. The form now contains the second And condition: "Rhode Island and Tour Operators." See Figure 5-51.

Figure 5-51	COMPLETED FILTER BY FORM

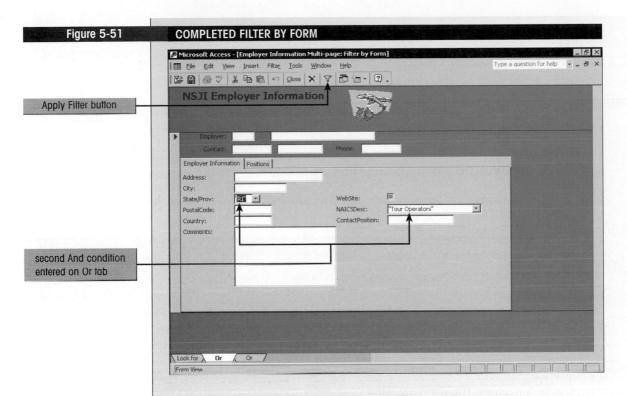

Apply Filter button

second And condition entered on Or tab

Combined with the Look for form, you now have the Or condition, and the complete Filter By Form conditions.

7. Click the **Apply Filter** button on the Filter/Sort toolbar. Access applies the filter and displays the first record that matches the selection criteria (Beantown Tours, a tour operator in Massachusetts). The bottom of the screen shows that the filter selected six records. See Figure 5-52.

Figure 5-52	FIRST RECORD THAT MATCHES THE SELECTION CRITERIA

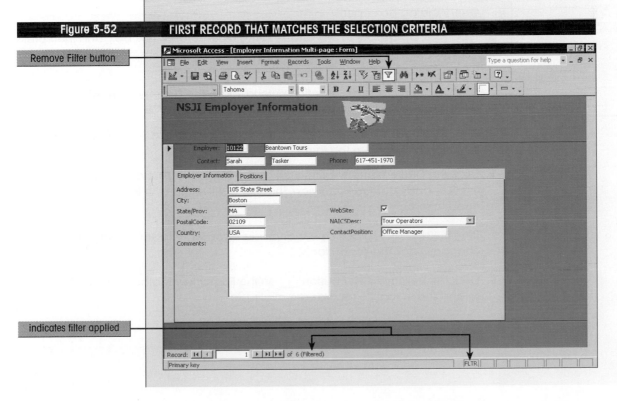

Remove Filter button

indicates filter applied

8. Click the main form's **Next Record** navigation button ▶ to display the second selected record (Newport Mansion Guided Tours, a tour operator in Rhode Island).

Now that you defined the filter, you can save it as a query, so that Elsa can easily view this information in the future.

Saving a Filter as a Query

By saving a filter as a query, you can reuse the filter in the future by opening the saved query.

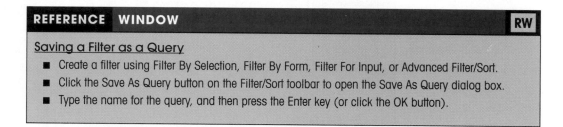

REFERENCE WINDOW   **RW**

Saving a Filter as a Query
- Create a filter using Filter By Selection, Filter By Form, Filter For Input, or Advanced Filter/Sort.
- Click the Save As Query button on the Filter/Sort toolbar to open the Save As Query dialog box.
- Type the name for the query, and then press the Enter key (or click the OK button).

Next, you'll save the filter you just created as a query named "Tour Operators in MA and RI."

To close the Form window and view the query list:

1. Click the **Filter By Form** button 🖹 on the Form View toolbar. Access displays the form with the selection criteria.

2. Click the **Save As Query** button 💾 on the Filter/Sort toolbar. The Save As Query dialog box opens.

3. Type **Tour Operators in MA and RI** in the Query Name text box, and then press the **Enter** key. Access saves the filter as a query in the Jobs database and closes the dialog box.

   Now you can clear the selection criteria, close the Filter by Form window, and return to Form view.

4. Click the **Clear Grid** button ✕ on the Filter/Sort toolbar. Access removes the selection criteria from the forms.

5. Click the **Close Window** button ✕ on the menu bar to close the Filter by Form window and return to Form view. The filter is still in effect in this window, so you need to remove it.

   TROUBLE? If a dialog box opens and asks if you want to save your form changes, click the Yes button.

6. Click the **Remove Filter** button ▽ on the Form View toolbar. The bottom of the screen shows that 45 records are available.

Next, to check that you saved the filter as a query, you'll close the Form window and view the list of queries on the Queries tab.

To save the filter as a query:

1. Click the **Close Window** button ☒ on the menu bar.

2. Click **Queries** in the Objects bar of the Database window to display the Queries list box. The query "Tour Operators in MA and RI" is now listed.

The next time Elsa wants to view the records selected by this query, she can apply the query to the form. If she simply runs the query, she will see the selected records, but they will not be shown in the Employer Information Multi-page form. Instead, she can open the form and apply the saved query to select the records she wants to view in the form.

Applying a Filter Saved as a Query

To see how to apply a query as a filter to a form, you will open the Employer Information Multi-page form and apply the Tour Operators in MA and RI query as a filter.

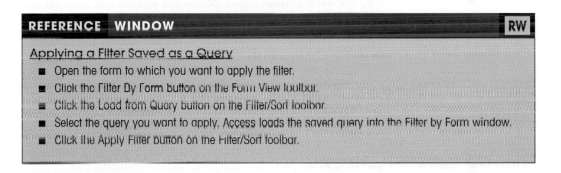

REFERENCE WINDOW | RW

Applying a Filter Saved as a Query
- Open the form to which you want to apply the filter.
- Click the Filter By Form button on the Form View toolbar.
- Click the Load from Query button on the Filter/Sort toolbar.
- Select the query you want to apply. Access loads the saved query into the Filter by Form window.
- Click the Apply Filter button on the Filter/Sort toolbar.

Now you'll open the Employer Information Multi-page form and apply the Tour Operators in MA and RI query as a filter.

To apply the filter saved as a query:

1. Open the Employer Information Multi-page form in Form view.

2. Click the **Filter By Form** button 🔲 on the Form View toolbar.

   TROUBLE? If your Filter by Form window already has the filter applied, skip to Step 5.

3. Click the **Load from Query** button 🔲 on the Filter/Sort toolbar. Access opens the Applicable Filter dialog box. See Figure 5-53.

Figure 5-53	APPLICABLE FILTER DIALOG BOX

your list might show the filters in a different order

Applicable Filter

Filter:
Selected Employer Info
508 Area Codes
Tour Operators in MA and RI

OK
Cancel

click to select filter saved as query

4. Click **Tour Operators in MA and RI** in the Filter list box, and then click the **OK** button. Access loads the saved query into the Filter by Form window.

5. Click the **Apply Filter** button on the Filter/Sort toolbar. Access applies the filter and displays the first filtered record in the form.

6. Click the **Close Window** button on the menu bar to close the form and return to the Database window.

   You can now close the Jobs database and exit Access.

7. Click the **Close** button on the Access window title bar to close the database and to exit Access.

The design changes you made to the Employer table and the new queries and form that you created will make it much easier for Elsa, Matt, and Zack to enter, retrieve, and view information in the Jobs database.

Session 5.3 QUICK CHECK

1. Describe how you would use a Control Wizard to add a tab control to a form.

2. How do you align a group of labels?

3. What is the purpose of Filter By Form?

4. How do you reuse a filter?

5. What is the difference between opening a query and applying a query to a form?

REVIEW ASSIGNMENTS

The **Students** database contains information about NSJI's recruiters and overseas students. The **Recruiter** table in the database contains records of the recruiters employed by NSJI to find students for seasonal work and match them with NSJI's client employers. The **Student** table contains student information. The database contains several other objects, including queries, forms, and reports. Elsa wants you to make changes to the design of the **Student** table, create some new queries, and create a custom form. Complete the following:

1. Make sure your Data Disk is in the appropriate disk drive, start Access, and then open the **Students** database in the Review folder on your Data Disk.

2. Open the **Student** table in Design view. Change the SSN field data type to Lookup Wizard. Look up values in the **Recruiter** table; select the SSN, FirstName, and LastName fields from the **Recruiter** table; use the label RecruiterName; and accept all other Lookup Wizard default choices. View the **Student** table datasheet, resize the RecruiterName column to its best fit, and then save and close the table.

3. Define data validation criteria for the Gender field in the **Student** table. Acceptable field values for the Gender field are F and M. Use the message, "Value must be F or M", to notify a user who enters an invalid Gender field value. Save your table changes, test the data validation criteria for the Gender field, and verify that the Lookup Wizard feature of the RecruiterName field works properly. Make sure the field values are the same as they were before you tested.

4. Modify the first record in the **Student** table datasheet by changing the FirstName, LastName, BirthDate, and Gender field values to your name, birth date, and gender. Close the table.

5. Use the Input Mask Wizard to add an input mask to the SSN field in the **Recruiter** table. Select the Social Security Number input mask, and then click the Finish button. Change the default input mask to 000\-00\-0000. Test the input mask by typing over an existing SSN field value, being sure not to change the value by pressing the Esc key after you type the last digit in the SSN field. Close the table.

6. Create a query to find all records in the **Student** table in which the Nation field value starts with either the letter A or the letter I. Include all fields in the query results. Save the query as **Students from Selected Countries**, run the query, and then print the query results. Keep the query open.

Explore 7. Modify the query you created in Step 6. Use the modified query to find all records in the **Student** table in which the Nation field value starts with neither the letter A nor the letter S. Save the query as **Students from Selected Countries Modified**, run the query, print the query results, and then close the query.

8. Create a query to find all records from the **Recruiter** table in which the BonusQuota field value is 40, 50, or 60. Use a list-of-values match for the selection criteria. Include all fields in the query results. Save the query as **Selected Bonus Quotas**, run the query, print the query results, and then close the query.

9. Create a query to select all records in the **Student** table for females from Australia or Germany. Display the FirstName, LastName, City, Nation, and Gender fields in the query results. Sort the query in ascending order by LastName. Save the query as **Females from Australia or Germany**, run the query, print the query results, and then close the query.

10. Create a parameter query to select the **Student** table records for a Nation field value that the user specifies. Include all fields in the query results. Save the query as **Nation Parameter**. Run the query and enter Ireland as the Nation field value. Print the query results and then close the query.

11. Use Figure 5-54 and the following steps to create a multi-page form based on the **Recruiter** and **Student** tables.

Figure 5-54

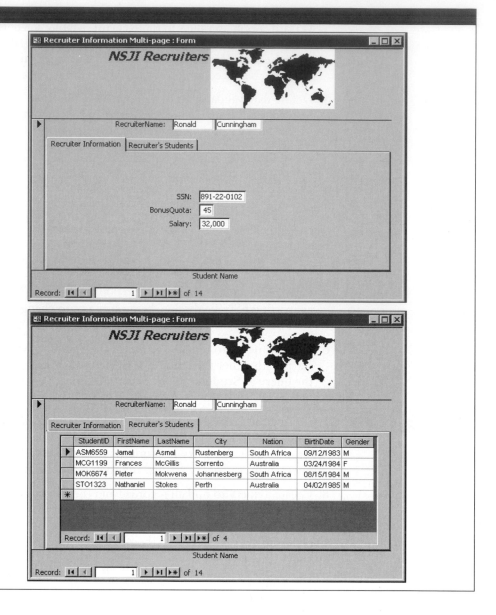

a. Place the FirstName and LastName fields from the **Recruiter** table at the top of the Detail section. Delete the LastName label and change the caption for the FirstName label to RecruiterName:.

b. Insert a Form Header section and a Form Footer section in the form. Place a title label in the Form Header section. Enter the title NSJI Recruiters, and change its font to 14-point bold italic.

c. Place the **WorldMap** picture in the Form Header section to the right of the title. The file containing this picture is in the Review folder on your Data Disk.

d. Place a label in the Form Footer section, and type your name in the label.

e. Place a tab control below the Recruiter Name label in the Detail section. On the first page of the tab control, place the remaining fields from the **Recruiter** table. Set the Caption property for each label, align the labels on the right, and move them closer to the text boxes. Resize the text boxes to appropriate widths.

    f. On the second page of the tab control, place a subform based on the **Student** table, include all fields from the table in the subform, and use SSN as the link field. Save the subform as **NSJI Student Subform**.

    g. Change the Caption property for each tab, and delete the subform label.

    h. Resize the form, the tab control, and the subform. You might need to resize one or more of these controls again as you complete the remaining steps.

Explore

    i. In Form view, hide the RecruiterName column in the subform datasheet.

    j. In Form view, change the text in the subform datasheet to 8 points, and then resize all datasheet columns to their best fit.

    k. Save the form as **Recruiter Information Multi-page**.

    l. View the form, and then print both pages for record 10. (*Hint:* Print the selected record after selecting one tab, and then repeat the procedure for the other tab.)

12. Use Filter By Form with the **Recruiter Information Multi-page** form to select all records in which the bonus quota is 40 and the salary is either 28,500 or 29,000. Apply the filter. How many records are selected?

13. Print the first page of the first selected record. Save the filter as a query named **Recruiter Information Multi-page Filter**. Close the filter and then close the form.

14. Close the **Students** database, and then exit Access.

CASE PROBLEMS

Case 1. Lim's Video Photography Youngho Lim owns a videography business, Lim's Video Photography. Located in San Francisco, California, the company specializes in digital video photography and offers customers the option of storing edited videos on CD or DVD. His video shoots include weddings and other special events, as well as recording personal and commercial inventories for insurance purposes. Youngho created an Access database named **Clients** to store data about his clients. He asks you to make changes to the design of the **Client** and **Shoot** tables in this database, to create several new queries, and to create a new form. You'll do so by completing the following steps.

1. Make sure your Data Disk is in the appropriate disk drive, start Access, and then open the **Clients** database in the Cases folder on your Data Disk.

2. Open the **Shoot** table in Design view. Change the ShootType field data type to Lookup Wizard. Look up values in the **ShootDesc** table, select the ShootType and ShootDesc fields from the **ShootDesc** table, use the label ShootDesc, and accept all other Lookup Wizard default choices. View the **Shoot** table datasheet, resize the ShootDesc column to its best fit, and then save and close the table.

3. Use the Input Mask Wizard to add an input mask to the Phone field in the **Client** table. Select the Phone Number input mask, and then click the Finish button. Change the default input mask to 999\/000\-0000. Test the input mask by typing over an existing Phone field value, being sure not to change the value by pressing the Esc key after you type the last digit in the Phone field.

4. Change the first record in the **Client** table datasheet so the ClientName field value is your name in the format: last name, comma, space, first name. Close the table.

5. Create a query to find all records in the **Client** table in which the Phone field value begins with 415. Include all fields from the **Client** table in the query results. Save the query as **415 Area Codes**, run the query, print the query results, and then close the query.

6. Create a query to find all records in the **Shoot** table in which the ShootDesc field value is AP, BP, or WE. Use a list-of-values match for the selection criterion, and include all fields from the **Shoot** table in the query results. Sort the query in ascending order by ShootDate and then in ascending order by ShootTime. Save the query as **Milestone Celebrations**, run the query, and then print the query results in landscape orientation. Keep the query open.

7. Modify the query you created in Step 6. Use the modified query to find all records in the **Shoot** table in which the ShootDesc value is not any of: AP, BP, or WE. Save the query as **Not Milestone Celebrations**, run the query, print the query results in landscape orientation, and then close the query.

8. Create a parameter query to select the **Shoot** table records for a ShootType field value that the user specifies. (*Hint:* Use the ShootDesc field from the Shoot table as the parameter field.) Include all fields from the **Shoot** table and the ContractAmt field from the **Contract** table in the query results. Save the query as **Shoot Type Parameter**. Run the query and enter SE as the ShootType field value. Print the query results in landscape orientation, and then close the query.

9. Use Figure 5-55 and the following steps to create a multi-page form based on the **Client** and **Contract** tables.

Figure 5-55

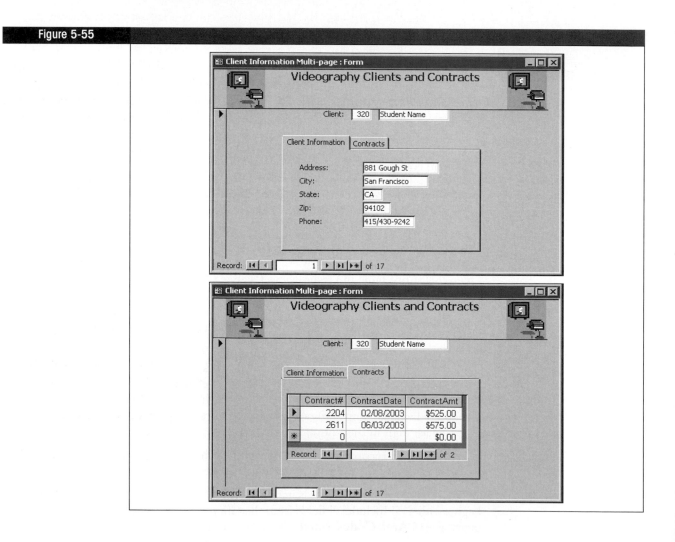

a. Place the Client# and ClientName fields from the **Client** table at the top of the Detail section. Delete the ClientName label, and change the caption for the Client# label to Client:.

b. Insert a Form Header section, but not a Form Footer section, in the form. Place a title label in the Form Header section. Enter the title and change its font to 12 points and bold.

c. Place the **TVandVCR** picture in the Form Header section to the right of the title. The file containing this picture is in the Cases folder on your Data Disk. Next, copy the picture, paste it to the left of the title, and then resize the section.

d. Place a tab control below the Client label in the Detail section. On the first page of the tab control, place the remaining fields from the **Client** table. Resize the text boxes to appropriate widths.

e. On the second page of the tab control, place a subform based on the **Contract** table, and include all fields except the Client# field from the table in the subform. Save the subform as **Contract Subform**.

f. Change the Caption property for each tab, and delete the subform label.

g. Resize the form, the tab control, and the subform. In Form view, resize all datasheet columns to their best fit.

h. Save the form as **Client Information Multi-page**.

i. View the form, print both pages for the first record, and then close the form.

10. Close the **Clients** database, and then exit Access.

Case 2. DineAtHome.course.com   DineAtHome.course.com in Naples, Florida, is an online service that lets people order meals from one or more area restaurants and delivers the meals to their homes. Participating restaurants offer everything from simple fare to gourmet feasts. Claire Picard, founder and owner, and her staff perform a variety of services, from simply picking up and delivering the meals to providing linens and table service for more formal occasions. Claire created the **Delivery** database to maintain information about participating restaurants and orders placed by customers. To make the database easier to use, Claire wants you to make changes to its design, create several queries, and design two new forms. To do so, you'll complete the following steps.

1. Make sure your Data Disk is in the appropriate disk drive, start Access, and then open the **Delivery** database in the Cases folder on your Data Disk.

2. Use the Input Mask Wizard to add an input mask to the OrderDate field in the **Order** table. Select the Short Date input mask, and then click the Finish button. Modify the default Short Date input mask by changing the two slashes to dashes. Next, set the Format property for the OrderDate field to mm-dd-yyyy. Test the input mask by typing over an existing OrderDate field value, being sure not to change the value by pressing the Esc key after you type the last digit in the OrderDate field. Resize the OrderDate column to its best fit, and then save and close the table.

3. Define data validation criteria for the DeliveryCharge field in the **Restaurant** table. Acceptable field values for the DeliveryCharge field are 0, 8, 10, and 15. Enter the message, "Value must be 0, 8, 10, or 15", so it appears if a user enters an invalid DeliveryCharge field value. Save your table changes and then test the data validation criteria for the DeliveryCharge field; make sure the field values are the same as they were before you tested.

4. Modify the first record in the **Restaurant** table datasheet by changing the OwnerFirstName and OwnerLastName field values to your name. Close the table.

5. Create a query to find all records in the **Order** table in which the Restaurant# field value is 108, 115, or 133. Use a list-of-values match for the selection criterion, and include all fields from the **Order** table in the query results. Sort the query in descending order by OrderAmt. Save the query as **Selected Restaurants**, run the query, and then print the query results. Keep the query open.

6. Modify the query you created in Step 5. Use the modified query to find all records in the **Order** table in which the Restaurant# field value is not any of: 108, 115, or 133. Save the query as **Selected Restaurants Modified**, run the query, print the query results, and then close the query.

7. Modify the **Marco Island Restaurants** query to select all records in which the City field value is Marco Island or Naples and the TakeoutOnly field value is No. Save the query as **Marco Island and Naples Restaurants**, run the query, print the query results, and then close the query.

8. Create a parameter query to select the **Restaurant** table records for a City field value that the user specifies. Include all fields from the **Restaurant** table in the query results, except for the State, Website, and TakeoutOnly fields. Save the query as **Restaurant City Parameter**. Run the query and enter Naples as the City field value. Print the first page of the query results in landscape orientation, and then close the query.

Explore ▶ 9. Create a custom form based on the **Large Orders** query. Display all fields from the query in the form. Create your own design for the form. Add a label to the bottom of the Detail section, and enter your name in the label. Change the label's font so that your name appears in bold blue text. Change the OrderAmt text box format so that the field value appears in bold red text. Save the form as **Large Orders**. In Form view, print the first record.

10. Use Filter By Form with the **Large Orders** form to select all orders placed in Naples or East Naples for more than $110. Apply the filter. How many records are selected?

11. Print the first selected record. Save the filter as a query named **Large Orders Filter**. Close the form.

12. Create a multi-page custom form named **Restaurant Multi-page** based on the **Restaurant** and **Order** tables by completing the following steps.

   a. Place a title label in the Detail section at the top of the form. Enter the title Restaurants. Change the title label font to 24-point bold Bookman Old Style, and then resize the title label to fit.

   b. Place the **PlaceSet** picture at the top of the form to the right of the title label. The file containing this picture is in the Cases folder on your Data Disk.

   c. Place the Restaurant# and RestaurantName fields below the title label and picture.

Explore ▶ d. Change the Restaurant# and RestaurantName label and text box formats so that the label and field values appear as red text set in 12-point, bold Bookman Old Style. Make sure each control box is appropriately sized.

   e. On the first page of the tab control, display the other fields from the **Restaurant** table. Make sure all field text boxes are left-aligned, all labels are right-aligned, and each field text box is appropriately sized. Change the Caption property for the first tab to Restaurant Information.

   f. On the second page of the tab control, display all fields from the **Order** table, except for Restaurant#, in a subform named **Order Multi-page Subform**. Resize the subform, change the Caption property for the second tab to Order Information, delete the subform label, and then resize the subform columns to their best fit in Form view.

   g. View the form, print both pages for the first record, and then save and close the form.

Explore ▶ 13. Open the **Restaurant Multi-page** form, and save it as **Enhanced Restaurant Multi-page**. Make and save the following changes to the design of the new form.

   a. Change the background color of the form's Detail section to light blue.

   b. Use the Line/Border Width button to place a border (weight 2) around the title label.

   c. Use the Font/Fore Color button to change the color of the title label to red.

   d. Print both pages of the finished form for the first record, save your changes, and then close the form.

14. Close the **Delivery** database, and then exit Access.

Case 3. Redwood Zoo The Redwood Zoo is a small zoo located in the picturesque city of Gig Harbor, Washington, on the shores of Puget Sound. The Redwood Zoo has some of the best exhibits of marine animals in the United States. Its newly constructed polar bear habitat is a particular favorite among patrons. The zoo relies heavily on donations to fund both permanent exhibits and temporary displays, especially those involving exotic animals. Michael Rosenfeld, director of fundraising activities, created the **Donors** database to track information about donors, their pledges, and the status of funds. Michael wants you to make changes to the database design, create several queries, and design two new forms. To do so, you'll complete the following steps.

1. Make sure your Data Disk is in the appropriate disk drive, start Access, and then open the **Donors** database in the Cases folder on your Data Disk.

2. Open the **Pledge** table in Design view. Change the FundCode field data type to Lookup Wizard. Look up values in the **Fund** table, select the FundCode and FundName fields from the **Fund** table, use the label FundName, and accept all other Lookup Wizard default choices. View the **Pledge** table datasheet, resize the FundName column to its best fit, and then save and close the table.

3. Define data validation criteria for the Class field in the **Donor** table. Acceptable field values for the Class field are B, D, and P. Enter the message, "Value must be B, D, or P", that appears if a user enters an invalid Class field value. Save your table changes and then test the data validation criteria for the Class field; make sure the field values are the same as they were before you tested.

4. Modify the first record in the **Donor** table datasheet by changing the Title, FirstName, MI, and LastName field values to your title and name. Close the table.

5. Create a query to find all records in the **Pledge** table in which the PaymentSchedule field value is M, Q, or S. Use a list-of-values match for the selection criterion, and include all fields from the **Pledge** table in the query results. Save the query as **Selected Payment Schedules**, run the query, and then print the query results in landscape orientation. Keep the query open.

6. Modify the query you created in Step 5. Use the modified query to find all records in the **Pledge** table in which the PaymentSchedule field value is not any of: M, Q, or S. Save the query as **Selected Payment Schedules Modified**, run the query, print the query results in landscape orientation, and then close the query.

7. Create a query to select all records from the **Pledge** table with fund codes of B11 or P15 in which the payment method is either C or E. (*Hint:* Use the FundName field from the Pledge table to set the criterion for fund codes.) Display all fields in the query results. Save the query as **Paid Bear Fund Pledges**, run the query, print the query results in landscape orientation, and then close the query.

8. Create a parameter query to select the **Pledge** table records for a FundCode field value that the user specifies. (*Hint:* Use the FundName field from the Pledge table as the parameter field.) Include all fields from the **Pledge** table in the query results. Save the query as **Fund Code Parameter**. Run the query and enter W13 as the FundCode field value. Print the query results in landscape orientation, and then close the query.

Explore 9. Create a custom form based on the **Costs** query. Display all fields in the form. Use your own design for the form. Change the FundName label and text box format, so the label and field values appear in 12-point bold, blue text on a yellow background. Add your name to the bottom of the form. Save the form as **Costs**, view the form, print the first record, and then close the form.

10. Close the **Donors** database, and then exit Access.

Case 4. Mountain River Adventures Connor and Siobhan Dempsey own Mountain River Adventures center, which offers clients their choice of outdoor activities, including white-water rafting, canoeing, hiking, camping, fishing, and rock climbing. To track their clients and bookings, they created the **Outdoors** database. Connor and Siobhan want you to make changes to the design of the database, create several queries, and design two new forms. To do so, you'll complete the following steps.

1. Make sure your Data Disk is in the appropriate disk drive, start Access, and then open the **Outdoors** database in the Cases folder on your Data Disk.

2. Open the **Booking** table in Design view. Change the Trip# field data type to Lookup Wizard. Look up values in the **Rafting Trip** table; select the Trip#, River, and Fee/Person fields from the **Rafting Trip** table; use the label River; and accept all other Lookup Wizard default choices. View the **Booking** table datasheet, resize the River column to its best fit, and then save and close the table.

3. Use the Input Mask Wizard to add an input mask to the Phone field in the **Client** table. Select the Phone Number input mask, and then click the Finish button. Change the default input mask to 999\-000\-0000. Test the input mask by typing over an existing Phone field value, being sure not to change the value by pressing the Esc key after you type the last digit in the Phone field.

4. Change the first record in the **Client** table datasheet, so the ClientName field value is your name in the format: last name, comma, space, first name. Close the table.

5. Create a query to find all records in the **Rafting Trip** table in which the River field value starts with the word Arkansas. Include all fields in the query results. Save the query as **Arkansas Trips**, run the query, and then print the query results. Keep the query open.

6. Modify the query you created in Step 5. Use the modified query to find all records in the **Rafting Trip** table in which the River field value starts with a word other than Arkansas. Save the query as **Non-Arkansas Trips**, run the query, print the query results, and then close the query.

7. Create a query to find all records in the **Client** table where the State/Prov field value is NE, UT, or WY. Use a list-of-values match for the selection criterion, and include all fields from the **Client** table in the query results. Save the query as **Selected Clients**, run the query, print the query results in landscape orientation, and then close the query.

8. Create a parameter query to select the **Client** table records for a State/Prov field value that the user specifies. Include all fields from the **Client** table in the query results. Save the query as **State/Prov Parameter**. Run the query and enter CO as the State/Prov field value. Print the query results in landscape orientation, and then close the query.

Explore ▶ 9. Create a custom form based on the **Costs** query. Display all fields in the form. Use your own design for the form, but place the title "Booked Trips," the **Kayak** picture (found in the Cases folder on your Data Disk), and your name in the Form Header section. Change the Booking# label and text box format so that the label and field value appear in 12-point bold text on a light blue background. Save the form as **Costs**, view the form, and then print the first form record.

10. Use Filter By Form with the **Costs** form to select all records that have a Fee/Person value of over $100 or include trips on the Arkansas River. Apply the filter. How many records does the filter select?

11. Print the first record. Save the filter as a query named **Costs Filter**, and then close the form.

12. Create a multi-page custom form named **Client Multi-page** based on the **Client** and **Booking** tables by completing the following steps.

   a. Place the ClientName field in the Detail section of the form.

   b. On the first page of a tab control, display the other fields from the **Client** table. Make sure each field text box is an appropriate size. Change the Caption property for the first tab to Client Information.

   c. On the second page of the tab control, display all fields from the **Booking** table in a subform named **Booking Multi-page Subform**. Resize the subform, change the Caption property for the second tab to Booking Information, delete the subform label, and resize the subform columns to their best fit.

   d. View the form, print both pages for the first record, and then save and close the form.

13. Make a copy of the **Client Multi-page** form, and save it as **Client Multi-page Enhanced**. Make the following changes to the design of the new form.

   a. Change the background color of the Detail section of the form (except the subform) to light blue.

   b. Use the Line/Border Width button to place a border (weight 2) around the ClientName label and field-value text box. Change the font size and weight for these controls, so that they stand out. Resize these controls, if necessary.

   c. Use the Font/Fore Color button to change the color of the Phone field value to red.

   d. Use the Special Effect button on the Form Design toolbar to change the display of the **Booking Multi-page Subform** subform to raised.

   e. Print both pages of the finished form for the first record, and then save and close the form.

14. Close the **Outdoors** database, and then exit Access.

Explore

Case 5. eACH Internet Auction Site Chris and Pat Aquino own a successful ISP (Internet service provider) and want to expand their business to host an Internet auction site. The auction site will let sellers offer items for sale, such as antiques, first-edition books, vintage dolls, coins, art, stamps, glass bottles, autographs, and sports memorabilia. After a seller posts an item for sale, the auction site sells it to the buyer who places the highest bid. Before people can sell and bid on items, they must register with the auction site. Each item will be listed by subcategory within a general category, so bidders can easily find items of interest. For example, the general category of antiques might consist of several subcategories, including ancient world, musical instruments, and general.

Chris and Pat registered their Web site name eACH, which stands for *electronic Auction Collectibles Host*. Now they need to create a database to track people registered, items for sale, and bids received for those items. The process of creating a complete database—including all fields, tables, relationships, queries, forms, and other database objects—for eACH is an enormous undertaking. So you start with just a few database components, and then you will create additional objects in subsequent tutorials.

Complete the following steps to create the database and its initial objects:

1. Read the appendix titled "Relational Databases and Database Design" at the end of this book.

2. Use your Web browser to gather information about other Internet auction sites, so that you become familiar with common rules and requirements, categories and subcategories, fields and their attributes, and entities. (*Hint:* Yahoo (www.yahoo.com) lists names of several auction sites, and eBay (www.ebay.com) is a popular Internet auction site.)

3. The initial database structure includes the following relations and fields.

   a. The **Category** relation includes a unique category number and a category (the category name or description).

   b. The **Subcategory** relation includes a unique subcategory number, subcategory name or description, and a category number.

    c. The **Registrant** relation includes a unique registrant number, last name, first name, middle initial, phone number, e-mail address, optional user ID, and password. Each person registers once and then can sell and bid on items.

    d. The **Item** relation includes a unique item number, the registrant who's selling the item, the subcategory number, a title (a short item description), a description (a fuller item description), a quantity (the number of identical items being sold separately, if there are more than one), a minimum bid amount in whole dollars, a duration (the number of days the site will accept bids for the item), an optional reserve price amount in whole dollars (the lowest sale price acceptable to the seller; this is not made available to bidders), and the date and time bidding started on the item.

4. Use the information in Step 3 to draw an entity-relationship diagram showing the entities (relations) and the relationships between the entities.

5. Build on Steps 3 and 4, creating on paper the initial database design for the eACH system. For each relation, identify all primary and foreign keys. For each field, determine attributes, such as data type, field size, and validation rules.

6. Create the database structure using Access. Use the database name **eACH**, and save the database in the Cases folder on your Data Disk. Create the tables with their fields. Be sure to set each field's properties correctly, select a primary key for each table, and then define the relationships between appropriate tables.

7. For each table, create a form that you'll use to view, add, edit, and delete records in that table.

8. For tables with one-to-many relationships, create a form with a main form for the primary table and a subform for the related table.

9. Design test data for each table in the database. You can research Internet auction sites to collect realistic values for categories, subcategories, and other fields, if necessary. Make sure your test data covers common situations. For example, your text data should include at least two sellers with multiple items for sale, one seller selling items in the same subcategory, another seller selling items in different subcategories, and at least one seller who currently has no items for sale. Each table should have at least 10 records. Include your name as one of the registrants, and include at least two items that you're selling.

10. Add the test data to your tables using the forms you created in Steps 7 and 8.

11. Open each table datasheet, resize all datasheet columns to their best fit, and then print each datasheet.

12. Set the option so Access compacts the **eACH** database when you close it.

13. Use the Input Mask Wizard to add an appropriate input mask to one field in any table. Print the table's datasheet after adding the input mask.

14. Define data validation criteria for any one field in any table. Make sure to set both the Validation Rule and the Validation Text properties for the field.

15. For one of the foreign key fields in one of the tables, change the field's data type to Lookup Wizard. (*Hint*: Before you change the data type to Lookup Wizard, you must delete the relationship for which the field serves as the foreign key.) If necessary, resize the table datasheet, and then print the datasheet.

16. Create, test, save, and print one parameter query.

17. Close the **eACH** database, and then exit Access.

INTERNET ASSIGNMENTS

Student Union

The purpose of the Internet Assignments is to challenge you to find information on the Internet that you can use to create effective documents. The actual assignments are updated and maintained on the Course Technology Web site. Log on to the Internet and use your Web browser to go to the Student Online Companion to accompany this text at **www.course.com/NewPerspectives/studentunion**. Click the Access link, and then click the link for Tutorial 5.

QUICK CHECK ANSWERS

Session 5.1

1. A Lookup Wizard field lets you select a value from a list of possible values, making data entry easier.
2. If two tables have a one-to-many relationship, when you display the primary table in Datasheet view, you can use a subdatasheet to display and edit the records from the related table.
3. input mask
4. The Validation Rule property specifies the valid values that users can enter in a field. For example, you could use this property to specify that users can enter only positive numeric values in a numeric field.
5. The Validation Text property value appears in a message box if the user violates the validation rule. For example, you could display the message, "Must be a positive integer", if the user enters a value less than or equal to zero.
6. Like
7. The asterisk is a wildcard that represents any string of characters in a pattern match query.
8. Use the In comparison operator to define a condition with two or more values.
9. Use the Not logical operator to negate a condition.
10. Use a parameter query when you want to prompt the user to enter the selection criterion when the query runs.

Session 5.2

1. A bound control is linked to a field in the underlying table or query; an unbound control is not.
2. grid
3. toolbox
4. move
5. Position the pointer anywhere on the border of the control (except not on a move or sizing handle), and then drag the control and its attached label.
6. Right-click the label, click Properties on the shortcut menu, click the All tab, edit the existing label in the Caption text box, or double-click it to select the current value, and then type a new caption.

7. Select the control, position the pointer on a sizing handle, and then drag the pointer in the appropriate direction to the new location.

8. The Form Header section lets you add titles, instructions, command buttons, and other information to the top of your form. This section of the form does not change as you navigate through the records.

9. Open the form in Design view, click the Image tool on the toolbox, position the pointer at the location for the upper-left corner of the picture, click the mouse button, select the picture file, and then click the OK button.

Session 5.3

1. Open the form in Design view, click the Tab Control tool on the toolbox, position the pointer in the form at the location for the upper-left corner of the tab control, and then click the mouse button.

2. Click a label, press and hold down the Shift key, click the other labels, release the Shift key, click Format on the menu bar, point to Align, and then click the appropriate alignment option.

3. Filter By Form finds records that match multiple selection criteria using the same Access logical and comparison operators that you use in queries.

4. Save the filter as a query, and then apply the query to an open form.

5. Opening a query runs the query and displays the results in Datasheet view. Applying a query to a form opens the query and displays the results in the open form.

OBJECTIVES

In this tutorial you will:

- Design and create a custom report

- Assign a conditional value to a calculated field

- Sort and group data in a report

- Add, move, resize, and align controls in a report

- Modify control properties

- Add a subreport to a main report

- Add lines to a report

- Hide duplicate values in a report

- Add calculated controls to a report

- Calculate group and overall totals in a report

- Define conditional formatting rules

- Use domain aggregate functions

- Add the date, page numbers, and title to a report

- Create and modify mailing labels

CREATING CUSTOM REPORTS

Creating a Potential Income Report

CASE

Northeast Seasonal Jobs International (NSJI)

At a recent staff meeting, Elsa Jensen indicated that she would like a new report created for the Jobs database. She wants a printed list of all positions for all NSJI employer clients. She also wants subtotals of the placement fee and potential income amounts from each employer and a grand total for all potential income amounts.

In this tutorial, you will create the report for Elsa. In building the report, you will use many Access report customization features—such as grouping data, adding a subreport, calculating totals, and adding lines to separate report sections. These features will enhance Elsa's report and make it easier to read.

SESSION 6.1

In this session, you will create a custom report. You will review two existing queries and create a new query that includes calculated fields and assigns conditional values. You will also add a Group Header section to the report and specify the sorting and grouping fields for the records. Finally, you will add, move, resize, and align controls in the report and change their captions and Can Grow properties.

Creating a Custom Report

A **report** is the formatted, printed contents of one or more tables from a database. Although you can format and print data using datasheets, queries, and forms, reports offer you greater flexibility and provide a more professional, custom appearance. For example, NSJI can create customized reports for billing statements and mailing labels.

An Access report is divided into sections. Each report can have the seven different sections described in Figure 6-1.

Figure 6-1	ACCESS REPORT SECTIONS
REPORT SECTION	**DESCRIPTION**
Report Header	Appears once at the beginning of a report. Use it for report titles, company logos, report introductions, and cover pages.
Page Header	Appears at the top of each page of a report. Use it for column headings, report titles, page numbers, and report dates. If your report has a Report Header section, it precedes the first Page Header section.
Group Header	Appears at the beginning of each new group of records. Use it to print the group name and the field value that all records in the group have in common. A report can have up to 10 grouping levels.
Detail	Appears once for each record in the underlying table or query. Use it to print selected fields from the table or query and to print calculated values.
Group Footer	Appears at the end of each group of records. It is usually used to print totals for the group.
Report Footer	Appears once at the end of the report. Use it for report totals and other summary information.
Page Footer	Appears at the bottom of each page of a report. Use it for page numbers and brief explanations of symbols or abbreviations. If your report has a Report Footer section, it precedes the Page Footer section on the last page of the report.

You don't have to include all seven sections in a report. When you design your report, you determine which sections to include and what information to place in each section. Figure 6-2 shows a sample report produced from the Jobs database; it includes all seven sections.

| Figure 6-2 | SAMPLE REPORT SHOWING THE SEVEN SECTIONS OF A REPORT |

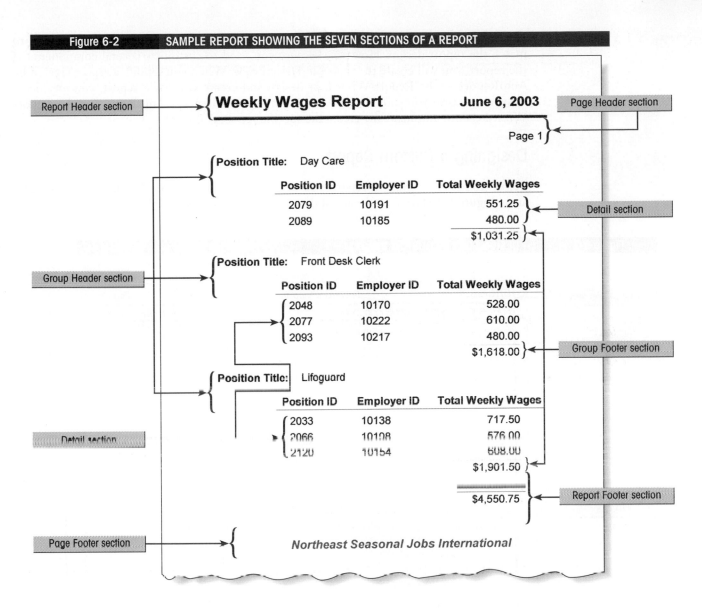

The report you need to create for Elsa will list the records for all employers and their positions. Elsa wants the report to group employers by values in the NAICSDesc field. The report will contain four sections:

- A Page Header section will show the current date, report title, and page number.
- A Group Header section will print the NAICS description and code.
- A Detail section will list all field values from the Employer table. Records within each NAICS group will appear in ascending order by employer name. Then for each employer's positions, the position title and ID, number of openings, and placement fee amount will print in ascending order by position title.
- A Report Footer section will print the grand total of the potential income amount.

From your work with AutoReport and the Report Wizard, you know that, by default, Access places the report title in the Report Header section and the date and page number in the Page Footer section. Elsa prefers the date, report title, and page number to appear at the top of each page, so you need to place this information in the Page Header section.

You could use the Report Wizard to create the report and then modify the report to match the report design. However, because you need to customize several components of the report, you will create the report in Design view. When you modify a report created by AutoReport or the Report Wizard, or design and create your own report, you produce a **custom report**. You should create a custom report whenever AutoReport or the Report Wizard cannot automatically create the specific report you need.

Designing a Custom Report

Before you create a custom report, you should first plan the report's contents and appearance. Figure 6-3 shows the design of the report you will create for Elsa.

Figure 6-3   DESIGN FOR THE CUSTOM REPORT

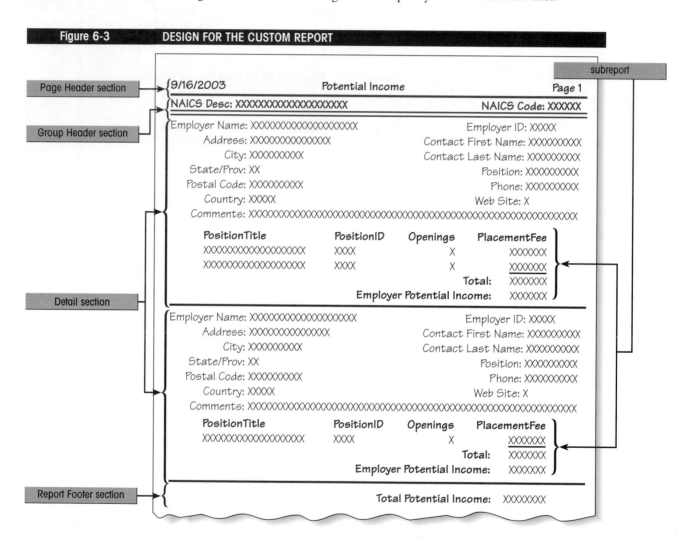

The Page Header section contains the report title ("Potential Income") centered between the current date on the left and the page number on the right. A thick blue horizontal line separates this section from the rest of the report page.

The NAICS description and code will appear in the Group Header section. Two thin, blue horizontal lines separate this section from the Detail section that follows.

In the Detail section, a series of Xs indicates the locations and relative lengths of the field values. The label for a field value will print to its left in the top portion of the Detail section and above the field value in the bottom portion of the Detail section. Employers with specific

NAICS codes will print in ascending order by employer name; a thick blue horizontal line will print at the bottom of the Detail section to separate each employer and its positions from the next employer's data. The position data in the Detail section will appear in a **subreport**, a report contained within another report.

The PlacementFee field in the Detail section is a calculated field based on the Openings, Hours/Week, and Wage field values in the Position table. The total for an employer's PlacementFee field values will appear in the Detail section after the employer's positions. Finally, two potential income values—a subtotal in the Detail section for each employer's positions and an overall total in the Report Footer section—will be calculated fields.

Reviewing and Creating Queries for a Custom Report

How does NSJI make the money it needs to run its business? It charges its employer clients a fee for each position filled. NSJI calculates this placement fee by multiplying the weekly wages for a position by two. Because the database does not contain a position's weekly wage amount, NSJI calculates the weekly wage value by multiplying the Hours/Week and Wage fields in the Position table. In addition to the placement fee, NSJI charges each employer a one-time search fee based on the total number of openings filled. For fewer than three openings filled, NSJI charges a $500 search fee; NSJI reduces the search fee to $200 if it fills three or more openings. Combining the search fee with the total placement fees for an employer produces the total income from the employer. The report you'll create for Elsa will show the placement fees and total income for each employer with the assumption that NSJI will fill all available openings for all positions. For this reason, the employer and overall income printed are considered potential income amounts.

The source data for a report (or form) can come from a single table, from a single query based on one or more tables, or from multiple tables and/or queries. Your report will contain data from the Employer, NAICS, and Position tables, but the report requirements are complicated enough that you'll need a total of three queries to supply the needed data. Elsa has already created two queries: the NAICS and Employers query and the Potential Placement Fees query. You'll create the third: the Potential Income by Employer query.

The first existing query, the NAICS and Employers query, lists all fields from the NAICS and Employer tables. This query will supply the data for the report's Group Header section and for the employer data in the Detail section.

The second existing query, the Potential Placement Fees query, lists the PositionID, PositionTitle, Openings, and EmployerID fields from the Position table. This query will provide the source data for the report's Detail section subreport, which is where the position data for an employer will print. The subreport also includes the PlacementFee column, which will print the calculated results of multiplying the Openings, Hours/Week, and Wage fields in the Position table by two. You can create a calculated field on a form or report, but then you wouldn't be able to calculate subtotals by employer and a grand total for the calculated field. However, you can calculate totals on a form or report for any field, including calculated fields, from a table or query used as the basis for the form or report. Because Elsa wants subtotals by employer for the PlacementFee field values on her report, the existing Potential Placement Fees query already includes the PlacementFee calculated field.

In most situations, the two existing queries would be the only data sources needed for Elsa's report. However, the report will list all employers, even those with no currently available positions. Elsa's report will not print the subreport for these employers for two reasons. First, printing a position-related column heading line and a subtotal in the subreport without any detail position data doesn't make sense and wouldn't look attractive. Second, for those employers without positions, Access will generate a data error for the subreport subtotals because Access doesn't let you calculate statistics when there are no records upon which to base the calculations. Because the subreport will not be printed for all employers, Access will generate a data error if you base your calculation for the grand total potential income on the individual employer potential incomes. Thus, you'll create a third query to serve as the source for the grand total of the new report's potential income value.

The query you'll create will be based on data from the Position table. It will be a statistical query, which you'll save as Potential Income by Employer, that will list the total number of openings, total placement fees, and total potential income by employer for those clients with available positions.

Before creating the new query, you'll review the two queries that Elsa already created for the report.

To review the NAICS and Employers query:

1. Place your Data Disk in the appropriate disk drive.

2. Start Access and open the **Jobs** database located in the Tutorial folder on your Data Disk.

3. Maximize the Database window, and then open the **NAICS and Employers** query. Forty-five records—one for each record in the Employer table—appear in the recordset.

4. Scroll right to view the fields in the recordset, and then switch to Design view. See Figure 6-4.

Figure 6-4   **NAICS AND EMPLOYERS QUERY IN DESIGN VIEW**

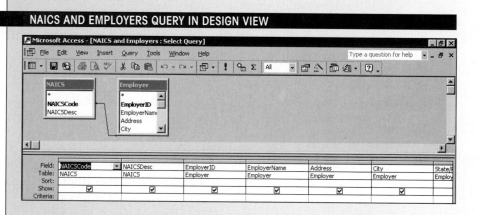

The NAICS and Employer tables are the source tables for the query. Both fields from the NAICS table—NAICSCode and NAICSDesc—appear in the design grid, as do all fields from the Employer table, except for the common NAICSCode field, which would be redundant if included in the query.

5. Close the query, and then restore the Database window.

Next, you'll review the design and recordset for the Potential Placement Fees query, the second query Elsa developed for the new report.

To review the Potential Placement Fees query:

1. Open the **Potential Placement Fees** query in Design view. The PositionID, PositionTitle, Openings, and EmployerID fields from the Position table appear in the design grid, along with the PlacementFee field, a calculated field.

2. Right-click the **PlacementFee Field** text box, click **Zoom** on the shortcut menu, and then position the insertion point to the right of the expression in the Zoom dialog box. See Figure 6-5.

Figure 6-5	CALCULATED FIELD IN THE ZOOM DIALOG BOX

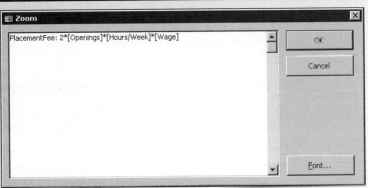

The **Zoom dialog box** has a large text box for entering text, expressions, and other values. The PlacementFee calculated field entry in the Zoom dialog box determines an employer's placement fee for a position by multiplying the weekly wages (Hours/Week field times the Wage field) by two, and then multiplying by the number of openings (Openings field) for the position.

3. Click the **OK** button, and then run the query. The recordset displays the four fields from the Position table and the calculated field, PlacementFee. See Figure 6-6.

Figure 6-6	RECORDSET DISPLAYING THE CALCULATED FIELD

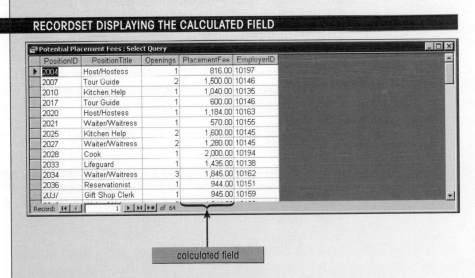

calculated field

4. Close the query, and then click the **No** button when asked if you want to save design changes to the query.

Next, you'll create the final query needed for Elsa's report.

Assigning a Conditional Value to a Calculated Field

You'll create the Potential Income by Employer query to list the total number of openings, total placement fees, and total potential income by employer. For the total potential income field calculation, you'll need to add either $200 (if the total number of openings is three or greater) or $500 (if the total number of openings is less than three) to an employer's total placement fees. To permit the calculated field to be one of two values based on a condition, you'll use the IIf function. The **IIf function** lets you assign one value to a calculated field or control if a condition is true, and a second value if the condition is false. The format of the IIf function you'll use is: *IIf (TotalOpenings>=3, PlacementFee+200, PlacementFee+500)*. You interpret this function as: If the TotalOpenings field value is greater than or equal to 3, then set the calculated field value equal to the sum of the PlacementFee field value and 200; otherwise, set the calculated field value equal to the sum of the PlacementFee field value and 500.

Now you are ready to create the statistical query.

To create the Potential Income by Employer query:

1. Double-click **Create query in Design view**, double-click **Position** in the Show Table dialog box, and then click the **Close** button.

   You need to add the EmployerID and Openings fields from the Position field list to the design grid, change the query to a statistical query, and then add two calculated fields—one to calculate the placement fees for an employer, and the other to calculate the potential income from the employer.

2. Add the **EmployerID** field to the first column of the design grid, add the **Openings** field to the second column of the design grid, and then click the **Totals** button Σ on the Query Design toolbar.

   Because you need the statistics grouped by employer, you'll use the default Group By operator for the EmployerID field. For the Openings field, you need to determine the total number of openings, so you'll use the Sum aggregate function and then enter the field name TotalOpenings.

3. Click the right side of the **Openings Total** text box, click **Sum**, position the insertion point to the left of Openings in the second column's Field text box, and then type **TotalOpenings:** (Make sure you type the colon.)

   Next, you'll add to the design grid's third column the PlacementFee calculated field that determines an employer's total placement fee. Once again, you'll use the Sum aggregate function for the calculated field that will multiply the product of the Openings, Hours/Week, and Wage fields in the Position table by two.

4. Right-click the **Field** text box in the third column, and then click **Zoom** on the shortcut menu.

   Because brackets must enclose field names containing spaces or special characters, you'll need to enclose the expression's Hours/Week field in brackets. If you omit brackets for other field names, Access adds them automatically when you close the Zoom dialog box.

5. Type **PlacementFee: 2*Openings*[Hours/Week]*Wage**. See Figure 6-7.

Figure 6-7 | **EXPRESSION FOR THE PlacementFee CALCULATED FIELD**

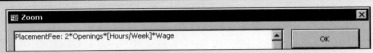

TROUBLE? If your calculated field differs from that shown in Figure 6-7, correct it so it matches.

The expression for the PlacementFee calculated field is the same as the expression in Elsa's Potential Placement Fees query for its PlacementFee calculated field.

6. Click the **OK** button, click the right side of the **PlacementFee Total** text box, and then click **Sum**.

Finally, you'll add to the design grid's fourth column the PotentialIncome calculated field that will determine an employer's total potential income using the IIf function.

7. Right-click the **Field** text box in the fourth column, click **Zoom** on the shortcut menu, and then type **PotentialIncome: IIf (TotalOpenings>=3, PlacementFee+200, PlacementFee+500)**. See Figure 6-8.

Figure 6-8 | **EXPRESSION FOR THE PotentialIncome CALCULATED FIELD**

For calculated fields that include functions, such as the IIf function, you must set the field's Total property to Expression.

8. Click the **OK** button, click the right side of the **PotentialIncome Total** text box, scroll down the list, and then click **Expression**.

9. Save the query as **Potential Income by Employer**, run the query, resize each column in the recordset to its best fit, and then deselect the columns. The recordset displays the statistical query that includes the two calculated fields for each employer with available positions in the Position table. See Figure 6-9.

Figure 6-9   RECORDSET DISPLAYING THE STATISTICAL QUERY

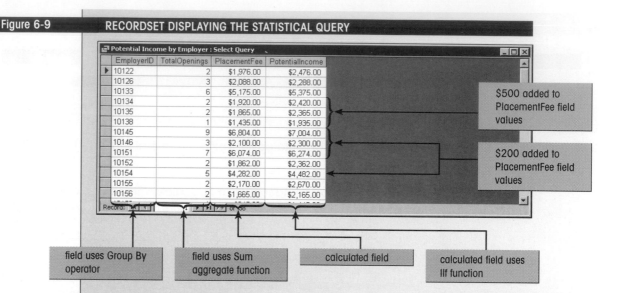

Records 4, 5, and 6 have PotentialIncome field values of $500 more than their PlacementFee field values because their TotalOpenings field values are less than three. Records with TotalOpenings field values equal to three or greater, such as records 7, 8, 9, and 11, have PotentialIncome field values of $200 more than their PlacementFee field values.

10. Save and then close the query.

You are now ready to create Elsa's report. To do so, you need to display a blank report in Design view.

Report Window in Design View

The Report window in Design view is similar to the Form window in Design view, which you used in Tutorial 5 to create a custom form.

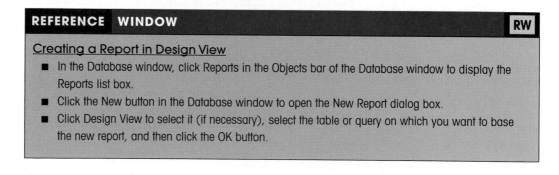

REFERENCE WINDOW   RW

Creating a Report in Design View
- In the Database window, click Reports in the Objects bar of the Database window to display the Reports list box.
- Click the New button in the Database window to open the New Report dialog box.
- Click Design View to select it (if necessary), select the table or query on which you want to base the new report, and then click the OK button.

The main source for the report you are creating is the NAICS and Employers query that you reviewed earlier in this tutorial. To begin, you need to create a blank report in Design view.

To create a blank report in Design view:

1. Click **Reports** in the Objects bar of the Database window to display the Reports list box, and then click the **New** button in the Database window to open the New Report dialog box.

2. Click **Design View** (if necessary), click the list arrow to display the list of tables and queries in the Jobs database, scroll down and click **NAICS and Employers** to select this query as the basis for your report, and then click the **OK** button. The Report window in Design view opens and displays a blank report.

3. Click the **Maximize** button ☐ on the Report window. See Figure 6-10.

Figure 6-10	REPORT WINDOW IN DESIGN VIEW

docked toolbox

Page Header section

Detail section

Page Footer section

Field List button

Toolbox button

field list

Properties button

Sorting and Grouping button

TROUBLE? If the rulers, grid, or toolbox do not appear, click View on the menu bar, and then click Ruler, Grid, or Toolbox to display the missing component. If the grid still does not appear, see your instructor or technical support person for assistance. If the toolbox is not positioned as shown in Figure 6-10, click the Toolbox window's title bar, and then drag it into position.

TROUBLE? If the field list does not appear, click the Field List 🗉 button on the Report Design toolbar to display it. If the field list is not positioned and sized as shown in Figure 6-10, click the field list title bar, and then drag it to the position shown; use the mouse to resize the field list.

TROUBLE? If the Report Design toolbar or the Formatting toolbar does not appear, click View, point to Toolbars, and then click Report Design or Formatting (Form/Report) to display the missing toolbar.

> TROUBLE? If the Report Design and Formatting toolbars appear as one toolbar or if the Formatting toolbar is positioned above the Report Design toolbar, drag the Formatting toolbar move handle ▯ below the Report Design toolbar to the position shown in Figure 6-10.

Notice that the Report window in Design view has many of the same components as the Form window in Design view. For example, the Report Design toolbar includes a Properties button, a Field List button, and a Toolbox button. Both windows also have horizontal and vertical rulers, a grid, and a Formatting toolbar.

Unlike the Form window in Design view, which initially displays only the Detail section on a blank form, the Report window also displays a Page Header section and a Page Footer section. Reports often contain these sections, so Access automatically includes them in a blank report.

According to Elsa's plan for the report (see Figure 6-3), the NAICSDesc and NAICSCode fields from the NAICS and Employers query will appear in a Group Header section, and the remaining 13 fields from the query will appear in the Detail section. Before you can add the NAICSDesc and NAICSCode fields to the report, you need to create the Group Header section by specifying the NAICSDesc field as a grouping field.

Sorting and Grouping Data in a Report

Access lets you organize records in a report by sorting them using one or more sort keys. Each sort key can also be a grouping field. If you specify a sort key as a **grouping field**, you can include a Group Header section and a Group Footer section for the group. A Group Header section typically includes the name of the group, and a Group Footer section typically includes a count or subtotal for records in that group.

You use the Sorting and Grouping button on the Report Design toolbar to select sort keys and grouping fields for a report. Each report can have up to 10 sort fields, and any of its sort fields can also be grouping fields.

REFERENCE WINDOW | **RW**

Sorting and Grouping Data in a Report
- Display the report in Design view.
- Click the Sorting and Grouping button on the Report Design toolbar.
- Click the first Field/Expression list arrow in the Sorting and Grouping dialog box, and select the field to use as the primary sort key. In the Sort Order text box, select the sort order.
- Repeat the previous step to select secondary sorting keys and their sort orders as necessary.
- To group data, click the field in the Field/Expression text box by which you want to group records. In the Group Properties section, set the grouping options for the field.
- Click the Close button on the Sorting and Grouping dialog box to close it.

Elsa wants records listed in ascending order based on the NAICSDesc field; the NAICSDesc and NAICSCode field values print at the beginning of each NAICSDesc group. For these reasons, you need to specify the NAICSDesc field as both the primary sort key and the grouping field. Elsa also wants the employer data listed in ascending order by EmployerName within each NAICSDesc group. So, you need to specify the EmployerName field as the secondary sort key.

To select the sort keys and the group field:

1. Click the **Sorting and Grouping** button [≣] on the Report Design toolbar. The Sorting and Grouping dialog box opens.

   The top section of the Sorting and Grouping dialog box lets you specify the sort keys for the records in the Detail section. For each sort key, the Group Properties section of the dialog box lets you designate the sort key as a grouping field and specify whether you want a Group Header section, a Group Footer section, and other options for the group.

2. Click the list arrow in the first **Field/Expression** text box to display the list of available fields, and then click **NAICSDesc**. Ascending is the default sort order in the Sort Order text box, so you do not need to change this setting.

   You can now designate NAICSDesc as a grouping field and specify that you want a Group Header section for this group. This section will contain the NAICS description and code labels and field values.

3. Click the right side of the **Group Header** text box to display a list arrow and a list of values, and then click **Yes**. Access adds a Group Header section named NAICSDesc Header to the Report window. See Figure 6-11.

Figure 6-11	ADDING A GROUP HEADER SECTION

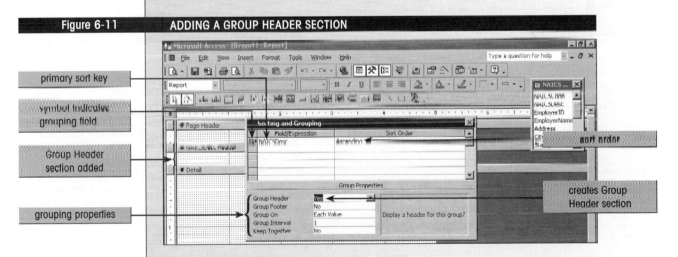

primary sort key

symbol indicates grouping field

Group Header section added

grouping properties

creates Group Header section

Notice the symbol placed to the left of the Field/Expression text box for NAICSDesc. That symbol indicates that you designated NAICSDesc as a grouping field.

You can now specify the secondary sort key and its sort order.

4. Click the right side of the second **Field/Expression** text box to display the list of fields, and then click **EmployerName**. Once again, you do not need to change the default sort order, so you've finished setting the sorting and grouping options for the main report.

5. Close the Sorting and Grouping dialog box.

Now that you've created the NAICSDesc Header section, you can add the fields from the field list to the correct sections of the report.

Adding Fields to a Report

Your next task is to add bound controls to the Group Header and Detail sections for all the fields from the NAICS and Employers query. Recall that a bound control displays field values from the table or query on which a form or report is based. You add bound controls to a report in the same way that you add them to a form.

REFERENCE WINDOW   **RW**

Adding Fields to a Report
- Display the report in Design view.
- If necessary, click the Field List button on the Report Design toolbar to display the field list.
- To place a single field on the report, position the pointer on the field name in the field list, drag the field name to the report, and then release the mouse button when the pointer is positioned correctly.
- To place all fields on the report, double-click the field list title bar to highlight them. Click anywhere in the highlighted area of the field list, and then drag the fields to the report. Release the mouse button when the pointer is positioned correctly.

First, you need to add bound controls for the NAICSCode and NAICSDesc fields to the Group Header section. Then you'll add bound controls for the other fields to the Detail section.

To add bound controls for all fields in the field list:

1. Click **NAICSCode** in the field list, hold down the **Shift** key, click **NAICSDesc** in the field list, and then release the **Shift** key to highlight both fields.

2. Click anywhere in the highlighted area of the field list (except the title bar), and then drag the fields to the NAICSDesc Header section. Release the mouse button when the pointer 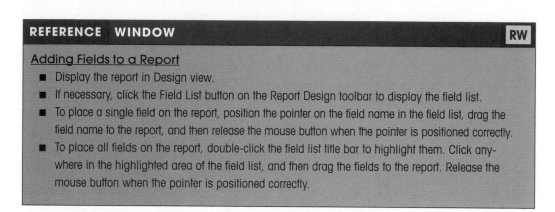 is positioned at the top of the NAICSDesc Header section and at the 3-inch mark on the horizontal ruler. You've added bound controls for the two selected fields. Each bound control consists of a text box and an attached label positioned to the left of the text box. See Figure 6-12. Notice that the text boxes are left aligned near the 3-inch mark; the labels are also left aligned.

   TROUBLE? If you did not position the bound controls properly in the NAICSDesc Header section, click the Undo button 🔄 on the Report Design toolbar, and then repeat Step 2. However, if the positioning of your controls differs just slightly from those shown in Figure 6-12, leave them where they are because you'll move all the controls later in this tutorial.

3. Double-click the field list title bar to highlight all the fields in the NAICS and Employers field list.

4. Hold down the **Ctrl** key, click **NAICSCode** in the field list, click **NAICSDesc** in the field list, and then release the **Ctrl** key. You've highlighted all fields in the field list, except the NAICSCode and NAICSDesc fields.

5. Drag the highlighted fields to the Detail section. Release the mouse button when the pointer 📋 is positioned at the top of the Detail section and at the 3-inch mark on the horizontal ruler. You've added bound controls to the Detail section for the 13 selected fields. See Figure 6-12.

Figure 6-12 | **ADDING BOUND CONTROLS TO THE REPORT**

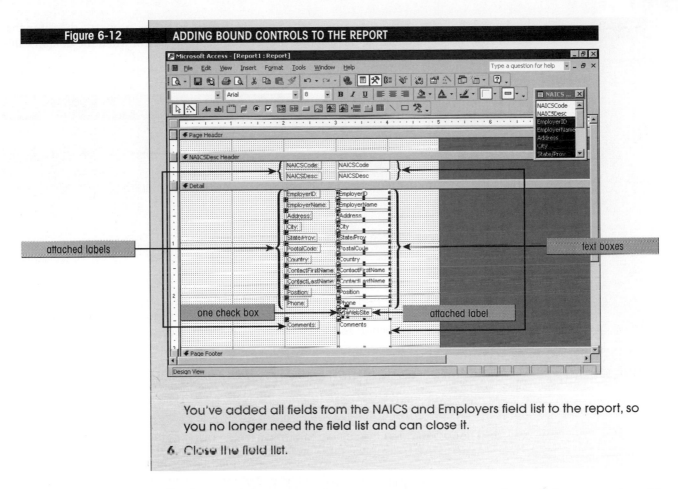

You've added all fields from the NAICS and Employers field list to the report, so
you no longer need the field list and can close it.

6. Close the field list.

Performing operations in the Report window in Design view will become easier with
practice. Remember, you can always click the Undo button one or more times immediately
after you make report design changes that produce unsatisfactory results. You can also click
the Print Preview button at any time to view your progress on the report.

Working with Controls

Two text boxes now appear in a column in the NAICSDesc Header section, and 12 text
boxes and one check box now appear in a column in the Detail section. Each box is a bound
control linked to a field in the underlying query and has an attached label box. The label
boxes appear to the left of the text boxes and to the right of the check box. The labels identify the contents of the text boxes and the check box; the text boxes and check box will display the field values from the database.

According to Elsa's plan for the report (see Figure 6-3), all multi-word labels, such as
EmployerName and ContactFirstName, have spaces between the separate words—for example,
EmployerName appears in the plan as Employer Name. You'll change the text of these labels by
changing each label's Caption property.

Changing the Caption Property

Each label has a **Caption property** that controls the text that appears in the label. The
default Caption property value for a bound control is the field name followed by a colon.
Other controls, such as buttons and tab controls, have Caption properties as well. You can

change the value of a Caption property for a control by using the property sheet for that control. You should change the Caption property value for a control when the default value is difficult to read or understand.

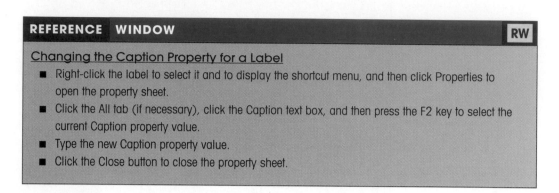

REFERENCE WINDOW   **RW**

<u>Changing the Caption Property for a Label</u>
- Right-click the label to select it and to display the shortcut menu, and then click Properties to open the property sheet.
- Click the All tab (if necessary), click the Caption text box, and then press the F2 key to select the current Caption property value.
- Type the new Caption property value.
- Click the Close button to close the property sheet.

The default Caption property values for several labels in the report do not match Elsa's report design. You need to change the Caption property for nine labels—two labels in the NAICSDesc Header section and seven labels in the Detail section.

To change the Caption property for the labels:

1. Right-click the **NAICSCode label** in the NAICSDesc Header section, and then click **Properties** to display the property sheet for the NAICSCode label.

2. If necessary, click the **All** tab to display the All page of the property sheet. You need to insert a space between "NAICS" and "Code."

   TROUBLE? If the property sheet blocks any controls in the report, drag the property sheet title bar down and to the right.

3. Position the insertion point between "NAICS" and "Code," and then press the **spacebar**. See Figure 6-13.

Figure 6-13	CHANGING THE CAPTION PROPERTY VALUE

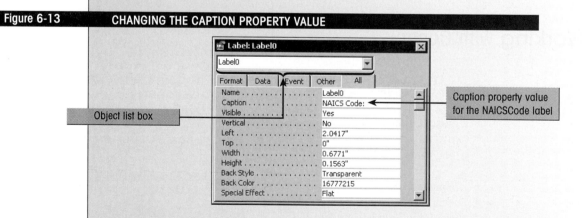

TROUBLE? The property sheet title bar, the Object list box, the Name property, and the label measurements on your screen might have values different than those shown in Figure 6-13. This causes no problems.

4. Click the **NAICSDesc label** in the NAICSDesc Header section to select it. The property sheet changes to show the properties for the NAICSDesc label.

5. Edit the text of the Caption property so that it displays the value **NAICS Desc:**.

6. Repeat Steps 4 and 5 for the EmployerID, EmployerName, PostalCode, ContactFirstName, ContactLastName, and WebSite labels. Change the Caption property to **Employer ID:**, **Employer Name:**, **Postal Code:**, **Contact First Name:**, **Contact Last Name:**, and **Web Site:**, respectively.

7. Close the property sheet.

8. Click an empty area of the grid to deselect any selected controls.

According to Elsa's report design, you need to reposition all labels and text boxes in the report. You'll also resize several text boxes, and you'll resize all labels to their best fit.

Moving and Resizing Controls

Just like with forms, you can move a text box and its attached label as a pair in the Report window. You can also move or resize any individual control or multiple selected controls. When you select a control, a move handle appears in its upper-left corner. This is the handle you use to reposition the selected control. Around its border, a selected control also displays sizing handles, which you can use to resize a control in different directions.

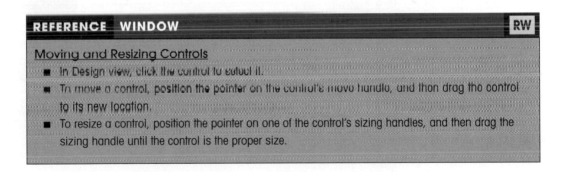

REFERENCE WINDOW RW

Moving and Resizing Controls

- In Design view, click the control to select it.
- To move a control, position the pointer on the control's move handle, and then drag the control to its new location.
- To resize a control, position the pointer on one of the control's sizing handles, and then drag the sizing handle until the control is the proper size.

You need to resize all labels to their best fit, and then reposition the text boxes, check box, and labels to match the report's design.

To resize the labels and move the controls in the NAICSDesc Header and Detail sections:

1. Click the **NAICSCode label**, hold down the **Shift** key, click all other labels in the NAICSDesc Header and Detail sections, and then release the **Shift** key. You've selected all the labels.

2. Click **Format** on the menu bar, point to **Size**, and then click **To Fit**. Access resizes all the label boxes to fit the captions.

   Next, you'll reposition all controls in the NAICSDesc Header and Detail sections.

3. Click an empty area of the grid to deselect all selected controls.

4. Click the **NAICSDesc label** in the NAICSDesc Header section, position the pointer on the move handle in the upper-left corner of the label so it changes to a ⬛ shape, and then drag the label to the upper-left corner of the NAICSDesc Header section.

5. Click the **NAICSDesc** text box in the NAICSDesc Header section, position the pointer on the move handle in the upper-left corner of the text box so it changes to a ✋ shape, and then drag the text box to the position shown in Figure 6-14.

6. Refer to Figure 6-14 and use the procedures in Steps 4 and 5 to move the other labels and text boxes in the NAICSDesc Header and Detail sections to match the figure as closely as possible. The report's width will widen automatically from 5 inches to approximately 5.5 inches when you move the NAICSCode text box in the NAICSDesc Header section. See Figure 6-14.

| Figure 6-14 | AFTER MOVING THE CONTROLS IN THE REPORT WINDOW |

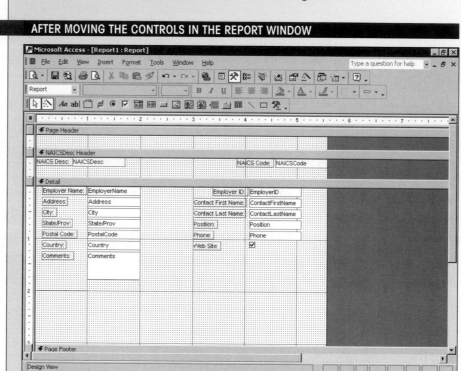

You've made many modifications to the report design and should save the report before proceeding.

To save the report design:

1. Click the **Save** button 🖫 on the Report Design toolbar. The Save As dialog box opens.

2. Type **Potential Income** in the Report Name text box, and then press the **Enter** key. The dialog box closes, and Access saves the report in the Jobs database.

Next, you'll resize four text boxes—the NAICSDesc, EmployerName, Address, and Comments text boxes—so their field-value contents will be completely visible. Because the Comments field in the Employer table is a memo field, the Comments text box is a special case; comments about an employer can range from none to many lines of text. Thus, you'll need to resize the Comments text box for the minimal case of one line, but you want the text box to expand to display the entire field value when multiple lines are needed. Setting the Can Grow property of the Comments text box to Yes will do exactly this. The **Can Grow property**, when set to Yes, expands a text box vertically to fit the field value when the report is printed.

To resize the text boxes and set the Can Grow property:

1. Click the **Comments** text box in the Detail section, position the pointer on its middle-right sizing handle so it changes to a shape, and then drag the right border to the right to the 5.5-inch mark on the horizontal ruler.

2. Position the pointer on the middle-bottom sizing handle of the Comments text box so it changes to a ↕ shape, and then drag the bottom border up until it's the same height as the bottom of the Comments label.

3. Refer to Figure 6-15 and repeat Step 1 to resize the width of the **EmployerName** and **Address** text boxes in the Detail section and the width of the **NAICSDesc** text box in the NAICSDesc Header section.

Figure 6-15	AFTER RESIZING FOUR TEXT BOXES

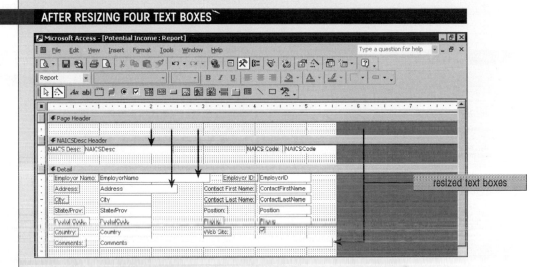

4. Click the **Comments** text box, press the **F4** key to open the property sheet, set the Can Grow property to **Yes**, and then close the property sheet.

Now you need to align the two columns of labels in the Detail section on their right edges.

Aligning Controls

You can align controls in a report or form using the **Align** command, which provides different options for aligning controls. For example, if you select controls in a column, you can use the Align Left option to align the left edges of the controls. Similarly, if you select controls in a row, you can use the Align Top option to align the top edges of the controls. The Align Right and Align Bottom options work the same way. A fifth option, Align To Grid, aligns selected controls with the grid dots in the Report window. To match Elsa's report design, you will use the Align Right option to align the labels in the Detail section. Then you'll save the modified report and preview it to see what it will look like when printed.

To align the labels in the Detail section and then save and preview the report:

1. Click an empty area of the grid to deselect all controls.

2. Click the **EmployerName label** in the Detail section, hold down the **Shift** key, click each of the six labels below the EmployerName label, and then release the **Shift** key. This action selects the seven labels in the left column of the Detail section in preparation for aligning them on their right edges.

3. Right-click one selected label, point to **Align** on the shortcut menu, and then click **Right** to right-align the selected labels on the right.

4. Repeat Steps 1 through 3 for the six labels in the right column of the Detail section to right-align them, and then click an empty area of the grid to deselect all controls. See Figure 6-16.

Figure 6-16	AFTER RIGHT-ALIGNING THE LABELS IN THE DETAIL SECTION

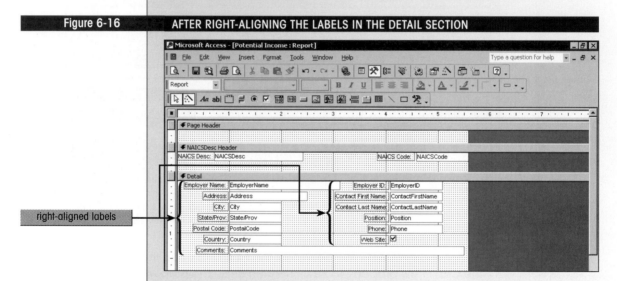

right-aligned labels

As you create a report, you should periodically save your modifications to the report and preview your progress.

5. Save your report design changes, and then switch to Print Preview.

6. Scroll the Print Preview window so that you can see more of the report on the screen. The field values for the first two employers follow the first pair of NAICS field values. See Figure 6-17.

Figure 6-17	REPORT IN PRINT PREVIEW

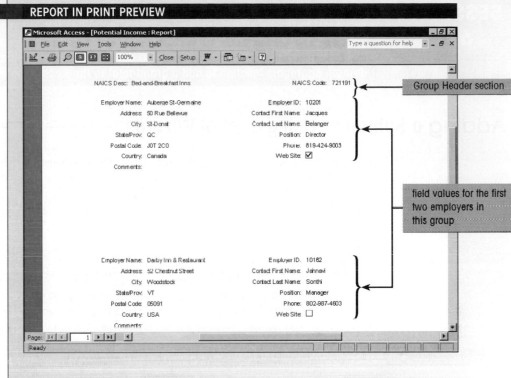

7. Navigate to Seaview Restaurant (page 7 or 8 of the Print Preview window). Notice that the Comments field value for Seaview Restaurant displays three lines of text, verifying that the Can Grow property is properly set for the field.

8. Click the **Close** button on the Print Preview toolbar to return to the Report window in Design view.

You have completed your initial work on the report. In the next session, you will continue developing the report according to Elsa's design.

Session 6.1 QUICK CHECK

1. Describe the seven sections of an Access report.

2. What is a custom report?

3. The _____ function lets you assign one value to a calculated field if a condition is true and a second value if the condition is false.

4. What does the Report window in Design view have in common with the Form window in Design view? How do the two windows differ?

5. What is a grouping field?

6. What is the Caption property for a control, and when would you change it?

7. The _____ property, when set to Yes, expands a text box vertically to fit the field value when a report is printed.

8. How do you right-align controls in a column?

SESSION 6.2

In this session, you will continue creating the Potential Income report. You will add a subreport to the Detail section, add a Group Footer section to the subreport, specify grouping and sorting fields for the subreport, and then add a line and group totals to the Group Footer section. Finally, you will define conditional formatting rules and use a domain aggregate function to add a grand total to the Report Footer section.

Adding a Subreport Using Control Wizards

According to Elsa's design, the Potential Income report uses a subreport in the Detail section to include an employer's position information. Similar to a subform, a Control Wizard can help you create a subreport. You will use the Subform/Subreport Wizard to add the subreport based on the data from the Potential Placement Fees query, which Elsa created and you reviewed at the beginning of Session 6.1.

To add the subreport to the report's Detail section:

1. If you took a break after the previous session, make sure that Access is running, that the **Jobs** database from the Tutorial folder on your Data Disk is open, and that the **Potential Income** report is open in Design view in a maximized window.

2. Make sure the **Control Wizards** tool ⬛ on the toolbox is selected, and then click the **Subform/Subreport** tool ⬛ on the toolbox.

3. Position the + portion of the pointer near the left edge of the Detail section, just below the 1.5-inch mark on the vertical ruler and in the third column of grid dots, and then click the mouse button. Access places a subreport control in the Detail section and opens the first SubReport Wizard dialog box.

   TROUBLE? If a dialog box opens and tells you that Microsoft can't start this Wizard, place your Office XP CD in the correct drive, and then click the Yes button. If you do not have this CD, ask your instructor or technical support person for help.

4. Make sure the **Use existing Tables and Queries** option button is selected, and then click the **Next** button. Access opens the next SubReport Wizard dialog box, from which you select the table or query on which the subreport is based and the fields from that table or query.

   You'll select all fields from the Potential Placement Fees query.

5. Click the **Tables/Queries** list arrow to display the list of tables and queries in the Jobs database, click **Query: Potential Placement Fees**, click the >> button to select all fields from the query, and then click the **Next** button to open the next SubReport Wizard dialog box.

   In this dialog box, you select the link between the main report and the subreport. You want to use the default option, which uses the EmployerID field as the common field between the two queries—the main report's NAICS and Employers source query includes the common field; so does the subreport's Potential Placement Fees source query.

6. Make sure the **Choose from a list** option button is selected and the first link is highlighted, and then click the **Next** button. The next SubReport Wizard dialog box lets you specify a name for the subreport.

7. Type **Potential Income Subreport**, and then click the **Finish** button. Access inserts a subreport control, which is where an employer's position records will appear, in the Detail section of the main report.

8. Save your report changes, maximize the Report window, and then close the field list. See Figure 6-18.

Figure 6-18	AFTER ADDING THE SUBREPORT TO THE MAIN REPORT

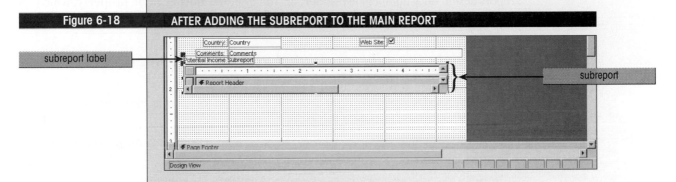

9. Switch to Print Preview to review the report. See Figure 6-19.

Figure 6-19	PRINT PREVIEW OF THE SUBREPORT IN THE MAIN REPORT

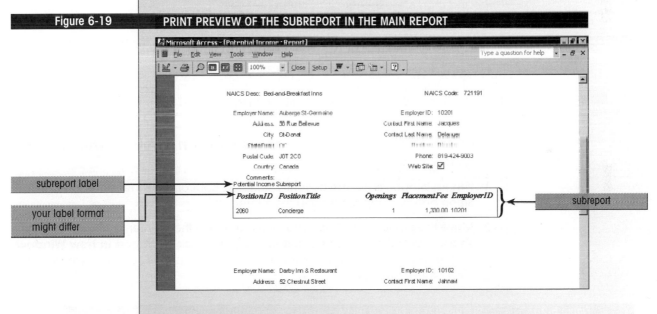

TROUBLE? If the format of your labels differs, don't worry. You'll change the label format later in this tutorial.

Based on Elsa's report design, you'll need to make several changes to the subreport.

Modifying a Subreport

In Elsa's report design (see Figure 6-3), the subreport includes columns for the PositionTitle, PositionID, Openings, and PlacementFee columns, but not for the EmployerID column. Also, the PositionTitle controls appear to the left of the PositionID controls. In addition, a line appears above the placement fee total. Before you open the subreport to modify it based on Elsa's report design, you'll delete the subreport label and change some subreport properties.

The subreport label does not appear in Elsa's report design, so you'll delete the label. In addition, you'll set the subreport's Can Shrink and Border Style properties. The **Can Shrink property**, when set to Yes, reduces the height of a control that contains no data to eliminate blank lines in the printed report. You'll set the subreport's Can Shrink property to Yes. When an employer has no available positions, Elsa wants to avoid printing the blank space occupied by the empty subreport. Finally, the subreport includes a rectangular border by default; Elsa's report design does not include this border. You'll set the **Border Style property**, which specifies a control's border type, to Transparent, so that the rectangle is invisible.

To delete the subreport label and set the Can Shrink and Border Style properties:

1. Switch to Design view, right-click the subreport label, and then click **Cut** on the shortcut menu to delete the label.

2. Right-click the subreport border to select it, and then click **Properties** to open the property sheet for the subreport.

3. If necessary, click the **Format** tab.

4. Set the Can Shrink property to **Yes**, set the Border Style property to **Transparent**, and then close the property sheet.

You could modify the subreport in the Report window of the Potential Income report. However, because the subreport is a separate report and making the subreport changes is easier in a separate window, you'll open the subreport in Design view in a new window. Then you'll modify the subreport design to match Elsa's design.

To open the subreport in Design view and modify the subreport design:

1. If the subreport is not the currently selected control, click the subreport border. Sizing handles appear around the subreport.

2. Move the pointer to the subreport border; when the pointer changes to a ✋ shape, right-click the mouse button, and then click **Subreport in New Window** on the shortcut menu. The Potential Income Subreport report opens in Design view. See Figure 6-20.

Figure 6-20	SUBREPORT IN DESIGN VIEW

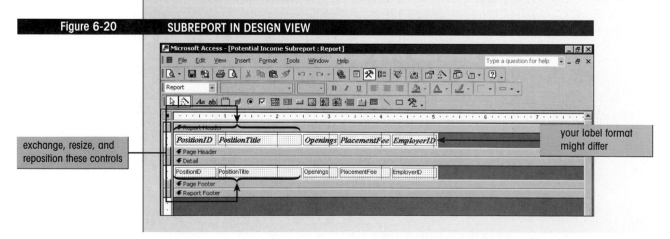

exchange, resize, and reposition these controls

your label format might differ

TROUBLE? If the labels in your Report Header section have different font properties than the labels shown in Figure 6-20, select the five labels, and then change
their properties to match. Figure 6-20 shows labels set in 11-point, bold, italic,
Times New Roman font; if you need to change these properties, use the buttons
on the Formatting toolbar.

TROUBLE? If the label captions in your Report Header section are not blue,
select the five labels, open the property sheet, click the Fore Color text box,
click the Build button [...] next to the Fore Color text box, click the blue color
(row 5, column 5), click the OK button, and then close the property sheet.

Unlike the main report, which initially contained Detail, Page Header, and Page
Footer sections when you created a blank report, the subreport contains a
Report Header section and a Detail section. (Although the Page Header, Page
Footer, and Report Footer sections appear in the subreport, their heights are set
to zero. As a result, these three sections do not appear in Print Preview or in the
printed subreport.) Labels appear as column headings in the Report Header
section, and field-value text boxes appear in the Detail section.

To match Elsa's design, you'll reduce the widths of the PositionID and
PositionTitle controls so that you can exchange their positions, and then you'll
resize and reposition the four controls.

3. Click an empty area of the grid to deselect any selected controls (if necessary),
   click the **PositionTitle label**, hold down the **Shift** key, click the **PositionTitle** text
   box, release the **Shift** key to select both controls, and then use the middle-right
   sizing handle of either control to reduce the widths of the selected controls to
   approximately 0.5 inches.

4. Click a blank area of the Report Header section to deselect the PositionTitle
   controls, and then repeat Step 3 for the **PositionID label** and the **PositionID**
   text box.

5. Position the pointer on the PositionID text box; when the pointer changes to a
   shape, drag the two selected controls to the right of the PositionTitle controls.

6. Refer to Figure 6-21 to resize and reposition the PositionID label and text box
   and the PositionTitle label and text box.

Figure 6-21	AFTER EXCHANGING, RESIZING, AND REPOSITIONING CONTROLS

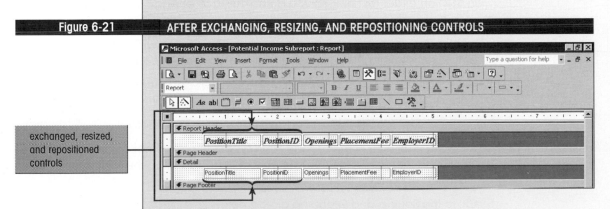

exchanged, resized,
and repositioned
controls

Because the EmployerID label and field value appear in the main report's
Detail section, you need to prevent them from printing in the subreport by setting their Visible property. You use the **Visible property** to show or hide a control.

7. Use the Shift key to select the **EmployerID label** and the **EmployerID** text box.

8. Press the **F4** key to open the property sheet. The text "Multiple selection" in the property sheet title bar and the empty Object list box both indicate that you'll set properties for two or more controls. See Figure 6-22.

Figure 6-22	PROPERTY SHEET FOR MULTIPLE CONTROLS

empty Object list box

properties for two (or more) selected controls

Visible property value

9. Set the Visible property to **No**, and then close the property sheet.

Elsa's report design includes subreport totals for the placement fee and employer potential income amounts, so you need to add a Group Footer section for the EmployerID field to the subreport. Thus, EmployerID will be the primary sort key using an ascending sort order. Because Elsa wants the positions to print in ascending order by the position titles for an employer, the PositionTitle field will be the secondary sort key.

To select the sort keys and the group field for the subreport:

1. Click the **Sorting and Grouping** button [icon] on the Report Design toolbar to open the Sorting and Grouping dialog box.

2. Click the list arrow in the first **Field/Expression** text box to display the list of available fields, and then click **EmployerID**. Ascending is the default sort order in the Sort Order text box, so you do not need to change this setting.

You can now designate EmployerID as a grouping field and specify that you want a Group Footer section for this group. This section will contain the employer totals for the placement fee and potential income amounts.

3. Click the right side of the **Group Footer** text box, and then click **Yes**. Access adds a Group Footer section named EmployerID Footer to the Report window.

You can now specify the secondary sort key and its sort order.

4. Click the right side of the second **Field/Expression** text box to display the list of fields, and then click **PositionTitle**. You've finished setting the sorting and grouping options for the subreport.

5. Close the Sorting and Grouping dialog box.

Next, you'll add a line to the EmployerID Footer section to separate the detail placement fees from the employer placement fee total.

Adding **Lines to a Report**

You can use lines in a report to improve the report's readability and to group related information. The **Line tool** on the toolbox lets you add a line to a report or form.

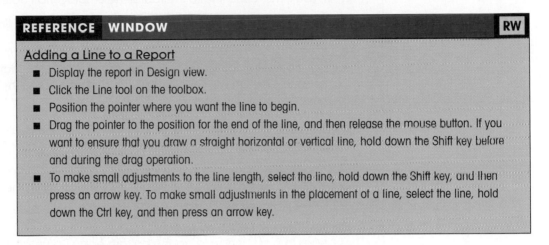

REFERENCE WINDOW   **RW**

Adding a Line to a Report

- Display the report in Design view.
- Click the Line tool on the toolbox.
- Position the pointer where you want the line to begin.
- Drag the pointer to the position for the end of the line, and then release the mouse button. If you want to ensure that you draw a straight horizontal or vertical line, hold down the Shift key before and during the drag operation.
- To make small adjustments to the line length, select the line, hold down the Shift key, and then press an arrow key. To make small adjustments in the placement of a line, select the line, hold down the Ctrl key, and then press an arrow key.

You will add a horizontal line to the top of the EmployerID Footer section under the PlacementFee text box to separate the total employer placement fee from the column of individual placement fees for the employer on the printed report.

To add a line to the report:

1. Click the **Line** tool ⬈ on the toolbox.

2. Position the pointer in the EmployerID Footer section. The pointer changes to a ╋⬈ shape.

3. Position the pointer's plus symbol (+) near the top of the EmployerID Footer section at the 3.75-inch mark on the horizontal ruler.

4. Drag a horizontal line from left to right, so the end of the line aligns with the right edge of the PlacementFee text box in the Detail section, and then release the mouse button. See Figure 6-23.

Figure 6-23	ADDING A LINE TO THE REPORT

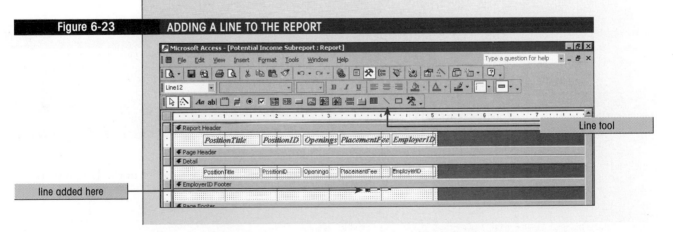

line added here

Line tool

TROUBLE? If the line is not straight or not positioned correctly, click the Undo button 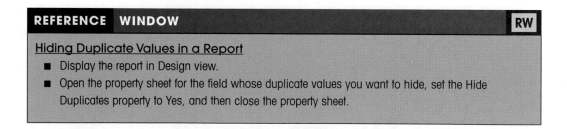 on the Report Design toolbar, and then repeat Steps 1 through 4. If the line is not the correct length, hold down the Shift key, and press one or more of the arrow keys until the line's length is the same as that of the line shown in Figure 6-23.

Next, you'll move the line to the top of the EmployerID Footer section.

5. Hold down the **Ctrl** key, and then press the ↑ key until the line reaches the top of the EmployerID Footer section.

TROUBLE? If the line jumps up to the bottom of the Detail section, hold down the Ctrl key and press the ↓ key until the line moves back to the top of the EmployerID Footer section.

Elsa asks you to remove the excess space above and below the five controls in the Detail section and to reduce the height of the Detail section.

6. Select all five controls in the Detail section and place the pointer on a selected control; when the pointer changes to a 🖐 shape, drag the controls straight up to the top of the Detail section.

7. Position the pointer on the bottom edge of the Detail section; when the pointer changes to a ╪ shape, drag the bottom edge up until it touches the bottom of the text boxes in the Detail section.

8. Save your subreport design changes.

Recall that the subreport's primary sort key is the EmployerID field and the secondary sort key is the PositionTitle field. For employers with several positions, it's possible that two or more positions could have the same PositionTitle field value. In these cases, Elsa wants the PositionTitle field value printed for the first position but not for subsequent positions because she believes that would make the position data easier to read.

Hiding Duplicate Values in a Report

You use the **Hide Duplicates property** to hide a control on a report when the control's value is the same as that of the preceding record.

REFERENCE WINDOW	RW
Hiding Duplicate Values in a Report	
■ Display the report in Design view. ■ Open the property sheet for the field whose duplicate values you want to hide, set the Hide Duplicates property to Yes, and then close the property sheet.	

Your next change is to hide duplicate PositionTitle field values in the Detail section.

To hide the duplicate PositionTitle field values:

1. Click an empty area of the grid to deselect all controls.

2. Open the property sheet for the PositionTitle text box.

3. Click the **Format** tab (if necessary), click the right side of the **Hide Duplicates** text box, and then click **Yes**. See Figure 6-24.

Figure 6-24	HIDING DUPLICATE FIELD VALUES

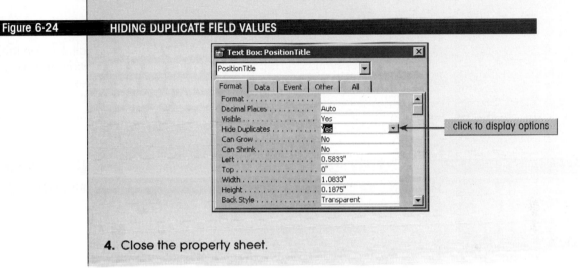

4. Close the property sheet.

You are now ready to calculate the group totals for the placement fee and employer potential income amounts.

Calculating Group Totals

Elsa wants the report to print each employer's subtotals for the placement fee and potential income amounts. To calculate subtotals and overall totals in a report, you use the **Sum function**. You place the Sum function in a Group Footer section to print each group's total. When placed in the Report Footer section, the Sum function prints the overall total. The format for the Sum function is =Sum([*fieldname*]). To create the appropriate text boxes in the footer sections, you use the Text Box tool on the toolbox.

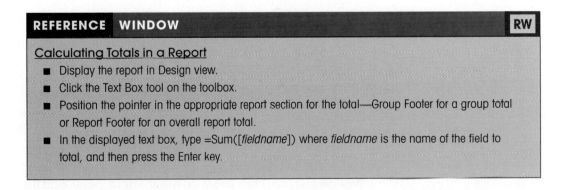

REFERENCE WINDOW   **RW**

Calculating Totals in a Report
- Display the report in Design view.
- Click the Text Box tool on the toolbox.
- Position the pointer in the appropriate report section for the total—Group Footer for a group total or Report Footer for an overall report total.
- In the displayed text box, type =Sum([*fieldname*]) where *fieldname* is the name of the field to total, and then press the Enter key.

To add the group totals to your report, you need to increase the height of the EmployerID Footer section to make room for the two text boxes that will contain the calculated fields. Then you need to add text boxes for the two calculated fields.

To resize the group footer section and add the two calculated fields for the group totals:

1. Use the ┼ pointer to increase the height of the EmployerID Footer section until the bottom of the section is at the 0.5-inch mark on the vertical ruler.

   Next, you'll add the first calculated field that will print the employer placement fee total.

2. Click the **Text Box** tool abl on the toolbox.

3. Position the pointer in the EmployerID Footer section, and click when the pointer's plus symbol (+) is positioned at the top of the section and aligns vertically with the left edge of the PlacementFee text box. Access adds a text box with an attached label box to its left. Inside the text box is the description "Unbound." Recall that an unbound control is a control that is not linked to a database table field. See Figure 6-25.

Figure 6-25	ADDING A TEXT BOX IN THE FOOTER SECTION

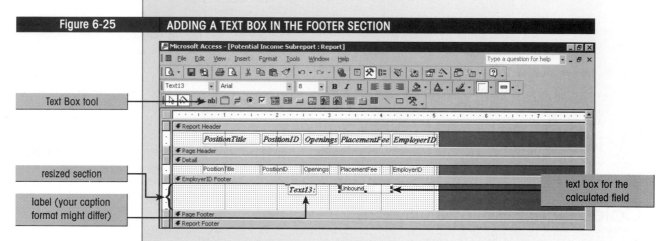

Text Box tool

resized section

label (your caption format might differ)

text box for the calculated field

TROUBLE? The label on your screen might have a caption other than the one shown in Figure 6-25. That causes no problems.

You'll now add the Sum function to the text box, which contains the name Unbound, and then set its Format property to Standard, which will print the values with two decimal places.

4. Right-click the **Unbound** text box, click **Properties** on the shortcut menu, click the **All** tab, type **=Sum([PlacementFee])** in the Control Source text box, set the Format property to **Standard**, and then close the property sheet.

   Now add a text box for the second calculated field. You'll use the IIf function for this calculated field.

5. Repeat Steps 2 and 3, clicking when the pointer's plus symbol (+) is positioned in the EmployerID Footer section two grid dots below the other text box and vertically aligned with its left edge.

6. Open the property sheet for the **Unbound** text box, right-click the **Control Source** text box, click **Zoom** on the shortcut menu, and then type **=IIf (Sum (Openings) >= 3, Sum (PlacementFee) + 200, Sum (PlacementFee) + 500)** in the Zoom box. See Figure 6-26.

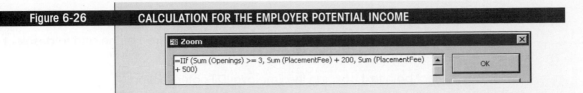

Figure 6-26 CALCULATION FOR THE EMPLOYER POTENTIAL INCOME

=IIf (Sum (Openings) >= 3, Sum (PlacementFee) + 200, Sum (PlacementFee) + 500)

The calculation is the same one you used in the Potential Income by Employer query, except it includes the Sum function. Depending on whether the total number of openings for an employer is three or more, either $200 or $500 is added to the employer total placement fee.

Next, you'll set the calculated field's Format property to Standard.

7. Click the **OK** button, set the Format property to **Standard**, and then close the property sheet.

8. Save your design changes, and then switch to Print Preview. See Figure 6-27.

Figure 6-27 PRINT PREVIEW OF THE SUBREPORT

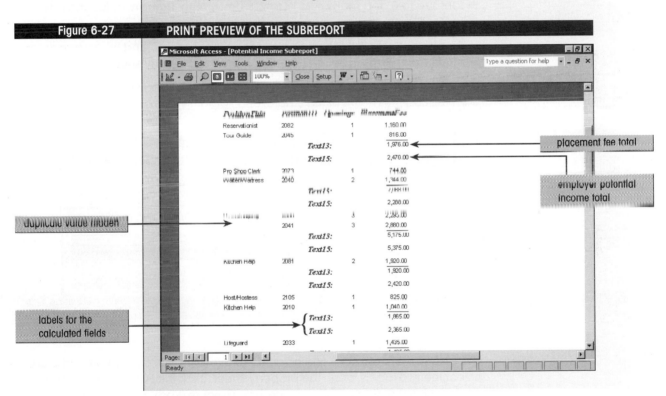

You still need to make several modifications to the subreport. The decimal points for the two calculated fields don't line up with the PlacementFee field values, so you'll need to resize the text boxes for the calculated fields. You'll set the Caption property for both labels, and then you'll resize and reposition them. Finally, Elsa wants to make it easier to use the report to find potential income amounts for employers with low- and high-income potential (under $2000 and over $5000, respectively).

First, you'll resize the text boxes and modify the properties for the two labels.

To resize the text boxes and modify the label properties:

1. Switch to Design view, and then click an empty area of the grid to deselect all controls.

2. Select both text boxes in the EmployerID Footer section.

3. Position the pointer on the middle-right sizing handle of either selected control so it changes to a ◄─► shape, and then drag the right borders to the left so that they align with the right border of the PlacementFee text box in the Detail section.

4. Using the middle-left sizing handle, repeat Step 3 to drag the left borders of the selected controls to the right until they are just to the right of the 3.5-inch mark on the horizontal ruler. (See Figure 6-28.)

5. Deselect the controls, open the property sheet for the top label in the EmployerID Footer section, set its Caption property to **Total:**, and then change its font size to **8** and make sure its font is **Times New Roman**, bold, and italic.

6. Click the bottom label in the EmployerID Footer section, set its Caption property to **Employer Potential Income:**, change its font size to **8** and make sure its font is **Times New Roman**, bold, and italic. Close the property sheet.

7. Resize and reposition both labels to match the labels shown in Figure 6-28, and then reduce the height of the EmployerID Footer section.

| Figure 6-28 | AFTER MODIFYING THE FOOTER LABELS AND TEXT BOXES |

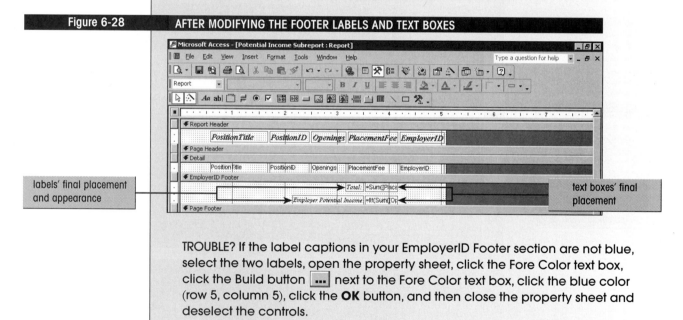

labels' final placement and appearance

text boxes' final placement

TROUBLE? If the label captions in your EmployerID Footer section are not blue, select the two labels, open the property sheet, click the Fore Color text box, click the Build button [...] next to the Fore Color text box, click the blue color (row 5, column 5), click the **OK** button, and then close the property sheet and deselect the controls.

Your final subreport modification will allow Elsa to more easily find employer potential income amounts under $2000 and over $5000.

Defining **Conditional Formatting Rules**

One way to make employer potential income amounts easier to spot on the report is to use conditional formatting for the calculated field's text box in the EmployerID Footer section.

Conditional formatting lets you change the format of a report or form control based on the control's value. For example, you can change the calculated field's font style or color when its value is more than $5000 and change the field's font to a different style or color when its value is less than $2000. All other values for the control print in the default font style or color. You can define up to a maximum of three conditional formats for each control.

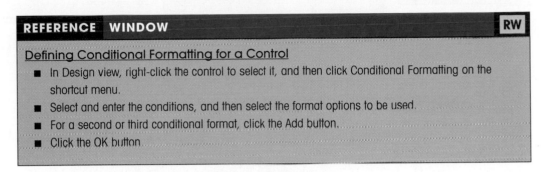

Defining Conditional Formatting for a Control
- In Design view, right-click the control to select it, and then click Conditional Formatting on the shortcut menu.
- Select and enter the conditions, and then select the format options to be used.
- For a second or third conditional format, click the Add button.
- Click the OK button.

You will use bold text for employer potential income amounts over $5000 and bold, italic text for values under $2000.

To define conditional formatting for the potential income amounts:

1. Right-click the **Employer Potential Income** text box in the EmployerID Footer section, and then click **Conditional Formatting** on the shortcut menu. The Conditional Formatting dialog box opens. See Figure 6-29.

Figure 6-29   CONDITIONAL FORMATTING DIALOG BOX

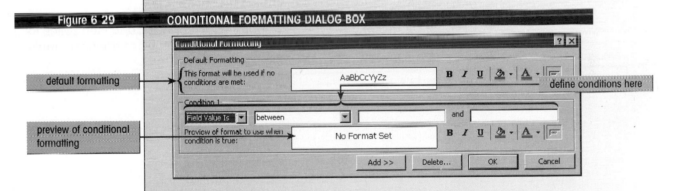

First, you'll define conditional formatting for employer potential income amounts under $2000.

2. In the Condition 1 section, click the list arrow for the second list box, click **less than**, press the **Tab** key, and then type **2000**. The condition will be true for all employer potential income amounts less than $2000.

Now you need to select the format that will be used for the first condition.

3. Click the **Bold** button **B** in the Condition 1 section, click the **Italic** button *I* in the Condition 1 section, and then click the **Add** button. You have defined the first condition and its format, and the Conditional Formatting dialog box expands so you can enter a second condition. See Figure 6-30.

Figure 6-30   AFTER DEFINING THE FIRST CONDITIONAL FORMAT

first condition completed

preview of conditional formatting for the first condition

define the second conditional format here

selected format options for the first condition

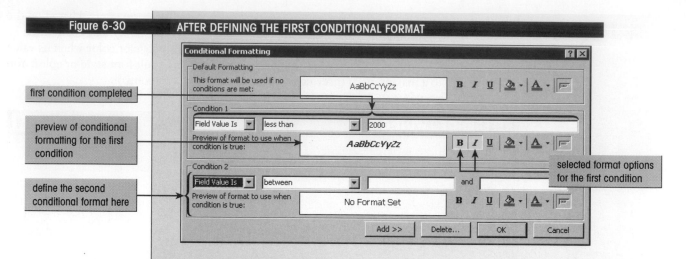

Next, you'll define the conditional formatting for employer potential income amounts over $5000.

4. In the Condition 2 section, click the list arrow for the second list box, click **greater than**, press the **Tab** key, and then type **5000**. The condition will be true for all employer potential income amounts greater than $5000.

5. In the Condition 2 section, click **B**. You have defined the second condition and its format.

You've finished defining the conditional formats for the employer potential income amounts. Next, you'll accept the conditional formats, save your work, and then show Elsa how the subreport looks.

6. Click the **OK** button, save your subreport design changes, and then switch to Print Preview to verify that the default format and the two conditional formats produce the results you expected. See Figure 6-31.

Figure 6-31   **PRINT PREVIEW SHOWING CONDITIONAL FORMATS**

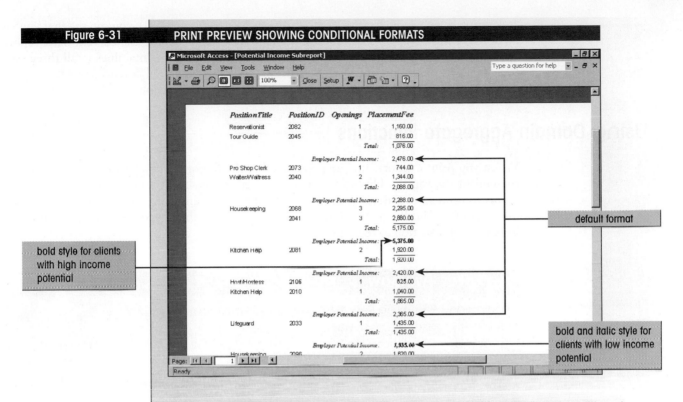

bold style for clients with high income potential

default format

bold and italic style for clients with low income potential

7. Preview the remaining pages of the report to verify that the two conditional formats are correct.

You've completed the subreport design, so you'll return to Design view and close the subreport.

8. Switch to Design view, and then click the **Close Window** button ☒ on the menu bar. The subreport closes, and you return to Design view for the main report.

Now that you've completed the subreport, you'll check the progress of your report design in Print Preview.

9. Switch to Print Preview. The Group Header and Detail sections are displayed for the first employer. See Figure 6-32.

Figure 6-32   **PRINT PREVIEW OF THE MAIN REPORT**

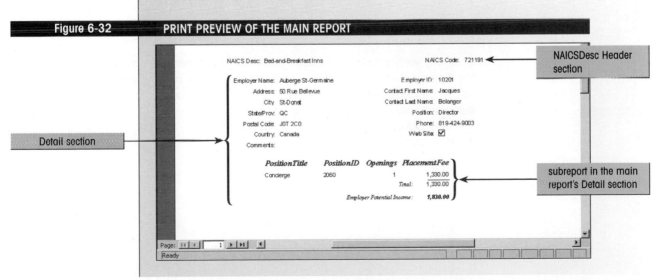

NAICSDesc Header section

Detail section

subreport in the main report's Detail section

Comparing your report with Elsa's report design (see Figure 6-3), you can see that you've completed most of the work. Your remaining tasks include adding the current date, report title, and page number to the Page Header section; adding horizontal lines to all three sections of the main report; and adding a calculated field for the total potential income.

First, you'll add the calculated field to the Report Footer section.

Using Domain Aggregate Functions

When you print a report, anything contained in the Report Footer section appears once at the end of the report. This section is often used to display overall totals. Elsa wants the report to print an overall total based on the employer potential income amounts. To include information in the Report Footer, you must first add both a Report Header section and a Report Footer section to the report.

REFERENCE WINDOW | **RW**

Adding and Removing Report Header and Report Footer Sections
- Display the report in Design view.
- To add the Report Header and Report Footer sections, click View on the menu bar, and then click Report Header/Footer.
- To remove a Report Header or Report Footer section, drag the bottom edge of that section up until the section area disappears.

Before adding the total potential income amount to the report, you need to add Report Header and Report Footer sections. Also, because you will not place any controls in the Report Header and Page Footer sections, you will remove these two sections.

To add Report Header and Report Footer sections and remove report sections:

1. Switch to Design view.

2. Click **View** on the menu bar, and then click **Report Header/Footer**. Access places a Report Header section at the top of the Report window and a Report Footer section at the bottom.

3. Scrolling vertically as necessary, use the ┿ pointer to decrease the height of the Report Header and Page Footer sections to 0, and to decrease the height of the Detail section to 2.5 inches. The new height of the Detail section will allow sufficient room to add a horizontal line in this section below the subreport control. See Figure 6-33.

Figure 6-33	REPORT SECTIONS ADDED AND REMOVED

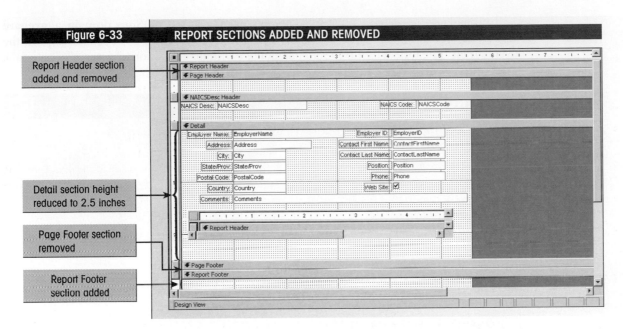

Report Header section added and removed

Detail section height reduced to 2.5 inches

Page Footer section removed

Report Footer section added

The subreport does not appear for those employers without available positions. Recall from Session 6.1 that this causes Access to generate a data error if you attempt to base your calculation for the total potential income amount on the individual employer potential incomes. For that reason, you created the Potential Income by Employer query in Session 6.1. To calculate the total potential income amount for Elsa, you'll use the Potential Income by Employer query as the data source and a domain aggregate function to perform the calculation.

Domain aggregate functions provide statistical information about a set of records (recordset), or **domain**. The set of records can be those records defined in a table or a query. Figure 6-34 describes the available domain aggregate functions. You use aggregate functions, such as the Sum function you used in the subreport, when the fields you're using for the function are bound fields that appear in text boxes in the report. In contrast, you use domain aggregate functions when the source data you're using for the function appear in a table or query recordset.

Figure 6-34	DOMAIN AGGREGATE FUNCTIONS

DOMAIN AGGREGATE FUNCTION	DESCRIPTION
DAvg	Calculates the average of the specified field values from the selected recordset.
DCount	Calculates the number of records with nonnull values in the specified field from the selected recordset.
DFirst	Provides the value in the specified field from the first physical record in the selected recordset.
DLast	Provides the value in the specified field from the last physical record in the selected recordset.
DLookup	Provides the value in the specified field from the selected recordset based on the specified criteria.
DMax	Provides the maximum value of the specified field from the selected recordset.
DMin	Provides the minimum value of the specified field from the selected recordset.
DStDev	Estimates a population sample standard deviation of the specified field from the selected recordset.
DStDevP	Estimates a population standard deviation of the specified field from the selected recordset.
DSum	Calculates the sum of the specified field values from the selected recordset.
DVar	Estimates a population sample variance of the specified field from the selected recordset.
DVarP	Estimates a population variance of the specified field from the selected recordset.

To calculate the total potential income amount, you use the **DSum domain aggregate function**. You place the DSum function in a text box in the Report Footer section to print the overall total. The format for the DSum function is =DSum("expression", "domain", "criteria").

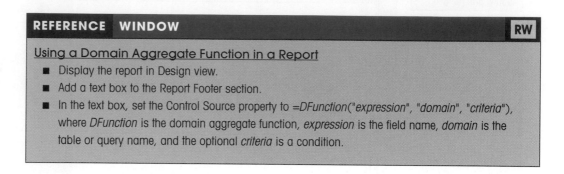

REFERENCE WINDOW   RW

Using a Domain Aggregate Function in a Report
■ Display the report in Design view.
■ Add a text box to the Report Footer section.
■ In the text box, set the Control Source property to =DFunction("expression", "domain", "criteria"),
  where *DFunction* is the domain aggregate function, *expression* is the field name, *domain* is the
  table or query name, and the optional *criteria* is a condition.

You need to add a text box for the DSum function in the Report Footer section.

To add a text box in the Report Footer section and add the DSum function:

1. Click the **Text Box** tool [abl] on the toolbox, position the pointer in the Report Footer section, and click when the pointer's plus symbol (+) is at the top of the Report Footer section and approximately at the 3.5-inch mark on the horizontal ruler. Access adds a text box with an attached label box to its left.

   You can now enter the DSum function for the text box.

2. Open the property sheet for the **Unbound** text box, click the **All** tab (if necessary), right-click the **Control Source** text box, and then click **Zoom** on the shortcut menu.

3. Type **=DSum("PotentialIncome", "[Potential Income by Employer]")** in the Zoom box. See Figure 6-35.

Figure 6-35	TOTAL POTENTIAL INCOME CALCULATION

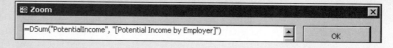

The DSum function will calculate the total of all the PotentialIncome field values in the Potential Income by Employer recordset.

Because Elsa wants the calculated value to print as a money field, you'll set the calculated field's Format and Decimal Places properties.

4. Click the **OK** button to close the Zoom box, set the Format property to **Currency**, and then set the Decimal Places property to **2**.

   Next, you'll set the label's Caption property, and then you'll format it similar to the other labels in the subreport—with blue, bold, italic Times New Roman font.

5. Click the label in the Report Footer section, and then set the Caption property to **Total Potential Income:**.

6. Scroll down the property sheet, click the **Fore Color** text box, and then click the **Build** button [...] next to the Fore Color text box. Access displays the palette of available colors. See Figure 6-36.

| Figure 6-36 | CHANGING THE LABEL'S FONT COLOR |

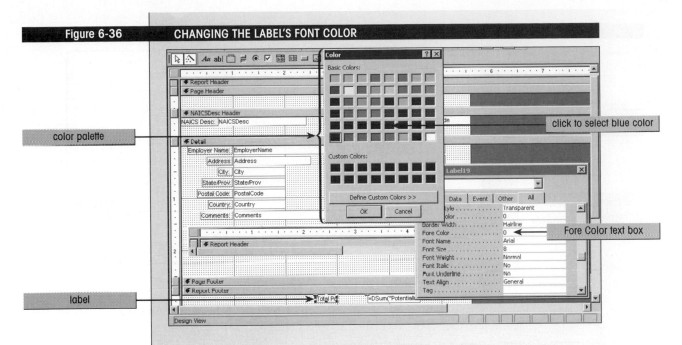

color palette

click to select blue color

label

Fore Color text box

7. Click the blue box in the color palette in row 5 and column 5 (see Figure 6-36), click the **OK** button, and then close the property sheet. The label text color changes to blue.

8. Click the **Bold** button **B** on the Formatting toolbar, click the **Italic** button *I* on the Formatting toolbar, click the **Font** list arrow on the Formatting toolbar, and then scroll down and click **Times New Roman**.

   Now you need to resize and reposition the label and text box in the Report Footer section.

9. Refer to Figure 6-37 to resize and reposition the DSum text box in the Report Footer section, and to size to fit and reposition the label in the Report Footer section.

| Figure 6-37 | FINAL SIZES AND POSITIONS OF REPORT FOOTER CONTROLS |

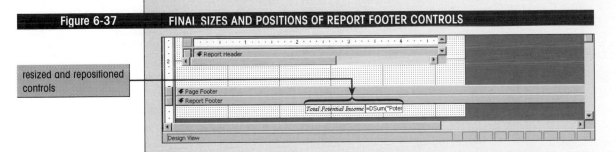

resized and repositioned controls

10. Save your report design changes, switch to Print Preview, and then navigate to the last page of the report. The total potential income and its associated label appear below the information for the last employer and its one available position. See Figure 6-38.

Figure 6-38   PRINT PREVIEW OF REPORT FOOTER CONTROLS

data for last employer and its position →

Employer Name:	NH Fall Foliage Tours		Employer ID:	10176
Address:	7 Alcott Road		Contact First Name:	Sam
City:	North Conway		Contact Last Name:	Bethel
State/Prov:	NH		Position:	Director
Postal Code:	03860		Phone:	603-468-7093
Country:	USA		Web Site:	☑
Comments:				

PositionTitle	PositionID	Openings	PlacementFee
Tour Guide	2065	1	600.00
		Total:	600.00

Employer Potential Income: **1,700.00**

label in the Report Footer section → Total Potential Income: $98,895.50   ← calculated control in the Report Footer section

Page: |◄ ◄ 19 ► ►| ◄
Ready

You have completed the Report Footer section of the report. In the next session, you will complete the report according to Elsa's design.

Session 6.2 QUICK CHECK

1. The _____ property, when set to Yes, reduces the height of a control that contains no data to eliminate blank lines from the printed report.

2. When you use Control Wizards to create a subreport, which non-empty sections does the Wizard create automatically?

3. You use the _____ property to show or hide a control.

4. To make small adjustments in the placement of a selected line, hold down the Ctrl key, and press a(n) _____ key.

5. Why might you want to hide duplicate values in a report?

6. What is the maximum number of conditional formats you can define for a control?

7. What is a domain?

SESSION 6.3

In this session, you will complete the Potential Income report. You will add a title and line, and add the date and page number to the Page Header section of the main report. You will also add lines to separate sections of the report visually. Finally, you will create and modify mailing labels.

Adding the Date to a Report

According to Elsa's design, the Potential Income report must include the date in the Page Header section. To add the date to a report, you insert the Date function in a text box. The **Date function** is a type of calculated control that prints the current date on a report. The format of the Date function is =Date(). The equals sign (=) indicates that what follows it is a calculated control; Date is the name of the function; and the parentheses () indicate a function rather than simple text.

REFERENCE WINDOW   **RW**

Adding the Date to a Report
- Display the report in Design view.
- Click the Text Box tool on the toolbox, position the pointer where you want the date to appear, and then click to place the text box in the report.
- Click the text box, type =Date(), and then press the Enter key.

You need to insert the Date function in the Page Header section so that the current date will print on each page of the report.

To add the Date function to the Page Header section:

1. If you took a break after the previous session, make sure that Access is running, that the **Jobs** database from the Tutorial folder on your Data Disk is open, and that the **Potential Income** report is open in a maximized Print Preview window.

2. Switch to Design view.

3. Click the **Text Box** tool [abl] on the toolbox, and then position the pointer in the Page Header section. The pointer changes to a $^{+}$[abl] shape.

4. Position the pointer's plus symbol (+) in the second row of grid dots in the Page Header section at the 1-inch mark on the horizontal ruler (see Figure 6-38), and then click the mouse button. Access adds a text box with an attached label box to its left.

5. Click the **Unbound** text box to position the insertion point and remove the word "Unbound," and then type **=Date()** and press the **Enter** key. See Figure 6-39.

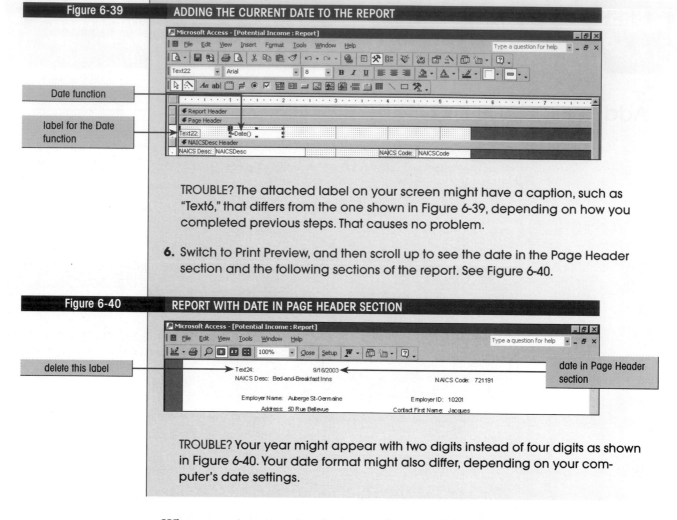

Figure 6-39   ADDING THE CURRENT DATE TO THE REPORT

Date function

label for the Date function

TROUBLE? The attached label on your screen might have a caption, such as "Text6," that differs from the one shown in Figure 6-39, depending on how you completed previous steps. That causes no problem.

6. Switch to Print Preview, and then scroll up to see the date in the Page Header section and the following sections of the report. See Figure 6-40.

Figure 6-40   REPORT WITH DATE IN PAGE HEADER SECTION

delete this label

date in Page Header section

TROUBLE? Your year might appear with two digits instead of four digits as shown in Figure 6-40. Your date format might also differ, depending on your computer's date settings.

When you print or preview the report, the current date appears instead of the Date function you entered in the text box. The date label is unnecessary, so you can delete it. You'll also move the text box to the left edge of the Page Header section and then left-align the date in the text box.

To delete the Date label and move and left-align the Date text box:

1. Switch to Design view.

2. Right-click the **Date label** located at the far left of the Page Header section, and then click **Cut** on the shortcut menu to delete the label.

3. Click the **Date** text box, drag its move handle to the left edge of the Page Header section, and then click the **Align Left** button on the Formatting toolbar to left-align the date in the text box.

4. Save your report design changes.

You are now ready to add page numbers to the Page Header section.

Adding **Page Numbers to a Report**

You can print page numbers in a report by including an expression in the Page Header or Page Footer section. You can type the expression in an unbound control, just as you did for the Date function, or you can use the Page Numbers option on the Insert menu. The inserted page number expression automatically prints the correct page number on each page of a report.

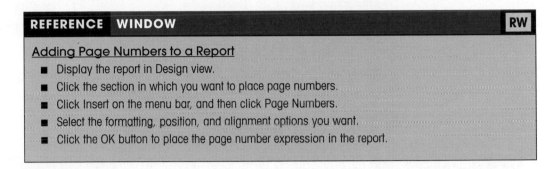

REFERENCE WINDOW   **RW**

Adding Page Numbers to a Report
- Display the report in Design view.
- Click the section in which you want to place page numbers.
- Click Insert on the menu bar, and then click Page Numbers.
- Select the formatting, position, and alignment options you want.
- Click the OK button to place the page number expression in the report.

Elsa wants the page number to be printed at the right side of the Page Header section, on the same line with the date. You'll use the Page Numbers option to insert the page number in the report.

To add page numbers in the Page Header section:

1. Click an empty area of the Page Header section to deselect the Date text box.

2. Click **Insert** on the menu bar, and then click **Page Numbers**. The Page Numbers dialog box opens.

   You use the Format options to specify the format of the page number. Elsa wants page numbers to appear as Page 1, Page 2, and so on. This is the Page N format option. You use the Position options to place the page numbers at the top of the page in the Page Header section or at the bottom of the page in the Page Footer section. Elsa's design shows page numbers at the top of the page.

3. Make sure that the **Page N** option button in the Format section and that the **Top of Page [Header]** option button in the Position section are both selected.

   The report design shows page numbers at the right side of the page. You can specify this placement in the Alignment list box.

4. Click the **Alignment** list arrow, and then click **Right**.

5. Make sure that the **Show Number on First Page** check box is checked, so the page number prints on the first page and all other pages as well. See Figure 6-41.

Figure 6-41   **COMPLETED PAGE NUMBERS DIALOG BOX**

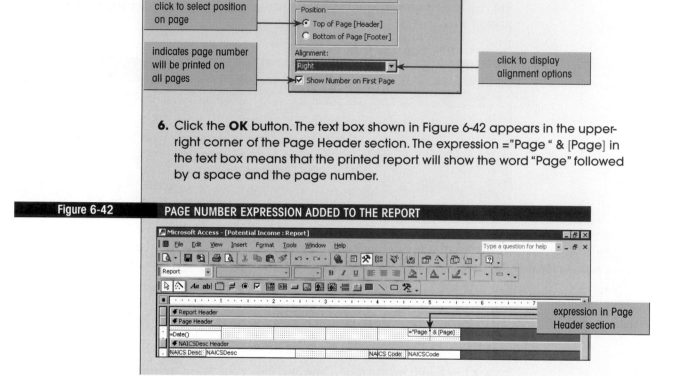

click to select format

click to select position on page

indicates page number will be printed on all pages

click to display alignment options

6. Click the **OK** button. The text box shown in Figure 6-42 appears in the upper-right corner of the Page Header section. The expression ="Page " & [Page] in the text box means that the printed report will show the word "Page" followed by a space and the page number.

Figure 6-42   **PAGE NUMBER EXPRESSION ADDED TO THE REPORT**

expression in Page Header section

Elsa wants the word "Page," the page number, and the date to be bold. You could select both controls and then set both to bold at the same time. Or you could select one of the two controls, set it to bold, and then duplicate the formatting for the other control. To duplicate a control's formatting, you can use the Format Painter. The **Format Painter** lets you copy the format of a control to other controls in the report. With the Format Painter, creating several controls with the same font style, size, color, and special effect is easy.

Elsa's report design also shows the page number's bottom edge aligned with the date in the Page Header section.

To use the Format Painter and to align controls:

1. Click the **Date** text box to select it, and then click the **Bold** button **B** on the Formatting toolbar to change the date to bold.

2. Click the **Format Painter** button on the Report Design toolbar.

3. Click the **Page Number** text box. The Format Painter automatically formats the Page Number text box like the Date text box, changing its font to bold.

   You'll now align the bottom border of the Date and Page Number text boxes.

4. Hold down the **Shift** key, click the **Page Number** text box, release the **Shift** key, click **Format** on the menu bar, point to **Align**, and then click **Bottom**. The bottom borders of the text boxes are now aligned.

5. Switch to Print Preview. See Figure 6-43.

Figure 6-43   DATE AND PAGE NUMBER IN THE PAGE HEADER SECTION

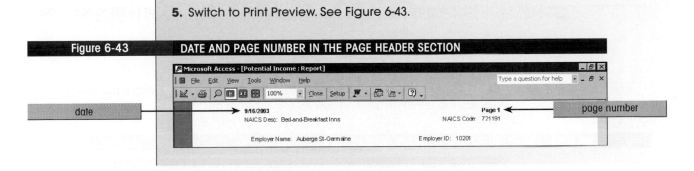

Now you are ready to add the title to the Page Header section.

Adding a Title to a Report

Elsa's report design includes the title "Potential Income," which you'll add to the Page Header section. To emphasize the report title, Elsa asks you to change it to bold and increase its font size from 8 points, the default, to 14 points.

To add the title to the Page Header section:

1. Switch to Design view.

2. Click the **Label** tool [Aa] on the toolbox, and then position the pointer in the Page Header section. The pointer changes to a ⁺A shape.

3. Position the pointer's plus symbol (+) at the top of the Page Header section and at the 1.75-inch mark on the horizontal ruler, and then click the mouse button. Access places a very narrow text box in the Page Header section. When you start typing in this text box, it will expand to accommodate the text.

4. Type **Potential Income**, and then press the **Enter** key. See Figure 6-44.

Figure 6-44   ADDING A LABEL FOR THE REPORT TITLE

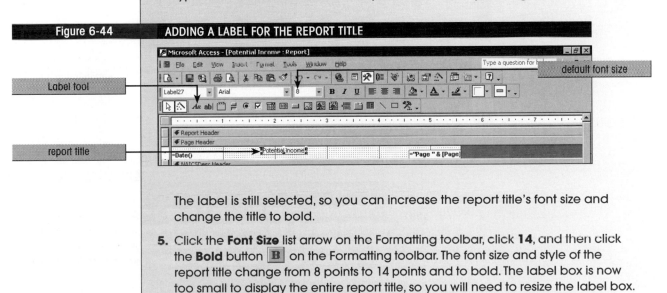

The label is still selected, so you can increase the report title's font size and change the title to bold.

5. Click the **Font Size** list arrow on the Formatting toolbar, click **14**, and then click the **Bold** button [B] on the Formatting toolbar. The font size and style of the report title change from 8 points to 14 points and to bold. The label box is now too small to display the entire report title, so you will need to resize the label box.

6. Click **Format** on the menu bar, point to **Size**, and then click **To Fit** to resize the report title text box.

Elsa wants to see how the report looks, so you'll switch to Print Preview to check the report against her design.

7. Save your report design changes, switch to Print Preview and, if necessary, scroll the Print Preview window to see more of the report. See Figure 6-45.

Figure 6-45 | **REPORT TITLE IN THE PAGE HEADER SECTION**

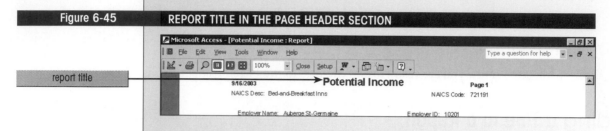

8. Review the first several pages of the report in Print Preview. Notice that the NAICSDesc Header section on page 5 appears near the bottom of the page, and the first employer name within this group appears at the top of the next page. See Figure 6-46.

Figure 6-46 | **GROUP HEADER SECTION ORPHANED FROM GROUP'S FIRST EMPLOYER**

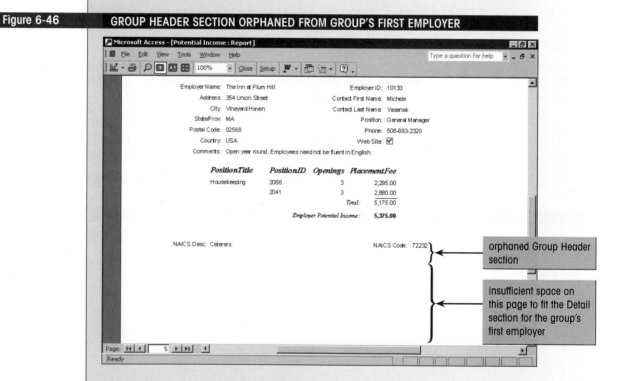

TROUBLE? If your Print Preview screen for page 5 doesn't match the one shown in Figure 6-46, navigate through the remaining Print Preview pages to find a similar Group Header section with the same problem. Depending on your printer driver, you might not find a similar Group Header section; in this case, simply continue with the tutorial.

The Group Header section shown in Figure 6-46 is an example of an orphaned header section. An **orphaned header section** appears by itself at the bottom of a page. Elsa prefers to see the NAICSDesc Header printed at the top of a page, just before the first employer name in the group. To do this, you'll set the Keep Together property for the NAICSDesc Header section. The **Keep Together property** prints a group header on a page only if there is enough room on the page to print the first detail record for the group; otherwise, the group header prints at the top of the next page.

Now you'll set the Keep Together property for the NAICSDesc Header section.

To set the Keep Together property for the NAICSDesc Header section:

1. Switch to Design view.

2. Click the **Sorting and Grouping** button [≣] on the Report Design toolbar to open the Sorting and Grouping dialog box. The NAICSDesc field is selected.

3. Click the right side of the **Keep Together** text box, and then click **With First Detail**. The NAICSDesc Header section will now print on a page only if the first detail record for the group can also print on the page.

4. Close the Sorting and Grouping dialog box.

5. Switch to Print Preview, and then navigate through the Print Preview pages to verify that the orphaned header section problem no longer exists.

6. Switch to Design view.

To make your report look like Elsa's report design, your final task is to add blue horizontal lines to the Page Header, NAICSDesc Header, and Detail sections. You'll first increase the height of the Page Header section so it will be easier to add the line below the three controls in the section.

To add lines to the report:

1. Use the ✛ pointer to increase the height of the Page Header section to the 0.5-inch mark on the vertical ruler. The new height of the Page Header section will allow sufficient room to add a horizontal line in this section below the three controls.

   You can now add a line under the controls in the Page Header section. If you want to make sure you draw a straight horizontal line, press the Shift key before you start drawing the line and release the Shift key after you've created the line.

2. Click the **Line** tool [◣] on the toolbox, position the pointer at the left edge of the Page Header section and on the bottom border of the Date text box, and then draw a horizontal line from left to right, ending at the 5-inch mark on the horizontal ruler.

   Elsa's report design shows a thick blue line in the Page Header section, so you'll now change the line to match the design.

3. Click the list arrow for the **Line/Border Color** button [✎] on the Formatting toolbar, and then click the dark blue box in the color palette in row 1 and column 6. The line's color changes to dark blue.

4. Click the list arrow for the **Line/Border Width** button ▢ on the Formatting toolbar, and then click width **3**. The line changes to a thick blue line. See Figure 6-47.

Figure 6-47

AFTER ADDING A THICK BLUE LINE IN THE PAGE HEADER SECTION

Line/Border Color button

Line/Border Width button

horizontal line

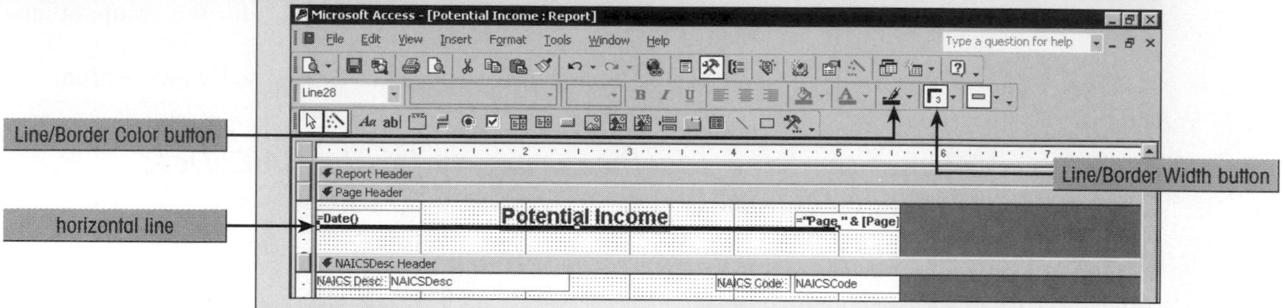

You need to place a copy of the thick blue line in the Detail section.

5. With the line selected, click the **Copy** button 📋 on the Report Design toolbar, click an empty area of the Detail section to make it the current section, and then click the **Paste** button 📋 on the Report Design toolbar. You've pasted a copy of the line at the top of the Detail section.

6. Position the pointer over the line in the Detail section; when it changes to a 🖐 shape, drag the line straight down to the 2.25-inch mark on the vertical ruler.

You can now reduce the height of the Page Header and Detail sections.

7. Use the ✛ pointer to decrease the height of the Page Header section so that the bottom of the section touches the blue line, and to decrease the height of the Detail section to the 2.375-inch mark on the vertical ruler.

Elsa's report design shows two thin, blue horizontal lines in the NAICSDesc Header section, so you'll now add these lines.

8. Click ╲ on the toolbox, position the pointer on the left edge of the NAICSDesc Header section and in the row of grid dots just above the 0.25-inch mark on the vertical ruler, and then draw a horizontal line from left to right, ending at the 5-inch mark on the horizontal ruler.

9. Click the **Line/Border Color** button 🖊 (not the list arrow) on the Formatting toolbar. The line changes to the dark blue color.

To draw the second line shown in Elsa's report design, you'll copy and paste the line you just drew.

10. Click 📋 on the Report Design toolbar, and then click 📋 on the Report Design toolbar. A copy of the line is positioned below it.

11. Drag the copied line straight up so that it's in the row of grid dots immediately below the original line. See Figure 6-48.

| Figure 6-48 | ADDING LINES TO THE REPORT |

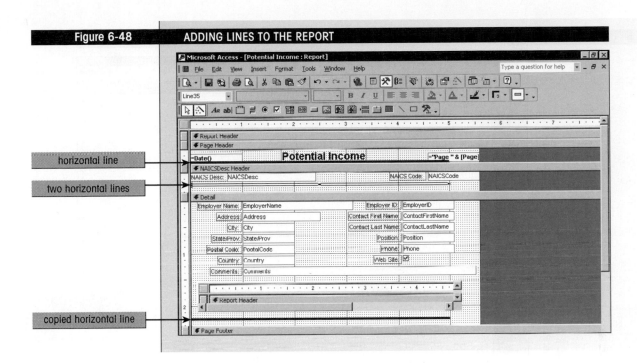

horizontal line

two horizontal lines

copied horizontal line

The Potential Income report is finished. You can now save the report and then preview its pages.

To save and preview the report:

1. Save your report changes, and then switch to Print Preview to display the first page of the report. See Figure 6-49.

| Figure 6-49 | PRINT PREVIEW OF PAGE 1 OF THE FINAL REPORT |

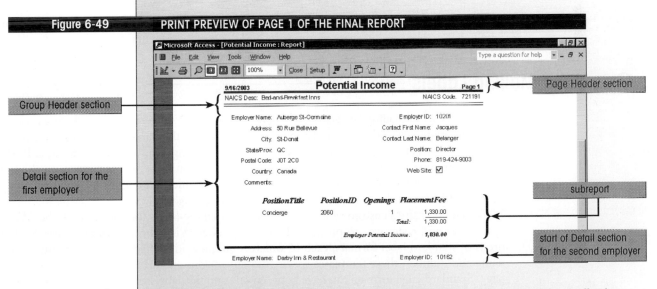

Group Header section

Detail section for the first employer

Page Header section

subreport

start of Detail section for the second employer

2. Use the navigation buttons to view the other pages of the report. In particular, note the information for Seaview Restaurant, which appears on approximately page 5. For this employer, the Comments field's Can Grow property has expanded its text box vertically to display its three lines of text. Also, because Seaview Restaurant has no available positions, the subreport's Can Shrink property removed the blank space for this control. See Figure 6-50.

Figure 6-50   CAN GROW AND CAN SHRINK PROPERTIES

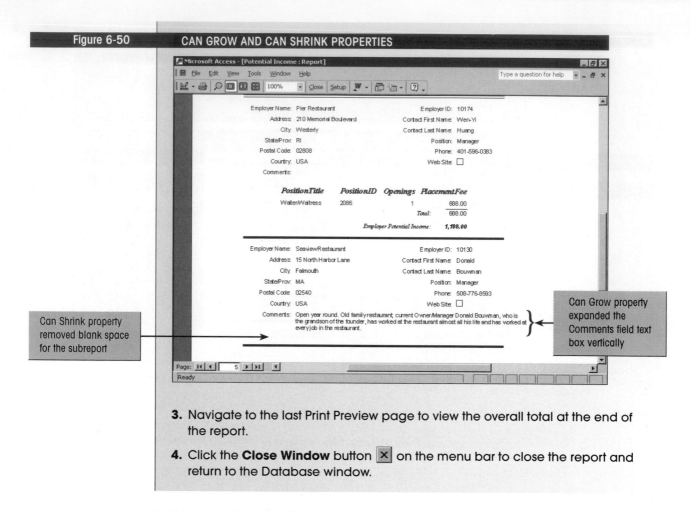

3. Navigate to the last Print Preview page to view the overall total at the end of the report.

4. Click the **Close Window** button ⊠ on the menu bar to close the report and return to the Database window.

Now that you've finished the Potential Income report, Elsa wants you to create mailing labels that can be used in mass mailings to NSJI's employer clients.

Creating Mailing Labels

Elsa needs a set of mailing labels printed for all employers, so she can mail a marketing brochure and other materials to them. The Employer table contains the name and address information that will serve as the source data for the labels. Each mailing label will have the same format: contact name on the first line; employer name on the second line; street address on the third line; city, state or province, and postal code on the fourth line; and country on the fifth line. In addition, Elsa wants the NSJI logo to appear on each mailing label.

You could create a custom report to produce the mailing labels, but using the Label Wizard is an easier and faster way to produce them. The **Label Wizard** provides templates for hundreds of standard label formats, each of which is uniquely identified by a label manufacturer's name and number; these templates specify the dimensions and arrangement of labels on each page. Standard label formats can have between one and five labels across a page; the number of labels printed on a single page also varies. Elsa's mailing labels are Avery number C2163; each sheet has 1.5-inch by 3.9-inch labels arranged in two columns and six rows on the page.

REFERENCE   WINDOW   RW

Creating Mailing Labels and Other Labels
- In the Database window, click Reports in the Objects bar of the Database window to display the Reports list box.
- Click the New button in the Database window to open the New Report dialog box.
- Click Label Wizard to select it, select the table or query that contains the source data for the mailing labels, and then click the OK button.
- Select the label manufacturer and its product number, and then click the Next button.
- Select the label font, color, and style, and then click the Next button.
- Construct the label content by selecting the fields from the data source and specifying their placement and spacing on the label, and then click the Next button.
- Select the sort fields, click the Next button, specify the report name, and then click the Finish button.

You'll use the Label Wizard to create a report to produce mailing labels for all employer clients.

To use the Label Wizard to create the mailing label report:

1. Make sure that **Reports** is selected in the Objects bar of the Database window, and then click the **New** button in the Database window to open the New Report dialog box.

2. Click **Label Wizard**, click the list arrow to display the list of tables and queries in the Jobs database, click **Employer** to select this table as the basis for your report, and then click the **OK** button. The first Label Wizard dialog box opens and asks you to select the standard or custom label you'll use.

3. Make sure that the **English** option button is selected in the Unit of Measure section, that the **Sheet feed** option button is selected in the Label Type section, that **Avery** is selected in the Filter by manufacturer list box, and then click **C2163** in the Product number list box. See Figure 6-51.

Figure 6-51	SELECTING A STANDARD LABEL

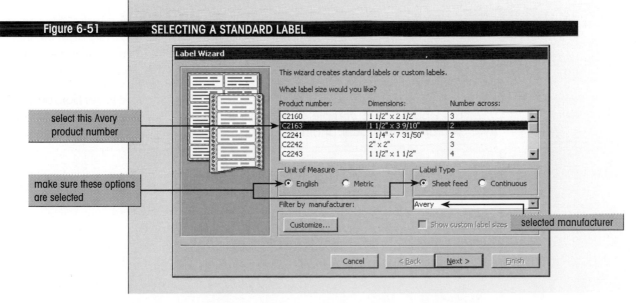

select this Avery product number

make sure these options are selected

selected manufacturer

Because you've filtered the labels by Avery as the manufacturer, the top list box shows the Avery product number, dimensions, and number of labels across the page for each of its standard label formats. If your label manufacturer or its labels do not appear in the list box, you can create your own custom format for them. You can display the dimensions in the list in either inches or millimeters by choosing the appropriate option in the Unit of Measure section. You can also specify in the Label Type section whether the labels are on individual sheets or are continuous forms.

4. Click the **Next** button to open the second Label Wizard dialog box, in which you choose font specifications for the labels.

   Elsa wants the labels to use 10-point Arial with a medium font weight and without italics or underlines. The font weight determines how light or dark the characters will print; you can choose from nine values ranging from thin to heavy.

5. If necessary, select **Arial** for the Font name, **10** for the Font size, and **Medium** for the Font weight; make sure the Italic and the Underline check boxes are unchecked and that black is the Text color; and then click the **Next** button to open the third Label Wizard dialog box, from which you select the data to appear on the labels.

   As you select fields from the Available fields list box or type text for the label, the Prototype label box shows the format for the label. Elsa wants the mailing labels to print the ContactFirstName and ContactLastName fields on the first line; the EmployerName field on the second line; the Address field on the third line; the City, State/Prov, and PostalCode fields on the fourth line; and the Country field on the fifth line. One space will separate the ContactFirstName and ContactLastName fields, the City and State/Prov fields, and the State/Prov and PostalCode fields.

6. Scroll down and click **ContactFirstName** in the Available fields list box, click the ⟩ button to move the field to the Prototype label box, press the **space-bar**, click **ContactLastName** in the Available fields list box (if necessary), and then click the ⟩ button (see Figure 6-52). The braces around the field names in the Prototype label box indicate that the name represents a field rather than text that you entered.

   TROUBLE? If you select the wrong field or type the wrong text, highlight the incorrect item in the Prototype label box, press the Delete key to remove the item, and then select the correct field or type the correct text.

7. Press the **Enter** key to move to the next line in the Prototype label box, and then use Figure 6-52 to complete the entries in the Prototype label box. Make sure you press the spacebar after selecting the City field and the State/Prov field.

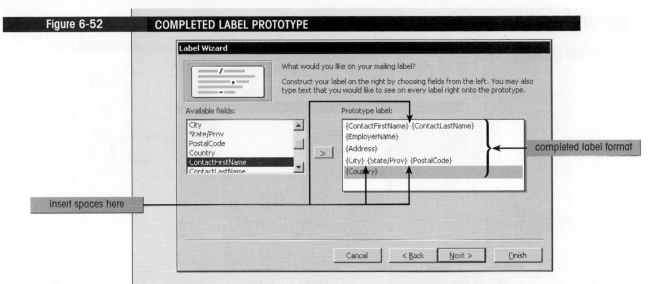

Figure 6-52   COMPLETED LABEL PROTOTYPE

8. Click the **Next** button to open the fourth Label Wizard dialog box, in which you choose the sort keys for the labels.

   Elsa wants the PostalCode to be the primary sort key and the EmployerName to be the secondary sort key

9. Select the **PostalCode** field as the primary sort key, select the **EmployerName** field as the secondary sort key, and then click the **Next** button to open the last Label Wizard dialog box, in which you enter a name for the report.

10. Type **Employer Mailing Labels**, and then click the **Finish** button. Access saves the report as Employer Mailing Labels and then opens the Report window in Print Preview.

11. Click the **Zoom** list arrow on the Print Preview toolbar, and then click **Fit**. The first page of the report appears. Note that two columns of labels appear across the page. See Figure 6-53.

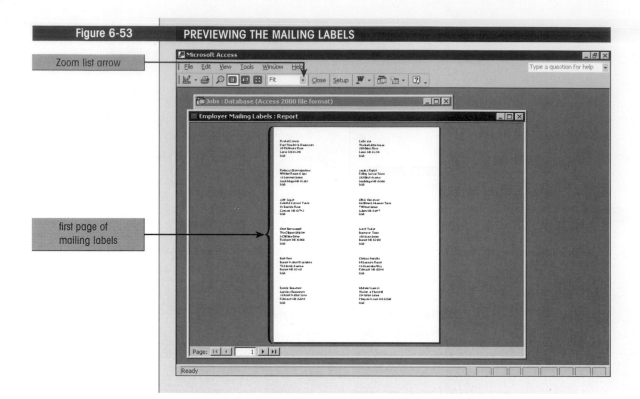

Figure 6-53   PREVIEWING THE MAILING LABELS

Zoom list arrow

first page of
mailing labels

Elsa wants the NSJI logo to appear on each mailing label, but first you'll review the mailing labels more closely to see if Elsa has other changes for you to make.

To preview the mailing label report in greater detail:

1. Click the **Zoom** list arrow on the Print Preview toolbar, and then click **75%** to preview the report in greater detail. See Figure 6-54.

Figure 6-54   PREVIEWING THE LABEL CONTENT AND SEQUENCE

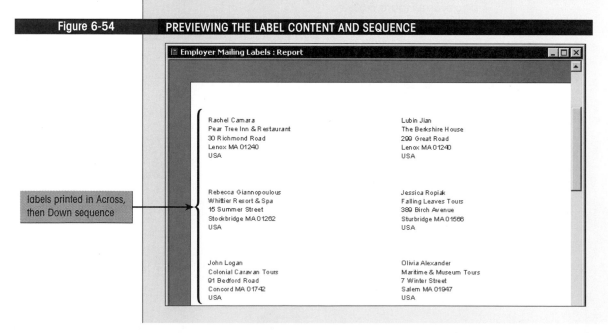

labels printed in Across,
then Down sequence

The Employer Mailing Labels report is a **multiple-column report**, one that prints the same collection of data fields in two or more sets across the page. The labels will print in ascending PostalCode order and then in ascending EmployerName order. The first label will print in the upper-left corner on the first page, the second label will print to its right, the third label will print under the first label, and so on. This style of multiple-column report is the "across, then down" layout. Instead, Elsa wants the labels to print with the "down, then across" layout—the first label prints, the second label prints under the first, and so on. After the bottom label in the first column is printed, the next label is printed at the top of the second column. The "down, then across" layout is also called **newspaper-style columns**, or **snaking columns**.

Elsa also wants the NSJI logo to print above the employer name and address information, so you'll add the logo as a picture in the report.

To change the layout and to add a picture to the mailing label report:

1. Switch to Design view. The Detail section, the only section in the report, is sized for a single label.

   First, you'll change the layout to snaking columns.

2. Click **File** on the menu bar, click **Page Setup**, and then click the **Columns** tab. The Page Setup dialog box displays the Columns options for the report. See Figure 6-55.

Figure 6-55	COLUMNS OPTIONS IN THE PAGE SETUP DIALOG BOX

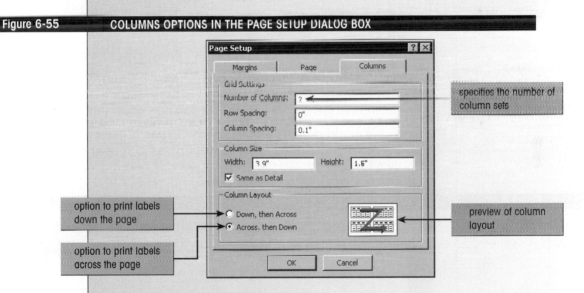

The Columns options in the Page Setup dialog box let you change the properties of a multiple-column report. In the Grid Settings section, you specify the number of column sets and the row and column spacing between the column sets. In the Column Size section, you specify the width and height of each column set. In the Column Layout section, you select between the "Down, then Across" and the "Across, then Down" layouts.

You can now change the layout for the labels.

3. Click the **Down, then Across** option button, and then click the **OK** button.

   Because Elsa wants the NSJI logo printed above the employer data, you'll select all controls and move them down the Detail section.

4. Click **Edit** on the menu bar, and then click **Select All** to select all controls in the Detail section.

5. Position the pointer over one of the selected controls; when the pointer changes to a ✋ shape, drag the controls straight down the Detail section until the top border of the top control is at the 0.375-inch mark on the vertical ruler.

Next, you'll add the NSJI logo above the employer information. You could add the logo to the report in the same way you added a picture to a form by using the Image tool on the toolbox. Instead, you'll use the Picture option on the Insert menu.

6. Click an empty area of the grid to deselect all controls, click **Insert** on the menu bar, and then click **Picture**. The Insert Picture dialog box opens.

7. Make sure **Tutorial** appears in the Look in list box, click **NSJILogo** to select the picture file, and then click the **OK** button. The Insert Picture dialog box closes and the picture is inserted in the upper-left corner of the Detail section.

8. Move the picture straight to the right until its left edge is at the 2-inch mark on the horizontal ruler. See Figure 6-56.

Figure 6-56   FINAL DESIGN FOR THE MAILING LABELS

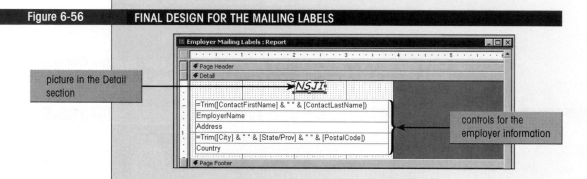

picture in the Detail section

controls for the employer information

You've finished Elsa's changes, so you can now save and preview the report.

9. Save your report design changes, and then switch to Print Preview. The logo will print on each label, and the labels appear in the snaking-columns layout. See Figure 6-57.

Figure 6-57   THE COMPLETED LABELS IN PRINT PREVIEW

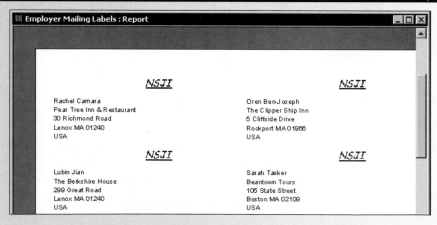

Because you've finished Elsa's reports, you can now close the Jobs database and exit Access.

10. Click the **Close** button ⊠ on the Access window title bar to close the Jobs database and to exit Access.

Elsa is very pleased with the two new reports, which will provide her with improved information and help expedite her written communications with NSJI's employer clients.

Session 6.3 QUICK CHECK

1. What do you type in a text box control to print the current date?

2. How do you insert a page number in the Page Header section?

3. You can use the _____ to copy the format of a control to other controls.

4. The Keep Together property prints a group header on a page only if there is enough room on the page to print the first _____ record for the group.

5. What is a multiple-column report?

REVIEW ASSIGNMENTS

Elsa wants you to create a custom report for the **Students** database that prints all recruiters and the students they've recruited. You will create the report by completing the following steps.

1. Make sure your Data Disk is in the appropriate disk drive, start Access, and then open the **Students** database in the Review folder on your Data Disk.

2. Create a custom report based on the **Recruiter** table. Figure 6-58 shows a sample of the completed report. Refer to the figure as a guide as you complete Steps 3 through 7.

Figure 6-58

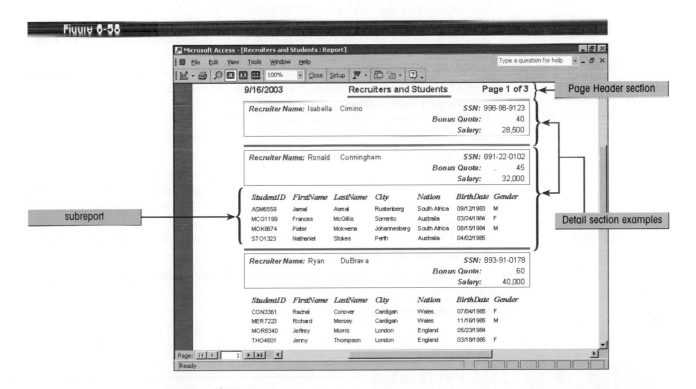

3. Use the **Recruiter** table as the source for the main report.

4. Make the following modifications to the main report:
   a. Include the following sections in the main report: Page Header, Detail, and Page Footer.
   b. At the top center of the Page Header section, enter the report title and format it with dark blue, 12-point, bold Arial font. Use the same format for the current date at the left edge of the section and for the page number at the right edge of the section. Use the "Page N of M" format for page numbers. Add a red line with a 3-point border width below the report title.
   c. Type your name in the top center of the Page Footer section with the same format that you used for the report title, and then save the report as **Recruiters and Students**.
   d. Add all fields from the **Recruiter** table to the Detail section, using Figure 6-58 as a guide.
   e. Delete the LastName label. Change the caption for the FirstName label to "Recruiter Name:", change the caption for the BonusQuota label to "Bonus Quota:", and resize both labels to fit.
   f. Change all labels and text boxes in the Detail section to 10-point Arial font; format all the labels with dark blue, bold, italic font; and then size all labels to fit.

Explore ▷   g. Draw a rectangle around the recruiter controls in the Detail section, and then change the rectangle's border color to red. Use the Send to Back option on the Format menu to position the rectangle.
   h. Sort the recruiter records in ascending order by the LastName field, and then in ascending order by the FirstName field.

5. Use the following instructions to add a subreport using Control Wizards to the Detail section:
   a. Select all fields from the **Student** table, link the main report and subreport using the SSN field, and name the subreport **Student Subreport**.
   b. Delete the subreport label.
   c. Open the subreport in a new window, and then delete the RecruiterName label and text box.
   d. Resize all labels to their best fit.
   e. By switching between Design view and Print Preview, resize each text box so that it's just wide enough to display the entire field value, and move and resize the labels and text boxes as necessary.
   f. Left-align all text boxes and their corresponding labels.
   g. Move all text boxes straight up to the top of the Detail section to eliminate all extra blank space above the text boxes, and then reduce the height of the Detail section until the bottom of the section touches the bottom of the text boxes.
   h. Reduce the subreport's width until the right edge touches the right edge of the Gender controls.
   i. Sort the student records in ascending order by the LastName field, and then in ascending order by the FirstName field.
   j. Hide duplicate values for the Gender field.
   k. Save the subreport design changes, and then close the subreport.

6. Make the following modifications to the main report:
   a. By switching between Design view and Print Preview, reduce the width of the subreport control in the Detail section from the right as much as possible (approximately 6 inches or less).
   b. Set the subreport border style to Transparent, and set its Can Shrink property to Yes.
   c. Add a red line with a 3-point border width below the subreport control.

Explore ▷   d. Set the Can Shrink property of the Detail section to Yes. (*Hint*: Click the Detail section bar to make the entire section the current control.)

7. Save your report design changes, switch to Print Preview, print the report's first page, and then close the report.

8. Close the **Students** database, and then exit Access.

CASE PROBLEMS

Case 1. Lim's Video Photography Youngho Lim wants you to create a custom report and mailing labels for the **Clients** database. The custom report will be based on the results of two queries you will create. You will create the queries, the custom report, and the mailing labels by completing the following steps.

1. Make sure your Data Disk is in the appropriate disk drive, start Access, and then open the **Clients** database in the Cases folder on your Data Disk.

2. Create two queries for the custom report following these instructions:
   a. For the first query, select (in order) the ShootDesc field from the **ShootDesc** table; and then select the ShootDate, Duration, Location, and Contract# fields from the **Shoot** table. Sort the query in ascending order by the Contract# field. Save the query as **Shoot Data**, run and print the query, and then close the query.
   b. For the second query, select all fields from the **Client** table; and then select all fields, except the Client# field, from the **Contract** table. Sort the query in ascending order by the Contract# field. Save the query as **Clients and Contracts**, run the query, print it in land-scape orientation, and then close the query.

3. Create a custom report based on the **Clients and Contracts** query. Figure 6-59 shows a sample of the completed report. Refer to the figure as a guide as you complete Steps 4 through 8.

Figure 6-59

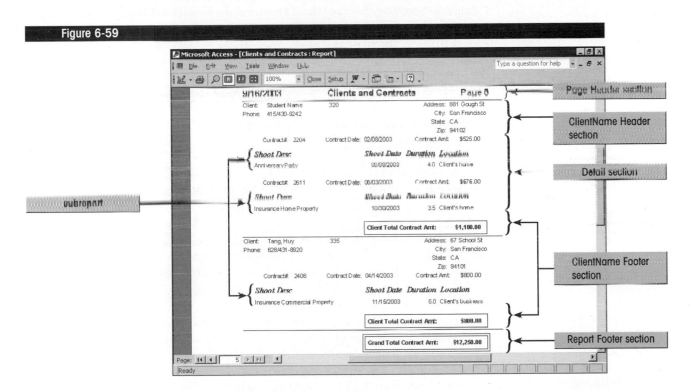

4. Use the **Clients and Contracts** query as the source for the main report.

5. Make the following modifications to the main report:
   a. You'll be directed to include the following sections in your report: Page Header, ClientName Header, Detail, ClientName Footer, Page Footer, and Report Footer.
   b. At the top center of the Page Header section, enter the report title and format it with Arial 12-point, bold font. Use the same format for the current date at the left edge of the section and for the page number at the right edge of the section. Below the controls in the Page Header section, add a dark blue line running from the left edge of the section to approxi-mately the 5-inch mark on the horizontal ruler.
   c. Enter your name in the top center of the Page Footer section with the same format that you used for the report title, and then save the report as **Clients and Contracts**.

    d. Sort the main report records in ascending order by the ClientName field, and then in ascending order by the Contract# field. Add Group Header and Group Footer sections for the ClientName field, and set its Keep Together property to "Whole Group."

    e. Add the ClientName, Client#, Phone, Address, City, State, and Zip fields from the **Clients and Contracts** query to the ClientName Header section. Delete the Client# label, and change the caption for the ClientName label to "Client:". Resize and reposition the labels and text boxes in the ClientName Header section as shown in Figure 6-59, positioning the Client# text box to the right of the ClientName text box.

    f. Add the Contract#, ContractDate, and ContractAmt fields from the **Clients and Contracts** query to the Detail section. Change the ContractDate label to "Contract Date:" and the ContractAmt label to "Contract Amt:". Resize and reposition the labels and text boxes in the Detail section as shown in Figure 6-59.

6. Use the following instructions to add a subreport using Control Wizards to the Detail section:

    a. Select all fields from the **Shoot Data** query, link the main report and subreport using the Contract# field, and name the subreport **Shoot Subreport**.

    b. Open the subreport in a new window, and then delete the Contract# label and text box.

    c. Change the ShootDesc label to "Shoot Desc" and the ShootDate label to "Shoot Date".

    d. By switching between Design view and Print Preview, resize each text box so that it's just wide enough to display the entire field value.

    e. Resize and reposition the labels in the Report Header section and the text boxes in the Detail section until they're positioned as shown in Figure 6-59.

    f. Move all text boxes straight up to the top of the Detail section to eliminate all extra blank space above the text boxes, and then reduce the height of the Detail section until the bottom of the section touches the bottom of the text boxes.

    g. If necessary, reduce the subreport's width until its right edge touches the right edge of the Location controls.

    h. Sort the subreport records in ascending order by the ShootDate field.

    i. Save the subreport design changes, and then close the subreport.

7. Make the following modifications to the main report:

    a. Delete the subreport label.

    b. By switching between Design view and Print Preview, reduce the width of the subreport control in the Detail section from the right as much as possible.

    c. Set the subreport border style to Transparent, and set its Can Shrink property to Yes.

    d. Reduce the height of the Detail section to just below the subreport control, and then reduce the width of the main report as much as possible.

    e. Add a text box to the ClientName Footer section, enter the function to calculate the total of the ContractAmt field values, format the calculated field as currency, change the label caption to "Client Total Contract Amt:", and then format both controls as bold. Resize and reposition the controls in the ClientName Footer section as shown in Figure 6-59.

Explore   f. Draw a rectangle around the controls in the ClientName Footer section, and then change the rectangle's border color to dark blue. Use the Send to Back option on the Format menu to position the rectangle.

    g. Add the Report Footer section, but not the Report Header section, to the main report. Add a text box to the Report Footer section, enter the function to calculate the total of the ContractAmt field values, and format the calculated field as currency. Change the label caption to "Grand Total Contract Amt:", and then format both controls as bold. Resize and reposition the controls in the Report Footer section as shown in Figure 6-59.

Explore   h. Draw a rectangle around the controls in the Report Footer section, and then change the rectangle's border color to dark blue. Use the Send to Back option on the Format menu to position the rectangle. Draw a second rectangle around the first rectangle, and then set its properties to match the properties for the inner rectangle.

    i. Add a dark blue line below the controls in the ClientName Footer section. Start the line at the left edge of the section and end it at approximately the 5-inch mark on the horizontal ruler.

j. If necessary, reduce the height of the ClientName Footer and Report Footer sections to the bottom of the controls in the section.

8. Save your report design changes, switch to Print Preview, print the first and last pages of the report, and then close the report.

9. Use the following instructions to create the mailing labels:
    a. Use the **Client** table as the source for the mailing labels.
    b. Use Durable 1452 labels, and use the default font and color. (*Hint*: Make sure the Metric option button is selected in the Unit of Measure section.)
    c. For the prototype label, place ClientName on the first line; Address on the second line; and City, a space, State, a space, and Zip on the third line.
    d. Sort by Zip and then by ClientName, and then enter the report name **Client Labels**.
    e. Print the first page of the report, and then close the report.

10. Close the **Clients** database, and then exit Access.

Case 2. DineAtHome.course.com Claire Picard wants you to create a custom report and mailing labels for the **Delivery** database. The custom report will be based on the results of a query you will create. You will create the query, the custom report, and the mailing labels by completing the following steps.

1. Make sure your Data Disk is in the appropriate disk drive, start Access, and then open the **Delivery** database in the Cases folder on your Data Disk.

2. Create a new query based on the **Restaurant** and **Order** tables. Select all fields from the **Restaurant** table, and select all fields except Restaurant# from the **Order** table. Add a calculated field named BillTotal that adds the OrderAmt and DeliveryCharge fields; use the IIf function to add an additional $2 to the BillTotal field if the City field value is Naples. Save the query as **Restaurant Orders**, and then close it.

3. Create a custom report based on the **Restaurant Orders** query. Figure 6-60 shows a sample of the completed report. Refer to the figure as a guide as you create the report.

Figure 6-60

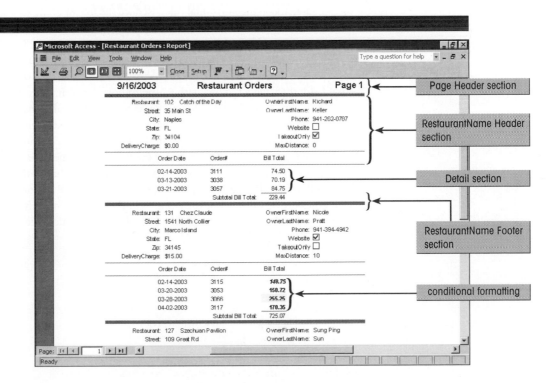

a. Sort the report records in ascending order by the RestaurantName field, and then in ascending order by the OrderDate field. Add Group Header and Group Footer sections for the RestaurantName field, and set its Keep Together property to "Whole Group."

b. In the RestaurantName Header section, add all fields from the **Restaurant Orders** query, except for the three **Order** table fields. Delete the Restaurant# label. Change the caption for the RestaurantName label to "Restaurant:", and then resize the label to fit. Resize and reposition the labels and text boxes as shown in Figure 6-60, placing the Restaurant# and RestaurantName text boxes to the right of the Restaurant label.

c. Add a red line to the RestaurantName Header section in the row of grid dots below the bottom controls. Start the line at the left edge of the section and end it at the 5-inch mark on the horizontal ruler. Save the report as **Restaurant Orders**.

Explore ▶ d. From the **Restaurant Orders** query, add the OrderDate, Order#, and BillTotal fields to the Detail section. Cut the three labels in the Detail section and paste them into the RestaurantName Header section. (*Hint*: Select the three labels, click the Cut button on the Report Design toolbar, click the RestaurantName Header bar, and then click the Paste button on the Report Design toolbar.) Change the captions for the OrderDate and BillTotal labels, resize them to fit, reposition the three labels, and then delete the colons from the label captions.

e. Add a second red line to the RestaurantName Header section in the row of grid dots below the three labels, and then reduce the height of the section to the row of grid dots below the line.

Explore ▶ f. Resize the three text boxes in the Detail section, move the text boxes to the top of the section, and then reduce the height of the section to the bottom of the text boxes. Define conditional formatting rules for the BillTotal field—use bold and italic font for values between 100 and 150, use bold for values between 150.01 and 200, and use a bold, dark blue font and a light yellow fill for values over 200. Set the BillTotal field's Format property to Fixed and its Decimal Places property to 2.

g. At the top center of the Page Header section, enter the report title and format it with 12-point Arial bold font. Use the same format for the current date at the left edge of the section and for the page number at the right edge of the section. Add a red line with a 4-point border width under the controls in the Page Header section. Start the line at the left edge of the section and end it at the 5-inch mark on the horizontal ruler. Reduce the height of the section to the row of grid dots below the line.

h. Add a text box to the RestaurantName Footer section, enter the function to calculate the total of the BillTotal field values, format the calculated field as Standard, and then change the label caption to "Subtotal Bill Total:". Add a short red line at the top of the section, above the calculated field; then add a red line with a 4-point border width below the controls in the section. Extend the line from the left edge of the section to the 5-inch mark on the horizontal ruler. Reduce the height of the section to the row of grid dots below the line.

i. Add the Report Footer section, but not the Report Header section, to the report. Add a text box to the Report Footer section, enter the function to calculate the total of the BillTotal field values, format the calculated field as Standard, and then change the label caption to "Grand Total Bill Total:". Resize and reposition the controls in the Report Footer. Add a red line with a 4-point border width below the controls in the section. Start the line at the left edge of the section and end it at the 5-inch mark on the horizontal ruler. See Figure 6-61.

Figure 6-61

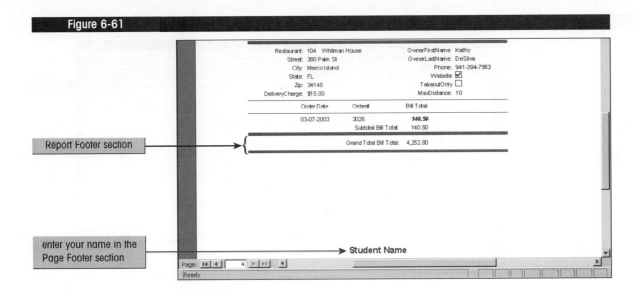

Report Footer section

enter your name in the Page Footer section

j. Enter your name in the top center of the Page Footer section with the same format you used for the report title.

4. Save your report design changes, switch to Print Preview, print the last page of the report, and then close the report.

5. Use the following instruction to create the mailing labels:

   a. Use the **Restaurant** table as the source for the mailing labels.

   b. Use Avery C2160 labels, and use the default font and color. (*Hint*: Make sure the English option button is selected in the Unit of Measure section.)

   c. For the prototype label, place OwnerFirstName, a space, and OwnerLastName on the first line; RestaurantName on the second line; Street on the third line; and City, a space, State, a space, and Zip on the fourth line.

   d. Sort by Zip and then by RestaurantName, and then type the report name **Restaurant Labels**.

   e. Select all controls in the Detail section, and then move them straight down until the top border of the top selected control is at the 0.75-inch mark on the vertical ruler.

   f. Add the **DineLogo** picture, located in the Cases folder on your Data Disk, to the upper-left corner of the Detail section.

   g. Save your report design changes, print the first page of the report, and then close the report.

6. Close the **Delivery** database, and then exit Access.

Case 3. Redwood Zoo Michael Rosenfeld asks you to create a custom report for the **Donors** database so that he can better track pledges made by donors to the zoo's funds. You'll create the report by completing the following.

1. Make sure your Data Disk is in the appropriate disk drive, start Access, and then open the **Donors** database in the Cases folder on your Data Disk.

2. Create a new query based on the **Donor** and **Pledge** tables. Select the FirstName and LastName fields from the **Donor** table; then select the FundName, PledgeDate, TotalPledged, and PaymentMethod fields from the **Pledge** table. Save the query as **Donor Pledges**, and then close it.

3. Create a custom report based on the **Fund** table. Figure 6-62 shows the completed report. Refer to the figure as a guide as you complete Steps 4 through 8.

Figure 6-62

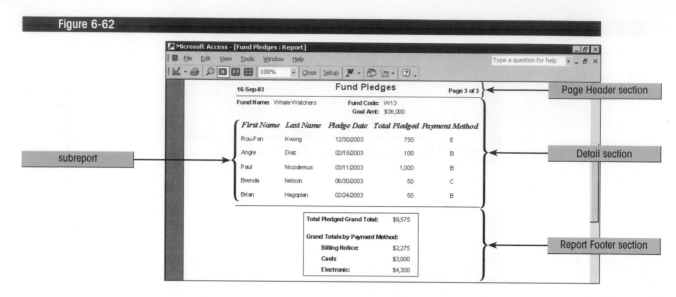

4. Use the **Fund** table as the source for the main report.

5. Make the following modifications to the main report:
   a. Sort the report records in ascending order by the FundName field.
   b. At the top center of the Page Header section, enter the report title and format it with 13-point Arial bold font. Add the current date at the left edge of the section, change it to bold, and then set the Format property to Medium Date. Add the page number at the right edge of the section, using the "Page N of M" format for the page numbers, and then change it to bold. Add a line to the section below the controls. Extend the line from the left edge of the current date text box to the right edge of the page number text box. If necessary, reduce the height of the Page Header section to the bottom of the controls in the section.
   c. Type your name in the top center of the Page Footer section with the same format you used for the report title, and then save the report as **Fund Pledges**.
   d. Add the three fields from the **Fund** table to the Detail section. Change the captions for the labels so that there's one space between each word, and make sure the labels are bold. Resize the labels to fit, and then resize and reposition the labels and text boxes in the Detail section as shown in Figure 6-62.

6. Use the following instructions to add a subreport using Control Wizards to the Detail section:
   a. Select all fields from the **Donor Pledges** query, link the main report and subreport using the FundCode field, and name the subreport **Fund Pledges Subreport**.
   b. Open the subreport in a new window, and then delete the FundName label and text box.
   c. Change the label captions by adding one space between each word, and then resize the labels to fit. Resize and reposition the labels and text boxes in the subreport as shown in Figure 6-62.
   d. If necessary, reduce the subreport width until its right edge touches the right edge of the PaymentMethod controls.
   e. Save the subreport design changes, and then close the subreport.

7. Make the following modifications to the main report:
   a. Delete the subreport label.
   b. By switching between Design view and Print Preview, reduce the width of the subreport control in the Detail section from the right as much as possible.
   c. Set the subreport border style to Transparent, and set its Can Shrink property to Yes.
   d. To the Detail section below the subreport, add a line that's the same length as the line in the Page Header section.
   e. Reduce the height of the Detail section to just below the line you drew below the subreport control, and then reduce the width of the main report as much as possible.

f. Add the Report Footer section, but not the Report Header section, to the main report. Add a text box to the Report Footer section, and then enter the DSum function to calculate the total of the TotalPledged field values from the **Donor Pledges** query. Format the calculated field as Currency with zero decimal places, and then change the label caption's text to "Total Pledged Grand Total:"and its font to bold. Resize and reposition the two controls in the Report Footer section, as shown in Figure 6-62.

Explore

g. Add a label below the two controls in the Report Footer section, using the caption value "Grand Totals by Payment Method:" and changing the text to bold. Below the label in the Report Footer section, add three text boxes. For each text box, enter the DSum function to calculate the total of the TotalPledged field values from the **Donor Pledges** query for each of the three PaymentMethod field values: B for a billing notice, C for cash, and E for electronic. (*Hint*: Use the same DSum function you used in Step 7f, but include the third optional *criteria* condition in the function. For example, use "PaymentMethod='B'" as the condition to calculate the total of the TotalPledged field values from billing notices as a payment method.) Set the captions for the three labels, format the text boxes as Currency with zero decimal places, and then resize and reposition the labels and text boxes.

Explore

h. Draw a rectangle around the controls in the Report Footer section, and then use the Send to Back option on the Format menu to position the rectangle.

i. If necessary, reduce the height of each section in the main report, and then reduce the width of the main report.

8. Save your report design changes, switch to Print Preview, print the first and last pages of the report, and then close the report.

9. Close the **Donors** database, and then exit Access.

Case 4. Mountain River Adventures Connor and Siobhan Dempsey want you to create a custom report and mailing labels for the **Outdoors** database. You will create the custom report and the mailing labels by completing the following steps.

1. Make sure your Data Disk is in the appropriate disk drive, start Access, and then open the **Outdoors** database in the Cases folder on your Data Disk.

2. Create a new query based on the **Rafting Trip** and **Booking** tables. Select all fields from the **Rafting Trip** table, and select all fields except River from the **Booking** table. Add a calculated field named TripFee that multiples the Fee/Person and People fields; use the IIf function to reduce the TripFee by 10% if the People field value is greater than six. Set the calculated field's Format property to Standard. Save the query as **Booked Rafting Trips**, and then close it.

3. Complete Steps 4 through 8 to create a custom report based on the **Client** table, saving the report as **Booked Trips**.

4. Use the **Client** table as the source for the main report.

5. Make the following modifications to the main report:
    a. Change the page orientation to landscape, and then change the width of the report to 7.5 inches.
    b. Sort the report records in ascending order by the Client# field.
    c. At the top center of the Page Header section, enter the report title of Booked Trips, and format it with 12-point Arial bold font. Use the same format for the current date at the left edge of the section and for the page number at the right edge of the section. Add a black line with a 3-point border width to underline the controls in the Page Header section. Extend the line from the left edge of the section to approximately the 7.5-inch mark on the horizontal ruler. If necessary, reduce the height of the Page Header section to the bottom of the controls in the section.
    d. In the top center of the Page Footer section, type your name. Use the same format for your name that you used for the report title, and then save the report.
    e. Add the eight fields from the **Client** table to the Detail section. Move the Client#, ClientName, Address, and City labels and text boxes in a column to the left. Move the State/Prov, and PostalCode, Country, and Phone labels and text boxes in a column to the right. Right-align the labels and left-align the text boxes.

6. Use the following instructions to add a subreport using Control Wizards to the Detail section:

   a. Select all fields from the **Booked Rafting Trips** query, link the main report and subreport using the Client# field, and name the subreport **Booked Trips Subreport**.

   b. Open the subreport in a new window, and then delete the Client# label and text box. Format the TripFee text box as Standard.

   c. Make sure the subreport page orientation is landscape, set its width to approximately 7.5 inches, and then resize and reposition its labels and text boxes. Switch between Print Preview and Design view to make sure that the labels and text boxes are aligned and that all field values are fully visible.

   d. Move all text boxes straight up to the top of the Detail section to eliminate all extra blank space above the text boxes, and then reduce the height of the Detail section until its bottom edge touches the bottom edges of the text boxes.

   e. Sort the subreport records in ascending order by the Client# field, and then sort in ascending order by the TripDate field. Add a Group Footer section for the Client# field, and set its Keep Together property to "Whole Group."

   f. Add a text box to the Client# Footer section, enter the function to calculate the total of the TripFee field values, format the calculated field as Standard, and then change the label caption to "Subtotal Trip Fee:". At the top of the section, add a short black line above the calculated field; then below the controls in the section, add a black line with a 3-point border width that extends from the left edge of the section to the 7.5-inch mark on the horizontal ruler. Reduce the height of the section to the row of grid dots below the line.

   g. Save the subreport design changes, and then close the subreport.

7. Make the following modifications to the main report:

   a. Delete the subreport label.

   b. Change the width of the subreport control in the Detail section so that it extends from the left edge of the section to the 7.5-inch mark on the horizontal ruler.

   c. Set the subreport border style to Transparent, and set its Can Shrink property to Yes.

   d. Reduce the height of the Detail section to just below the subreport control.

   e. Add the Report Footer section, but not the Report Header section, to the main report. Add a text box to the Report Footer section, and then enter the DSum function to calculate the total of the TripFee field values from the **Booked Rafting Trips** query. Format the calculated field as Standard with two decimal places, and then change the label caption to "Grand Total Trip Fee:". Change the label font to 11-point Times New Roman, change its style to bold and italic, and change its color to blue. Resize and reposition the two controls in the Report Footer section so that the calculated field right-aligns with the subtotal amount.

Explore

   f. In the Report Footer section, add two text boxes below the text box you added in Step 7e. In the first text box that you added, use the DAvg function to calculate the average of the TripFee field values from the **Booked Rafting Trips** query. Format the DAvg text box as Standard with two decimal places. In the other text box, use the DCount function to calculate the total number of trips booked. (*Hints*: The DAvg and DCount functions use the same format as the DSum function. You can use the TripFee field for the DCount function.) Format the DCount text box as Standard with zero decimal places. Use the label captions "Average Trip Fee:" and "Total Trips:", and then change the labels to bold. Resize and reposition the labels and text boxes in the Report Footer section.

   g. If necessary, reduce the height of the Report Footer section in the main report.

8. Save your report design changes, switch to Print Preview, print the first and last pages of the report, and then close the report.

9. Use the following instructions to create the mailing labels:

   a. Use the **Client** table as the source for the mailing labels.

   b. Use Avery C2163 labels, and use the default font and color settings. (*Hint*: Make sure the English option button is selected in the Unit of Measure section.)

   c. For the prototype label, place ClientName on the first line; Address on the second line; City, a space, State/Prov, a space, and PostalCode on the third line; and Country on the fourth line.

   d. Sort by PostalCode and then by ClientName, and then enter the report name **Client Labels**.

e. Change the column layout to "Down, then Across," print the first page of the report, and then save and close the report.

10. Close the **Outdoors** database, and then exit Access.

Explore **Case 5. eACH Internet Auction Site** Chris and Pat Aquino want you to continue developing their Internet auction site for collectibles. Their auction site is now a proven success, with tens of thousands of bids placed daily. However, their costs have increased because they've had to install additional servers and high-speed communication lines to support the growing traffic at eACH. Income they earn from eACH offsets their costs—they charge a seller $2 to post an item plus an additional 3% of the item's final sale price. The number of items for sale varies dramatically each day, so Chris and Pat want you to design and then create a custom report to project income from the **eACH** database; the basis for the report will be a query you'll need to create. You will create the necessary query and report by completing the following steps.

1. Make sure your Data Disk is in the appropriate drive, start Access, and then open the **eACH** database in the Cases folder on your Data Disk.

2. Create a select query based on all four tables in the database. Display the subcategory name from the **Subcategory** table; the category name from the **Category** table; the title from the **Item** table; the seller's last name and first name from the **Registrant** table; and the minimum bid from the **Item** table, in that order. Create a calculated field named ProjectedIncome that displays the results of adding $2 to 3% of the minimum bid. Format the calculated field as Standard with two decimal places. Sort the query in descending order by the ProjectedIncome field. Save the query as **Projected Income**, run the query, resize all columns to their best fit, print the query in landscape orientation, and then save and close the query.

3. On a piece of paper, sketch the design for a custom report based on the **Projected Income** query. The report must include at least the following features:
   a. A Page Header section that includes the report title, the current date, the page number, and column headings.
   b. A Group Header section that includes the subcategory name and category name, both sorted in ascending order.
   c. A Detail section that includes the title, seller's first name and last name, minimum bid, and ProjectedIncome field. (Hide duplicate values for the title.)
   d. A Group Footer section that includes an appropriate label and totals by subcategory for the minimum bid and ProjectedIncome field.
   e. A Report Footer section that includes an appropriate label and totals for the minimum bid and ProjectedIncome field.

4. Building on Step 3, create, test, and print the custom report. Save the report as **Projected Income Based on Minimum Bid**. You might need to add records to your tables and modify existing records so that you have enough data and a sufficient level of variety to test your report features.

5. Close the **eACH** database, and then exit Access.

INTERNET ASSIGNMENTS

Student Union

The purpose of the Internet Assignments is to challenge you to find information on the Internet that you can use to create effective documents. The actual assignments are updated and maintained on the Course Technology Web site. Log on to the Internet and use your Web browser to go to the Student Online Companion to accompany this text at **www.course.com/NewPerspectives/studentunion**. Click the Access link, and then click the link for Tutorial 6.

QUICK CHECK ANSWERS

Session 6.1

1. The Report Header section appears once at the beginning of a report. The Page Header section appears at the top of each page of a report. The Group Header section appears once at the beginning of a new group of records. The Detail section appears once for each record in the underlying table or query. The Group Footer section appears once at the end of a group of records. The Report Footer section appears once at the end of a report. The Page Footer section appears at the bottom of each page of a report.

2. A custom report is a report you make by modifying a report created by AutoReport or the Report Wizard, or by creating a report from scratch in Design view.

3. IIf

4. The Report window in Design view has many of the same components as the Form window in Design view, including a Properties button, a Field List button, and a Toolbox button on the toolbar. Both windows also have horizontal and vertical rulers, a grid, and a Formatting toolbar. Unlike the Form window in Design view, which initially displays only the Detail section on a blank form, the Report window also displays a Page Header section and a Page Footer section.

5. A grouping field is a field from the underlying table or query by which records are grouped in a report.

6. The Caption property for a control determines the text displayed for the control. You would change the Caption property value for a control when the default value is difficult to read or understand.

7. Can Grow

8. Click a control, hold down the Shift key, click the other controls, release the Shift key, right-click a selected control, point to Align, and then click Right.

Session 6.2

1. Can Shrink

2. Report Header and Detail sections

3. Visible

4. arrow

5. Hiding duplicate values makes a report easier to read; duplicate values clutter the report.

6. three

7. a recordset or set of records

Session 6.3

1. =Date()

2. Click Insert on the menu bar; click Page Numbers; specify the format, position, and alignment of the page number; and then click the OK button.

3. Format Painter

4. detail

5. A multiple-column report prints the same collection of data in two or more sets across the page.

OBJECTIVES

In this tutorial you will:

- Export an Access table to an HTML document

- View an HTML document using a Web browser

- Use a Wizard to create a data access page for an Access table

- Update a data access page using a Web browser

- Sort and filter data access page records

- Create a custom data access page

- Create and use a PivotTable on a data access page

- Create and use a PivotChart on a data access page

- Import an XML file as an Access table

- Export an Access table as an XML file

- Export an Access query as an Excel worksheet

- Add a hyperlink field to an Access table

- Create hyperlinks to Office documents

INTEGRATING
ACCESS WITH THE WEB AND WITH OTHER PROGRAMS

Creating Web-Enabled and Integrated Information for the Jobs Database

CASE

Northeast Seasonal Jobs International (NSJI)

Elsa Jensen, Zack Ward, and Matt Griffin are pleased with the design and contents of the Jobs database. Their work has been made much easier because they are able to quickly obtain the information they need from the database. Matt feels that others in the company would benefit from gaining access to the Jobs database. Elsa asks Matt if he can make information in the database available to employees using the company network. That way, employees could obtain company information using their desktop and portable computers rather than using printouts and paper forms.

Zack mentions that most employees, such as the recruiters, do not need access to the entire database, nor should they be able to make changes to all the database objects. He proposes publishing the necessary Access data on the company's intranet, or internal network, as Web pages.

In this tutorial, you will use Access to make objects in the Jobs database available to employees on NSJI's internal network. You will use Access to import and export XML files and integrate Access with other Office programs.

SESSION 7.1

In this session, you will export an Access query to an HTML document and then view the HTML document using a Web browser. You'll use a Wizard to create a data access page for an Access table, and use your Web browser to update the data and to sort and filter records on the data access page. Finally, you'll create a custom data access page.

Using the Web

The **World Wide Web (WWW)**, commonly called the **Web**, is a vast collection of digital documents available over the **Internet**, which is a worldwide network consisting of millions of interconnected computers. Each electronic document on the Web is called a **Web page**. Individuals and companies store their Web pages on special computers called **Web servers**. Each Web page is assigned an Internet address called a **Uniform Resource Locator (URL)**; the URL identifies where the Web page is stored—the location of both the Web server and the Web page filename on that server. To view a Web page, you start a special program called a **Web browser**, such as Microsoft Internet Explorer or Netscape Navigator. After you start the Web browser, you enter the Web page's URL. The Web browser uses the URL to find and retrieve the Web page, and then displays it on your computer screen.

Each Web page contains the necessary instructions for your Web browser to display its text and graphics. These instructions, called **tags**, describe how text is formatted, position graphic images, and set the document's background color and other visual characteristics of the Web page. Certain tags, called **hyperlinks**, link one Web page to another. When you click hyperlink text, the linked page opens. Hyperlinks connect Web pages throughout the Internet, and these connections form the Web. Hyperlinks are the primary means of navigation on the Web.

Most Web pages are created using a programming language called **HTML (HyperText Markup Language)**. You can create a Web page by typing all the necessary HTML code into a text document, called an **HTML document**, and saving the document with the .htm or .html file extension. Some programs, including Access, have built-in tools that convert objects to HTML documents for viewing on the Web.

When you use Access to create a Web page, the page can be either static or dynamic. A **static Web page** shows the state of the database object at the time the page was created. Any subsequent changes made to the database object, such as updates to field values in records, are not reflected in a static Web page. A **dynamic Web page** is updated automatically each time the page is viewed and therefore reflects the current state of the database at that time. When you use a browser to open a Web page created from an Access database, you cannot make changes to the database using a static Web page, but you can change database data for certain types of dynamic Web pages. The type of Web page you create depends on how you want other users to be able to share and manipulate its information. In this tutorial, you'll work with both static and dynamic Web pages.

Exporting an Access Query to an HTML Document

Matt has asked you to create an HTML document for the Employer Positions query. He wants this data to be available to the recruiters when they work outside the office to interview and screen students for available positions. The recruiters will access the company's intranet from laptop computers connected to telephone lines. The recruiters usually wait until they have completed all interviews for available positions before matching qualified applicants with appropriate jobs. For this reason, the recruiters only need to reference the available positions data, so Matt asks you to create a static Web page for the recruiters to use as a resource during the interview process.

Creating the necessary HTML document is not as difficult as it might appear at first. You will use the Export command on the shortcut menu, which automatically converts the selected database object to an HTML document.

REFERENCE WINDOW   RW

Exporting an Access Object to an HTML Document
- In the Database window, right-click the object (table, query, form, or report) you want to export, and then click Export on the shortcut menu.
- Enter the filename in the File name text box, and then select the location where you want to save the file.
- Click the Save as type list arrow, and then click HTML Documents.
- Click the Save formatted check box (if using a template), and then click the Export button.
- Select the template (if necessary), and then click the OK button.

To complete the following steps, you need to use Access and a Web browser. The steps in this tutorial are written for Internet Explorer, the Web browser used at NSJI. If you use Navigator or another browser, the steps you need to complete will be slightly different.

You'll export the Employer Positions query as an HTML document.

To export the Employer Positions query as an HTML document:

1. Place your Data Disk in the appropriate disk drive, start Access, and then open the **Jobs** database in the Tutorial folder on your Data Disk.

2. Click **Queries** in the Objects bar of the Database window, right-click **Employer Positions** to display the shortcut menu, and then click **Export**. The Export dialog box opens, displaying the type and name of the object you are exporting in its title bar—in this case, the Employer Positions query.

   In this dialog box you specify the filename for the exported file and its type and location. You'll save the Employer Positions query as an HTML document in the Tutorial folder on your Data Disk.

3. Make sure the Save in list box displays the **Tutorial** folder on your Data Disk.

4. Click the **Save as type** list arrow, and then scroll down the list and click **HTML Documents**. The query name is added to the File name text box automatically. See Figure 7-1.

Figure 7-1

EXPORT DIALOG BOX

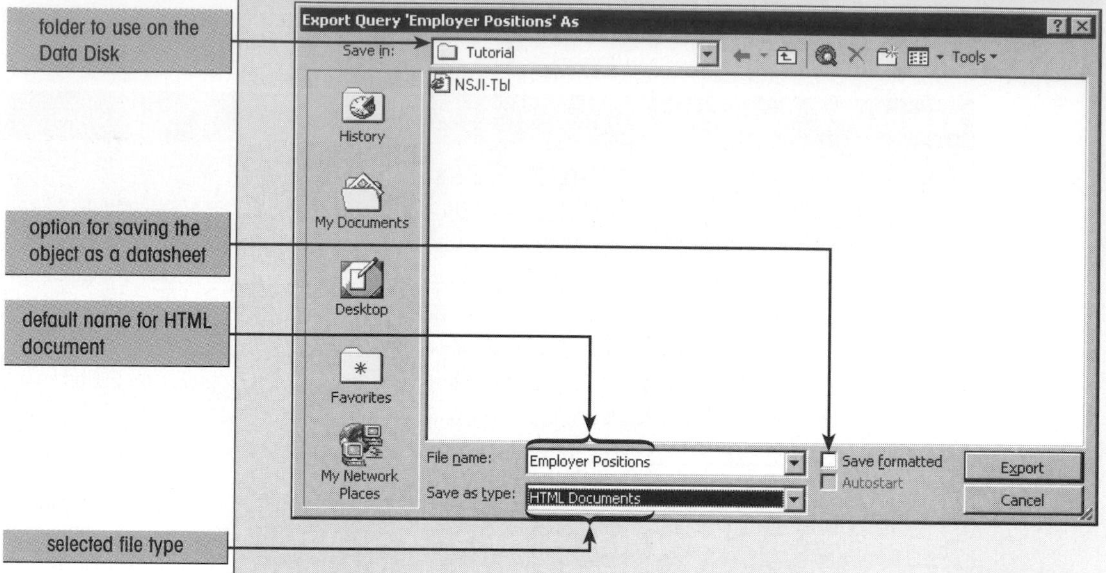

folder to use on the Data Disk

option for saving the object as a datasheet

default name for HTML document

selected file type

Export Query 'Employer Positions' As

Save in: Tutorial

NSJI-Tbl

History

My Documents

Desktop

Favorites

My Network Places

File name: Employer Positions

Save as type: HTML Documents

Save formatted
Autostart

Export

Cancel

The Save formatted option lets you save the object formatted as a datasheet. If you do not choose this option, the object will appear without the field names as column headings. Matt wants the query saved in datasheet format.

5. Click the **Save formatted** check box, and then click the **Export** button. The HTML Output Options dialog box opens.

This dialog box lets you specify an HTML template or use the default format when saving the object. An **HTML template** is a file that contains HTML instructions for creating a Web page with both text and graphics, together with special instructions that tell Access where to place the Access data on the Web page. Matt used a text-editing program to create an HTML template, named NSJI-Tbl, that you'll use. This template will automatically include the NSJI logo in all Web pages created with it. You need to locate Matt's template file on your Data Disk.

6. Make sure the **Select a HTML Template** check box is checked, and then click the **Browse** button. The HTML Template to Use dialog box opens.

7. If necessary, use the Look in list box to display the contents of the **Tutorial** folder on your Data Disk, click **NSJI-Tbl**, and then click the **OK** button. Access closes the HTML Template to Use dialog box, returns to the HTML Output Options dialog box, and displays the location and filename for the HTML template. See Figure 7-2.

Figure 7-2   **HTML OUTPUT OPTIONS DIALOG BOX**

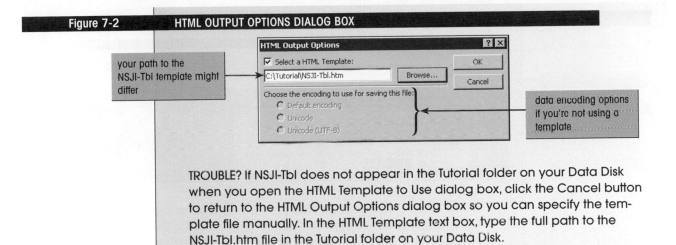

your path to the
NSJI-Tbl template might
differ

HTML Output Options

☑ Select a HTML Template:

C:\Tutorial\NSJI-Tbl.htm   Browse...   OK   Cancel

Choose the encoding to use for saving this file:
○ Default encoding
○ Unicode
○ Unicode (UTF-8)

data encoding options
if you're not using a
template

TROUBLE? If NSJI-Tbl does not appear in the Tutorial folder on your Data Disk when you open the HTML Template to Use dialog box, click the Cancel button to return to the HTML Output Options dialog box so you can specify the template file manually. In the HTML Template text box, type the full path to the NSJI-Tbl.htm file in the Tutorial folder on your Data Disk.

8. Click the **OK** button. The HTML Output Options dialog box closes, and the HTML document named Employer Positions is saved in the Tutorial folder on your Data Disk.

Now you can view the Web page.

Viewing an HTML Document Using Internet Explorer

Matt asks to see the Web page you created. You can view the HTML document that you created using any Web browser. You'll view it using Internet Explorer next.

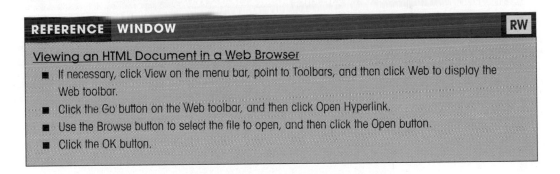

REFERENCE WINDOW   **RW**

Viewing an HTML Document in a Web Browser
- If necessary, click View on the menu bar, point to Toolbars, and then click Web to display the Web toolbar.
- Click the Go button on the Web toolbar, and then click Open Hyperlink.
- Use the Browse button to select the file to open, and then click the Open button.
- Click the OK button.

You can now view the Employer Positions query Web page.

To view the Employer Positions query Web page:

1. If necessary, click **View** on the menu bar, point to **Toolbars**, and then click **Web**. Access displays the Web toolbar. See Figure 7-3.

Figure 7-3 **DISPLAYING THE WEB TOOLBAR**

Web toolbar

Go button

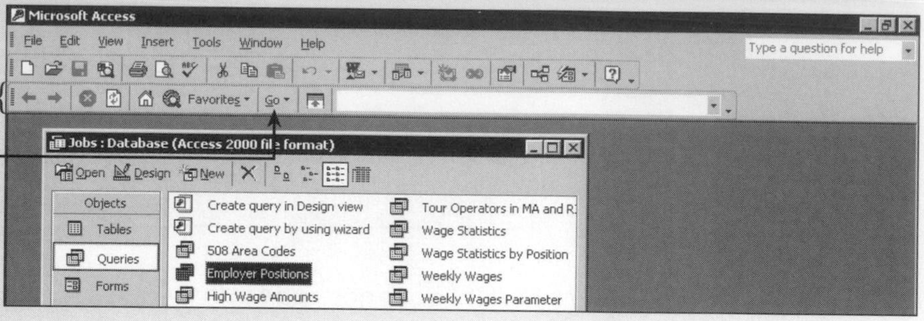

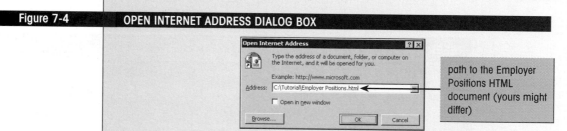

TROUBLE? If the Database and Web toolbars appear on the same line or the Web toolbar appears above the Database toolbar, drag the Web toolbar's move handle below the Database toolbar to the position shown in Figure 7-3.

2. Click the **Go** button on the Web toolbar, and then click **Open Hyperlink**. Access opens the Open Internet Address dialog box, in which you can specify or browse for the URL of the Web page or the path and filename of the HTML document you want to view.

3. Click the **Browse** button. Access opens the Browse dialog box.

4. Make sure the Look in list box displays the **Tutorial** folder on your Data Disk, click **Employer Positions** in the list, and then click the **Open** button. The Browse dialog box closes, and the Address text box in the Open Internet Address dialog box now displays the path and filename for the Employer Positions HTML document. See Figure 7-4.

Figure 7-4 **OPEN INTERNET ADDRESS DIALOG BOX**

path to the Employer Positions HTML document (yours might differ)

5. Click the **OK** button. Internet Explorer starts and opens the Employer Positions Web page. See Figure 7-5.

TROUBLE? If a dialog box opens and tells you that an unexpected error has occurred, click the OK button, click the Start button on the taskbar, point to Programs, click Internet Explorer, type the path to the Employer Positions.html file in the Tutorial folder in the Address bar, and then press the Enter key.

Figure 7-5	EMPLOYER POSITIONS QUERY IN THE INTERNET EXPLORER WINDOW

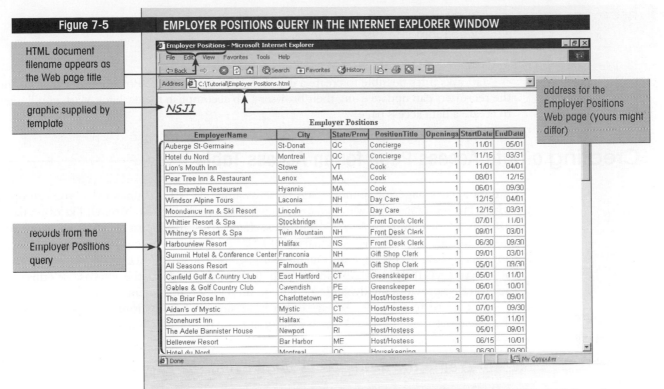

HTML document filename appears as the Web page title

graphic supplied by template

records from the Employer Positions query

address for the Employer Positions Web page (yours might differ)

Inside the Internet Explorer window:

Address: C:\Tutorial\Employer Positions.html

NSJI

Employer Positions

EmployerName	City	State/Prov	PositionTitle	Openings	StartDate	EndDate
Auberge St-Germaine	St-Donat	QC	Concierge	1	11/01	05/01
Hotel du Nord	Montreal	QC	Concierge	1	11/15	03/31
Lion's Mouth Inn	Stowe	VT	Cook	1	11/01	04/01
Pear Tree Inn & Restaurant	Lenox	MA	Cook	1	08/01	12/15
The Bramble Restaurant	Hyannis	MA	Cook	1	06/01	09/30
Windsor Alpine Tours	Laconia	NH	Day Care	1	12/15	04/01
Moondance Inn & Ski Resort	Lincoln	NH	Day Care	1	12/15	03/31
Whittier Resort & Spa	Stockbridge	MA	Front Desk Clerk	1	07/01	11/01
Whitney's Resort & Spa	Twin Mountain	NH	Front Desk Clerk	1	09/01	03/01
Harbourview Resort	Halifax	NS	Front Desk Clerk	1	06/30	09/30
Summit Hotel & Conference Center	Franconia	NH	Gift Shop Clerk	1	09/01	03/01
All Seasons Resort	Falmouth	MA	Gift Shop Clerk	1	05/01	09/30
Canfield Golf & Country Club	East Hartford	CT	Greenskeeper	1	05/01	11/01
Gables & Golf Country Club	Cavendish	PE	Greenskeeper	1	06/01	10/01
The Briar Rose Inn	Charlottetown	PE	Host/Hostess	2	07/01	09/01
Aidan's of Mystic	Mystic	CT	Host/Hostess	1	07/01	09/30
Stonehurst Inn	Halifax	NS	Host/Hostess	1	05/01	11/01
The Adele Bannister House	Newport	RI	Host/Hostess	1	05/01	09/01
Belleview Resort	Bar Harbor	ME	Host/Hostess	1	06/15	10/01
Hotel du Nord	Montreal	QC	Housekeeping	3	06/30	09/30

Done   My Computer

TROUBLE? If another program opens, such as Microsoft Word, then Internet Explorer might not be installed on your computer. If the title bar on your screen displays "Microsoft Word," you can continue with the steps, but your screens will look different from those shown in the figures.

TROUBLE? If your computer has Navigator installed as its default browser, Navigator will start automatically and open the Employer Positions Web page. If Navigator opens, your screens will look slightly different from those shown in the figures.

TROUBLE? If a Web browser is not installed on your computer, ask your instructor or technical support person for help.

Changes that NSJI employees make to the Jobs database will not appear in the Employer Positions Web page that you created because it is a static page—that is, it reflects the state of the Employer Positions query in the Jobs database at the time you created it. If data in the Employer Positions query changes, Matt will have to export the Employer Positions Web page again.

Because this static Web page is not linked to the Employer Positions query on which it is based, you cannot use your browser to make changes to its data. Before closing the Employer Positions Web page, you'll try to change one of its field values.

To attempt to change a field value, and then close the browser:

1. Double-click **QC** in the State/Prov column for the first record (Auberge St-Germaine), and then type **NS**. The value of QC remains highlighted and unchanged, because the Employer Positions Web page is a static page.

2. Click the **Close** button ⊠ on the Internet Explorer window title bar to close it and to return to the Database window.

3. Click **View** on the menu bar, point to **Toolbars**, and then click **Web** to close the Web toolbar.

Matt asks if it's possible to create a dynamic Web page for the Position table that he and the recruiters can update using their browsers. To accomplish this task for Matt, you'll need to create a data access page.

Creating a Data Access Page for an Access Table

A **data access page** (or simply a **page**) is a dynamic HTML document that you can open with a Web browser to view or update current data in an Access database. Unlike other database objects stored in an Access database, such as forms and reports, data access pages are stored outside the database as separate HTML documents. Like other database objects, however, a data access page also includes a page object in the Access database; this page object connects the HTML document with the bound fields from the database. It's this connection that provides the dynamic element to the HTML document.

You can create a data access page either in Design view or by using a Wizard. To create the data access page for the Position table, you'll use the Page Wizard.

To create the data access page using the Page Wizard:

1. Click **Pages** in the Objects bar of the Database window to display the Pages list. The Pages list box does not contain any data access pages.

2. Click the **New** button in the Database window to open the New Data Access Page dialog box. This dialog box is similar to the ones you've used to create tables, queries, forms, and reports.

3. Click **Page Wizard** to select this Wizard, click the list arrow for choosing the table or query on which to base the page, scroll down and click **Position**, and then click the **OK** button. The first Page Wizard dialog box opens, in which you select the fields you want to display on the data access page. You'll include all of the fields from the Position table.

4. Click the ⟩⟩ button to select all of the fields from the Position table, and then click the **Next** button to open the next Page Wizard dialog box, in which you select the grouping levels for the data access page. See Figure 7-6.

Figure 7-6	SELECTING GROUPING LEVELS FOR A DATA ACCESS PAGE

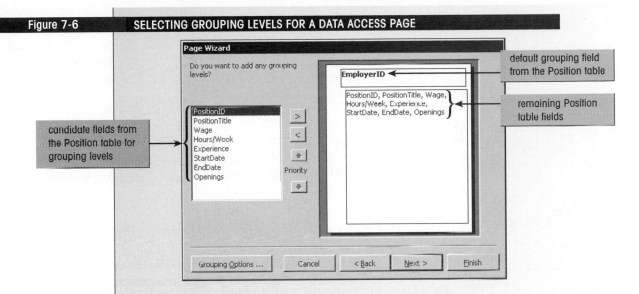

The Wizard selected the EmployerID field for a grouping level. Matt doesn't need any grouping levels for this data access page, so you'll delete the EmployerID field grouping level.

5. Click the **EmployerID** field on the right side of the dialog box, click the < button to delete the EmployerID grouping level and to place the field with the other Position table fields, and then click the **Next** button. In this Page Wizard dialog box, you select the sort fields for each data access page. Matt wants the records sorted in descending order by the EmployerID field, and then in ascending order by the PositionTitle field.

6. Select the **EmployerID** field as the primary sort key and the **PositionTitle** field as the secondary sort key, and then click the **Next** button to open the last Page Wizard dialog box, in which you enter a name for the data access page. You'll use the default name, and then open the data access page in Access.

7. Click the **Open the page** option button, and then click the **Finish** button. Access opens the data access page in Page view. See Figure 7-7.

Figure 7-7	DATA ACCESS PAGE CREATED BY THE PAGE WIZARD

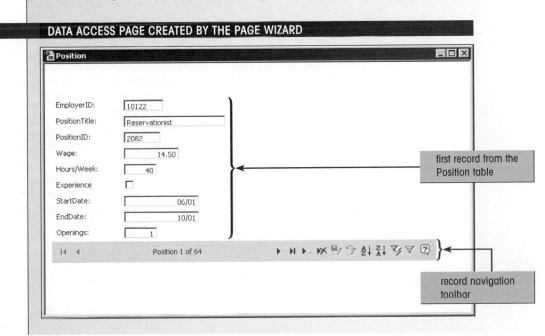

This data access page, which has an appearance similar to a form, displays a record's field values from the Position table one at a time. The **record navigation toolbar**, which appears below the record, lets you move between records in the table, add and delete records, edit and undo entries, sort and filter data, and request Help. ScreenTips for each button on the record navigation toolbar will appear if you position the pointer on a button, and 11 of the 13 buttons are familiar because you've seen them on other Access toolbars. The Save button and the Undo button are the two new buttons on the record navigation toolbar.

Matt wants to make sure that he can update the Position table using the data access page that you created. You can use a data access page to update data in Page view or with a Web browser, so you'll show Matt how to use both update methods. First, you'll save the data access page, and then you'll update a field value in Page view.

To save the data access page, and then update a Position table field value in Page view:

1. Click the **Save** button on the Page View toolbar. The Save As Data Access Page dialog box opens. You'll save the data access page using the default name (Position) and type (Microsoft Data Access Pages).

2. Make sure the Save in list box displays the **Tutorial** folder on your Data Disk, and then click the **Save** button. Unless it has been disabled, a message box opens to warn you that the page's connection string is an absolute path. See Figure 7-8.

Figure 7-8	CONNECTION STRING WARNING

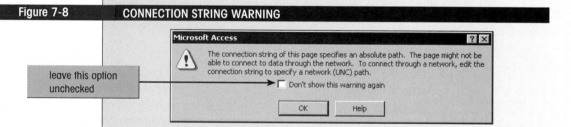

leave this option unchecked

TROUBLE? If the message box doesn't open, a previous user has disabled it. Continue with Step 4.

The **connection string** is a string, or text, expression that specifies the disk location and the database name used to connect a page to an Access database. When you specify a specific file on a specific disk drive, you've provided what is called an **absolute path**. For example, if your Tutorial folder is located on drive C when you save the Position page, C:\Tutorial\Jobs.mdb would be the connection string expressed as an absolute path. If you want others to use the page, you must make sure the disk drive specified in the absolute path represents a Web server or network drive that others can access. After saving the page, if you want to change the connection string to a different disk drive, switch to Design view, right-click the data access page title bar, click Page Properties on the shortcut menu, click the Data tab, click the ConnectionString text box, click its Build button, click the Connection tab, modify the absolute path in the first text box, and then click the OK button.

You won't be changing the connection string because Matt won't be moving the Jobs database to NSJI's Web server until after you've completed all your work with it. Also, it's a good idea to view the message box every time you create a page as a reminder that you need to update the connection string if you move the database, so you'll leave the "Don't show this warning again" check box unchecked.

3. Make sure the **Don't show this warning again** check box is unchecked, and then click the **OK** button to save the page with the default name and type.

Next, you'll show Matt how to update position data on the page.

4. Double-click **40** in the Hours/Week text box, type **35**, and then press the **Tab** key. The value of the Hours/Week field is now 35. Note that several buttons on the record navigation toolbar changed from dimmed to active.

Next, you'll close the page.

5. Click the **Close** button ☒ on the Position window title bar. A message opens and warns you that your change to the Hours/Week field will be discarded because you didn't save it. You can save changes to a record automatically by navigating to another record or by clicking the Save button on the record navigation toolbar. You'll cancel the message, and then save your change.

6. Click the **Cancel** button, and then click the **Save** button ▣ on the record navigation toolbar. Your change to the record is saved in the database, and the Save button and other buttons on the record navigation toolbar changed from active to dimmed.

You've completed working in Page view, so you can close the page.

7. Click ☒ on the Position window title bar. The page closes and you return to the Database window. Notice that the Position page is listed in the Pages list box.

Next, you'll view the page with your browser. Then you'll show Matt how to update data on a page using a browser; you'll change the Hours/Week field value for the first position for EmployerID 10122 back to 40.

Updating Data on a Data Access Page Using Internet Explorer

You can view a data access page using any Web browser. However, if you want to update data on a data access page, you must use Internet Explorer 5.0 or higher, or another browser that supports data access pages.

Viewing and Updating Data on a Data Access Page Using Internet Explorer

- If necessary, click Pages in the Objects bar of the Database window.
- Right-click the data access page name, and then click Web Page Preview to start Internet Explorer and open the data access page.
- If changing an existing record, navigate to the desired record, make changes to the record, and then click the Save button on the record navigation toolbar.
- If deleting an existing record, navigate to the desired record, click the Delete button on the record navigation toolbar, and then click the Save button on the record navigation toolbar.
- If adding a record, click the New button on the record navigation toolbar, enter the field values for the record, and then click the Save button on the record navigation toolbar.

You can now view and update data on the page using Internet Explorer.

To view and update data on the page using Internet Explorer:

1. Right-click **Position** in the Pages list box, and then click **Web Page Preview** to start Internet Explorer and open the Position page. See Figure 7-9.

   TROUBLE? If an Internet Explorer dialog box opens and indicates that the Position page is unavailable offline, click the OK button to close the dialog box. In Internet Explorer, click File on the menu bar, and then click Work Offline. You do not need an Internet connection to complete these steps.

Figure 7-9   PAGE IN THE INTERNET EXPLORER WINDOW

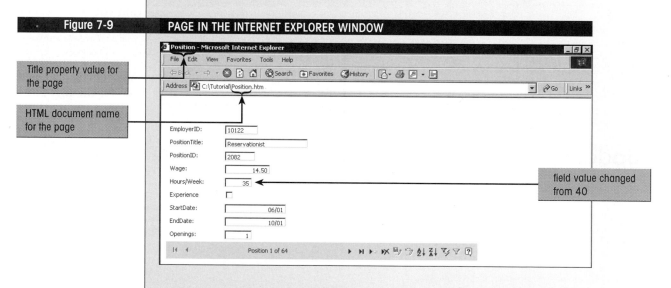

Title property value for the page

HTML document name for the page

field value changed from 40

You'll change the Hours/Week field value for position 2082 back to 40.

2. Double-click **35** in the Hours/Week text box, type **40**, press the **Tab** key, and then click the **Save** button 🖫 on the record navigation toolbar. The value of the Hours/Week field is changed to 40 in the database.

Matt asks about the other buttons on the record navigation toolbar. Next, you'll show him how to sort and filter records using a data access page.

Using a Data Access Page to Sort and Filter Records

The buttons on the record navigation toolbar for sorting and filtering data work the same for data access pages as they do for forms. You'll show Matt how to sort and filter records using a data access page based on a value in the StartDate field.

To use a data access page to sort and filter records:

1. Click the **StartDate** text box, and then click the **Sort Descending** button ![ZA] on the record navigation toolbar. Access rearranges the records in descending order by start date—records for 12/15 appear first, followed by records for 12/01, and so on.

   You can now filter records, selecting just the records for those positions with a 12/15 start date.

2. Click the **StartDate** text box, and then click the **Filter by Selection** button ![icon] on the record navigation toolbar. Access filters the position records, displaying the first of four records having a start date field value of 12/15. See Figure 7-10.

Figure 7-10	USING FILTER BY SELECTION ON A DATA ACCESS PAGE

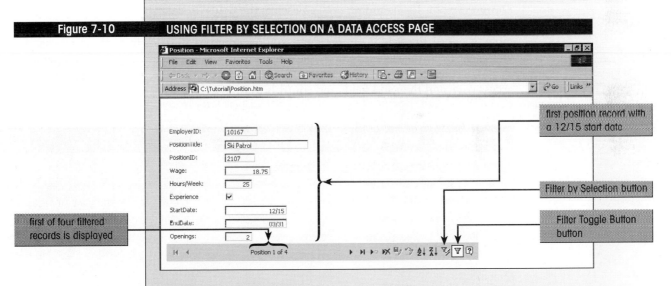

- first position record with a 12/15 start date
- Filter by Selection button
- Filter Toggle Button button
- first of four filtered records is displayed

Now you can redisplay all the customer records by clicking the Filter Toggle Button button.

3. Click the **Filter Toggle Button** button ![icon] on the record navigation toolbar. Access makes all 64 records from the Position table available on the page.

4. Click the **Close** button ![X] on the Internet Explorer window title bar to close it and return to the Database window.

When visiting employers, the recruiters frequently require access to current information about employers and their positions at the same time. Elsa asks if it's possible to create a data access page that the recruiters can use to view and update current Jobs database information about employers and their positions. To do this, you'll create a custom data access page in Design view.

Creating a Custom Data Access Page

Because of its connection to the database object on which it is based, every data access page is a dynamic HTML document. When you open a data access page, you are viewing current data from the Access database that produced it. To create a data access page that recruiters can use to view and update data, you'll create a data access page that includes data selected from the Employer table and from the related Position table.

Just as with forms and reports, you could use a Wizard to create a basic data access page and then customize it in Design view, or you could create a data access page from scratch in Design view. To create the data access page with the employer and position information for Elsa and the recruiters, you'll create the entire data access page in Design view.

Creating a Blank Data Access Page in Design View

You use the Page window in Design view to create and modify data access pages. Similar to Design view for forms and reports, you select the fields for a data access page in Design view from the field list. Unlike previous field lists, which contain only the fields from the source table or query, the field list in the Page window contains all fields from the database. Thus, you don't need to select a source table or query for a data access page before opening the Page window in Design view. To create Elsa's data access page, you'll create a blank data access page and then add fields and controls to it.

REFERENCE WINDOW   **RW**

Creating a Data Access Page in Design View

- If necessary, click Pages in the Objects bar of the Database window to display the Pages list.
- Click the New button to open the New Data Access Page dialog box, click Design View (if necessary), click the OK button, and then if necessary click the OK button to close the warning message and to create a blank data access page.
- Place the necessary controls in the Page window in Design view. Modify the size, position, and other properties of the controls as necessary.
- Click the Save button on the Page Design toolbar, enter a name for the data access page, select a location for the data access page, and then click the Save button.

To create the data access page, you'll first create a blank data access page in the Page window in Design view.

To create a blank data access page in Design view:

1. Maximize the Database window, and then click the **New** button in the Database window. The New Data Access Page dialog box opens.

2. Click **Design View** in the list box (if necessary), and then click the **OK** button. Access displays the Page window in Design view. See Figure 7-11.

Figure 7-11	PAGE WINDOW IN DESIGN VIEW

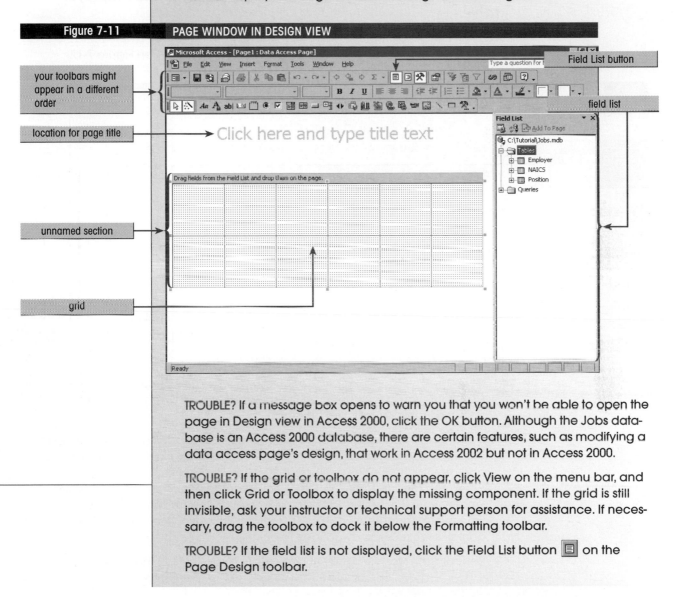

your toolbars might appear in a different order

location for page title

unnamed section

grid

Field List button

field list

TROUBLE? If a message box opens to warn you that you won't be able to open the page in Design view in Access 2000, click the OK button. Although the Jobs database is an Access 2000 database, there are certain features, such as modifying a data access page's design, that work in Access 2002 but not in Access 2000.

TROUBLE? If the grid or toolbox do not appear, click View on the menu bar, and then click Grid or Toolbox to display the missing component. If the grid is still invisible, ask your instructor or technical support person for assistance. If necessary, drag the toolbox to dock it below the Formatting toolbar.

TROUBLE? If the field list is not displayed, click the Field List button 📋 on the Page Design toolbar.

The Page window in Design view has many of the same components as the Form and Report windows in Design view. For example, these windows include a Formatting toolbar, a grid, a Properties button, a Field List button, and a Toolbox button.

Unlike the Form and Report windows in Design view, however, the Page window initially contains only one unnamed section, which is named after you place controls in it, and placeholder text for the title of your data access page. Also, the Field List window, which is also called the field list, contains all of the tables and queries in the database; you can select fields from one or more tables and queries to include in the data access page.

Adding Fields to a Data Access Page

Because Elsa wants to see employers and their positions, your first task is to use the field list to add fields from the Employer table to the grid.

To add fields to the grid from the field list for the Employer table:

1. Click ⊞ next to Employer in the field list. The fields from the Employer table and a folder for related tables are now visible in the field list. See Figure 7-12.

Figure 7-12	FIELDS AND RELATED TABLES FOLDER FOR THE EMPLOYER TABLE

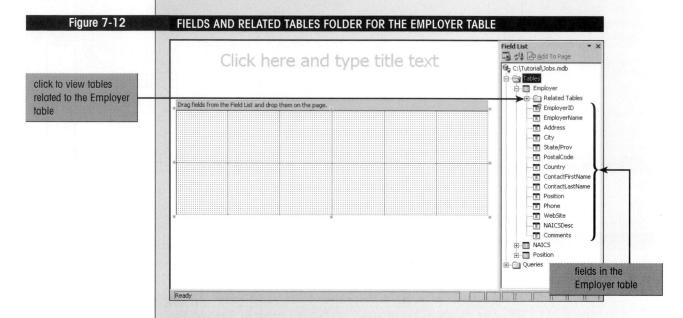

Elsa wants you to include only the EmployerName, City, and State/Prov fields from the Employer table on the page.

2. Double-click **EmployerName** in the field list. Access adds a bound control for the EmployerName field to the grid. The bound control consists of a text box and an attached label, similar to the bound controls you've used previously for forms and reports. Notice that the section name has changed to Header: Employer, which is referred to as the Employer Header section. Below the Employer Header section, Access adds the Employer Navigation section, which contains the record navigation toolbar.

3. Repeat Step 2 to select the **City** and **State/Prov** fields, in that order.

Elsa wants you to include the PositionTitle, Wage, Hours/Week, and Openings fields from the Position table on the page. To display the fields in the Position table, you'll expand the Employer table's Related Tables entry in the field list, which will display the NAICS and Position tables, and then expand the Position table. (If you had first selected fields from the Position table instead of from the Employer table, you would have expanded the Position table at the bottom of the field list.)

To add fields to the grid from the field list for the Position table:

1. Click ⊞ next to Related Tables in the field list, and then click ⊞ next to Position in the field list. The NAICS and Position tables, which are related to the Employer table, are now visible in the field list, as are the fields from the Position table.

2. Click **PositionTitle** in the field list, press and hold the **Ctrl** key, click **Wage**, **Hours/Week**, and **Openings** in the field list, and then release the **Ctrl** key. All four fields are selected.

3. Drag the selected Position table fields from the field list to the bottom of the Employer Header section so that the text "Create new section below Employer" appears within a rectangle with a blue border. See Figure 7-13.

Figure 7-13	ADDING SELECTED POSITION TABLE FIELDS TO THE GRID

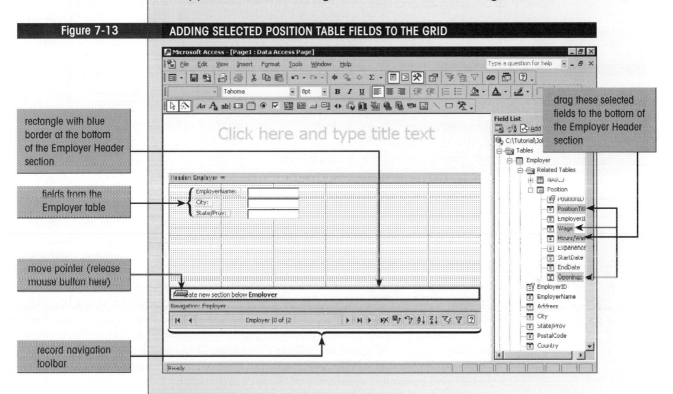

rectangle with blue border at the bottom of the Employer Header section

fields from the Employer table

move pointer (release mouse button here)

record navigation toolbar

drag these selected fields to the bottom of the Employer Header section

4. Release the mouse button. The Layout Wizard dialog box opens, in which you can choose a columnar or tabular layout for the new Position section.

5. Click the **Tabular** option button, click the **OK** button, and then scroll down the Page window. The four fields from the Position table are added to the grid in a new Position Header section, a new Position Navigation section is added above the Employer Navigation section, and a Position Caption section is added above the Position Header section. See Figure 7-14.

Figure 7-14   PAGE AFTER ADDING ALL REQUIRED FIELDS TO THE GRID

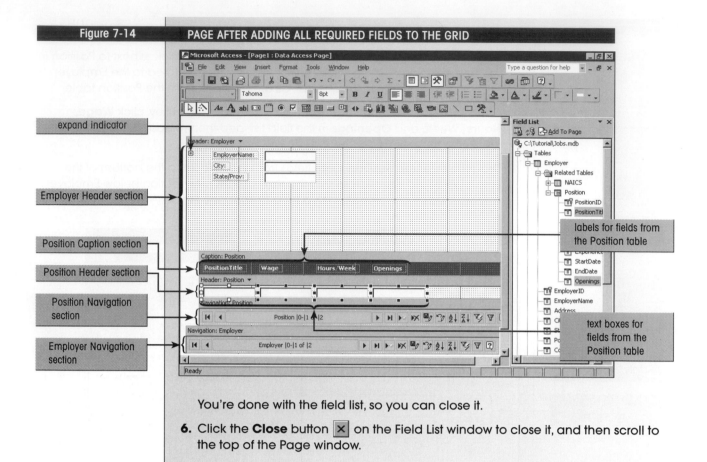

You're done with the field list, so you can close it.

6. Click the **Close** button ☒ on the Field List window to close it, and then scroll to the top of the Page window.

Notice that an expand indicator ⊞ appears to the left of the EmployerName label in the Employer Header section. When you view the page in Page view or with a browser, the Employer Header and Employer Navigation sections will be displayed, but the Position Caption, Position Header, and Position Navigation sections will be hidden. Each employer record has an expand indicator, and clicking this control opens a band below the employer record that contains the position data for that employer. At the same time, the ⊞ changes to ⊟, which you can click to collapse or hide the employer's positions. The expand indicator (⊞ and ⊟) provides the same features as the expand indicators you used with subdatasheets in Tutorial 5.

Next, you'll add a title to the page above the Employer Header section.

To add a title to the page:

1. Click anywhere in the **Click here and type title text** placeholder at the top of the page. The text disappears and is replaced by a large insertion point.

2. Type **Employers and Positions**. Your typed entry becomes the title for the page.

   Elsa wants the title left aligned.

3. Click the **Align Left** button ▤ on the Formatting toolbar.

Next, you'll modify the controls in the Employer Header section.

Deleting, Moving, and Resizing Controls on a Data Access Page

Elsa wants you to delete the labels and to move and resize the text boxes in the Employer Header section. She feels that the field values without labels are self-explanatory, and she'd prefer to view the data for as many employers as possible at one time.

To delete the labels, and then move and resize the text boxes in the Employer Header section:

1. Right-click the **EmployerName label** in the Employer Header section, and then click **Cut** on the shortcut menu to delete the label.

2. Repeat Step 1 to delete the **City label** and the **State/Prov label**.

   TROUBLE? If the Office Clipboard Task Pane opens, click the **Close** button ☒ on the Task Pane to close it.

   TROUBLE? If the Office Assistant opens, right-click it to open the shortcut menu, and then click Hide to close it.

   Next, you'll move and resize the three text boxes. You usually identify some design changes, such as resizing text boxes to best fit the data they contain, on a data access page when you switch to Page view. You then switch back to Design view to make the changes and continue changing views and identifying and making changes to the data access page until you are satisfied with its appearance. When you create your own data access pages, you will need to use Page view and Design view to identify changes you need to make to increase the effectiveness of the data access page.

3. Click the **EmployerName** text box (the top text box), and then use the 🖐 pointer to drag the text box into position. (See Figure 7-15.)

4. Use the ↔ pointer on the middle-right sizing handle to resize the **EmployerName** text box. (See Figure 7-15.)

5. Repeat Step 3 for the two remaining text boxes, repeat Step 4 to reduce the width of the State/Prov text box, and then click an empty area of the Employer Header section. See Figure 7-15.

Figure 7-15	AFTER DELETING LABELS AND MOVING AND RESIZING TEXT BOXES

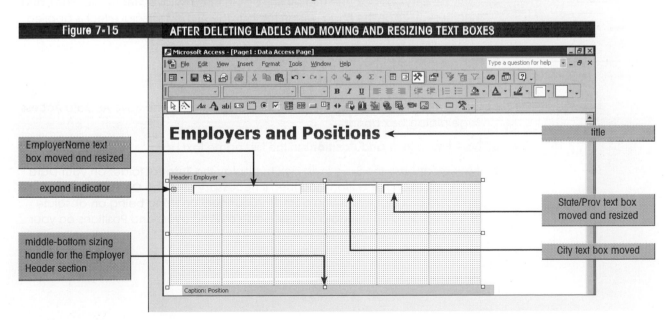

EmployerName text box moved and resized

expand indicator

middle-bottom sizing handle for the Employer Header section

title

State/Prov text box moved and resized

City text box moved

Next, you'll finish your changes to the Employer Header section by reducing the section's height and applying a special effect to the text boxes.

Resizing a Section and Applying a Special Effect

Elsa prefers a different special effect for the three text boxes in the Employer Header section. She also asks you to reduce the height of the section.

To resize the Employer Header section, and then change the special effects for the text boxes:

1. Position the pointer on the middle-bottom sizing handle of the Employer Header section; when the pointer changes to a ↕ shape, drag the bottom up until it's just below the text boxes. See Figure 7-16.

Figure 7-16	AFTER RESIZING THE EMPLOYER HEADER SECTION

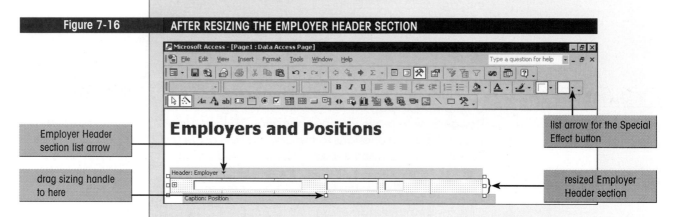

Employer Header section list arrow

drag sizing handle to here

list arrow for the Special Effect button

resized Employer Header section

Next, you'll change the special effect for each of the text boxes.

2. Click the **EmployerName** text box (the leftmost text box in the Employer Header section), click the list arrow for the ▭ on the Page Design toolbar, and then click the **Special Effect: Etched** button ▭. The etched special effect is applied to the EmployerName text box.

3. Click the **City** text box (the middle text box in the Employer Header section), and then click ▭ on the Page Design toolbar. The etched special effect is applied to the City text box.

4. Repeat Step 3 for the **State/Prov** text box.

   You've made many changes to the page, so you'll save it.

5. Click the **Save** button ▤ on the Page Design toolbar. The Save As Data Access Page dialog box opens.

6. Type **Employers and Positions** in the File name text box.

7. If necessary, use the Save in list box to display the **Tutorial** folder on your Data Disk, click the **Save** button, and then if necessary click the **OK** button in the message box that warns you about the connection string being an absolute path. Access saves the data access page as Employers and Positions on your Data Disk.

Elsa asks if you can change the number of employer records displayed on the page in Page view. The **DataPageSize property** specifies the number of records displayed on a data access page for a group. The default value is 10 for a grouped data access page and one for a non-grouped data access page. A **grouped data access page** uses two or more group levels to display information from general categories to specific details. For the Employers and Positions page, the first group level is data from the Employer table, and the second group level is data from the Position table. Data from the Employer table represents the general category, and data from the Position table represents the specific details.

Elsa asks you to increase the number of displayed employer records from 10 to 12.

To set the DataPageSize property for the Employer Header section:

1. Click the **Employer Header section** list arrow (see Figure 7-16), and then click **Group Level Properties** on the shortcut menu to open the property sheet for the group.

2. Select the value in the DataPageSize text box, and then type **12**. Access will display 12 employers on each page. See Figure 7-17.

| Figure 7-17 | PROPERTY SHEET FOR THE EMPLOYER HEADER SECTION |

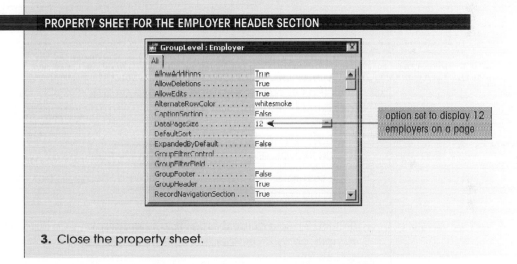

option set to display 12 employers on a page

3. Close the property sheet.

Elsa is pleased with the data access page that you have created. She asks if there's a way to format the page to have a more interesting and professional appearance. Next, you'll select a theme for the page.

Selecting a Theme

Before viewing the completed form, Elsa wants to know if you can easily change the overall style of the page. You can select a **theme**, which is a predefined style for a page, to add visual interest to the page.

To select a theme for a page:

1. Click **Format** on the menu bar, and then click **Theme**. The Theme dialog box opens. See Figure 7-18.

Figure 7-18   THEME DIALOG BOX

available themes (your
themes might differ)

sample of theme
appears here

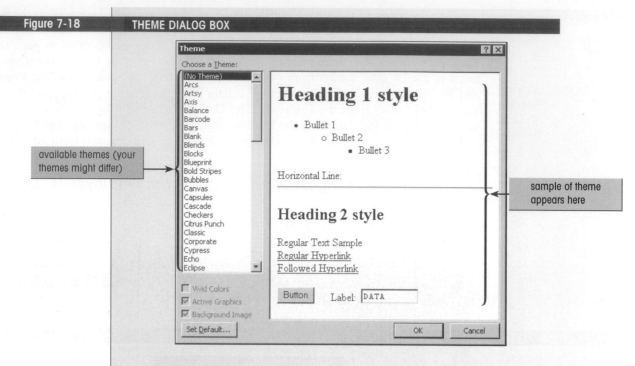

TROUBLE? If a dialog box opens and tells you that the Theme feature is not currently installed, insert your Microsoft Office XP CD in the correct drive, and then
click the OK button. If you do not have an Office XP CD, ask your instructor or
technical support person for help.

A sample of the default theme, the selected "(No Theme)" in the Choose a
Theme list box, appears in the box on the right.

2. Click several of the styles in the Choose a Theme list box, and view the corresponding sample.

TROUBLE? If one of the themes you select displays an Install button instead of a
sample, choose another theme from the list box.

3. Click **Axis** in the Choose a Theme list box, and then click the **OK** button. The
selected theme is applied to the page.

TROUBLE? If an Install button appears in the sample box for the Axis theme,
choose another theme that's already installed on your system.

Next, you'll save and view the completed page.

Saving and Viewing a Data Access Page

Elsa wants to view and update the completed data access page, but first you'll save the
changes you made to it.

To save, view, and update the completed page:

1. Save your design changes, and then click the **Close Window** button ☒ on the
Page Design window menu bar. The page closes and you return to the Database
window. Notice that the Employers and Positions page is listed in the Pages list box.

2. Right-click **Employers and Positions** in the Pages list box, and then click **Web Page Preview**. Internet Explorer starts and opens the Employers and Positions page. See Figure 7-19.

Figure 7-19 COMPLETED DATA ACCESS PAGE

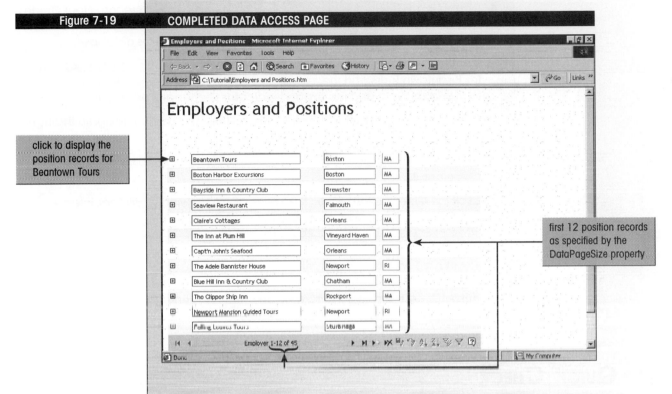

click to display the position records for Beantown Tours

first 12 position records as specified by the DataPageSize property

Next, you will show Elsa how to view an employer's position records.

3. Click the **expand indicator** ⊞ to the left of Beantown Tours (the first record). The two positions for Beantown Tours are displayed between Beantown Tours and the next employer record, the record navigation toolbar for positions appears, and the expand indicator ⊞ changes to ⊟. See Figure 7-20.

Figure 7-20 DISPLAYING THE POSITIONS FOR BEANTOWN TOURS

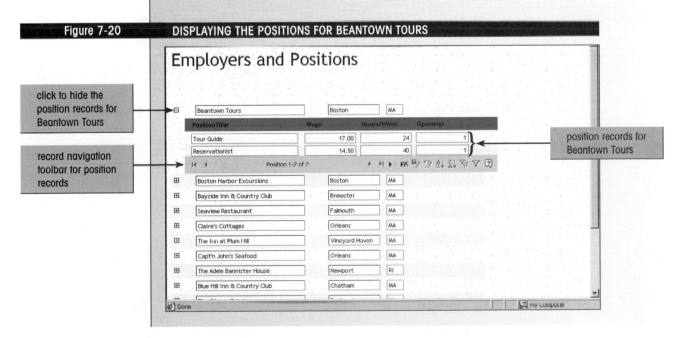

click to hide the position records for Beantown Tours

record navigation toolbar for position records

position records for Beantown Tours

Elsa recently heard from Beantown Tours that they now have two Tour Guide openings, so you'll change the Openings field value for the first position record from 1 to 2.

4. Double-click **1** in the Openings column for the first position record (Tour Guide), type **2**, and then click the **Save** button 🖫 on the record navigation toolbar. The value of the Openings field is changed to 2 in the Jobs database.

5. Click the **expand indicator** ⊟ to the left of Beantown Tours. The two positions for Beantown Tours and the record navigation toolbar for positions are no longer displayed, and the expand indicator ⊟ changes back to ⊞.

6. Use the navigation buttons (First, Previous, Next, and Last) to navigate through the pages.

   You've completed your work with the Employers and Positions page, so you can close it.

7. Click the **Close** button ✕ on the Internet Explorer window title bar. Internet Explorer closes, and you return to the Database window.

Elsa is pleased with the HTML documents and the data access pages that you created. Your work will make it easy to distribute important Jobs database information on the company's intranet. In the next session, you will continue working with data access pages to enhance the database further.

Session 7.1 QUICK CHECK

1. What is the World Wide Web?

2. What is the purpose of a Web browser?

3. What is a hyperlink?

4. What is HTML?

5. What is an HTML template?

6. What is a static Web page?

7. What is a data access page?

8. A _____ string is a string, or text, expression that specifies the disk location and database name used to connect a data access page to an Access database.

9. What is a grouped data access page?

10. What is a theme?

SESSION 7.2

In this session, you will create two new data access pages: one that uses a PivotTable, and a second that uses a PivotChart.

Creating and Using a PivotTable on a Data Access Page

Elsa would like to expand the use of Web pages for the Jobs database. In particular, she wants to be able to use Web pages to analyze her business in a flexible way. You can use PivotTables on data access pages to provide the flexible analysis that Elsa needs. When used on a data access page, a **PivotTable**, also called a **PivotTable list**, is an interactive table that lets you analyze data dynamically using a Web browser. You can use a PivotTable on a data access page to view and organize data from a database, look for summary or detail information, and dynamically change the contents and organization of the table. Figure 7-21 shows a PivotTable on a data access page.

Figure 7-21   PivotTable ON A DATA ACCESS PAGE

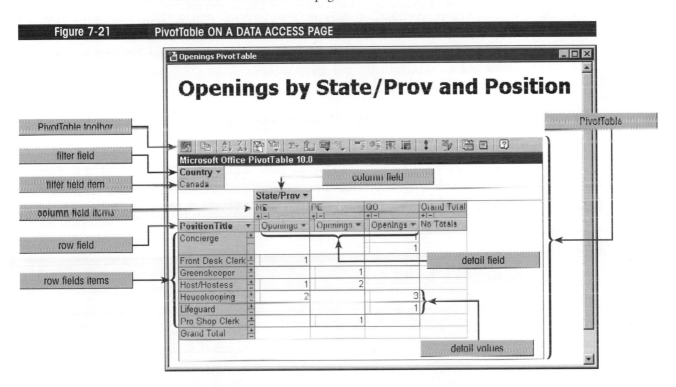

A PivotTable contains the following basic components:

- The **PivotTable toolbar** lets you perform actions such as sorting and filtering when viewing the PivotTable as a Web page.
- The **main body**, consisting of a **detail field** and **detail values**, provides details or totals from a database. In Figure 7-21, the detail field is the Openings field from the Position table, and the detail values are the Openings field values.

- The **row area**, consisting of a **row field** and **row field items**, provides row groupings for the PivotTable. In Figure 7-21, the row field is the PositionTitle field from the Position table, and the row field items are the PositionTitle field values.

- The **column area**, consisting of a **column field** and **column field items**, provides column groupings for the PivotTable. In Figure 7-21, the column field is the State/Prov field from the Employer table, and the column field items are the State/Prov field values.

- The **filter area**, consisting of a **filter field** and **filter field items**, lets you restrict which data appears in the PivotTable. In Figure 7-21, the filter field is the Country field from the Employer table, and the filter field item is "Canada"—only Canadian provinces appear in the PivotTable.

- All the PivotTable areas—main body, row area, column area, and filter area—can have multiple fields with associated field items.

When you use PivotTables on data access pages, you are not using Access 2002 features. Instead, the PivotTable uses the **Office PivotTable Component**, one of the **Office XP Web Components** that are part of Office XP. Therefore, PivotTables can be used with other programs, such as Excel and FrontPage. You can also use PivotTables with Access forms and with Access table and query datasheets; the PivotTable view with these Access objects provides this capability.

Adding a PivotTable to a Data Access Page

Matt and the recruiters have been very successful finding overseas students interested in the seasonal jobs NSJI brokers. To place all these students, Elsa and Zack need to find more employers with seasonal jobs. To help them determine which positions are popular and where they are popular, Elsa wants to analyze position openings by location (state/province) and by position title. You'll create a PivotTable on a data access page to let her perform this analysis.

REFERENCE WINDOW   **RW**

Adding a PivotTable to a Data Access Page

- If necessary, click Pages in the Objects bar of the Database window to display the Pages list.
- Click the New button to open the New Data Access Page dialog box, click Design View (if necessary), click the OK button, and then if necessary click the OK button to close the warning message and to create a blank data access page.
- Click the Office PivotTable tool on the toolbox, and then click the mouse button in the location on the page where you want to position the upper-left corner of the PivotTable.
- Use the fields from the field list to drag and drop the filter, row, column, and detail fields on the PivotTable. Add calculated and total fields to the PivotTable as needed.
- Modify the size of the PivotTable, and modify the size and other properties of the controls on the PivotTable.
- Click the Save button on the Page Design toolbar, enter a name for the data access page, select a location for the data access page, and then click the Save button.

You'll first create a blank data access page and add a PivotTable to the page.

To create a PivotTable on a data access page:

1. If you took a break after the previous session, make sure that Access is running, that the **Jobs** database in the Tutorial folder on your Data Disk is open, that **Pages** is selected in the Objects bar of the Database window, and that the Database window is maximized.

2. Click the **New** button in the Database window to open the New Data Access Page dialog box, click **Design View** in the list box (if necessary), click the **OK** button, and then if necessary click the **OK** button if you're warned about the Access 2000 Design view issue.

   You'll use the Office PivotTable tool on the toolbox to add a PivotTable control to the page.

3. Click the **Office PivotTable** tool 🖽 on the toolbox. The pointer changes to a ⁺🖽 shape when you move it over the data access page.

4. Move the pointer to the grid, and when the center of the pointer's plus symbol (+) is positioned on the grid dot in the upper-left corner, click the mouse button. Access adds a PivotTable control to the page. See Figure 7-22.

| Figure 7-22 | AFTER ADDING A PIVOTTABLE CONTROL TO THE PAGE |

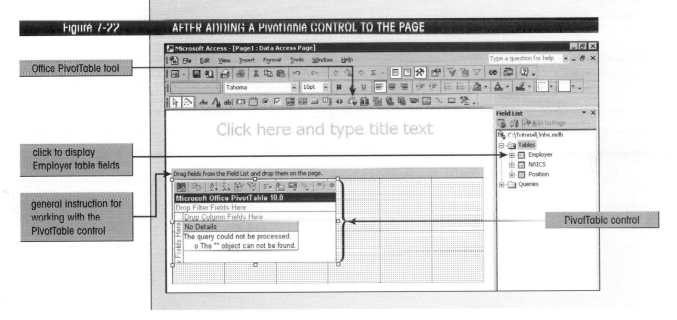

Labels: Office PivotTable tool; click to display Employer table fields; general instruction for working with the PivotTable control; PivotTable control

If you do not select a table or query as the basis for a page when you create a new page in Design view, the message "The query could not be processed: The " " object can not be found." appears inside the PivotTable control. After you add fields to the PivotTable, the message will disappear.

Adding Fields to a PivotTable

For Elsa's analysis, she will need the Country and State/Prov fields from the primary Employer table and the PositionTitle and Openings fields from the related Position table. Within the PivotTable, the Country field will be the filter field, the State/Prov field will be the column field, the PositionTitle field will be the row field, and the Openings field will be the detail field.

First, you'll expand the Employer table in the field list to display its fields, and then you'll add the required fields from the field list to the PivotTable.

To add fields to a PivotTable:

1. Click ⊞ next to Employer in the field list to display the fields from the Employer table and a folder for related tables.

2. Drag the **Country** field from the field list to the "Drop Filter Fields Here" section on the PivotTable so that the section's border color changes to blue. See Figure 7-23.

Figure 7-23	ADDING THE COUNTRY FIELD AS THE FILTER FIELD

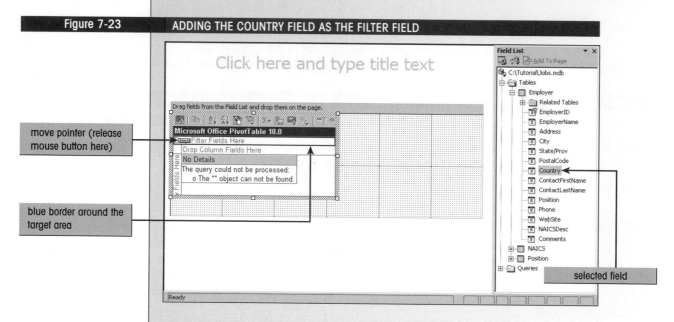

move pointer (release mouse button here)

blue border around the target area

selected field

3. Release the mouse button. A control for the Country field now appears in the filter section of the PivotTable. "All" below the Country field indicates that all country values will appear in the PivotTable—that is, no filter is currently applied. (See Figure 7-24.)

   TROUBLE? If you move the wrong field to a PivotTable section or move a field to the wrong PivotTable section, right-click the field name in the PivotTable, click Remove Field on the shortcut menu, and then drag and drop the correct field to the correct section.

   Next, you'll specify the State/Prov field as the column field.

4. Drag the **State/Prov** field from the field list; when the "Drop Column Fields Here" section's border color changes to blue, release the mouse button. A control for the State/Prov field now appears in the column section of the PivotTable. The State/Prov field is the column field, and its field values (CT, MA, and so on) are the column field items. See Figure 7-24.

Figure 7-24	AFTER ADDING THE COUNTRY AND STATE/PROV FIELDS TO THE PivotTable

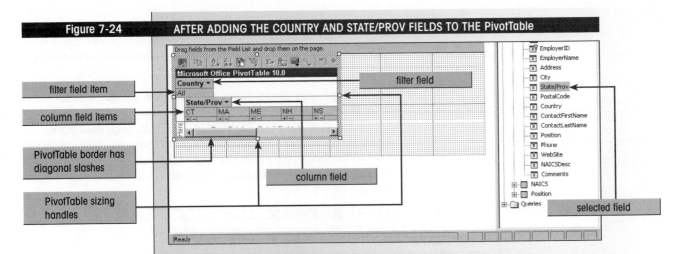

5. Use the ←→ pointer on the PivotTable's middle-right sizing handle to increase its width, and then use the ↕ pointer on the control's middle-bottom sizing handle to increase its height. See Figure 7-25.

After adding the filter and column fields to the PivotTable, you no longer can see the drop areas for the row area and main body, so you need to increase the PivotTable control's height and width. The border of the PivotTable has diagonal slashes, which indicates that the control's content is activated, so that you can manipulate its inner controls, such as the filter and column fields. You use the PivotTable's sizing handles to change the control's size.

Figure 7-25	AFTER RESIZING THE PivotTable

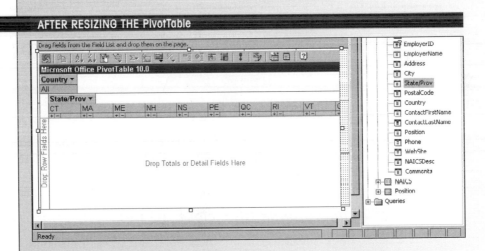

You need to drag and drop the PositionTitle and Openings fields from the related Position table into the PivotTable, so you'll expand the Related Tables entry in the field list and then expand the Position table.

6. Click ⊞ next to Related Tables in the field list, and then click ⊞ next to Position in the field list. The NAICS and Position tables, which are related to the Employer table, are now visible in the field list, as are the fields from the Position table.

7. Drag the **PositionTitle** field from the field list and drop it in the "Drop Row Fields Here" section on the PivotTable. A control for the PositionTitle field now appears in the row section of the PivotTable. The PositionTitle field is the row field, and its field values (Concierge, Cook, and so on) are the row field items. (See Figure 7-26.)

8. Drag the **Openings** field from the field list and drop it in the "Drop Totals or Detail Fields Here" section on the PivotTable. A control for the Openings field now appears in the detail section of the PivotTable. The Openings field is the detail field. The values in the body of the PivotTable are Openings field values from records in the Position table; for example, two Massachusetts (MA) employers each have one available position for a cook. See Figure 7-26.

| Figure 7-26 | AFTER ADDING THE FIELDS FROM THE JOBS DATABASE TO THE PivotTable |

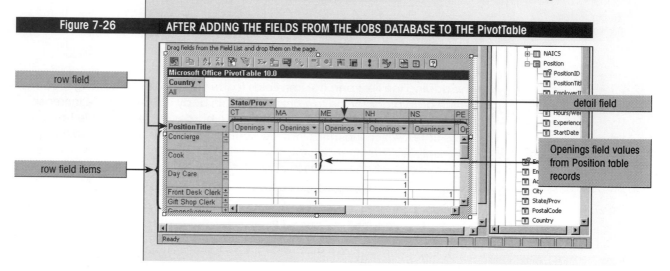

The PivotTable control is finished. Elsa wants you to add a title to the page and then open it in Page view.

Using a PivotTable in Page View

Before viewing and using the PivotTable in Page view, you'll add a page title and then save the page. Also, because you've added all the required fields to the PivotTable, you'll close the field list.

To add a page title, close the field list, and save the page:

1. Click anywhere on the **Click here and type title text** placeholder at the top of the page, and then type **Openings by State/Prov and Position**.

2. Close the field list, and then save the page as **Openings PivotTable** in the Tutorial folder on your Data Disk. If necessary, click the **OK** button to close the dialog box containing the connection string warning message.

Next, you'll view the page in Page view.

To view and use a PivotTable in Page view:

1. Click the **View** button for Page view 🔳 on the Page Design toolbar. The Page window opens in Page view. See Figure 7-27.

Figure 7-27   INITIAL VIEW OF THE PivotTable IN PAGE VIEW

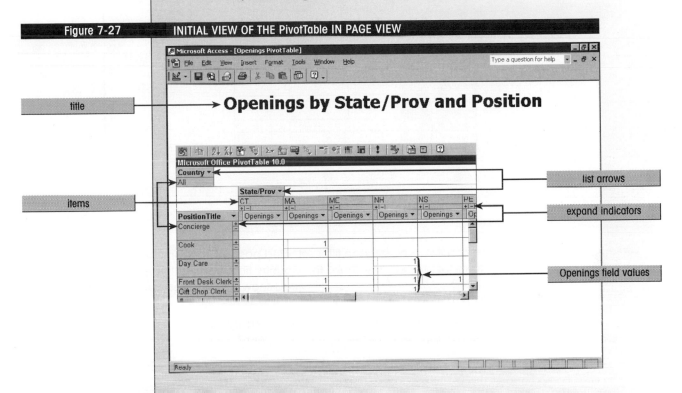

title

list arrows

items

expand indicators

Openings field values

Elsa asks you to explain the purpose of the list arrows next to each field name. The list arrows let you filter the data displayed in the PivotTable. You can filter which countries, position titles, and states/provinces you want to view in the PivotTable. You'll filter to display openings in Canada.

2. Click the **Country** list arrow, click the **All** check box to clear all selections, click the **Canada** check box, and then click the **OK** button. Access applies the Country filter and displays openings in the provinces of Nova Scotia (NS), Prince Edward Island (PE), and Quebec (QC). See Figure 7-28.

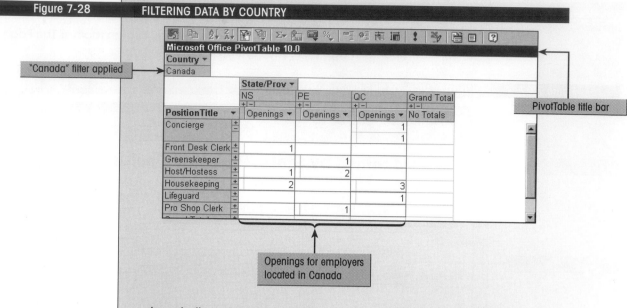

Figure 7-28   FILTERING DATA BY COUNTRY

"Canada" filter applied

PivotTable title bar

Openings for employers located in Canada

In a similar way, you can filter selected position titles and selected states/provinces. To remove the Country filter, you could repeat Step 2 and click the All check box. You'll instead show Elsa a faster way to remove and then reapply the filter.

3. Click the **AutoFilter** button ![icon] on the PivotTable toolbar. Access removes the Country filter and displays employers in all locations.

4. Click ![icon] again to reapply the Country filter to display only employers in Canada.

The PivotTable expand indicators ⊞ and ⊟ provide the same functionality as the expand indicators used with subdatasheets and data access pages. Unlike datasheets and data access pages, which display one expand indicator at a time, both PivotTable expand indicators appear for each row field item and column field item. However, clicking the expand indicator ⊞ has no effect if the item is already expanded, and clicking ⊟ has no effect if the item is already collapsed.

5. Click the **Concierge expand indicator** ⊞. Because the Concierge item is already expanded, clicking ⊞ did not change the PivotTable.

6. Click the **Concierge expand indicator** ⊟. The Concierge item collapses to a single line, and its two Openings field values are now hidden.

7. Click the **Concierge expand indicator** ⊞ again to show its details, and then click the rightmost column **Grand Total expand indicator** ⊞. See Figure 7-29.

Figure 7-29	SHOWING ROW GRAND TOTALS

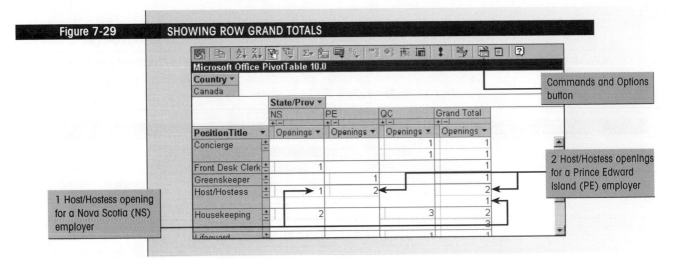

A PivotTable automatically includes a grand total column and a grand total row. However, the grand total values do not function as you might expect when the PivotTable's main body displays field values from a database. For example, instead of a grand total value of 3 openings appearing for the Canadian Host/Hostess position, each of the two individual Openings detail values appears in a separate row in the Grand Total column; the same happens in the grand total row. However, the grand total column and row values work as expected when the PivotTable's main body displays total field values.

Adding a Total Field to a PivotTable

A **total field** summarizes field values from a source field. For example, Elsa prefers to view the total number of openings for each position and location in the PivotTable instead of each individual Openings field value. For Elsa's request, you'll add a total field to the PivotTable's main body that will calculate the sum of the Openings field values for each position in each state/province. Before adding the total field, you'll switch to Design view to increase the width and height of the PivotTable, and then you'll change the caption for the PivotTable title bar. Both of these design changes will make the PivotTable easier to use for identifying and viewing the data that Elsa needs.

To change the PivotTable's dimensions and title bar caption:

1. Switch to Design view, click anywhere outside the PivotTable control to deselect it, and then click the PivotTable control to select the outer control. Sizing controls appear on the control's border, which does not have diagonal slashes.

2. Use the middle-right sizing handle to increase the width of the PivotTable until you can see the entire QC column field item, and then use the middle-bottom sizing handle to increase the height of the PivotTable until you can see the entire Housekeeping row field item.

   TROUBLE? If you increase the PivotTable's width or height too much, drag the sizing handle back to its correct position, click the grid that extends beyond the PivotTable, and then drag the grid's sizing handle so that its edge overlaps the PivotTable's edge.

   You can now change the PivotTable title bar caption.

3. Click the PivotTable title bar and, if the PivotTable border does not have diagonal slashes, click the PivotTable title bar until the control's border has diagonal slashes.

4. Click the **Commands and Options** button on the PivotTable toolbar to open the Commands and Options dialog box, and then if necessary click the **Captions** tab. See Figure 7-30.

Figure 7-30   COMMANDS AND OPTIONS DIALOG BOX

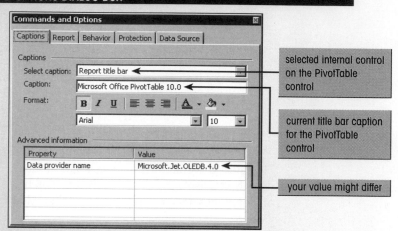

Serving a function similar to the property sheet, the Commands and Options dialog box lets you set property values, such as fonts and captions, for the internal controls on the PivotTable control.

5. Make sure the Select caption list box is set to **Report title bar**, select **Microsoft Office PivotTable 10.0** in the Caption text box, type **Openings PivotTable** in the Caption text box, and then close the Commands and Options dialog box. The PivotTable title bar caption changes to Openings PivotTable.

Next, you'll add the total field to display the total number of openings in the PivotTable's main body.

To add the total field to the PivotTable's main body:

1. Click one of the Openings column headings (but not a list arrow for an Openings column heading) to select the detail column heading row, right-click the same Openings column heading, point to **AutoCalc** on the shortcut menu, and then click **Sum**. Access adds a new row for each position in the PivotTable that displays the total number of openings for the position in each state/province. See Figure 7-31.

Figure 7-31   AFTER ADDING THE TOTAL FIELD

changed PivotTable
title bar caption

total field rows
displaying the total
number of openings

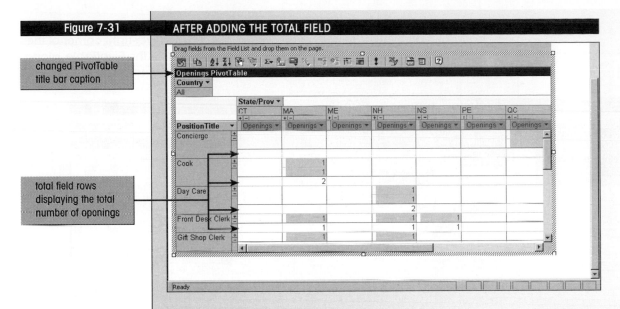

Elsa wants to view only the new total field, so you'll hide the detail number of openings values in the PivotTable.

2. Click the **Hide Details** button 📷 on the PivotTable toolbar. The detail values are now hidden, and only the total field values appear in the PivotTable's main body. See Figure 7-32.

Figure 7-32   AFTER ADDING THE TOTAL FIELD TO THE DETAIL SECTION

Hide Details button

default total field
caption

total field values for
each positon in each
state/province

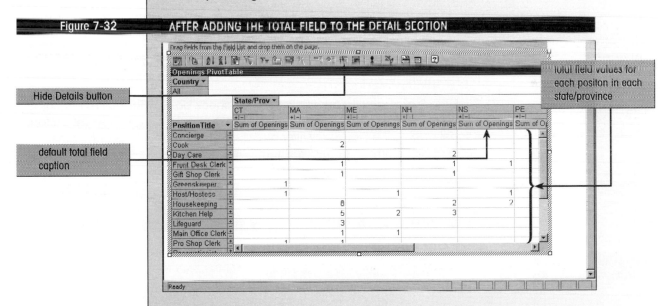

You can now change the default total field caption to a shorter, more meaningful description of the field's contents.

3. Right-click one of the Sum of Openings column headings, click **Commands and Options** on the shortcut menu to open the Commands and Options dialog box for the total field column heading, and then if necessary click the **Captions** tab.

4. Make sure that **Total** appears in the Select caption list box, change the Caption property to **Total Openings**, and then close the Commands and Options dialog box. The total field column headings change to the new Caption property value.

5. Save your design changes, switch to Page view, and then use the PivotTable's horizontal and vertical scroll bars to scroll down to the lower-right corner of the PivotTable. The Total Openings total field values appear in the PivotTable, along with a grand total row and a grand total column. See Figure 7-33.

Figure 7-33   COMPLETED PivotTable IN PAGE VIEW

grand total column (total number of openings for each position)

grand total row (total number of openings for each state/province)

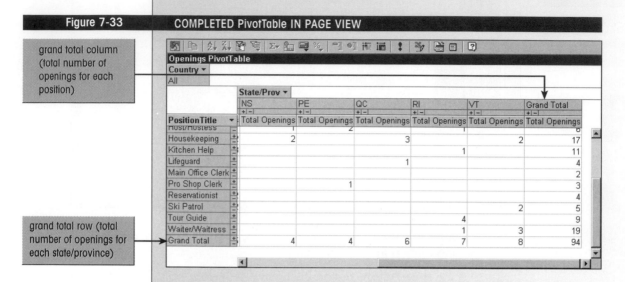

PositionTitle	NS Total Openings	PE Total Openings	QC Total Openings	RI Total Openings	VT Total Openings	Grand Total Total Openings
Host/Hostess	1	2		1		6
Housekeeping	2		3		2	17
Kitchen Help				1		11
Lifeguard			1			4
Main Office Clerk						2
Pro Shop Clerk		1				3
Reservationist						4
Ski Patrol					2	5
Tour Guide				4		9
Waiter/Waitress				1	3	19
Grand Total	4	4	6	7	8	94

You've completed the PivotTable for Elsa, so you can close the data access page and open it using your browser.

6. Close the data access page, right-click **Openings PivotTable** in the Pages list box, and then click **Web Page Preview**.

Elsa wants to view a summary of the total openings in New Hampshire (NH) and Vermont (VT).

7. Click the **State/Prov** list arrow, click the **All** check box to clear all selections, click the **NH** check box, click the **VT** check box, and then click the **OK** button. Access applies the State/Prov filter and displays total openings only in the states of New Hampshire and Vermont. See Figure 7-34.

Figure 7-34   COMPLETED PivotTable IN THE INTERNET EXPLORER WINDOW

New Hampshire and Vermont selected

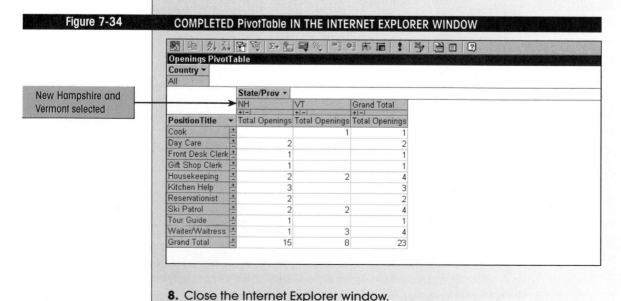

PositionTitle	NH Total Openings	VT Total Openings	Grand Total Total Openings
Cook		1	1
Day Care	2		2
Front Desk Clerk	1		1
Gift Shop Clerk	1		1
Housekeeping	2	2	4
Kitchen Help	3		3
Reservationist	2		2
Ski Patrol	2	2	4
Tour Guide	1		1
Waiter/Waitress	1	3	4
Grand Total	15	8	23

8. Close the Internet Explorer window.

Elsa is so pleased with the PivotTable that you created for her that she immediately thinks of another data access page that would be helpful to her. She asks if you can create a data access page with a chart showing the total openings for each state/province. You'll create a PivotChart on a data access page to satisfy Elsa's request.

Creating and Using a PivotChart on a Data Access Page

Office XP provides the **Office PivotChart Component** to assist you in adding a chart to a data access page, form, or datasheet. Using the Office PivotChart Component, you can create a **PivotChart**, an interactive chart that provides capabilities similar to a PivotTable. Figure 7-35 shows a PivotChart on a data access page.

Figure 7-35   PivotChart ON A DATA ACCESS PAGE

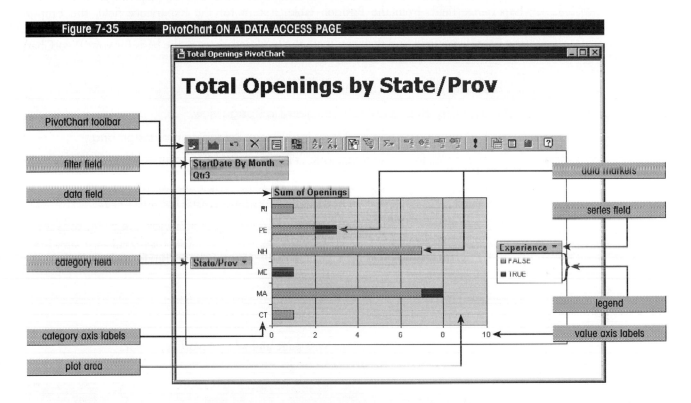

A PivotChart contains the following basic components:

- The **PivotChart toolbar** lets you perform actions such as sorting and filtering.
- The **plot area** provides a background for the data markers and gridlines. A **data marker** is a bar, dot, segment, or other symbol that represents a single data value. The **data field**, which is the Sum of Openings field in Figure 7-35, identifies which values the data markers represent and which values are shown as **value axis labels**. The **gridlines**, which appear in Figure 7-35 as vertical lines in the plot area, make it easier to see the values represented by the data markers.
- The **category field** determines which values appear as **category axis labels**. In Figure 7-35, the State/Prov field is the category field; and CT, MA, and the other states/provinces are the category axis labels. Therefore, the data markers show the total number of openings for each state/province.

■ The **series field** identifies the data markers' subdivisions. In Figure 7-35, the Experience field is the series field, and the data markers show the portion of the total number of openings that require experienced workers. The **legend** provides a list of the series field values and how these values are indicated on the data markers.

■ The **filter field** lets you restrict which data appears on the PivotChart. In Figure 7-35, the filter field is StartDate by Month, and a filter has been applied to include only those openings with start dates in the third quarter (Qtr3).

Using the Office PivotChart Component, you'll create a PivotChart on a data access page to let Elsa analyze total openings for each state/province. The data for a PivotChart can come from either a single table or from a query based on one or more tables. Elsa wants the chart to include the State/Prov field from the Employer table and the Openings, StartDate, and Experience fields from the Position table. Except for the Experience field, the Employer Positions query contains the fields needed for the PivotChart. You will modify the query to add the Experience field, and then you'll use the modified query as the basis for your PivotChart.

To modify the Employer Positions query:

1. Open the **Employer Positions** query in Design view.

2. Add the **Experience** field from the Position field list to the design grid.

   You'll save the query as Employer Positions with Experience.

3. Click **File** on the menu bar, click **Save As**, change the query name to **Employer Positions with Experience**, and then press the **Enter** key.

4. Run the query. Access displays the query results, which show the 64 records with the EmployerName, City, and State/Prov fields from the Employer table, and the PositionTitle, Openings, StartDate, EndDate, and Experience fields from the Position table.

5. Close the query.

Next, you'll create a new data access page and add a PivotChart to it.

REFERENCE WINDOW   RW

Adding a PivotChart to a Data Access Page

■ If necessary, click Pages in the Objects bar of the Database window to display the Pages list.

■ Click the New button to open the New Data Access Page dialog box, click Design View (if necessary), click the OK button, and then if necessary click the OK button to close the warning message and to create a blank data access page.

■ Click the Office Chart tool on the toolbox, and then click the mouse button in the location on the page where you want to position the upper-left corner of the PivotChart.

■ Click the PivotChart control to open the Commands and Options dialog box. Select the data source, data link connection, table or query, and chart type for the PivotChart.

■ Close the Commands and Options dialog box.

■ From the field list add the category, data, filter, and series fields to the PivotChart.

■ Modify the size of the PivotChart, and modify the size and other properties of the controls on the PivotChart.

■ Click the Save button on the Page Design toolbar, enter a name for the data access page, select a location for the data access page, and then click the Save button.

You'll first create a blank data access page and add a PivotChart to the page.

To create a PivotChart on a data access page:

1. Click **Pages** in the Objects bar of the Database window to display the Pages list.

2. Click the **New** button in the Database window to open the New Data Access Page dialog box, click **Design View** in the list box (if necessary), click the **OK** button, and then if necessary click the **OK** button if you're warned about the Access 2000 Design view issue.

   You'll use the Office Chart tool on the toolbox to add a PivotChart control to the page.

3. Click the **Office Chart** tool 📊 on the toolbox. The pointer changes to a $^+$📊 shape when you move it over the data access page.

4. Move the pointer to the grid, and when the center of the pointer's plus symbol (+) is positioned on the grid dot in the upper-left corner, click the mouse button. Access adds a PivotChart control to the page.

5. Click the PivotChart control. The Chart Wizard opens the Commands and Options dialog box. See Figure 7-36.

Figure 7-36	SPECIFYING THE DATA SOURCE FOR THE PivotChart

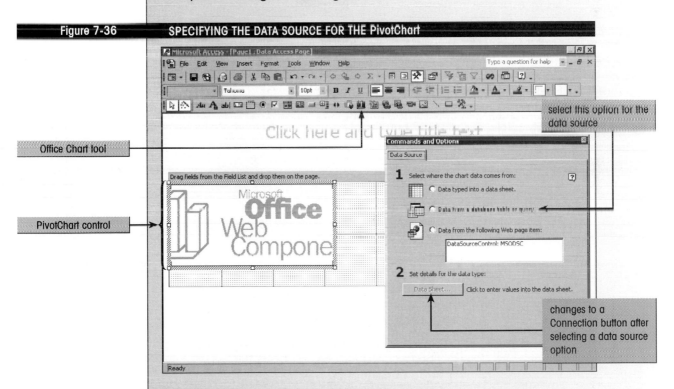

Your first step is to choose the data source for the PivotChart. The data source for a PivotChart can be data you type into a datasheet, data from a table or query, or data from a Web page. Because the Employer Positions with Experience query is the data source, you'll choose the second option.

6. Click the **Data from a database table or query** option button, and then click the **Connection** button. The Commands and Options dialog box expands to include the Data Details and Type tabs, in addition to the original Data Source tab, and the Data Details tab is selected. You need to set the Connection text box to the Jobs database on your Data Disk. Notice that as you make selections in the dialog boxes, the PivotChart control on the data access page changes to reflect your selections.

7. Click the **Edit** button, use the Look in list box to open the **Tutorial** folder on your Data Disk, click **Jobs** (if necessary), and then click the **Open** button. The Data Link Properties dialog box opens and displays the Jobs database as the selected database name. See Figure 7-37.

Figure 7-37	SPECIFYING THE CONNECTION TO THE DATABASE

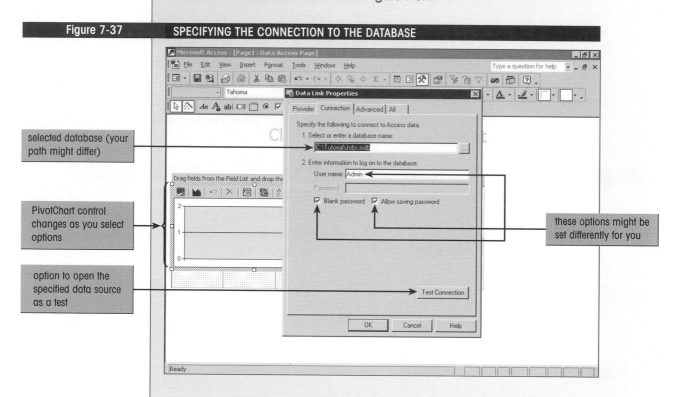

selected database (your path might differ)

PivotChart control changes as you select options

option to open the specified data source as a test

these options might be set differently for you

The second section of the dialog box contains a user name (yours might differ from the user name shown in Figure 7-37) and two check boxes. Because you don't want to type a password to establish a connection to the Jobs database and because the default user name is acceptable to Elsa, you won't change anything in the dialog box. If you click the Test Connection button, the Office PivotChart Component will test the accuracy of your data source settings by attempting to open the Jobs database. This test will fail because you already have the database open; the Office PivotChart Component can open the data source only if it's not currently in use. (You would use this option when you have started the Office PivotChart Component but have not opened the data source.)

8. Click the **OK** button to close the Data Link Properties dialog box and open the next dialog box. This dialog box displays the options you've previously selected, so you do not need to make any changes to it.

9. Click the **OK** button to close the dialog box and open the Select Table dialog box, click **Employer Positions with Experience**, click the **OK** button, and then click the **Type** tab on the Commands and Options dialog box. See Figure 7-38.

Figure 7-38   SELECTING THE CHART TYPE

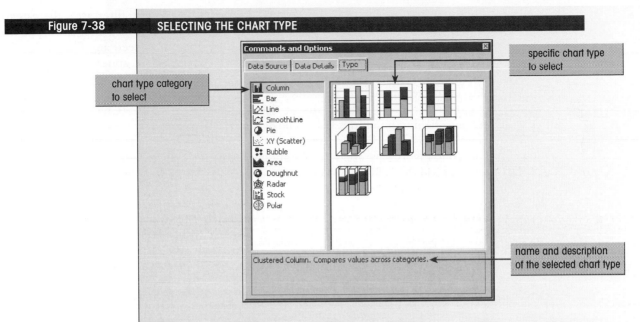

Next, you need to select the specific chart type you'll use for the PivotChart. Elsa suggests using a stacked column chart.

10. Click **Column** in the left list box, click the stacked column chart type (row 1, column 2), and then close the Commands and Options dialog box. The PivotChart control now appears with the settings you selected in the dialog boxes, and the data access page field list might be open on your screen. See Figure 7-39.

Figure 7-39   AFTER ADDING THE PivotChart CONTROL TO THE PAGE

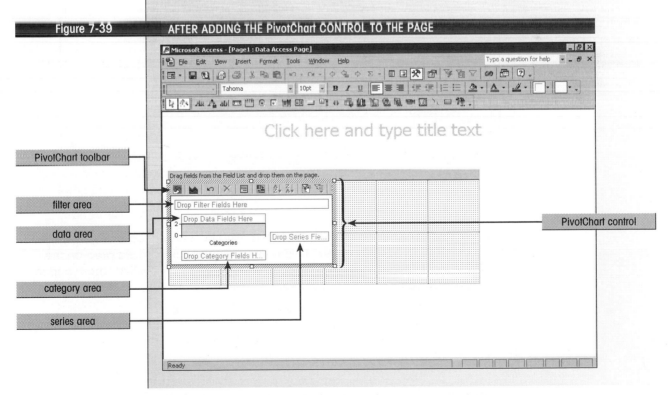

The PivotChart control contains a toolbar and four areas: the filter area, the category area, the data area, and the series area. The filter area will contain any filter fields you need to filter data displayed in the PivotChart; Elsa initially doesn't need any filter fields. The category area will contain the category field whose values will appear as labels on the PivotChart's category axis where "Categories" currently appears; Elsa wants the State/Prov field to be a category field. The series area will contain any series fields you need to represent groups of related data points or data markers on the PivotChart; Elsa wants the Experience field to be a series field. The data area will contain the data fields that will serve as data markers on the PivotChart; Elsa wants the Openings field to be the data field.

The four PivotChart areas are empty until you add fields from the field list to them. Before you add the fields to the PivotChart, you'll enlarge the PivotChart.

To resize and add fields to a PivotChart:

1. Use the ↔ pointer on the PivotChart's middle-right sizing handle to increase its width so that its right edge touches the right edge of the page grid.

2. Use the ↕ pointer on the control's middle-bottom sizing handle to increase its height until you can see 1.25 at the top of the y-axis. (See Figure 7-40.)

3. Click the PivotChart so that border has diagonal slashes, and then click the **Field List** button ▤ on the PivotChart toolbar to open the field list. See Figure 7-40.

Figure 7-40	AFTER ENLARGING THE PivotChart AND OPENING THE FIELD LIST

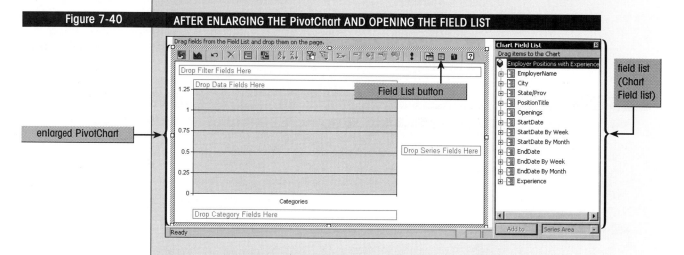

4. Drag the **State/Prov** field from the field list to the category area on the PivotChart. The State/Prov field is now a category field on the PivotChart.

5. Drag the **Experience** field from the field list to the series area on the PivotChart, and then drag the **Openings** field from the field list to the data area on the PivotChart. The Experience field is now a series field on the PivotChart, and the Openings field is now a data field on the PivotChart.

Next, you'll add a left-aligned page title and save the page.

6. Click anywhere on the **Click here and type title text** placeholder at the top of the page, type **Total Openings by State/Prov**, and then click the **Align Left** button ▤ on the Formatting toolbar. Note that the field list no longer appears in the Page Design window.

7. Save the page as **Total Openings PivotChart** in the Tutorial folder on your Data Disk; if necessary, click the **OK** button if the connection string warning message appears. See Figure 7-41.

Figure 7-41	COMPLETED PivotChart IN DESIGN VIEW

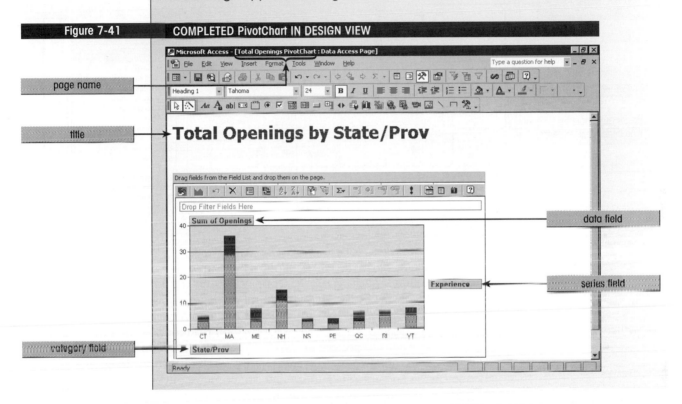

Elsa wants to view the PivotChart in Internet Explorer.

To view the PivotChart in Internet Explorer:

1. Click the list arrow for the **View** button 🗐 on the Page Design toolbar, and then click **Web Page Preview**. Internet Explorer starts and displays the Total Openings PivotChart page.

2. Click the **Show/Hide Legend** button 🗐 on the PivotChart toolbar to display the legend for the Experience series field. See Figure 7-42.

Figure 7-42   COMPLETED PivotChart IN WEB PAGE PREVIEW

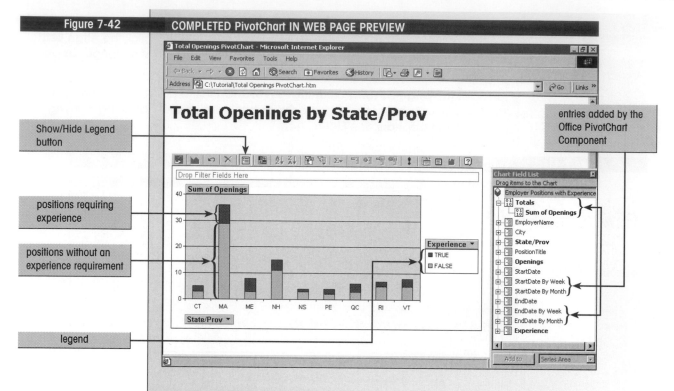

Show/Hide Legend button

positions requiring experience

positions without an experience requirement

legend

entries added by the Office PivotChart Component

The field list contains the eight fields from the Employer Positions with Experience query and the Sum of Openings summary field, created automatically by the Office PivotChart Component when you added the Openings field as the data field to the PivotChart; the summary field appears as a Totals subentry. In addition, the Office PivotChart Component automatically added two field list entries (StartDate By Week and StartDate By Month) based on the StartDate field, and two entries (EndDate By Week and EndDate By Month) based on the EndDate field. These four date entries let you filter date fields by time divisions such as year, quarter, month, and day.

Elsa asks if she can view the total openings for a specific quarter of the year.

3. Click ⊞ next to StartDate By Month in the field list, and then drag **Quarters** to the filter area on the PivotChart to add it as a filter field to the PivotChart.

4. Click the **StartDate By Month** list arrow, click the **All** check box to clear all selections, click ⊞ next to 2003, click the **Qtr3** check box so that it's the only checked entry, and then click the **OK** button. Access applies the StartDate By Month filter and displays total openings in only those states/provinces that have openings with start dates in the third quarter. See Figure 7-43.

Figure 7-43	AFTER APPLYING THE FILTER

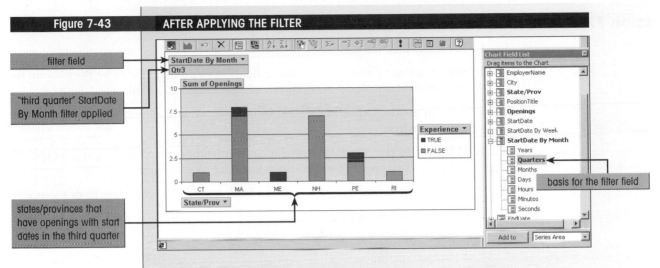

filter field

"third quarter" StartDate By Month filter applied

states/provinces that have openings with start dates in the third quarter

basis for the filter field

After viewing the filter, Elsa now wants to remove the filter field from the PivotChart.

5. Click the **StartDate By Month** filter field in the PivotChart control to make it the current selection, and then click the **Delete Selection** button ⊠ on the PivotChart toolbar to remove the filter field from the PivotChart.

Elsa now wants to replace the stacked column chart with a stacked bar chart. You need to change the chart type in Design view.

To change the chart type of the PivotChart:

1. Close Internet Explorer, and then click the PivotChart control until the field list appears. You've selected the PivotChart control and activated the PivotChart toolbar.

2. Click the **Chart Type** button 🔲 on the PivotChart toolbar. The Commands and Options dialog box opens with the Type tab selected.

3. Click **Bar** in the left list box, and then click the stacked bar chart type (row 1, column 2). The chart changes to a stacked bar chart.

4. Close the Commands and Options dialog box.

   Elsa has no further changes to the PivotChart, so you'll save your design changes and close the page.

5. Save your changes, and then close the data access page.

You have completed the data access pages for Elsa. In the next session, you will help Elsa use XML files and integrate Access data with other programs.

Session 7.2 QUICK CHECK

1. What is a PivotTable?

2. Within a PivotTable you can choose fields from the field list to be the column field, the row field, the detail field, and the _____ field.

3. You can use the Office PivotTable Component to add a PivotTable to which three Access objects?

4. What's different about a PivotTable's expand indicators compared to the expand indicators that appear for datasheets and data access pages?

5. On a PivotTable, the _____ field summarizes field values from a source field.

6. On a PivotChart, the _____ field identifies which values are shown as value axis labels.

7. You can show/hide a legend for the _____ field on a PivotChart.

SESSION 7.3

In this session, you will import data from an XML file into an Access table and export an Access table to an XML file. You will also export Access data to an Excel worksheet. Finally, you'll add a hyperlink field to a table and enter hyperlink values that link records to Word documents.

Using XML

Matt has been tracking positions and the students hired for those positions. Elsa wants to add this data to the Jobs database; in response to her request, Matt has made the data available to Elsa in an XML document. **XML (Extensible Markup Language)** is a programming language similar in format to HTML that is more customizable and suited to the exchange of data between different programs. Unlike HTML, which uses a fixed set of tags to describe how a Web page should look, developers can customize XML code to describe the data it contains and how that data should be structured.

Importing an XML File as an Access Table

Access can import data from an XML file directly into a database table. Matt's XML file is named Job, and you'll import it as a table with the same name into the Jobs database.

REFERENCE WINDOW	RW

Importing an XML File as an Access Table

- Click File on the menu bar, point to Get External Data, and then click Import.
- Click the Files of type list arrow, and then click XML Documents.
- Use the Look in list box to select the XML document to import.
- Click the Import button to open the Import XML dialog box, click the Options button, select the desired import option, and then click the OK button.

Now you will import the Job.xml document as an Access database table.

To import the XML document as an Access table:

1. Make sure that Access is running, that the **Jobs** database in the Tutorial folder on your Data Disk is open, that the Database window is maximized, and that **Tables** is selected in the Objects bar of the Database window.

2. Click **File** on the menu bar, point to **Get External Data**, and then click **Import**. The Import dialog box opens.

3. If necessary, click the **Files of type** list arrow, scroll down, and then click **XML Documents**.

4. Make sure the Look in list box displays the **Tutorial** folder on your Data Disk, and then click **Job** to select it.

5. Click the **Import** button to open the Import XML dialog box, and then click the **Options** button. See Figure 7-44.

Figure 7-44	IMPORT XML DIALOG BOX

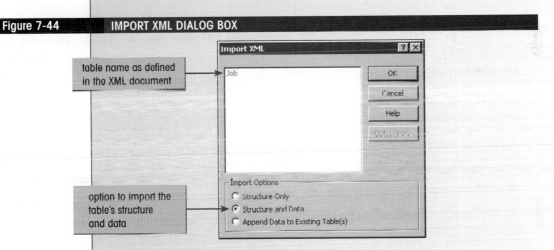

table name as defined in the XML document

option to import the table's structure and data

From the XML file, you can import just the table structure to a new table, import the table structure and data to a new table, or append the data in the XML file to an existing table. You'll import the table structure and data to a new table named Job.

6. Make sure the **Structure and Data** option button is selected, click the **OK** button, and then click the **OK** button when the import confirmation message box appears. The Job table has been imported to the Jobs database and its data has been saved in a new table named Job. This table is now listed in the Tables list box of the Database window.

Elsa asks to view the data in the Job table.

7. Open the **Job** table in Datasheet view. Access displays the PositionID, StudentID, StartDate, and EndDate fields from the Job table, which contains 31 records. See Figure 7-45.

Figure 7-45   JOB TABLE IN DATASHEET VIEW

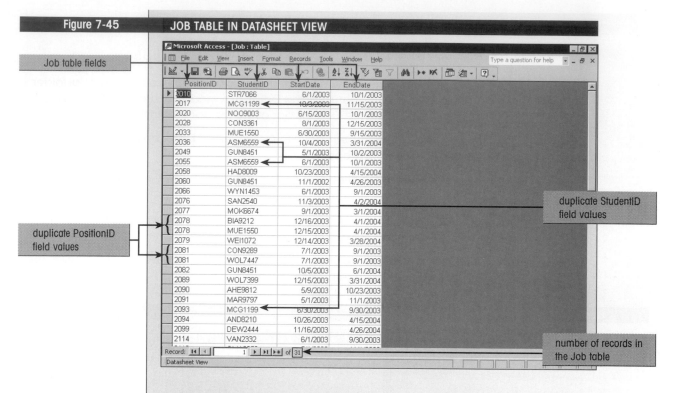

Job table fields

duplicate StudentID field values

duplicate PositionID field values

number of records in the Job table

Notice the duplicate PositionID field values (2078 and 2081) and the duplicate StudentID field values (MCG1199 and ASM6559). Because of these duplicate field values, neither field can be the table's primary key. The StartDate or EndDate fields cannot serve as the table's primary key either because they also contain duplicate field values. So what's the primary key for the Job table? It's the combination of the PositionID and StudentID fields; each pair of values for these two fields is unique. You'll verify the primary key by viewing the Job table in Design view.

8. Switch to Design view. Both the PositionID field and the StudentID field have the key symbol in their row selectors, so the combination of values in these two fields serves as the primary key for the Job table. See Figure 7-46.

Figure 7-46   JOB TABLE IN DESIGN VIEW

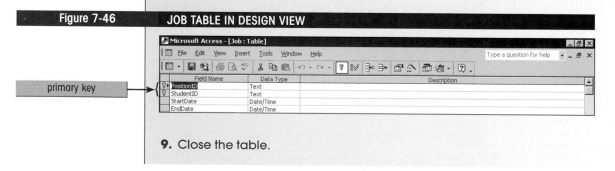

primary key

9. Close the table.

Elsa just received a request that requires you to export the Position table as an XML file.

Exporting an Access Table as an XML File

A regional nonprofit agency, which coordinates housing for international students, recently contacted Elsa and requested job-opening information for NSJI's client employers. The agency uses a specialized computer program, and the agency representative asked Elsa to provide the data as an XML file to make it easier for the agency to identify and process the data.

Just as you did when you exported the Employer Positions query as an HTML document earlier in this tutorial, you'll use the Export command on the shortcut menu to export the Position table as an XML file.

REFERENCE WINDOW   **RW**

Exporting an Access Object as an XML File
- In the Database window, right-click the object (table, query, form, or report) you want to export, and then click Export on the shortcut menu.
- Enter the filename in the File name text box, and then select the location where you want to save the file.
- Click the Save as type list arrow, click XML Documents, and then click the Export button.
- Click the Advanced button on the Export XML dialog box; set the data, schema, and presentation options; and then click the OK button.

You can now export the Position table as an XML file.

To export the Position table as an XML file:

1. Right-click **Position** in the Tables list to display the shortcut menu, and then click **Export**. The Export dialog box opens, displaying the type and name of the object you are exporting in its title bar—in this case, the Position table.

   You'll save the Position table as an XML file in the Tutorial folder on your Data Disk.

2. Make sure the Save in list box displays the **Tutorial** folder on your Data Disk.

3. Type **NSJI Employer Positions** in the File name text box, click the **Save as type** list arrow, scroll down the list and click **XML Documents**, and then click the **Export** button. The Export XML dialog box opens.

   Clicking the Advanced button in the Export XML dialog box lets you view and change detailed options for exporting a database object to an XML file.

4. Click the **Advanced** button to reveal detailed export options in the Export XML dialog box. See Figure 7-47.

Figure 7-47   DATA TAB OF THE EXPORT XML DIALOG BOX

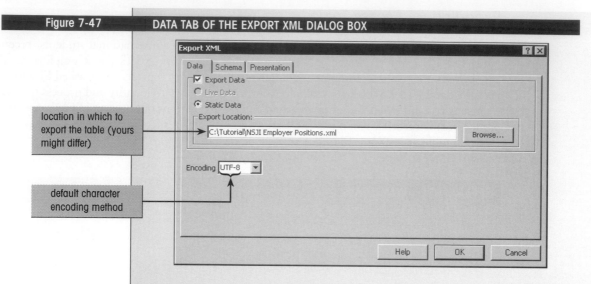

location in which to
export the table (yours
might differ)

default character
encoding method

The Export Data check box and the Export Location text box display the selections you made in the previous step. You're exporting the table data, so the data is static, not dynamic. The encoding option determines how characters will be represented in the exported XML file. The encoding choices are UTF-8, which uses 8 bits to represent each character, and UTF-16, which uses 16 bits to represent each character.

The Data tab settings are correct, so you'll verify the Schema tab settings.

5. Click the **Schema** tab. See Figure 7-48.

Figure 7-48   SCHEMA TAB OF THE EXPORT XML DIALOG BOX

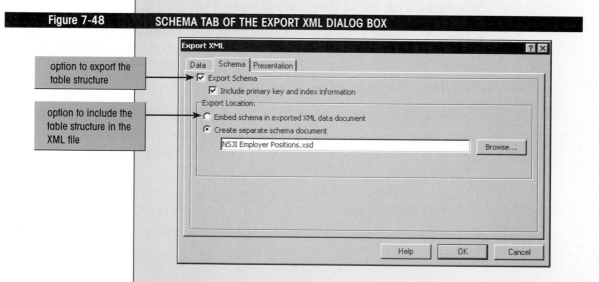

option to export the
table structure

option to include the
table structure in the
XML file

Along with the data from the Position table, you'll be exporting its table structure, including information about the table's primary key and indexes. You can include this information in a separate **XSD (XML Structure Definition)** file, or you can embed the information in the XML file. The agency wants a single XML file, so you'll embed the structure information in the XML file.

6. Click the **Embed schema in exported XML data document** option button to select that option and to dim the "Create separate schema document" list box, and then click the **Presentation** tab.

The Presentation tab options let you export a separate **XSL (Extensible Stylesheet Language)** file containing the format specifications for the Position table data. Unlike HTML, XML provides no screen formatting information. An XSL file provides formatting instructions so that a browser or another program can display the data in the XML file in a readable way. The agency will import the Position table data directly into its computer program, which contains its own formatting instructions, so you will not export an XSL file.

7. Make sure that the **Export Presentation (HTML 4.0 Sample XSL)** check box is unchecked, and then click the **OK** button. Access closes the Export XML dialog box, creates the XML file in the Tutorial folder on your Data Disk, and returns you to the Database window.

When contacted in the future, Elsa now knows how to create an XML file to give to the agency.

Elsa next wants to perform a detailed analysis on potential income data. To do so, she wants to work with the data in a Microsoft Excel worksheet.

Exporting an Access Query as an Excel Worksheet

A spreadsheet (or worksheet) program, such as Microsoft Excel, is designed to assist you in analyzing data. Although a database management program provides some data analysis capabilities, it is primarily designed for storing and retrieving records. A worksheet program has many more powerful tools for analyzing data to create budgets, projections, and models.

You can export the contents of most Access objects, including tables, forms, and reports, to other Windows programs, including Excel.

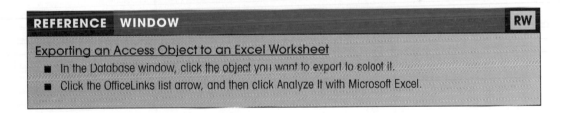

REFERENCE WINDOW   RW

Exporting an Access Object to an Excel Worksheet
- In the Database window, click the object you want to export to select it.
- Click the OfficeLinks list arrow, and then click Analyze It with Microsoft Excel.

Like many business owners, Elsa uses a worksheet program as a planning and budgeting tool for her business. She would like to use the potential income information to analyze the company's future income. She asks you to transfer the results of the Potential Income by Employer query to an Excel worksheet so that she can use Excel to perform the necessary analysis that she cannot perform using Access.

To export the query results to an Excel worksheet:

1. Click **Queries** in the Objects bar of the Database window to display the queries list.

2. Click **Potential Income by Employer**, click the list arrow for the **OfficeLinks** button on the Database toolbar, and then click **Analyze It with Microsoft Excel**. Access automatically starts Excel and places the query results in a new worksheet. See Figure 7-49.

   TROUBLE? Depending on your Access settings, your OfficeLinks button might look different than the one shown in Figure 7-49.

   TROUBLE? If Excel is not installed on your computer, another spreadsheet program might start. The specific program that starts and opens the query results is not important. Simply continue with the steps. If a spreadsheet program is not installed on your computer, ask your instructor or technical support person for help.

Figure 7-49	QUERY RESULTS IN THE EXCEL WORKSHEET

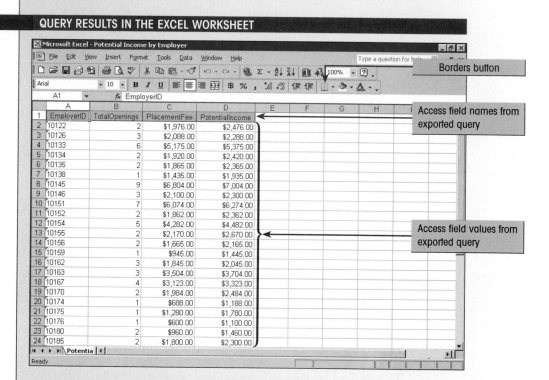

Notice that each field value is placed in a single cell in the worksheet. The field names are entered in the first row of cells in the worksheet. You can now use this data just as you would any other data in an Excel worksheet.

Elsa wants to see the total of the potential income amounts, so she asks you to create a grand total for the data in column D. You'll first add a line to separate the grand total amount from the other potential income amounts.

To create the grand total amount:

1. Scroll down the worksheet, and then click cell **D39** to select the rightmost cell in the last row of data in column D (see Figure 7-50).

2. Click the list arrow for the **Borders** button ▢ on the Formatting toolbar to display the list of border options, click the **Thick Bottom Border** button (the second choice in row two), and then click cell **E39**. Excel places a heavy border on the bottom of cell D39. See Figure 7-50.

Figure 7-50	ADDING A BOTTOM BORDER TO THE CELL

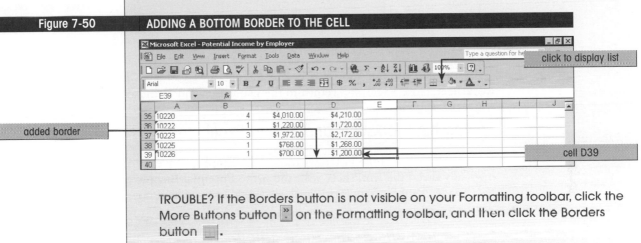

TROUBLE? If the Borders button is not visible on your Formatting toolbar, click the More Buttons button ▸ on the Formatting toolbar, and then click the Borders button ▢.

TROUBLE? Your Borders button might look different from the one shown in Figure 7-50 and might be in a different position on the Formatting toolbar.

3. Click cell **D40** to select it, and then click the **AutoSum** button Σ on the Standard toolbar. Excel automatically creates the formula to sum the contents of the cells above cell D40. See Figure 7-51.

Figure 7-51	FORMULA TO SUM THE CONTENTS OF CELLS D2 THROUGH D39

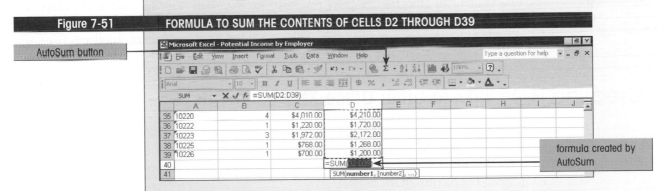

4. Press the **Enter** key to enter the formula. Excel displays the sum of the contents of cells D2 through D39 in cell D40. See Figure 7-52.

Figure 7-52   **TOTAL ADDED TO CELL D40**

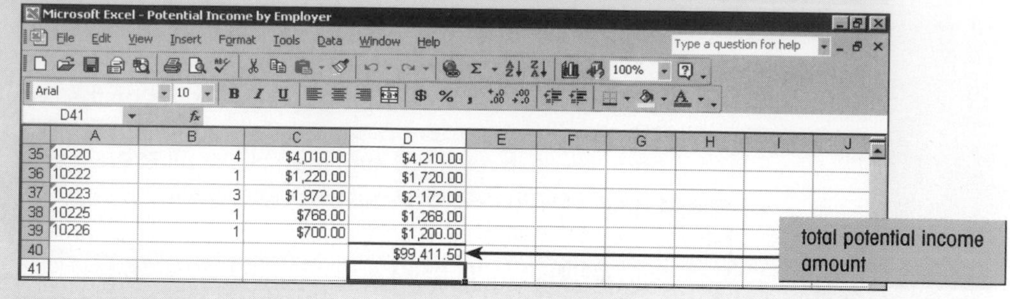

total potential income amount

Elsa plans on doing more work with the data in Excel later. For now, you can save the worksheet, close Excel, and return to the Database window in Access.

Saving the Worksheet and Exiting Excel

When you exported the Potential Income by Employer query results to Excel, Excel automatically saved the worksheet with the name Potential Income by Employer. Because you have made changes to the worksheet, you need to save them now before exiting Excel.

> ### To create the grand total amount:
>
> 1. Click the **Save** button 🖫 on the Standard toolbar.
>
> 2. Click the **Close** button ☒ on the Excel window title bar to close the worksheet, exit Excel, and return to the Database window in Access.

When you exported the query results to Excel, Access placed a copy of the query results in the worksheet. The query results in the Excel worksheet are static, so any later changes made to the Access data will not be reflected in the Excel worksheet. Similarly, any changes made in the worksheet will not affect the Access data.

Creating Hyperlinks to Other Office XP Documents

When Zack visits client employers, he keeps field notes about their positions in Word documents. Now he would like some way of connecting these notes with the corresponding records in the Position table. This connection would allow him to review his notes when he views the records in the table.

Each position's set of notes is a separate Word document. For example, Zack created a Word document named Aidan to enter his notes on the host/hostess position at Aidan's of Mystic. Similarly, his notes for the tour guide position at Newport Mansion Guided Tours are in a file named Newport, and the file for the cook position at Pear Tree Inn & Restaurant is named PearTree. To connect Zack's notes with the corresponding records in the Position table, you need to create a hyperlink field in the Position table.

Creating a Hyperlink Field in a Table

Access lets you create a hyperlink field in a table. The field value in a hyperlink field is a hyperlink or pointer to another object. These objects can be database objects (such as tables or forms), a Word document, a named range in an Excel worksheet, or even a URL for a Web page. When you click a hyperlink field value, the associated program starts and opens the linked object.

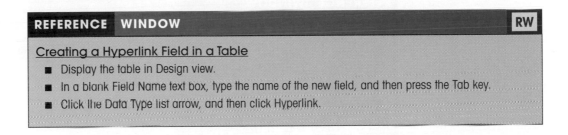

REFERENCE WINDOW RW

Creating a Hyperlink Field in a Table
- Display the table in Design view.
- In a blank Field Name text box, type the name of the new field, and then press the Tab key.
- Click the Data Type list arrow, and then click Hyperlink.

You will create a hyperlink field in the Position table. The hyperlink field value will be a hyperlink to one of Zack's Word documents. When Zack clicks a hyperlink, Word will start and open the Word document that contains his notes.

To add a hyperlink field to the Position table:

1. Open the **Position** table in Design view.

2. Click the **Field Name** text box in the first empty row, type **FieldNotes**, and then press the **Tab** key.

3. Click the **Data Type** list arrow, and then click **Hyperlink**. See Figure 7-53.

Figure 7-53	ADDING A HYPERLINK FIELD TO A TABLE

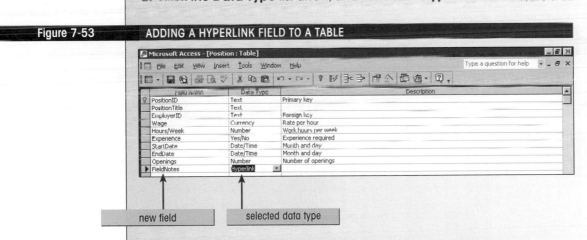

4. Save your table design change, and then switch to Datasheet view.

Now you can add the hyperlink field values to the new FieldsNotes field in the Position table datasheet. These field values will be hyperlinks to the Word documents Zack created.

Entering Hyperlink Field Values

When you add a field value in a hyperlink field, you can enter the name of an object, such as a table, form, worksheet, or document, or you can enter a URL to a Web page. You can type the field value directly into the field or you can use the Insert Hyperlink dialog box to enter it.

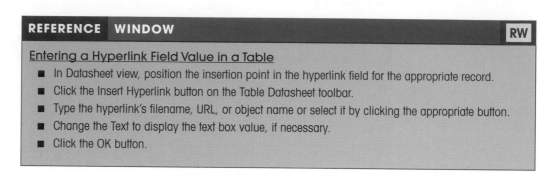

REFERENCE WINDOW   RW

Entering a Hyperlink Field Value in a Table
- In Datasheet view, position the insertion point in the hyperlink field for the appropriate record.
- Click the Insert Hyperlink button on the Table Datasheet toolbar.
- Type the hyperlink's filename, URL, or object name or select it by clicking the appropriate button.
- Change the Text to display the text box value, if necessary.
- Click the OK button.

You will use the Insert Hyperlink dialog box to enter the necessary hyperlink field values.

To enter field values in the hyperlink field:

1. In Datasheet view, click the **FieldNotes** text box for the PositionID 2004 record (record 1).

2. Click the **Insert Hyperlink** button 📖 on the Table Datasheet toolbar. The Insert Hyperlink dialog box opens.

3. If necessary, use the Look in list arrow to display the contents of the **Tutorial** folder on your Data Disk in the Look in list box. See Figure 7-54.

Figure 7-54   **INSERT HYPERLINK DIALOG BOX**

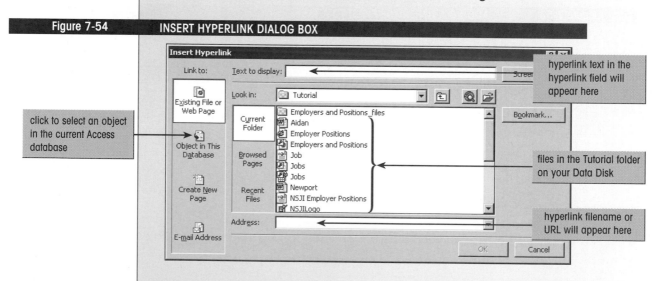

In the Insert Hyperlink dialog box, you can type the hyperlink, select the link from the Look in list box, or select the link by using one of the buttons. You can click the Bookmark button or the Object in This Database button to select an object in the current Access database as the hyperlink.

The hyperlink for the first record is the file named Aidan.

4. Click **Aidan** in the Look in list box. The name of the Aidan file appears in the Address text box with a .doc extension, which is the extension for a Word document. This is the file that will open when you click the hyperlink field for record 1 in the Position table.

   The Text to display text box shows what will be displayed as a field value in the database hyperlink field for record 1. You'll change the value of the Text to display text box to "Aidan's of Mystic" so that it is more descriptive.

5. Select **.doc** in the Text to display text box, and then type **'s of Mystic**. See Figure 7-55.

Figure 7-55   **ENTERING A HYPERLINK FIELD VALUE AND FILENAME**

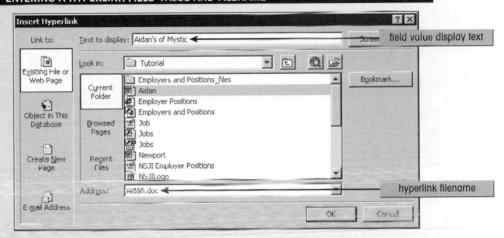

6. Click the **OK** button to close the Insert Hyperlink dialog box. The display text for the hyperlink field value appears in the FieldNotes field for the first record. See Figure 7-56.

Figure 7-56   **AFTER ENTERING THE HYPERLINK FIELD VALUE**

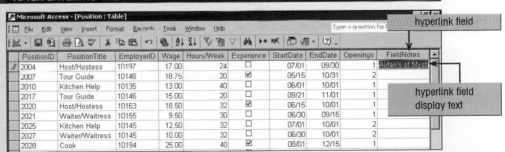

TROUBLE? If you selected the wrong hyperlink value, right-click the hyperlink field value, point to Hyperlink on the shortcut menu, click Edit Hyperlink, and then repeat Steps 4 through 6.

7. Use the same procedure to enter hyperlink field values for the records for PositionID 2007 (record 2) and PositionID 2028 (record 9). Select **Newport** as the filename and type **Newport Mansion Guided Tours** as the display text value for the PositionID 2007 record; select **PearTree** as the filename and type **Pear Tree Inn & Restaurant** as the display text value for the PositionID 2028 record.

8. Resize the FieldNotes column to its best fit and, if necessary, scroll to the right to view the entire column. Click in any empty FieldsNotes text box to deselect the FieldNotes column. When you are finished, the Datasheet window should look like Figure 7-57.

Figure 7-57   HYPERLINK FIELD VALUES ENTERED FOR THE THREE RECORDS

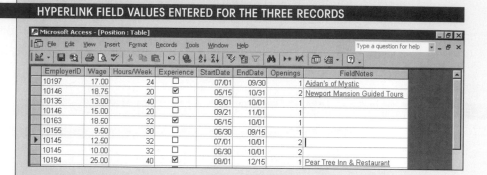

TROUBLE? If you click a hyperlink in the datasheet, instead of an empty FieldNotes text box, Access will start Word and open the hyperlinked file. Click the Close button ⊠ on the Word title bar to close Word.

Notice that the hyperlink field values have a different appearance from the other field values. The hyperlink field values are shown in a different color and are underlined, indicating that they are hyperlinks.

Zack wants to test one of the new hyperlink fields in the Position table. You'll use a hyperlink to view his corresponding field notes for the Pear Tree Inn & Restaurant.

Using a Hyperlink

When you click a hyperlink field value, its associated program starts and opens the linked object. When you click a value in the FieldNotes field, for example, Word will start and open the linked document.

To use a hyperlink to open a Word document:

1. Click the **Pear Tree Inn & Restaurant** FieldNotes hyperlink. Word starts and opens the PearTree document, which contains Zack's field notes for Pear Tree Inn & Restaurant. See Figure 7-58.

| Figure 7-58 | FIELD NOTES FOR PEAR TREE INN & RESTUARANT IN THE PEARTREE DOCUMENT |

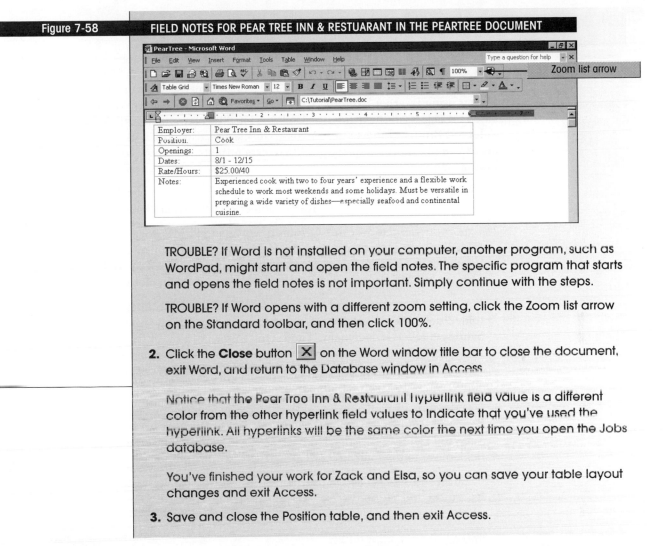

TROUBLE? If Word is not installed on your computer, another program, such as WordPad, might start and open the field notes. The specific program that starts and opens the field notes is not important. Simply continue with the steps.

TROUBLE? If Word opens with a different zoom setting, click the Zoom list arrow on the Standard toolbar, and then click 100%.

2. Click the **Close** button [X] on the Word window title bar to close the document, exit Word, and return to the Database window in Access.

Notice that the Pear Tree Inn & Restaurant hyperlink field value is a different color from the other hyperlink field values to indicate that you've used the hyperlink. All hyperlinks will be the same color the next time you open the Jobs database.

You've finished your work for Zack and Elsa, so you can save your table layout changes and exit Access.

3. Save and close the Position table, and then exit Access.

Elsa, Zack, and Matt are very pleased with the data access pages and integration work you completed for them. They've learned enough to be able to do similar work on their own.

Session 7.3 QUICK CHECK

1. _____ is a programming language that describes how a Web page should look; _____ is a programming language that describes the data it contains and how that data should be structured.

2. When you import or export an XML file using Access, is the data in the XML file static or dynamic?

3. When you use Access to export an XML file and an accompanying XSD file, what information is stored in the XSD file?

4. How do you export a table or query datasheet to Excel?

5. What does the field value of a hyperlink field represent?

6. How do you view a hyperlink that is named in a hyperlink field?

REVIEW ASSIGNMENTS

Elsa wants you to export the data selected by the **Selected Bonus Quotas** query and the **Recruiters and Students** report as HTML documents so she can view these Access objects using Internet Explorer. In addition, she asks you to create additional Web pages based on objects in the **Students** database. Finally, she wants to use the data in the **Selected Bonus Quotas** query as an XML file and also work with the data in Excel, so she needs you to export the query into these data formats. To do so, you'll complete the following steps.

1. Make sure your Data Disk is in the appropriate disk drive, start Access, and then open the **Students** database in the Review folder on your Data Disk.

2. Export the **Selected Bonus Quotas** query as an HTML document in the Review folder on your Data Disk, using the HTML template file named **NSJI-Tbl**, which is located in the Review folder. Use Internet Explorer to open the **Selected Bonus Quotas** HTML document, print the document, and then close Internet Explorer.

Explore ▷ 3. Export the **Recruiters and Students** report as an HTML document in the Review folder; do not use a template. Use Internet Explorer to open the **Recruiters and Students** HTML document. Then scroll to the bottom of the document; use the First, Previous, Next, and Last links to navigate through the Web page; print the first page of the report; and then close Internet Explorer. (*Note:* The report title and some labels will appear truncated on the right when you view the HTML document.)

Explore ▷ 4. Use the AutoPage: Columnar Wizard to create a data access page based on the **Selected Bonus Quotas** query. Save the data access page in the Review folder as **Selected Quotas**, sort the data access page in descending order based on the Salary field, move to the fourth record, print this record, and then close the data access page.

5. Create a custom data access page named **Recruiters with Students** based on the **Recruiter** and **Student** tables. Use the design in Figure 7-59 as a guide.

Figure 7-59

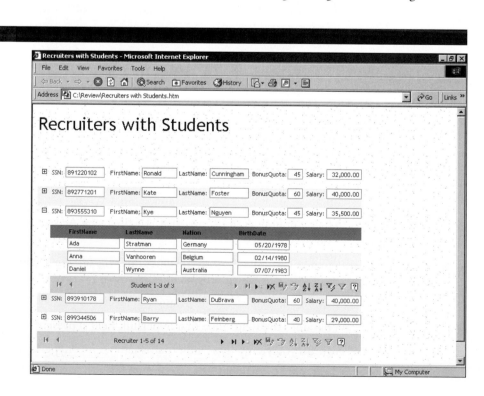

a. Place the five fields from the **Recruiter** table in the Recruiter Header section.

Explore

b. Place the FirstName, LastName, Nation, and BirthDate fields from the **Student** table in the Student Header section.

c. Select the Axis theme.

Explore

d. In the Recruiter Header section, move and resize the labels and text boxes.

e. Reduce the height of the Recruiter Header section, and set its DataPageSize property to 5.

f. Use Recruiters with Students as the title for the data access page, and then left align the title.

g. Save the data access page as **Recruiters with Students** in the Review folder.

h. Close the data access page, use the Web Page Preview command to view the data access page, expand the third record (Kyle Nguyen), print the Web page, and then close Internet Explorer.

6. Create a PivotChart on a new data access page as follows:

a. Use the **Student** table as the data source for the PivotChart, and select the stacked column chart type.

b. Increase the width of the PivotChart control so that you can see the control's Field List button. Select Nation as the category field, Gender as the series field, LastName as the data field, and RecruiterName as the filter field.

c. Increase the height and width of the PivotChart control so that you can see the nation values in the chart and all columns of data.

d. Use Students by Nation as the title for the data access page.

e. Save the data access page as **Students by Nation** in the Review folder, and then close the data access page.

f. Use the Web Page Preview command to view the data access page, display the legend, and then print the page.

g. Use the RecruiterName filter to select the first five recruiters, print the page, and then close Internet Explorer.

7. Export the **Selected Bonus Quotas** query as an XML file named **Selected Bonus Quotas** in the Review folder; do not create a separate XSD file.

8. Export the **Selected Bonus Quotas** query as an Excel worksheet. In the worksheet, add a calculation in cell E12 for the grand total salary, print the worksheet, and then save and close the worksheet.

9. Close the **Students** database, and then exit Access.

CASE PROBLEMS

Case 1. Lim's Video Photography Youngho Lim wants to be able to use his Web browser to view data stored in the **Clients** database. He asks you to export table data and a report as Web pages, create data access pages, and export data to an XML file. To do so, you'll complete the following steps.

1. Make sure your Data Disk is in the appropriate disk drive, start Access, and then open the **Clients** database in the Cases folder on your Data Disk.

2. Export the **ShootDesc** table as an HTML document in the Cases folder; do not use a template. Use Internet Explorer to open the **ShootDesc** HTML document, print the page, and then close Internet Explorer.

Explore

3. Export the **Clients and Contracts** report as an HTML document in the Cases folder; do not use a template. Use Internet Explorer to open the **Clients and Contracts** HTML document. Then scroll to the bottom of the document; use the First, Previous, Next, and Last links to navigate through the Web page; print page 4 of the report; and then close Internet Explorer. (*Note:* The report title will appear truncated on the right when you view the HTML document.)

4. Use the Page Wizard to create a data access page based on the **Client** table as follows:

   a. Select all fields from the **Client** table, do not select any grouping levels, sort in ascending order by the ClientName field, use Client Page as the title, and then open the page.

   b. Use the data access page to add a new record to the **Client** table with these values: ClientName of "Trent, Brenda," Client# of 982, Address of 18 Sunset Rd, City of Hurley, State of CA, Zip of 94449, and Phone of 6286312041. Save the record.

   c. Close the page, saving it as **Client Page** in the Cases folder.

   d. Open the **Client** table datasheet, print the datasheet, and then close the table.

5. Create a custom data access page named **Clients and Their Contracts** based on the **Client** and **Contract** tables. Use the design in Figure 7-60 as a guide.

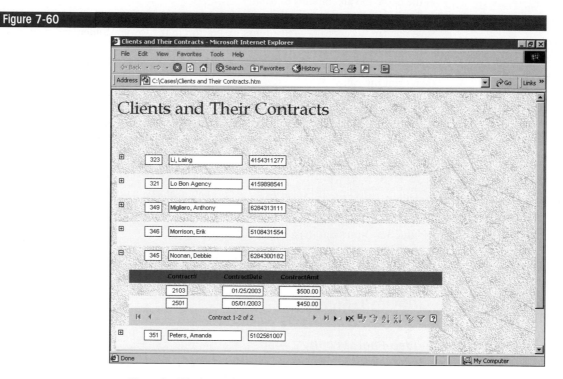

   a. Place the Client#, ClientName, and Phone fields from the **Client** table in the Client Header section.

   b. Place the Contract#, ContractDate, and ContractAmt fields from the **Contract** table in the Contract Header section.

   c. Select the Expedition theme.

   d. Delete the labels, and move and resize the text boxes in the Client Header section. Reduce the width of the text boxes in the Contract Header section.

Explore

   e. Reduce the height of the Client Header section, set its DataPageSize property to 6, and then change its default sort to an ascending sort based on the ClientName field. (*Hint:* Set the DefaultSort property for the Client Header section in the Group Level Properties dialog box; use Help if you need more information about setting the DefaultSort property.)

      f. Use Clients and Their Contracts as the title for the data access page, and then left align the title.

      g. Save the data access page as **Clients and Their Contracts** in the Cases folder.

      h. Close the data access page, use the Web Page Preview command to view the data access page, navigate to the page that contains the client record with your name, expand that record, print the Web page, and then close Internet Explorer.

6. Create a PivotTable on a new data access page as follows:

      a. Select City from the **Client** table as the row field, ContractAmt from the **Contract** table as the detail field, ContractDate from the **Contract** table as the filter field, and ShootDesc from the **Shoot** table as the column field.

      b. Increase the height and width of the PivotTable control so that you can see Grand Total row and the entire GR column. Set the PivotTable title bar caption to City and Shoot PivotTable.

      c. Use City and Shoot Table as the title for the data access page.

      d. Save the data access page as **City and Shoot Table** in the Cases folder.

      e. Switch to Page view.

      f. Use the ContractDate filter to select all April dates, print the page, and then close the page.

7. Export the **Client Contract Amounts** query as an XML file named **Client Contract Amounts** in the Cases folder; do not create a separate XSD file.

8. Export the **Client Contract Amounts** query as an Excel worksheet. In the worksheet, add a calculation in cell D22 for the grand total contract amount, print the worksheet, and then save and close the worksheet.

9. Close the **Clients** database, and then exit Access.

Case 2. DineAtHome.course.com   Claire Picard wants to be able to use her Web browser to view data stored in the **Delivery** database. She asks you to export data retrieved by a query and a report as HTML documents, create data access pages, and export data as XML documents and Excel worksheets. To do so, you'll complete the following steps.

1. Make sure your Data Disk is in the appropriate disk drive, start Access, and then open the **Delivery** database in the Cases folder on your Data Disk.

2. Export the **Large Orders** query as an HTML document in the Cases folder; do not use a template. Use Internet Explorer to open the **Large Orders** HTML document, print the page, and then close Internet Explorer.

Explore   3. Export the **Restaurant Orders** report as an HTML document in the Cases folder; do not use a template. Use Internet Explorer to open the **Restaurant Orders** HTML document. Then scroll to the bottom of the document; use the First, Previous, Next, and Last links to navigate through the Web page; print the last page of the report; and then close Internet Explorer. (*Note:* The report title and some labels will appear truncated on the right when you view the HTML document.)

4. Use the AutoPage: Columnar Wizard to create a data access page based on the **Order** table, and then do the following:

      a. Save the data access page in the Cases folder as **Order Page**.

      b. Sort the data access page in descending order based on the OrderDate field.

      c. Change the OrderAmt field value for Order# 3123 from 45.42 to 55.77, and then print this record.

      d. Filter the page, selecting all records with a Restaurant# field value of 131. (*Hint:* The second record should have that field value.) Print the last filtered record.

      e. Close the data access page.

      f. Open the **Order** table datasheet, print the datasheet, and then close the table.

5. Create a custom data access page named **Orders for Restaurants** based on the **Restaurant** and **Order** tables. Use the design in Figure 7-61 as a guide.

Figure 7-61

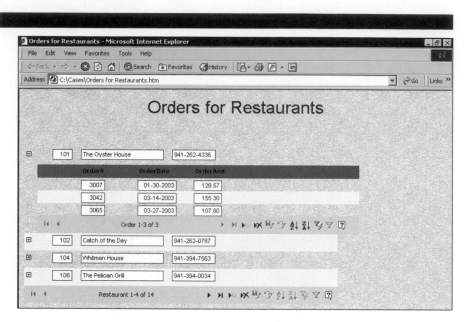

a. Place the Restaurant#, RestaurantName, and Phone fields from the **Restaurant** table in the Restaurant Header section.

b. Place the Order#, OrderDate, and OrderAmt fields from the **Order** table in the Order Header section.

c. Select the Sandstone theme.

d. In the Restaurant Header section, delete the labels, and then move and resize the text boxes to match Figure 7-61. Reduce the width of the text boxes in the Order Header section.

e. Reduce the height of the Restaurant Header section, and then set its DataPageSize property to 4.

f. Use Orders for Restaurants as the title for the data access page.

g. Save the data access page as **Orders for Restaurants** in the Cases folder.

h. Close the data access page, use the Web Page Preview command to view the data access page, expand the first record (The Oyster House), print the Web page, and then close Internet Explorer.

6. Create a PivotChart on a new data access page as follows:

a. Use the **Restaurant Orders** query as the data source for the PivotChart, and select the pie chart type.

b. Increase the width of the PivotChart control so that you can see the control's Field List button. Select City as the category field, BillTotal as the data field, and OrderDate By Month as the filter field.

c. Increase the height and width of the PivotChart control so that you can see the entire PivotTable toolbar and the pie chart is a readable size.

d. Use Restaurant Orders as the title for the data access page.

e. Save the data access page as **Restaurant Orders Chart** in the Cases folder.

f. Use the Web Page Preview command to view the data access page, display the legend, and then print the page.

g. Use the OrderDate By Month filter to select only the March orders, print the page, and then close the page.

7. Import the data and structure from the XML file named **Choices**, located in the Cases folder, as a new table in the **Delivery** database. Open the imported **Selection** table, resize all columns to their best fit, print the first page, and then save and close the table.

8. Export the **Order** table as an XML file named **Order** in the Cases folder; do not create a separate XSD file.

9. Export the **Order** table as an Excel worksheet. In the worksheet, add a calculation in cell D39 for the order grand total, print the worksheet, and then save and close the worksheet.

10. Claire has created a Web page in the Cases folder containing a description about one of the meal selections. Add a hyperlink field named SelectionDetails to the **Selection** table. Add a hyperlink with the text "Sunshine Skillet" to the record for the Sunshine Skillet field value that opens the **Skillet** file located in the Cases folder. Resize the SelectionDetails column to its best fit, and then click the hyperlink. View the short description in the Web page, print the description, and then close the browser.

11. Save and close the **Selection** table, close the **Delivery** database, and then exit Access.

Case 3. Redwood Zoo   Michael Rosenfeld wants you to create Web pages for the **Donors** database so he can use his Web browser to access and view data. To do so, you'll complete the following steps.

1. Make sure your Data Disk is in the appropriate disk drive, start Access, and then open the **Donors** database in the Cases folder on your Data Disk.

2. Export the **Donor** table as an HTML document in the Cases folder; do not use a template. Use Internet Explorer to open the **Donor** HTML document, print the page, and then close Internet Explorer.

Explore 3. Export the **Fund Pledges** report as an HTML document in the Cases folder; do not use a template. Use Internet Explorer to open the **Fund Pledges** HTML document. Then scroll to the bottom of the document; use the First, Previous, Next, and Last links to navigate through the Web page; print the last page of the report; and then close Internet Explorer.

Explore 4. Use the AutoPage: Columnar Wizard to create a data access page based on the **Fund** table, and then do the following:

   a. Save the data access page in the Cases folder as **Fund Page**.
   b. Sort the data access page in descending order based on the GoalAmt field.
   c. Change the GoalAmt field value for record 2 (Kodiak Bear Exhibit) from $65,000 to $95,000.
   d. Close the data access page.
   e. Open the **Fund** table datasheet, print the datasheet, and then close the table.

5. Create a custom data access page named **Pledges for Zoo Funds** based on the **Fund**, **Donor**, and **Pledge** tables. Use the design in Figure 7-62 as a guide.

Figure 7-62

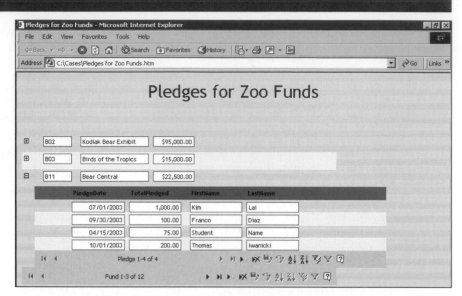

a. Place the FundCode, FundName, and GoalAmt fields from the **Fund** table in the Fund Header section.

b. Place the PledgeDate and TotalPledged fields from the **Pledge** table, and the FirstName and LastName fields from the **Donor** table in the Pledge Header section.

c. Select the Profile theme.

d. In the Fund Header section, delete the labels, and then move and resize the text boxes.

e. Reduce the height of the Fund Header section, and then set its DataPageSize property to 3.

f. Use Pledges for Zoo Funds as the title for the data access page, and then change its font color to blue.

g. Save the data access page as **Pledges for Zoo Funds** in the Cases folder.

h. Close the data access page, use the Web Page Preview command to view the data access page, expand the third record (Bear Central), print the Web page, and then close Internet Explorer.

6. Create a PivotChart on a new data access page as follows:

a. Use the **Donor Pledges** query as the data source for the PivotChart, and select the stacked bar chart type.

b. Increase the width of the PivotChart control so that you can see the control's Field List button. Select FundName as the category field, TotalPledged as the data field, PaymentMethod as the series field, and PledgeDate By Month as the filter field.

c. Increase the height and width of the PivotChart control so that you can see the entire PivotChart toolbar and all rows in the chart.

d. Use Donor Pledges Chart as the title for the data access page.

e. Save the data access page as **Donor Pledges Chart** in the Cases folder.

f. Close the data access page, use the Web Page Preview command to view the data access page, display the legend, and then print the page.

g. Use the PledgeDate By Month filter to select pledges in the last two quarters, print the page, and then close the browser.

7. Export the **Pledge** table as an XML file named **Pledge** in the Cases folder; do not create a separate XSD file.

8. Export the **Pledge** table as an Excel worksheet. In the worksheet, add a calculation in cell E30 for the total pledged grand total, print the worksheet in landscape orientation, and then save and close the worksheet.

9. Close the **Donors** database, and then exit Access.

Case 4. Mountain River Adventures   Connor and Siobhan Dempsey travel frequently and need to access data from the **Outdoors** database using their Web browsers. They ask you to export a query and a report as HTML documents, and to create data access pages based on database tables. Finally, they need to use the data in a query in Excel and also in another application that requires XML data. To make these changes, you'll complete the following steps.

1. Make sure your Data Disk is in the appropriate disk drive, start Access, and then open the **Outdoors** database in the Cases folder on your Data Disk.

2. Export the **Trip Dates** query as an HTML document in the Cases folder; do not use a template. Use Internet Explorer to open the **Trip Dates** HTML document, print the page, and then close Internet Explorer.

 **Explore**

3. Export the **Bookings** report as an HTML document in the Cases folder; do not use a template. Use Internet Explorer to open the **Bookings** HTML document. Then scroll to the bottom of the document; use the First, Previous, Next, and Last links to navigate through the Web page; print the last page of the report; and then close Internet Explorer.

4. Use the Page Wizard to create a data access page based on the **Costs** query as follows:

   a. Select all fields from the **Costs** query, select River as a grouping level, sort in ascending order by the TripDate field, use Costs Page as the title, and then open the page.
   b. Navigate to the last record (South Platte River), navigate to the second record for that group, and then print the page.
   c. Close the page, saving it as **Costs Page** in the Cases folder.

5. Create a custom data access page named **Bookings for Clients** based on the **Client** and **Booking** tables. Use the design in Figure 7-63 as a guide.

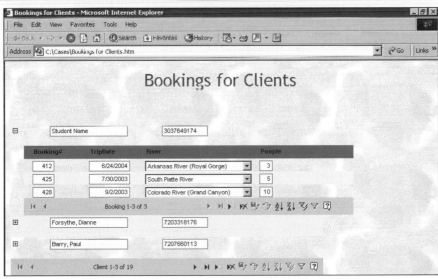

Figure 7-63

a. Place the ClientName and Phone fields from the **Client** table in the Client Header section.
b. Place the Booking#, TripDate, River, and People fields from the **Booking** table in the Booking Header section.
c. Select the Nature theme.
d. In the Client Header section, delete the labels, and then move and resize the text boxes.

e. In the Booking Header section, modify the width of the text boxes, and then move the People label and text box to the right to make room for the River text box.

f. Reduce the height of the Client Header section, and then set its DataPageSize property to 3.

g. Use Bookings for Clients as the title for the data access page.

h. Save the data access page as **Bookings for Clients** in the Cases folder.

i. Close the data access page, use the Web Page Preview command to view the data access page, expand the record that contains your name, print the Web page, and then close Internet Explorer.

6. Create a PivotChart on a new data access page as follows:

a. Use the **Booked Rafting Trips** query as the data source for the PivotChart, and select the stacked bar chart type.

b. Increase the width of the PivotChart control so that you can see the control's Field List button. Select TripDays as the category field, TripFee as the data field, People as the series field, and River as the filter field.

c. Increase the height and width of the PivotChart control so that you can see the entire PivotChart toolbar and 5,000.00 on the vertical axis.

d. Use Booked Rafting Trips Chart as the title for the data access page.

e. Save the data access page as **Booked Rafting Trips Chart** in the Cases folder.

f. Close the data access page, use the Web Page Preview command to view the data access page, display the legend, and then print the page.

g. Use the River filter to select trips for all rivers except those occurring on the Arkansas River, print the page, and then close Internet Explorer.

7. Export the **Booked Rafting Trips** query as an XML file named **Booked Rafting Trips** in the Cases folder; do not create a separate XSD file.

8. Export the **Booked Rafting Trips** table as an Excel worksheet. In the worksheet, add a calculation in cell J24 for the grand total trip fee, print the worksheet, and then save and close the worksheet.

9. Close the **Outdoors** database, and then exit Access.

Explore **Case 5. eACH Internet Auction Site**   Chris and Pat Aquino want you to continue your development of their Internet auction site for collectibles. They want you to export some of the **eACH** database data as HTML documents for their registrants to view. They also want you to create two data access pages, an XML file, and then create a hyperlink field that's linked to Word documents. One of the data access pages will allow buyers to view categories with their subcategories when they're searching for items that might be of interest to them. They ask you to make the following changes to the **eACH** database.

1. Make sure your Data Disk is in the appropriate drive, start Access, and then open the **eACH** database in the Cases folder on your Data Disk.

2. Export the **Item** table to an HTML document in the Cases folder, using the HTML template named **eACH-Tbl**, which is located in the Cases folder. Use Internet Explorer to open the **Item** HTML document, print the page, and then close Internet Explorer.

3. Export the custom report you created in Tutorial 6 to an HTML document in the Cases folder, using the HTML template named **eACH-Rpt**, which is located in the Cases folder. Use Internet Explorer to open the HTML document that you created, print the report, and then close Internet Explorer.

4. Use the AutoPage: Columnar Wizard to create a data access page based on the **Registrant** table, and then complete the following:

a. Use the data access page to add a new record with your name to the **Registrant** table with additional data that you create.

b. Sort the data access page in ascending order based on the field that contains the registrant's last name.

   c. Print the first record.

   d. Close the data access page, saving it as **Registrant Page** in the Cases folder.

5. Design and then create a custom data access page that satisfies the following requirements:

   a. Place all the fields from **Category** table in the Category Header section.

   b. Place all the fields, except for the common field, from the **Subcategory** table in the Subcategory Header section.

   c. Select the Edge theme.

   d. In the Category Header section, move the labels and text boxes into a row, and then resize the text boxes. Resize the text boxes in the Subcategory Header section.

   e. Reduce the height of the Client Header section, and then set its DataPageSize property to 4.

   f. Use an appropriate title for the page.

   g. Save the data access page as **Categories and Subcategories Page** in the Cases folder.

   h. Close the page, use the Web Page Preview command to view the page, expand a record with related records, print the Web page, and then close Internet Explorer.

6. Export the **Registrant** table as an XML file named **Registrant** in the Cases folder; do not create a separate XSD file.

7. Given the test data you created in Tutorial 5, you should have at least two items you've posted for sale on eACH. To attract bidders to those items, you should include visuals and short descriptions of them by completing the following:

   a. Create at least three Word documents and save them with appropriate filenames in the Cases folder. In each document, write a short description for one of the items in your database. Also, include an appropriate graphic or picture (that you locate in the Microsoft Clip Gallery or download from the Internet) for the item. Save each document.

   b. Add a hyperlink field named Visual to the **Item** table. Add hyperlink field values for each item that has a corresponding Word document.

   c. Click the hyperlink for one of the items. View the Word document, print the document, and then close Word.

8. Close the **eACH** database, and then exit Access.

INTERNET ASSIGNMENTS

Student Union

The purpose of the Internet Assignments is to challenge you to find information on the Internet that you can use to create effective documents. The actual assignments are updated and maintained on the Course Technology Web site. Log on to the Internet and use your Web browser to go to the Student Online Companion to accompany this text at **www.course.com/NewPerspectives/studentunion**. Click the Access link, and then click the link for Tutorial 7.

QUICK CHECK ANSWERS

Session 7.1

1. The World Wide Web is a vast collection of digital documents stored on Web servers linked through the Internet.

2. A Web browser is a program used to view Web pages.

3. A hyperlink links one Web document to another.

4. HTML (HyperText Markup Language) is the language used to create most Web documents.

5. An HTML template is a file that contains HTML instructions for creating a Web page with both text and graphics, together with special instructions that tell Access where to place the Access data on the page.

6. A static Web page shows the state of the database object at the time the page was created. Any subsequent changes made to the database object, such as updates to field values in records, are not reflected in a static Web page.

7. A data access page is a dynamic HTML document that you can open with a Web browser to view or update current data in an Access database.

8. connection

9. A grouped data access page is a data access page that uses two or more group levels to display information from general categories to specific details.

10. A theme is a predefined style for a data access page.

Session 7.2

1. A PivotTable is an interactive table that lets you analyze data dynamically from within a Web browser.

2. filter

3. data access pages, forms, datasheets

4. For datasheets and data access pages, only one expand indicator appears at a time and is active; clicking the expand indicator causes the data to expand or collapse and to change to the other expand indicator. For PivotTables, both expand indicators appear, even though only one is active at any given time.

5. total

6. data

7. series

Session 7.3

1. HTML; XML

2. static

3. The XSD (XML Structure Definition) file contains table structure information, including information about the table's primary key and indexes.

4. Select the table or query in the Database window, click the OfficeLinks list arrow, and then click Analyze It with Microsoft Excel.

5. a hyperlink or pointer to another object in the database, file, or Web page

6. Click the hyperlink field value to start the associated program and open the hyperlinked document or object.

OBJECTIVES

In this appendix you will:

- Learn the characteristics of a relation

- Learn about primary, candidate, alternate, foreign, and composite keys

- Study one-to-one, one-to-many, and many-to-many relationships

- Learn to describe relations and relationships with entity-relationship diagrams and with a shorthand method

- Study database integrity constraints for primary keys, referential integrity, and domains

- Learn about determinants, functional dependencies, anomalies, and normalization

RELATIONAL DATABASES AND DATABASE DESIGN

This appendix introduces you to the basics of database design. Before trying to master this material, be sure you have an understanding of the following concepts: data, information, field, field value, record, table, relational database, common field, database management system (DBMS), and relational database management system.

Relations

A relational database stores its data in tables. A **table** is a two-dimensional structure made up of rows and columns. The terms table, row, and column are the popular names for the more formal terms **relation** (table), **tuple** (row), and **attribute** (column), as shown in Figure 1.

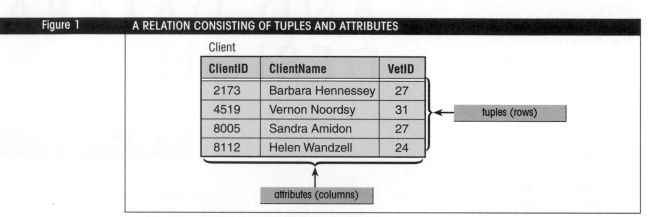

Figure 1   **A RELATION CONSISTING OF TUPLES AND ATTRIBUTES**

Client

ClientID	ClientName	VetID
2173	Barbara Hennessey	27
4519	Vernon Noordsy	31
8005	Sandra Amidon	27
8112	Helen Wandzell	24

tuples (rows)

attributes (columns)

The Client table shown in Figure 1 is an example of a relation, a two-dimensional structure with the following characteristics:

- Each row is unique. Because no two rows are the same, you can easily locate and update specific data. For example, you can locate the row for ClientID 8005 and change the ClientName value, Sandra Amidon, or the VetID value, 27.

- The order of the rows is unimportant. You can add or view rows in any order. For example, you can view the rows in ClientName order instead of ClientID order.

- Each table entry contains a single value. At the intersection of each row and column, you cannot have more than one value. For example, each row in Figure 1 contains one ClientID, one ClientName, and one VetID.

- The order of the columns is unimportant. You can add or view columns in any order.

- Each column has a unique name called the **attribute name**. The attribute name allows you to access a specific column without needing to know its position within the relation.

- The entries in a column are from the same domain. A **domain** is a set of values from which one or more columns draw their actual values. A domain can be broad, such as "all legitimate names of people" for the ClientName column, or narrow, such as "24, 27, or 31" for the VetID column. The domain of "all legitimate dates" could be shared by the BirthDate, StartDate, and LastPayDate columns in a company's employee relation.

- Each row in a relation describes, or shows the characteristics of, an entity. An **entity** is a person, place, object, event, or idea for which you want to store and process data. For example, ClientID, ClientName, and VetID are characteristics of the clients of a pet-sitting company. The Client relation represents all the client entities and their characteristics. That is, the sets of values in the rows of the tblClient relation describe the different clients of the company. The Client relation includes only characteristics of a client. Other relations would exist for the company's other entities. For example, a Pet relation might describe the clients' pets and an Employee relation might describe the company's employees.

Knowing the characteristics of a relation leads directly to a definition of a relational database. A **relational database** is a collection of relations.

Keys

Primary keys ensure that each row in a relation is unique. A **primary key** is an attribute, or a collection of attributes, whose values uniquely identify each row in a relation. In addition to being *unique*, a primary key must be *minimal* (that is, contain no unnecessary extra attributes) and must not change in value. For example, in Figure 2 the State relation contains one record per state and uses StateAbbrev as its primary key.

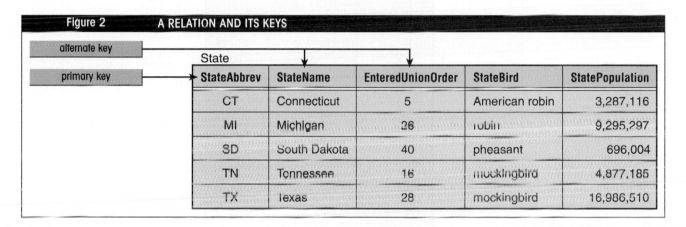

Figure 2   **A RELATION AND ITS KEYS**

alternate key

primary key

State

StateAbbrev	StateName	EnteredUnionOrder	StateBird	StatePopulation
CT	Connecticut	5	American robin	3,287,116
MI	Michigan	26	robin	9,295,297
SD	South Dakota	40	pheasant	696,004
TN	Tennessee	16	mockingbird	4,877,185
TX	Texas	28	mockingbird	16,986,510

Could any other attribute, or collection of attributes, be the primary key of the State relation?

- Could StateBird serve as the primary key? No, because the column does not have unique values (for example, the mockingbird is the state bird of more than one state).
- Could StatePopulation serve as the primary key? No, because the column values change periodically and are not guaranteed to be unique.
- Could StateAbbrev and StateName together serve as the primary key? No, because the combination is not minimal. Something less, StateAbbrev by itself, can serve as the primary key.

■ Could StateName serve as the primary key? Yes, because the column has unique values. In a similar way, you could select EnteredUnionOrder as the primary key for the State relation. One attribute, or collection of attributes, that can serve as a primary key is called a **candidate key**. The candidate keys for the State relation are StateAbbrev, StateName, and EnteredUnionOrder. You choose one of the candidate keys to be the primary key, and the remaining candidate keys are called **alternate keys**.

Figure 3 shows a City relation containing the attributes StateAbbrev, CityName, and CityPopulation.

Figure 3	A RELATION WITH A COMPOSITE KEY

City

primary key

StateAbbrev	CityName	CityPopulation
CT	Hartford	139,739
CT	Madison	14,031
CT	Portland	8,418
MI	Lansing	127,321
SD	Madison	6,257
SD	Pierre	12,906
TN	Nashville	488,374
TX	Austin	465,622
TX	Portland	12,224

What is the primary key for the City relation? The values for CityPopulation periodically change and are not guaranteed to be unique, so CityPopulation cannot be the primary key. Because the values for each of the other two columns are not unique, StateAbbrev alone cannot be the primary key and neither can CityName (for example, there are two Madisons and two Portlands). The primary key is the combination of StateAbbrev and CityName. Both attributes together are needed to identify, uniquely and minimally, each row in the City relation. A multiple-attribute primary key is called a **composite key** or a **concatenated key**.

The StateAbbrev attribute in the City relation is also a **foreign key**. A **foreign key** is an attribute, or a collection of attributes, in one relation whose values must match the values of the primary key of some relation. As shown in Figure 4, the values in the City relation's StateAbbrev column match the values in the State relation's StateAbbrev column. Thus, StateAbbrev, the primary key of the State relation, is a foreign key in the City relation. Although the attribute name StateAbbrev is the same in both relations, the names could be different. Most people give the same name to an attribute stored in two or more tables to broadcast clearly they are really the same attribute.

Figure 4	STATEABBREV AS A PRIMARY KEY (STATE RELATION) AND A FOREIGN KEY (CITY RELATION)

State

StateAbbrev	StateName	EnteredUnionOrder	StateBird	StatePopulation
CT	Connecticut	5	American robin	3,287,116
MI	Michigan	26	robin	9,295,297
SD	South Dakota	40	pheasant	696,004
TN	Tennessee	16	mockingbird	4,877,185
TX	Texas	28	mockingbird	16,986,510

primary key
primary key
foreign key

City

StateAbbrev	CityName	CityPopulation
CT	Hartford	139,739
CT	Madison	14,031
CT	Portland	8,418
MI	Lansing	127,321
SD	Madison	6,257
SD	Pierre	12,906
TN	Nashville	488,374
TX	Austin	465,622
TX	Portland	12,224

A **nonkey attribute** is an attribute that is not part of the primary key. In the two relations shown in Figure 4, all attributes are nonkey attributes except StateAbbrev in the State and City relations and CityName in the City relation. *Key* is an ambiguous word because it can refer to a primary, candidate, alternate, or foreign key. When the word key appears alone, however, it means primary key and the definition for a nonkey attribute consequently makes sense.

Relationships

The Capital relation, shown in Figure 5, has one row for each state capital. The CapitalName and StateAbbrev attributes are candidate keys; selecting CapitalName as the primary key makes StateAbbrev an alternate key. The StateAbbrev attribute in the Capital relation is also a foreign key, because its values match the values in the State relation's StateAbbrev column.

Figure 5	A ONE-TO-ONE RELATIONSHIP

State

StateAbbrev	StateName	EnteredUnionOrder	StateBird	StatePopulation
CT	Connecticut	5	American robin	3,287,116
MI	Michigan	26	robin	9,295,297
SD	South Dakota	40	pheasant	696,004
TN	Tennessee	16	mockingbird	4,877,185
TX	Texas	28	mockingbird	16,986,510

Capital

CapitalName	StateAbbrev	YearDesignated	PhoneAreaCode	CapitalPopulation
Austin	TX	1845	512	465,622
Hartford	CT	1662	860	139,739
Lansing	MI	1847	517	127,321
Nashville	TN	1843	615	488,374
Pierre	SD	1889	605	12,906

(primary key → State.StateAbbrev; foreign key → Capital.StateAbbrev; primary key → Capital.CapitalName)

One-to-One

The State and Capital relations, shown in Figure 5, have a one-to-one relationship. A **one-to-one relationship** (abbreviated 1:1) exists between two relations when each row in one relation has at most one matching row in the other relation. StateAbbrev, which is a foreign key in the Capital relation and the primary key in the State relation, is the common field that ties together the rows of each relation.

Should the State and Capital relations be combined into one relation? Although the two relations in any 1:1 relationship can be combined into one relation, each relation describes different entities and should usually be kept separate.

One-to-Many

The State and City relations, shown once again in Figure 6, have a one-to-many relationship. A **one-to-many relationship** (abbreviated 1:M) exists between two relations when one row in the first relation matches many rows in the second relation and one row in the second relation matches only one row in the first relation. Many can mean zero rows, one row, or two or more rows. StateAbbrev, which is a foreign key in the City relation and the primary key in the State relation, is the common field that ties together the rows of each relation.

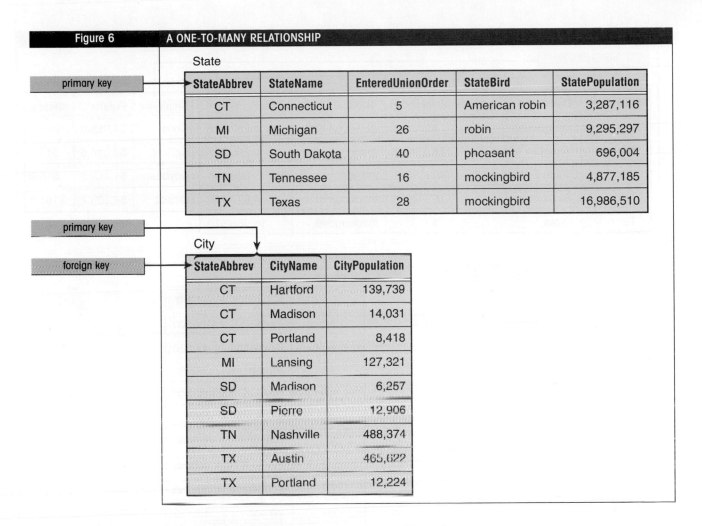

Figure 6	A ONE-TO-MANY RELATIONSHIP

State

StateAbbrev	StateName	EnteredUnionOrder	StateBird	StatePopulation
CT	Connecticut	5	American robin	3,287,116
MI	Michigan	26	robin	9,295,297
SD	South Dakota	40	pheasant	696,004
TN	Tennessee	16	mockingbird	4,877,185
TX	Texas	28	mockingbird	16,986,510

City

StateAbbrev	CityName	CityPopulation
CT	Hartford	139,739
CT	Madison	14,031
CT	Portland	8,418
MI	Lansing	127,321
SD	Madison	6,257
SD	Pierre	12,906
TN	Nashville	488,374
TX	Austin	465,622
TX	Portland	12,224

(labels at left: primary key, primary key, foreign key)

Many-to-Many

In Figure 7, the State relation with a primary key of StateAbbrev and the Crop relation with a primary key of CropName have a many-to-many relationship. A **many-to-many relationship** (abbreviated as M:N) exists between two relations when one row in the first relation matches many rows in the second relation and one row in the second relation matches many rows in the first relation. In a relational database, you must use a third relation to serve as a bridge between the two M:N relations; the third relation has the primary keys of the M:N relations as its primary key. The original relations now each have a 1:M relationship with the new relation. The StateAbbrev and CropName attributes represent the primary key of the Production relation that is shown in Figure 7. StateAbbrev, which is a foreign key in the Production relation and the primary key in the State relation, is the common field that ties together the rows of the State and Production relations. Likewise, CropName is the common field for the Crop and Production relations.

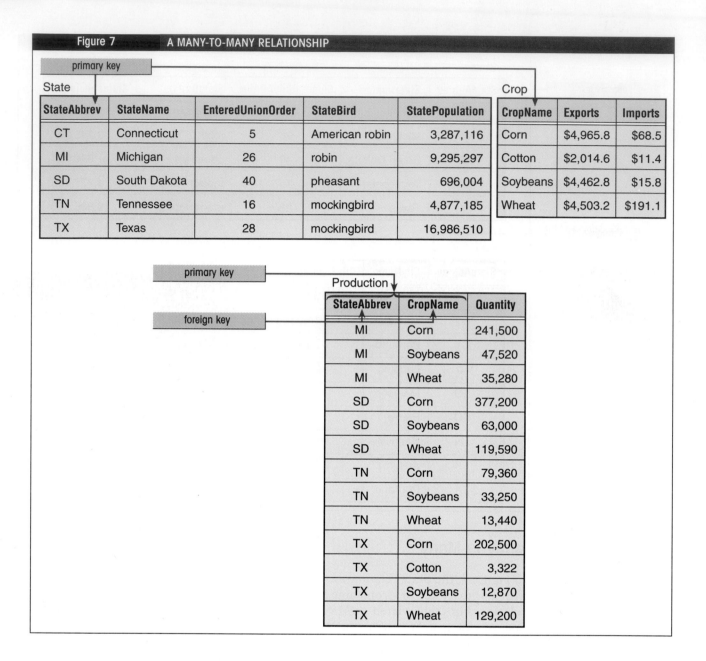

Figure 7   A MANY-TO-MANY RELATIONSHIP

primary key

State

StateAbbrev	StateName	EnteredUnionOrder	StateBird	StatePopulation
CT	Connecticut	5	American robin	3,287,116
MI	Michigan	26	robin	9,295,297
SD	South Dakota	40	pheasant	696,004
TN	Tennessee	16	mockingbird	4,877,185
TX	Texas	28	mockingbird	16,986,510

Crop

CropName	Exports	Imports
Corn	$4,965.8	$68.5
Cotton	$2,014.6	$11.4
Soybeans	$4,462.8	$15.8
Wheat	$4,503.2	$191.1

primary key

foreign key

Production

StateAbbrev	CropName	Quantity
MI	Corn	241,500
MI	Soybeans	47,520
MI	Wheat	35,280
SD	Corn	377,200
SD	Soybeans	63,000
SD	Wheat	119,590
TN	Corn	79,360
TN	Soybeans	33,250
TN	Wheat	13,440
TX	Corn	202,500
TX	Cotton	3,322
TX	Soybeans	12,870
TX	Wheat	129,200

Entity Subtype

Figure 8 shows a special type of one-to-one relationship. The Shipping relation's primary key is StateAbbrev and contains one row for each state having an ocean shoreline. Because not all states have an ocean shoreline, the Shipping relation has fewer rows than the State relation. However, each row in the Shipping relation has a matching row in the State relation with StateAbbrev serving as the common field; StateAbbrev is the primary key in the State relation and is a foreign key in the Shipping relation.

Figure 8	AN ENTITY SUBTYPE

State

StateAbbrev	State Name	EnteredUnionOrder	StateBird	StatePopulation
CT	Connecticut	5	American robin	3,287,116
MI	Michigan	26	robin	9,295,297
SD	South Dakota	40	pheasant	696,004
TN	Tennessee	16	mockingbird	4,877,185
TX	Texas	28	mockingbird	16,986,510

primary key

Shipping

primary key

foreign key

StateAbbrev	OceanShoreline	ExportTonnage	ImportTonnage
CT	618	3,377,466	2,118,494
TX	3,359	45,980,912	109,400,314

The Shipping relation, in this situation, is called an **entity subtype**, a relation whose primary key is a foreign key to a second relation and whose attributes are additional attributes for the second relation. You can create an entity subtype when a relation has attributes that could have null values. A **null value** is the absence of a value. A null value is not blank, nor zero, nor any other value. You give a null value to an attribute when you do not know its value or when a value does not apply. For example, instead of using the Shipping relation, you could store the OceanShoreline, ExportTonnage, and ImportTonnage attributes in the State relation and allow them to be null for states not having an ocean shoreline. You should be aware that database experts are currently debating the validity of the use of nulls in relational databases and many experts insist that you should never use nulls. Part of this warning against nulls is based on the inconsistent way different relational DBMSs treat nulls and part is due to the lack of a firm theoretical foundation for how to use nulls. In any case, entity subtypes are an alternative to the use of nulls.

Entity-Relationship **Diagrams**

A common shorthand method for describing relations is to write the relation name followed by its attributes in parentheses, underlining the attributes that represent the primary key and identifying the foreign keys for a relation immediately after the relation. Using this method, the relations that appear in Figures 5 through 8 are described in the following way:

State (StateAbbrev, StateName, EnteredUnionOrder, StateBird, StatePopulation)
Capital (CapitalName, StateAbbrev, YearDesignated, PhoneAreaCode,
    CapitalPopulation)
    Foreign key: StateAbbrev to State relation
City (StateAbbrev, CityName, CityPopulation)
    Foreign key: StateAbbrev to State relation
Crop (CropName, Exports, Imports)

Production (<u>StateAbbrev</u>, <u>CropName</u>, Quantity)
   Foreign key: StateAbbrev to State relation
   Foreign key: CropName to Crop relation
Shipping (<u>StateAbbrev</u>, OceanShoreline, ExportTonnage, ImportTonnage)
   Foreign key: StateAbbrev to State relation

Another popular way to describe relations *and their relationships* is with entity-relationship diagrams. An **entity-relationship diagram (ERD)** shows a database's entities and the relationships among the entities in a symbolic, visual way. In an entity-relationship diagram, an entity and a relation are equivalent. Figure 9 shows an entity-relationship diagram for the relations that appear in Figures 5 through 8.

Figure 9	AN ENTITY-RELATIONSHIP DIAGRAM

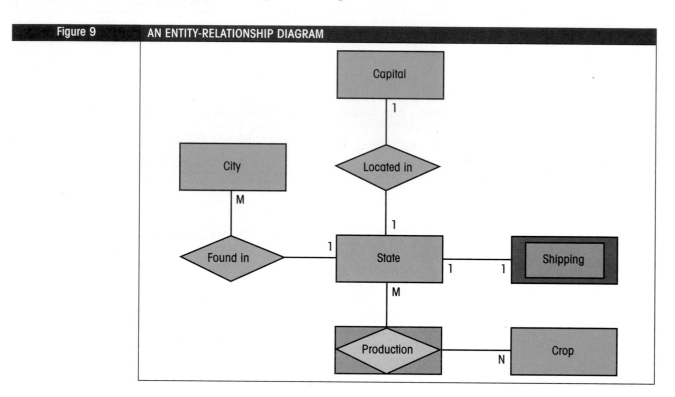

Entity-relationship diagrams have the following characteristics:

- Entities, or relations, appear in rectangles and relationships appear in diamonds. The entity name appears inside the rectangle and a verb describing the relationship appears inside the diamond. For example, the City rectangle is connected to the State rectangle by the Found in diamond and is read: "a city is found in a state."

- The 1 by the State entity and the M by the City entity identify a 1:M relationship between these two entities. In a similar manner, an M:N relationship exists between the State and Crop entities and 1:1 relationships exist between the State and Capital entities and between the State and Shipping entities.

- A diamond inside a rectangle defines a composite entity. A **composite entity** is a relationship that has the characteristics of an entity. For example, Production connects the State and Crop entities in an M:N relationship and acts as an entity by containing the Quantity attribute, along with the composite key of the StateAbbrev and CropName attributes.

- An entity subtype, for example, Shipping, appears in a double rectangle and is connected without an intervening diamond directly to its related entity, for example, State.

You can also show attributes in an ERD by placing each individual attribute in a bubble connected to its entity or relationship. However, typical ERDs have large numbers of entities and relationships, so including the attributes might confuse rather than clarify the ERD.

Integrity Constraints

A database has **integrity** if its data follows certain rules, known as **integrity constraint**s. The ideal is to have the DBMS enforce all integrity constraints. If a DBMS can enforce some integrity constraints but not others, the other integrity constraints must be enforced by other programs or by the people who use the DBMS. Integrity constraints can be divided into three groups: primary key constraints, referential integrity, and domain integrity constraints.

- One primary key constraint is inherent in the definition of a primary key, which says that the primary key must be unique. The **entity integrity constraint** says that the primary key cannot be null. For a composite key, none of the individual attributes can be null. The uniqueness and nonnull properties of a primary key ensure that you can reference any data value in a database by supplying its table name, attribute name, and primary key value.

- Foreign keys provide the mechanism for forming a relationship between two tables, and referential integrity ensures that only valid relationships exist. **Referential integrity** is the constraint specifying that each nonnull foreign key must match a primary key value in the related relation. Specifically, referential integrity means that you cannot add a row with an unmatched foreign key value. Referential integrity also means that you cannot change or delete the related primary key value and leave the foreign key orphaned. In some relational DBMSs, if you try to change or delete a primary key value, you can specify one of these options: restricted, cascades, or nullifies. If you specify **restricted**, the DBMS updates or deletes the value only if there are no matching foreign key values. If you choose **cascades** and then change a primary key value, the DBMS changes the matching foreign keys to the new primary key value, or, if you delete a primary key value, the DBMS also deletes the matching foreign-key rows. If you choose **nullifies** and then change or delete a primary key value, the DBMS sets all matching foreign keys to null.

- A domain is a set of values from which one or more columns draw their actual values. **Domain integrity constraints** are the rules you specify for an attribute. By choosing a data type for an attribute, you impose a constraint on the set of values allowed for the attribute. You can create specific validation rules for an attribute to limit its domain further. As you make an attribute's domain definition more precise, you exclude more and more unacceptable values for an attribute. For example, in the State relation you could define the domain for the EnteredUnionOrder attribute to be a unique integer between 1 and 50 and the domain for the StateBird attribute to be any name containing 25 or fewer characters.

Dependencies and Determinants

Relations are related to other relations. Attributes are also related to other attributes. Consider the StateCrop relation shown in Figure 10. Its description is:

StateCrop (StateAbbrev, CropName, StateBird, BirdScientificName, StatePopulation, Exports, Quantity)

| Figure 10 | A RELATION COMBINING SEVERAL ATTRIBUTES FROM OTHER RELATIONS |

null value

primary key

StateCrop

StateAbbrev	CropName	StateBird	BirdScientificName	StatePopulation	Export	Quantity
CT	Corn	American robin	Planesticus migratorius	3,287,116	$4,965.8	
MI	Corn	robin	Planesticus migratorius	9,295,297	$4,965.8	241,500
MI	Soybeans	robin	Planesticus migratorius	9,295,297	$4,462.8	47,520
MI	Wheat	robin	Planesticus migratorius	9,295,297	$4,503.2	35,280
SD	Corn	pheasant	Phasianus colchicus	696,004	$4,965.8	277,200
SD	Soybeans	pheasant	Phasianus colchicus	696,004	$4,462.8	63,000
SD	Wheat	pheasant	Phasianus colchicus	696,004	$4,503.2	119,590
TN	Corn	mockingbird	Mimus polyglottos	4,977,185	$4,965.8	79,360
TN	Soybeans	mockingbird	Mimus polyglottos	4,977,185	$4,462.8	33,250
TN	Wheat	mockingbird	Mimus polyglottos	4,977,185	$4,503.2	13,440
TX	Corn	mockingbird	Mimus polyglottos	16,986,510	$4,965.8	202,500
TX	Cotton	mockingbird	Mimus polyglottos	16,986,510	$2,014.6	3,322
TX	Soybeans	mockingbird	Mimus polyglottos	16,986,510	$4,462.8	12,870
TX	Wheat	mockingbird	Mimus polyglottos	16,986,510	$4,503.2	129,200

The StateCrop relation combines several attributes from the State, Crop, and Production relations that appeared in Figure 7. The StateAbbrev, StateBird, and StatePopulation attributes are from the State relation. The CropName and Exports attributes are from the Crop relation. The StateAbbrev, CropName, and Quantity attributes are from the Production relation. The BirdScientificName attribute is a new attribute for the StateCrop relation, whose primary key is the combination of the StateAbbrev and CropName attributes.

Notice the null value in the Quantity attribute for the state of Connecticut (StateAbbrev CT). If you look back to Figure 7, you can see that there were no entries for Quantity for the state of Connecticut, which is why Quantity is null in the StateCrop table. However, note that CropName requires an entry because it is part of the composite key for the relation. If you want the state of CT to be in the relation, you need to assign a dummy CropName for the CT entry, in this case, Corn.

In the StateCrop relation, each attribute is related to other attributes. For example, a value for StateAbbrev determines the value of StatePopulation, and a value for StatePopulation depends on the value of StateAbbrev. In database discussions, the word functionally is used, as in: "StateAbbrev functionally determines StatePopulation" and

"StatePopulation is functionally dependent on StateAbbrev." In this case, StateAbbrev is called a determinant. A **determinant** is an attribute, or a collection of attributes, whose values determine the values of another attribute. We also state that an attribute is functionally dependent on another attribute (or collection of attributes) if that other attribute is a determinant for it.

You can graphically show a relation's functional dependencies and determinants in a bubble diagram. Bubble diagrams are also called data model diagrams and functional dependency diagrams. Figure 11 shows the bubble diagram for the StateCrop relation.

Figure 11	A BUBBLE DIAGRAM FOR THE STATECROP RELATION

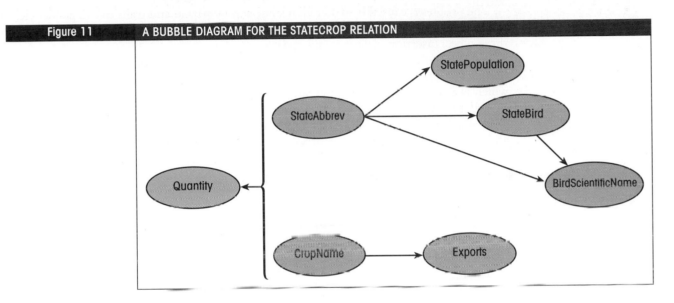

- StateAbbrev is a determinant for StatePopulation, StateBird, and BirdScientificName.
- CropName is a determinant for Exports.
- Quantity is functionally dependent on StateAbbrev and CropName together.
- StateBird is a determinant for BirdScientificName.

Only Quantity is functionally dependent on the relation's full primary key, StateAbbrev and CropName. StatePopulation, StateBird, and BirdScientificName have partial dependencies, because they are functionally dependent on StateAbbrev, which is part of the primary key. A **partial dependency** is a functional dependency on part of the primary key, instead of the entire primary key. Does another partial dependency exist in the StateCrop relation? Yes, Exports has a partial dependency on CropName.

Because StateAbbrev is a determinant of both StateBird and BirdScientificName, and StateBird is a determinant of BirdScientificName, StateBird and BirdScientificName have a transitive dependency. A **transitive dependency** is a functional dependency between two nonkey attributes, which are both dependent on a third attribute.

How do you know which functional dependencies exist among a collection of attributes, and how do you recognize partial and transitive dependencies? The answers lie with the questions you ask as you gather the requirements for a database application. For each attribute and entity, you must gain an accurate understanding of its meaning and relationships in the context of the application. **Semantic object modeling** is an entire area of study within the database field devoted to the meanings and relationships of data.

Anomalies

When you use a DBMS, you are more likely to get results you can trust if you create your relations carefully. For example, problems might occur with relations that have partial and transitive dependencies, whereas you won't have as much trouble if you ensure that your relations include only attributes that are directly related to each other. Also, when you remove data redundancy from a relation, you improve that relation. **Data redundancy** occurs when you store the same data in more than one place.

The problems caused by data redundancy and by partial and transitive dependencies are called **anomalies**, because they are undesirable irregularities of relations. Anomalies are of three types: insertion, deletion, and update.

To examine the effects of these anomalies, consider the Client relation that is shown in Figure 12. The Client relation represents part of the database for Pet Sitters Unlimited, which is a company providing pet-sitting services for homeowners while they are on vacation. Pet Sitters Unlimited keeps track of the data about its clients and the clients' children, pets, and vets. The attributes for the Client relation include the composite key ClientID and ChildName, along with ClientName, VetID, and VetName.

Figure 12	THE CLIENT RELATION WITH INSERTION, DELETION, AND UPDATE ANOMALIES

primary key

Client

ClientID	ChildName	ClientName	VetID	VetName
2173	Ryan	Barbara Hennessey	27	Pet Vet
4519	Pat	Vernon Noordsy	31	Pet Care
4519	Dana	Vernon Noordsy	31	Pet Care
8005	Dana	Sandra Amidon	27	Pet Vet
8005	Dani	Sandra Amidon	27	Pet Vet
8112	Pat	Helen Wandzell	24	Pets R Us

- An **insertion anomaly** occurs when you cannot add a row to a relation because you do not know the entire primary key value. For example, you cannot add the new client Cathy Corbett with a ClientID of 3322 to the Client relation when you do not know her children's names. Entity integrity prevents you from leaving any part of a primary key null. Because ChildName is part of the primary key, you cannot leave it null. To add the new client, your only option is to make up a ChildName, even if the client does not have children. This solution misrepresents the facts and is unacceptable, if a better approach is available.

- A **deletion anomaly** occurs when you delete data from a relation and unintentionally lose other critical data. For example, if you delete ClientID 8112 because Helen Wandzell is no longer a client, you also lose the only instance of VetID 24 in the database. Thus, you no longer know that VetID 24 is Pets R Us.

- An **update anomaly** occurs when you change one attribute value and either the DBMS must make more than one change to the database or else the database ends up containing inconsistent data. For example, if you change the ClientName, VetID, or VetName for ClientID 4519, the DBMS must change multiple rows of the Client relation. If the DBMS fails to change all the rows, the ClientName, VetID, or VetName now has two different values in the database and is inconsistent.

Normalization

Database design is the process of determining the precise relations needed for a given collection of attributes and placing those attributes into the correct relations. Crucial to good database design is understanding the functional dependencies of all attributes; recognizing the anomalies caused by data redundancy, partial dependencies, and transitive dependencies when they exist; and knowing how to eliminate the anomalies.

The process of identifying and eliminating anomalies is called **normalization**. Using normalization, you start with a collection of relations, apply sets of rules to eliminate anomalies, and produce a new collection of problem-free relations. The sets of rules are called **normal forms**. Of special interest for our purposes are the first three normal forms: first normal form, second normal form, and third normal form. First normal form improves the design of your relations, second normal form improves the first normal form design, and third normal form applies even more stringent rules to produce an even better design.

First Normal Form

Consider the Client relation shown in Figure 13. For each client, the relation contains ClientID, which is the primary key; the client's name and children's names; the ID and name of the client's vet; and the ID, name, and type of each client's pets. For example, Barbara Hennessey has no children and three pets, Vernon Noordsy has two children and one pet, Sandra Amidon has two children and two pets, and Helen Wandzell has one child and one pet. Because each entry in a relation must contain a single value, the structure shown in Figure 13 does not meet the requirements for a relation, therefore it is called an **unnormalized relation**. ChildName, which can have more than one value, is called a **repeating group**. The set of attributes that includes PetID, PetName, and PetType is a second repeating group in the structure.

Figure 13	REPEATING GROUPS OF DATA IN AN UNNORMALIZED CLIENT RELATION

repeating group

Client

ClientID	ClientName	ChildName	VetID	VetName	PetID	PetName	PetType
2173	Barbara Hennessey		27	Pet Vet	1 2 4	Sam Hoober Sam	Bird Dog Hamster
4519	Vernon Noordsy	Pat Dana	31	Pet Care	2	Charlie	Cat
8005	Sandra Amidon	Dana Dani	27	Pet Vet	1 2	Beefer Kirby	Dog Cat
8112	Helen Wandzell	Pat	24	Pets R Us	3	Kirby	Dog

First normal form addresses this repeating-group situation. A relation is in **first normal form (1NF)** if it does not contain repeating groups. To remove a repeating group and convert to first normal form, you expand the primary key to include the primary key of the repeating group. You must perform this step carefully, however. If the unnormalized relation has independent repeating groups, you must perform the conversion step separately for each.

The repeating group of ChildName is independent from the repeating group of PetID, PetName, and PetType. That is, the number and names of a client's children are independent of the number, names, and types of a client's pets. Performing the conversion step to each independent repeating group produces the two 1NF relations shown in Figure 14.

Figure 14	AFTER CONVERSION TO 1NF

primary key

Child

ClientID	ChildName	ClientName	VetID	VetName
4519	Pat	Vernon Noordsy	31	Pet Care
4519	Dana	Vernon Noordsy	31	Pet Care
8005	Dana	Sandra Amidon	27	Pet Vet
8005	Dani	Sandra Amidon	27	Pet Vet
8112	Pat	Helen Wandzell	24	Pets R Us

primary key

Client

ClientID	PetID	ClientName	VetID	VetName	PetName	PetType
2173	1	Barbara Hennessey	27	Pet Vet	Sam	Bird
2173	2	Barbara Hennessey	27	Pet Vet	Hoober	Dog
2173	4	Barbara Hennessey	27	Pet Vet	Sam	Hamster
4519	2	Vernon Noordsy	31	Pet Care	Charlie	Cat
8005	1	Sandra Amidon	27	Pet Vet	Beefer	Dog
8005	2	Sandra Amidon	27	Pet Vet	Kirby	Cat
8112	3	Helen Wandzell	24	Pets R Us	Kirby	Dog

The alternative way to describe the 1NF relations is:

Child (<u>ClientID</u>, <u>ChildName</u>, ClientName, VetID, VetName)
Client (<u>ClientID</u>, <u>PetID</u>, ClientName, VetID, VetName, PetName, PetType)

Child and Client are now true relations and both have composite keys. Both relations, however, suffer from insertion, deletion, and update anomalies. (Find examples of the three anomalies in both relations.) In the Child and Client relations, ClientID is a determinant for ClientName, VetID, and VetName, so partial dependencies exist in both relations. It is these partial dependencies that cause the anomalies in the two relations, and second normal form addresses the partial-dependency problem.

Second Normal Form

A relation in 1NF is in **second normal form (2NF)** if it does not contain any partial dependencies. To remove partial dependencies from a relation and convert it to second normal form, you perform two steps. First, identify the functional dependencies for every attribute in the relation. Second, if necessary, create new relations and place each attribute in a relation, so that the attribute is functionally dependent on the entire primary key. If you need to create new relations, restrict them to ones with a primary key that is a subset of the original composite key. Note that partial dependencies occur only when you have a composite key; a relation in first normal form with a single-attribute primary key is automatically in second normal form.

Figure 15 shows the functional dependencies for the 1NF Child and Client relations.

Figure 15	A BUBBLE DIAGRAM FOR THE 1NF CHILD AND THE CLIENT RELATIONS

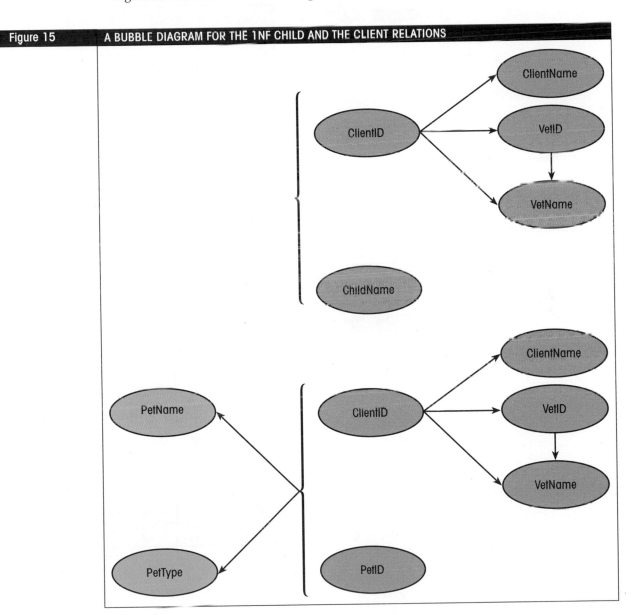

ClientID is a determinant for ClientName, VetID, and VetName in both relations. The composite key ClientID and PetID is a determinant for PetName and PetType. ChildName is not a determinant, nor is PetID. Is the composite key of ClientID and ChildName a determinant? No, it is not a determinant. What happens, however, if you do not have a relation with this composite key? You lose the names of the children of each client. You need to retain this composite key in a relation to preserve the important 1:M attribute relationship between ClientID and ChildName. Performing the second conversion step produces the three 2NF relations shown in Figure 16.

Figure 16   AFTER CONVERSION TO 2NF

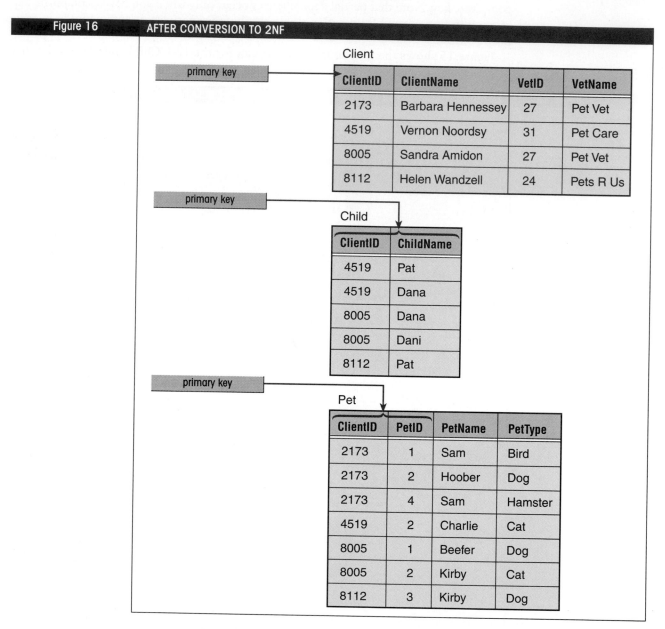

Client

primary key

ClientID	ClientName	VetID	VetName
2173	Barbara Hennessey	27	Pet Vet
4519	Vernon Noordsy	31	Pet Care
8005	Sandra Amidon	27	Pet Vet
8112	Helen Wandzell	24	Pets R Us

primary key

Child

ClientID	ChildName
4519	Pat
4519	Dana
8005	Dana
8005	Dani
8112	Pat

primary key

Pet

ClientID	PetID	PetName	PetType
2173	1	Sam	Bird
2173	2	Hoober	Dog
2173	4	Sam	Hamster
4519	2	Charlie	Cat
8005	1	Beefer	Dog
8005	2	Kirby	Cat
8112	3	Kirby	Dog

The alternative way to describe the 2NF relations is:

Client (<u>ClientID</u>, ClientName, VetID, VetName)
Child (<u>ClientID</u>, <u>ChildName</u>)
    Foreign key: ClientID to Client relation
Pet (<u>ClientID</u>, <u>PetID</u>, PetName, PetType)
    Foreign key: ClientID to Client relation

All three relations are in second normal form. Do anomalies still exist? The Child and Pet relations show no anomalies, but Client suffers from anomalies caused by the transitive dependency between VetID and VetName. (Find examples of the three anomalies caused by the transitive dependency.) You can see the transitive dependency in the bubble diagram shown in Figure 15; VetID is a determinant for VetName and ClientID is a determinant for VetID and VetName. Third normal form addresses the transitive-dependency problem.

Third Normal Form

A relation in 2NF is in **third normal form (3NF)** if every determinant is a candidate key. This definition for 3NF is referred to as **Boyce-Codd normal form (BCNF)** and is an improvement over the original version of 3NF.

To convert a relation to third normal form, remove the attributes that depend on the non-candidate-key determinant and place them into a new relation with the determinant as the primary key. For the Client relation, you remove VetName from the relation, create a new Vet relation, place VetName in the Vet relation, and then make VetID the primary key of the Vet relation. Note that only VetName is removed from the Client relation; VetID remains as a foreign key in the Client relation. Figure 17 shows the database design for the four 3NF relations.

Figure 17   AFTER CONVERSION TO 3NF

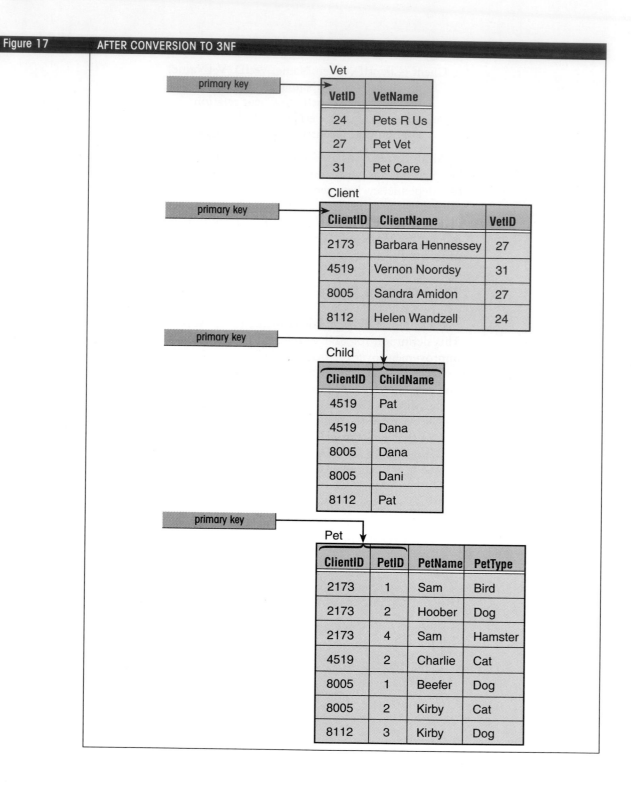

The alternative way to describe the 3NF relations is:

Vet (<u>VetID</u>, VetName)
Client (<u>ClientID</u>, ClientName, VetID)
    Foreign key: VetID to Vet relation
Child (<u>ClientID</u>, <u>ChildName</u>)
    Foreign key: ClientID to Client relation
Pet (<u>ClientID</u>, <u>PetID</u>, PetName, PetType)
    Foreign key: ClientID to Client relation

The four relations have no anomalies, because you have eliminated all the data redundancy, partial dependencies, and transitive dependencies. Normalization provides the framework for eliminating anomalies and delivering an optimal database design, which you should always strive to achieve. You should be aware, however, that experts often denormalize relations to improve database performance—specifically, to decrease the time it takes the database to respond to a user's commands and requests. When you denormalize a relation, you reintroduce redundancy to the relation. At the same time, you reintroduce anomalies. Thus, improving performance exposes a database to potential integrity problems. Only database experts should denormalize relations, but even experts first complete the normalization of their relations.

REVIEW QUESTIONS

1. What are the formal names for a table, for a row, and for a column?

2. What is a domain?

3. What is an entity?

4. What is the relationship between a primary key and a candidate key?

5. What is a composite key?

6. What is a foreign key?

Explore

7. Look for an example of a one-to-one relationship, an example of a one-to-many relationship, and an example of a many-to-many relationship in a newspaper, magazine, book, or everyday situation you encounter. For each one, name the entities and select the primary and foreign keys.

8. When do you use an entity subtype?

9. What is a composite entity in an entity-relationship diagram?

10. What is the entity integrity constraint?

11. What is referential integrity?

12. What does the cascades option, which is used with referential integrity, accomplish?

13. What are partial and transitive dependencies?

14. What three types of anomalies can be exhibited by a relation, and what problems do they cause?

15. Figure 18 shows the Vet, Client, and Child relations with primary keys VetID, ClientID, and both ClientID and ChildName, respectively. Which two integrity constraints do these relations violate and why?

Figure 18

Vet

VetID	VetName
24	Pets R Us
27	Pet Vet
31	Pet Care

Client

ClientID	ClientName	VetID
2173	Barbara Hennessey	27
4519	Vernon Noordsy	31
8005	Sandra Amidon	37
8112	Helen Wandzell	24

Child

ClientID	ChildName
4519	Pat
4519	Dana
8005	
8005	Dani
8112	Pat

16. The State and Capital relations, shown in Figure 5, are described as follows:

    State (StateAbbrev, StateName, EnteredUnionOrder, StateBird,
      StatePopulation)
    Capital (CapitalName, StateAbbrev, YearDesignated, PhoneAreaCode,
      CapitalPopulation)
      Foreign key: StateAbbrev to State relation

    Add the attribute CountyName for the county or counties containing the state capital to this database, justify where you placed it (that is, in an existing relation or in a new one), and draw the entity–relationship diagram for all the entities. The counties for the state capitals shown in Figure 5 are Travis and Williamson counties for Austin TX; Hartford county for Hartford CT; Clinton, Eaton, and Ingham counties for Lansing MI; Davidson county for Nashville TN; Hughes county for Pierre SD.

17. Suppose you have a relation for a dance studio. The attributes are dancer's identification number, dancer's name, dancer's address, dancer's telephone number, class identification number, day that the class meets, time that the class meets, instructor name, and instructor identification number. Assume that each dancer takes one class, each class meets only once a week and has one instructor, and each instructor can teach more than one class. In what normal form is the relation currently, given the following shorthand description?

    Dancer (DancerID, DancerName, DancerAddr, DancerPhone, ClassID, ClassDay, ClassTime, InstrName, InstrID)
    Convert this relation to 3NF and then draw an entity–relationship diagram for this database.

18. Store the following attributes for a library database: AuthorCode, AuthorName, BookTitle, BorrowerAddress, BorrowerName, BorrowerCard Number, CopiesOfBook, ISBN (International Standard Book Number), LoanDate, PublisherCode, PublisherName, and PublisherAddress. A one-to-many relationship exists between publishers and books. Many-to-many relationships exist between authors and books and between borrowers and books.

    a. Name the entities for the library database.
    b. Create the relations for the library database and describe them using the shorthand method. Be sure the relations are in third normal form.
    c. Draw an entity–relationship diagram for the library database.

A

absolute path, connection string, AC 7.10–7.11

Access. *See also* database; table, database
exiting, AC 1.13
in general, AC 5.03, OFF 6
starting, AC 1.07–1.10, AC 3.03

Access database. *See* database

Access table. *See* table

Access window, AC 1.10

aggregate functions, in query, AC 3.38–3.40

Align command. *See also* controls
controls, AC 6.19–6.21

alternate key, RD 4. *See also* key

And logical operator, AC 3.28, AC 3.29–3.30. *See also* logical operator
use in query, AC 3.19–3.20

anomalies. *See also* dependencies
deletion anomaly, RD 14
in general, RD 14–15
insertion anomaly, RD 14
update anomaly, RD 14

Ask a Question box, OFF 21

asterisk, use as wildcard character, AC 5.15, AC 5.16

attribute, RD 2, RD 12
nonkey attribute, RD 5

attribute name, RD 2

AutoForm Wizard, AC 1.18

B

background color modification, form control, AC 5.40–5.42

backup, database, AC 1.23

BCNF. *See* Boyce-Codd normal form

Border Style property, AC 6.24

bound control, AC 5.26. *See also* controls

Boyce–Codd normal form (BCNF), RD 19

button, Office, OFF 13

C

calculated control, AC 5.27. *See also* controls

calculated field. *See* field

calculations, with query, AC 3.33

Can Shrink property, AC 6.24

candidate key, RD 4. *See also* key

caption. *See also* text
changing for label, AC 5.31–5.33
changing for title bar, AC 7.33–7.34

Caption property, changing, AC 5.46–5.47, AC 6.15–6.17

category axis label, AC 7.37. *See also* label

category field. *See also* field
PivotChart, AC 7.37

character. *See also* text
literal display character, AC 5.10

color, background color modification, AC 5.40–5.42

column
multiple-column report, AC 6.55
newspaper-style columns, AC 6.55
resizing, AC 5.52

column selector, AC 1.11

compacting, database AC 1.24–1.25

comparison operator, AC 3.22
In comparison operator, AC 5.17
using to match values, AC 3.26–3.28

composite key, AC 2.03, RD 4. *See also* key

concatenated key, RD 4. *See also* key

conditional formatting rules, reports, AC 6.32–6.36

connection string, absolute path, AC 7.10–7.11

Control Wizard
adding subform with, AC 5.48–5.52
adding subreport with, in general, AC 6.22–6.23

controls. *See also* form; tab controls
aligning, AC 6.19–6.21, AC 6.44 6.45
background color modification, AC 5.40–5.42
bound control, AC 5.26
adding to field list, AC 6.14–6.15
calculated control, AC 5.27
Caption property changes, AC 6.15–6.17
deleting, AC 7.19–7.20
for forms, AC 5.26–5.27
in general, AC 6.15
label, AC 5.26
moving, AC 6.17–6.19, AC 7.19 7.20
resizing, AC 5.33–5.35, AC 6.17–6.19, AC 7.19 7.20
selecting and moving, AC 5.29–5.31
move handle, AC 5.29
sizing handles, AC 5.29, AC 5.30
toolbox, AC 5.27
unbound control, AC 5.26

custom form, AC 5.23. *See also* form

custom report. *See also* report
adding date to, AC 6.41–6.42
adding fields, AC 6.14–6.15
adding lines to, AC 6.27–6.28
adding page numbers, AC 6.43–6.45
adding title to, AC 6.45–6.50
calculating group totals, AC 6.29–6.32
conditional formatting rules, AC 6.32–6.36

controls, AC 6.15–6.21
data sorting and grouping,
AC 6.12–6.13
design considerations,
AC 6.04–6.05
domain aggregate functions,
AC 6.36–6.40
in general, AC 6.02–6.04
hiding duplicate values in,
AC 6.28–6.29
query creation for,
AC 6.05–6.10
Report Window in Design
view, AC 6.10–6.12

D

data
filtering, AC 3.19–3.21
finding with form,
AC 4.08–4.10
maintaining in form,
AC 4.12–4.14
sorting
in general, AC 3.14–3.15
grouping and, AC 6.12–6.13
updating, AC 3.07
with Internet Explorer,
AC 7.11–7.13
data access page. *See also*
HTML document; Web page
creating
adding fields to,
AC 7.16–7.18
controls manipulation on,
AC 7.19–7.20
in Design view, AC 7.14–7.15
in general, AC 7.14
resizing section,
AC 7.20–7.21
special effects application,
AC 7.20–7.21
theme selection,
AC 7.21–7.22
DataPageSize property,
AC 7.21
grouped, AC 7.21
PivotChart use with,
AC 7.37–7.45

PivotTable use with
adding fields, AC 7.28–7.30
adding PivotTable,
AC 7.26–7.27
adding total field,
AC 7.33–7.37
in general, AC 7.25–7.26
Page view use, AC 7.30–7.33
saving and viewing,
AC 7.22–7.24
sorting and filtering records
with, AC 7.13–7.14
for table, AC 7.08–7.11
updating data on,
AC 7.11–7.13
data field. *See also* **field**
PivotChart, AC 7.37
data organization, AC 1.04
data redundancy
avoiding, AC 2.03
occurrence, RD 14
data type, field data types,
AC 2.05–2.06
data validation criteria,
defining, AC 5.13–5.15
database, OFF 6. *See also*
Access; database
backup and restoration,
AC 1.23
compacting and repairing,
AC 1.24
automatically, AC 1.24–1.25
converting, AC 1.25–1.26
copying records from,
AC 2.29–2.31
creating, AC 2.07–2.08
data organization, AC 1.04
common field, AC 1.05
field, AC 1.04
field value, AC 1.04
record, AC 1.04
table, AC 1.04
design guidelines, AC 2.02–2.04
editing mode, AC 2.34
in general, AC 1.04
primary key, AC 1.05
importing table from,
AC 2.32–2.33
management, AC 1.23

navigation mode, AC 2.34
opening, AC 1.07–1.10
record modification, AC 2.35
relational database,
AC 1.04–1.08
relational database management system, AC 1.06
saving, AC 1.12–1.13
updating
changing records,
AC 2.34–2.35
deleting records, AC 2.33–2.34
in general, AC 2.33
database design, RD 15
database management system
(DBMS), discussed,
AC 1.06–1.07
database program, OFF 6
database window, AC 1.10
DataPageSize property,
AC 7.21
datasheet, AC 1.11
changing appearance,
AC 3.25–3.26
navigating, AC 1.11–1.12
current record symbol,
AC 1.11
navigation buttons, AC 1.11
Specific Record box, AC 1.12
subdatasheet, AC 5.09–5.10
datasheet view, table, AC 1.11
date, adding to report,
AC 6.41–6.42
Date function, AC 6.41
DBMS. *See* **database**
management system
deleting
field, AC 2.23–2.24
record, AC 2.33–2.34
dependencies. *See also*
anomalies; relations
determinants and, RD 12–13
partial dependency, RD 13
semantic object modeling,
RD 13
transitive dependency, RD 13
design grid, AC 3.04

Design view.
See also **Page view**
data access page creation in,
AC 7.14–7.15
form modification,
AC 4.19–4.22
Report window in Design
view, AC 6.10–6.12
subreport opening in,
AC 6.24–6.26
detail record, AC 4.22.
See also **record**
Detail section
Form window, AC 5.28
resizing, AC 5.43
**determinants, dependencies
and, RD 12–13**
document. *See also* **HTML
document; report**
entering text into, OFF 16–17
Word, OFF 4
domain, AC 6.37, RD 2
domain aggregate function
DSum domain aggregate
function, AC 6.38
reports, AC 6.36–6.40
**domain integrity constraints,
RD 11**
**DSum domain aggregate
function, AC 6.38**
DSum function.
See also **Sum function**
adding, AC 6.38–6.40

E

editing, database, AC 2.34
entity, RD 2
entity integrity, AC 2.16
**entity integrity constraint,
RD 11**
**entity-relationship diagram
(ERD).** *See also* **relationships**
composite entity, RD 10
discussed, RD 9–11
ERD. *See* **entity-relationship
diagram**

Excel
exiting, AC 7.54
exporting query as Excel
worksheet, AC 7.51–7.54
in general, OFF 4
saving worksheet, AC 7.54
starting, OFF 10–11
exiting
Access, AC 1.13
Excel AC 7.54
Office, OFF 23
**expand indicator, sub-
datasheet, AC 5.09**
expression, AC 3.33
Expression Builder, AC 3.34
**Extensible Markup Language
(XML)**
exporting XML file as table,
AC 7.49–7.501
in general, AC 7.46
importing XML file as table,
AC 7.16–7.48

F

field. *See also* **field list; field
properties; Lookup Wizard
field**
adding, AC 2.24–2.26
to data access page,
AC 7.16–7.18
to form, AC 5.28–5.29
to PivotChart, AC 7.42–7.43
to PivotTable, AC 7.28–7.30
to report, Ac 6.14–6.15
to tab control, AC 5.44–5.46
calculated, AC 3.33
assigning conditional value
to calculated field,
AC 6.08–6.10
creating, AC 3.34–3.38
IIf function, AC 6.08
common field, AC 1.05
data field, AC 7.37
defining, AC 2.09–2.16
deleting, AC 2.23–2.24
entering hyperlink field values,
AC 7.56–7.58
in general, AC 1.04, AC 2.02,
AC 2.03

grouping field, AC 6.12
hyperlink field in table,
AC 7.55
moving, AC 2.24
null value, AC 2.16
properties, AC 2.04
series field, AC 7.38
sorting, AC 3.16–3.19
total field, adding to
PivotTable, AC 7.33–7.37
field list
adding bound controls to,
AC 6.14–6.15
closing, AC 7.30
query, AC 3.04
field properties
changing, AC 2.26–2.27
field data types, AC 2.05–2.06
Field Size property,
AC 2.06–2.07
guidelines, in general, AC 2.04
naming fields and objects,
AC 2.04–2.05
setting, AC 2.04
field selector, table, AC 1.11
**Field Size property,
AC 2.06–2.07**
field value, database, AC 1.04
file
closing, OFF 18
modifying, OFF 18
opening, OFF 18–20
printing, OFF 20–21
saving, OFF 18
switching between, OFF 12–13
file extension, OFF 16
filename, OFF 16
filter
Advanced Filter/Sort, AC 5.53
data, AC 3.19–3.21
defined, AC 5.53
in general, AC 5.53
saving filter as query,
AC 5.56–5.57
application, AC 5.57–5.58
**Filter By Form, AC 3.20,
AC 5.53**
using, AC 5.53–5.56

**Filter By Selection, AC 3.20,
AC 5.53**
**filter field, PivotChart,
AC 7.38**
Filter For Input, AC 5.53
Find command, AC 4.08
 wildcard character, AC 4.09
first normal form (1NF).
 See also **normalization**
 in general, RD 15–16
  repeating group, RD 15
  unnormalized relation,
   RD 15
font size. *See also* **text**
 changing, AC 5.38–5.39
footer. *See* **Form
 Header/Footer**
foreign key, AC 1.05, RD 4.
 See also **key**
form. *See also* **form record**
 adding fields to, AC 5.28–5.29
 adding label to, AC 5.37–5.39
 adding picture to,
  AC 5.39–5.40
 AutoForm Wizard, AC 1.18
 AutoFormat changes,
  AC 4.05–4.08
 controls for, AC 5.26–5.27
  background color
   modification,
   AC 5.40–5.42
 creating
  with Form window in
   Design view,
   AC 5.25–5.28
  with Form Wizard,
   AC 4.02–4.05,
   AC 4.16–4.19
  main form and subform,
   AC 4.16–4.22
  navigating and, AC 1.18–1.20
  with tab controls,
   AC 5.42–5.48
 custom form creation
  design considerations,
   AC 5.23–5.25
  in general, AC 5.23
 detail record, AC 4.22

 filter use with, in general,
  AC 5.53
 finding data using,
  AC 4.08–4.10
 form record, previewing and
  printing, AC 4.11–4.12
 Form view, switching to,
  AC 5.33
 modifying, in Design View,
  AC 4.19–4.22
 multi–page, creating with
  tab controls,
  AC 5.42–5.48
 Position Data form, changing
  the record, AC 4.12.–4.13
 saving, AC 5.33
 subform, AC 5.24
  adding with Control
   Wizard, AC 5.48–5.52
 table data
  maintenance, AC 4.12–4.14
  spell checking, AC 4.14–4.15
Form Header/Footer.
 See also **header**
 adding label to form,
  AC 5.37–5.39
 adding picture to form,
  AC 5.39–5.40
 in general, AC 5.35–5.37
Form window, closing, AC 5.56
Form window in Design view.
 See also **Design view; Report
 window in Design view**
 using, AC 5.25–5.28
  Detail section, AC 5.28
  grid, AC 5.28
  ruler, AC 5.28
Form Wizard, AC 1.18
 form creation with,
  AC 4.02–4.05, AC
  4.16–4.19
**Format Painter, reports,
 AC 6.44–6.45**
 formatting, conditional for-
  matting rules definition,
  AC 6.32–6.36

G

graphics. *See* **picture**
grid, Form window, AC 5.28
gridline, PivotChart, AC 7.37
Group By operator, AC 3.40
**Group Header, orphaned
 header section, AC 6.47**
grouping field. *See also* **field**
 data, AC 6.12
Groups bar, AC 1.10

H

header. *See also* **Form
 Header/Footer**
 Group Header, AC 6.47
 orphaned header section,
  AC 6.47
  Keep Together property,
   AC 6.47
 Report Header/Footer,
  AC 6.36–6.40
Help, Office, OFF 21–23
**Hide Duplicates property,
 reports, AC 6.28–6.29**
HTML. *See* **Hypertext
 Markup Language**
HTML document, AC 7.02.
 See also **data access page;
 document; Web page**
 exporting query to,
  AC 7.02–7.05
 viewing with Internet
  Explorer, AC 7.05–7.08
hyperlinks, AC 7.02
 creating
  entering hyperlink field val-
   ues, AC 7.56–7.58
  in general, AC 7.54
  hyperlink field in table,
   AC 7.55
 using, AC 7.58–7.59
**Hypertext Markup Language
 (HTML), AC 7.02**

I

IIf function, calculated field, AC 6.08
In comparison operator, AC 5.17
input mask, creating, AC 5.10–5.13
Input Mask Wizard, using, AC 5.10–5.13
integration, Office, OFF 7–9
integrity, RD 11
  cascades, RD 11
  nullifies, RD 11
  referential, RD 11
  restricted, RD 11
integrity constraints, RD 11
  domain integrity constraints, RD 11
  entity integrity constraint, RD 11
Internet, AC 7.02. *See also* **World Wide Web**
Internet Explorer
  updating data access page with, AC 7.11–7.13
  viewing HTML document with, AC 7.05–7.08

J

join, tables, AC 3.08

K

Keep Together property, AC 6.47
key
  alternate key, RD 4
  candidate key, RD 4
  composite key, AC 2.03, RD 4
  concatenated key, RD 4
  foreign key, AC 1.05, RD 4
  in general, RD 3–5
  nonkey attribute, RD 5
  primary key, AC 1.05, AC 2.03, RD 3
    specifying, AC 2.16–2.17
  sort key, AC 3.14, AC 3.16
keyboard shortcut, Office, OFF 13

L

label
  adding to form, AC 5.37–5.39
  aligning, AC 6.20–6.21
    right-aligning, AC 5.46–5.48
  category axis label, AC 7.37
  changing Caption property, AC 5.31–5.33, AC 6.16–6.17
  defined, AC 5.26
  editing, deleting, AC 5.51
  mailing label creation, AC 6.50–6.57
  resizing, moving, right-aligning, AC 5.46–5.48
  value axis label, AC 7.37
Label Wizard, AC 6.50
legend, PivotChart, AC 7.38
Like comparison operator, AC 5.15
line. *See also* **report**
  adding to report, AC 6.27–6.28, AC 6.47–6.49
Line tool, AC 6.27
links. *See* **hyperlinks**
list-of-values match. *See also* **value**
  use in query, AC 5.17–5.18
literal display character, AC 5.10
logical operator, AC 3.28
  And logical operator, AC 3.28, AC 3.29–3.30, AC 5.19–5.20
  Not logical operator, AC 5.18
  Or logical operator, AC 3.28, AC 3.31–3.33, AC 5.19–5.20
Lookup Wizard field. *See also* **field**
  creating, AC 5.04–5.07

M

mailing label report. *See also* **label; report**
  adding picture to, AC 6.55–6.57
  changing layout, AC 6.55–6.57
  creating, AC 6.51–6.54
  multiple-colum report, AC 6.55
  newspaper-style columns, AC 6.55
mask, input mask, AC 5.10
menu
  Office, OFF 13–16
  personalized, OFF 13–14
menu command, OFF 13
Microsoft Access 2002. *See* **Access**
Microsoft Excel 2002. *See* **Excel**
Microsoft Internet Explorer. *See* **Internet Explorer**
Microsoft Office XP. *See* **Office**
Microsoft Outlook 2002. *See* **Outlook**
Microsoft PowerPoint 2002. *See* **PowerPoint**
Microsoft Word 2002. *See* **Word**
move handle, controls, AC 5.29

N

NAICSCode field, changing, AC 5.04–5.07
NAICSCode field value, changing, AC 5.07–5.09
navigation
  database, AC 2.34
  datasheet, AC 1.11–1.12
  form, AC 1.18–1.20
  query, AC 1.15–1.18
  record navigation toolbar, AC 7.10
navigation buttons, AC 1.11
nonmatching value. *See also* **value**
  use in query, AC 5.18–5.19
normalization
  first normal form, RD 15–16
    repeating group, RD 15
    unnormalized relation, RD 15
  in general, RD 15
    database design, RD 15
    normal form, RD 15
  second normal form, RD 17–19
  third normal form, RD 19–21

Not logical operator, AC 5.18.
See also logical operator
null value, AC 2.16.
See also value
number field. *See also* field
property settings, AC 2.06
number symbol, use as wildcard character, AC 5.15

O

object, naming, AC 2.04–2.05
Objects bar, AC 1.10
Office
closing, OFF 16–18
exiting programs, OFF 23
in general, OFF 4–7
Help, OFF 21–23
menus and toolbars,
OFF 13–16
opening file, OFF 18–20
program integration,
OFF 7–9
saving, OFF 16–18
speech recognition, OFF 15
starting, OFF 9–12
switching between programs
and files, OFF 12–13
Office Assistant, OFF 21
Office PivotChart
Component, AC 7.37
Office PivotTable
Component, AC 7.26.
See also **PivotTable**
Office XP Web Components,
AC 7.26
1NF. *See* **first normal form**
opening
database, AC 1.07–1.10
query, AC 1.13–1.15
Or logical operator, AC 3.28,
AC 3.31–3.33
use in query, AC 5.19–5.20
Outlook, in general, OFF 6

P

page numbers, adding to
report, AC 6.43–6.45

Page view.
See also **Design view**
PivotTable use in,
AC 7.30–7.33
parameter query.
See also **query**
creating, AC 5.20–5.22
pattern match, use in query,
AC 5.15–5.17
picture
adding to form, AC 5.39–5.40
adding to mailing label
report, AC 6.55–6.57
inserting in report,
AC 4.30–4.34
PivotChart
adding fields to, AC 7.42–7.43
category axis labels, AC 7.37
category field, AC 7.37
changing chart type, AC 7.45
data field, AC 7.37
data marker, AC 7.37
filter field, AC 7.38
gridlines, AC 7.37
legend, AC 7.38
plot area, AC 7.37
resizing, AC 7.42–7.43
series field, AC 7.38
use with data access page,
AC 7.37–7.45
PivotChart toolbar, AC 7.37
PivotTable. *See also* **data**
access page
column area, AC 7.26
column field, AC 7.26
column field items, AC 7.26
filter area, AC 7.26
filter field, AC 7.26
filter field items, AC 7.26
main body, AC 7.26
detail field, AC 7.26
detail values, AC 7.26
Office PivotTable
Component, AC 7.26
row area, AC 7.26
row field, AC 7.26
row field items, AC 7.26
use with data access page
adding fields, AC 7.28–7.30
adding PivotTable,

AC 7.26–7.27
adding total field,
AC 7.33–7.37
changing dimensions,
AC 7.33–7.34
in general, AC 7.25–7.26
Page view use, AC 7.30–7.33
PivotTable toolbar, AC 7.26
PowerPoint, in general, OFF 5
presentation, in general, OFF 5
presentation graphics program,
OFF 5
primary key, AC 1.05, AC 2.03.
See also **key**
specifying, AC 2.16–2.17
printing
file, OFF 20–21
form record, AC 4.11–4.12
programs. *See also* ***specific***
programs
switching between, OFF 12–13
properties. *See* **field properties**

Q

QBE. *See* **query by example**
query. *See also* **query window;**
table
And, Or operator use in,
AC 5.19–5.20
assigning conditional value
to calculated field,
AC 6.08–6.10
for calculations
aggregate functions,
AC 3.38–3.40
calculated field creation,
AC 3.34–3.38
in general, AC 3.33
record group calculations,
AC 3.40–3.41
creating, AC 3.05–3.07
for custom report,
AC 6.05–6.10
multi-table, AC 3.13–3.14
creating, sorting, navigating,
AC 1.15–1.18

exporting
  as Excel Worksheet,
    AC 7.51–7.54
  to HTML document,
    AC 7.02–7.05
filter as, AC 5.56–5.57
  application, AC 5.57–5.58
for data updating, AC 3.07
in general, AC 1.13, AC 3.02
list-of-values match in,
    AC 5.17–5.18
modifying, AC 7.38
multiple selection criteria
  AND logical operator,
    AC 3.29–3.30
  in general, AC 3.28
  multiple Undo and Redo,
    AC 3.30–3.31
  OR logical operator,
    AC 3.31–3.33
nonmatching value use in,
    AC 5.18–5.19
opening, AC 1.13–1.15
parameter query creation,
    AC 5.20–5.22
pattern match use in,
    AC 5.15–5.17
record selection criteria
  changing datasheet appear-
    ance, AC 3.25–3.26
  comparison operator use,
    AC 3.26–3.28
  in general, AC 3.22
  specifying exact match,
    AC 3.22–3.25
recordset, AC 3.02
running, AC 3.04,
    AC 3.05–3.07
select query, AC 3.02
sorting data
  in general, AC 3.14–3.15
  multiple fields in design
    view, AC 3.16–3.19
  toolbar button for,
    AC 3.15–3.16
**query by example (QBE),
  AC 3.02**
query list, viewing, AC 5.56

query window
  discussed, AC 3.02–3.05
    design grid, AC 3.04
    field list, AC 3.04
Query Wizard, AC 1.15
**question mark, use as wild-
  card character, AC 5.15**

R

record. *See also* **form; form
  record; table**
adding to table, AC 2.19–2.22
changing, AC 2.34–2.35
  in form, AC 4.12.–4.13
copying, AC 2.29–2.31
current record symbol, AC 1.11
database, AC 1.04
deleting, AC 2.33–2.34
detail record, AC 4.22
displaying, in subdatasheet,
    AC 5.09–5.10
domain and, AC 6.37
modifying, AC 2.35
orphaned, AC 3.09
record group calculations,
    AC 3.40–3.41
related, displaying,
    AC 5.09–5.10
  selecting, with Filter By
    Form, AC 5.54–5.56
sorting, AC 3.14
  filtering and, AC 7.13–7.14
Specific Record box, AC 1.12
**record navigation toolbar,
  AC 7.10**
record selector, AC 1.11
recordset, AC 3.02
**Redo command, multiple,
  AC 3.30–3.31**
referential integrity, AC 3.09
relational database. *See also*
  database; relations
defined, RD 3
discussed, AC 1.04–1.08
relations. *See also* **dependencies; relationships**
attribute, RD 2
attribute name, RD 2

domain, RD 2
entity, RD 2
in general, RD 2–3, RD 12
table, RD 2
tuple, RD 2
unnormalized relation, RD 15
relationships. *See also* **table
  relationships**
entity subtype, RD 8–9
  null value, RD 9
entity–relationship diagrams,
    RD 9–11
in general, RD 5–6
many–to–many, RD 7–8
one–to–many, RD 6–7
one–to–one, RD 6
report. *See also* **custom
  report; document; mailing
  label report; Report Wizard**
adding date to, AC 6.41–6.42
adding field to, AC 6.14–6.15
adding lines to, AC 6.27–6.28,
    AC 6.47–6.49
closing and saving,
    AC 1.23–1.24
creating
  custom report, AC 6.02–6.05
  previewing and navigating,
    AC 1.20–1.21
  with Report Wizard,
    AC 4.22–4.30
data sorting and grouping,
    AC 6.12–6.13
defined, AC 6.02
hiding duplicate values in,
    AC 6.28–6.29
inserting picture in,
    AC 4.30–4.34
previewing, AC 6.49–6.50
saving, AC 6.49–6.50
  design, AC 6.18
sections, AC 6.02
subreport, AC 6.05
**Report Header/Footer, adding
  and removing, AC 6.36–6.40**
**Report window in Design
  view.** *See also* **Form window
  in Design view**
discussed, AC 6.10–6.12

Report Wizard
report creation, AC 4.22–4.30
detail record, AC 4.22
row, relations, RD 2
row selector, AC 1.11
ruler, Form window, AC 5.28

S

saving
database, AC 1.12–1.13
Office, OFF 16–18
report, AC 1.23–1.24
table, AC 2.17–2.18
ScreenTip, Office, OFF 21
search. *See* **Find command**
second normal form (2NF), in general, RD 17–19
semantic object modeling, RD 13
series field. *See also* **field**
PivotChart, AC 7.38
sizing handles, controls, AC 5.29, AC 5.30
sort key, AC 3.14. *See also* **key**
nonunique, AC 3.16
primary, AC 3.16
secondary, AC 3.16
unique, AC 3.16
sorting
data, AC 3.14–3.15
fields, AC 3.16–3.19
query, AC 1.15–1.18
Sort Ascending, AC 3.15
Sort Descending, AC 3.15
special effects, application to data access page, AC 7.20–7.21
speech recognition, Office, OFF 15
spell checking, table data, AC 4.14–4.15
spreadsheet program, OFF 4
starting
Excel, OFF 10–11
Office, OFF 9–12
Word, OFF 11–12

subdatasheet.
See also **datasheet**
displaying related records in, AC 5.09–5.10
expand indicator, AC 5.09
subform, AC 5.24.
See also **form**
adding with Control Wizard, AC 5.48–5.52
resizing columns in, AC 5.52
subreport, AC 6.05.
See also **report**
adding using Control Wizards, AC 6.22–6.23
modifying, AC 6.23–6.24
opening in Design view, AC 6.24–6.26
Sum function
DSum function, adding, AC 6.38–6.40
reports, AC 6.29–6.32

T

tab controls. *See also* **controls**
form creation with, AC 5.42–5.48
table. *See also* **query; record; table; table relationships**
adding records to, AC 2.19–2.22
creating
field definition, AC 2.09–2.16
in general, AC 2.08–2.09
primary key specification, AC 2.16–2.17
saving, AC 2.17–2.18
data access page for, AC 7.08–7.11
data maintenance with form, AC 4.12–4.14
database, AC 1.04, AC 2.02, AC 2.03
defined, RD 2
entity integrity, AC 2.16
exporting, XML file, AC 7.49–7.51
in general, AC 1.10–1.11
column selector, AC 1.11
datasheet view, AC 1.11

field selector, AC 1.11
record selector, AC 1.11
row selector, AC 1.11
hyperlink field in table, AC 7.55
importing, AC 2.32–2.33
XML file, AC 7.46–7.48
modifying
adding field, AC 2.24–2.26
changing field properties, AC 2.26–2.29
deleting field, AC 2.23–2.24
in general, AC 2.22–2.23
moving field, AC 2.24
table relationships. *See also* **relationships**
defining, AC 3.09–3.12
in general, AC 3.08
join, AC 3.08
one–to–many, AC 3.08–3.09
orphaned record, AC 3.09
primary table, AC 3.09
related table, AC 3.09
referential integrity, AC 3.09
cascade deletes, AC 3.09
cascade updates, AC 3.09
text. *See also* **caption; character; text box; title**
entering in document, OFF 16–17
font size modification, AC 5.38–5.39
label for, AC 5.26
Validation Text property value, AC 5.13
Zoom box, AC 3.34
text box
adding in Report Footer, AC 6.38–6.40
resizing, AC 5.34–5.35, AC 6.19, AC 6.32
special effects application to, AC 7.20–7.21
theme. *See also* **data access page**
selecting, AC 7.21–7.22
third normal form (3NF)
discussed, RD 19–21
Boyce–Codd normal form, RD 19

3NF. *See* **third normal form**
title. *See also* **text**
  adding to page, AC 7.18,
    AC 7.30
  adding to report, AC 6.45–6.50
  changing caption,
    AC 7.33–7.34
  changing font size and weight,
    AC 5.38–5.39
toolbar
  Office, OFF 13–16
  personalized, OFF 14–15
toolbox, AC 5.27
total field. *See also* **field**
  adding to PivotTable,
    AC 7.33–7.37
tuple, RD 2
2NF. *See* **second normal form**

U

unbound control, AC 5.26.
  See also **controls**
Undo command, multiple,
  AC 3.30–3.31
Uniform Resource Locator
  (URL), AC 7.02
URL. *See* **Uniform Resource**
  Locator

V

validation criteria, defining,
  AC 5.13–5.15
Validation Rule, AC 5.13
Validation Text, AC 5.13
value
  assigning conditional value to
    calculated field,
    AC 6.08–6.10
  entering hyperlink field values,
    AC 7.56–7.58
  hiding duplicate values in
    report, AC 6.28–6.29
  list-of-values match, use in
    query, AC 5.17–5.18
  nonmatching value,
    AC 5.18–5.19
value axis label, AC 7.37.
  See also **label**

W

Web browser, AC 7.02
Web page, AC 7.02. *See also*
  data access page; HTML
  document
  dynamic, AC 7.02
  static, AC 7.02
Web. *See* **World Wide Web**

What's This? command,
  OFF 21
wildcard character, AC 4.09,
  AC 5.15
Word
  in general, OFF 4
    documents, OFF 4
  starting, OFF 11–12
word processing program,
  OFF 4
workbook, Excel, OFF 4
World Wide Web (WWW),
  AC 7.02
WWW. *See* **World Wide Web**

X

XML. *See* **Extensible Markup**
  Language

Z

Zoom box, AC 3.34

TASK REFERENCE

TASK	PAGE #	RECOMMENDED METHOD
Access, exit	AC 1.13	Click ☒ on the program window
Access, start	AC 1.07	Click Start, point to Programs, click Microsoft Access
Aggregate functions, use in a query	AC 3.38	Display the query in Design view, click Σ
And operator, enter selection criteria for	AC 5.19	Enter selection criteria in the same Criteria row in the design grid
AutoFormat, change	AC 4.05	See Reference Window: Changing a Form's AutoFormat
Calculated field, add to a query	AC 3.34	See Reference Window: Using Expression Builder
Caption, change for a form label	AC 5.31	See Reference Window: Changing a Label's Caption
Caption, change for a report label	AC 6.16	See Reference Window: Changing the Caption Property for a Label
Color, change an object's background	AC 5.41	See Reference Window: Changing the Background Color of a Control
Column, resize width in a datasheet	AC 2.29	Double-click ↔ on the right border of the column heading
Conditional formatting rules, define	AC 6.33	See Reference Window: Defining Conditional Formatting for a Control
Control, align	AC 5.46	See Reference Window: Aligning Controls on a Form
Control, apply special effect	AC 7.20	Select the control, click the list arrow for ▭, click the special effect
Control, delete	AC 7.19	Right-click the control, click Cut
Control, hide	AC 6.26	Set Visible property to No
Control, move in a form	AC 5.29	See Reference Window: Selecting and Moving Controls
Control, move in a report	AC 6.17	See Reference Window: Moving and Resizing Controls
Control, resize in a form	AC 5.34	See Reference Window: Resizing a Control
Control, resize in a report	AC 6.17	See Reference Window: Moving and Resizing Controls
Control, select	AC 5.29	See Reference Window: Selecting and Moving Controls
Data, check spelling of	AC 4.15	Click ✓
Data, find	AC 4.08	See Reference Window: Finding Data in a Form or Datasheet
Data, group in a report	AC 6.12	See Reference Window: Sorting and Grouping Data in a Report
Data, sort in a report	AC 6.12	See Reference Window: Sorting and Grouping Data in a Report
Data access page, create a custom	AC 7.14	See Reference Window: Creating a Data Access Page in Design View

TASK	PAGE #	RECOMMENDED METHOD
Data access page, display related records	AC 7.23	Click ⊞
Data access page, filter records	AC 7.13	Click filter field text box, click 🔽
Data access page, hide related records	AC 7.24	Click ⊟
Data access page, select theme	AC 7.22	In Design view, click Format, click Theme, select desired theme, click OK
Data access page, sort records	AC 7.13	Click sort field text box, click either ⬇ or ⬆
Data access page, update with a browser	AC 7.12	See Reference Window: Viewing and Updating Data on a Data Access Page Using Internet Explorer
Data access page, use Page Wizard to create	AC 7.08	Click Pages in the Objects bar, click New, click Page Wizard, choose the table or query to use, click OK, choose Wizard options
Data access page, view with a browser	AC 7.12	See Reference Window: Viewing and Updating Data on a Data Access Page Using Internet Explorer
Database, compact and repair	AC 1.24	Click Tools, point to Database Utilities, click Compact and Repair Database
Database, compact on close	AC 1.25	See Reference Window: Compacting a Database Automatically
Database, convert to another Access version	AC 1.26	Close the database to convert, click Tools, point to Database Utilities, point to Convert Database, click the format to convert to
Database, create a blank	AC 2.07	Click ▢ on the Database toolbar, click Blank Database in the Task Pane, type the database name, select the drive and folder, click Create
Database, create using a Wizard	AC 2.07	Click ▢ on the Database toolbar, click General Templates in the Task Pane, click the Databases tab, select a template, click OK, type the database name, select the drive and folder, click Create, follow the instructions in the Wizard
Database, open	AC 1.07	Click 📂
Datasheet view, switch to	AC 2.19	Click ▦
Date, add to a report	AC 6.41	See Reference Window: Adding the Date to a Report
Design view, switch to	AC 2.23	Click ⬚
Domain aggregate function, add	AC 6.38	See Reference Window: Using a Domain Aggregate Function in a Report
Duplicate values, hide	AC 6.28	See Reference Window: Hiding Duplicate Values in a Report
Field, add to a data access page or form	AC 5.28	Drag the field from the field list to the object in Design view

TASK REFERENCE

TASK	PAGE #	RECOMMENDED METHOD
Field, add to a report	AC 6.14	See Reference Window: Adding Fields to a Report
Field, add to a database table	AC 2.25	See Reference Window: Adding a Field Between Two Existing Fields
Field, define in a database table	AC 2.10	See Reference Window: Defining a Field in a Table
Field, delete from a database table	AC 2.23	See Reference Window: Deleting a Field from a Table Structure
Field, move to a new location in a database table	AC 2.24	Display the table in Design view, click the field's row selector, drag the field with the pointer
Filter, save as a query	AC 5.56	See Reference Window: Saving a Filter as a Query
Filter, saved as a query, apply	AC 5.57	See Reference Window: Applying a Filter Saved as a Query
Filter By Form, activate	AC 5.55	Click
Filter By Form, using	AC 5.53	See Reference Window: Selecting Records Using Filter By Form
Filter By Selection, activate	AC 3.20	See Reference Window: Using Filter By Selection
Form, create a custom	AC 5.25	See Reference Window: Creating a Form in Design View
Form Footer, add	AC 5.36	See Reference Window: Adding and Removing Form Header and Form Footer Sections
Form Footer, remove	AC 5.36	See Reference Window: Adding and Removing Form Header and Form Footer Sections
Form Header, add	AC 5.36	See Reference Window: Adding and Removing Form Header and Form Footer Sections
Form Header, remove	AC 5.36	See Reference Window: Adding and Removing Form Header and Form Footer Sections
Form Wizard, activate	AC 4.02	Click Forms in the Objects bar, click New, click Form Wizard, choose the table or query for the form, click OK
Group totals, calculating in a report	AC 6.29	See Reference Window: Calculating Totals in a Report
HTML document, export an Access object as	AC 7.03	See Reference Window: Exporting an Access Object to an HTML Document
HTML document, view	AC 7.05	See Reference Window: Viewing an HTML Document in a Web Browser
Hyperlink, use	AC 7.58	Click the hyperlink field value
Hyperlink field, create	AC 7.55	See Reference Window: Creating a Hyperlink Field in a Table
Hyperlink field value, enter	AC 7.56	See Reference Window: Entering a Hyperlink Field Value in a Table

TASK	PAGE #	RECOMMENDED METHOD
Input Mask Wizard, activate	AC 5.11	Click the field's Input Mask text box, click ..., specify your choices in the Input Mask Wizard dialog boxes
Label, add to a form or report	AC 5.37	See Reference Window: Adding a Label to a Form
Line, add to a report	AC 6.27	See Reference Window: Adding a Line to a Report
Lookup Wizard field, create	AC 5.04	Click the Data Type list arrow, click Lookup Wizard, specify your choices in the Lookup Wizard dialog boxes
Mailing labels, create	AC 6.51	See Reference Window: Creating Mailing Labels and Other Labels
Multiple-column report, modify	AC 6.55	In Design view, click File, click Page Setup, click Columns, set multiple-column options
Object, export as an Excel worksheet	AC 7.51	See Reference Window: Exporting an Access Object to an Excel Worksheet
Object, open	AC 1.10	Click the object's type in the Objects bar, click the object's name, click Open
Object, save	AC 1.20	Click 🖫, type the object name, click OK
Overall totals, calculating in a report	AC 6.29	See Reference Window: Calculating Totals in a Report
Page numbers, add to a report	AC 6.43	See Reference Window: Adding Page Numbers to a Report
Parameter query, create	AC 5.21	See Reference Window: Creating a Parameter Query
Picture, add to a form or report	AC 5.39	See Reference Window: Adding a Picture to a Form
Picture, insert on a report	AC 4.31	Select the report section in which to insert the picture, click Insert, click Picture, select the picture file, click OK
PivotChart, add to data access page	AC 7.38	See Reference Window: Adding a PivotChart to a Data Access Page
PivotTable, add a total field	AC 7.33	Click a detail field's column heading, right-click it a second time, point to AutoCalc, click an aggregate option
PivotTable, add to data access page	AC 7.26	See Reference Window: Adding a PivotTable to a Data Access Page
Primary key, specify	AC 2.16	See Reference Window: Specifying a Primary Key for a Table
Property sheet, open	AC 3.37	Right-click the object or control, click Properties
Query, define	AC 3.03	Click Queries in the Objects bar, click New, click Design View, click OK
Query, run	AC 3.06	Click 🗈
Query results, sort	AC 3.17	See Reference Window: Sorting a Query Datasheet
Record, add a new one	AC 2.28	Click ▶*

TASK	PAGE #	RECOMMENDED METHOD
Record, delete	AC 2.33	See Reference Window: Deleting a Record
Record, move to a specific one	AC 1.11	Type the record number in the Specific Record box, press Enter
Record, move to first	AC 1.12	Click ⏮
Record, move to last	AC 1.12	Click ⏭
Record, move to next	AC 1.12	Click ▶
Record, move to previous	AC 1.12	Click ◀
Records, redisplay all after filter	AC 3.21	Click ▽
Redo command, use to redo multiple operations in a database object	AC 3.31	Click the list arrow for ↻ , click the action(s) to redo
Relationship, define between database tables	AC 3.10	Click ⛁
Report, create a custom	AC 6.10	See Reference Window: Creating a Report in Design View
Report Footer, add	AC 6.36	See Reference Window: Adding and Removing Report Header and Report Footer Sections
Report Footer, remove	AC 6.36	See Reference Window: Adding and Removing Report Header and Report Footer Sections
Report Header, add	AC 6.36	See Reference Window: Adding and Removing Report Header and Report Footer Sections
Report Header, remove	AC 6.36	See Reference Window: Adding and Removing Report Header and Report Footer Sections
Report Wizard, activate	AC 4.23	Click Reports in the Objects bar, click New, click Report Wizard, choose the table or query for the report, click OK
Sort, specify ascending in datasheet	AC 3.15	Click ᴬ↓
Sort, specify descending in datasheet	AC 3.15	Click ᶻ↓
Subdatasheet, display related records	AC 5.09	Click ⊞
Subdatasheet, hide related records	AC 5.10	Click ⊟
Subform/Subreport Wizard, activate	AC 5.48	Make sure ⬚ is selected, click ▦ , click in the grid at the upper-left corner for the subform/subreport

TASK	PAGE #	RECOMMENDED METHOD
Subreport, open in a new window	AC 6.24	Right-click the subreport, click Subreport in New Window
Tab Control, add to a form	AC 5.43	Click ▣, click in the grid at the upper-left corner for the tab control
Table, create in a database	AC 2.08	Click Tables in the Objects bar, click New, click Design View, click OK
Table, export as an Excel worksheet	AC 7.51	See Reference Window: Exporting an Access Object to an Excel Worksheet
Table, Import from another Access database	AC 2.32	Click File, point to Get External Data, click Import, select the folder, click Import, select the table, click OK
Table, open in a database	AC 1.10	Click Tables In the Objects bar, click the table name, click Open
Table structure, save in a database	AC 2.18	See Reference Window: Saving a Table Structure
Template, use an HTML	AC 7.04	Click the Save formatted check box in the Export dialog box, click Export, select template, click OK
Title, add to a form or report	AC 5.37	Click Aa, click in the grid at the upper-left corner for the title, type the title, click anywhere outside the label box
Totals, calculate in a report	AC 6.29	See Reference Window: Calculating Totals in a Report
Undo command, use to undo multiple operations in a database object	AC 3.30	Click the list arrow for ↺, click the action(s) to undo
Validation Rule property, set	AC 5.13	Display the table in Design view, select the field, enter the rule in the Validation Rule text box
Validation Text property, set	AC 5.13	Display the table in Design view, select the field, enter the text in the Validation Text text box
XML file, export an Access object to an	AC 7.49	See Reference Window: Exporting an Access Object as an XML File
XML file, import as a table	AC 7.46	See Reference Window: Importing an XML File as an Access Table

Standardized Coding Number	Certification Skill Activity		End-of-Tutorial Practice	
	Activity	**Tutorial Number (page numbers)**	**Exercise**	**Step Number**
AC2002-1	**Creating and Using Databases**			
Ac2002-1-1	Create Access databases	2 (2.07)	Review Assignment	2
Ac2002-1-2	Open database objects in multiple views	1 (1.10-1.11, 1.13-1.14, 1.18-1.19, 1.20-1.21) 2	1: Review Assignment Case Problem 1 Case Problem 2 Case Problem 3 Case Problem 4 2: Review Assignment Case Problem 1 Case Problem 2 Case Problem 3 Case Problem 4	5 3-6 3, 4, 6-9 3-9 3-9 3-6, 9 3, 6-10 3-11 5-7 4-6, 8-12
Ac2002-1-3	Move among records	1 (1.11-1.12, 1.17-1.18, 1.20-1.22) 2 4 (4.07-4.08) 5 (5.33)	1: Review Assignment Case Problem 2 Case Problem 3 Case Problem 4 2: Review Assignment Case Problem 1 Case Problem 2 Case Problem 3 Case Problem 4	9 6, 7 8 16 9 7, 11 7 6
Ac2002-1-4	Format datasheets	2 (2.29) 3 (3.25-3.26)	2: Review Assignment Case Problem 1 Case Problem 3 Case Problem 4 3: Review Assignment Case Problem 2 Case Problem 3 Case Problem 4	11, 15 8, 10, 12 6 12 10-12 8 6, 7 3, 6
Ac2002-2	**Creating and Modifying Tables**			
Ac2002-2-1	Create and modify tables	2 (2.09)	Review Assignment Case Problem 3 Case Problem 4	3, 13 3 3
Ac2002-2-2	Add a pre-defined input mask to a field	5 (5.10-5.13)	Review Assignment Case Problem 1 Case Problem 2	5 3 2

Standardized Coding Number	Certification Skill Activity		Tutorial Number (page numbers)	End-of-Tutorial Practice	
	Activity			Exercise	Step Number
				Case Problem 4	3
				Case Problem 5	13
Ac2002-2-3	Create Lookup fields		5 (5.01-5.09)	Review Assignment	2
				Case Problem 1	2
				Case Problem 3	2
				Case Problem 4	2
				Case Problem 5	15
Ac2002-2-4	Modify field properties		2 (2.22-2.27)	2: Review Assignment	5, 10, 14
			5 (5.10-5.13)	Case Problem 1	7
				Case Problem 2	6
				Case Problem 3	5
				Case Problem 4	5
				5: Review Assignment	5
				Case Problem 1	3
				Case Problem 2	2
				Case Problem 4	3
Ac2002-3	**Creating and Modifying Queries**				
Ac2002-3-1	Create and modify Select queries		1 (1.13-1.17)	1: Review Assignment	7
			3 (3.02-3.07, 3-23-3.24)	Case Problem 1	4
			5 (5.15-5.16)	Case Problem 2	4
				Case Problem 3	4
				Case Problem 4	5
				3: Review Assignment	2, 5, 9, 12
				Case Problem 1	3
				Case Problem 2	3, 5-8
				Case Problem 3	3, 5-7
				Case Problem 4	3-7
				5: Review Assignment	6, 8-10
				Case Problem 1	5, 6, 8
				Case Problem 2	5, 8
				Case Problem 3	5, 7, 8
				Case Problem 4	5, 7, 8
Ac2002-3-2	Add calculated fields to Select queries		3 (3.34-3.38, 3.38-3.39)	Review Assignment	10
				Case Problem 2	8
				Case Problem 3	6, 7
				Case Problem 4	4
Ac2002-4	**Creating and Modifying Forms**				
Ac2002-4-1	Create and display forms		1 (1.18-1.20)	1: Review Assignment	8
			4 (4.02-4.07, 4.16-4.19)	Case Problem 1	5
			5 (5.23-5.58)	Case Problem 2	7

Certification Skill Activity

End-of-Tutorial Practice

Standardized Coding Number	Activity	Tutorial Number (page numbers)	Exercise	Step Number
			Case Problem 3	6
			Case Problem 4	8
			4: Review Assignment	3, 6, 7
			Case Problem 1	2, 6
			Case Problem 2	2
			Case Problem 3	3, 6
			Case Problem 4	2
			5: Review Assignment	11
			Case Problem 1	9
			Case Problem 2	9, 12, 13
			Case Problem 3	9
			Case Problem 4	9, 12, 13
			Case Problem 5	8
Ac2002-4-2	Modify form properties	5 (5.31-5.32, 5.33-5.35, 5.37-5.39, 5.40-5.42, 5.46-5.47, 5.51)	Review Assignment	11
			Case Problem 1	9
			Case Problem 2	9, 12, 13
			Case Problem 3	9
			Case Problem 4	9, 12, 13
			Case Problem 5	8
Ac2002-5	**Viewing and Organizing Information**			
Ac2002-5-1	Enter, edit, and delete records	2 (2.19-2.22, 2.23-2.24, 2.28)	2: Review Assignment	4, 6, 16
			Case Problem 1	5, 9, 12
		3 (3.07)	Case Problem 2	5, 7, 11
		4 (4.12-4.13)	Case Problem 3	7
			Case Problem 4	6, 10
			3: Review Assignment	3
			Case Problem 2	4
			Case Problem 3	4
			4: Review Assignment	5
			Case Problem 1	5
			Case Problem 2	4, 5
			Case Problem 3	4
			Case Problem 4	4, 5
Ac2002-5-2	Create queries	1 (1.15-1.18)	1: Review Assignment	7
		3 (3.02-3.07, 3.13-3.14, 3.23-3.24, 3.32-3.33, 3.39-3.41)	Case Problem 1	4
			Case Problem 2	4
			Case Problem 3	4
		5 (5.15-5.16)	Case Problem 4	5

| Standardized Coding Number | Certification Skill Activity | | End-of-Tutorial Practice | |
	Activity	Tutorial Number (page numbers)	Exercise	Step Number
			3: Review Assignment	2, 5, 9, 12
			Case Problem 1	3
			Case Problem 2	3, 5-8
			Case Problem 3	3, 5-7
			Case Problem 4	3-8
			5: Review Assignment	6, 8-10
			Case Problem 1	5, 6, 8
			Case Problem 2	5, 8
			Case Problem 3	5, 7, 8
			Case Problem 4	5, 7, 8
Ac2002-5-3	Sort records	3 (3.14-3.20, 3.33)	Review Assignment	5, 10
			Case Problem 1	3
			Case Problem 2	3, 7
			Case Problem 3	3
			Case Problem 4	3-5
Ac2002-5-4	Filter records	3 (3.20-3.21) 5 (5.53-5.58)	3: Review Assignment	6-9
			Case Problem 1	4
			5: Review Assignment	12, 13
			Case Problem 2	10, 11
			Case Problem 4	10, 11
Ac2002-6	**Defining Relationships**			
Ac2002-6-1	Create one-to-many relationships	3 (3.08-3.13)	Review Assignment	4
			Case Problem 1	2
			Case Problem 2	2
			Case Problem 3	2
			Case Problem 4	2
Ac2002-6-2	Enforce referential integrity	3 (3.09, 3.11-3.12)	Review Assignment	4
			Case Problem 1	2
			Case Problem 2	2
			Case Problem 3	2
			Case Problem 4	2
Ac2002-7	**Producing Reports**			
Ac2002-7-1	Create and format reports	1 (1.20-1.23) 4 (4.22-4.30) 6 (6.02-6.57)	1: Review Assignment	12
			Case Problem 1	6
			Case Problem 2	8
			Case Problem 3	7
			Case Problem 4	9

| | **Certification Skill Activity** | | **End-of-Tutorial Practice** | |
Standardized Coding Number	*Activity*	*Tutorial Number (page numbers)*	*Exercise*	*Step Number*
			4: Review Assignment	8
			Case Problem 1	8
			Case Problem 2	7
			Case Problem 3	8
			Case Problem 4	7
			6: Review Assignment	2-7
			Case Problem 1	3-9
			Case Problem 2	3-5
			Case Problem 3	3-8
			Case Problem 4	3-9
			Case Problem 5	3-4
Ac2002-7-2	Add calculated controls to reports	6 (6.08-6.10, 6.29-6.32, 6.36-6.40)	Case Problem 1	7e, 7g
			Case Problem 2	3h, 3i
			Case Problem 3	7f, 7g
			Case Problem 4	6f, 7e, 7f
			Case Problem 5	3
Ac2002-7-3	Preview and print reports	4 (4.27-4.30, 4.32-4.33) 6 (6.20-6.21, 6.49-6.50, 6.54)	4: Review Assignment	11
			Case Problem 1	10
			Case Problem 2	11
			Case Problem 3	11
			Case Problem 4	11
			6: Review Assignment	7
			Case Problem 1	8, 9e
			Case Problem 2	4, 5g
			Case Problem 3	8
			Case Problem 4	8, 9e
			Case Problem 5	4
Ac2002-8	**Integrating with Other Applications**			
Ac2002-8-1	Import data to Access	2 (2.29-2.33) 7 (7.46-7.48)	2: Review Assignment	8
			Case Problem 1	6
			Case Problem 2	8
			Case Problem 3	3
			Case Problem 4	3, 11
			7: Case Problem 2	7
Ac2002-8-2	Export data from Access	7 (7.02-7.05, 7.49-7.54)	Review Assignment	2, 7, 8
			Case Problem 1	2, 7, 8
			Case Problem 2	2, 8, 9
			Case Problem 3	2, 7, 8
			Case Problem 4	2, 7, 8
			Case Problem 5	2, 6
Ac2002-8-3	Create a simple data access page	7 (7.08-7.11)	Case Problem 4	4

Access Level I File Finder

Note: *The Data Files supplied with this book and listed in the chart below are starting files for Tutorial 1. You will begin your work on each subsequent tutorial with the files that you created in the previous tutorial. For example, after completing Tutorial 1, you begin Tutorial 2 with your ending files from Tutorial 1. The Review Assignments and Case Problems also build on the starting Data Files in this way. You must complete each tutorial, Review Assignment, and Case Problem in order and finish them completely before continuing to the next tutorial, or your Data Files will not be correct for the next tutorial.*

Location in Tutorial	Name and Location of Data File	Student Creates New File
Tutorial 1		
Session 1.1	Disk1\Tutorial\Seasonal.mdb	
Session 1.2	Disk1\Tutorial\Seasonal.mdb *(continued from Session 1.1)*	
Review Assignments	Disk2\Review\Seasons.mdb	Disk2\Review\Seasons2002.mdb Disk2\Review\Seasons97.mdb
Case Problem 1	Disk3\Cases\Videos.mdb	Disk3\Cases\Videos2002.mdb Disk3\Cases\Videos97.mdb
Case Problem 2	Disk4\Cases\Meals.mdb	Disk4\Cases\Meals2002.mdb Disk4\Cases\Meals97.mdb
Case Problem 3	Disk5\Cases\Redwood.mdb	Disk5\Cases\Redwood.mdb Disk5\Cases\Redwood.mdb
Case Problem 4	Disk6\Cases\Trips.mdb	Disk6\Cases\Trips2002.mdb Disk6\Cases\Trips97.mdb
Tutorial 2		
Session 2.1		Disk1\Tutorial\Northeast.mdb
Session 2.2	Disk1\Tutorial\Northeast.mdb *(continued from Session 2.1)* Disk1\Tutorial\NEJobs.mdb Disk1\Tutorial\Seasonal.mdb *(continued from Tutorial 1)*	
Review Assignments	Disk2\Review\Elsa.mdb	Disk2\Review\Recruits.mdb
Case Problem 1	Disk3\Cases\Videos.mdb *(continued from Tutorial 1)* Disk3\Cases\Events.mdb	
Case Problem 2	Disk4\Cases\Meals.mdb *(continued from Tutorial 1)* Disk4\Cases\Customer.mdb	
Case Problem 3	Disk5\Cases\Redwood.mdb *(continued from Tutorial 1)* Disk5\Cases\Pledge.mdb	
Case Problem 4	Disk6\Cases\Trips.mdb *(continued from Tutorial 1)* Disk6\Cases\Rafting.xls Disk6\Cases\Groups.mdb	
Tutorial 3		
Session 3.1	Disk1\Tutorial\Northeast.mdb *(continued from Session 2.2)*	
Session 3.2	Disk1\Tutorial\Northeast.mdb *(continued from Session 3.1)*	
Review Assignments	Disk2\Review\Recruits.mdb *(continued from Tutorial 2)*	
Case Problem 1	Disk3\Cases\Videos.mdb *(continued from Tutorial 2)*	
Case Problem 2	Disk4\Cases\Meals.mdb *(continued from Tutorial 2)*	
Case Problem 3	Disk5\Cases\Redwood.mdb *(continued from Tutorial 2)*	
Case Problem 4	Disk6\Cases\Trips.mdb *(continued from Tutorial 2)*	
Tutorial 4		
Session 4.1	Disk1\Tutorial\Northeast.mdb *(continued from Session 3.2)*	
Session 4.2	Disk1\Tutorial\Northeast.mdb *(continued from Session 4.1)* Disk1\Tutorial\Globe.bmp	
Review Assignments	Disk2\Review\Recruits.mdb *(continued from Tutorial 3)* Disk2\Review\Travel.bmp	
Case Problem 1	Disk3\Cases\Videos.mdb *(continued from Tutorial 3)* Disk3\Cases\Camcord.bmp	
Case Problem 2	Disk4\Cases\Meals.mdb *(continued from Tutorial 3)* Disk4\Cases\Server.bmp	
Case Problem 3	Disk5\Cases\Redwood.mdb *(continued from Tutorial 3)* Disk5\Cases\Animals.bmp	
Case Problem 4	Disk6\Cases\Trips.mdb *(continued from Tutorial 3)* Disk6\Cases\Raft.gif	
Creating Web Pages with Access		
Tutorial	Disk1\Tutorial\Northeast.mdb *(continued from Session 4.2)*	Disk1\Tutorial\Employer Positions.html Disk1\Tutorial\Employer.htm
Review Assignments	Disk2\Review\Recruits.mdb *(continued from Tutorial 4)*	Disk2\Review\Recruiter.html

Access Level II File Finder

Location in Tutorial	Name and Location of Data File	Student Creates New File
Tutorial 5		
Session 5.1	Disk1\Tutorial\Jobs.mdb	
Session 5.2	Disk1\Tutorial\Jobs.mdb *(continued from Session 5.1)*	
	Disk1\Tutorial\Plane.gif	
Session 5.3	Disk1\Tutorial\Jobs.mdb *(continued from Session 5.2)*	
Review Assignments	Disk1\Review\Students.mdb	
	Disk1\Review\WorldMap.gif	
Case Problem 1	Disk2\Cases\Clients.mdb	
	Disk2\Cases\TVandVCR.gif	
Case Problem 2	Disk2\Cases\Delivery.mdb	
	Disk2\Cases\PlaceSet.gif	
Case Problem 3	Disk2\Cases\Donors.mdb	
Case Problem 4	Disk2\Cases\Outdoors.mdb	
	Disk2\Cases\Kayak.gif	
Case Problem 5		Disk2\Cases\eACH.mdb
Tutorial 6		
Session 6.1	Disk1\Tutorial\Jobs.mdb *(continued from Session 5.3)*	
Session 6.2	Disk1\Tutorial\Jobs.mdb *(continued from Session 6.1)*	
Session 6.3	Disk1\Tutorial\Jobs.mdb *(continued from Session 6.2)*	
	Disk1\Tutorial\NSJILogo.gif	
Review Assignments	Disk1\Review\Students.mdb *(continued from Tutorial 5)*	
Case Problem 1	Disk2\Cases\Clients.mdb *(continued from Tutorial 5)*	
Case Problem 2	Disk2\Cases\Delivery.mdb *(continued from Tutorial 5)*	
	Disk2\Cases\DineLogo.gif	
Case Problem 3	Disk2\Cases\Donors.mdb *(continued from Tutorial 5)*	
Case Problem 4	Disk2\Cases\Outdoors.mdb *(continued from Tutorial 5)*	
Case Problem 5	Disk2\Cases\eACH.mdb *(continued from Tutorial 5)*	
Tutorial 7		
Session 7.1	Disk1\Tutorial\Jobs.mdb *(continued from Session 6.3)*	Disk1\Tutorial\Employer Positions.html
	Disk1\Tutorial\NSJI-Tbl.htm	Disk1\Tutorial\Position.htm
		Disk1\Tutorial\Employers and Positions.htm and related Disk1\Tutorial\Employers and Positions_files folder
Session 7.2	Disk1\Tutorial\Jobs.mdb *(continued from Session 7.1)*	Disk1\Tutorial\Openings PivotTable.htm
		Disk1\Tutorial\Total Openings PivotChart.htm
Session 7.3	Disk1\Tutorial\Jobs.mdb *(continued from Session 7.2)*	Disk1\Tutorial\NSJI Employer Positions.xml
	Disk1\Tutorial\Job.xml	Disk1\Tutorial\Potential Income by Employer.xls
	Disk1\Tutorial\Aidan.doc	
	Disk1\Tutorial\Newport.doc	
	Disk1\Tutorial\PearTree.doc	
Review Assignments	Disk1\Review\Students.mdb *(continued from Tutorial 6)*	Disk1\Review\Selected Bonus Quotas.html and related Disk2\Review\Selected Bonus Quotas_files folder
	Disk1\Review\NSJI-Tbl.htm	Disk1\Review\Recruiters and Students.html
		Disk1\Review\Recruiters and StudentsPage2.html
		Disk1\Review\Recruiters and StudentsPage3.html
		Disk1\Review\Recruiters and StudentsPage4.html

Access Level II File Finder

Location in Tutorial	Name and Location of Data File	Student Creates New File
		Disk1\Review\Selected Quotas.htm
		Disk1\Review\Recruiters with Students.htm and related Disk1\Review\Recruiters with Students_files folder
		Disk1\Review\Students by Nation.htm
		Disk1\Review\Selected Bonus Quotas.xml
		Disk1\Review\Selected Bonus Quotas.xls
Case Problem 1	Disk2\Cases\Clients.mdb *(continued from Tutorial 6)*	Disk2\Cases\ShootDesc.html
		Disk2\Cases\Clients and Contracts.html
		Disk2\Cases\Clients and ContractsPage2.html
		Disk2\Cases\Clients and ContractsPage3.html
		Disk2\Cases\Clients and ContractsPage4.html
		Disk2\Cases\Clients and ContractsPage5.html
		Disk2\Cases\Clients and ContractsPage6.html
		Disk2\Cases\Client Page.htm
		Disk2\Cases\Clients and Their Contracts.htm
		Disk2\Cases\City and Shoot Table.htm
		Disk2\Cases\Client Contract Amounts.xml
		Disk2\Cases\Client Contract Amounts.xls
Case Problem 2	Disk2\Cases\Delivery.mdb *(continued from Tutorial 6)*	Disk2\Cases\Large Orders.html
	Disk2\Cases\Choices.xml	Disk2\Cases\Restaurant Orders.html
	Disk2\Cases\Skillet.htm	Disk2\Cases\Restaurant OrdersPage2.html
		Disk2\Cases\Restaurant OrdersPage3.html
		Disk2\Cases\Restaurant OrdersPage4.html
		Disk2\Cases\Order Page.htm
		Disk2\Cases\Orders for Restaurants.htm and related Disk2\Cases\Orders for Restaurants_files folder
		Disk2\Cases\Restaurant Orders Chart.htm
		Disk2\Cases\Order.xml
		Disk2\Cases\Order.xls
Case Problem 3	Disk2\Cases\Donors.mdb *(continued from Tutorial 6)*	Disk2\Cases\Donor.html
		Disk2\Cases\Fund Pledges.html
		Disk2\Cases\Fund PledgesPage2.html
		Disk2\Cases\Fund PledgesPage3.html
		Disk2\Cases\Fund Page.htm
		Disk2\Cases\Pledges for Zoo Funds.htm and related Disk2\Cases\Pledges for Zoo Funds_files folder
		Disk2\Cases\Donor Pledges Chart.htm
		Disk2\Cases\Pledge.xml
		Disk2\Cases\Pledge.xls
Case Problem 4	Disk2\Cases\Outdoors.mdb *(continued from Tutorial 6)*	Disk2\Cases\Trip Dates.html
		Disk2\Cases\Bookings.html
		Disk2\Cases\BookingsPage2.html
		Disk2\Cases\BookingsPage3.html
		Disk2\Cases\BookingsPage4.html
		Disk2\Cases\Costs Page.htm
		Disk2\Cases\Bookings for Clients.htm and related Disk2\Cases\Bookings for Clients_files folder

Access Level II File Finder

Location in Tutorial	Name and Location of Data File	Student Creates New File
		Disk2\Cases\Booked Rafting Trips Chart.htm
		Disk2\Cases\Booked Rafting Trips.xml
		Disk2\Cases\Booked Rafting Trips.xls
Case Problem 5	Disk2\Cases\eACH.mdb *(continued from Tutorial 6)* Disk2\Cases\eACH-Rpt.htm	Disk2\Cases\Item.html
		Students will export a report that they created and named in Tutorial 6 to an HTML document.
		Disk2\Cases\Registrant Page.htm
		Disk2\Cases\Categories and Subcategories Page.htm
		Disk2\Cases\Registrant.xml
		Students will create at least three Word documents to use as the target of hyperlinks.